AN HISTORICAL INTRODUCTION
TO MODERN PHILOSOPHY

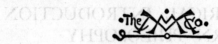

THE MACMILLAN COMPANY
NEW YORK · BOSTON · CHICAGO
DALLAS · ATLANTA · SAN FRANCISCO

MACMILLAN AND CO., LIMITED
LONDON · BOMBAY · CALCUTTA
MADRAS · MELBOURNE

**THE MACMILLAN COMPANY
OF CANADA, LIMITED**
TORONTO

AN HISTORICAL INTRODUCTION TO MODERN PHILOSOPHY

by Hugh MILLER

UNIVERSITY OF CALIFORNIA *at Los Angeles*

THE MACMILLAN COMPANY

1947   *New York*

PREFACE

THIS BOOK IS INTENDED TO LEAD THE READER TO AN
understanding of contemporary philosophy, allowing
him to play his full part in the intellectual life of this time.

Recent advances in science and logic have effected a radical
reorientation of thought, necessitating profound readjustments
in our conceptions of the individual, society, and nature. So
deep do these changes go that they seem to cut through the
living tissue which binds the present to the past. We face unprecedented tasks, to the solution of which the past brings little
or no help; yet the tasks are so urgent that only immediate
action, unhindered by time-consuming thought, seems to be of
avail. To this pressure of urgent and unprecedented tasks comes
the modern habit of mind, which assumes that problems arising
out of present conditions must and can be solved by a better
perception of present activities. How should history help meet
the emergency which history has precipitated?

The publication of an historical introduction to philosophy
therefore calls for some defense. The full defense of this historical approach must be left to the chapters which follow.
These chapters indicate the nature of the problem which has
stimulated the development of the western intellect, a problem
which has become steadily more insistent, until today its solution is in literal fact a matter of life and death. The problem

v

concerns the relationship of theory to practice, or, more concretely, of science to government. This relationship becomes clear only when we observe how the intellectual development proceeding in science and philosophy and the social development of political economy have conditioned each other. To grasp the relationship between science and society is to discover the moral progress, of which the intellectual and political-economic developments are complementary aspects.

This relationship might possibly be revealed by an analysis of contemporary society; but its portrayal in this way would be difficult and unconvincing. It takes more than a cross-section of social evolution to disclose the deeper lying movements of progress and decline. We know today that the forms of organic nature can be explained only as the contemporary phase of a long organic evolution. How much more necessary is this historical explanation in regard to social evolution, which proceeds so much more rapidly! No one can understand the social process today, no one can even understand the terms in which it is described and debated, without more than a casual knowledge of the intellectual evolution which forged this vocabulary in the crucibles of human history and on the anvil of human faith.

It seems to us, in this fifth decade of the twentieth century, that man holds in his hand henceforth the instruments which may either restore him to Eden or blast him along with all other life into eternal oblivion. This is a fact which should shock us into philosophical reflection, if we have time to reflect. Why has time brought us to these dreadful alternatives, and how shall we implement our decision between them? Only the most rapid and resolute creation of the political instrumentalities able to secure peace and good will among men, it would seem, can save us from present annihilation. But on what foundation, and in the strength of what political intelligence, shall we establish these institutions? What is political wisdom? Inquiry into the nature of justice is still, as it was for Plato in the *Republic,* inquiry into the moral foundations of the universe. Today, in the strength of those very advances in science and logic which initially threw us into intellectual confusion, it is possible to discern the moral foundation on which must be erected the commonwealth of man.

It is the task of philosophy to discern and to promulgate this moral truth, making itself the center and container of all education. For of what profit is science, or art, or any industrial or professional technique, if there be none alive to put it to use?

The bibliographies appended to all but the later chapters are meant to be suggestive rather than exhaustive, directing the students to reading-matter which should be available in college and public libraries. The concurrent reading of one or more short histories of philosophy will amplify what is presented in this book, and provide a basis for its critical estimate. Especially recommended are the selections from the philosophers themselves. It is by coming to grips with these men whose thought has shaped the human intellect that the student will discover and develop his own intellectual power. These men too must be viewed critically, with understanding of the time which conditioned them. For it is still and always true that

"Who reads
Incessantly, and to his reading bring not
A spirit and judgment equal or superior,
Unsettled and uncertain still remains,
Deep versed in books but shallow in himself."

May the ready spirit of Milton, who knew that thought must translate itself into action, be with this age! To you who are this age, and who read this book, I dedicate what follows.

HUGH MILLER

Los Angeles

TABLE OF CONTENTS

AN HISTORICAL INTRODUCTION
TO MODERN PHILOSOPHY

1 THE PLACE OF PHILOSOPHY
IN CONTEMPORARY LIFE

THE RECENT WAR AND ITS AFTERMATH MAKE CLEAR to us the radical transition which has just occurred. Western Europe, the source of western civilization, is no longer its center. Western civilization has now two centers, one located in North America and the other in Russia. These two peoples head the van of human progress because they most explicitly base their social constitutions upon political theory. A political theory expounds some concept of justice. It therefore involves initially an ethical or social philosophy, and finally a complete philosophy of nature and man.

It is apparent to most of us that we are entering a new political epoch, an era in which government becomes to an unprecedented degree the agency by which man seeks to control his destiny, and especially to regulate conduct which directly affects other human individuals. Government tends today to replace the religious, educational, charitable, and other institutions which earlier helped to ameliorate human relations. It is evident that this empowerment of government will proceed further, and that the United States and Soviet Russia loom so large in world affairs not only because of their size, but because

3

they have undertaken most deliberately and most successfully this development of man's political resources. But it is not so evident that this political evolution is also a philosophical evolution. We tend to forget that political principles involve wider philosophical principles, and that to enter a political era is also to enter a philosophical era.

If the most important event of our century is its advance to a larger political control of human destiny, the most important fact at this moment is that the United States and Soviet Russia apply two very different political theories, involving opposed philosophies of life and nature. The philosophy of communist Russia looks back to Marx, Hegel, Rousseau, and Descartes, and beyond them to medieval and Greek philosophies. The philosophy of democratic America is close to what is known as empirical philosophy, an outlook which was inaugurated in modern times by Bacon and Locke and Hume. While we welcome the new political era as an age in which men will use governmental agencies to reach higher powers of self-control and control of nature, we must also recognize that this political evolution remains in its outcome uncertain, so long as it points in two directions and threatens to divide humanity against itself. Democratic theory makes the human individual an absolute. It affirms the right of the individual to determine his economic condition, in the strength of political powers invested inalienably in himself. More or less implicit in all democratic practice is the assumption that the social economy may be politically controlled. Communistic doctrine, on the contrary, assumes that economic conditions determine the distribution and use of political power. This means that the political power of an individual is a function of his economic power, which is determined in its turn by the prevalent economic system. Where democracy enthrones liberty, or the power of the individual to regulate the social economy through government, the communist makes his objective the economic security of society at large, and believes that this is to be achieved by establishing the right economic system. The controversy seems to turn on the question whether political history determines economic history, or vice versa; and it is not perceived that the real issue is whether or not the individual shall possess political-economic power of any sort whatsoever. Very evidently, political history is economically conditioned; but it is equally evident that at the same time the course of economic development is politically regulated. By focusing our attention upon the pseudo-problem of which sphere exclusively conditions the other, the absolutist deflects attention from the real problem, which is whether the individual should determine the political economy, *i.e.* the state, or be wholly determined by it. The question of liberty goes by default.

Behind absolutistic doctrine, and supporting it, stands universalistic or rationalistic philosophy, the most authoritative intellectual tradition of the past. Rationalism may be roughly defined as the view that all particular or individual character necessarily conforms to some definable system of natural law. Communism is perhaps the most thoroughgoing application to social and political life of this philosophy of natural law or universal necessity. Once we accept the premise of natural necessity, we are directly led to the conclusion that the human individual necessarily conforms to some pattern of social necessity, and that our aim should be the full realization of this pattern in the state or political economy. The state becomes identified with "universal being," over which the individual has no control.

What is the defense of the democrat against this rationalistic doctrine, which leaves to the human individual neither inviolable rights, nor political competence, nor in the last resort any intelligible status? The democrat must affirm the absoluteness of the individual, the ultimacy and the effectiveness of individual character. What socially transpires, he must say, is the end-result of a sum of individual actions, and not of any universal necessity; and he must affirm this to be true also of nature at large, not only of human affairs. There is, he must insist, no natural or universal necessity.

This democratic philosophy has never been sufficiently explicit. The American revolution looked back to the first English revolution, which made use of a religious terminology, and to the writings of John Locke, who was never able to free his liberal thought from rationalistic elements. Jefferson in his Preamble to the Declaration of Independence, following Locke, based democratic theory and practice upon the concept of inalienable rights invested in the individual by "the laws of Nature and of Nature's God." If inalienable rights are in any way invested, there would seem to be needed some process of investiture and some investing authority. What might be the investing power? It seemed reasonable to locate it in nature itself. But what is nature? If nature is everywhere subject to universal necessity, the human individual too must be subject; and why should we not discover this universal necessity, which imposes itself upon human life, in the actuality of some civic order effectively governing individual behavior? The law of the state, we may conclude, only makes specific, in human affairs, the absolute law of nature.

This was the creed of Aristotle, who defined man as a rational and political animal. He meant that men exist as men only where they are citizens or subjects of a political state. This doctrine was restated in the seventeenth century by Hobbes, often called the founder of modern political science, who ostensibly distinguished natural law from the law of reason. Animals, he thought, live by natural law in continual conflict and brutishness, whereas men live by rational law in civic peace. But Hobbes meant that it is the natural law of the human species to live by reason under civic law. Civic law only specifies natural law relatively to man. This doctrine implies that the human individual owes all that he humanly is to the state, which becomes the source and authority for everything good in human life. It leaves the individual with no intrinsic rights, no inherent value. Conduct becomes moral only as it conforms to civic law. This doctrine provides no rationale for democracy, which conceives the individual to be the creator of law and the master of the state. The doctrine of Hobbes has supported every sort of political absolutism, and has finally issued in the totalitarian state against which our wars were fought. It is the creed of political 'absolutism.

But today, even amongst ourselves, this absolutistic doctrine propagates itself in a new and powerful form. Is not government an agency of the people, is not law the instrument by which society imposes its will upon all? If so, should we not look behind government to those popular or social movements which arise by natural necessity, and which proceed by this same necessity to surmount or overturn every obstacle to their progress? Must not the individual either conform to this social necessity or be destroyed by it? And are not they who perceive this inevitable trend of social change, and who identify their effort with its direction, at once authorized and compelled to assume the powers of government and to become the agents of natural necessity? Is not their ability to seize and maintain government the proof of their right and duty to do so? This is the conception of natural necessity which today undermines our faith in individual rights, and prepares the way for tyranny.

How escape this conception? We should see that the concept of natural necessity is simply incompatible with democratic faith. According to this concept the individual person or thing only seems to act freely—in truth, every individual reaction is determined by some universal necessity. The individual reacts in his own character, but his individual character is only the local and transient manifestation of a universal form or natural law. Individual character only seems to be individual, in reality it is generic or universal. Here, in this depreciation of individual character as unreal or unimportant, and in this elevation of generic character as real and important, lies the premise of every authoritarian doctrine aimed at the destruction of human freedom.

The foregoing paragraph may suffice to show the dependence of political theory upon a large philosophy concerned with the relation of individual character to general character. What democratic doctrine has to establish is the primacy or ultimacy of individual character, and its determination in some way of all general or universal character. The true inaugurator of modern political theory was therefore David Hume, who first successfully challenged the dogma of natural necessity, and not Hobbes with his authoritarian successors, who only perpetuated the authoritarian past. The "natural law" according to which the individual possesses inherent rights or just powers is simply the fact that nature is composed of real individual things, the interactions of which determine all that occurs. From this fact it follows that the political responsibility of the individual is not his responsibility to government, nor is it his freedom from government. It is his responsibility *for* government. More generally, the moral responsibility of the individual derives from the fact that every occurrence is the result of individual actions or reactions. Only individuals effect anything.

How is the reality or effectiveness of individual being to be established? We implied above that the concept of universal necessity is a dogma, which means that it is incapable of being derived from some wider truth. But the concept of individual freedom is also a dogma in this sense. We may call the two dogmas *philosophical postulates*. Such postulates cannot be derived from any more ultimate truth, but must be judged in terms of their consequences for thought and action. For example, the rationalistic concept of natural necessity is authoritarian and despotic in its social consequences, whereas the empirical postulate, affirming the freedom of the individual from universal necessity, is liberal and democratic in its implications.

Must we, therefore, simply announce our preference for democratic government, saying that we just happen to like it better than totalitarian government; and should we affirm the postulate of individual freedom merely because it is logically compatible with democratic government, whereas the postulate of natural necessity is not? Is reason just a rationalization which makes explicit the implications of an irrational choice? No, we can elaborate the moral consequences or the ethical theories flowing from the two postulates. We may see that the very conception of value or goodness implies the power of the individual to make decisions and to acknowledge their effect upon his own and other lives. We may find that society is healthful only if the energies and intelligence of its individual members are morally and politically exercised. We may conclude that the democratic participation of each and every individual in government is the sole means of keeping government sensitive to the social pressures exerted upon it, so that all nondemocratic government is inherently unstable. These and other theoretical considerations may influence our choice of the postulate of freedom.

But what if the postulate, however preferable on moral grounds, should be simply untrue? Is not human society part and parcel of the larger world? Did not man emerge as the inevitable result of an evolution of planetary life? Did not organic nature merely complicate certain physical processes which antedated the appearance of life? And is not physical nature wholly necessitated, wholly uniform in its obedience to physical laws? Can we suppose that freedom emerged with man, or perhaps with the amoeba? Must we not conclude that the appearance of freedom is an illusion, hiding from us the fact of physical necessity?

It may seem farfetched to make our faith in a certain form of government depend upon a general philosophy which inquires into the character of everything that exists. Surely we are more cognizant of the nature and needs of man than we are of the ultimate pattern of universal nature? Protagoras, living in the fifth century B.C., taught that "man is the measure of all things"; and ever since Protagoras there have been sophists assuring us that human faith neither needs nor allows of philosophical support. Today, our world is more than ever full of such sophistry. Yet it is a fact, and the fact is witness to something profound and truthful in man, that men have never been willing to cut the tie that binds them to larger nature, in order to avoid the difficult task of making intelligible their relation to nature. It was in pursuit of this intelligence that originated first religion, and later, science and philosophy; and today no less than in former times those movements prosper which establish their social and political teaching upon some philosophical basis. An age of political faith is always a philosophical age.

The contradictory postulates of natural freedom and natural necessity must therefore be judged in terms of their whole consequence, not merely in terms of their social and political consequence. What does everything we know of nature imply with respect to the postulates? Which postulate, this means, makes possible our science of nature? Which does natural science itself affirm, freedom or necessity?

For twenty-five centuries, which is as far back as the record goes, science seemed to require the postulation of natural necessity. How can science correctly predict the course of particular events, if it does not possess, in its theoretical formulas, knowledge of a universal structure to which events necessarily conform? Must we not conclude that the character of particular events and of individual things is finally necessitated by universal structure, and that individual behavior, in spite of its seeming spontaneity, is really determined in every respect by natural necessity?

Until very recently, the whole weight of theoretical science seemed to support the principle of natural necessity. In modern times, the principle has been maintained with special stringency in the requirement that particular fact shall yield itself exactly and without residue to theoretical analysis. Things must be completely subject to natural necessity, it seemed, since otherwise we could not discover this necessity working in particular occurrence, nor define it in theoretical formulas. The real character of things must be their uniformity or like-ness, and the apparent differences which individuate things must be illusory or meaningless. The human individual, a part of nature, cannot escape this necessity. Men, too, under their apparent individuality, must really be uniform and without essential difference. We are justified, therefore, in seeking the formulas which specifically define human character, and in imposing these formulas upon all individuals; for just insofar as an individual departs from the formulas, he cannot be said to be really human. He becomes unnatural or monstrous—if he can be said to exist at all.

In this way, by means of the concept of natural necessity, modern science has been employed to support political and other absolutism, and to discredit liberal theory and practice. Science has increasingly become the real faith of modern man, steadily displacing all other faiths; and if our faith in science commits us to the tenets of political absolutism, there is little point in continuing our lip service to liberty. This is why all moral, philosophical, and political controversy finally centers on a single issue: Upon which concept is science established, that of necessity or that of freedom?

The thought of the past, we said, inclined to the conclusion that science involves the postulation of natural necessity. The modern intellect derives from ancient Greece, and the great thinkers of Greece who inaugurated this philosophical inquiry into the implications of natural science were able to do small justice to individuality and freedom. In its main current, which flows through Plato and Aristotle, philosophy attributed to existing things only a small measure of freedom. Things might depart from universal form, it was held, only at the price of their annihilation. According to this doctrine, whatever is individual and nonuniform becomes scientifically unintelligible and morally worthless. But even this residual freedom vanished in the modern philosophy inaugurated by Descartes, who inquired into the implications of modern science as this was developed by Galileo and later extended by Newton. This modern science seemed to deny all chance or freedom, and to require an exact mathematical conformity of particular occurrence to physical necessity. The great development of exact science in modern times seemed to be irrefutable testimony that nature, in its astronomical reaches as in its microscopic grain, is ruled by mathematical necessity; and the tremendous industrial revolution consequent upon this development of exact science seemed to show that the whole social economy of modern man similarly stands upon this postulate of natural necessity. The postulate seemed to govern all theory and all practice. It seemed to be the truth generative of modern civilization.

Yet, directly contrary to this intellectual development, there proceeded a political development which was authentically liberal in its affirmation of the reality, power, and goodness of the human individual, and in its creation of political institutions implementing this individual power and responsibility. Thus the great schism was widened which paralyzes the modern intellect, and which today threatens the civilization dependent upon it. In our scientific and economic activities we do obeisance to natural necessity, but in our political practice we still affirm freedom. This inner contradiction has long defeated thought, and today it endangers human sanity. The advocates of liberty have been tempted to reject science, impugn reason, and explicitly extol unreason. The last decades increasingly exhibit traits familiar to us in the psychopathic ward. Whole peoples go berserk.

Liberal thinkers tried to save the postulate of freedom, in the

interests of morality and justice, by turning to criticism of the
rationalistic philosophy which affirms the postulate of necessity. But criticism without positive construction soon degenerates into skepticism. It is not an accident that Hume, who
first clearly saw the real issue and boldly questioned the dogma
of natural necessity, is still known as a skeptic. It is not an
accident that liberal and empirical philosophy has become increasingly confused, until today the very name of liberalism is
in bad repute among intellectuals. Has the great tradition of
liberty, which in the revolutions of the seventeenth and eighteenth centuries moved to the establishment of free institutions,
lost substance, aim, and momentum? Is liberalism really discredited? Must we conclude that democracy is only the transition from monarchical tyranny to some other form of despotism?

It almost began to seem so. But, fortunately for ourselves
and for civilization, there have occurred within this century
certain revolutionary advances in the fields of logic and science,
which turn the tables upon the authoritarian advocates of
natural necessity, and which reestablish, we must believe conclusively, the philosophical principle upon which is grounded
all liberty of thought and practice. These recent advances show
the belief in mathematical and physical necessity to be ground-
less; and without the support of this basic necessity, the notions
of chemical, biological, social, and other forms of necessity
have little plausibility. We know today that not men alone, but
all things, are free, even as Hume surmised. What looks like
physical or other necessity is something else, the true identity
of which awaits discovery. The postulate of natural necessity,
we now perceive, was only a cover for ignorance of the causes
of natural uniformity, and an excuse for not inquiring into
these causes. Things are necessarily uniform, we said, and that
is all there is to it. We can no longer say this. Every uniformity
or conformity of individuals constitutes a specific scientific

problem. Why do or should individuals conform in certain specific ways?

The revolutionary studies we refer to are so new that the general public is little aware of them, and still less aware of their tremendous philosophical implications. These implications are so radical and startling, indeed, that some professional philosophers fail to perceive them, and perpetuate in their thinking the nineteenth-century approach to problems which these discoveries now make obsolete. It takes a generation or more, as a rule, before a profound revolution in science or logic reveals its largest implications.

Yet there is no question that we witness today an intellectual revolution as thorough as that which occurred when Descartes established modern philosophy upon the postulate of mathematical necessity, or when Greek thinkers established theoretical science upon the principle of natural law. Inevitably, the thought of the future will in many respects diametrically reverse the directions of past thought. We stand at the portals of a cultural reformation which must affect every department of life and every phase of conduct. The conclusive refutation of the postulate of natural necessity removes certain basic prepossessions which for twenty-five centuries have confined imagination and disabled thought. New vistas open to science and art; we are urged to move to new conceptions of the world and man.

The largest consequence of this intellectual revolution is its rehabilitation of the human individual. Modern thought, whatever might be its moral estimate of the significance of the individual, was intellectually constrained to see in the individual only the local and transient appearance of some universal form. For three centuries we have seen the individual emptied of real content, to become a cipher attached to, but adding nothing to, the single fact of universal necessity. Today we know the individual for what the individual is—an ultimate being, subject to no necessity, substance and creator of all that is. After three thousand years of philosophical effort we arrive at philosophical truth; and we find it to be the truth which was already realized in the long evolution to a liberal culture and a democratic society. Practice anticipated theory.

It is to this philosophical truth, generative of a liberal and just civilization, that the student of philosophy is brought today. To convince oneself of its veracity, and to begin to grasp its intellectual and practical consequence, one must know something of the social and philosophical evolution leading up to its establishment. So studied, in the light of its issue in present truth, the history of western thought becomes much more than a chronology of thinkers, systems, and ideas. It resembles the dramatic history of some special science, each epochal stage of which is illuminated and made significant by the further advance to which it leads. The past is not just the past. In this world where time can have no stop, the past is the movement which issues in the present; and only in the light of its present issue can the past be known.

So we turn to an outline of the movement of western thought, disclosing the evolution of the human intellect. The issue of this progress is truth; but the passion which motivated the long progress was the passion for justice. That passion, which created all the worlds, now creates the world to come.

Notes for Further Reading

This book presents philosophy as a study seeking to establish a broad intellectual foundation for political faith. There are other approaches to philosophy, for example from science, art, mathematics, religion.

The prefaces or initial chapters of various histories of philosophy, and also the contents of various introductions to philosophy, may be used to study such varieties of approach. Several of these books will be found in any good college or city library, and the list below is intended to be suggestive only. Russell's recently published

History of Western Philosophy excels in its relation of philosophical to social history, its mature judgment, and its lucid and readable style.

1. Russell, B., *The History of Western Philosophy*. New York, Simon and Schuster, 1945.
2. Fuller, B. A. G., *A History of Philosophy*. New York, Henry Holt and Company, 1938, revised 1945.
3. Randall, J. H., *The Making of the Modern Mind*. Boston, Houghton Mifflin Company, 1926.
4. Windelband, W., *A History of Philosophy*, trans. J. H. Tufts. New York, The Macmillan Company, 1923.
5. Patrick, G. T. W., *Introduction to Philosophy*. Boston, Houghton Mifflin Company, 1924.
6. Jerusalem, W., *An Introduction to Philosophy*, trans. C. F. Sanders. New York, The Macmillan Company, 1910, revised 1932.
7. Paulsen, Fr., *Introduction to Philosophy*, trans. F. Thilly. New York, Henry Holt and Company, 1926.
8. Thilly, F., *A History of Philosophy*. New York, Henry Holt and Company, 1914.

I THE GREAT BEGINNINGS

2 THE STRUGGLE FOR JUSTICE

THE GREEKS OF ANTIQUITY ARE OUR INTELLECTUAL
progenitors; yet almost everything we look back to in
Greek antiquity was the work of two short centuries, lying
between 550 B.C. and 350 B.C., when Greek sculpture, architecture, drama, science, and philosophy reached their zenith.
From that great and decisive beginning proceeded the continuous, remarkably self-conscious development which issues
in the social and intellectual culture of today. Time and again,
when men have lost their bearings, they have returned to that
limpid stream of Greek life for guidance and assurance; and
seldom have they come away unrefreshed. We may even do
this still. Ancient Greece lives in us yet, in more ways than
we know. Still the Greek thinker stands, a guide-post pointing
the way we have come and the way we must go.

We have been taught, not least by the Greeks themselves,
to think of the Greek truth as something timeless, suddenly
appearing to hang forever like a great star in the firmament
of the past. "There," we say, "was Greece!" as if we too believed that Athena had sprung in all her cool maturity from
the head of Zeus. But Greece also, of course, had its origins, its
infancy and adolescence. Of this long growth we know little.
Suddenly the Greek genius found voice; and even as it sang, in

the midst of its new song, came catastrophe no less sudden, followed by long decline.

We do know that a long period of political evolution preceded these articulate centuries. Some centuries earlier the Greek people had put away their kings, and established their free or self-governed city-states. Democratic in our present sense we could scarcely call those communities, since they distinguished between men born to citizenship and others within the city who remained unfranchised. High office and virtual rulership usually remained the privilege of the notable families. But in theory, and to a real degree in practice, those cities knew self-government. They conceived of a government not by persons but by law; and every citizen was held to be a trustee of the city's law, and was expected to take his turn in administrative office. That the Greeks clearly understood their government to be of this constitutional sort is indisputable. They distinguished themselves from other peoples by reference to their form of government; and when they started out to establish new colonies, the colonists would sometimes set forth the constitution which should govern them in their new home. This might be the constitution of the mother city; but it might be a new charter, promising greater or surer liberty. The first and last art of the Greeks, source of all their other art, was their political science.

The beginnings of this political development are lost in prehistory. The sort of political invention just mentioned presumably perpetuated, or sought to recover, the free practices of the Achaean forefathers of the Greeks, who had come down from central or northern Europe much as did Norsemen in later times, first to harass and then to settle these Mediterranean lands. Accepting much of the indigenous culture, these barbarians from the north evidently strove to retain certain characteristics which distinguished them from the peoples with whom they now mingled. They never lost their geographical venturesomeness, which made them the great seafarers and merchants of the inland sea. They kept alive their curious wonder at the strange customs of other peoples, a wonder which was to make them the observant analytical people they became and the creators of natural science. Above all they cherished their conception of what is right and proper in human government. They were fiercely individualistic, in the right sense of this word signifying a respect for individual being everywhere, a sentiment which is the contrary of mere egoism. This sense of the value of the human individual they translated into the political conviction that government should be by law. They believed that individuals may subject themselves with dignity to a common law, but only with indignity to the fiat or whim of a personal ruler.

Settled on sea-girt islands and promontories, or in mountain-girt valleys and narrow littorals, the Greeks never became a nation. Their creation of governmental mechanisms was never so far developed as to show individual liberty to be compatible with large community. Only in the small sovereign city-state, they agreed, could a citizen actively participate in his government. So the fierce love of liberty became identified with a fierce loyalty to the city, precluding all larger political unity; and upon this rock of isolationism the Greek people foundered.

When the historical record begins, Greek society was already suffering from the consequences of this limitation. Cities economically favored by location had grown great; they had become wealthy in trade; and they had attracted increasing numbers of resident aliens who remained unfranchised, so that citizenship became an hereditary privilege and a segregative power. There appeared in such cities two factions whose political opposition reflected a radical divergence of economic interests. The landholders and farmers, citizens impoverished by a commerce which enriched all but them, were conservative or reactionary, resistant to change, doggedly jealous of their ancient rights and privileges, and convinced that they alone truly represented civic tradition and just law. They upheld the ancient religion, and they did not distinguish piety from civic loyalty, since the guardian diety symbolized the political community. The other faction was that which benefited by trade, and which cultivated close relations with similar groups in other cities. The commendable outcome of this economic development would have been some form of political union, supporting and supported by this economic interdependence; but local loyalties and the intransigeance of the conservative faction prevented a federation. The unification of Greece, long overdue, was never consummated, and Greek society was torn to pieces by factional dispute. Within each city there appeared the division between a more aristocratic and conservative group and a more democratic and progressive group, each struggling for control of the civic government. Athens became the recognized leader of the more democratically ruled cities; and Sparta organized against Athens the more reactionary cities. Much as contemporary Europe divided into irreconcilable fascist and communist camps, the Greek people were divided by their aristocratic and democratic factions; and this dissension finally carried them into the Peloponnesian War, which ruined all of them and left them ready to be subjugated by an alien conqueror.

This development was complicated and probably accelerated by the war with Persia. Persia, a young and vigorous empire, represented all that was most feared and abhorred by the liberty-loving Greeks. In 546 B.C. Cyrus the Great delivered Persia from the Medes and set out upon larger conquest. The Greek cities of Ionia on the west coast of Asia Minor were one by one reduced. Thales of Miletus, whose name begins our roster of Greek science, pleaded in vain for a Greek confederation to oppose the Persian menace. Around 500 B.C. Persia mobilized an enormous force for the onslaught upon further Greece.

The advance of Persia, which sent Ionian refugees into every part of Greece, quickened in the Greek people a sense of their cultural unity. The cities now formed a loose confederation, at first under the direction of Sparta, whose militant way of life seemed to qualify it for this leadership; but it was the flexible genius of the Athenians, with their stout and clever sailors, which at Salamis in 480 B.C. secured definitive victory over great Persia. Athens was now commissioned by the confederation to keep intact the naval power, since Persia still threatened. After a brief struggle against jealous Sparta, Athens assumed what was virtually a hegemony over the Greek cities, placing their contributions in its own treasury and seeking to bring cases of dispute to its civic courts. Sparta, militant and reactionary, was able to foment rebellion against progressive Athens on the ground, apparently justified, that Athens abused its commission and was aiming to subject all of Greece to its imperial self.

The brilliant, unforgettable half century following the Persian War produced the architectural masterpieces, the deathless tragedies, the incomparable sculptures that still symbolize classical Greece. Then, in the long, increasingly brutal, and ruinous Peloponnesian War, which according to realistic Thucydides changed the very soul of Greece, that lyrical, gracious, energetic, and free spirit was darkened and all but destroyed. The cities which Persia could not conquer destroyed one another; and the Macedonian who waited in the north came down to subjugate them all, and turn the world barbarian again.

One must not draw too close a parallel between the rise and fall of the Greek cities and the present ruin of Europe after a century rich in achievement. Yet it would be a worse error to recognize the forces which first stimulated and then destroyed Greece, and not to see these same forces working similar destruction in the modern world. The basic failure of Greece was its inability to advance to a just and stable political union, giving to all of the Greek cities a due share of political power and economic benefit. This failure in its turn was due in part to the imperialistic presumptions of Athens, and in part to the jealousy of Sparta and its associates. But we must look deeper than these causes, since similar difficulties attend all efforts at political union. If there had not been in every Greek city an invincible core of moral resistance to the political unification which might have saved all, union would have been achieved. Intransigeant groups controlled the cities aligned with Sparta, and intrigued as a fifth column within Athens and its confederate cities. To understand the Greek debacle we must know wherein the progressive party was weak and the reactionary party strong.

The strength of the reactionary group was its sincere conviction that it alone represented, in each city, the authentic tradition of Greek life. Its adherents saw in fidelity to the interests and institutions of their particular city their whole duty—moral, civic, and religious. They were patriots whose narrow loyalty was their whole ethical code and their effective religion. They looked back with pride and humility upon their noble civic histories; they believed that their civic codes, even as they stood, constituted the essential life and health of their cities; and they could not conceive of a world in which Athens and Sparta, Corinth and Megara were something less than sovereign independent powers. They could see no virtue, but only moral vacuity and religious blasphemy, in the libertarian and universalistic outlook of their political opponents. They identified justice with the letter of the law, righteousness with a pious conservation of old custom, and religion with fidelity to the religious past. In their clear and narrow faith they were strong; and in their strength lay the ruin of Greece.

The weakness of the progressive group was their lack of an explicit political, moral, and religious faith, definite enough to direct fixed policies, inspiring enough to weld them together into an organization crossing civic boundaries. That this group had the support of majorities in all the larger cities is probable; but they lacked discipline, unity of purpose, and organization. They were unable, until it was too late, to present their program in definitely moral and religious terms, and to distinguish their pursuit of liberty from license and laissez-faire. Their opponents, on the other hand, could point to an explicit ideal, realized in civic history and civic practice, and calling only for an obstinate fidelity.

Thus the fall of Greece is a major demonstration of the importance of political, moral, and religious forces in social evolution. If Greek history had been merely an economic development, the Greek people would have been irresistibly drawn to political unity. It seems evident that the majority of Greek citizens were so impelled, their economic interests driving them that way. But the small groups whose economic interests were endangered by this movement were able to call into play very definite political and moral forces which worked against the economic trend. They were able to persuade the Greek people to sacrifice economic interest to patriotic pride, moral integrity, and religious piety. And they succeeded, in spite of the narrowness of their social ideal, in holding back the tide of progress.

How could the progressives have undermined and overcome the resolute, uncompromising fundamentalism of their conservative opponents? Only by advancing to a larger political, moral, and religious vision, retaining what was strong, clean, honest, and true in the old faiths. The Athenians, for example, believed that their austere and beloved Pallas Athene was the daughter of Zeus, sprung from the very head and intelligence of that father of the gods. How could the Greek people be brought to worship Zeus himself, their common god, without these local intermediaries? How could they advance to a justice, a law, a morality and religion that was one and the same for all Greeks? This was the question to which the ancient Greek philosophers applied themselves; and out of their thought proceeded Greek science and ethics.

These men were not able to save Greece; but they began the movement which may save posterity. Their work falls into two distinct phases. The earlier thinkers had in mind primarily

the salvation of the city-states, in their separateness as independent polities. Their essential teaching was that the city-
state represented a particular and local manifestation of a universal constitution which is the universal justice of nature. This
earlier phase culminates in Plato, who could still believe, with
inhuman effort, in the viability of the small sovereign city-state.
The later thinkers renounced allegiance to this civic ideal. The
individual person, they taught, is the citizen of a universal city
of God, prior to and independent of his local political allegiance. It is this doctrine, brought down to earth again as a
result of its inclusion in Christianity, that was to provide the
basis for modern government. It is still, in one or another clarified and enlarged form, all our hope for the future.

What, finally, did the Greek people have, and other peoples
lack, that made them the progenitors of the long political and
intellectual evolution which has brought us as far as we have
come? We must suspect that the Achaean forefathers of the
Greeks brought with them the distinctive tradition which later
made them the great protagonists of justice and science; and
we may believe that the same customs qualified those peoples
who later recognized what was essential and distinctive in the
Greek culture, and made it very deliberately an expression of
their own character. This distinctive character has often been
discovered, not without reason, in the deep humanism of classical Greece. The Greeks honored man, man as such, as he had
never before been honored. They held that man is too dignified
a being to be ruled by man, and that all government must therefore be government by law, to which all men without loss of
dignity may be subject. This humanism appears in all their art,
which is an adoration of the human personality in its bodily
beauty and poise. It is the secret of all their science, which
dared to conceive of vast nature as but the larger extension of
that natural law which man, conscious and intelligent, preserves in his self-subjection to civil law.

But we should not suppose this Greek humanism to have

implied, as does some contemporary humanism, a repudiation, implicit or explicit, of the religious foundations of being. All Greek literature, all truly Greek science, is repeated warning against the thought that human life can be humanly lived in neglect of its religious sources, and that respect for man excludes religious faith. Most intellectual of all the ancient peoples, the Greeks were also the most deeply religious. We can best understand this Greek outlook, at once humanistic and religious, by a study of the work of Aeschylus, greatest poet of the Greeks, in whose bold thought lies an insight common to all the great prophets of the past.

Aeschylus, who fought at Marathon against the Persians in 490 B.C., returned to Athens to create the Greek theater and to establish his own fame as one of the supreme dramatic poets of all time. Of his many dramas, most are lost; but we possess the great trilogy portraying the death of Agamemnon and its fateful consequence. The story really begins earlier, when Agamemnon, king of Mycenae and leader of the fabulous expedition against Troy, sacrifices his daughter Iphigenia to win a favorable wind for his fleet. His wife Clytemnestra does not forgive this ambitious violation of domestic love. She takes a lover, sets him on the throne beside her, orders the destruction of Agamemnon's son Orestes, and demeans his daughter Electra. When Agamemnon returns victorious after the ten-year siege of Troy, his wife murders him in the ceremonial bath. Orestes, saved from death, grows up in exile under the admonishments of the god Apollo to avenge his father. Come to manhood, he returns secretly to Mycenae, and meets Electra at their father's tomb. In the most moving and profound moment of the drama, these youngsters pledge themselves to their dreadful task. Orestes slays his mother's paramour, and then, on those same palace steps up which Agamemnon had gone to his doom, he lets quick death cut short his mother's appeal to filial duty. Driven now by the Furies of remorse, Orestes wanders mad over Greece. Apollo leads him to Athens, and there defends him before the Athenian court against the just but merciless Furies. The deadlock is broken by an appeal to mercy, enlarging a literal or legal justice.

What was the purpose of this tale of blood and horror? Aeschylus used a familiar and dreadful theme to expound his new insight into the moral and religious issues of contemporary Greek history. The real theme of the drama is the old concept of a cosmic justice, requiring for every violation of justice its equal and opposite penalty. But how can a crime be corrected by an equal crime perpetrated on the criminal? A crime is a falling away from the law; but is the law restored by balancing the old injustice with a new? What is the consequence of this antique legalism? With every new crime, that crime must be duplicated, its duplicate duplicated, and so on forever. The "law" becomes the pattern of crime, crime and its criminal avengement become the law, injustice sits in the seat of justice, morality is a fullness of blood. Such "law" must sink under its own weight.

And see how bold is Aeschylus—he does not mince the truth! The horrid Furies, those crawling but winged creatures of night, do not essentially differ in their moral blindness from Apollo, the great deity of intelligence and light, sun-god and king-god. The harpies cried for blood for Clytemnestra, the blood of her matricide son; but Apollo incited and defended the slaughter of Clytemnestra, whose blood assuaged Agamemnon. To oblivion, Aeschylus cries, with these ghastly gods and their bloody libations! Let us have mercy, sanity, human justice! Let Athena, true daughter of Zeus, Athena who is close to us, Athena who lives in us, cleanse a corrupt world and dispense a law that transcends all its violations. A political pamphlet as well as a moral sermon and a religious iconoclasm, the trilogy pleads with the Greek people to forget their local vendettas, and to accept an Athenian hegemony that will deal mercy with impartial hand. The trilogy has its important place in the long tradition of the prophetic literature which refuses to divorce justice from righteousness, politics from religion. The laws of human society are not just if they are less merciful than the law of Zeus, giver of life.

What Aeschylus said in great drama and high verse, Greek science repeated in sober but convincing prose. A century before Aeschylus, great Anaximander had written that things "return of necessity" to the chaos whence they had come as "punishment and reparation to one another for their injustice, according to the order of time." This is still the law of tooth for tooth, of crime for crime; but Anaximander is already pointing in his cosmology to a larger law, which Socrates and Plato would show to transcend the earthly passage of crime and punishment.

Notes for Further Reading

A wealth of literature exists to illustrate the Greek milieu in which science and philosophy developed. There is a dearth of studies, however, relating the development of science and philosophy to the political achievement in which the Greek intellect had its first exercise and expression.

1. Murray, Gilbert, *Five Stages of Greek Religion*. New York, Columbia University Press, 1925.
2. ――― *Aeschylus, the Creator of Tragedy*. Toronto, Oxford University Press, 1940.
3. Aeschylus. *The Tragedies of Aeschylus,* trans. G. Murray and others. New York, The Macmillan Company, 1908.
4. Cornford, F. M., *From Religion to Philosophy*. Boston, Longmans, Green and Company, 1912.
5. Barker, E., *Greek Political Theory*, 2nd ed. London, Methuen and Company, Ltd., 1925.
6. Bury, J. B., "The Age of Illumination," *The Cambridge Ancient History*. New York, The Macmillan Company, 1927, Vol. V.
7. Sabine, G. H., *A History of Political Theory*. New York, Henry Holt and Company, 1937, Part I.
8. Zimmern, A. E., *The Greek Commonwealth*. London and New York, Oxford University Press, 1922.
9. Dickinson, G. L., *The Geek View of Life*. Garden City, Doubleday Doran and Company, 1925.

3   THE BIRTH OF SCIENCE

A GOOD DEAL OF CONTEMPORARY DISCUSSION IS devoted to the causes and conditions of scientific progress; and it is usual today to emphasize the economic forces which stimulate and advance the development of science. It is well to recognize these practical motivations moving in business, industry, warfare, etc., which stimulate new advance in science. However, man has always and everywhere been economically motivated; yet he has pursued science only in certain epochs and places. If science arises solely as a result of economic forces, why did it not arise in China, where these economic forces have worked unceasingly for many thousands of years? The truth would seem to be that science, once it exists, may be pursued for its economic returns; but the notion that science appears and develops as a sublimation of economic forces cannot be established.

The intellectual activity which issues in the pure and applied science of today arose in ancient Greece, in the Ionian cities studding the western coast of Asia Minor, in the sixth century B.C. There is no doubt that its development, even its origin, was industrially and otherwise economically stimulated, those Ionian cities being active commercial centers. But to repeat, since science did not develop in the great Phoenician and Egyptian industrial cities, its development cannot be explained as an economic phenomenon.

Science of a sort, we know, existed earlier and elsewhere. *Thales of Miletus*, the father of western science, is said to have learned his geometry in Egypt; and his prediction of the solar eclipse of 585 B.C. testifies to his access to astronomical records covering some centuries, accumulated perhaps in Mesopotamia, where astrologer-priests had long plotted the sky. But we ascribe the creation of science to Ionian Greece because it was there that the study of natural phenomena was undertaken, as we say, "for its own sake," with an increasing recognition of the universal scope, the theoretical unity, and the distinctive method of science. Science arose, in short, as a philosophical enterprise which pursued nothing less than a comprehensive knowledge of the universe in its entirety.

It is unfortunate that we have so little firsthand knowledge of these great Ionian pioneers. Of their actual writings and sayings we possess next to nothing, all our knowledge being hearsay. Our chief source is Aristotle, who included in his writings a short account of his more important predecessors; and Aristotle wrote not as an historian, but as a special pleader who wished to show how all earlier science pointed to his own conception of nature, or miserably failed where it did not. His account of his predecessors is consequently somewhat misleading. Unfortunately this work of Aristotle was religiously accepted as an impartial record until very recently, and its misinterpretation has colored every conception of Greek thought down to the present time.

Aristotle believed that his own most important contribution to science was his doctrine of substance; and he accordingly interpreted each of his predecessors as presaging, more clearly or more dimly, his own view. Thus the history of Greek science became in his hands the account of a search for the underlying and universal substance which inheres in all things. But to understand the Ionian pioneers of science as merely seekers after the "universal substance" is to misunderstand them, and to fail to grasp their real purpose and achievement.

To understand these men we must know how they departed from earlier thought, and why. Earlier thought about nature had been of the sort we call "mythological." We are familiar with Greek mythology through the poems of Homer and Hesiod. We characterize its conceptions as animistic and anthropomorphic, because they symbolize the controlling powers of nature as living beings and as quasi-human divinities. Thus there was gorgeous Apollo, god of the sun and intelligent light; there was ethereal Aphrodite, goddess of love and pro-creation; and there was Zeus, austere father and king of lesser gods. We should not be too scornful of these mythological fantasies. Their authors did not, as we usually suppose them to have done, take these anthropomorphic symbols literally; and the symbols did service in their day, as an expression of man's religious love and awe before the foundations of nature. The powers symbolized were real enough. Who scorns Aphrodite will still pay dear for his mockery, since there is some meed of divinity in the fruitful and poignant love of man and woman; and who refuses homage to Zeus under every name will sooner or later lose all the faith which is his strength and zest of life.

In the sixth century B.C., however, these symbols were no longer adequate to express the maturing insight of the Greeks. Even ancient Homer, whose *Iliad* and *Odyssey* had become the scripture and schoolbook of the Greek peoples, was less than serious in his treatment of the gods. For Homer the gods were but supplementary to man, providing a supporting and ghostly background for the concrete and vivid human drama. Man in his diverse types, in his virtue and cunning, in his deeds of love and friendship and war, was Homer's theme. Sophistry had already worked when Homer sang. Hesiod, a little later, took his gods more seriously. More plebeian and less sophisti-cated than his great predecessor, he strove to incorporate into the aristocratic Homeric pantheon some of the ancient local deities, indigenous to Greek soil and dear to the farmers for whom he wrote. But Hesiod too, even by his effort to revitalize the Olympian myth, betrayed his awareness of its inadequacy and assisted in its obsequies.

The Milesian progenitors of science boldly departed from this venerable but decadent mythology. They sought a new vehicle for the expression of their religious faith and for their perception of the religious unity and meaning of the world. Of this moral and religious motive, in them become realistic, was born their science. They used their extended knowledge of fact, and their deep concern for the moral and political well-being of man, to create a new form of religion, so different from other religious symbolisms that it has usually been contrasted with religion. Yet it was religion, because its motive was religious. Let us examine for a few moments the thought of Thales, Anaximander, and Anaximenes, citizens of Miletus, who initiated the development which was to become science and philosophy.

Of *Thales*, who "flourished," as the Greeks were wont to say, about 600 B.C., we know little. A leader who vainly appealed for a confederation of Greek cities to meet the menacing power of Persia, a navigator and astronomer, he evidently elaborated a cosmology the chief lines of which were retained by his Milesian and later successors. If, as reported, he said, "All things are full of gods," he presumably was proposing a realistic and empirical study of the forces inherent in things, since "gods" meant nothing less than "effective powers." If he said, "The lodestone is alive, because it has the power to move iron," he presumably pointed to a rather striking instance of this power inherent in all things. Thales proposed, in short, that we should recognize and acknowledge effective and forceful being wherever it appears, and not only on Mount Olympus, the home of the Homeric divinities. If he said, "All things are water," he evidently had in mind a cosmic process in which the elements of nature are transmuted one into another. And if he added, "The earth floats on water," he evidently conceived the earth to be suspended in a gaseous medium—to wit, water vapor which he confused with air.

In the above paragraph, we have understood the sayings credited to Thales in the light of the successors who developed his views. *Anaximander*, the first of these, is the giant of this Milesian succession. Of his writings we have but one indubitably authentic fragment; but it is all-important. It states: *"Things pay a penalty and recompense to each other for their injustices in the fixed order of time, out of which things is birth for the things that are, into which things is also death as is proper."* This rather cryptic statement we can understand in the light of other indirect evidence. The cosmology developed by Anaximander has been called "meteorological," because it described the whole movement of our galactic universe by analogy with the terrestrial cycle of rainfall, evaporation, cloud formation, and rainfall again. Thus Anaximander supposed this cycle to be only part of a larger cycle, in which what is solid gives place to what is liquid, this to vapor, and this to fire or light. This process is balanced by an opposite movement from fire to earth. The universe is the solid earth, enveloped successively by spheres of water, air, and fire; and there is real or apparent movement from the center to the periphery and back. This conception remains somewhat obscure, for two reasons. First, Anaximander did not teach the transmutation of these four elements one into another, as might be supposed. He taught that the four elements separate out of a characterless being which he called *"the indefinite,"* again returning to this matrix after due season. And secondly, the Greek words for the four elements might be translated adjectivally as the solid, the liquid, the vaporous, the ethereal or luminous, rather than as "earth, water, air, and fire." When we today ponder on "the indefinite" of Anaximander, it seems to become almost a fourth dimension, an invisible yet ubiquitous realm out of which everything articulate proceeds, and into which it again returns.

But we need not be too much concerned with how Anaximander developed his conception, nor even with what the conception exactly was. More important is the sort of conception, the general approach and method, involved in this new speculation. We see here a sustained effort to conceive of nature as a single, continuous, and self-regenerating process. We see, in short, the inauguration of mechanistic science. The mechanism of natural change, Anaximander taught, is always and everywhere simply that of separation and commingling, *i.e.* of spatial displacement. Physical science has followed this direction of thought from that day to the present.

Anaximander developed his mechanistic hypothesis on a grand scale, with superb genius. He conceived not only things, but worlds or "universes," to generate and disappear again *"in the fixed order of time."* The initial separation of heavier from lighter elements, he thought, would generate a great vortex or whirlpool, with the moist earth at the center and the fiery sun at the periphery. The action of heat on moist earth would then generate living organisms, first simple but increasingly complex, man appearing as a late mutation from the fish. Unfortunately this evolutionary conception was later submerged by a more static conception of nature, and not recovered until the close of our eighteenth century.

But most important and revealing in Anaximander's cosmology, and as a rule least emphasized, is the teaching contained in the authentic fragment which we have quoted. *"Things pay a penalty and recompense to each other for their injustice in the fixed order of time."* The conception of the change and movement of nature as only a spatial separation and commingling is a purely mechanistic conception; but this conception of spatial process is only one half of Anaximander's science. It needs to be supplemented by an appreciation of "the fixed order of time," *i.e.* the temporal dimension of fact;

and here the mechanical process of spatial displacements is explained as the working of a universal justice, which gives to each thing its due meed of existence, removing it again in order to give other things their turn. Anaximander would seem to be conceiving of a limited space, too small to include at one and the same time all the articulate forms of nature; but the infinite dimension of time corrects this inadequacy of space by providing for every such form its just habitation, turn and turn about.

Rudimentary as was the science of Anaximander, and inadequate as is our acquaintance with it, we can see that it gave expression to the three great thoughts which have directed and stimulated the intellectual progress of the centuries to follow. First was the conception of a mechanistic science, intent upon the observation and calculation of the spatial displacements of the parts of nature. Second was the conception of universal evolution—a conception which had to wait twenty-five centuries for its astonishing confirmation. Third, and most important, although also most difficult, was the conception of an eternal and implacable justice which underlies and determines these mechanical and evolutionary processes of nature—a justice of which accordingly all science is the revelation and confirmation. It is no accident that the just and implacable "order of time," which consigned to oblivion the spoken and written word of Anaximander, spared from oblivion this one word, with its homage to eternal justice. The eternal moral structure of the world, Anaximander said, lies under and determines, and is not constituted by, the mechanical processes of nature; and we shall see that science today is more than ever faithful to the prophetic and moral genius which grasped that truth.

Anaximenes, a short generation later, modified his predecessor's doctrine in at least one important respect, namely in that he assumed the reciprocal transmutation of the four sorts of being, not merely their mixing and separation. He speaks of the process as one of condensation and rarefaction; and this would suggest that he really conceived of a single substance, appearing in four different degrees of density. It must be remembered that these Milesian thinkers had no idea of empty space. They believed that the atmosphere extended indefinitely, until it reached the celestial firmament or "fire." Nor did they distinguish air from water vapor, the latter being for them only very moist air, and air only very dry vapor. So the clouds were "felted air," according to Anaximenes.

Aristotle says that Anaximenes made air the original element, the others being formed by its rarefaction or condensation. There seems no reason why one element should be so distinguished, since the cycle of transmutation goes on eternally. But Anaximenes probably started with air, since for him it occupied most of space, in his description of the cyclical change. He may have further characterized air, since he said *"Just as our soul, being air, holds us together, so do breath and air encompass the universe."* This statement informs us that these Milesian scientists did not distinguish organic from inorganic processes, as we do. They did not conceive of a physical world devoid of life and organic character. Yet apart from the above statement, we would call Anaximenes' description of nature a purely physical description.

We have concerned ourselves here only with the largest conceptions of these Milesian thinkers. We know that they were active and productive scientists, pursuing special studies and advancing special hypotheses in many fields. Thus Anaximenes elaborated hypotheses on the origins of wind, rainbows, and earthquakes; he developed an astronomy according to which the heavens rotate like a cap or bowl about a disc-shaped earth, to produce the apparent rotation of the constellations about the pole-star. But we shall not refer to such special studies except where they involve a new direction of thought and a new approach or method in the prosecution of science. What distinguished these Milesian thinkers from earlier speculators was their combination of a realistic observation of matters of fact with large cosmological speculation, leading them to a new and realistic conception of the world.

After we have done full justice to these men as the progenitors of the realistic and observant study which has developed into the science of today, in how far and in what respect, we must ask, did these thinkers differ from their mythological forebears? Implicit in all their large speculation upon the cosmic process was the conception familiar to ourselves as that of *natural law*. The mechanical process of the universe, they tell us, is the working of a deeper necessity which gives to each thing its due span of existence in time, "as is just and proper." Whence was derived this conception of a universal and eternal justice, a law conditioning all the processes of nature? Was it not the projection into nature of the moral code which they recognized in their human relations? Was not this natural and universal law only the extrapolation into nature of the civic law which they honored in their self-government? The Olympian mythology which these thinkers rejected, with its highest and higher and lesser and least deities, was really appropriate only to a feudal society, which thus imaginatively projected into nature its own feudal institutions. Here we can see the intimate relation between political pattern and thought about nature. Shall we not say, therefore, that the new science arose as a consequence of the development of self-government in the Greek cities, and as the unconscious understanding of nature by analogy with Greek institutions? This would partly explain why science first arose and developed in Greece, and not elsewhere. And to explain why it arose just when it did, we should point to the menace to these free institutions which came directly from Persia, and indirectly from the difficulties internal to Greek society of which we have spoken. Only in ancient and self-governed Greece, and only when Greek liberty was threatened, did there arise a natural science which replaced all personal deities by a divine and natural law, even as personal rulers had earlier been displaced by the sovereignty of civic law. It was incumbent upon these Greeks, when their free institutions were menaced by external attack and internal crisis, to assure themselves of the righteousness and propriety to nature of these institutions; and they sought this assurance in a conception of nature which affirmed nature to be everywhere governed by "natural law," a conception which stretched Greek justice to the end of infinite space.

Was this procedure, which has been justified by the continuous development of the natural science it initiated, really less anthropomorphic than the earlier mythology? If the Olympian pantheon saw in nature a feudal hierarchy of personal divinities, did not this new cosmology extend to all of nature the pattern of human relations characteristic of the Greek city-state? We shall see that the concept of nature, even in its most objective and scientific elaboration, has never ceased to be intimately related to the social and political habits of men. We shall find, indeed, that our conception of external nature so overlaps our conception of human nature that it is impossible to draw a sharp line dividing man from his natural environment, or to make our studies of man and of nature reciprocally exclusive. The studies of man and of nature have mutually and profitably conditioned each other. The perception of human relations first quickened the perception of the connections among things, and a better understanding of things then implemented our understanding of man. The word "anthropomorphic" is used to discredit any conception which interprets nature by analogy with human and social processes; but it is doubtful whether we can ever reach a concept of nature not open to this criticism. Such criticism is perhaps hypercriticism, in that it overlooks the continuity which relates man to his larger environment. "No art but nature makes that art," said Shakespeare.

This Milesian science initiated directions of thought which it could not follow very far, and raised theoretical problems which it did not clearly see. Its crucial problem was the relation between the constant structure attributed to the cosmic process and the ubiquitous fact of change. This is the largest and continuing problem of all Greek thought, so that we shall be concerned with it through several chapters. A secondary problem was the relation of qualitative character to quantitative character. The Milesians spoke of qualities such as hot and cold and moist and dry, or of qualitied "elements" such as earth, water, fire; but it is evident that they thought, rather vaguely perhaps, in quantitative terms. They conceived the universe to be continuously generated in time, yet to preserve in all of its processes a certain balance or symmetry, much as a fountain moves in all its parts yet preserves its definite shape. The expansion and application of any such conception, we well know today, requires a mathematical treatment; and the Milesians evidently had recourse to mathematical methods. They do not seem to have realized, however, how basic to their whole conception and approach were quantitative character and mathematical theory. The appreciation of the role of quantity in nature, and of mathematical theory in natural science, was the achievement of Pythagoras and his school.

Pythagoras was *of Samos*, an island to the northwest of Miletus; and there is every reason to believe that Pythagoras appropriated the Milesian science, and developed it with new method and in a new direction. He departed from his city rather than live under tyranny, and wandered as a refugee over Greece, to settle finally in southern Italy, where he expounded his new faith and established the famous Pythagorean lodges. In the Pythagorean cult the close relation between scientific interest and moral or social-political ideals is most strikingly illustrated. Pythagoras was a religious visionary who found a theoretical expression of his vision in mathematical science, and carried its practical application into a puritan discipline and a communal form of economy.

Scholars have recently revealed to us the vigorous and widespread religious ferment which worked under the political surface of sixth and fifth century Greece. It was a period which saw many new forms of religious expression and organization, but these movements break through the surface of recorded history only here and there. They appear in some of the great tragedies, *e.g.* in the *Bacchantes* of Euripides, and in certain otherwise obscure developments of science and philosophy; and they must be called upon to explain the steady drift of Greek thought toward its issue in mystical Neoplatonism and Christianity. The movement was a popular one, constituting an appropriation of religious authority by the people at large, and suggesting withdrawal from the established faiths which had become identified with certain political institutions and ruling groups. These "mystery-religions," as we call them because they usually centered in some purifying and redeeming sacrament, often claimed only to recover faiths immemorially old; but there is little doubt, whatever their historical origins, that they constituted new developments of religious speculation appropriate to their age. An important shrine was at Eleusis, outside of Athens; and it is interesting to observe that official Athens tried to identify the Eleusinian mysteries with itself, as a means of influence over the Greek people.

Pythagoras does not seem to have made any claim to antiquity for his cult, but seems rather to have presented it as a new revelation of truth. In the lodges which he founded, communities of men and women embraced a strict discipline of life and thought, accepting the authority of their tutors, and seeking to advance through well-defined stages of moral and intellectual illumination. In their self-government and self-discipline they resembled a medieval monastery, as they did also in their communistic economy. Less clear is the relation of the lodges to the society outside of them. For a time they exercised authority over the cities of southern Italy; but then came revolt, with Pythagoras forced into exile. Later they regained power, but only to be destroyed by a persecution which dispersed their members and their beliefs over much of Greece.

Yet the movement always had its notable adherents in southern Italy, which was in antiquity a vigorous part of the Greek world.

Pythagoras taught the immortality of the soul, its separateness from the body, and its need of redemption from the world. He used music and mathematical science as means to spiritual salvation. The cult was the great forerunner of Christian otherworldliness, and of the puritanism which has been our occidental strength. "We are strangers in this world, and the body is the tomb of the soul, which we may not seek to escape by self-murder; for we are chattels of God our herdsman, and without his command we have no right to make our escape." This is not the creed usually identified with the spirit of Greece, which we like to associate with a somewhat complacent satisfaction in the rounded natural life. Pythagoras was a cry in the night, a call for more than nature had yet given, a bursting of bonds by a human spirit more intense and avid than any earlier recorded; and it was this Pythagorean cry, and not the easy naturalism we today impute to the Greeks, that would penetrate the centuries to shape the imagination and work of man.

But was there any connection, except perhaps of the most accidental sort, between this otherworldly Pythagorean puritanism and the development of natural science? Indeed there was, and it is important to acknowledge it. Three sorts of people, the Pythagoreans said in a parable, come to the Olympic games. There are those who come to buy and sell for a profit, those who come to compete for the honor of their city, and those who come to observe (*theorein*, to look on); and these last are the best. But so are we all divided, or perhaps each of us is divided, by our desires for material reward, for the love and plaudits of our fellows, and for understanding and religious truth. Pythagoras has here distinguished and named the motive, the disinterested love of knowledge, which supports the pursuit of science. But he has also identified this motive with religion, something we no longer find it easy to do. For Pythagoras the scientific pursuit of knowledge was a religious pursuit of truth, bringing emancipation to the soul. And still it is, if we would but know science in its wholeness again.

Music served in this Pythagorean doctrine to bridge the distance between moral and aesthetic art and descriptive science. The lilt and fall of melody, the thrill of harmony, depend on intervals of pitch which in their turn are conditioned by the mathematical proportions of the instruments used—by the lengths of string in the lute, by the spaced holes of the flute. The form and substance of music is its proportion, its measured pattern of tone. Similarly Greek architecture, sculpture, and verse were of the classical sort which looks to symmetry, proportion, and repeated measure. It was this classical art which Pythagoras pursued in his puritan discipline of the individual life, in his disposition of the communal life of the lodge, and finally in his scientific exploration of earth and heaven. The essential form of every sort of being, he taught, is its mathematical form. Mathematics is the key to every secret of nature and of life.

So, with the Pythagoreans, science became consciously and emphatically quantitative, mathematical, precise. Exact science was born; and even among the Pythagoreans this mathematical science, both pure and applied, advanced to most notable achievements. Nor may we believe that any spiritual hunger less acute, less intense, or less abstracted from the world than this Pythagorean quest of supreme deliverance would have sufficed to establish firmly, so that it should never again be lost, this so theoretical and "impractical" wisdom, this mathematical science which has revolutionized human practice, and which has made of our modern industrialized world a monument to pure theory.

From that day onward, the study of mathematics would foster the belief in a realm of ideal and purely intelligible being, a rational realm not of this world, yet required in every explanation of this world. Thus the otherworldliness of the Pythagorean mystery-religion left behind it, after its religious sources were forgotten, the otherworldliness of philosophical rationalism, which has always found in the exact and universal certainties of mathematical theory its broad foundation. We shall finally, in our study of modern thought, reject this rationalistic philosophy with its mathematical basis, although not without acknowledging its partial insight. But we should appreciate here, in our survey of Greek thought, the great service and the partial truth of this mathematical rationalism, which gave to natural science its method or logic, and therewith its systematic and theoretical form.

The realm of mathematical entities, it seemed to those Greeks, is everything this everyday world is not. That realm is perfect order, symmetry, design; this world is by contrast chaotic and unpatterned; that realm is immutable, this world is flux; that realm is invisible to the eye but wholly transparent to thought; this visible world is muddy, formless, opaque to thought. So Pythagoras, and after him the great intellectual tradition of antiquity, saw in observable nature not reality itself, but the shadow or sepulcher of an intelligible reality which is disclosed only to the mind. Why else should mathematics, child of pure reason, provide the key to visible nature? Today we realistically reject this transcendentalism, which sees in visible nature only the shabby replica of an eternal but remote being; but our real problem is to correct the transcendental error without loss of the truth which it distorted.

The Pythagoreans themselves, however, did not perceive the full implication of their mathematical faith. They did not perceive, that is to say, the purely ideal and abstract character of mathematical entities, for they still confused numbers with things. Our own school training, which presents mathematics abstractly, makes the Pythagorean concept of number somewhat difficult to grasp. They conceived of every number as having a definite geometrical shape. For example, there were "square" and "oblong" numbers; and the number ten was conceived as a pyramid, made up of four levels containing respectively four, three, two, and one units. The unit of number was conceived as a volume possessed of spatial size; and they accordingly did not sharply distinguish arithmetic from geometry. Indeed, they took all science to be essentially the science of numbers, since they supposed every distinct sort of thing, and even every distinct sort of natural occurrence, to have "its number," to know which was to know the essential character or true form of the thing. Thus there was one number which was the horse, another which was man, another which was marriage, and so forth. But we should expect these errors, to us whimsical, in the first groping but prescient sketch of what was to become the universal mathematical science of today. Nor were the Pythagorean scientists prevented by their quaint numerology from mighty achievements in arithmetic, geometry, and astronomy. The mathematics and astronomy with which modern science began was essentially their creation. From the Milesians, and through these mathematical Pythagoreans, came the systematic study of nature of which modern science is the faithful development; and about this backbone of authentic theoretical science was incorporated all later thought. One can hardly overestimate, therefore, the influence of Pythagoras upon the intellectual development of man.

Scarce.y less important was his influence upon human practice. His communal ideal was developed by Plato, through whom, as well as more directly, it influenced all later political thought. This ideal was variously pursued in the monastic movements of later antiquity, in the ecclesiastical system of medieval Christianity, and in the orders of the Knights Templar and Rosicrucians, through which it came into Freemasonry and even into the college fraternity, which still curiously preserves in its esoteric symbolism the Pythagorean lore. But the most tremendous of its contemporary applications, of course, is the communism of Soviet Russia.

Let us sum up and estimate this great inauguration of natural science! The Milesians moved to the concept of a single universal process, namely a cycle or oscillation of change between the periphery and the center of nature. They moved to this conception from the observable facts of nature, which they sought to systematize by means of large hypothesis into a unitary and consistent design. This constructive and intellectual effort, as we shall see, involved many new concepts which the Milesians left undefined and implicit. Above all, it involved the concept of a universal structure or form of natural law, which remains stable, universal, and fixed within the changing and diversified panorama of natural occurrence. The Milesians identified this structure with an eternal and universal justice which ultimately controls all generation and decay, all natural occurrence. We shall see, but only at the end of this study, how profound and eternally true was this moral insight which directed the first growth of science.

The Pythagoreans converted this systematic cosmology into a mathematical science applying precise measurements. This development made two great contributions. First, it encouraged accurate and precise observation, and created new ways and new fields of study. Secondly, it established a purely mathematical theory which has never ceased to generate new and increasingly powerful instruments of analysis and hypothesis. We shall discover that mathematics has been the agency through which was developed the capacity for logical analysis, *i.e.* for the theoretical construction of great systems of knowledge. The Pythagoreans did not realize this logical character of their science, because they thought of numbers as the concrete and distinct forms of things. But it was implicit in their science; and Parmenides, their disciple and great critic, was to make it almost explicit.

Notes for Further Reading

Prior to this century, the historian chiefly depended for his knowledge of early Greek thought upon Aristotle's account of his predecessors. Today he has at his disposal the "fragments" consisting of quotations and references to the earlier thinkers gathered from later writings. The task of reconstructing the thought of the philosopher from these fragments is a difficult one, comparable with that of the zoologist who "reconstructs" an extinct animal on the evidence of a few fossils. The best introduction to this field of scholarship for the English reader is probably the writings of John Burnet.

1. Bakewell, C. M., *Source Book in Ancient Philosophy*. New York, Charles Scribner's Sons, 1907.
2. Nahm, M. C., ed., *Selections from Early Greek Philosophy*. New York, F. S. Crofts and Company, 1934.
3. Burnet, J., *Greek Philosophy*. New York, The Macmillan Company, 1914, Vol. I.
4. —— *Early Greek Philosophy*, 3rd ed. New York, The Macmillan Company, 1920.
5. McClure, M. T., *The Early Philosophers of Greece*. New York, Appleton-Century Company, 1935.
6. Gomperz, Th., The Presocratics, *Greek Thinkers*, trans. L. Magnus. London, J. Murray, 1905, Vol. I.
7. Cherniss, H. F., *Aristotle's Criticism of Presocratic Philosophy*. London and New York, Oxford University Press, 1935.
8. Zeller, Ed., *Outlines of the History of Greek Philosophy*, trans. L. R. Palmer. New York, Henry Holt and Company, 1931, Part I.

4 REFLECTION DEEPENS

THE INAUGURATION OF NATURAL SCIENE DESCRIBED
in the preceding chapter occurred in the sixth century B.C. Thales "flourished" around 600 B.C.; Anaximander's
life covered the first half of the century; that of Anaximenes,
probably, the second half. Pythagoras, it is believed, was an
older contemporary of Anaximenes. In the fifth century, when
Athens became the political and cultural capital of the Greek
world, this new science came with disturbing effects upon general thought. One might almost speak of the fifth century as the
sophistic age of antiquity, since its most apparent feature, although not its most important feature, was the spread of a
superficially educated but increasingly skeptical attitude of
mind. Skepticism resulted from the clash of older and newer
ways of thought, each of these ways being used to invalidate
the other.

We have presented the new science of the Milesians as an
effort to discover in nature a constitution or structure similar
to that which these thinkers already knew in their civic constitutions. We need not suppose that these men consciously and
deliberately read into nature their own civic constitution. It
was by an unconscious analogy, which turned out to be a very
successful hypothesis, that they conceived nature to be a single

48

vast economy, things being subject to a universal law even as Greek citizens were willingly subject to their civic laws. All change, Anaximander taught, is the working in nature of universal justice, which keeps things within their proper bounds of space and time, yet gives to each its due. This moral conception was given a more concrete and material expression in the notion of a world the constituents of which are in flux, always coming and going, yet which preserve in their totality a constant balance and design. Thus the measures of water which become air are balanced by measures of air which become water or fire, the quantitative distribution of nature remaining unaltered. This notion is not easy to work out in detail. Anaximander, we saw, needed a sort of fourth dimension, the indefinite, in order to explain change. In his view there is no change except that by which things emerge from or vanish into this medium. Anaximenes had explained all change as rarefaction or condensation—but a rarefaction and condensation of what? Of some one of the four types of being, or of some underlying stuff with four recognizable densities? Is ice frozen water, or is water melted ice? Or are ice and water both phases of some underlying substance? And in the last case, what is this substance in distinction from its variable appearances? The Milesian science raised several problems of this sort, because of the desire to see in nature, at one and the same time, both a process of change and a preservation of something elemental and changeless.

Heraclitus of Ephesus, a city which lay to the south of Miletus on that same Ionian coast, early in the fifth century concerned himself with these problems; and the conclusion he reached makes him the first consistently *dynamic* thinker in history. It is neither necessary nor possible, Heraclitus concluded, to conceive of ultimate substance. If there is real and universal change in the world, and there evidently is, there can be no real substance; for by "substance" we mean just what does not change. What is conserved within change, Heraclitus taught, is the rate and direction of change—something quite definite yet quite unsubstantial. Thus the Milesian science, consistently worked out into its whole implication, must mean that change or motion alone is real, the apparently substantial and solid character of nature being an illusion due to the presence of fixed measures of change. All is motion, but there is a constant pattern of motion.

This idea, familiar to ourselves, was then new; and Heraclitus had difficulty in expressing it, even in steadily conceiving it. To express his idea he used the familiar phenomenon of fire or flame, perhaps the most transient of things. In a candle flame, melted wax is rarefied into vapor and then burned into invisible particles and gases. What we see is the visible *process* of oxidation or burning. Process means a recognizable sort of change. If the flame is steady, this is because the process proceeds at a fixed rate. Everything, Heraclitus generalized, must be really a sort of burning, a process or a change. Even the eternal rocks are really in continuous and steady transformation. All nature is a sort of diversified fire or process of change, *"with measures kindling and measures going out."* Because Heraclitus used fire to symbolize the universal process, Aristotle superficially understood him to say that fire in some literal way is the stuff out of which all things are made. Truly, Heraclitus taught that there is no elemental stuff. In the light of modern science, which has steadily appropriated this dynamic concept of nature first entertained by Heraclitus, this thinker might appear as the mightiest scientific intellect of all antiquity, whose thought far outran his age. Whether the purely dynamic conception of nature is wholly adequate we will not here discuss; but certainly Heraclitus had some reason to claim discovery of a truth until then unknown—so new, he said, that when men first hear it, they react just as if they had not heard it at all. Nor indeed, although the later Greeks did much honor to Heraclitus, were they ever to perceive the full implication of his dynamic doctrine, or cease to find him anything but "obscure."

The full implications of dynamism, indeed, are scarcely clear today, as we shall discover in our concluding chapters. What does it imply when we make change the most basic and ir-reducible character of nature? Something we call *A* becomes something we call *B*. If *A* and *B* constitute our perspectives upon this change, *A* being our view as we look back to its be-ginnings, *B* our view as we look forward to its terminus, then the sole reality confronting us is the process *AB*. But now let us universalize this conception, and think of vast reality itself as a process which is known only in its forward sweep, *AB!* We reach a conception of evolution so radical that neither Darwin nor any other scientist has yet thought to embrace it, and so dis-turbing that no philosopher has yet steadily contemplated it!

Heraclitus did not proceed so far along the trail he was the first to blaze. He still subscribed to the Milesian cosmogony, which conceived the solid earth to be enclosed in permanent envelopes of water, air, and ethereal "fire." To get back to this self-contained cosmos, he conceived all changes to proceed reversibly, between two poles or opposites. *"Fire lives the death of air, air lives the death of fire,"* he said, meaning that there is in nature a downward and an upward movement, a reversible process, which we call "fire" in its upper limits and "air" in certain lower stages. Heraclitus also said, much as did Anaxi-mander, *"Mortals are immortals, the one living the other's death and dying the other's life."* This would seem to imply the immortality of a nonsubstantial soul, our birth and growth being our gradual transference from some other shadowy realm; and similarly our aging and death would restore sub-stance to something in that other realm.

Heraclitus' controlling purpose, we must believe, was to save and give force to the conception of universal justice which Anaximander had magnificently affirmed. According to Anax-imenes, all change is the condensation or rarefaction of some-thing indestructible; and this would mean that all change is merely the redisposition in space of this indestructible matter. But a science which reduces all change to material displacement would apparently be devoid of moral significance. Heraclitus moves in the opposite direction from that taken by Anaximenes, when he denies the existence of immutable stuff, and affirms the absoluteness of change. The truly substantial, lasting, effective and all-regulative factor in nature now becomes the great law or justice which holds all change to fixed rates, and imposes on all things their limits of existence. *"The sun will not overstep his measures,"* said Heraclitus, *"because if he does, the Furies will get after him."* He thought of this universal law very concretely, as a great system of tensions or forces, which he likened to those in the strung bow of the archer.

The difficulty or danger in this dynamic, mobile concept of nature is its relativism. To determine ratios of change we need a measure of change; and if change is radical and universal, our very measures must be changes or motions too. It is this dynamic conception of nature which has recently led the physical scientist to the theory of relativity, accepting this consequence. All knowledge, it follows, presupposes some standard of measurement, and varies with the standard selected; yet our selection of this standard seems to be arbitrary. Knowledge thus becomes only a peculiar perspective upon nature, revealing nature from some one point of view. Many of the sayings of Heraclitus refer to this relativity of knowledge, upon which he evidently brooded long. *"To God,"* he said, *"all things are fair and good and right; but men hold some things wrong and some things right . . . The way of man has no wisdom, but that of God has."* The way of man? Man's whole experience is but one strand of the radical change, his measure of nature is perforce only the change which he himself is. Insofar as man is something distinct in nature, his knowledge of nature is peculiarly anthropomorphic and subjective. So the relativism of Heraclitus became a source of sophistic skepticism.

In Heraclitus himself this tendency to skepticism was more

than outweighed by an intense and, in terms of his own doctrine, literally burning faith in the intellectual power of man. All being, he taught, is some sort of flame; and in man this flame burns brightest in the intelligence. We know, he said, three stages of being. There is sleep, there is ordinary waking, and there is the completely awakened life of intelligence, which has to ordinary experience the relation this latter has to the fitful dream-life of sleep. "*All things we see when awake are death, even as those we see in slumber are sleep . . . It is not meet to act and speak like men asleep.*" In its full wakefulness, the spirit of man knows the cosmos and its divine tension. But man seems to fear this dry, flamelike life of intelligence. He prefers even to quench the flame in liquor, and to "*go tripping, having his soul moist.*" The call to intelligence is also a call to moral living. In dream, each man enters an idiosyncratic world private to himself, woven of his personal memories and desires; in ordinary waking, he shares a common perceptual world with his fellows; only in the elevated life of thought does he fully enter into "*what is common.*" "*The many live as if they had each an understanding of his own . . . Those who speak with understanding must hold fast to what is common as a city holds fast to its law, and even more strongly; for all human laws are fed by the one divine law . . . Wisdom is one thing, it is to know the thought by which all things are steered through all things.*"

Heraclitus established no school, perhaps because his conception outranged the accustomed limits of the Greek mind; but his thought had broad influence upon all the later intellectual development. His most important contribution, the concept of an intelligible form which is the measure of change, and which is itself nonsubstantial, was recovered and firmly established by Plato.

Parmenides of Elea, living, it is believed, a generation later than Heraclitus, until about the middle of the fifth century, was the other outstanding thinker of that age. He was the able and respected ruler of his city in southern Italy; and there is little doubt that Parmenides was fully acquainted with the methods and teachings of the Pythagoreans, one account being that he had belonged to that school before he criticized its doctrine. Parmenides wrote in verse, fragments of his poem being preserved. The poem had two parts, one entitled "*The Way of Truth*," and the other "*The Way of Opinion*"; and this second part, it is thought, may have presented the Pythagorean views which he now publicly renounced.

It seems not unlikely, if we may judge by its subsequent developments, that this Eleatic movement had in fact its origin in certain criticisms of the Pythagorean science. The Pythagoreans, we saw, conceived of forms which they identified somehow with numbers, and which they again discovered in the visible manifestations of nature. They had theories concerning the generation of numbers; and they were active and competent geometers who conceived geometrical figures to be constituted of units identical with those which constitute numbers. This valuable idea, which ties together geometry and number-theory, met certain obstacles when it was persistently applied. We can conceive a right-angled triangle to have two sides respectively of 3 and 4 units each, when its hypotenuse will be 5 units; but how can we conceive a triangle with sides each of 1 unit, the hypotenuse of which must measure $\sqrt{2}$, an irrational quantity which cannot be reduced to any set of integers. Legend says that one Pythagorean was liquidated for having betrayed this breakdown of the Pythagorean system, and revealing the falsity of the assumption that everything is analyzable into some pattern of discrete integers.

Underlying all problems of this sort is the single large question which inquires whether nature and its motions are properly conceived to be continuous in character, or discontinuous— a question which is never answered, since it reappears in some new form with every advance of science. The Pythagoreans were committed to the view that nature is discontinuous, since they understood all things to be numbers made up of discrete units possessed of volume. The Eleatic followers of Parmenides elaborated arguments which reduced this view to self-contradiction and absurdity. Whether or not the Eleatic system originated in these mathematical problems, it certainly carried to its extreme conclusions the opposite view, which denies the discrete or discontinuous character of nature. The Eleatics believed that nature is truly one, solid, infinite, without vacuum, without diversity, without change, without motion. Any other conception of nature, they taught, ulimately leads to the affirmation of discontinuity, with all its consequent absurdities.

The writings of Parmenides, taken by themselves, would suggest another origin of this Eleatic philosophy. "*What is,*" goes the refrain of his poem, "*is identical with what can be thought.*" "*The way of truth,*" in short, is the way of the intellect; and "*the way of opinion,*" *i.e.* of error, is that which puts its trust in the senses. The evidence of the senses and the evidence of reason conflict; we must choose between the senses and reason; the senses lead us to self-contradiction, reason gives us coherent knowledge; so we must resolutely reject sense evidence, and cleave only to reason. The Eleatics dismissed, as a realm wholly made up of illusions, the world which appears to us in ordinary perception. So Parmenides may have been only too loyal to the most essential doctrine of the otherworldly Pythagoras. It is not easy, in our empirical and naturalistic age, to sympathize with this sheer, uncompromising Eleatic rationalism—only an occasional thinker subscribes to its logic today. But we should appreciate its service to the development of science and thought. In the fifth century B.C., it must be remembered, science was still struggling to establish itself as a method of inquiry reaching authentic natural knowledge; and it was becoming evident that science reaches conclusions far removed from those of current opinion, and sometimes rather directly contrary to common sense. Would men accept or tolerate such a science? Would they prefer the conclusions of logic and careful analysis to the apparent evidence of their senses? The Eleatics boldly attacked this danger by making a virtue out of the remoteness of science from ordinary opinion. Science, they resolutely asserted, reaches a wholly incredible truth; and they were able to relate this incredible truth to the religious insight of man, although not to his more casual experience.

We shall be busy with this problem until the close of this book. Parmenides might be called, indeed, the founder of logic, and the founder also of philosophy in its distinction from science. When Parmenides said: "*What is, must be what can be thought*," he showed that he had clearly distinguished knowledge-of-nature from nature-the-object-of-knowledge; he had reached certain conclusions regarding the character or form of knowledge; and he required our conception of nature to conform to this character of knowledge, since nature must correspond to our knowledge of it. The study of the form of knowledge, in distinction from the content of knowledge, is what is called "logic"; and the study of the relationship which holds between this logical form and nature or fact itself is the peculiar responsibility of philosophy. Since we touch here the living core of the whole long development of thought, the nucleus out of which all intellectual growth has proceeded, let us pause for a moment to appreciate this Parmenidean insight.

Ordinarily, the scientist does not stop to observe what he is himself doing. He observes things, events, and processes outside of himself, where they can be sensibly observed. Automatically he compares, generalizes, elaborates hypotheses, applies these, confirms or rejects their statements. In this way he reaches a science of geometry or astronomical physics. But now let him turn around and reflect upon his own procedure! He will find that he always and of necessity brings to his study of nature two presuppositions. One is that the facts he observes may and must be incorporated into some self-consistent theory. The other, which is really only the first differently stated, says that a theory is acceptable only where it violates none of the known facts. But what is "self-consistent theory"? Logic is the large answer to this question. And by what right does the theoretical scientist require the facts of nature to fit into some theory? Why should they not refuse to conform to any and every theory? Philosophy is the long answer to this question. It is no wonder that Plato, the greatest intellect of antiquity, esteemed Parmenides the most among all his predecessors; for Parmenides was the first thinker clearly to perceive the four following facts: one, man always and necessarily brings certain presuppositions to his perception and understanding of nature; two, these presuppositions are somehow included in all his description of nature; three, these presuppositions constitute a purely rational, nonempirical or nonobservable factor in all natural knowledge; four, these presuppositions point to some peculiar and profound relationship between nature and the mind of man.

What can be, said Parmenides, is what can be thought. And what can be thought? Thought, said the Greek, is theoretical science, reaching a theory which defines, we may believe, the real, permanent, and universal character of nature. In appearance nature is diverse, variable, shifting, particular, chaotic. To theoretical study, however, nature is one, same, constant, universal, perfectly formed. Which shall we believe, the senses or the intellect? If you are going to think at all, said Parmenides, think consistently and believe in your thought! Believe that nature is in truth that one, same, inflexible, and whole Being which your theory describes! This conclusion, which identifies thought with *theoretical* knowledge, which prefers reason to the senses, which attributes "real being" only to universal character and which dismisses particular and transient character as sense-illusion, we properly call *rationalism*. Parmenides inaugurated rationalistic philosophy. In so doing, he only stated with unusual and magnificent clarity the essential bias of all Greek science and philosophy, which had been and remained rationalistic in its pursuit of a purely theoretical knowledge.

Modern science, it may be remarked, has been on the whole anti-rationalistic and *empirical*, subordinating to particular fact its general theory. But modern philosophy has wavered between scientific empiricism and the rationalistic doctrines retained from the Greek and medieval past. The modern thinker would like to be rationalistic and empirical at once. We shall find that he may be so, if he will reflect deeply enough upon empirical science and its method.

Parmenides, in presenting his rationalistic faith, was limited by the science of his time, which compelled him to present his view too specifically and narrowly. Science, he said, seeks to define Being, that which is; and yet it also supposes motion and change to be real. This is impossible, he argued. All change is a sort of motion; all motion presupposes something which moves from where it was to where it was not. To move, there must be empty space for it to move into. Parmenides calls empty space "nothing" or "non-Being." But "nothing" cannot be thought, since it is by definition just the absence of all definite and thinkable character. Thus empty space is a fiction. The only reality is that one, fixed, immutable, eternal, universal Being, which somehow dwells in illusory change; for "*it is the same thing that can be thought and that can be*." Only that Being, "*immovable in the bonds of mighty chains, without beginning and without end*," is real. It is the object of all scientific thought, and also of our religious awe.

The thought of Parmenides was to control the whole direction of Greek philosophy; but its most immediate consequence, aside from its reiteration by his Eleatic followers, was a movement almost diametrically opposed to its own. The doctrine of Parmenides implied the falsity of all earlier science, in both its Milesian and its Pythagorean forms; and it was especially directed against the dynamic conception of Heraclitus. The older science found defenders, however, in the atomists, who turned the edge of the Eleatic criticism by stoutly affirming what Parmenides had called inconceivable, the existence of empty space.

A certain *Leucippus*, who journeyed from Miletus to Elea and later settled in Abdera in northern Greece, first clearly enunciated the principle of atomism. *"What is not,"* he said, is as real as *"what is."* There is empty space; and the positively characterized sort of Being required by Parmenides exists in the form of small atoms, indivisible and eternal as Parmenides supposed, but moving in the void. Of Leucippus and his teaching we know little; but the doctrine was elaborated in much detail by his great disciple, *Democritus of Abdera.*

Atomistic theory has been of great importance in modern science, because it can be applied with quantitative methods allowing mathematical calculation. To what degree the Greek atomism was mathematical we do not know; it did not establish any mathematical tradition. It did presuppose, however, the reduction of all qualitative character to quantitative spatial differences. The atoms, Democritus taught, are all of the same stuff; but they differ in size and shape, which results in differences of motion. All the observable qualitative difference and change of nature, excepting of course the qualitative difference between this atomic stuff and pure space, is due to the various dispositions of atoms in space. Some of the atoms have jagged edges and cohere firmly together; others are smooth, and flow freely as liquid or air. Smallest and smoothest of all, and therefore speediest and most penetrating, are the atoms of light, the movement of which Democritus identified with consciousness or intelligence.

In this atomistic doctrine, Greek science approached as near as it was to come to the mechanistic science of today. It postulated only "atoms and the void," the atoms being endowed with self-motion, and being deflected from their self-determined paths only by collisions or other direct contacts. We have some evidence that Democritus was aware that his atomism implied the effective presence in all nature of general mechanical laws, since he conceived all that happens in nature to happen of necessity. But there seems to have been no explicit recognition of such laws, the properties of the atoms themselves being supposed to determine their motions and their reactions upon each other. The doctrine was accordingly completely materialistic, in the modern sense of this word. All growth, all living activity, and all human behavior is to be understood as an appearance to our senses of the motions, the conjunctions, and the dispersions of these changeless and deathless atoms, which alone are real. Human thought itself, which penetrates through these illusory appearances to find only "atoms and the void," is only a motion of those speediest atoms which constitute light. Yet Democritus does not seem to have felt that his doctrine did violence to the aesthetic, moral, and religious beliefs of man. There really are these differences of atomic size, shape, and speed which result in all the differences we know in nature, and which we variously esteem or disparage. In the lucid spaces between the worlds, Democritus supposed, there may dwell the ethereal beings we call "divine," and quite properly worship.

The materialistic character of the doctrine lies in its failure to conceive of any large and effective rule in nature, and in its consistent explanation of the larger movements of nature as determined by microscopic inertias. A world may be conceived to generate itself, Democritus taught, merely out of a collection of atoms. The atoms will fall because they have weight; collisions will occur because some weigh more and move faster. Such contacts will generate a vortex which will constantly be enlarged by new atoms falling into it, until it becomes a world centered in a solid earth with rings of progressively lighter atoms about it. This whole conception, we know today, is based upon false suppositions. Heavy atoms would not fall faster than light atoms, atoms would not "fall" at all in empty space. But there was one presupposition that entitles this Greek atomism to respect, and which made it the influential and profitable conception it was to become in modern science. This was its demand for completeness of explanation. Everything in nature, it insisted, happens of necessity, with adequate cause. Each stage of nature is *completely* determined by the preceding stages, and *completely* determines the succeeding stages. This insistence upon the complete and perfectly intelligible determination of events by events outweighs all the errors of the Greek atomism. It was this rigorous requirement, suggested certainly in part by Greek atomism, which made modern science the rigorous and effective mode of analysis it is. The doctrine that there is no chance in nature has recently come into question; but it was this doctrine that chiefly aided modern science in its advance beyond Greek and medieval science. We owe much to these men.

There were two other forms of atomism, or at least approaches to atomism, of sufficient importance to warrant mention here. *Empedocles of Acragas* in Sicily, a younger contemporary of Parmenides, elaborated a system which supposed that four different kinds of being (the familiar earth, water, air, and fire of the Milesians) might be conceived to be eternal and indestructible, yet to be finely divided into parts which move concurrently, without the supposition of empty space, much as the parts of water may be swilled in a bowl. All things would be explained, in this prototype of modern chemistry, as compositions of these four elements, atomically divided. Empedocles had discovered by experiment that air, which the ancients conceived to fill the space between earth and the "fiery" heavens, is a material body; and this encouraged him to believe, in spite of Parmenides, that motion is not incompatible with a solid or filled Being, and with the denial of a vacuum. Earth may move in air. He still required some source of motion, however; and he therefore postulated two agencies which he called *Love* and *Strife,* the former commingling the elements and the latter separating them out. Empedocles evidently thought of these agencies as immaterial forces, although he is betrayed by his inadequate vocabulary into speaking of them as things which mix with the elements in different proportions. Empedocles stayed as close as he could to the system of Anaximander. He conceived the world to pass through a cycle of four stages, Love generating a perfectly blended cosmos, and Strife reversing the process to produce separation and ultimate chaos. He is the last Greek thinker of importance to subscribe to an evolutionary doctrine. The present world, he believed, is in the unhappy grip of Strife, and we should make the most of any Love that still remains. Empedocles seems to have been a generous, ardent, and lovable soul. He was a great orator, "the founder of rhetoric"; a great and sincere democrat, who led a successful revolt against tyranny and then refused a crown; a lover and student of living things, "the founder of medicine." In all of these ways he established influential traditions; but he cannot be said to have grasped the implications of the critical teaching of Parmenides, which he thought to have escaped. An observant scientist, prolific of fruitful hypothesis, he had little perception of the logical presuppositions of science, and perhaps little interest in them.

The other near-atomist was *Anaxagoras of Clazomene* in Ionia, who lived at about the same time. Anaxagoras spent his middle years in Athens, where the liberal leader Pericles and the dramatist Euripides were his pupils. However, even the protection of Pericles could not save him from persecution for his opinions, and he finally returned to his native city where he was given much honor.

Parmenides had denied the possibility of substantial change. Anaxagoras accepts this reasoning, yet will not renounce the Milesian science which assumed change to be real. Like the atomists he proceeds to a conception of nature as finely divided, indeed he holds it to be infinitely divisible, which was the logical alternative allowed by the Eleatic argument. This bold step allowed him, he believed, to save all the change and apparent diversity of nature from the destructive Eleatic criticism. The substantial being of the world, he agrees, cannot change; but this being may exist in infinite qualitative modes, in all sorts of mixtures of these modes, and in changing mixtures of them. Everything will contain some proportion of every mode; but it will appear to us as that mode of which it contains most. Thus a white object contains much white, but also a trace of every other color, even of black. Copper is mostly copper, but everything has in it a little copper, and copper has in it a little of everything. This seems to us a rather curious and scientifically useless theory. Its virtue, apparently, was that it allowed the scientist to trust his senses, while at the same time it admitted that there could be no change of substance, since Parmenides had shown such change to be inconceivable. Like Empedocles, Anaxagoras needed some agency, distinct from these immutable qualities of nature, to mix and unmix things. He postulated therefore *Nous* or intelligence, a nonsubstantial agency responsible for all motion, and the true ruler of the world. Plato makes Socrates complain that Anaxagoras called *Nous* the controller of the world, but that when he treated of any actual occurrence he explained it mechanically, as a result merely of the push and pull of things. Perhaps we should understand Anaxagoras to have subscribed in general to the science of Anaximander, with some additions of his own which were intended to meet the Eleatic criticism.

In truth, the Milesian science seemed to be self-contradictory. It supposed that the happenings of nature are at once the result of a cosmic purpose, and the necessary and intelligible result of the impingement of the parts of nature against or in each other. Since our own science also shows this apparent contradiction, we cannot be too rough with the Milesians and their apologists. Science, we shall find, does not and cannot explain itself, if we mean by science any special hypothesis or even the sum of special hypotheses descriptive of nature. In antiquity, only Plato was to offer a consistent solution of this problem; and even his solution, we believe to-day, requires radical modification.

Only Plato, too, grasped the larger import of the Parmenidean criticism. Much as in modern thought Hume has been fully understood only by Kant, so in ancient thought Parmenides was fully understood only by Plato. Parmenides taught that the presuppositions supporting all thought, those logical presuppositions which are involved in all consistent description, must necessarily be predicated of nature, because they are inevitably incorporated into every theoretical description. Then he gave a special application of this teaching, in terms of substance. If thought seeks a single, universal, and logically unified theory of nature, explaining natural change as a manifestation of some constancy of Being which is defined by the stable theory, we evidently believe that nature does not really change, but only seems to do so. The Being or substance which we define in science must be immutable and indivisible, in order to correspond to the theory which defines it. This post-Milesian thought looked for a theory of nature which would recognize the immutability of substance, yet allow substance to move. The extreme atomists were most consistent, since they defined very substance or Being, *i.e.* the atoms, as mobile and divided. But they have missed the point of Parmenides' criticism. Parmenides would say that any theory describing these atomic motions, if it defines the laws of the motions, *i.e.* the structure of motion which does not itself change nor move, describes only immobile Being. Parmenides knew very well that there is observable motion and change. He pointed out that when we *think* about what we see, the motion and change vanish, to become only the visible clue to an intelligible Being which is immobile, immutable, and therefore theoretically definable. What Parmenides and his followers failed to explain was the "illusion" of change. Change is real enough, it is a feature of the world. Plato, understanding Parmenides, would correct this failure.

It may seem strange that in all antiquity there should have been only two or three men able to grasp this large but simple thought of Parmenides. But we shall find, as we proceed with this study, that there have been only some half-dozen basic thoughts in all of this intellectual history—the bulk of philosophical speculation is the weaving of these few thoughts into new combinations and modes.

5   SOCRATES: THE WISEST
        AND BEST OF MEN

Upon SOCRATES THE THOUGHT AND THE SPIRITUAL
life of the Greeks were to be centered, so that all roads
seem to lead to and from him. Yet Socrates can be understood
only in the context of his age.

In the preceding chapter, we considered the outstanding
thinkers of the first half of that most glorious fifth century.
We saw reflection deepen, in Heraclitus and Parmenides, until
it grasped something of the implications and presuppositions
of the new science; and then in the atomists we saw the first
repercussions of this deeper reflection upon science itself. But
the dynamism of Heraclitus and the rationalism of Parmenides
were in some ways very disturbing. Both challenged common
sense, the first with its denial of permanent substance, the
second with its denial of real change. The foundations of the
old familiar world seemed to be in volcanic convulsion, much
as they are today. And atomism offered, in place of the once
familiar abode of gods and men, a new and flat world, intelligible only in its microscopic detail and devoid of large design.

In this development the profounder purposes which had
motivated science seemed to have been betrayed. Instead of

restoring in new and powerful form the moral insight of free Greece, instead of showing that the just law of the city-state only administered the larger law of nature, the new science seemed to issue in something unintelligible and morally vacuous. During the second half of the fifth century there spread over the Greek world a blight of sophistry that was in part an enthusiastic but superficial absorption of the new science, in part an open or furtive rebellion which used the new science to discredit what was sober and sane in Greek life. Heraclitus was employed to justify a cheap subjectivism or relativism, making each individual his own truth and his own law. Parmenides was used as a model for clever logic-chopping, which reduced every familiar or established truth to apparent absurdity. The atomistic science could be used to discredit everything but the crassest egoism. This sophistry and skepticism threatened the very existence of Greek society, and consequently it produced a strong reaction against science. Now that the old religion was no longer effective, only science remained to save Greek society. There had to arise, if science and society were to be saved, a man who could make clear the moral foundations of science. Such a man was Socrates.

The sophistry and skepticism of the later fifth century would have not been so dangerous, if Greek society had not already been thrown into economic and political ferment. Their high optimism, which had carried the Greek cities to economic expansion and to victory over Persia, became confused and reckless when the Greeks found themselves confronted with problems of political and economic reconstruction, now acute and not to be postponed; and the forces which should have carried Greece to political unity were dissipated in civic conflict and abortive revolution. The sophists exploited these social and political tensions. They were usually clever but irresponsible men, often without fixed political or other ties, who traveled as teachers, publicists, and dispensers of the new learning from city to city, turning their little knowledge to pecuniary profit.

Their patrons were usually the wealthier residents, and they took their political color from these groups, often serving as the apologists of reaction. Their direct political influence was probably small; but their indirect influence, in undermining the bases of political and intellectual faith, was great and pernicious.

Of most of these itinerant lecturers we need say little; but there runs through their teachings a familiar and sinister refrain. As might be expected from men who put the fruits of disinterested scientific research to personal use, they required of scientific knowledge some immediate utilitarian profit. This requirement was as ambiguous then as it is now. Truth is gained only when it is pursued for its own sake; but to pursue truth for its own sake means to pursue it for the moral direction it gives to human life. Greek science seemed, to these superficial purveyors of science, devoid of such significance. Empty of deep scientific motive, caring nothing for what science revealed of great nature, and without religious interest, they could not grasp the truth which science did reveal; and consequently their justifiable demand that science should serve man became a narrow utilitarianism, or even an immoral opportunism.

Protagoras of Abdera, the contemporary of his fellow townsman Democritus, was perhaps the noblest of this sophistic strain, and may represent his profession. The true value of science, Protagoras asserted, lies in its moral use as an education for youth. Just as arithmetic teaches us to calculate, grammar to speak correctly, and rhetoric to speak persuasively, so a larger science must teach us how to live well. His own teaching, he intimated, would morally enlighten the youth entrusted to him. And what was his teaching? It began with a skeptical argument against universal truth, derived from the relativism of Heraclitus. Each man's "truth" is his individual insight, determined by his individual character and therefore peculiar to himself. Truth, in all literalness, is just someone's opinion—beyond opinion we cannot go. But whose opinion? That of the expert, surely. And who is the expert in this matter of the good life? Well, Protagoras suavely suggested, the expert in this domain is the able and personable individual whose savoir-faire is his fortune; and for a goodly fee, Protagoras would transmit his own worldly wisdom to the children of his auditors. Protagoras with his eloquence and engaging personality moved through the wealthier Greek cities, filling his lecture hall and his purse.

Not a bad fellow, as Plato allows in his satire, was Protagoras. Bluffly kind and shrewdly suave, he used a superficial skepticism to expound the truth that what a man can teach, in the last analysis, is only himself. But what is man—an opinion, or a truth? "Man is the measure of all things" can be a profound saying, as Socrates was to show. But in the mouth of Protagoras the phrase was something less than profound, since it elevated personal talent above a common truth and a common faith.

Another sophist, the Sicilian *Gorgias*, also famous for his oratory, carried this relativism to its final implications in a skepticism virtually complete. If knowledge is only the opinion induced in us by temperament and environment, what basis of judgment among differing opinions can we find? Why is expert opinion best, or today's opinion better than yesterday's? The only criterion Gorgias could find was that of immediacy. We are certain of what we now immediately sense or feel. But such sensation, stripped of all conceptual understanding, is incommunicable, ineffable. We can know the truth only if we do not speak it; to speak is necessarily to lie.

Socrates was by many of his contemporaries, almost certainly by those who encompassed his death, accounted just another sophist. He resembled the sophists in his love of logical acrobatics, in his love and distrust of the new science, and in his demand that knowledge should have practical use. He differed from the sophists in his refusal to exploit intellectual talent for pecuniary or personal gain, in his deep and sincere piety, in his respect for the civic institutions of Greece, and in his faith in the power of the intellect to overcome the obstacles raised by the intellect itself. Having said this much, we might be wise to say no more, because Socrates left no written word; and no man will ever know with certainty just what was that truth which he inspired in those who opened themselves to his influence. Socrates stands in Greek intellectual history like a sun, the radiance of which can be guessed from what it illuminates, but which cannot be directly examined. Some scholars believe that Plato in his writings inscribed, as literally as he could, the teachings of Socrates his master; and it is hard to believe that Plato dramatically concocted the words he made Socrates speak in the famous trial for his life, or when drinking the hemlock. Some scholars do not agree that Plato made himself the mouthpiece of a greater than he; they prefer to leave mystery inscrutable and Socrates unknown. But something of Socrates must be said, at whatever risk, because he is the hinge on which this whole Greek history swings.

An Athenian citizen, son of a stonemason and a midwife, squat and ugly with protruding eyes and snub nose, Socrates first pursued with zeal the new science, only to find in its astronomical speculation nothing of the wisdom he sought. He next ranged over all the arts and crafts for the clue to knowledge, finding much that was sound and good for its purpose, but no moral or political wisdom. He next submitted himself to the visiting sophists, but found them to be windbags, easily deflated by persistent questioning. This practice brought him some notoriety; and a young admirer brought back from a famous shrine the oracular judgment that Socrates was "the wisest of the Greeks." Aware of his ignorance, Socrates concluded that this very consciousness of ignorance must be his wisdom. His own reliance was an inner voice, or conscience, that warned him when he was about to do wrong. Loving

Athens and seeing it bent upon false courses, he devoted his life to arousing in others, especially in the Athenian youth who looked to him for entertainment and guidance, a moral fervor for the salvation of themselves and their city. In this work he neglected his private fortune, but found great satisfaction. Like his mother, who brought bodies to birth, he said, he was midwife to men's thoughts. He wrote nothing because he believed that a disciple is a living book, much more effective than a written word that cannot answer back.

What was his teaching? The soldier-author Xenophon gives us anecdotes about the man. Plato puts a whole philosophy into his mouth. Aristotle, whose biased reports of his predecessors usually misrepresent something factual, says that Socrates invented the method of definition; and this is a real clue. We know that Socrates was famous for his irony, that he was addicted to dialogue with short questions and answers, avoiding rhetoric, and that he identified virtue with understanding, vice with ignorance. When we study clues of this sort in the light of the philosophical development which he so powerfully influenced, we are led to certain broad conclusions concerning the Socratic teaching.

His purpose, it is clear, was to carry to success the intention of the great pioneers of science, by showing how an independent and comprehensive study of nature does in fact reveal the moral foundation of being, which Greek society was apt to call "justice." The Milesian cosmology had failed in this purpose, because it developed into the mechanistic science of the atomists, and supported the skeptical relativism of the sophists. Two errors, Socrates believed, were responsible for this failure. The first was an exaggerated interest in celestial nature, to the neglect of human affairs. The second was the failure, in part corrected by Parmenides, to realize the presuppositions or first principles of scientific study. It was this second error, Socrates saw, that led to relativism and skepticism. To correct these errors, it was necessary to discover the method

which distinguishes scientific research from casual opinion, and
then to apply this method to the problems of human life.

The initial objective of science, Socrates found, is correct
definitions. To say what in general is a correct definition, however, requires understanding of the nature of knowledge, of
the nature of nature, and of the relationship between knowledge and nature. Geometry, the most articulate, exact, and
certain science, provides a model for all science. The method
of geometry is to discern certain recurrent elements such as
the circle, the straight line, the triangle, the point, etc., and
to define these elements in terms of one another. Definitions of
this sort possess a self-evident certainty, an immediate appeal
to the intellect which just cannot be denied. Who could deny
that a straight line is the shortest distance between two points?
Cannot an integrated set of such axiomatic definitions, therefore, comprise a truth which is invincible to skeptical criticism?
The definitions together comprise a theory which, when it is
applied to particular situations, gives us rational and real insight into observable fact.

Later, Plato would proceed from this study of scientific
method to a completed philosophy of nature and man. How
far Socrates had already traveled this road we do not know.
It is likely that Socrates was more concerned to apply the
scientific method as he understood it to human affairs, than
to elaborate a metaphysical system. In making this application,
he started from conceptions famiilar to all the Greeks, who in
their literature and casual discussions were wont to distinguish
certain strengths or "virtues," proper to man but unequally
distributed. Heracles was notable for his resolute strength,
Ulysses for his shrewdness, Solon for his statesmanlike insight
into justice, and so forth. Socrates recognized these "virtues"
as the forces which shape individual character, and which in
their outcome determine social and political history. He found,
however, that each "virtue" only specifies in certain ways,
proper to certain sorts of situation, a single basic virtue, much

as all geometrical figures only specify what we call "geometrical form." Geometrical theory, although it consists of definitions of specific forms, is tied up by these definitions into a unitary knowledge, which in its totality defines geometrical form; and the development of geometry presupposes an initial insight, which all geometrical science only makes explicit, into geometrical form as such. What, therefore, is the basic insight and the constitutive form of our knowledge of man?

It is, Socrates concluded, the insight and the form which are justice, though perhaps it matters little what we call it. All the virtues—piety, modesty, courage, prudence, shrewdness, poise, etc.—arise from an understanding of the objective pattern of permanent and healthy human relationships within which we necessarily live. There are laws of human behavior, not in the modern sense which would explain every human act, however abnormal, as the instance of some law, but in the Greek sense which recognized certain permanent facts to respect which is to succeed and to violate which is to fail in all our doing. The basic virtue, consequently, is an insight into this universal norm of human behavior and social structure. There is a moral pattern which is proper to human life itself, and which can be departed from only with disaster to oneself and society. It is only in appearance that we can "get away with" violations of this moral law. Since the violation is of our own nature, as well as of social morality, it inevitably exacts its penalty. The sole wisdom is an understanding of this justice, the sole good is the doing of it. And really to know justice is automatically to do it, because we necessarily seek our own well-being. All wrongdoing is just confusion of mind or ignorance.

This teaching is so simple that it is easy to overlook its profundity. To impart it, Socrates had to pursue and pin down with endless patience the ambiguities and evasions which arise in human discourse. To discover it, he had to plunge deeper into the mechanism of human thought than anyone before him. The Eleatics had discovered logic; but Socrates attacked the more difficult problem of the relation of logic to fact. The Eleatics were right, he found, in their emphasis upon logic, but wrong when they simply identified the theoretical or logical unity of knowledge with that of intelligible reality. The relation of logic to fact is more complex. The logical form is that which unites a number of definitions into a unitary theory; but the definitions are still plural in number, and they indicate a real plurality in intelligible nature. The definitions are a halfway house, so to speak, between the chaotic plurality of particular facts and the austere but empty unity of logic.

Socrates also clarified the confusion which had demoralized the Milesian science. Anaximander conceived of a universal law which is the eternal justice of the universe; but he conceived of this law as completely and perfectly manifested in all the detail of nature. His "justice" thus became that dread fatality which in Greek legend required the expiation of crime by new crime. The development of the Milesian science into atomism, following this conception of law as natural necessity, had issued in an amoral science, explaining everything, good or bad, as the necessary and inevitable issue of the permanent characters of atoms. Nature is thus voided of value and moral significance. Good and bad, right and wrong, health and disease, beauty and hideousness become subjective illusions, expressing only a human bias. Socrates may have learned from Aeschylus his deeper ethics; in any case, he provided scientific foundation for the higher morality of Aeschylus. The great law of nature, he taught, is not to be identified with the cause of all that happens. It is the cause only of what is good, healthy, wholesome, and normal; it is the destroyer of what is abnormal and aberrant. It transcends the shifting flux of fact in which it appears. The forms of nature, grasped in scientific definitions, provide the *norms* of nature, from which the actualities of nature fall somewhat short. Yet this *normative* science, defining the true and permanent form of nature, is also our only *descriptive* science—we have no other science. In man, Socrates concluded, this universal norm becomes the norm of human behavior, a moral habit incorporated into good custom and true law.

Socrates paid for this teaching with his life. Born ten years after the final defeat of Persia, he saw Athens rise to power, rebuild itself in incomparable beauty, and make itself the brilliant but hectic metropolis of that world. He loved Athens as he loved nothing else under God, not for its glory but for its stout courage and humaneness. He belonged to a group who were critical of the new imperialistic Athens; who believed that Pericles, compelled to depend increasingly upon chauvinistic and radical support for his liberal leadership, was leading Athens astray; who wished somehow to preserve the sober, homespun Athens of the past, even in building the new. Then Socrates and his friends saw these fears realized in the debacle and horror of the long war, and in the disruption of Athens between its "democratic" and "aristocratic" factions. When the reactionary faction revolted and seized power, Socrates incurred its anger by refusing to participate in its purge of innocent opponents. When the more democratic faction regained power, Socrates incurred its anger too by refusing, as officer for the day, to let the aristocratic generals who had lost a battle be made scapegoats for administrative inefficiency. So Socrates himself became the scapegoat. The most truly pious of men was charged with impiety or blasphemy, the man who had devoted his life to restore in Athenian youth the old faith was charged with perverting youth. In vain the fathers and brothers of these youths spoke for Socrates. In a packed court and in one day he was indicted, tried, and condemned to death.

Plato has given us an account of that trial. He did this in the *Apology*, in which surely only a scholarship become hypercritical can see anything but verbatim report. Socrates, writes Plato, undertook his own defense, because his inner voice had prevented him from preparing a set speech, and he refused to make any emotional appeal to the crowded court. After some ironical questioning of his accusers, whose hypocrisy he quickly laid bare, he gave a short review of his life and work, which he described as a public service to his city. Was it for this voluntary service, in which he had impoverished himself, he ironically asked, that he was brought to trial?

Having by a near vote been found guilty, he further angered his accusers by refusing to be serious in the discussion of his penalty. Condemned to death, he thanked his friends and forgave the enemies who had brought him to this end. Whether death is an evil or a blessing, he said, he did not know; but he was glad that evil, which is the real death of man, had not caught up with him, as it had with his young accusers.

In the *Apology* we have one of the great portraits of all time. The picture breathes and speaks. We see a man whose sole concern under threat of death was to do nothing out of character, nothing that would compromise his life's work. Another Platonic writing, the *Crito*, casts light upon this conduct. Importuned by friends who had arranged his escape, Socrates refuses to cooperate. The law, he implied, is altogether more important than its miscarriages of justice. There is really no escape from the legal and political conditions of human existence. Man is a citizen by nature, and owes all that he is to law and government. The failure of justice is cosmic tragedy, not a local incident merely. Because we honor justice and law, we must bear with the human error which miscarries law. Loving Athens, Socrates could not seek to escape its law, and so bring contumely upon his city.

The death of Socrates was destined to be one of the two great martyrdoms which have directed the course of western political evolution. In his trial, when he refused to make use of the degenerate legal practices of the Athenian court, and in his acceptance of its unjust judgment, Socrates attempted to raise Athenian justice to the justice which was in himself.

His intention was successful, but not in the way he hoped. When justice errs, the accused becomes judge and the court is the accused. The Greek people, learning that the most just of men had been destroyed in the name of justice, renounced their allegiance to the state and its law, and looked to another law, not mediated by man, for their salvation. They put law into the skies, and made God their judge. It is we later peoples who, after twenty centuries, reap the fruits of Socrates' martyrdom, by honoring again a human law that can, if man will, dispense the awful yet merciful justice that is God.

We should spend more thought today upon the life, work, and death of this man; for time has brought our larger civilization through half its circle, to that selfsame place where stood in antique civilization the upright figure of Socrates. Our political, practical, and theoretical problems are almost identically those which he and Greece encountered. We too have established a great society upon a political constitution. We have not yet, as did the Greeks, read that constitution into the larger universe, to find in that universe, by scientific study, a larger law. We have proceeded rather in the other direction. Having received from the Greeks their science, with its high vision of a universal and natural justice, we established our political constitution upon that faith, in the doctrine of inalienable rights invested in the individual "by the laws of Nature and of Nature's God." But popular science has repeated in the modern period, only more slowly and relentlessly, the downward curve which it described in earlier antiquity. It has translated the natural law which is the divine justice of the world into a formula which is but the summary of what things do and are, a law which is obeyed in death as in life, in disease as in health, in crime as in community, in madness as in sanity. Once again, as in the later fifth century B.C., the foundations of the world are convulsed, and sophists thrive upon moral and intellectual confusion. Truth, we are told, is just someone's opinion, the perspective upon fact of some economic or other bias. Justice, our sophists tell us, is but preponderant weight of opinion, pressing upon and shaping the law and its interpretation. Law, they say, is only what some pressure-group makes it—an injustice which a later injustice may balance. And human society, under such teaching, strains again toward those irreconcilable factions whose unstable government is legalized persecution or murderous purge. If the sophists are right, if their clamor cannot be silenced by great truth, we are undone as surely as Greece was undone. Nor can we return simply, as some would have us do, to the truth of Socrates and his great succession. Modern criticism has gone too deep, and needs a cure more potent than any truth inherited from Greek antiquity. The method of Socrates we accept. His method was to inquire into those presuppositions of science which are the breath of science, and the condition of all intellectual vigor. But we cannot stop where Socrates and Plato stopped. We know too well that the definitions of theoretical science do not of themselves define that justice which is the norm of being, and the ground of sanity in man and nature.

Notes for Further Reading

The shorter Socratic dialogues, such as the *Charmides, Laches, Lysis,* and *Euthydemus,* show Socrates at work as a teacher. The *Euthyphro, Apology, Crito,* and *Phaedo* show him at his trial, imprisonment, and death. The *Protagoras* presents him in debate. The *Symposium* or *Banquet* sets him in relief against the brilliant intellectual background of fifth-century Athens.

If we accept the dialogues of Plato as a portrait of Socrates by an intimate, competent, and truthful disciple, we may see in the *Memorabilia* of Xenophon a portrait of the homespun moralist as he appeared to the world.

1. Plato, *The Socratic Dialogues.* New York, The Macmillan Company, 1907.
2. Xenophon, *Memorabilia.* New York, G. P. Putnam Sons, 1923.

3. Gomperz, Th., *Greek Thinkers,* trans. G. G. Berry. London, J. Murray, 1914.

4. Zeller, Ed., *Outlines of the History of Greek Philosophy.* New York, Henry Holt and Company, 1931, Part II, Chaps. I and II.

5. Taylor, A. E., *Socrates.* New York, Thomas Nelson and Sons, 1939.

6 PLATO: THE MASTERMIND

BY BIRTH AND TRAINING PLATO SHOULD HAVE SUC-
ceeded Pericles, the liberal leader who ruled Athens at
the zenith of its power. Descended from the great emancipator
Solon, who first reconciled the factions which ultimately
destroyed the city, and descended also from the last Athenian
king, Plato grew up in the circle most responsible for the governmental policies of Athens; his mother's second marriage
had been to a close adviser of Pericles. Two things deflected
Plato from this political career. One was his perception that
factionalism could no longer be overcome. There no longer
existed, he wrote, a group devoted to civic and not to partisan
interest. The other was his inability to identify himself with a
government which had put to death Socrates, its noblest citizen
and his beloved friend and teacher. For some years after
Socrates' death Plato removed himself from Athens, presumably so as not to look upon scenes which reminded him of
that loss. When he returned it was to establish himself outside
of the city, in a school which he hoped would restore to
Greece its political faith. Thus Plato made the controlling
purpose of Socrates his own. If ever a man devoted his life to
the propagation of a master's teachings, Plato did this. It was
no literary convenience that made Plato put his almost every

word into the mouth of Socrates. Those who have assumed that Plato wished merely to exploit the fame of Socrates in order to advance his own doctrines forget that this fame was still infamy when the earlier dialogues of Plato were written; and one wonders a little at certain scholars who imply that the work of the greatest intellect of antiquity was built upon a literary deceit.

Although Plato was given to writing, he shared with Socrates a distrust of the written word. *"One statement,"* he wrote when he was already old, *"I can make in regard to all who have written or may write with a claim to knowledge of the subjects to which I devote myself. . . . Such writers can, in my opinion, have no real acquaintance with the subject. I certainly have composed no work in regard to it, nor shall I ever do so; for there is no way of putting it into words like other studies. Acquaintance with it must come rather after a long period of attendance or instruction in the subject itself and of close companionship, when suddenly, like a blaze kindled by a leaping spark, it is generated in the soul and becomes self-sustaining."* Without pretending to knowledge of this esoteric teaching, we can learn the steps by which it was approached, since Plato tells us of these himself in his many dialogues.

The most important of Plato's writings for our knowledge of the man and his thought is the book-length dialogue *The Republic*, in which he discourses of justice and presents his picture of the good and healthy state; and the first importance of this work is its frank association of philosophical speculation with a practical political purpose. The primary purpose of Plato, and of the Academy which he founded, was political education; nor did Plato ever conceive of a science not inspired and controlled by a political ideal. It is one and the same faith, he knew, which promotes the pursuit of justice and the pursuit of truth; and the *Republic* of Plato, perpetuating this faith which had created Greek science and for which Socrates had lived and died, has molded all subsequent history, by inculcating in us all this realistic association of scientific and political faith. Whenever and wherever this identity has been perceived, there has been great life, progress, social and intellectual growth.

The *Republic* begins its discussion of justice with a consideration of the prevalent sophistries, which taught that justice and law are only the will of the stronger imposed upon the weaker, or the will of the many weak imposed upon the few strong, or the fear of the individual that his contemplated crime may be discovered and punished. Plato discusses, in short, the conception now called "political realism," which finds law and government to be only the resultant of certain forces exerted by the parts of society upon one another. The final consequence of all such "realism" is to identify justice and law with the device by which a part of society forcibly imposes its will upon the rest—a view which robs law of all moral sanction. If justice is only a species of coercion, Plato admits the discussion might as well be closed; but perhaps a wider study reveals a truer justice. The justice which does not disclose itself to a study of relations among human individuals may be "writ large" in nature as a whole. Rather abruptly, the discussion gives way to the exposition of Plato's Utopia. What sort of a state will achieve stability for itself and true well-being for its citizens?

To our democratic minds, Plato's ideal community can be little less than revolting. Let this be frankly confessed! He divides society functionally into three classes, responsible respectively for the productive, administrative, and legislative activities of society. The large productive class would comprise, apparently, a bourgeoisie without political or other ambition and interested in stable government only as the condition of its free pursuit of domestic happiness and economic security. The second class, made up of soldiers and administrative officers, is composed of those whose dominating impulse is social loyalty, and who are happy only when they are identified in some way with the state and its institutions. They seek fame, honor, recognition; and their courage and dutifulness express this civic loyalty and ambition. This class Plato would house in a closed community, with no private property and without separate families. It would undergo a rigorous physical training and be liberally educated in the culture and ideals of its people. Its annual matings, scientifically managed to produce an optimum progeny, would be ritualized so as to become a civic and religious sacrament; and the children from these unions would be fostered as wards of the state. Plato, astonishingly in that day, was a convinced feminist who would open every office to both sexes. The third class of citizens, so small as to constitute a council, would be obtained by selecting the best of the second class, and subjecting them to further scientific training and to trials in practical administrative work. This council, self-perpetuated, would shape administrative policies and be the absolute rulers of the state. Plato would have the state remain small, not exceeding a few thousand citizens. He would keep it poor, in order not to incite envy, and warlike, in order to discourage aggressors.

In this ideal and secure state, Plato says, we can at last discover the seat of justice. Justice is the form or unitary pattern of this ideal society, in its proper balance of the three classes, a balance which secures the smooth fulfilment of the functions upon which society depends for its existence and health. Where the middle group is too strong, the state becomes a Sparta wholly geared for war. Where the bourgeoisie is too powerful, one gets an Athens or Corinth intent only upon economic ends and neglectful of the political needs of the state. But the well-balanced society will be a secure and truly prosperous polity.

The democrat of today can scarcely take seriously this Platonic utopia, which would permanently locate the common responsibility of government in a self-perpetuating privileged class. To sympathize in any way with Plato's conception we have to remember the sorrow and disappointment which engendered it. Plato failed to perceive the liberal political ideals of the Greeks in abstraction from the limited civic forms in which those ideals had been realized. He would not see that the small city-state had outlived its day, and had to make room for some larger form of polity. He therefore became the most extreme of isolationists. First he inquires into the conditions necessary to perpetuate the city-state in a world no longer adapted to it and largely hostile to it; and then he wholeheartedly embraces these monstrous conditions. He had seen Athens grow corrupt and degenerate; he had observed with a keen eye the internal processes of this ruin, but either overlooked or discounted their external causes; and he proposed by sheer rigor to prevent such processes. We who find even national loyalties confining to our growth may see many negative lessons to be learned here.

But after all criticism is done, we should appropriate certain positive insights in Plato's political analysis. Has he not correctly discerned the motivating forces constitutive of society and everywhere working within it? Are there not in each of us, in differing proportions, the three sorts of motivation which he mistakenly segregated into three classes? Do we not each of us respond in some degree to our environment in these three ways, as good bourgeois, as patriots socially ambitious, and as scientific and religious minds? And do these not comprise the three forces on which we must build the human community? Plato's social psychology would seem to be as discerning as his use of it was reactionary and perverse; and it is for us to put it to better service.

This analysis, observe, is at once a behavioristic psychology and a field psychology. The individual is understood by way of his responses to several environments. The narrowest environment stimulates his appetites, his love of home and creature comforts, his love of family and friends. The life stimulated by this immediate environment is essentially bourgeois, whether it be the life of French peasants, of Middletown, of Washington or London "society," or of a Czarist nobility that has lost its honor.

The next wider environment, which differs from the narrower more importantly in its structure than in its size, is that of politically organized society. Many men and women are of that soldierly and administrative type which spontaneously identifies itself with some large institution and is happy only in its service. These people are loyal, reliable, dutiful, but essentially stereotyped and unstatesmanlike, so that a people ruled by its bureaucrats is never well governed. They are reactionary because their whole response is to the actuality of the state or church or other visible institution. They serve the law in its letter, they revere the state in its de facto governors. They are the sticklers for privilege, for custom, for a morality that is uncritical of itself.

But finally there are those who respond to a widest environment, wider than society, embracing all humanity and whatever is more than that. This response to the largest environment is expressed in creative art, science, and religion—not, be it emphasized, in the stereotyped art, science, or religion which reveres the established forms of these interests more than the reality which they seek to embrace. All three interests are really a worship of truth, or of That Nameless which to know is truth—this is why Plato said that the knowledge he was concerned with could not be put in a book. These creative people are apt to be rather oblivious of political, economic, and domestic affairs; but it is their creative power alone, brought into our political economy, which lets us see society in its larger international context, so that we can observe its controlling conditions and its health or disease, and in the light of this dispassionate and disinterested vision steer it aright. Part of this vision, of course, is the perception of the structure of society itself, in its constituent elements of which Plato tries to tell us; but really to understand, to hold fast, and to

apply this structural conception of society requires an understanding of structure everywhere, in all its forms; for it is the
deepest pattern of natural occurrence itself, that which makes
science possible and justice an achievable end. So Plato is compelled, in order to elucidate human justice, to discuss the just
and divine order of the world.

For our summary of Plato's general philosophy, we should
not confine ourselves to the *Republic*; but before we leave this
book, let us appreciate its most essential teaching and its lasting influence. In spite of the fact that Plato would put all
authority in the hands of a ruling council, or even in a
"philosopher-king," the *Republic* is the classical defense of
impersonal and constitutional government, or of government
by law. The religious devotees of science who are appointed
to govern his ideal state do not govern in their own right.
Their qualification is their intelligent obedience to the universal law, which is at once the object of all scientific truth
and the model of all human justice. What actually governs the
Republic is the natural moral law, which Plato assumed to be
known only to scientist-philosophers, an error which a later
generation would correct. Through Plato chiefly—through
his academy for legislators, which perpetuated his teaching for
nearly a thousand years, and through his writings which preserve it still—the concept of constitutional justice came to
dominate western thought; and it would be a bold man who
would claim that without Plato, his school, and his book, we
should enjoy constitutional democracy today.

At one point in the *Republic* the question is raised whether
a society so utopian, making such drastic demands upon its
citizens, could ever be established. We know that Plato hoped,
and at Syracuse in Sicily twice vainly attempted, to establish
such a state; but the answer given to this question in the
Republic is more germane for our understanding of Plato's
general philosophy. Whether such a republic can be realized
or not, Socrates is made to say, it still remains the ideal to

which we should aspire, the standard by which we must appraise existing conditions, and the guide to whatever justice we can achieve. We cannot aspire, appraise, or strive without a clear and intelligible ideal.

This idealism is the key to Plato's general philosophy. Look again at the psychology of the *Republic*! The bourgeois citizen enjoys a good life only if the conditions of domestic and industrial economy are secured by stable government and just law. The soldier-administrator can pursue his ambition and have an object for his loyalty only in a firmly established and wisely governed state. The wise governor owes his wisdom to an intelligence of that universal law which his science discovers and his statesmanship applies. Universal law makes science possible, science makes the statesman possible, the statesman makes the state possible, the state and its order make industry and the family possible. The individual can function properly and hope to secure health and happiness only in an ordered community and an ordered world. In an unjust community the just man must choose, as Socrates had to choose, between doing injustice and suffering disgrace and death. The good life is not merely an individual matter. It presupposes a good society and a good world. The nearer and the remoter environments both condition individual existence; and life can be lived intelligently only if the environment can be understood and its conditions met. Knowledge and a knowable world are presupposed by even the most individual human effort. Justice and law must rule the world—yet not rule it absolutely, because the individual must still be free to deal justly or unjustly, to act intelligently or blindly. The law of nature must be a persuasive law, a norm which conditions prosperity and which ultimately conditions existence, but which does not immediately compel.

This is Plato's idealism. The law of nature, it says, is not just the summary of what goes on in nature. The law of nature is the law of health, of life, and of existence. (Much of nature is moribund.) The law of nature is a structure of just the opposite sort from that affirmed by the atomists, who supposed the larger patterns of nature to result wholly from the microscopic motions of nature. The true structure of nature is that vast economy in which universal nature conditions all of its parts, these parts their parts, and so on downwards or inwards. The freedom of the part may transgress, but it cannot destroy, the lasting structure of the whole.

This Platonic metaphysic has been called "Plato's Theory of Ideas." The name is very misleading. In the first place, Plato's metaphysic is not so much a theory as it is a conception of nature intended to make theories possible and profitable. Secondly, it does not postulate "ideas," but it postulates something which allows us to have ideas and to pursue a true science. The world, Plato taught, is at once many and one, it has individual plurality and cosmic unity. At first sight nature appears to us as a chaos of individual things, each wholly self-determined; but study reveals a pattern or law to which these things must on the whole conform. In the physical world we find a law of inertia, in the organic world a law of self-preservation; and we notice that in their approximate conformity to these laws, things tend to conform in specific ways. Thus an animal does not merely seek to preserve its individual existence, but it seeks to preserve that specific form of life and that specific pattern of behavior which is its own; and it will usually die rather than depart from that specific norm. The inertia of a physical body or a chemical substance, its resistance to change, is similarly an adherence to some specific character which only external force can overcome. And a man, or a society, strives to maintain a characteristically human and just way of life. Along with all the change in nature, there is this conservative bias against change, resulting in the perpetuation of natural species or constant types, and setting a limit to the diversity of nature. When this limit is trespassed, we have the abnormal and moribund. Thus the law works to preserve the vast economy which is the cosmos. In the physical realm, certain constancies of setting and rhythm provide the conditions of organic life; and animal and vegetable life reciprocally condition each other. Each natural species, indeed, is conditioned by many and perhaps by all other species, so that each species has its place, supporting and supported, within the universal economy. All existence is a commerce or symbiosis. Simply by remaining true to its type and by perpetuating its type, each individual thing subscribes to the cosmic order. Fidelity to type is obedience to cosmic law.

Man's true law is his fidelity to man, *i.e.* to his human character. Man is distinguished from the higher animals by his social nature—society is a form and condition of humane living. But man is even more basically differentiated from all other species by his intellectual faculties, arising from his sensitiveness to the largest environment about him, which is what makes human society possible. It is his scientific intellect that makes him moral; for it is through intellect alone that he perceives the universal plan, and learns that his integrity to human nature is his whole and sufficient health. To do evil is quite literally to die, since it is to become what one is not. And Socrates was therefore right when he equated righteousness with understanding and identified vice with ignorance.

In the cosmos, the law appears as the great conservator, perpetuating the species of physical and organic nature and holding them within their appropriate bounds and to their mutual service. But in the individual, the law appears as a creative force, since it is through the individual alone that the cosmic pattern is continually regenerated in existent nature. Plato's most compelling paragraphs are his descriptions of the creative working of the law in ourselves. Even in its healthy appetite for good food, he might have said, the body seeks its re-creative sustenance. In the passion of sex, he does say, it seeks its reproduction in the beautiful mate, with unconscious forethought for sound and healthy progeny. When appetite or passion is controlled and directed, it becomes a cognitive activity leading to a perception of general forms. Both art and science are sublimated appetite. Thus an artist is led to perceive, and to reproduce in works of art, the beauty which is proper to flower and fruit, animal forms, and the human figure. With larger experience we advance beyond the perception of physical beauty, and respond to the beauty of human character; and in the cultivation of friendship we re-create our own character by assuming something of the character of the friend. Friendship, controlled and broadened, leads us into the group of friends, a true society; and society stimulates our love and loyalty to our own people and its distinctive pattern of being. If we are fortunate, we may be led further to a knowledge of other cultures and to an understanding of what is common to all human society. This social response of the individual is of course what perpetuates society; it is the mother of nations and peoples. Thus we are always guided by a creative response to the form which is beauty, and by an unconscious purpose we reproduce and immortalize ourselves in that beauty, moving towards an ever-widening cognition and a growing wisdom and power; until at last, Plato says, we suddenly find ourselves immersed in a sea of beauty, of beauty one and unparalleled; and we know that we have known, for a moment, the beauty of holiness, which is the eternal and universal creator of all that is. From such an insight, we might add, come those supreme and deathless acts of individuals which continue through the ages to shape the life and thought of man, even as these immortal dialogues of Plato, born of such communion with truth, were to inform the civilization which was and is to come, making Plato immortal in Platonic man.

Thus Plato restored to science the moral insight which had earlier initiated and empowered science. He did this by distinguishing in nature two sorts of causal influence or force—the first exerted by the cosmos as a whole upon its parts, the second having its source in the local and transient things which are the constituents of nature. At some risk we may call this conception a dualism of *Form and matter*—this name at least is preferable to "The Theory of Ideas." In the *Timaeus,* an important dialogue in which Plato is careful not to make use of Socrates, but advances his teaching merely as an hypothesis incapable of strict demonstration, a dualism of this sort is presented. The topic discussed is the creation of the world. The creative process of nature may be understood, we are told, as the working of a great *demiurge,* a creative god immanent to the world. This divine artisan has at his disposal a material stuff, which is described somewhat atomistically. In incessant and chaotic motion, and divided into small and inert particles, matter is ruled by mechanical necessity and is devoid of all large and intelligible design. Matter is in itself neither good nor bad, it is aesthetically and morally characterless or neutral. Matter is the "formless" not because it has no character whatsoever, but because its character is so local, shifting, and infinitely diversified that it cannot be steadily contemplated nor intelligibly defined. The creative demiurge has, however, a model accessible to his intelligent vision. This model is a transcendent Form, wholly beautiful, constant, and supremely intelligible. Gazing upon this Form, he shapes mechanical matter, *so far as necessity allows,* into a material replica of the Form. What results is the existent cosmos, compounded of Form and matter, of stability and motion, of sameness and difference, of universal intelligible character and particular visible character, of beauty and defect, of success and failure, of goodness and decay, of truth and error. This divinity immanent to the world, Plato makes clear in other writings, indwells all things. It works in each thing as the response of that thing to the cosmic Form, and as a striving of that thing to be its true self, in fidelity to its type. In man, this response and this effort are enlarged to become a creative adoration of the cosmic Form. Man's fidelity to type is his fidelity to his reason, which is his cognition of

Cosmic Being itself. His intelligence and service of this Form is his science, which is also his truest art and his religion.

Here, in its essential outline, is the metaphysic which was to direct the development of the human intellect from that day to this; for modern thought, which has been a sustained, six-century long criticism of Platonism, nevertheless must and does in all its criticism somehow preserve and enlarge, and not repudiate, the essential Platonic truth. For what is true and in its acceptance obligatory in this Platonic metaphysic does not arise from Plato, and it remains with us after all criticism of Plato is done. The Platonic metaphysic only tried to make explicit the assumptions implicit in any and every theoretical knowledge. Such knowledge postulates and attempts to discover in nature a more or less permanent structure which appears in particular transient fact and which is susceptible of theoretical definition. The Platonic metaphysic can be modified, reformulated, reinterpreted, enlarged; but it cannot be flatly rejected unless we are willing to repudiate our faith in theoretical knowledge, and finally in everything that we call human intelligence.

We will not conclude this chapter without indicating certain limitations in this Platonic conception; but first let us appreciate more fully Plato's version of this formalistic realism, which gathered up into itself all of the important insights of earlier science and philosophy. Plato accepted the science of Anaximander, who looked for a universal law which is at once the justice of the world and a pattern discernible within the observable processes of nature. He seems to have accepted the main insight of the Pythagoreans, who identified universal law with the mathematical structure of nature, but who mistakenly looked to their number-theory for the definition of this structure. He accepted also the criticism of the Eleatics, which indicated that the Pythagorean science necessitated an advance to a more purely logical science, going beyond arithmetic to an understanding of those super-mathematical entities out of which number itself devolves. But in accepting this Eleatic insight, Plato did not renounce the Milesian science, which Heraclitus had shown to presuppose the radical and irreducible reality of change and motion. He accepted something also from the atomists, who had made clear the effectiveness of even the smallest and most particular constituents of nature in the determination first of their own destinies, and through these of the larger courses of nature. All of these apparently contradictory insights Plato recovered, reconciled, and conserved for posterity in that stupendous, simple, and in some respects irrefutable doctrine of Form and matter. At one stroke, leaning upon Socrates, Plato established again a theoretical science that was about to dissipate into paradox, sophistry, and skepticism. At one blow, Plato restored faith in the human intellect and its power to know truth, and propelled science up all the centuries to ourselves and the ages to come. And in restoring to man his intellectual faith, Plato restored to him also his moral faith, by showing that the world known to the intellect is a world compact of beauty and goodness, and contracted indissolubly with justice. After six centuries of modern criticism, criticism which in certain of its conclusions is altogether cogent, Plato looms larger today in human history than ever before; for criticism, finally, can only enlarge, not minimize, that Platonic truth. More than Plato man may hope to be; but to be less than Plato is degenerate. Such is the irreversibility of creative thought.

It was necessary, of course, not only to devise this great conception compounding existent nature out of Form and matter, but to demonstrate its truth. The arguments used to do this were of two kinds. One of them applied the Socratic irony; it pretended to accept the skeptical or sophistical conceptions of those who denied truth or justice, and proceeded to show how even these conceptions illicitly assumed what they denied. Thus in the opening books of the *Republic* the sophist who insists that justice is only the legitimization by social convention of the will of a tyrant is compelled by logical argument to admit that the tyrant who hopes to preserve his power must use skill and understanding in his management of the people, and at least give the appearance of administering justice. Thus he does lip service to truth. More generally, the skeptical view which dismisses all intellectual knowledge as illusion, mere opinion, or appearance, is shown to be based upon an unacknowledged realism able to distinguish truth from illusion. Skepticism of necessity contradicts itself, because it necessarily appeals to realistic criteria the authenticity of which it finally denies. If we knew only illusion, we would not know it for illusion.

The other sort of argument was more systematic and constructive. Although Plato's primary interest was political, he was also an active scientist interested in natural knowledge for its intrinsic value. His Academy was a center of scientific research as well as a school of law; and Plato, endowing and directing its researches, was himself a productive scientist, especially active it is believed in the development of solid geometry. Like so many who have devoted themselves to mathematical study, Plato was convinced of the self-evident, purely rational character of mathematical axioms; and he did not perhaps clearly distinguish these mathematical axioms from the descriptive formulas in which the axioms are applied to natural phenomena. In mathematics, consequently, he found a systematic knowledge established upon self-evident truth and universally applicable to nature. All other natural knowledge, including perhaps a good deal of aesthetic insight which we would ordinarily relegate to art, Plato believed to be an approach to this mathematical physical science; for science, he believed, is the development of an apprehensive faculty which is confusedly applied in all our thinking and imagining, and even in animal perception. This is why, in the *Republic*, he will educate youth first in the liberal arts and in gymnastics, developing their perception of beauty or Form, and only then introduce them to mathematical science, *i.e.* to natural science.

Mathematics is not, however, the end for Plato of our intellectual study. Just as we can break down the visible patterns of things into a few elementary geometrical figures, and then reduce our definitions of these to a number of axioms, so we can proceed upwards from this set of mathematical axioms to a still smaller number of metaphysical principles; and ultimately, Plato believed, one reaches an insight into that ineffable Being out of which all articulate and definable form proceeds. Into this *dialectic*, which was the culmination of Plato's teaching, and which carries the thinker to a religious vision of the Good, we will not go, since it is that truth which Plato said could not be imparted by words. But it is evident that Plato found in mathematical science, with its rational certainty and its universal applicability, the great bastion of his moral and intellectual faith.

In both of these arguments Plato leans to the rationalism of Parmenides, who first perceived clearly the theoretical form of science, and showed that it presupposes a unity of character in nature which is the object of science. But Plato combines the Eleatic insight with the insight of Heraclitus, and refuses to deny reality to motion, change, and diversity. These three thinkers, Heraclitus, Parmenides, and Plato, showed the limits within which all theoretical speculation about nature and man must move. Change and constancy, individual and universal character, motion and immobility must all be allowed reality.

The Platonic metaphysics implies a Platonic theory of knowledge, or *epistemology*. Plato's epistemology is a modified rationalism, not the stark rationalism of Parmenides. Reason, he taught, is the faculty which discloses to us, within the transient actualities apprehended by the senses, the true forms of things. Between ordinary sensation and scientific intuition there are intermediate stages in common sense, ordinary understanding, and artistic vision. Plato did not despise the senses. He made them a condition of all natural knowledge, providing the particular data which science must transmute; and the scientist in applying his rational formulas must, he said, "save the appearances," *i.e.* conform to the pattern of observable fact. With certain reservations, it would be possible to present contemporary physical science—which remains our most developed, systematic, and universal science of nature—as the exemplification of Plato's doctrine concerning human knowledge and the ultimate structure of nature.

This brings us to our concluding topic, namely the limitations of this Platonic conception of nature and knowledge. In the writer's opinion, most of the criticisms which from the time of Aristotle have been brought against this conception have either misinterpreted Plato, or failed to refute his essential teaching. Conclusive evidence against the Platonic rationalism has appeared only in this twentieth century; and even this evidence might be turned aside, if it were desirable to turn it aside. It might still be argued, that is to say, that natural science carries into all of its analysis—for example, in its principle of the conservation of energy—certain presuppositions, especially of a mathematical sort, which seem necessary to thought and which nature everywhere respects. Once this conclusion is reached, one might establish upon it the whole Platonic system.

There is, however, important evidence against Platonism, in a weakness which is internal to the system itself. It lies in the unintelligibility of the relationship between the two elements, Form and matter. How does the Form of nature, either in its unity or in the many specific forms in which it is visibly manifested in nature, come into conjunction with the shifting, incorrigibly heterogeneous matter which makes Form manifest and existent? Theoretical science necessarily understands individual things and particular events as "instances" of electrons or atoms, as "instances" of copper or carbon, as exemplifications of this physical process or that biological type. Doubtless, individual things do manifest such general characters; and we are practically justified in understanding particular events as

instances of general laws or specific processes, since this is the
only way we can initially understand them. But why do individuals so conform? What is our explanation of this deference
of particular events to universal norms or general forms?

Again and again in his writings Plato takes up this problem,
only to let it fall again unsolved. There is no solution, he concludes, to this mystery upon which all theoretical knowledge
and all intelligent conduct is established. Nor, we know after
two thousand years of meditation upon this problem, is any
solution possible so long as we identify knowledge, as did
Plato, with a purely theoretical science or a purely theoretical
philosophy. We can say with Plato that things "participate"
somehow in general forms; but how they do so, whether the
general form molds the individual thing or the individual thing
pursues the general form, we cannot say. Only ask this question and inquiry is balked, reason is stopped in its tracks.

But this core of opaque unintelligibility at the very heart of
the Platonic system has serious consequences. We do not get
natural science simply out of mathematical axioms and their
applications. To apply mathematics we must have prepared
the way for it by an initial analysis of observable fact, in which
we distinguish by means of qualitative differences certain
types of things or processes. How can we be sure that the
types we distinguish are the real forms, the authentic "species"
of physical or organic nature? The Platonic rationalism presupposes, we see, a kind of foreknowledge of the "real" constitution of nature, prior to all experience of the individual
constituents of nature and their behavior. This implication
Plato duly recognized in his doctrine of reminiscence. Somehow, he suggested, we must bring with us, perhaps from an
earlier existence, our infallible insight into the true forms of
nature. Science is not a discovery, but only a rediscovery in
particular situations of a cosmic structure the knowledge of
which is given to us with intelligence itself.

Thus Plato did not avoid, in the last resort, certain errors

which science had arisen to bring to an end. The pioneers of
science proposed to go to observable nature for their understanding of the world and man, and in this way to make themselves independent of earlier opinion, often erroneous and
superstitious. But if Plato is right, the most that science can
do is to confirm, in newly observed nature, a rational knowledge which has eternally invested the mind. Just observe the
implication of this Platonic rationalism, which ascribes to the
reason an intuition of the eternal and universal structure of
being! Once this reason has truly spoken, its dictum must stand
forever as authoritative truth! Thus Plato is the chief propagator of a dogmatic rationalism which has never, even after six
centuries of criticism, been wholly eliminated from western
thought. This dogmatism appears occasionally in Plato's writings, in a harsh authoritarianism which is foreign to his essentially genial and generous nature. But its most deplorable consequence was to give to the results of Greek science, as they
existed in Plato's day or a little later, an absolute authority
which discouraged and even prohibited further scientific progress. What reason had once discerned, it was concluded, could
never be denied. Thus Plato, hoping to justify the faith of
theoretical science in an intelligible Form of nature, also helped
to fixate fourth-century Greek science into a dogma which
was to imprison thought for two thousand years. Yet this
rationalistic dogmatism which issued from Plato was a necessary deduction from the assumption, common to all Greek and
much modern thought, that theoretical knowledge alone and
of itself constitutes our whole natural knowledge.

To sum up, then, our too brief study of the consummatory
thought of Greece, and of that immortal mind which has shaped
all later political and intellectual development: Plato, following Socrates, established in more explicit language and in
sharper conception the central Greek insight into the constitutional forms of human society and universal nature. Justice,
he showed, is the political form which constitutes the func-

tional mechanism of society, and which appears as a balance or proportion sustained amongst the parts of society. It is within this constitutional form that must proceed all of the life of society, if society is to remain healthy and not decay nor rupture. Further, this constitutional form appears on a larger scale as the constitution of the cosmos itself, in a functional mechanism which preserves the cosmic economy by stabilizing, "in the fixed order of time," the species of nature and their reciprocal dependence. This cosmic constitution is revealed to the human reason as a knowledge of universal Form, which allows man to pursue a theoretical science, discovering and defining that Form in its specific manifestations and its causal sequences. Finally, we found a crucial inadequacy in Plato's thought, the consequence of which is an inescapable dogmatism. Plato's error, we shall discover at the close of our review of modern philosophy, was to fail to distinguish the forms of society and science with sufficient rigor from the content which is conditioned by those forms. He did not distinguish the political constitution from the changing body of custom and law; and he did not distinguish theoretical form from the changing content of specific hypothesis. He did not discover, in short, a cosmic law which lies beyond the specific processes of nature. But this is to anticipate.

There was another Plato, whose aesthetic and religious insight always impelled, yet could never completely contain itself within, the scientific studies of this supreme Greek intellect. This other Plato occasionally took the pen from the scientist's fingers, and adjoined to the rigorous conceptual analysis a parable or myth, using artistic or religious symbolism to suggest a vision that intellect could approach but not communicate. The myths of Plato may have preserved some of the imaginative conceptions used in the Pythagorean cult or in the mystery-religions. They treat of the immortality of the individual soul, of the day of judgment in which each individual life is weighed and assigned a new career appropriate to the desire it has pursued in the life just past, and of the divine hunger of man for redemption from a world that is shadow and death. These parables, probably far more than we suspect, supported and propagated the intellectual teaching of Plato, adding to the latter a religious significance it might not otherwise seem to possess. It was Plato the artist who carried Plato the mathematical realist down the ages. The myths of Plato became part of the religious development of the later centuries of antiquity, and prepared the way for Christianity. They point, indeed, to the direction of thought which modern man would follow in order to transcend the science of Greece; and they show us that Plato could define forever the limits of the classical Greek mind only because he had himself, in incommunicable ways, already passed beyond those limits. It is not an accident that Plato's Academy became later a stronghold of Greek skepticism. Intelligence is more, he knew, than its explicit statement. Intelligence is a faith that goes beyond the known to discover the yet unknown. Even where we think to leave Plato, he is with us still. If he could return today he would observe with respect and delight the achievement of modern thought, which begins to make explicit the truth which he obscurely knew, but which he could intimate only in a parable and apply only in a utopian fantasy.

Notes for Further Reading

It is difficult to make a selection from the embarrassingly rich literature on Plato and Platonism. The histories of Greek philosophy by Gomperz and Zeller contain good accounts of Plato. Available are monographs by Taylor, Ritter, Demos, and others.

Plato's later dialogues are our best clue to his thought, but they are not easy reading. The *Parmenides* is most important for its reserved acceptance of the so-called "theory of ideas," the doctrine central to Platonism. The *Theatetus*, the *Philebus*, and the *Sophist* also concern themselves with this doctrine. The *Timaeus* is impor-

tant for its influence on medieval thought, and for its conception of
the relation of eternal form to moving existence.

The *Republic*, whether we attribute its teaching to Socrates or
to Plato, remains the supreme Greek classic and the best introduction to Plato himself. The *Epistles*, especially the seventh, shed light
on Plato's political activity.

1. *The Dialogues of Plato*, trans. B. Jowett. New York, Random
   House, Inc., 1937.
2. Field, G. C., *Plato and His Contemporaries*. New York, E. P.
   Dutton and Company, Inc., 1930.
3. Taylor, A. E., *Plato*. New York, Dial Press, Inc., 1936.
4. Ritter, C. *The Essence of Plato's Philosophy*, trans. A. Alles.
   New York, Dial Press, Inc., 1933.
5. Gomperz, Th., *Greek Thinkers*, trans. G. G. Berry. London,
   J. Murray, 1912, Vols. II, III.
6. Zeller, Ed., *Outlines of the History of Greek Philosophy*, trans.
   L. R. Palmer, New York, Henry Holt and Company, 1931,
   Part II, Chap. III.
7. Woodbridge, F. J. E., *The Son of Apollo*. Boston, Houghton,
   Mifflin Company, 1929.
8. Demos, R., *The Philosophy of Plato*. New York, Charles Scribner's Sons, 1939.
9. Post, L. A., *Thirteen Epistles of Plato*. London and New York,
   Oxford University Press, 1925.

7   THE SCIENCE OF ARISTOTLE

THE DUALISM OF ETERNAL FORM AND SHIFTING matter, by which Plato synthesized and illuminated earlier Greek science, was destined to be the largest tradition of western thought for more than two thousand years; but this dualistic metaphysic, so long preserved and so authoritative, was later conceived in the form given to it by Aristotle rather than in the original Platonic version. Only recently has scholarship begun to emancipate itself from an Aristotelian interpretation of Plato's teaching; and in attempting to present the science of Aristotle in sharp distinction from that of his great predecessor, we enter a controversial zone in which almost any statement is subject to correction. Yet it is indispensable, whatever the difficulties, to distinguish these two most influential thinkers of Greek antiquity, and come to some definite estimate of their relationship. It has long been a truism that Plato and Aristotle represent, and consequently appeal to, almost diametrically opposite temperaments and habits of mind; yet the sources or consequences of this difference, which presumably lie in their respective philosophies, have never been satisfactorily clarified. An obstacle to clarification is that Aristotle first accepted the Academic doctrine, at least in its major features, but then attempted to make it the vehicle of a totally different conception of nature; and with Plato Aristotelianized, and Aristotle Platonized, it becomes well-nigh impossible to demarcate clearly the two thinkers.

Aristotle entered Plato's Academy at the age of eighteen. He came from Macedon, the rising monarchy to the north, where his father was court physician; and he resided at the Academy no less than twenty years. It is astonishing, therefore, to find in Aristotle's many allusions to Plato only what might have been derived from Plato's published writings, as we know them today, and little reference to that intimate esoteric teaching which Plato held to be incommunicable in books. Aristotle does record, it is true, a public lecture given by Plato on the subject of the Good; but he tells us only that Plato became very mathematical, mystifying his audience. Aristotle's statements about Plato are those of a hostile, unsympathetic, and not too well-informed critic. The twenty years he spent at the Academy covered the last years of Plato's long life, when the aged thinker may well have retired from active teaching, and been immersed in public affairs.

We should emphasize perhaps the early training of these two men, which inspired totally different interests and approaches to science. Plato was by birth a free and aristocratic Greek citizen, whose life and thought were dominated by his political purpose, which was the redemption of the city-state, and whose scientific training was in the mathematical tradition of Socrates, the Eleatics, and the Pythagoreans. Aristotle was a Macedonian subject who spent most of his life as an alien resident of Greek cities, whose admiration of the city-state was that of a disinterested outsider and beneficiary, and whose earliest scientific training was biological, with probably some knowledge of atomistic and Milesian theory. Aristotle, moreover, came to Athens when that city had definitely failed in its struggle for power, and when the city-states were overshadowed by the rising monarchy to the north. Libertarian sentiment, we may believe, became somewhat academic and less than realistic when the Greeks had lost confidence and were losing interest in their political ideals. It is not difficult, therefore, to understand and distinguish the two men temperamentally, in the light of these different contexts which produced them. What is difficult is to state the whole consequence of this temperamental difference in their theoretical systems and their methods.

Aristotle has usually been regarded as the more scientific and empirical, Plato as the more mystical and rationalistic of the two thinkers. The distinction is undeniable, yet it is misleading. Aristotle certainly lacked the mystical tendency which we observed in Plato; yet the intellectual difference between the two men was that which still divides the mathematical physicist from the biological naturalist, and one would hardly say that mathematical physics is less scientific, or even less empirical and observant, than is botany or zoology. The strongest current of modern empirical science has centered itself in mathematical physics and astronomy. The difference between the Platonic and Aristotelian habits of mind would seem to fall within science, and not to distinguish the scientist from the nonscientist.

There is no doubt that Aristotle's whole thought and method were dominantly directed by his major scientific interest, which lay in biology. This was probably instilled very early by his physician-father, and it bred in him a dislike and distrust of mathematical science. But Aristotle's interest in the living organism was also a positive and productive force, as well as an obstacle to his appreciation of the Platonic and Pythagorean science. It provided the central and controlling concept, namely the concept of development, of all his thought; and his criticism of mathematical science was justified, in that such science did not obviously assist the study and understanding of organic nature. But Aristotle's great error, initiating centuries of confusion, was to think that the Platonic science could be converted by a simple modification into a nonmathematical system adapted to his own interest and method.

What we do mean by a *development*? A development is a temporal change having a beginning and an end. It is a unit of process, a real unit of change. Secondly, it is a recognizable and describable process, one that recurs again and again at different times and places. And thirdly, it is a cumulative or directed process, one which points throughout its course to a certain definable goal or terminus. In organic nature developments are everywhere evident and often striking. Every living creature proceeds through such a development from its inception to its maturity. Those organisms which pass through one and the same type of development we classify as a *species*. Thus the diverse species of organic nature indicate the different sorts of organic development known to us. Today we do not usually speak of species when studying physical, geological, or astronomical fact, because we conceive physical nature to be inorganic. But Aristotle wished to establish his whole science upon organic concepts such as development, species, etc.; and he accordingly applied the concepts in every field, to physical as well as to organic phenomena.

It is by comparing individual animals and plants, in their visible anatomies and developmental processes, that we classify them into species. We may then compare these species, placing those which are most like each other in groups which we call *genera* (plural of *genus*). We can then compare genera, to reach higher "orders," "families," "kingdoms." The animal and vegetable "kingdoms" have been very exhaustively classified in this way. The complete classification has the appearance of a genealogical tree, which Darwin showed it literally to be, because the observable similarities among animals and plants, especially their similarities of development, are clues to their evolutionary origins. But imagine this specific and generic classification extended over all of nature, to cover also inorganic nature! Each organic and inorganic thing will now be understood and defined as the specimen of some species; this species will be a member of some genus, this genus a member of some higher or more inclusive genus, and so on. Ultimately we must reach a highest genus; and from this summit we can then look back and down upon descending tiers of higher and lower genera, arriving again finally at the species, made up of individual but specifically similar animals, plants, or other things. This, broadly speaking, is the concept of nature and of science which Aristotle advocates. *This hierarchy of specific and generic forms he conceives to constitute the fixed and eternal structure of nature.* Change occurs only on the ground level of individual being, in which the eternal structure is materialized in visible things.

Aristotle saw, correctly we should say, that the crucial level in this hierarchical structure of forms, that which determines the whole superstructure, is the level of specific forms. An error in our distinction of species will be carried into all our classification of genera; and the distinction of species, moreover, must precede all further classification. He therefore ascribed to specific forms a special importance and reality; and he held up the definition and differentiation of species as the primary task of the scientist. We might say that Aristotle compromised between Plato and the atomists. He broke up the universal Form of Plato into this plurality of specific forms; but these are still general forms, standing above the ground floor of individual things or atoms.

It has not been sufficiently remarked how far Aristotle departed here from the major tradition of Greek science, initiated by the Milesians and consummated in Plato, all of whom subscribed to the concept of a universal Form or natural law. The Aristotelian view, which gives primacy to the specific forms of nature, is an important and defensible alternative to the concept of universal law. It may turn out to be a better and truer view—in any case, it is a conception supported by all our knowledge of organic nature, the study of which can never overlook specific differences. It is a fact that the science of living organisms cannot ignore the specific forms of nature.

But we know today that this study of the specific forms of organic nature leads us onward to the concept of evolution, and to an evolutionary science discovering the origins and mutations of the species of life. Return for a moment to the concept of development, which is the generative idea in Aristotle's science, and try to universalize this concept! A development is a directed succession of stages a b c d, d being regarded as the definitive stage towards which a, b, and c are directed. To universalize this concept, you must conceive of the universe in its entirety, and in its whole history, as a vast directed advance A B C D. You must conceive, that is to say, of a single vast universal evolution, advanced by every occurrence that is or was or will be. Such a conception is impossible, you may say, since every evolution requires a context or environment conditioning it and causally explaining it. The universe as an entirety cannot evolve, since by definition it has no external context which might condition its evolution. It may be argued that universal evolution *is* conceivable; but this is irrelevant to our topic, which is the science of Aristotle. Aristotle did not only reject the notion of a universal evolution, he rejected the hypothesis of an evolution even of species. He allows, that is to say, only individuals to develop; and he allows them to develop only within the limits of their specific forms. Any individual aberration from the normal line of development, or from the fixed form and behavior characteristic of the species, is for him an accident devoid of scientific significance, and defying explanation. Aristotle's controlling conception is that of a world composed of a large number of eternal and immutable species, made up of successive individuals which can only be understood as instances or specimens of these species; and so to understand things, allocating them to species and defining these species, he took to be the sum of science.

In strictness, this Aristotelian conception would multiply the all-governing Form of Plato into as many absolute forms as there are species; and in his very theological astronomy Aristotle is apparently ready to accept this implication. There would now be no reason, however, for any relation among species; and it is impossible to deny all significance to the relations which tie the vegetable and animal species into higher genera and orders. The science of Aristotle is therefore confused by two incompatible tendencies, one of which would allow ultimacy and causal effectiveness only to specific forms, whereas the other would explain the specific forms more Platonically as the constituent parts of a universal design and as the agents of a universal Form. We can sympathize with Aristotle's purpose, if this was to allow real efficacy and importance to individual being as well as to universal Being or Form; but this purpose was defeated by his ascription of fixity and ultimacy to specific forms, which would confine and determine individual existence no less effectively, and more narrowly, than would universal Form. Plato's conception of Form is quite compatible with the hypothesis of an evolution of species engineered by individual mutations, although there is nothing in Plato's writings to suggest that he entertained this hypothesis. The above discussion may serve to make clear how seriously, and in what way, the modern hypothesis of evolution must affect our estimate of Greek science and philosophy.

Aristotle wished to modify the Platonic science so as to allow a greater role to specific forms. Plato's insuperable problem, we remember, was the relation of universal Form to transient and shifting existence. Aristotle believed, not without some reason, that his doctrine of specific development pointed to a solution of this problem. In the Platonic science the first principles of natural occurrence were prescribed by a purely rational knowledge, namely mathematical theory. Reason provided an abstract knowledge of universal principles, which the senses then again discovered in particular instances. But Aristotle can insist that the specific forms of nature are apparent to the eye, even as they inform individual things. We actually see dog or cat, and immediately recognize the individual as a member of its species, although reasoning may be required to reach a satisfactory definition of the species. In this doctrine Aristotle is more empirical than Plato, in that he enlarges the role of sense-observation in science. Aristotle also believed, however, that the problem of the relation of form to matter disappeared in his mode of explanation. He held that the specific form appears in the development of the individual thing; and this would mean that specific forms are already resident in the matter which is informed by them. Aristotle, we earlier mentioned, believed his concept of substance, by which he meant this union of form and matter in existent things, to be his greatest contribution to science; and we must examine this teaching more closely.

The specific forms of nature, he says, although they are immutable and eternal, do not exist apart from the things they inform. They are not transcendent, like the Form of Plato, but have their whole being within the existent and material world. Form exists only in some material realization; and matter exists only in some specifically organized form. This would mean that the process of development is really the development of matter into some specific form; and this would seem to require the assumption of as many sorts of matter as there are specific forms or species. Aristotle is moving towards a materialistic philosophy in which form would be only the complete manifestation of matter. He accepts this implication when he says that matter is *potential* of form, form being the realization of these potentialities, or potencies, of matter. Yet he never relinquishes the Platonic view, which gave to form a being in its own right, and which saw in matter only the material which is shaped by form. He swings between, or overlaps, the opposed views of "formism" and materialism. Thus his science remains ambiguous and inconsistent, and cannot be brought into logical unity. This lack of coherence in Aristotle should perhaps be excused, if it arose from a desire to do justice to the facts.

Matter, Aristotle says, is the principle of individuation in nature. It is what gives to the general specific forms their additional character as living forces within individual things. Such individuation of specific form results in *substances*. Substances are always individuals, identical with nothing else; yet they are also the manifestants of some general and specific character, *i.e.* of form. Aristotle is led, therefore, to postulate two very different sorts of causation. On the one hand are *material* causes, namely the effective characters which inhere in matter as such, and which limit and determine what matter may become; and on the other hand are *formal* causes due to the efficacy of specific forms upon or in matter. Aristotle further subdivides formal causes into efficient, formal, and final causes. The *efficient* cause is what starts a body of matter upon its specific development. The *formal* cause is the specific form as it directs this development. The *final* cause is the goal, the specific form in its full realization, which terminates the development.

The value of this complicated doctrine was its closeness to common sense. It distinguished the various ways in which men are wont to use the concept of cause. Its defect was its vagueness and ambiguity. The efficient, formal, and final causes seem to be only different stages in the working of the specific form; and since this working of specific form in matter may also be regarded as only the realization by matter of its own potentiality, all four causes threaten to collapse into one, which may be called material or formal as we please. This would mean, however, that the development of a material substance is wholly self-caused, which is to say uncaused. Modern science rejects this ambiguous Aristotelian concept of causation. In its place it puts the view that all causes are particular causes (*i.e.* not formal), at least two particular causes being required to bring about a particular change. Thus it is stated that a body will change its velocity only if some other body exerts a force upon it. Aristotle's doctrine, it was finally perceived, really precludes and defeats causal analysis. A "specific form" is initially just the similarity between individuals "of the same species"; and we cannot suppose that the similarity of a thing with other things is what determines its behavior. A pup does not develop into a dog because there are other pups, similarly developing into dogs. If this were the case, the death of all other pups would require the death of this pup. However, it remains true that we *discover* the particular causes of natural occurrence by taking note of such similarities. If we want to know the particular causes of a particular pup's death, we look around for other instances of animal mortality, similar to and illuminative of this instance. This suggests that there is some mysterious connection between the two large facts of similarity and causation in nature. We may not discuss the nature of this connection here, since our purpose is only to show how Aristotle confused the concept of causation.

These very general doctrines concerning substance, potentiality, development, causation, and the relation of form to matter are presented by Aristotle in an introductory work which he entitled "first philosophy." We will understand the doctrines better by noting Aristotle's application of them in special fields; but before we turn to these special applications we should take note of Aristotle's *logic*, which in its prescription of the method to be used in all scientific research constituted a most general application of his metaphysical teaching or "first philosophy." Aristotle has often been called "the founder of logic," presumably because his logical treatises were long regarded as the definitive manual of this study, which they remained until the close of the nineteenth century. The Eleatics who followed Parmenides have probably more title to the fame of having originated logic; but Aristotle systematized logical study, and gave to it a form peculiarly his own, which it was long to retain.

The chief doctrines of Aristotle's logic are those of definition, the syllogism, and the categories. An adequate *definition*, he said, defines a species. It states the next higher class, the proximate genus to which the species belongs, together with the differentia, or distinguishing characters, which mark that species off from others of the same genus. The student of botany is very familiar with this type of definition, which provides the basis of botanical nomenclature. For example, the plant *rosa rugosa* belongs to the genus *rosa*, and it is distinguished from other species of rose by the characters connoted by the term *rugosa*.

The *syllogism* is a set of three propositions, the first two of which are premises, the third being the conclusion necessitated by those premises. For example: (1) all felines are mammals, all cats are felines, so all cats are mammals; (2) no mammals live in the sea, all whales live in the sea, so no whale is a mammal. These are valid syllogisms. They are called "valid" because the conclusions follow necessarily from the premises. The conclusion of the second syllogism happens to be false; but it is nevertheless a valid conclusion, its falsity arising from the false premise, "no mammals live in the sea." Logic allows us to abstract from questions of truth and untruth, and to consider only the *formal* properties of sentences. Formal properties are appealed to in all argument and are used in all analysis. Logic is essentially a study of implication. It is best studied by means of special symbols allowing us to neglect the special content of sentences, and to consider only their forms. Thus the first syllogism above is of the form: all S is M, all M is P, so all S is P. This syllogism remains valid whatever values we give to S, M, and P. We might even say: all berbs are slampions, all slampions are prooters, so all berbs are prooters. This sequence is meaningless until we provide significant meanings for the three terms; but its form is that of a valid syllogism. The second syllogism may be symbolized: All S is M, no P is M, so no S is P. Aristotle regarded the first type of syllogism, that of the form: All S is M, all M is P, so all S is P, as the correct scientific form of argument or exposition, to which all the other forms are auxiliary. The only reason for preferring this type would seem to be its conformity with the doctrine of definition. If the members of a group S belong to a certain species M, and the species M belongs to the genus P, then the conclusion of the syllogism will state that the group S belongs to the genus P. The letters S and P are chosen to indicate respectively the Subject and the Predicate of the conclusion; and M indicates the Middle term, which by appearing twice, once in each premise, relates the premises to each other. Aristotelian logic is essentially an exhaustive survey of the syllogisms which arise when we abide by certain formal requirements, limiting us to sentences of the forms: All S is M, no S is M, some S is M, some S is not M. These syllogisms can then be classed as valid or invalid, according as the conclusion is or is not required by the premises.

The third doctrine is that of the *categories*. Aristotle held that all sentences can be classified into eight or perhaps ten sorts of sentence, according as to whether they predicate of some subject its substance, its quantity, its quality, its position in space or time, its action, its exposure to action, etc. The categories would seem to indicate the ways in which the verb *to be* was used in the Greek language (this *is* a cat, here *are* fourteen, this *is* black, it *is* on the table, etc.). The doctrines of definition and of the syllogism support one another; but the doctrine of the categories seems to be independent, and to presuppose a different conception of nature and scientific method.

The Aristotelian logic remained authoritative until a generation ago, and it still has its adherents. Most contemporary logicians regard it as a very limited, wooden, and artificial exposition of the formal properties of language. It is not true, they say, that we need think, or ordinarily do think, in these stilted forms: All *S* is *M*, etc. Logic must be as flexible and various as is meaningful language. If mathematics has mightily developed since antiquity, why should logic not also develop? As a matter of fact, modern symbolic logic grew out of a study of the logical properties of mathematical sentences and formulas. This study showed that mathematics, and not the inadequate logic of Aristotle, has really provided the logical instrument of modern science.

Those who still hold the Aristotelian logic to be adequate do so presumably because they wish to preserve the conceptual limitations which the Aristotelian logic reflected and imposed. They remain faithful to certain metaphysical preconceptions, similar or identical with those which governed Aristotle when he constructed and enforced his logic. We have seen how the doctrines of definition and of the syllogism, as prescribed by Aristotle, presupposed and implemented the Aristotelian science, with its dominating concern for specific and generic forms. It is the view of many contemporary students of philosophy that modern logic is a valuable aid to the emancipation of thought from such traditional limitations. Aristotle was quite right when he presented logic as an *organon, i.e.* a scientific instrument or methodology. It is all the more important, accordingly, that the method which is prescribed by logic should be as powerful, and as little confined by prejudice and intellectual prepossession, as is humanly possible. Limitations of logic confine speech and thought.

Let us turn now to some of Aristotle's special studies, since these at once illustrate the method and reveal the man. The method was most successful, as we should expect, in the field of biology. Aristotle shows profound discernment of organic process and great knowledge of organic morphology. He remains one of the greatest biologists of all time. Most remarkable were his studies of embryonic development. His descriptions of living activity are dynamic and functional, since they always illustrate his basic concept of organic deveiopment. He distinguished some organic functions as vegetative, others as animal because they involve locomotion and sensaton. In man, he tells us, the vegetative functions support the locomotive and sensitive animal functions, which in turn support the intellectual functions distinguishing man from his fellow creatures. Aristotle thinks of the development of the vegetative, animal, and intellectual functions as resulting from three distinct potencies. The matter which enters into living organisms, he says, is of a special sort, being composed of the four material elements (earth, air, water, fire) together with a portion of a special sort of matter, the quintessence, which otherwise appears only in celestial bodies. Thus Aristotle explicitly postulates at least three sorts of matter. There is the ordinary terrestrial matter which we should call inorganic; there is the celestial quintessence; and then there is organic matter, blended of these two.

Aristotle's biology is basic to his psychological, ethical, and political studies. We remember Plato's psychology, which distinguished in human individuals three sorts of response to three successively larger environments: The response to the immediate environment stimulates the productive and procreative functions, the response to the state stimulates the social and political functions, and the response to the universe stimulates those scientific and religious interests which are the prerequisite, Plato believed, of true statesmanship. Aristotle seems initially to accept this psychology. In his biology he defined man as "the animal endowed with reason," *i.e.* the species which adds to the vegetative and animal faculties that of reasoning; and when he comes to discuss man further, he defines him as "the political animal," which would imply that he, like Plato, saw in man's political activity his distinctive character. Further, Aristotle presents ethics, the inquiry into what is right and wrong in human behavior, as only a part of the larger study of man which is political theory. We are accordingly surprised to find in Aristotle little appreciation of the moral responsibility which inheres in citizenship.

Aristotle's ethical writings were apparently inscribed at different periods of his life. One essay, thought to be written quite early, is submissively Platonic; but the major treatises contain two or three distinct theories which show little Platonic influence. One theory formulates the familiar Greek ethics of moderation, the doctrine of the Golden Mean, which advocates the maintenance of a balance between spendthrift and miserly character, cowardice and recklessness, and other extremes of behavior. This is a good empirical starting point for ethics; but since it presupposes a prior and correct estimate of what is extreme, and consequently of what is moderate, it does not provide a basis for estimating values. Socrates proceeded from this starting point to the conception of a whole or single virtue, a justice or righteousness which is the perception of the eternal and whole design of life.

A second theory proposes the pursuit of what is "noble and elevated" in human behavior, this character being recognizable as a poise maintained under all or most conditions. Perhaps this is not a separate theory, but only another way of putting the doctrine of the Golden Mean. But the theory which is most characteristic of Aristotle, in that it follows from his biology and psychology and seems to have been incorporated in his own practice, is that which made scientific research the essential and characteristic activity of man, and which set forth the conditions prerequisite to this pursuit of scientific knowledge. These conditions include domestic comfort, wife, family, friends, and a secure estate managed by slaves. Given, that is to say, complete and secure satisfaction of his vegetative and animal needs, the individual has leisure for the scientific studies in which he realizes his human and intellectual potency. This is a very comfortable doctrine; but one does not find, on the whole, that the provision of domestic bliss and economic security suffices to convert an individual into an ardent seeker

after scientific truth. Science, like art, has been as creative in
the garret or tenement as in the manor or mansion. Aristotle's
ethics are undeniably egoistic. They teach that the first duty
of a man is the fullest realization of his individual powers; and
they do not say that such realization involves the fullest responsibility of the human individual for his fellows. Human
affection, in Aristotle's teaching, is limited to family affection
and personal friendship. About friendship Aristotle writes
enthusiastically and convincingly.

After this ethical introduction we are not surprised to find in
Aristotle's political treatises a certain obliviousness to the moral
foundations of government, which lie in the assumption by the
individual of moral responsibility to and for his fellows. The
Politics of Aristotle initiates an exhaustive study and an impartial estimate of the diverse sorts of governments that are to
be found in the world. Aristotle collected "constitutions" much
as he collected specimens of botanical and geological species;
but his classification of types of government is less successful
than his classification of species, being confused by what
the logician calls a "cross-division." On the one hand he distinguishes states according to whether they are ruled by one
individual (monarchy), by a few (aristocracy), or by many
(democracy). On the other hand he distinguishes between
states as good or bad. He accordingly finds both good and bad
versions of all three types of state, the bad versions being respectively tyranny, oligarchy, and demagoguery or mob-rule.
A Platonic note enters when Aristotle finds good states to be
those which are subject to constitutional limitations, whatever
their forms; but he does not show why constitutionality is good.
He says that the best state is the good and constitutional
monarchy, and that tyranny, which is unconstitutional autocracy, is the worst state. Democracy is not so good as monarchy,
but demagoguery is not so bad as tyranny. Still another leading
idea in Aristotle's analysis conceives the best form of the state
to be that most appropriate to prevailing conditions; and in

line with this thought he sometimes suggests that a mixed type of government, including elements of monarchy, aristocracy, and democracy, is best adapted to survive and prosper, because each element will contribute its function yet hold the others in check.

It is difficult to pass judgment upon Aristotle's *Politics*, partly because no clear political theory is presented. Aristotle is often called "the founder of political science." If by "political science" we mean a study which merely collects, compares, and analyzes the diverse types of government which have appeared among men, without care for the deeper issues and principles of politics, then Aristotle has claim to this title. This would make political science, however, only a branch of anthropology. Aristotle was a wide and shrewd observer of the political history of his time; and his political treatises are full of penetrating observations, with clever and sometimes unscrupulous suggestions as to their use. Thus his *Politics* was a model for the immoral political realism of Machiavelli; yet it also propagated respect for constitutional government, and it suggested, in its praise of mixed government, the notion of a limitation of governing power. Compared with Plato's *Republic*, the *Politics* of Aristotle is a confused, irresolute, even a rather trivial work, the chief virtue of which, perhaps, was to familiarize later generations with the idea of political theory. But we view these defects more sympathically when we remember that Aristotle was virtually a man without a country, who spent most of his life as a resident in alien cities, who impersonally admired the cultural achievement of the Greek city-state, yet who also perceived the large political and economic movement which overwhelmed and submerged the Greek cities. It says a great deal for Aristotle that although he was tutor for some years to the prince who became Alexander the Great, the "conqueror of the world," he always preserved his formal admiration of Greek liberty, and continued to register hatred of tyrannical government.

We have not yet considered Aristotle's physical science, where the limitations of his method are most apparent. Modern science has not recognized species in physical nature; and Aristotle's insistence upon finding them there takes him to strange conclusions. He fell back upon the popular view, rejected at least in principle by the earlier scientists, that the character of celestial nature is altogether different and more perfect than that of earthly nature. This allowed him to postulate new and different principles in his explanation of celestial processes. For example, he calls upon a very special sort of matter, the quintessence, which is described as being peculiarly amenable to form, in order to explain the remarkable regularity of the movements of sun and stars; and he supposes that in the celestial realm species are normally constituted of but one individual member. This is really to confess the inapplicability of the Aristotelian science to astronomical phenomena. Finally, the process of development becomes, in all of its physical realizations, only a movement of things in space, to or from their "proper" places in the cosmos. All motion is said to derive ultimately from the original circular motion which we perceive in the "sphere" of fixed stars. This motion is caused by God, who by his transcendent yet immobile Being outside of the sphere stimulates its rotation. Circular motion is said to be most perfect because it is most like immobility, and does not involve linear displacement. This perfect motion is transferred with increasing irregularity and imperfection to interior spheres, the innermost of which is that of the moon's orbit. Aristotle thinks of the heavenly bodies as the visible conjunctions of these otherwise invisible "crystalline spheres." More than one sphere was usually required to explain the motion of a heavenly body. All in all, fifty-five spheres were called upon to explain the lunar, solar, planetary, and sidereal motions; and Aristotle spoke of the spheres as divinities, so that they constituted a pantheon of fifty-five gods.

Below the moon the circular celestial motion is broken up

into mere fragments, and we leave astronomy to study sub-
lunary nature. The four elements normally abide in their
proper places, a core of earth with envelopes of water, air,
and fire; but the celestial bodies influence terrestrial motions,
producing weather, stimulating growth, etc. As we noted, the
celestial "quintessence" is also needed to support terrestrial
organic developments. We should not believe that this Aristotelian astronomy and physics adequately represented the
science of that day. Some half century after Aristotle lived
Aristarchus of Samos, who used the mathematical methods of
the Pythagoreans and the Academy to reach, apparently on good
evidence, a true conception of the earth's movement about the
sun. But Aristotle's crude astrophysics won the day, and the
world had to wait seventeen centuries for Copernicus to revive
the solar-centric hypothesis, and bring to a close this geocentric
astronomy of Aristotle and Ptolemy.

How shall we estimate Aristotle and his science? We have
observed that his emphasis upon specific form and developmental process raised insoluble problems, multiplied meaningless verbal distinctions, and retarded physical science. Plato's
science was admirably clear in its pursuit of a single universal
pattern, summarized by mathematical theory and indicative of
the unity of nature in the worshipful economy of the Good.
Aristotle emphatically rejects mathematical method and transcendent Form, in order to bring form and matter closer together, and to show how rational knowledge only better ap-
preciates the visible characters of things. Is Aristotle able to
make good his criticism of Plato, or does he only introduce
confusion into what was clear? His doctrine involves the relativity of form and matter. In man, for example, the vegetative
activities provide matter for the realization of the animal activities, and these two activities together provide matter for the
realization of man's intellectual functions. But since these material conditions are present in all animals, why do not all
animals also think rationally and pursue scientific research?

Further, not only must there be as many sorts of matter as there are forms, but there must also be, one would conclude, a most basic or rudimentary matter out of which develop the most general forms. Nor does Aristotle escape the transcendentalism for which he so emphatically indicts Plato. Not only are his eternal specific forms really transcendent, inasmuch as one and the same specific form stimulates the development of a given species not only here and now, but always and everywhere throughout space and eternity; but all the motion of nature is finally attributed by Aristotle to the stimulating and effective presence of a God who is outside of the universe and no part of it. One might continue this indictment for many pages. One might show how Aristotle's science, steadily displacing better science, finally resulted in intellectual stagnation and a scientific coma which lasted until the pioneers of modern science returned to Plato for their method and inspiration, and so overcame the sterilities of Aristotelian thought. One might also point to the long struggle of modern scientists against an ever resurgent vitalism, vitalism being nothing else than a return to Aristotle's ascription of causal power to specific forms.

Yet after all this is said and done, we shall have to return to do justice to Aristotle, for three reasons. In the first place, there are indeed natural species, they do exist, and we cannot study nature without full recognition of them. Physical science does not really, as it may seem to do, rest its whole theory upon mathematical axioms. It, too, needs concepts of natural types, which are really species although they are not so called. It requires its electrons, its atoms, its chemical elements, its organized and specific kinds of energy. Secondly, the study of organic species has led to the discernment of an evolution of species; and the hypothesis of evolution, since it cannot be confined to organic nature on this earth, must ultimately give to all of our science a new evolutionary and organic character. And thirdly, if Aristotle introduced confusion into the magnificently clear Platonic science, he did so not without cause; for that science rested upon a mystery, namely the mystery of the relation of individual being to universal Being, which involves the relation of particular fact to universal theory; and here modern science must side with Aristotle against Plato, while still rejecting that hypostatization of specific forms which in Aristotle was a confused and groping step toward the acknowledgment of individual potency. Modern science is established upon Aristotle's dictum that only individual being is substantial and real.

The reader is now excusably confused. We have just said: first, that modern science was initiated when men left Aristotle and returned to Plato, and secondly, that modern science has followed Aristotle in his rejection of Plato's universalism. We cannot remove this confusion here, but can only say that modern science itself has been and largely remains in this confusion. Modern science makes universal theory its chief objective, and thus does homage to Plato and to universal Form; yet it makes particular fact, or observed individual being, its whole criterion of truth; and herein it leans toward Aristotle. This raises a problem, an apparent contradiction, which later thought must elucidate and remove. But if we justify Aristotle's confused metaphysics, at least in respect to its intention to do justice to individual being, we may also be able to sympathize with his political and social teaching. Against the stark communism of Plato, with its identification of religious, moral, and political loyalty, Aristotle favored an uncertain, experimental, and rather casual attitude toward government. He vaguely felt, in spite of his lip service to the Platonic definition, that man is not only, nor perhaps most essentially, "a political animal." Here too we moderns, especially in America, have accepted both of these contradictory attitudes. With Plato we have risked our whole destiny and existence upon a political constitution; yet with Aristotle we know that government is a means to life and an agency of life, but not the end and purpose of life. This apparent contradiction too we must resolve.

Notes for Further Reading

The best and most scholarly rendering of Aristotle's works in English is the Oxford Translation, recently completed. The *Metaphysica* (Vol. VIII) and the logical treatises (Vol. I) present his basic philosophy. Volume IX comprises his ethical, Volume X his political treatises. The *De Anima* (in Vol. III) is epistemologically important. The *De Poetica*, aesthetic criticism dealing with tragedy, will be found in Volume XI.

There are earlier translations of many of the works. The student might do better to read first some studies of Aristotle by modern scholars.

1. *The Oxford Translation of Aristotle*, ed. W. D. Ross and J. A. Smith. London and New York, Oxford University Press, various dates.
2. Ross, W. D., *Aristotle*. New York, Charles Scribner's Sons, 1924.
3. Gomperz, Th., *Greek Thinkers*, trans. G. G. Berry. London, J. Murray, 1914, Vol. IV.
4. Mure, G. R. G., *Aristotle*. London and New York, Oxford University Press, 1932.
5. Jaeger, W. W., *Aristotle; Fundamentals of the History of his Development*, trans. R. Robinson. London and New York, Oxford University Press, 1934.
6. Taylor, A. E., *Aristotle*. A short summary. New York, Thomas Nelson and Sons, 1943.
7. Zeller, Ed., *Outlines of the History of Greek Philosophy*, trans. L. R. Palmer. New York, Henry Holt and Company, 1931, Part II, Chap. IV.

8   HELLENISTIC PHILOSOPHY

WE ARE ACCUSTOMED TO THINK OF THE CENTURIES following Aristotle as a long decline, in which Greek art, literature, and science flattened out into something stereotyped and mediocre. It is true that the period of great intellectual achievement ends with Aristotle; yet these later centuries saw the spread and the appropriation by a large public of the earlier insights. Aristotle himself in his Lyceum furthered this transition from the high and intensive cultivation of science by a few to its broad, more matter of fact acceptance by the many. He popularized science, making it a business of common sense, deprecating esoteric, otherworldly, and difficult doctrines, and dividing science up into easily digestible portions. We distinguish earlier classical Greece as *Hellenic* from these later *Hellenistic* centuries, when Greek culture spread and merged with Syrian, Egyptian, Persian, and other traditions. Aristotle was already somewhat Hellenistic. He looked at the classical Greek forms from outside, acknowledging them with admiration, but with little sense of their origins in living culture.

The thought of the later period lacks realism. Historians have sometimes designated these centuries "the moral period," in order to distinguish them from the earlier "scientific period."

This nomenclature is misleading, not to say erroneous, in that the earlier period was often more rigorous and puritanical in its moral ideal. We might say, perhaps, that the later period pursued philosophy for its emotional inspiration, without scientific and moral concern for the truthful description of fact. The source of this shift of interest, in the writer's opinion, is to be found in the changed political condition of Greece. Hellenic Greece was free and self-governing; its moral and intellectual life found realistic expression in political activities, and it therefore required a realistic science. But later Greece was politically subject, first to Macedon and then to Rome; and it accordingly cultivated a "reason" which elevated the individual as the citizen of a universal and divine polity, but which encouraged him to be indifferent to the social and political actualities about him. The living cord of liberty which had tied the intellectual life of Greece to actuality had been cut; and the Greek intellect increasingly gave itself to a dream.

Nothing illustrates this movement to unrealism better than the uncritical homage brought to Socrates in those later centuries. Socrates had in all things tried to be a man, claiming no more than man might claim, dismissing the wisdom attributed to him as only his awareness of its lack; but the later centuries made of Socrates a god, attributing to him faculties beyond the range of common man. Further, Socrates had died to save the faith of the Greeks in their political institutions, *i.e.* in the civic law; but these later centuries made Socrates the martyr of the law, and the patron saint of a moral idealism that looked away from human government to a divine justice in the skies. So, for many centuries, men sought a moral salvation in no way related to government, and became indifferent or even hostile to law. What else could they do, so long as one or another imperialistic power deprived them of moral responsibility and of its exercise in self-government?

The broadest movement through which Socratic and other

Greek thought permeated this Hellenistic world was that of
Stoicism. The Stoics made contact with Socrates chiefly
through *Antisthenes*, proponent of the doctrine which gives
us our word "cynicism." The Greek *Cynics* who followed
Antisthenes were cynical only about conventional morality.
They were anything but cynical about duty and conscience.
If we rightly understand Socrates, he had taught that the moral
conventions of society express, sometimes perhaps superficially
and too woodenly, a moral insight into nature which the individual by reflection and self-knowledge may appropriate in
its fullness. Antisthenes, at once Socratic and sophistic, contrasted individualistic insight with social convention. The
individual alone is moral, he taught; and all cultural norms and
social *mores* are but artifice and semblance, a drag and disturbance to moral freedom. Salvation lies, accordingly, in
cutting oneself free from society with its demands and false
standards, and living unperturbed by public opinion. All conventional goods—honor, fame, position, loyalty, wealth, pleasure—are false and artificial. Only the completely self-reliant
soul is good. Salvation is to be one's true and natural self.

We may understand these Greek Cynics by way of Thoreau,
a modern Cynic. There is no doubt of their earnestness, nor
of their real insight into certain essential characters of moral
man. Morality is an individual matter, it makes of the individual a real and true unit of being; and moral judgment is
individual judgment. But this does not mean that the moral
life is unsocial. Wherever in history we see a society grown
artificial, hectic, and diseased, there we find also the Cynics
who seek a purely individual salvation, and cultivate a "natural" morality deeper and more spontaneous than "convention." Where can the individual look, when society has lost
its moral bearings and its moral impetus, except to his own
moral sense of what is healthy, natural, and sane? Every society
tottering to its fall has worshipped nature, and found sanity
in woods and field.

But Cynicism is really a transitional attitude, marking a shift or expansion of loyalties. If it does not develop into something more than this antisocial revulsion, it degenerates into mere boorishness. So Diogenes, we read, lived in a hogshead, scorning every human amenity not directly provided by nature. That he was honest in his fashion we know from the boon he asked of Alexander, called "the Great," who would have willingly pensioned him. "Just stand," Diogenes said, "from between me and the sun." Said Alexander: "If I were not Alexander, I would be Diogenes!" A pretty tableau! The sycophantic reporters hastily jot down the great man's words, and rush off to telephone their editors!

In *Stoicism*, what was true in Cynicism was broadened and elevated into a noble metaphysics, which became perhaps the best and broadest faith of that pagan world. Stoicism gets its name from the *Stoa* or Porch, the place in Athens where Zeno, a Semitic merchant of Cyprus, first preached this faith around 300 B.C. Throught the writings of Epictetus, a crippled Greek slave, through the great Roman stylists Cicero and Seneca, and through the *Meditations* of Marcus Aurelius, who was Emperor of Rome at Rome's imperial height, Stoicism came down to modern times. For some six centuries it was the chief faith of intellectual antiquity.

Stoicism translated the political faith of earlier Greece into a "moral" faith, making the individual a citizen of the universe, subject only to universal and divine law. In its metaphysics it looked back of Socrates to the earlier science, although its emphasis was Socratic. The human reason, it taught, discovers the vast economy or divine plan of the world, in which each individual thing has its proper place and function. Not a sparrow falls to earth except by divine ordination, they said. A man's whole duty is to preserve himself intact from more proximate stimuli, which mislead and destroy him, and to live wholly in the light of this rational knowledge of universal nature; for man's integrity is his reason, at once theoretical and practical. The integrity of the individual is that of the universe, rationally intuited. The constitution of the universe is reflected in the constitution of the moral individual. Stoicism paid little attention to science and society, although its conception originated, as we have seen, in speculations which were at once scientific and socially motivated.

The strength of Stoicism was its catholicity. It broke through all political, racial, and religious boundaries, and ignored all distinctions of class and birth. It honored man as such, as the specific vehicle of divine reason. Rather deliberately it made itself all things to all men, absorbing into itself the prevalent philosophical and religious cults, in which it ostensibly found allegorical versions of its own more literal truth. Its objectives were breadth, inclusiveness, and ethical single-mindedness.

The ethical teaching of Stoicism seems to us moderns rather negative in its warning against all commonly accepted goods. It did not, like Cynicism, abhor all ordinary contentments and pleasures; but it accepted these as incidental to the true business of life, which is the pursuit of moral integrity. Least to our liking is the Stoic distrust of the human affections, first those of family life, and finally all pity and sympathy. The ideal condition, the Stoic taught, is an apathy purified of all feeling, as cold and intellectual as white light. There is only this one virtue and righteousness, to lose which even for a moment is folly. Tortured on the rack, the rational man will be calm and at peace.

By placing virtue so high, the Stoics narrowed the company of the elect who might achieve it. They credited Socrates with having perfectly achieved wisdom, and doubted whether a second man could do this. So they made a place for those who might humbly strive toward wisdom, without claiming to be wise; and herein they came closer than they knew to their Socratic ideal, since Socrates had taught that wisdom is indeed the love and pursuit of truth, and not its sure possession.

Although in Stoicism the political motivations which had

earlier directed Greek philosophy were no longer remembered, they persisted subconsciously; and they come strangely and importantly to light in the Stoic vocabulary. The universe, said the Stoic, is the great City of God, a realm of moral individuals ruled by divine justice. The Stoics were not transcendentalists like Plato. Their City of God did not exist only in the skies or beyond. It is the actual material universe which now and everywhere exists, but which only reason discerns. It is a City without a written code, a divine community needing neither church nor priesthood, and which no earthly catastrophe can harm. All men are by birth the citizens of this visible-invisible realm, so replete with light, beauty, law, goodness. The eternal and divine constitution of the world is wholly realized in every part of the world. The sole evil is our failure to recognize this goodness. Stoicism reacted to the political failure of antique society with a renewed confession of faith. The free cities had fallen; but the free City of God, which is the universe itself, remained undisturbed, and provided a home for man. Spinoza would later dream this dream again.

This tremendous loyalty, one might argue, excuses every defect of Stoicism—its confused metaphysic, in which nature is at once natural law and what conforms to natural law; its bankruptcy of affection, excused by moral casuistry; its facile catholicity, allegorizing every teaching into its own. Stoicism first consoled the Greek who had lost his freedom, restoring his self-respect; then it broadened Roman justice; finally it prepared the way for universalistic Christianity. It was the widest channel through which there flowed to posterity the Greek faith in a justice which is truth. Yet our appreciation of the nobility and generosity of this Stoic faith, and of its ennobling influence upon the later centuries and our consequent debt to it, should not blind us to its great defect, which was its moral unrealism. The Stoic taught that the world is even now perfect, in spite of all apparent evil. The difference between good and evil, this suggests, is subjective and illusory;

it arises from our failure to see the larger plan of nature which is at every moment wholly realized, and which transmutes local evil into universal good. But why abhor and resist evil, if evil is but the fragmentary perception of good? The Stoic optimism was too facile, too verbal. It disguised a real and paralyzing pessimism, whistling in the dark.

From this gravest defect proceeded other inadequacies. The moral unrealism, which assumed that local evils may compound to a general good, bred an intellectual unrealism ready to overlook the challenge of particular fact to dogmatic assertion. (We shall discover these same errors in modern idealism, which is Stoic in its largest thesis.) This dogmatic universalism, overriding all particularity, was also presumably the source of the Stoic belittlement of the human affections, and the justification of its political indifference. The realistic idealism of Plato, who admitted the presence in nature of a matter neutral to form and value, avoided these errors and did not have to explain away apparent evil as disguised good. But the source of the scientific and moral unrealism of the Stoics was their initial political unrealism. They were willing to forego political liberty, and to tolerate tyranny, in return for a merely verbal acknowledgment of their moral freedom. Yet what is a moral freedom that is without power to direct the courses of human society, and that must willingly suffer the knout of tyranny, swallowing indignation and reproving pity?

The Stoics were often better than their doctrine. In their elaborate *theodicy*, which is the effort to justify an absolute deity in spite of the abundant evils of this world, they really excused the lesser evil as a condition of the larger good; and this was to deny, by implication, their principle that whatever is, is good. Where their doctrine called for a relentless fatalism, asserting that whatever happens is inescapably ordained, they tried inconsistently to save a little room for human freedom by teaching that the rational soul may freely will what is ordained, where unreason must struggle and be compelled.

Some of their scholars took advantage of the wide and eclectic character of Stoic doctrine to develop a very empirical theory of knowledge. All knowledge, these men taught, comes from experience, the mind being initially a blank tablet upon which impressions are left by observed particular things; and memory and inference then allow the advance from these particular impressions to the general concepts of a universal science. This epistemology was revived at the beginning of the modern age to support the philosophy of *empiricism*; and it led some of the Stoics, as it was later to lead Berkeley and Hume, to skeptical conclusions. To avoid these, they vaguely appealed to "common sense," by which they meant a faculty to apprehend general forms. Here they followed Aristotle. Stoic thinkers also developed the Aristotelian logic, in particular the doctrine of the categories, and the important properties of conditional sentences of the form: If A, then B. The Stoic epistemology and logic helped the pioneers of modern thought to break away from the scholastic philosophy of the Middle Ages, and they have continued to play an important part in later philosophy.

The great virtue of Stoicism, we said, was its universalistic humanism. The earlier Greeks were humanistic in their respect for the human "essence" which dwells in every human individual; but they tended to identify humanity with the Greek people, leaving "barbarians" outside the pale. These Hellenistic Greeks made no such distinction. Semite and Greek, slave and master, commoner and emperor, halt and whole were equally citizens of "the blessed City of God," and children of the God in whom all things "live and move and have their being." This hospitable humanism, however, was facilitated and made futile by political indifference. They affirmed human equality, but they did not draw the political implications of this doctrine. They tolerated every sort of economic and political disfranchisement. Nevertheless this merely verbal equalitarianism was not without some realistic consequence. The slave was finally admitted into the community of men, and a liberal personal attitude softened institutional injustice. The Stoic liberalism, looked back to by later centuries which took it more literally, became during the later Middle Ages one of the important factors in the movement to the realistic liberalism of today. We see the beginning of this movement, indeed, in certain Roman applications of the Stoic principles.

Cicero, greatest of Roman orators and stylists, was the spokesman in the Senate for senatorial privileges threatened by a rising Caesarism. He defended these privileges as the inalienable rights of free citizens exercising their responsible function of self-government; and he used in his argument the Stoic conception of natural and divine law, Stoicism being his professed faith as it was of most Roman intellectuals. However, Cicero conjoined with Stoicism the earlier Greek philosophy, which conceived the universal law of nature to have its most important realization in the political constitution of human society. Thus Stoic ethics became realistic in the concept of *natural rights, i.e.* political powers invested in the individual by natural and divine law. It was upon this conception, sixteen hundred years later, that modern society was to establish its political theory. Cicero, as we said, neither intended nor imagined so democratic an application of his doctrine. He defended a Roman oligarchy and its vested rights. The Senate was an hereditary aristocracy ruling a vast empire primarily to fill its personal coffers; and the Caesarian dictatorship which robbed the Senate of its powers was an inevitable and in some ways an emancipating reform. But medieval Europe, unaware of that history, read Cicero literally. It saw in him the defender of popular rights against tyranny, with the result that the eloquent apologist for vested interests became the great protagonist of the rights of man. Such is the virtue of universal principles, that even those who prostitute them help finally to establish their authority.

In another way Roman Stoicism was politically realistic.

Under the Empire, the city of Rome became increasingly a court of last appeal for cases not covered by provincial laws. The Roman jurists used Stoic principles in their creation of a law of equity, the *jus gentium* or "law of peoples." This Roman jurisprudence—not to be confused with the old civic law of Rome—was codified under Justinian in the sixth century A.D.; and as "Roman law," never forgotten in the Italian law schools, it deeply influenced the development throughout Europe of the concept of justice. Through Cicero and through Roman law, the Stoic concept of equalitarian and universal citizenship began its descent to earth, to become after many centuries the theory of democratic society.

A second Socratic development, existing alongside of Stoicism through these later centuries of antiquity, was *Epicureanism*. Much as Stoicism corrected and enlarged Cynicism, the Epicureans elaborated the hedonistic doctrine of *Aristippus of Cyrene*. (*Hedonism* is any doctrine which finds pleasure to be the substance or criterion of goodness.) Aristippus had come to Socrates from Protagoras, and he seems to have seen in Socrates only a more able sophist, appealing against convention and law to some purely individual and subjective insight into truth. Whereas the Cynics found this criterion in the individual's moral sense of self-integrity, Aristippus found it in the immediate conscious apprehension of value, *i.e.* in pleasure. Man's reason, Aristippus implied, is his ability to calculate, aided by memory and anticipation, the consequences of his conduct; but his criterion of what is good for him must be a deeper, personal, and natural instinct, common to man and the animals. Every creature is endowed with sensitivity to pleasure and pain, which tells it what to pursue and what to avoid; but man, by means of his reason, is able to apply this instinctive faculty widely and precisely, by weighing pleasures and pains and calculating an optimum synthesis. Hedonism usually has received hard treatment from moralists, who are apt to find in it only a defense of license. The present writer believes that hedonism is an inadequate doctrine, but one which contains a truth which will break any theory that neglects it. This truth is its empiricism, the demand that moral ideals shall support themselves by an appeal to human experience. Moral knowledge, like any other knowledge, must finally depend upon immediate experience, which includes our immediate reactions to situations as pleasurable or painful. A moral theory which rejects this empirical criterion becomes harsh, uncritical, inhumane. But hedonism is inadequate as it stands, just as empiricism is inadequate if it fails to realize its own presuppositions. Both hedonism and empiricism assume, as theories respectively of conduct and knowledge, a second criterion other than that of immediacy. This second criterion is that of totality or comprehensiveness—the criterion one-sidedly emphasized by cynicism and by rationalism. Why should we remember yesterday's sorrow or be concerned for tomorrow's pleasure, in our reaction to a present stimulus? Why not take at any cost the moment's joy, avoid at any cost the moment's pain? Because we are concerned, in action as in thought, for more than the moment. And once we have admitted this, where shall our concern stop? It cannot be stopped short of all creation.

If this is true, one must allow to reason itself, to pure logic if you will, a moral constitution, and not dismiss it as a mere calculating machine. Because the Cyrenaics divorced intellect from feeling, they failed really to apply their intellectual calculus. They pursued the more intense pleasure as the better pleasure; and this pursuit resulted, as it still must result, in a breakdown of the bodily and mental faculties, accompanied by a moral nausea or ennui which could become a suicidal aversion to life. One of the later Cyrenaics was called "the counselor of death," because of the wake of suicides he left in his train. It is because life and nature are moral in their innermost structure, not merely in their apparent quality, that the divorce of reason and feeling abets neurosis. We should observe, by comparing and contrasting the Cyrenaic and Cynic doctrines, their common error, which was their isolation of the individual from his moral context in society. This isolation left their ethics arbitrary and wilful. The Cyrenaic could equate the good with pleasure, the Cynic could equate it with aloofness from pleasure. Each of the doctrines confused reality with one or the other of the two criteria of reality, with immediate experience or with logic.

Epicurus rescued the truth which lay in the Cyrenaic hedonism by replacing the individual in his social and natural context. Born and brought up like Pythagoras in the isle of Samos off the Ionian coast, Epicurus came to the mainland of Greece for his education. Samos had earlier escaped the horrors of the long war; but on his return he found it ruined and desolate. Epicurus evidently experienced a deep revulsion against the cultured, educated, but hectic and irresponsible world which bred these wars. He hated the great world with its grandiloquent and deadly superstitions—its idols religious, political, scientific. He taught sobriety, and established his "gardens" in which humble, sane, and loving people could take refuge from the world, scorning its prizes and its feverish ambition. In these Epicurean groves all was plainness, simplicity, and friendship. Men and women lived as nature intended them to live, satisfied with normal pleasures, healthy with work, blessed with human community.

The essential doctrine of Epicurus was that of human freedom. There is no just power, he taught, which has authority over man. The human individual is properly a natural unit, a self-determined and self-controlled absolute. His whole duty is to himself, since there is no higher unit of which he is a part. His virtue is self-preservation and self-discipline; and he is wholly responsible to himself for his conduct. Virtue, therefore, even as Socrates taught, is just sane and intelligent living.

To establish this doctrine Epicurus appropriated the atomistic science, rejecting all other Greek science. His intention was to invalidate the concept of universal law, which was being used to support political and other authority over the individual. Things do not obey laws, he taught. There is no universal structure, there are only transient collocations of atoms. Such a collocation is the human individual, who will enjoy life and health just so long as he preserves his material integrity, cultivating and strictly controlling his appetites, *i.e.* his relations and responses to what immediately affects him. Only the calmer pleasures, it is evident, conduce to well-being and health. (Epicurus was diabetic, and required a strict regimen.) Pains and intense pleasures equally destroy the organism; and it is incipient destruction of this sort, leading to fear and a sense of guilt, that drives people who fail to control their passions to superstitious faith and idolatry. Over and above the simple and healthy animal appetites, the one pleasure which man may safely and unreservedly pursue is that of friendship or companionship. This costs nothing, it has no evil residues, it is the truly human condition.

Too little honor has been done Epicurus. He did not perceive some of the inescapable conditions of human existence, nor properly appreciate its potentialities; but he did clearly perceive and stoutly affirm the absolute reality and the underived moral responsibility of the human individual. No other Greek thinker so uncompromisingly affirmed this truth, that the individual is not the creature of law but is indeed the source of law, all true discipline being self-discipline.

The weaknesses of the Epicurean doctrine are rather apparent. There is nothing in atomistic science which would explain, or in any way require, the effort of the living organism to preserve its existence or its health. The naturalistic ethics of hedonism assumes the living organism to be of greater value than the corpse disintegrating into atomic dust; but for atomism, in strictness, the organism is really only its atomic constituents; and to allow higher value to life than to death is eventually to affirm a vast faith of the Platonic type. More obviously, of course, atomism fails to account for the existence of a life cognitive of its own conditions. The ascription of consciousness to atoms or atomic collocations would cause the collapse of the atomistic view, if this consciousness is allowed to influence their behavior. The failure of Epicurus to see the social and metaphysical implications of his individualistic creed caused the degeneration of Epicureanism. When memory of the noble life of its founder waned, there was left the cult of refined sensuality which the name "Epicurean" connotes today. But we may believe that Epicurus had truer descendants in the early Christians, whose cult of the community of friends bound by mutual love revived his central teaching.

A secondary Epicurean doctrine was to have important uses in later times. The early Epicureans withdrew from the world, but they still had to adjust themselves to politically organized society. To guide or justify their dealings with governments they developed the sophistic view, which held law to be but convention imposed upon the individual by force, into the more self-respecting and reasonable theory that government arises out of a business contract, entered into by individuals for the performance of certain specific common functions such as police duty and military protection. The intention of this contract-theory was to deprive government of all intrinsic authority, especially religious and moral authority, yet to justify government as an economic utility. Recovered in the later Middle Ages and curiously associated with biblical ideas of a covenant binding God and man, this contract-theory became an important element of modern political thought, where it supports the doctrine of government by consent and the insistence upon moral limitations upon government.

It was chiefly through the Roman poet *Lucretius* that knowledge of Epicurean doctrine came to later Europe. In his great Latin epic *De Rerum Natura* Lucretius gave to the doctrine a new and ennobling purpose. The rejection of superstition becomes a positive adoration of scientific truth, and the provin-

cial and narrow Greek atomism becomes a healthy naturalism
standing in awe and worship before great nature. Lucretius is
the chief source of a modern naturalism which has corrected
and widened the concept of nature, and prevented the identification of science with the conceptual systems which science
creates. So, by another of life's ironies, Epicurus who dismissed "science for its own sake" became through his latest
and greatest disciple one of those to whom we owe a disinterested science.

Stoicism and Epicureanism, along with the other philosophical traditions earlier established, continued down the later centuries into the Christian era, often in acrimonious controversy;
but even in this controversy they propagated the widest conceptions of Greek science. It is an error to think of this current of ideas as completely cut off by the rise of Christianity
and the "dark ages." Narrowed and in part submerged it
was; but in eastern Europe it continued into and through the
Moslem culture; and in western Europe, at least in the south,
it was never completely dammed. One finds concrete historical
continuity between late antiquity and the Italian Renaissance.
Until the sixth century or later, many a perfectly sincere
Greek or Latin "Christian" was in truth a Stoic or a Platonist,
who found his philosophical faith allegorized in the Christian
symbolism. In one of its forms, indeed, Greek philosophy has
always threatened what is most distinctive in Christian faith,
not by attacking Christianity from without, but by devouring
it from within. This form is Neoplatonism, which in the third
century was to establish itself firmly in Christian theology.
Although Neoplatonism arose concurrently with Christianity,
it was essentially Greek in its conceptions and method; and in
taking note of it we close this survey of Greek thought.

Neoplatonism originated, so far as is known, with *Philo
Judaeus*, a Jewish scholar in Alexandria who was the contemporary of Jesus Christ. Philo had given his heart to Plato; but he
saw Plato from the perspective of his Judaic tradition, and he

emphasized especially the mystical elements in the Platonic teaching. Further, Philo was influenced by the method of interpretation developed by the Stoics, who accepted many religious creeds as allegorical versions of their more theoretical faith. Thus Philo believed (as Roger Bacon much later was to believe) that Plato and Moses offered different versions of one and the same truth. The hospitable but uncritical attitude of mind supporting this belief is characteristic of these later centuries of antiquity, when men were seeking a faith which might unite into cultural homogeneity that motley Mediterranean world. The deepest cleft in the cultural landscape was the chasm between Greek and Semitic cultures, as we shall observe in our discussion of Christianity; and it was this chasm that Philo wished to bridge.

Similarly characteristic of all of these centuries is the lack of scientific interest which marked Neoplatonism. The dominating interest is moral and religious, in the unfortunate sense which divorces morality and religion from science. Philo's interest was intellectual, since he required a conceptual approach to truth; but his dominating objective was the moral and religious salvation of the individual, to which the conceptual approach must lead. He is no scientist like Plato, who required reason to "save the appearances," *i.e.* to illuminate particular and observable fact; but he used the largest framework of Platonic and Aristotelian science as a conceptual ladder, up which the inquiring mind might ascend in order, from its highest rung, to leap off into a mystical communion or mergence with absolute Being, this ecstatic vision being the sole motive and reason of the intellectual effort of man.

Argument as to whether Plato was correctly understood by Philo would be inconclusive, since the difference is essentially one of emphasis. Plato established a school of science and law, the Neoplatonists established theology. But more important than this epistemological difference was the shift in metaphysical doctrine. Plato was uncompromisingly dualistic in his distinction of Form or Being from matter, or "non-being" as he called it. Matter for Plato was altogether real, as real as Form, since it was the actuality of all observable mobility and change, as also of the infinite diversity and imperfection of visible nature. But in Neoplatonism matter is divested of all positive character, to become identified, it would seem, with extension or space. This required a change in the concept of Form, which must now initiate, somewhat as Aristotle would have God do, all the motion of nature. In Neoplatonism, the existing universe is pictured as the progressive emanation or evolution of Being first into a logical configuration, finally into the spatial configuration which is the visible world of things.

If this Neoplatonic metaphysics renounced a conception of matter without which the Platonic philosophy collapses, it is also true that Plato's dualism was inherently unstable, since it left unintelligible the relation between Form and existing things. Aristotle had tried, impossibly, to bridge the duality of Form and matter, by supposing matter to be at once the source of individual character and the source of general form. This line of thought, logically carried to its conclusion, would finally erase the difference between matter and Form. Neoplatonism similarly moved away from Plato's dualism by robbing matter of all save spatial character. The motive impelling this direction of thought was religious. The Hebraic religion made God an omnipotent Creator transcending His creation, an infinite Being transcending all definite form. Philo brings this intense monotheism into the Platonic system; and the Platonic Form becomes a Jacob's ladder upon the rungs of which the angels stand, and up which the soul may climb to lose itself in infinite godhead. Philo speaks of the last rung, corresponding to the superlative Form of Plato, as God's Word, His Wisdom, Thought, Regent, Instrument, First-born Son. The *Logos, i.e.* science, becomes the intermediary or savior, reconciling man with infinite God. Perhaps half a century after Philo a certain John would open his Christian gospel with the lines: "*In the beginning was the Word* [*Logos*], *and the Word was with God, and the Word was God . . . And the Word was made flesh, and dwelt among us* (*and we beheld his glory, the glory as of the only begotten of the Father*), *full of grace and truth.*" So, of Philo and of John, elder of the church at Alexandria, was born Christian theology.

Evidently, this Neoplatonic version of Plato persisted in Alexandrian thought from the beginning of the Christian era; but it reached its full elaboration only in the third century A.D., through Plotinus and Origen, pupils both of one Ammonius Saccas of Alexandria. *Plotinus* is usually regarded as the authoritative exponent, his writings being edited and published by his pupil Porphyry in a work since called the *Enneads* from its division into nine books. The work is a beautiful fantasy, full of light and color and suggestive metaphor, warm with moral aspiration and religious anticipation. It is certainly not science, and scarcely philosophy, since its speculation is almost wholly uncritical, and weaves together with eclectic liberality half a dozen brilliant strands of earlier Greek speculation. The method is wholly deductive and nonempirical, moving from the intuition of ultimate Being downward (whereas empirical thought moves upward from observed particulars to ever more general principles); and very much as Hegel later was to weave into his speculative fantasy the concepts of contemporary science, so Plotinus finds room on his celestial ladder of form for Ionian, Pythagorean, Stoic, Aristotelian, Eleatic, and other concepts. From God, the infinite and ineffable, there moves *nous* or reason, the articulate thought of God with its plurality of forms or ideas. (It is from Neoplatonism that the word "idea" gets its present meaning. Earlier it had meant "form" or even "shape," something objective which might be known but which was not peculiarly mental in itself.) The divine ideas are eternal or timeless, they define the five categories or ways of being, and they generate a cloud of mystical numbers, of which there is one for each species, and one for each immortal human soul, each soul being a species to itself. This purely logical realm is then spatialized to constitute the "world-soul" or universal life, a pure rational consciousness; and from the world-soul emanate in infinite number other individual immortal souls, which finally are materialized, *i.e.* they cast into space the flitting shadows we call "bodies." Difficulties of exposition in this system are relieved by metaphor, the emanation of forms being likened to the radiance of the sun dissipated into darkness, or to a cascading fountain. The work is an aesthetic creation, and a very lovely one, but devoid of rigorous logic and scientific cogency.

Yet it was chiefly through Neoplatonism that Greek philosophy was to be known to later centuries. Partly because of its absorption into Christian theology, partly because of its domination over subsequent pagan writings, Neoplatonism came to be identified with philosophy as such. Little distinction, indeed, was sometimes made between this pagan system and Christian doctrine. Two Neoplatonic works, apparently quite free from Christian influence, became important items in the Christian library. One was the *Consolations* of Boethius. *Boethius* was a minister of state in Constantinople around A.D. 500, who came under the Emperor's suspicion. Disgraced, imprisoned, his family destroyed and his wealth confiscated, Boethius awaits execution when he is visited by a lady called Philosophy, who persuades him of the worthlessness of all he had lost, since only the immortal soul has real being. King Alfred of England translated this work into Anglo-Saxon, thinking to provide a religious manual for his nobles. Boethius was supposed to be a Christian, yet one searches the book in vain for evidence of Christian knowledge or Christian sentiment. Another Neoplatonic work which found its way into Christian libraries was that attributed to Dionysius the Areopagite. Of this we will speak in a later chapter.

Through *Origen*, fellow pupil of Plotinus under Ammonius Saccas, and chief of the early Fathers who created Christian theology, Neoplatonism was incorporated bodily into the

Christian creed. There were, further, numerous encyclopedias of Greek thought, and commentaries on earlier Greek thinkers, written by Neoplatonists between the third and the sixth centuries, and preserved by the church when earlier writings were lost. Thus it was that philosophy came to be identified with Neoplatonic mysticism; and although after a millennium Europe was to enjoy again a firsthand knowledge of classical Greece, it still read the Greek originals through Neoplatonic spectacles. Nor has it ever fully emancipated itself from that influence. To this day philosophy remains either shaped by the Neoplatonic tradition, or in a revulsion against it so violent that the Platonic insight is often rejected along with the Neoplatonic fantasy; and seldom, except amongst a few scholars versed in Greek, does one find any adequate knowledge and just estimate of Greek science.

The result is that in spite of our professed admiration for the Greek achievement, we have never done justice to it nor appropriated its greatest values. We look back to Greek art with its delicacy and poise, its lyrical poignancy, its sense of the audacious right word, its Homeric complacency; but we do not see clearly the Greece that gave us a realistic science and a realistic ethics, the Greece that nursed Socrates and Plato and their great predecessors. Plotinus was not Greece, even Aristotle was no true Greek. That other Greece was rugged, plain, sober; yet it too was poignant in its moral hunger, and more audacious than any Greek simile in its demand for a religion that served justice first and last. There was in the greatest Greek thinkers an incomparable honesty, a realism that has never been surpassed; and the honesty of Greece is half of the great heritage which is the source of all our blessing. Only in Plato do we know with some familiarity and completeness the superb mind and spirit, the sublime truthfulness that was early Greece.

From Greece came theoretical science, the mother of all science, and one of the two great bulwarks of the modern world. There is no reason to believe that factories and dynamos and scientific industries would exist if Greece had not created theoretical science. Science has not arisen elsewhere, nor anywhere except where early Greek thought was recovered and expanded. And from Greece came also our realistic faith in political justice, actualized in constitutional democratic government, without which the great dynamo of applied science must destroy man. The march of time, so majestic, is as intelligible as it is royal. Did not Greece create theoretical science and a just political system in one breath, as twin halves of a single thought? Why should they not stand or fall together forever? This truth needs new establishment today, when national life totters where it has not already fallen; but it is not a new truth, it is the old truth, freshly and more largely turned, that we must seek. Once again we reach the crisis, twenty-three centuries after Socrates, when science and political theory blindly grope for each other, aware that truth and justice cannot exist apart, yet each only half aware of its other half. Once again, under whatever name, there must arise that realistic philosophical truth which is their union, if we would save not only the civilization we now enjoy, but that of all the future. Where there is no truth, it has been said, the people perish; but truth is not truth if it be not also justice.

So we leave Greece, the parent of our thought, holding fast to its truth, but turning now to that larger movement of creative life which has given us the modern world, and also this near-debacle of the modern world. And the new story begins with a new gospel and a great hope.

Notes for Further Reading

1. Zeller, Ed., *Outlines of the History of Greek Philosophy*, trans. L. R. Palmer. New York, Henry Holt and Company, 1931, Parts III, IV.
2. Gomperz, Th., *Greek Thinkers*, trans. G. G. Berry. London, J. Murray, 1914, Vol. IV, later chapters.

3. Fuller, B. A. G., *A History of Ancient and Medieval Philosophy*. New York, Henry Holt and Company, 1938, revised 1945, Chaps, VI, VII.
4. Bevan, E. R., *Stoics and Sceptics*. London and New York, Oxford University Press, 1913.
5. *The Meditations of Marcus Aurelius Antoninus*. Many editions.
6. Wenley, R. M., *Stoicism and Its Influence*. Boston, Longmans, Green and Company, 1927.
7. Inge, W. R., *Plotinus*. Boston, Longmans, Green and Company, 1918.
8. Patrick, M. M., *The Greek Sceptics*. New York, Columbia University Press, 1929.
9. Lucretius, *De rerum natura*, trans. P. Bailey, London and New York, Oxford University Press, 1904, also translations by Munro, Leonard, and others.
10. Santayana, G., *Three Philosophical Poets*. Cambridge, Harvard University Press, 1910.
11. Taylor, A. E., *Epicurus*. New York, Dodge Publishing Company, 1910.
12. Wallace, W., *Epicureanism*. London, Society for Promotion of Christian Knowledge, 1880.

II THE ANTECEDENTS OF MODERN PHILOSOPHY

9 A NEW HEAVEN AND A NEW EARTH

Is the intellectual and moral confusion of today the result of our erroneous belief that we can continue to enjoy the fruits of a religious past without acknowledging their religious source? Was it religion that gave to this modern era its great impetus, generated by a millennium of great faith? It was necessary, in order to allow this faith to reach its full realization, to emancipate religion from its institutional forms, its dogmatic creeds, and its closed ecclesiastical organization. This emancipation required the disestablishment of institutions which for many had become identified with religion itself. But might it not be argued that what was emancipated and empowered by the Reformation and the Renaissance was just religious truth itself, in its essential sanity and power? Should we imagine that a purely secular culture has expressed itself in the social and scientific achievements of the last four centuries? It may be that the virtues of tolerance, kindness, justice, and mercy will not persist in individual and social life if we no longer remember their historical evolution and their religious source. It is scarcely to be denied that what there is of culture or civilization in modern society is of Christian origin; and the penalty for failure to acknowledge our cultural origins may be the loss of culture itself.

We shall find, when we come to the discussion of dialectical philosophy, that there is no dialectic of truth; but there is most assuredly a dialectic of error, in that every error must generate its contradictory complement. If we reject religious insight in our effort to escape dogma, casting out the seed of truth along with its dead protective husk, we really only repeat the medieval error, which was to confuse religious truth with its theological and ecclesiastical wrappings. It was a crime against religious truth itself when certain powers attempted to make that truth an institutional monopoly, and to raise it above common understanding and critical inquiry. Thereby they hardened flexible and living insight into dogma, and placed religion outside of the intellectual pale. "You claim," said the inquiring thinker to the dogmatist, "to possess intellectual and moral authority over me, on the ground of your monopoly of religious truth? In that case I will abjure religion, and so undercut the foundations of your power!" And this was all too simply done. The modern thinker has subscribed to a secular science, and given to that science his largest trust. Since the Renaissance the human intellect has accepted every formula offered to it in the name of science. It has made science its active faith; and by science is usually meant a knowledge indifferent to religious truth, and often contrasted with it.

Yet, whether we admit the fact or not, modern society in all its evolution has been shaped by religious belief and religious purpose. To ignore this religious motivation is to fail to understand past history, and without some understanding of history there can be no adequate social theory. Failure to appreciate the religious past has in this way defeated social analysis, and left society prey to pseudosciences and verbal myths, some of which are more pernicious than anything in dogmatic theology.

The first purpose of science is a clear perception of facts

and their causal connections. Neither religious indifference nor religious unbelief should deter the social scientist from impartial study and objective estimate of the working of religion in human history. It is a fact that for nearly two thousand years, religious faith chiefly determined the direction of social evolution in the western world; and the effort to recover this history without full acknowledgment of its religious stimulation merely leaves the historian impotent and his narrative trivial and tedious. Religious beliefs impelled or conditioned all the moral, political, and economic history of the west. One cannot set forth the long movement of western man to his present form of society without continuous reference to Christian tenets. This does not mean, of course, that the historian should identify his own faith with that of Christianity. As a historian, he must remain free from every religious prepossession. But he does not obtain this freedom by ignoring the degree to which religious faith, for better or for worse, has molded history. His business as a historian is to state what actually occurred, and to discover what caused what. It is accordingly his duty to register and estimate the effects of religion upon political and other history, where religion had such effects. He may properly abstain from any explicit conclusion regarding the truth or error of the faith which had these effects; but he will scarcely find it possible to avoid all estimate of those effects as good, bad, or indifferent. In any case, those who read his history will draw such conclusions, since the good or evil fruits of a faith are evidence for or against its truth. A faith that destroys or weakens society cannot be true; a faith that strengthens and invigorates society may be true. Historical impartiality means honest judgment, not abstention from judgment, with respect to religion. Complete reservation of judgment is just intellectual cowardice.

By any historical measure, the rise and spread of Christianity was a social revolution of the first magnitude. The Roman empire, the greatest and stablest political organization human society had yet created, was undercut and displaced by a non-political organization, the Christian church, which during these early centuries enjoyed no political or military power, and little or no prestige of any sort. Early Christianity was a humble, persecuted, furtive faith. Yet by A.D. 325, although its adherents numbered still only a minority of one fifth of the population, imperial Rome found itself forced to make common cause with this minority; and henceforward the declining imperial power steadily flowed over into the church, which finally assumed universal authority, and actively exerted authority for well-nigh a thousand years. Will the political historian ignore this millennial fact?

The rise of Christianity was the enormous event that balanced the books of antiquity. It liquidated the pagan past, and ushered in the age that was to become the modern world. The historian Gibbon could see in the rise of Christianity only the corruption of that imperial Rome which he perversely loved. Gibbon was both right and wrong. Rome died, yet did not die. Its political genius lived on in Roman ecclesiasticism, whence it was transferred when the time was ripe to modern society, which has developed it again.

The source of Rome's political power was its relative freedom from racial and religious pride. Rome did not stigmatize peoples as "barbarian" because they were not Roman. It put no people outside the human pale. It respected all cultures, borrowing from them avidly; and it left to the peoples which it politically ruled their languages, their religions, and their local customs. Tribute it exacted, but it gave in return a real measure of peace and economic security. Only by the Semitic peoples of Carthage and Judaea, and by certain Teutonic tribes in the north, was this exchange resolutely refused. The challenge of Carthage was bloodily answered, but only after a mortal struggle which unnerved Rome. Judaea also persistently rebelled, until it likewise was destroyed in a bloody campaign. Rome paid dearly for these victories. The penalty for the destruction of Judaea was Rome's final abdication, and the passage of power from imperial to papal hands.

Roman history is an object lesson in the sources of political power, and the conditions of its retention. The Jewish people were set apart from other peoples by a rigid and fierce loyalty to their religious and national past. For more than three centuries, however, ever since the conquests of Alexander, they had been directly exposed to foreign influences, including that of the Greek mystery-religions. Among Grecianized Jews there appeared a new cult which combined the intensity of the Jewish faith, focused now upon a Messiah who would carry Judaea to victory, with the more personal ardor of the mystery-religions, which offered salvation to the individual through the mediation of a divine Savior or Christ. The new faith was Pythagorean, at once individualistic and social. It taught the redemption of a Christian community, composed of all those individuals who accepted the atonement of Christ. After a sharp struggle, this Christian faith was carried by some of its Jewish proponents to the gentile world. Because the Jewish people had established important colonies in all of the larger Mediterranean cities, the propagation of Christianity proceeded from many centers and was accordingly rapid. With the destruction of Judaea in A.D. 70 Christianity became definitely hostile to Rome, this attitude finding its earliest expression in the *Book of the Revelation* of John, later included in the Christian Bible. This writing was dedicated to the seven churches of Asia Minor, the chief center of early Christianity; and it foretells the destruction of "Babylon," meaning Rome, to make room for "a new heaven and a new earth."

Very rapidly this Christian cult spread, until it reached the remote outposts of the far-flung Roman world; and steadily it gathered into itself what was best in that world. What did it offer to its faithful, whom it exposed to contempt, ostracism, persecution, and death? Why did it gain ground in spite of the opposition of politically organized power? It is evident that

Rome itself, by establishing peaceful intercourse among the Mediterranean peoples, had prepared the way for their deeper cultural unification. Somewhere, somehow, there would form, in that turbid and agitated mother liquor which was Mediterranean life, the first crystal establishing a new cultural pattern. Christianity was the successful candidate among the many faiths which aspired to unify the Mediterranean culture. We must conclude that Christianity best met the requirements of human community, as they existed in that world; and a study of early Christianity should accordingly reveal something of the permanent conditions of large association, at every place and time.

The early Christian community demanded from its members something else than the overt, external, political obedience required of its subjects by Rome. It demanded an unreserved and heartfelt loyalty, a spiritual or affectionate allegiance. More fully and forcibly than Rome or Stoicism it erased distinctions of race, birth, wealth. It was in almost every way the most radical of the competing faiths. Its requirement of unreserved and heartfelt devotion was the condition of an emancipation of affectional life, liberating the human heart from confining restrictions of race and class. Christianity gave far more than it took. It offered "rebirth" into a universal community that promised a new upsurge of human life, even a mutation of the human species. It required abnegation of all the past, and directed the eye and heart of man towards the future. This was the great revolution effected by Christianity, source of all the revolutions that were to come. It was most emphatically an intellectual revolution, involving a new conception and evaluation of the temporal dimension of nature and fact, and thereby inaugurating a new era of science and philosophy. The character of this intellectual reorientation was to become clear only many centuries later, in the development of modern thought; but even the earliest Christians indicated it, when they exhorted men to turn from obedience to "the

law" and to follow instead the admonitions of "the spirit."
What was this "spirit," which transcended all law and all the
past?

The spirit, said *Paul of Tarsus*, who first carried this radical
gospel to the gentile world, is the faith, hope, and love which
transforms a group of random individuals into a living community, solid and impulsive yet free. Here were three new
"virtues"; and their establishment as such constituted a new
theory of human nature. You must throw off your old nature,
said Paul, and put on a new nature. Was this doctrine less
momentous two thousand years ago than today, when it is
revived in perverted forms? To appropriate the new nature,
concluded Paul, you need only accept the atonement and
example of Jesus Christ, the new man who is also God. Faith
in the godhead of Jesus Christ is the sufficient condition of the
three virtues of faith, hope, and love, which in their turn are
the constitutive properties of the new man and the new society. Did Paul merely use the figure of Jesus, as Plato is
sometimes held to have used the figure of Socrates, to express
his own ideas and to advance his own purposes? Or shall we
too say that Jesus Christ was the divine and creative seed out
of which grew a new civilization? This was not the only time
that such claims have been made for a human individual; but
it was perhaps the only time in human history that such claims,
widely allowed, have revolutionized civilization.

It is fairly well agreed among exegetical scholars that the
earliest Christian conceptions, even those presented in the New
Testament, are an inseparable amalgam of historical fact and
imaginative interpretation. In one sense there is nothing new
in the New Testament. No dictum there that has not its
analogue in earlier wisdom, no incident that is not reminiscent
of earlier myth, no concept that is not implicit in some earlier
train of thought! The New Testament could conceivably be
the imaginative creation of a gifted group of audacious seekers
after religious truth. It could be a synthesis of earlier religious

conceptions which required, over and above those materials, only imagination or insight. But this scholarly acknowledgment of the continuity of Christian teaching with earlier religious vision only serves to emphasize the new and radical realism which allowed Christianity to establish itself as a world religion; and this realistic power forbids us to deny the historical reality of its originator. That there did occur the movement we call "Christianity" is, of course, an historical fact; but it is also a fact that the movement differentiated itself from other faiths chiefly in this, that it identified God with the individual Jesus, friend and teacher of the first Christians. The weight of evidence, moreover, is that the first Christian community came together just to preserve the memory and carry out the instructions of this Jesus. What Jesus was we may debate; but that he lived, and taught, and originated Christianity is scarcely debatable. The historian, whatever his own religious confession, must find in this historical actuality of the object of Christian worship the most distinctive and significant feature of this religion. It was this religious realism, which identified God with a man who walked this earth, that gave to Christianity its victory, that carried it beyond all earlier religious conception, and that made it the source of the scientific and moral realism characteristic of the civilization which issued from it.

Time has made too familiar the spiritual and intellectual audacity of the founder of Christianity. We should remember that Jesus was arraigned, judged, and executed as a freethinker and blasphemer; and surely he was just that, to every pagan mind. Pagan piety had confined deity within some supernatural dimension, other than that of everyday human existence. Even Plato had been compelled to make the Good transcendent over the world. But Jesus preferred the naturalistic realism of the Ionian thinkers, whose moral insight he advanced in the far bolder claim that man himself might be God. The early Greeks had accorded to man a high measure of dignity and power.

The Stoics had allowed that man might live and move and have his being in God; but only Jesus, carrying to its full conclusion the Socratic teaching that piety is the love of God, dared to teach that God might live and move and have his being in individual man. Perhaps this is blasphemy still. Whatever it be, it is nevertheless the creed by which Jesus Christ brought to an end the pagan world, and announced the religious basis upon which our modern world is established; for what Jesus revealed is the truth that man is in his own nature divine, free, and creative, even as is God. How, except on this awful, audacious, and sobering assumption, should the human individual exercise moral and intellectual responsibility? Yet upon this exercise of individual responsibility we have established our society and our science. Let the modern thinker make explicit the religious and metaphysical implications of the fact of individual responsibility, which is the foundation and presupposition of modern life!

The first of the Christian virtues, accordingly, is faith in the divinity of man. Christianity was a humanism which affirmed God even in its affirmation of human rights. It saw in Jesus, whom it called "Christ," the protagonist and exemplar of this faith that man is in his incalculable measure God. It taught that we shall find God if we will look for Him in the lineaments of men and women, boys and girls. The kingdom of heaven is within man, not in the sky.

The second of the Christian virtues was its optimism, its hope. This optimism is once again our faith in creative man, relieved of the intolerable burden of past failure. Hope is our natural orientation upon the future; for to be so oriented is to recognize, intelligently and explicitly, the instinctive momentum of our flesh and blood, and to affirm, and not obstruct, our essential nature. We have forgotten, just because Christianity is still our teacher, how afflicted with nostalgia and pessimism was all antiquity. Before Christ all goodness was residue, the golden age was a remote past, the present was a decline preceding death. (Bertrand Russell, a contemporary philosopher, returns to this pagan pessimism when he tells us, in his essay *A Free Man's Worship*, to warm ourselves at each other's hearts awaiting the day when universal nature must annihilate itself.) Christianity put glory in the future, it believed that the millennium was imminent, next week, tomorrow. The Stoic City of God became the Christian heaven, something to be possessed some day in material actuality. Christianity made utopianism a permanent character of western thought; and society began realistically to require the progressive actualization in time of its moral ideal. The Christian duty of hope put humanity on the march; and marched it has, ever since, in one direction.

The third of the three virtues was *caritas* or loving-kindness, the affectional aspect of the faith affirming the divine character of man. This caritas is the supreme virtue, Paul wrote; for love is in truth the source, substance, and actuality of the divinity which is man. It was initially the immeasurable love which Jesus brought to man that so established the worth and the desert of man; and if we today find man to be innately good and worthy of self-government, it is because we intellectually endorse the warm and passionate judgment upon man of Jesus Christ. Democracy is just Christian practice. Modern society has taken Christian truth out of the theological wrappings in which a still pagan society had fearfully swaddled it, and applied it in social institutions.

So invincibly armed with faith, hope, and love, the early Christians conquered their world. They had purpose, self-respect, confidence; above all, they had the friendly approach that disarms hostility, and the generous trust in mankind which guarantees successful organization. We know today that this organizing ability is the ruling power of the world. A truly Christian society is invincible.

Early Christianity, composed of loosely linked proselytizing communities inspired and governed by their religious leaders, transformed itself within a few centuries into a closed ecclesiastical system, which from the fifth to the fifteenth century was to be the chief agency of government in Europe, exercising powers coordinate with or superior to those of secular rulers. Since ecclesiasticism, like feudalism, has been a stage or tendency in every large social evolution, we need not suppose that there is any especially close bond between ecclesiastical form and Christian tenets. What most strikingly distinguishes Christianity from other faiths, indeed, is its explosive exodus, after a thousand years of vigorous development, from the eccelesiastical institution which had so long protected and directed its growth.

The historian should not, of course, overlook the great achievements of ecclesiastical Christianity, and the inestimable service it rendered to the long Middle Ages and through them to ourselves. When the Roman economy collapsed, and the peoples of central and northern Europe came tumbling into what had been the Empire, it was the church that educated this new Europe, not only in literary arts and in religious symbolism, but also in agriculture, building, and every economic skill. For a thousand years the church educated Europe. It preserved and propagated the political genius inherited from imperial Rome, providing ministers of state more educated and humane than their royal masters. For a thousand years it guided and moderated secular governments. And during this long period it firmly inculcated the truth, which Europe was not to forget until this twentieth century, that there stands above all kings and governments a moral authority which no political power may exert. Modern society could establish itself only after the disestablishment of ecclesiastical authority; but the free modern society which replaced medieval ecclesiasticism was, even in its libertarian rebellion, the child of that church, to which we must still owe a filial gratitude. Not to bring this gratitude is to lack spiritual maturity, and to have no claim to religious and intellectual liberty. Only what honors its origins lives long on this earth.

But the chief concern of this chapter is the intellectual

outlook which characterized Christianity. This required a departure from the most basic conceptions that had governed pagan thought. Christianity entertained a concept of nature so new that it has still eluded philosophical definition. Even after nineteen centuries there exists no satisfactory philosophical exposition of the Christian concept of nature, in spite of the revolutions this concept has inspired in natural science and social theory. Except in its theological elaborations, Christianity looked away from the concepts and ideals we have studied in classical Greek thought. Its largest concept it took from Judaism, which defined its faith partly in terms of the Mosaic law, partly by means of an imaginative historical retrospect upon the origins, development, and religious experience of the Jewish nation, which had prospered or suffered, the Jews believed, according to its fidelity to its theistic faith. In Christianity this dramatic history was widened to become a universal history of man. Adam's fall from grace, it was taught, had depraved the human race, which progressively declined until redeemed by the sacrifice and atonement of Jesus Christ, who would continue to abide with man until the completion of his work in a final salvation ending "the world" and inaugurating an era of perfect grace. In this doctrine Christianity substituted for the eternalistic or nontemporal metaphysic which had become identified with Greek science a temporal or evolutionary conception, in which nature was conceived to be a progressive creation in time; and this conception was pivoted upon the life and death of Jesus Christ, a dated historical event. The subsequent movement of science and philosophical thought has been a long transition, at first very slow, recently more rapid, from the Greek concept of eternal form to this Christian concept of temporal progress.

With this shift to a progressive or temporalistic concept of nature went a new perception of the primacy in nature of individual character. Greek thought had always placed a high evaluation upon the human individual and had distinguished men from other individuals on the ground of their rational faculty. But this emphasis upon human individuality had always been a sort of joint or hinge in Greek philosophy, because it could not be derived from the still more basic conception which saw in individual things only the local and imperfect appearances of eternal and universal Being. Christianity went still further in its high evaluation of the human individual; and it did not identify what is eternal in the human individual with the theorizing intellect. Its conception of nature as a great drama of temporal creation required the attribution of some sort of absoluteness to individual being, in that it made individuals, and not specific or other eternal forms, the directive agencies of natural occurrence.

But the opposition between the new Christian concept of nature and the old Greek eternalism, although it was doubtless vividly felt, could not be easily stated, or immediately grasped in its tremendous implication; and the new faith had to make some sort of contact with the long intellectual tradition of antiquity, which still dominated the intellectual life of that time. So we find Christianity seeking to adapt its language to that of traditional Greek philosophy, and even to present its very different conception in terms of that philosophy. Neoplatonism, as the form of Greek philosophy most familiar to educated Christians, provided the vocabulary used to introduce Christian thought to intellectual society. At the beginning of the third century there was elaborated, chiefly by *Origen*, the pupil of Neoplatonist Ammonius Saccas in Alexandria, the Christian theology which for many centuries would largely replace, as authoritative Christian creed, the simpler and mightier faith affirmed in the earlier scriptures. The junction between Christian faith and Greek philosophy was effected by means of the doctrine of the Trinity, which interpreted the relation of Jesus Christ to God and to man in terms of the three highest forms of the Neoplatonic hierarchy of being. The supreme Being became God the Father or Jehovah; the Logos or divine mind became God the Son, or Jesus Christ; and the world-soul became the Holy Ghost, the divine community of the church. Whether and in what degree this Neoplatonic theology expressed the insight of the founders of Christianity is a question we will not here debate. We may agree perhaps that any new faith projected into those last centuries of antiquity would have reached some sort of compromise reconciling the new faith with Greek thought. There seems to be little doubt that this Alexandrian theology aided the spread of the Christian gospel in the Roman world; but the price paid for this assistance was high. The insoluble epistemological and metaphysical problems of Greek philosophy were thereby injected into Christian doctrine, where they have properly no place; and when science and philosophy moved to new concepts of nature and knowledge, the Neoplatonic theology was left high and dry, without contact with modern life and thought.

But there was at least one early Father of the Church who was prescient of the revolutionary intellectual shift which was involved in the Christian outlook upon the world. This great thinker was *Augustine*, a fourth-century scholar. Born near Carthage in A.D. 354, of a pagan father and a Christian mother, Augustine in his earlier life was prey to moral and intellectual conflicts, which drove him to a pursuit of spiritual illumination so intense as to be almost morbid. Impelled first to skepticism, he escaped this by embracing Manichaean views which portrayed the existent world as an interminable struggle between God and Satan, or good and evil. From this dreadful creed he advanced to Neoplatonism, with its too facile optimism; and by Neoplatonism he was led to Christianity, of which he became the leading apologist.

Christianity solved Augustine's moral problem by its portrayal of evil as the consequence of human freedom. Evil is real enough; yet it is not a necessary, eternal condition of existence, since man has the power to eliminate it. But Christianity gave Augustine far more than this theoretical solution of his intellectual difficulties. It is evident to the reader of his *Confessions* that Augustine's problem was a personal one. A man of exceptional intellectual power, he had found no great work to do, no lasting and cumulative purpose which would give substance and perhaps immortality to his achievements. The young and vigorous church offered the vehicle for his talents that he needed. What he gave to that church would go far, and be conserved perhaps forever. Just because Augustine was individualistic to the point of egoism, it was altogether essential for him to lose himself in a life greater than his own. In the church, he tells us, he found the release for his energies and the serenity of mind he had sought elsewhere in vain; and the egoist of the *Confessions* became the immortal author of *The City of God*.

Looking back to Augustine today, we see in him the prototype of modern man. He stands alongside Plato as the second of the two thinkers who have most forcefully determined our intellectual evolution; and with each year, as we more clearly grasp the constitution of this modern age, the figure of Augustine increases in stature. Unlike Plato, who consummated the thought of Greece, Augustine stands at the beginning of the intellectual age which is our own. No great systematist, his greatness lay in his grasp, seldom clear but ultimately effective, of the new conception of reality which moved in the Christian faith. Limited though he was by the vocabulary of Greek philosophy, Augustine was nevertheless able to indicate a new sort of apprehension of actuality. He accomplished this by implication and suggestion. He gave to old concepts new meanings, he bluntly rejected certain hitherto dominant concepts, and he created some new concepts. In their sum, these changes successfully communicated the new concept of reality which engendered them. It is scarcely too much to say that the history of thought since Augustine, especially the thought of the last six centuries, has been the struggle between Greek eternalism and Augustinian creationism; and today we must acknowledge Augustine the victor in this struggle.

The concept of creation itself is the chief Augustinian doctrine. This concept is possibly the oldest of all philosophical ideas. Man's first anticipation of science was his mythical description of the creation of the world. The movement of Greek thought to a purely theoretical science had required the rejection of this primitive concept. Anaximander and Empedocles could teach the evolution of nature; but Aristotle taught, consistently with his method, that nature in all its specific form is eternal, and that there neither was nor is creation, except the perpetual re-creation of individual vehicles bearing the eternal specific forms. Augustine rejected this eternalistic theory; and in so doing he challenged the whole tradition of Greek theoreticism. The universe was literally created, he insisted, by God at a certain date. God first created matter, by a sheer benevolent act, in order to have a vehicle for form. To the question why a benevolent God so long delayed this benevolent creation, Augustine sturdily replied that there was no eternity prior to creation. Time appeared only with the creative act. Most remarkable is the confidence with which Augustine maintained this new and astonishing doctrine, which flatly collided with the earlier doctrine, still maintained by some, that time is only an empty and infinite medium in which events are simply located, even as events are located in space. Until quite recently Augustine's doctrine of a creation of time was opposed to scientific orthodoxy, and seemed almost unintelligible; but today, relativistic physical science is compelled to embrace it, intelligible or not. Leibnitz in the seventeenth century was the first modern thinker to hold that time and space are adjectival, not substantial. Augustine's conception of time would seem to be involved in any radically evolutionary conception of nature.

The notion of an original creation of the world leads to that of a continuous creation, still proceeding in present occurrence. Augustine did believe, of course, that God had continued providentially to direct nature, after His original creation of it; and he looked forward confidently to the re-creation and salvation of the human race through the creative agency of Jesus Christ and the church. Yet he never quite rejected the eternalistic theology of the earlier Fathers, who spoke of the world as the materialization of the timeless ideas of the *Logos* or the mind of God. However, Augustine's greatest and best-known work, *The City of God*, very definitely advanced a temporalistic or historical conception of reality. In this book the biblical story of the creation, fall, and redemption of man is expanded into a philosophy of history, which uses the narrative and prophecy of the Old Testament to portray a long struggle of earthly empires as the prelude to the advent of the true and divine government of man in the church. The Roman Empire is depicted as the latest embodiment of the powers of error and evil in the world; and Augustine hopefully anticipated, as well he might early in the fifth century, its final collapse. Augustine was not the first thinker to make use of history as a vehicle of philosophical truth; but he was the thinker through whom this philosophical approach, which earlier ages called "prophecy," was chiefly developed and transmitted to later times.

Augustine's reading of history as a long progress from more secular to more spiritual government is often dismissed by modern critics as a flagrant example of fatalistic or *teleological* explanation. Whereas science mechanistically explains later events as effects of earlier events which are their causes, the teleologist explains earlier events as the necessary antecedents of certain later events, their goal. Teleology, in short, extends the concept of purposive behavior to wider nature, as if vast nature revealed some purpose of its own. Thus for Augustine material nature was created to provide a home for the human spirit, and the long centuries of human error are shown to be the working of the will of God, who has determined man's salvation. It cannot be denied that Augustine does explain the history of nature teleologically, as leading up to its divinely intended goal or terminus; but the critic is incautious when he hastily assumes that such explanation is necessarily unscientific. As will be shown in the concluding chapters of this book, mechanistic science is not so directly opposed to teleological explanation as has been thought. The mechanistic scientist finally understands earlier and later events in terms of their causal relationships, which means in terms of one another. The later events are called the effects of the earlier events; but the earlier events themselves are finally described in terms of their causal consequences. Also, Augustine's teleology is of a rather curious sort, since the creation of the world is portrayed as a free act of God, *i.e.* as determined by nothing outside of itself; and the salvation of man, likewise, results from the free acts of freely willing individuals. Augustine did not always grasp the full implications of his own teaching. For example, he supposes that each human individual must have been preordained, even at its creation, to will its own salvation or damnation. This unhappy doctrine of predestination, according to which men are born saved or damned, shows that Augustine did not fully grasp what is implied by his doctrine of human freedom. The problem of the meaning and nature of causal determination, it is perhaps clear, requires an analysis of causal connection more penetrating than anything attempted in antiquity. Augustine, it may be said, did better with this problem than anyone before him, when he insisted upon the freedom of the individual, and consequently looked for a teleological pattern in events.

All of these problems of freedom, causation, determinism, etc., pivot on the relation of the individual thing or person to its larger context, "the world." If the individual is a real and effective being, then none of our traditional concepts of causation can be quite correct, because they finally preclude such effective reality in the individual thing. Augustine maintained the doctrine of determinism, which requires adequate cause for every event; and we shall find this doctrine to be presupposed in any and every intelligent inquiry into fact. He also maintained the freedom of the human will, a doctrine which only clearly states the concept of individual moral responsibility.

Since all science and society are established upon these two apparently contradictory doctrines, it is for the honest and courageous thinker to attempt their reconciliation, by showing how their apparent contradiction can be removed. We do not further understanding by affirming one of the two doctrines, while glibly ignoring the other.

The intention of early Christianity was to extol spontaneous goodness, immediate responsiveness, ready feeling. It advocated more "life," *i.e.* more sensitiveness to the immediate present. It opposed "the spirit" to "the law," the claim of the present or future to the claim of the dead past. This attitude was and is deeply philosophical—however, it is philosophical in a sense directly opposed to ancient philosophy, which had always deprecated the present in the interests of the "eternal," *i.e.* the past. Therefore Christianity in its most essential doctrine, that of the spirit which fulfils and transcends the law, could not be absorbed into Greek philosophy; and it has always reacted with and upon Greek philosophy in significant and profitable ways. One of these ways has been its emphasis upon individual character. To subordinate the law to the needs of living men and women is ultimately to make individuals the source and criterion of law.

This individualism appears both implicitly and explicitly in Augustine's writings. It is implicit in his autobiographical *Confessions*. These, with their unrelieved and somewhat egoistic concern for the salvation of their author, are the prototype of the psychological literature widely current in our own day. No other work of antiquity is so modern in quality as this. Augustine shows here little awareness of the society around him, the well-being of which is the real goal of all his moral effort. He is concerned only with his own soul and its redemption; yet the solution of his private problem is his entrance into the Christian community, in which his individual life is identified, by an act of free will, with the larger life of the church.

More explicit is the individualism of Augustine's theory of

knowledge. Where early Greek philosophy had separated the reason, as the only true cognitive faculty, from the other mental processes, Augustine finds cognition to involve the three faculties of will, intellect, and memory. Intellect had guided him to Neoplatonism, and through that doctrine to the contemplation of the Christian outlook; but an effort of will, in which he freely consigned himself to divine grace, was needed to take him into the Christian faith. One must believe, he said, in order to understand. William James would revive this doctrine early in the present century.

How does this theory of knowledge escape the pitfalls of skepticism? Greek rationalism, we saw, was a reply to the skeptics who had argued that the subjectivity and diversity of private experience leaves each individual with a knowledge peculiar to himself and without cogency for others. The rationalist had replied that reason, unlike perceptual experience, is identical in all men, and discovers in nature a self-identical and universal structure. Augustine is not willing to discount individual and perceptual experience in this way. The conceptual forms of the intellect become real, he implies, only when we positively and by an act of will translate them into personal experience; and it is this latter, with its immediate quality, that sanctions and confirms our intellectual formulas. Thus the reason, since it must wait in this way upon experience, is no refuge from skepticism. As a matter of fact, Augustine argues, skepticism is not something to be avoided, it is something to be embraced and overcome in personal combat. It is unavoidable that the individual mind should doubt, and doubt everything— that is its privilege and duty. One can and should, at some time or other, doubt one's reason, one's senses, God, the world, everything! Why should not all our personal experience be a nightmare, a private lunacy? But however far this process of doubt may go, we cannot doubt the reality of the person doubting—self-doubt implies a doubter. Having established in this way the reality of the individual self, characterized by its need and love of truth, Augustine is able to argue the reality of God who created the world and implanted in us our love of truth. Descartes, early in the seventeenth century, revived this Augustinian doctrine, which has given to all modern thought its distinctive subjective character.

Augustine was the first great and original thinker, if we except Lucretius, who used the Latin language. The use of Latin affected western thought, since Greek concepts undergo some modification even in their nearest Latin rendering; but more important is the great influence which this use of Latin gave to Augustine in the west, where Latin was to be the language of scholarship for more than a thousand years It is difficult to overemphasize this Augustinian influence in the development of western thought and life. The earlier Church Fathers had tied Christian theology to the rationalistic Neoplatonic philosophy. Augustine did not repudiate the earlier theology; yet he liberated himself from it, and liberated finally the thought of the west, by appending to it the individualistic, empirical, and creationistic doctrines we have noted.

The greatness of Augustine, and the enormous part he played in the shaping of western thought, are becoming recognized today. The positive and revolutionary character of his thought was not immediately apparent, for he usually said less than his doctrines implied. He retained the older theology alongside his own radical tenets; and he never, because he could not have done so, adds up his radical innovations and emphases to produce a total picture. But when, fifteen hundred years later, we try to sum up the modifications introduced by this remarkable thinker, in order to grasp the integral concept of reality which inspired and emboldened his thought, we are startled to find how different from that of any earlier thinker, and how like our own, was Augustine's vision of the world. This man, we conclude, was the first "modern"! And then we discover how, in historical fact, the thought of Augustine stimulated the late medieval movements which ushered in modern science and philosophy. But surprise becomes something like consternation when we realize that Augustine was led to these modern ways of thought only because he most literally and persistently adhered to the primary concepts of his religious faith, and to the facts of religious conversion as he had experienced these. It is scarcely too much to say that the modern mind, in its characteristic method and thought, is the extension of Augustine's theory of knowledge and his concept of nature, both of which he drew from his religion.

Notes for Further Reading

What is needed here is a presentation of Christian texts and early Christian history in a new sociological light, without sentimental and traditional coloring. The literature listed below may aid such presentation.

1. Goodspeed and Smith, *The Short Bible*. Chicago, University of Chicago Press, 1933.
2. Goodspeed, E. J., *An Introduction to the New Testament*. Chicago, University of Chicago Press, 1937.
3. ———— *The Story of the New Testament*. Boston, Beacon Press, and Chicago, University of Chicago Press, 1916, 1919.
4. Hitchcock, F. R. M., *St. Augustine's Treatise on the City of God*, abridged. S. P. C. K. Translations of Christian Literature, Series 2, 1931.
5. Healey, J., *St. Augustine's City of God*, introd. E. Barker. London and Toronto, J. M. Dent and Sons, Ltd., 1931, 1934.
6. McKeon, R., *Selections from Medieval Philosophies*. New York, Charles Scribner's Sons, 1929, Chap. I.
7. Augustinus, Aurelius, *The Confessions*. New York, Sheed and Ward, 1943. Especially Book XI.
8. Gilson, E., *The Spirit of Medieval Philosophy*. New York, Charles Scribner's Sons, 1936.
9. Bailey, C., ed., *The Legacy of Rome*. Oxford, The Clarendon Press, 1928, Oxford Series.
10. Figgis, J. N., *The Political Aspects of St. Augustine's City of God*. Boston, Longmans, Green and Company, 1921.
11. Miller, H., *Christian Truth in History*. New York, Harper and Brothers, 1941.

10   THE LONG MIDDLE AGE

WE HAVE NOW OBSERVED THE DEVELOPMENT OF Greek science, in its effort to establish a universal knowledge grounding a just civic constitution; we have seen how realistic thought, following Aristotle, became idealistic, natural science becoming a moral system and the ideal constitution becoming a city of the sky; and we have finally noted how Christianity cut across this Greek movement at an oblique angle, retaining and even accentuating its moral emphasis, yet requiring a realistic actualization of the moral ideal in a redeemed human community. The final result of the long development was the establishment of a universal church, armed with a moral or spiritual authority which claimed precedence over secular power. To Caesar should be rendered what is Caesar's, and to God what is God's. To God, announced the Christian prayer, belongs the kingdom, the power, and the glory forever! Just what was assigned to Caesar?

For a thousand years the ecclesiastical organization centered at Rome retained this authority, and western Europe developed under a dual government of church and state. The complex relationship between the ecclesiastical and secular governments is the central theme of the long medieval history; and this relationship continues to play a much larger part than is usually recognized in the history of the last five centuries—witness its importance in the convulsions of France and Spain today! The deeper issue, that of the relationship between moral authority and political power, is the central theme of western history from early Greece to the present. Western history is the long and successful effort to create political institutions which will be subject to, and progressively expressive of, the moral genius of man.

Some contemporary thinkers and publicists, incurably pessimistic about the present world, would have us go back of the Reformation and Renaissance to that golden age when a great established church, wielding the sword of the spirit, dominated every part of human life and channeled every human activity toward its sublime ideal. In point of fact one seeks in vain in the pages of history for that medieval paradise. One can be enthusiastic about many phases of the great work of the medieval church; but one cannot be enthusiastic about the social and political life of the Middle Ages, which conditioned and required medieval ecclesiasticism. Only where political power is unenlightened and oppressive, only where society is ignorant and oppressed, is an authoritative church a palliative for social evils. We agree with these critics that modern society too often forgets the moral and religious sources of its present liberty; but we also remember that only through the Reformation and the Renaissance were great aspirations, fostered by a thousand years of medieval religion, realized in an emancipated modern world. Long though they lasted, the medieval institutions were inherently transitional and unstable. The first three quarters of the Middle Ages saw vigorous development of the great ecclesiastical system; but the last quarter, from the thirteenth century to the fifteenth, saw the explosive exodus of Christian society from its medieval chrysalis into modern life—since which time all feudal and ecclesiastical systems have been anachronisms, retained at the price of social and intellectual stagnancy, and not to be revived except by a return to the social and political poverty out of which they arose.

Feudalism appears at an early stage of many a developing civilization. When the western Roman Empire, separated now from the eastern Empire centered at Constantinople, fell into chaos as the result of turbulent migrations from northern and central Europe, a measure of order and stability was reached where local chieftains could establish their power by rigid military rule. As chaos lessened and migrating peoples turned to settlement and agriculture, military discipline became a system of land tenure, the ownership of land carrying military responsibilities. This was feudalism, a loose system of personal government which could and did develop into the great feudal hierarchy of emperor, kings, princes, lords, knights, squires, yeomen, and serfs. Normally, *i.e.* with peace and the development of artisanship and commerce, feudal government is steadily transformed into something else, even where the feudal forms and titles are retained. It should be observed that feudal government, although personal, is not absolute government. Each level of the feudal hierarchy has its rights as well as its responsibilities, and it is the duty of the individual to maintain these feudal rights, established by use or common law, against aggression from above and invasion from below. When war and the constant threat of war gave way to more peaceful prospects, the feudal system became artificial and self-destructive, corrupting into "chivalry" and bloody vendettas between noble families. The Wars of the Roses illustrate this dying feudalism in England. When the rival factions had sufficiently destroyed each other, Henry Tudor, as Henry VII, backed by the urban nonfeudal population, was able to establish monarchy in place of feudalism. The English people tolerated, indeed heartily supported, this Tudor dynasty in its usurpation of absolute power, until feudal claims had become obsolete; yet when the people rebelled against royal absolutism, they justified their rebellion in part on the ground of ancient feudal rights which monarchy had overridden.

The medieval church developed within or alongside this feudal system, as in certain respects itself a feudal institution. Its assumption of institutional powers corresponding to its responsibility for the spiritual well-being of the community was intelligible within this feudal context; and its hierarchical organization paralleled that of feudalism, although it was a hierarchy not so much of birth as of talent. The medieval church realized in a striking degree the vision of Plato's *Republic*, and it offered for many centuries some escape from the harsh restrictions of the landed feudalism based upon inherited privilege; but it is only in a feudal system, characterized by a distribution of governmental responsibilities and powers among self-perpetuating classes, that moral authority can be the monopoly of an established clergy. Democracy forbids the allocation of authority to any institution, since it places authority wholly in the people. Instead, therefore, of proposing to reestablish authoritative religion, the moral reformer should show us how the great religious and moral vision inculcated by the medieval church inspired the movement to a democratic form of government, which would make possible, it was believed, the full realization of that vision in a moral society. During the long Middle Ages the church upheld the principle that might is subject to right, and that political power is therefore eternally subject to moral authority. That principle we must still enforce; and when we do enforce it, we are the true and loyal children of the medieval church. We place this authority in the individual conscience.

By the thirteenth century, which saw the greatest achievement of the medieval church, the feudal system with its divided powers had become impracticable and intolerable. The ecclesiastical domains had expanded until they included a large portion of the arable land of Europe, so that they constituted a great and self-sufficient economy, indeed an independent empire with its own government, code of law, and courts. In many respects this great ecclesiastical state which crossed all feudal boundaries offered to the individual a life more free, more inspired, and more humane than might be found elsewhere. It was a question, indeed, whether this clerical government might not become the sole government of Europe. Yet the church itself, since its clergy was celibate, could not be identified with European society; and the great expansion of its economic and political responsibilities increasingly affected the character of the church, secularizing it and prejudicing its religious work. Thus the Middle Ages produced a well-nigh insoluble problem, a problem that was to convulse Europe in century-long wars and that has never ceased to disturb continental Europe. The problem was to keep religion authoritative while divesting it of secular powers.

Having brought this problem to an acute stage, the Middle Ages came to an end, the feudal and ecclesiastical systems crashing down together. Strong kings with the support of their commoners usurped the feudal power; the great ecclesiastical estates were confiscated and distributed, the clerical orders were disbanded. But the deeper problem was not solved by these strong-arm measures. Where was now the moral authority, the rule of the spirit, which ever since Emperor Constantine's recognition of the church had in theory limited tyrannous government? I am that spirit, said the absolute king; I am the head and fount of the church. And where was the common law, the inborn rights and powers that inhered in some measure in every feudal class? I am the law, said the king; all powers derive from me. So the fall of feudalism and ecclesiasticism, precipitated by strong kings who could sincerely and reasonably appeal to the crying need for radical political and economic reform, was followed by a period of revolutions, needed to establish once again the authority of moral man over established power. And we observe that such revolution was successful, permanent in its political establishments, and beneficial in its consequence, only where it was motivated by religious hope and sustained by religious conviction.

The great stream of medieval life and letters moved through the church. Recent scholarship makes much of the secular arts of the Middle Ages—the charming romance, the quaint ballad with its prehistoric allusions, and the shrewd folklore; but the historian must always return to the central river of intellectual life which proceeded, even where it challenged and undermined the church, within the cloister. There, clerics working in ecclesiastical libraries and teaching in the great ecclesiastical schools slowly engendered those political, scientific, and philosophical conceptions which provided the framework or anatomy of modern society. Modern society is the child of that medieval clericalism, which was perhaps less cloistered than it appears to us today.

With much of this medieval scholarship we are not here concerned. The chief intellectual labor of the first six or seven centuries was the definition of Christian dogma, this definitive statement of creed being designed to ensure the unity and effectiveness of the ecclesiastical organization. Later it was necessary to defend these Christian tenets in face of the newly arisen and rapidly expanding Mohammedan world, which enclosed Christian Europe in a great crescent from Spain to the Near East. Through Araby came the science and philosophy of Aristotle, avidly sought after by European scholars and leading to a reformulation of Christian philosophy. Finally came a flood of pre-Christian and Arabic texts which no theology could make orthodox, and the Renaissance carried science and philosophy out of the church into the secular world. But the cloistered centuries had left their mark, indeed they had given momentum and form to a European mind which was to be satisfied with no earlier wisdom, and which was to deliver itself of a science peculiarly its own, outranging anything bequeathed to it by antiquity.

Western scholars have lamented the vandalism with which

early Christianity destroyed or allowed to rot the great libraries of later antiquity. That early Christianity prohibited the pagan literature is unquestionable; but since this literature was never lost in eastern Europe, where the Greek language remained in common use, it seems to have been the use of Latin rather than any deliberate prohibition that cut western Christianity off from Greek science and scholarship. However this may be, there is no doubt that the small library of writings which was retained by the western church had all the more influence in its determination of a distinctively occidental way of thought. This library contained the works of Augustine and other Latin Fathers in their Latin originals, and also portions of the writings of Cicero, Seneca, and Lucretius. In translation from the Greek there was of course the New Testament, and also portions of the Greek Fathers, a fragment fror the *Timaeus* of Plato, parts of Aristotle's logic with a commentary by the Neoplatonist Porphyry, the *Consolations* of Boethius, and some philosophical commentaries. For some centuries the mind of western Europe was whetted on these few texts, which gave to western culture a vocabulary, a style of speech, and an orientation of thought which are still discernible. Just as a boy today might be better educated by the rigorous study of a few well-selected texts than by a large amount of casual reading, so it is possible that western Europe was blessed and not cursed by its isolation from the vast literature of later antiquity. One effect of this isolation was that the great systems of Greek science and metaphysics became known only when western society had developed itself far enough, in exercises logical and theological, to be able to meet Greek thought with a measure of independence. So there could arise and maintain itself that critical attitude of mind which is the chief mark of the western intellect. Our concern therefore with these Middle Ages will be the movement to this critical attitude of mind, as this movement was stimulated by increasing contact with the original thought of Greece.

The first contact of this kind was a strange one, occurring

early in the ninth century. *John Scotus Eriugena* was called from northern Britain or Ireland to the continent of Europe to teach in the court school newly established by Charlemagne. In his remote mission, founded presumably very early by Greek-speaking Christians, the Greek language was still remembered, and Eriugena could read the Greek Fathers in the original. He was also deeply influenced by a late Neoplatonic work, mistakenly attributed to Dionysius the Areopagite, a person mentioned in the New Testament but otherwise unknown. Eriugena's Latin translation of this work gave to Europe its first considerable knowledge of Greek thought. In his own writings, Eriugena displayed an independence of mind as praiseworthy as it was remarkable. One must read even the Bible and the Christian Fathers, he wrote, with independent judgment, because faith must lead reason and not displace it. While it is important to descend from universal truths to their manifestations in observable fact, he further said, we must also ascend from observed fact to universal truth. Here in the ninth century, in the mouth of a Scotch or Irish monk, is the first indication of the critical and empirical faith which will characterize modern thought. Although the church formally condemned Eriugena's declaration of intellectual independence, it does not seem to have effectively prohibited the study of his works.

There followed this first revival of scholarship a century of turmoil, due to the incursions over Europe of the Norsemen; but the educational movement begun by Charlemagne weathered the storm, and in the eleventh century there began that development which made the schools at Paris a great center of intellectual development, which they remained until the Renaissance. It is remarkable how soon the clerical scholars, examining their scanty literary bequest, fastened upon that crucial problem which was to remain the nub of scientific and philosophical controversy down to this day. This was the *problem of universals*, the word "universal" being the Latin translation of the Greek "idea" or "form." Porphyry in his commentary upon Aristotle's logic had asked: Are universals prior to the things which instance them, or in things, or after things, *i.e.* in our minds? Roscellinus answered flatly: in our minds, and only there, because all actual things are individual beings, and there is no being that is not ineradicably individual. This is the doctrine of *nominalism*, which affirms that universal or general terms are but names. We can give the same name, *e.g.* "dog," to any member of a class of similar things; but these things are individual beings, and we may not suppose that there is some nonindividual sort of being, *i.e.* universal Being, corresponding to universal terms.

This doctrine is at first sight plausible, and we shall see that it withstands criticism; yet the nominalist must explain why, if general terms refer to nothing real in nature, they are indispensable to all study and explanation of nature. Does theoretical science, which defines certain very general structures such as physical structure, chemical structure, etc., describe not a structure in nature but only a structure in our minds? The nominalist will always raise an adversary in the *realist*, who insists that universal terms refer to realities, not to names merely. So *Anselm of Canterbury*, the older and much respected contemporary of Roscellinus, rose to the latter's challenge with an able defense of realistic metaphysics. To deny the reality of universal Being, Anselm argued, is to forego all rational knowledge. To know the universal forms which reside in individual things is to understand things. It is to know why things behave as they do, and to understand their place and function in the universal system of the cosmos. Individual things are therefore intelligible and "real" only in virtue of these universal forms which they manifest, which forms therefore are most real. It is through these universal forms, moreover, that we are led to religious truth, since to pursue these causal and formal relations is to be led finally to the supreme Form and First Cause of everything, which is God. Thus to affirm universals is to affirm at once the intelligible structure and the divine governance of the world. Anselm pointed out that the nominalist must eventually deny the doctrine of the Trinity. If only individuals are real, the three individual persons of the Trinity can never be one, a real Being present in all three. Roscellinus might have replied that the realist has an equal but opposite difficulty with the doctrine of the Trinity. If individual being only manifests real universal Being, the three persons of the Trinity are real only as one, and not in their separateness.

Christian dogma did in fact preclude both extremes of nominalism and realism. It implied that individual being and universal Being are equally real; but it was usually satisfied to see in this double affirmation a truth transcending purely logical analysis. In this compromise it pointed the way to modern empirical science, and also indicated the central problem of modern philosophy, which is still focused upon this crucial relationship between particular and general fact.

The most striking and fruitful intellect of this period was that of *Peter Abelard*. Abelard got rid of the controversy over universals by agreeing with the nominalist that only individual beings are real, yet also holding with the realist that these individual beings are informed with genuinely universal characters. Thus there are only individual dogs; yet there is an authentic canine form, identical in all of these individuals and making of them a real species. But Abelard's more important contribution was his development of the method of critical and constructive analysis, which became the foundation of all later medieval scholarship. This method requires the clear statement of a problem or topic, and the collection of all authoritative statements by earlier thinkers bearing upon this subject. Then it undertakes the analysis and clarification of this body of evidence, and finally advances to a solution or definitive statement required by the weight of evidence. Later writers have heaped much contumely upon this scholastic method; and we must recognize that it fell short of the scientific method of the modern period, in that it confined itself to book knowledge and traditional learning, and did not advance to conclusions based upon new evidence reached by original observation and experiment. Yet we should do justice to the scholastic method, even in recognizing its limitations. It was not subservient, since it required the scholar to weigh his textual authorities and to depend upon his own judgment. It proposed to advance beyond earlier opinion, by finding in the contradictions of past authorities an injunction to independent thought. Scholastic method at its best, for example in Abelard or Aquinas, was in truth a preparation for modern critical science; and without this first stage there could not have developed the second stage. In this first stage, the scholar aimed to master past thought, accepting its conclusions as evidence yet not as finality, in order to reach a higher and truer illumination. Such scholarly analysis, comprehending and weighing all existing knowledge, must always form an important part of research. In the second stage of this development, properly called "science," the thinker turns to observable fact and experiment for new evidence, derived not from books and past authorities but from nature itself. However, a true science will always comprehend the insight of the past; and the scholastic method was a proper and necessary prelude of the independent natural science of today.

Abelard's tragic history is a profound commentary on medieval society. The most brilliant young scholar of his century, he could anticipate a clerical career leading to the highest and most responsible offices in Europe. This career required celibacy; and Abelard fell in love with his lovely and gifted pupil Heloise. Heloise, vowing that she would rather be Abelard's mistress than the spouse of an emperor, refused to allow her lover to sacrifice his career by regularizing their union; and she retired with their daughter to a convent, where she wrote those letters which still make this story the most authentic and moving of the medieval romances. Abelard, emasculated by the indignant family of Heloise and publicly disgraced, never made good his broken career. He was given charge of wild monks in remote monasteries, and his great abilities were never adequately used.

This twelfth century saw the first important incursion into Europe of Arabic science and scholarship, at first through Spain, later by other routes. With this Moslem learning came a knowledge of Aristotle, at first only in Arabic and Hebrew translations. Both the Arabs and the Jews, who were honored in the Moslem world, produced great syntheses of Aristotelian philosophy and religious doctrine, and their scholastic systems were at once challenge and model to Christian scholasticism. The new knowledge of Aristotle produced an intellectual revolution among European scholars, especially at the schools of Paris, where the teaching of Aristotle, at first prohibited, could not really be discountenanced. *Albertus Magnus* (Albert of Cologne) studied in the original Greek each of Aristotle's treatises, and made translations with explanations which allowed the European reader, confused by many centuries of misinterpretation of Greek thought, entrance into the true thought of Aristotle—a very remarkable achievement; and *Thomas Aquinas* (St. Thomas, the Angelic Philosopher), Albert's pupil, incorporated the science and metaphysics of Aristotle into a great Christian synthesis.

Both directly through the translation into Latin of Aristotle's treatises, and indirectly through the scholastic system of Aquinas, the science and philosophy of Aristotle now became the framework of formal education, and to a very large degree possessed itself of European thought, a position it retained for several centuries. Because modern science arose, as we shall presently see, largely by contrast and in combat with this Aristotelian scholasticism, we seldom perceive how great is the debt Europe owed to these scholastic disciples of Aristotle. It was through this recovery of Aristotelian science that Europe obtained its first conception of a natural science reached by rational analysis of observable fact. The scholastics, it is true, read Aristotle subserviently, as if the human reason had uttered in Aristotle its whole thought and must ever after only think that thought again. Yet it was nevertheless Aristotle who taught Europe to see in nature a great array of natural domains, each accessible to the natural light of reason and each delivering its appropriate science. And the rebellion against Aristotle, necessary and fruitful as it was, was never able to confine the broadened mind of Europe to a single narrow discipline.

It would take too long, nor does it belong within the purpose of this book, to try to portray the great system of Aquinas, which erects upon the flat architectonic of Aristotelian science the towering spire of Christian theology. *Thomism*, as we call this system today, became very quickly the unofficial, and much later the official, philosophical code of the Roman Church, which it remains to this day, when it is experiencing a vigorous revival in certain Catholic centers. The largest movement of modern science and philosophy, however, whatever may be its final or future constitution, has proceeded independently of scholastic thought, and to a considerable degree in hostile opposition to it. We will note, therefore, only some of the largest and most generally influential doctrines of the scholastic philosophy.

First, Aquinas defined the boundaries and legitimate functions of faith and reason, *i.e.* of revealed religion and theoretical science. Faith, he taught, reveals the goal toward which reason must strive, but which reason cannot of itself attain. Because the world is the creation of God's free and omnipotent will, it is a contingent world, *i.e.* it is a world the character of which cannot be deduced from any purely rational premises. This principle of the contingency of nature, which Aquinas derives from Christian doctrine, is truly the principle which calls for an empirical science, reaching its conclusions from observed fact, to replace the rationalistic science of antiquity. Aquinas concludes further that scientific knowledge must be less than complete, because the world, as the creature of an infinite Creator, must be infinite and incomprehensible. It is the duty of the reason, however, to carry its purely rational and unaided study as far as it can, and then, having reached this point, to use the truths of revealed religion as a guide and aid to a further rationalization of fact. In this way, reason and faith will support, complete, and confirm one another.

This doctrine is of importance for the later development of thought, first because it set aside a domain for the natural reason, *i.e.* for a science moving from sensible fact, by way of logical analysis, to natural principles; and secondly because it recognized that the widest principles of natural knowledge, for example those which affirm the world to be an intelligible domain, transcend anything that can be certainly inferred by logic from observable fact. Aquinas intimated what Hume and Kant were later to establish—the fact that science issues from an act of faith in the unity and intelligibility of nature. In Christianizing Aristotle, Aquinas went beyond Aristotle. It is only our faith in the intelligent creation of the world, a faith derived from revealed religion, Aquinas believed, that justifies the rational demands we make upon nature. Experience provides the matter for knowledge; reason undertakes the organization of this matter into knowledge; and faith assures reason of its powers and guides their exercise. We shall see that the profoundest of modern thinkers have still required a threefold analysis of mind, somewhat of this sort.

The great social problem of the later Middle Ages was the relation of ecclesiastical government to the secular governments of Europe, *i.e.* the relation between church and state. Aquinas was orthodox, yet liberal and forward-looking, in his treatment of this problem. His purpose was to secure to both church and state their due powers, appropriate to their functions in that medieval world; and he did this by means of certain political concepts that were to dominate later political thought, and help to determine the political foundations of modern society. There are, he taught, four kinds of law. *Eter-*

nal law is the infinite and unknowable will of God. *Natural law* is the part of eternal law accessible to the human reason through its scientific study of nature. *Divine law* is the part revealed to man in transmitted religion. *Human law* is the realization of natural and divine law in legal codes, *e.g.* Roman and canon law, and in the *jus gentium*, the unwritten law regulating relations among nations or peoples. By means of this elastic or compendious doctrine Aquinas established the concept of a divine or natural law, supporting and realized in the actualities of government. This was a return to the Greek and Platonic ideal of government by law, which Aquinas thus helped to make a commonplace of political thought. Aquinas followed Aristotle in his conception of the state as a natural outgrowth of human sociability. He favored monarchy, as did in the thirteenth century most forward-looking thinkers, weary of the failures of feudal government. Also forward-looking was Aquinas' doctrine that the state, responsible at once to God and to the people, must secure the economic welfare of its citizens.

We should see in the scholastic system of Aquinas one of the great achievements and emancipating influences of medieval thought. It established the authority of a free natural science, proceeding from observable fact by way of rational analysis; it secured the authority of secular government, yet subjected this power to limitations both moral or spiritual and popular or legal; and it showed the dependency of both science and society upon moral foundations. The later centuries owe much to this great and liberal thinker, who combined breadth of classical scholarship with intensity of religious faith. Yet the work of Aquinas had very definite limitations, which leave it an achievement peculiarly medieval and unmodern.

Its most obvious limitation was its fidelity to the logic and science of Aristotle, whose method, as we noted earlier, constituted only one movement of Greek science, and not the most fruitful approach to fact. In the hands of men of less genius

than Aquinas this Aristotelian method produced a very stereotyped and sterile sort of analysis, which was often little more
than a pretentious systematization of verbal usage. Aquinas
died young, he was almost wholly the pupil of Albertus, and
he seems to have been ignorant of vital currents moving in
other clerical circles. Nor does he seem to have realized the
significance of certain deep stirrings in the religious world of
his day, leading to the Reformation. These limitations might
have been overcome, perhaps, if the church had appropriated
the liberal spirit and intention of Aquinas, instead of the letter
of his doctrines; but the church, able to accept this synthesis
of Christian doctrine and Aristotelian science, was disturbed
by the increasing ferment which was stirred by the recovery
of pagan literature, and refused to move further. It equated
natural science with the science of Aristotle. The result was to
make of modern science, which looked away from Aristotle,
a heresy separating its adherents from established religion.

There occurred during the thirteenth century radical
changes in the ecclesiastical and religious life of Europe. St.
Thomas belonged to the Benedictine order, which had always
been closely identified with the tradition of ecclesiastical authority; but there arose in the thirteenth century the lay order
of Franciscan friars, which spread rapidly across Europe and
propagated a new conception of the Christian faith. *St. Francis
of Assisi* had received a spontaneous and independent apprehension of Christ, unmediated by ritual and ecclesiastical discipline. In poverty, in humility, in simple and unreserved adoration and passionate obedience, Francis expressed his unassum-
ing protest against the institutionalism that had incorporated
Christian faith into a vast political, economic, and intellectual
system. More powerfully than any systematic thinker might
have done, Francis through his incomparable simplicity and
infectious ardor restored to Christianity the naturalism which
is so evident in the scriptural record of its founder.

The rapid growth of the Franciscan movement among the

lay membership of the church testified to the desire of the people of Europe to appropriate to themselves the religious insight which earlier had been the prerogative of the ecclesiastical priesthood. Very soon, it is true, the Franciscans organized themselves into a clerical order similar to that of the Dominicans; and only two centuries later did the Protestant Reformation erase in northern Europe the line between the priesthood and society at large. But the Franciscan movement foreshadowed, in its unpretentious and simple practice of religion and in its philosophical and theological leanings, the modern society that issued from the Middle Ages. Franciscan theology looked chiefly to Augustine, and gave to the creative thought of that great mind an influence greater than it had enjoyed; and the memory of St. Francis was preserved in a naturalistic mysticism which made the visible world an immediate experience of God. Thus *Buonaventura,* a contemporary of Aquinas and the first Franciscan philosopher, tells us to see in our immediate experience the small analogue of the universal and divine process by which God creates the world. Earlier theology had looked to the authority of tradition, derived from revelation in the past; but St. Francis, in the power of his direct experience of God, taught his followers a new way of truth, a new confidence in their powers of immediate apprehension, and a new conception of that ultimate Being which is at every time accessible to the earnest and illuminated mind. Following the lives and words of these thirteenth-century Franciscans, we feel that we are attending the birth of a new mentality, one that is modern, democratic, and empirical; and we are not surprised to discover in the writings of certain Franciscan scholars the initial steps of the science and philosophy of today. This modern way of thought we call "empirical" or "empiricistic," because it emphasizes experience rather than reason, even at the expense of reason. By "experience" is meant the immediate perception of sensible fact, and by "reason," in this context, is meant the conceptual formulations and explicit theories of the intellect.

The essential result of this emphasis upon experience, consequently, is the subjection of conceptual knowledge to the test
of observable fact, and the utilization of presently observable
fact as a source of new knowledge. Such empiricism, critical of
conceptual theory, is the distinctive character of the modern
mind; and we should recognize in the religious empiricism of
the Franciscans its historical beginnings.

Originating in Italy, the Franciscan order had its most important development further north. It seems to have quickly
gathered into its intellectual outlook much of the mystical,
nominalistic, and other speculative thought which found no
place in the great Thomistic synthesis, so that its scholars prepared the chief opposition to this scholastic development. Even
in the thirteenth century there arose Roger Bacon, the Franciscan thinker whose teaching directed thought into new chan-
nels which, running alongside or underneath the more orthodox scholastic tradition, were to deepen and broaden into the
great current of modern science.

Bacon was the pupil of *Robert Grosseteste*, a remarkably
well-read cleric who was familiar with the Arabic learning,
an early translator of Aristotle, and the progenitor of a mathematical study of nature which apparently looked back to
Plato for its inspiration. Grosseteste, influenced perhaps by
Arabic science, rejected the Greek view that circular motion
is the original form of all natural motion. He held original motion to be rectilinear, and circular motion to be derivative.
This change was to be of drastic importance for all later
science. The new view encouraged the study of terrestrial
motions in their own right, and the extension of this terrestrial
physics to celestial phenomena. This approach led to the science
of Galileo and Newton, and through them to the theoretical
science and philosophy of the modern period.

Roger Bacon devoted himself to the development of this new
science, which recovered, he rather astonishingly believed, the
eternal truth revealed by Moses, by Plato, and by Christ. The

whole business of science, he said, is to know clearly the small set of primary and universal principles basic to mathematical science, and to apply these principles, directly or through experimentation, to the observable phenomena of nature, which will everywhere reveal their perfect fidelity to mathematical pattern. He mercilessly castigated the loose and haphazard "learning" of his time, and was especially critical of Aristotelian science. He professed adherence to the established religion; but he called upon the church to cast out its unscientific philosophy, and to encourage this mathematical and experimental research. It is the virtue of this true science, he said, to give man power over nature; and this great instrument, if the church neglects its use, will fall into the hands of the enemies of the church and be used to destroy the church. The church did not respond to these vehement exhortations. It imprisoned the hot old genius during the last decade or more of his long life, none other than the saintly and gifted Buonaventura signing the order for his incarceration; and we shall never know what the church might have become if instead of repudiating its great son it had united the development of modern science with its own religious aspiration, and not required posterity to choose between scientific truth and religious orthodoxy.

The complete teaching of Roger Bacon is a matter of some obscurity. Only fragments of his writings are preserved, some of his works being inscribed in a curious cipher not yet decoded. But it is established that he was a great initiator of experimental theoretical science, looking to experience and attempting an independent analysis of observed fact. He seems to have united the mathematical faith of Plato with the new Franciscan and Augustinian insight into the potentialities of our immediate experience of nature. Just how Bacon united reason and experience we do not know; but that he did bring them together into a most fruitful union is shown by the long development of science and philosophy, reaching down to ourselves, which issued from him. In Bacon first was the great impetus of

Greek science recovered, and science was reestablished in its more powerful modern form. Just what this modern science is, only another six centuries of philosophical analysis will at last make clear. We should not feel scornful nor superior, therefore, with respect to Bacon's large claim to have rediscovered the great vision of Hebrew, Greek, and Christian antiquity. What his whole vision was, we do not know; but that he had vision, all subsequent thought is proof. He is the gigantic progenitor of modern science, if that claim may be made for any man.

From Roger Bacon there proceeded an intellectual tradition, developed first in England and later on the continent of Europe, which would define itself by way of its divergence from the Aristotelian scholasticism, and by way of its opposition to every form of rationalistic and dogmatic thought. Its first English proponents were Duns Scotus and William of Occam. *Duns Scotus* was a brilliant young theologian who immediately followed Bacon at Oxford. His chief teaching was that of the contingent or irrational character of nature, its infinite diversity, and its completely individual character, these qualities deriving from its origin as the creation of the infinite will of God. From this characterization of nature, Scotus proceeded to a critique of rational knowledge. Rational knowledge, of necessity general and abstract, must fail of exhaustiveness, because it does not grasp the concrete individual character of things. The human will, Scotus pointed out, limits human knowledge, in that it directs our intellectual attention upon certain abstract characters to the neglect of others. Only the infinite will of God can wholly comprehend nature. This profound study, startling in its foreshadowing of Kant, was the work of a young man who died in his thirty-fourth year.

The new tradition was carried forward by *William of Occam* (or Ockham), the greatest mind of the fourteenth century, whose theory of knowledge clearly defined the lines which empirical philosophy has subsequently followed. There are, Occam taught, two criteria or tests of knowledge, not merely one. The first is the rational criterion—our conclusions must be deducible from basic self-evident principles, such as the axioms of mathematics. The second is the empirical criterion, which requires that general knowledge must confirm itself in all observable particular fact. We saw how Eriugena in the ninth century first set forth this double requirement, which Occam in the fourteenth century restates in clearer language. It is this double requirement that distinguishes modern empirical science from all earlier science, which was rationalistic because it emphasized the first requirement to the neglect of the second. We must believe that Occam publicized in this way the scientific theory and practice proposed by his predecessor Roger Bacon. This means that modern science was inaugurated in its essential principles in the thirteenth century.

Equally important for the rise of empirical science was a second doctrine promulgated by Occam. The objective of science, he taught, is the discovery of causal relations among particular things. Medieval learning, following Aristotle, had found the causes of individual things in their specific forms, *i.e.* in the conformity of particular fact to general forms, which constitute in this view the general causes of particular events. (So today we might explain the motion of the moon as a particular instance of the general "law" of gravitation.) In a slashing attack upon the scholastic science, Occam rejected this sort of explanation as merely verbal. To classify a thing as a member of a certain species, or to classify an event as a certain sort of event or as the instance of some law, does not inform us concerning the cause of that thing or that event. The causes of a particular thing or event lie in other *particular* things or events. (Thus although we say that the motion of the moon is an instance of the law of gravitation, we mean that the moon is determined in its motion by the action upon it of particular forces exerted by particular bodies, chiefly the earth and sun.) There are in every occurrence or change, it follows, at least two particular causes, namely the nature of the particular thing acted upon, and the particular character of what acts upon it. Occam recognized this fact in his principle of the *plurality of causes*. One might say, therefore, that modern science is the explanation of events as resulting from a plurality of particular causes, according to some law or principle. This principle of particular and plural causation, perhaps the most basic and distinctive principle of modern science, has been too little studied in its tremendous implications for our concept of nature.

Empirical philosophy, which Occam first elaborated and which continues and broadens to become the dominant modern outlook, tends to overlook an important fact. Causal interactions, however particular their component factors may be (*e.g. this* moon, *this* earth, *this* sun exerting just *these* particular forces upon one another) still conform to general laws or principles. If they did not do so, there could be no theoretical science, explaining particular interactions as instances of general scientific formulas. Occam too easily dismissed this important fact because he was a nominalist, which means that he supposed all universal or general forms to exist only in the mind, as names assignable to collections of individual things or particular events. The whole great tradition of universal science, he said, was only a pretentious fiction, since the universal forms which it postulated as the "causes" of natural occurrence have no existence. The definitions of these forms, he further concluded, are only verbal, trivial, or *nominal* definitions, not the real definitions of things. This debate concerning the reality of general and universal forms is the theme of all later philosophy, and we must not enter it here; but we may anticipate what follows so far as to say that later thought has widely accepted Occam's description of scientific explanation as bent upon particular causes, but not as a rule his nominalistic dismissal of general laws as only mental. If a general formula allows the prediction of individual behavior, there must be something in individual things which corresponds to the general formula and is truly indicated by it. But we forgive Occam's error because of the value and truth of his positive account of science. Occam's strictures upon scientific method became a deathblow to all forms of scholastic, merely rationalistic science, and the foundation of an empirical science which derives its hypotheses from experienced fact and confirms them again therein.

We have given considerably more space and importance to these medieval Franciscans than is usually accorded to them. Our purpose is to correct the still prevalent superstition that modern science suddenly appeared, without notable antecedents, at the time of the Renaissance. We must insist that modern science in its distinctive character was initiated by these clerics working in the thirteenth and fourteenth centuries. What was the deep and obscure feeling which motivated these men, whose thought was to transform the human intellect, and through this the human world? What compelled them to rebel against all the scientific and philosophical authority of the past? What insight gave them their moral courage and their scientific power? In their own day, remember, they could appeal to no great body of empirical achievement such as exists today. For their scientific experiments they were suspect in the public eye, as devotees of the "black art" of magic. For their philosophical teachings they were persecuted, ostracized, despised by their learned fellows. Bacon languished in prison; and the name of Duns Scotus became the scornful epithet "dunce," hurled by orthodox scholars at these subversive nonconformists. Did these followers of St. Francis see a new world because they strained toward a new society, a society emancipated from the political bonds of feudalism and the intellectual bonds of medieval ecclesiasticism? Was their intellectual rebellion the van of a social and religious rebellion? The early Greeks established Greek science because they insisted that nature, like Greek society, must manifest a legal constitution, and comprise a realm of "natural law." Did these Franciscans propose to make nature the domain of a new liberty? Did they enfranchise individual things in preparation for the revolution that would enfranchise individual men?

Occam, we know, sided with the Emperor in that struggle against papal authority out of which later was to proceed the Reformation. Something new, something pure, free, common, holy, and omnipotent was born in that thirteenth century, when Grosseteste and Bacon stood entranced before a world compacted of holy light, and when St. Francis saw God in trees and birds and flowers and Christ revealed in every human lineament. There mightily stirred again in that century the force that in Augustine—or was it in Jesus Christ?—had put humanity on the march. It was an irresistible force that moved now slowly, now tumultuously, here creatively, there catastrophically, but that always moved and still moves. It was the force, clearly cognizable only in its outcome, that moved through intellectual and political revolution to create the modern world. In these last pages, all too obscurely and incompletely, we have reported the birth of modern society.

Notes for Further Reading

1. McKeon, R., *Selections from Medieval Philosophies*. New York, Charles Scribner's Sons, 1929, Vol. I; 1930, Vol. II.
2. Gilson, E., *La Philosophie au Moyen Age*. Strasbourg, The University of Strasbourg, 1925. The best short account, in easy and clear French.
3. —— *The Spirit of Medieval Philosophy*. New York, Charles Scribner's Sons, 1936.
4. De Wulf, M., *History of Medieval Philosophy*. Boston, Longmans, Green and Company, 1926, 1935.
5. —— *Philosophy and Civilization in the Middle Ages*. Princeton, N. J., Princeton University Press, 1922.
6. Sabine, G. H., *A History of Political Theory*. New York, Henry Holt and Company, 1937, Part II.
7. Taylor, H. O., *The Medieval Mind*. New York, The Macmillan Company, 1925.

8. —— *The Classical Heritage of the Middle Ages*. New York, The Macmillan Company, 1923.

9. Crump, C. G., and Jacob, E. F., *The Legacy of the Middle Ages*. Oxford, The Clarendon Press, 1943, Oxford Series.

10. Coker, F. W., *Readings in Political Philosophy*. New York, The Macmillan Company, 1938, Chap. V.

11. McIlwain, C. H., *The Growth of Political Thought in the West*. New York, The Macmillan Company, 1932, Chap. V.

11 THE BIRTH OF
MODERN SOCIETY

WHAT DO WE MEAN BY "MODERN SOCIETY"? Not, surely, any society that has existed during the last two centuries. Much of Asia remains steeped in pre-antiquity. Does "modern society" mean Europe with its outgrowths in other continents? During the later nineteenth century Japan "modernized" itself, using scientific technology to industrialize a people which in its new culture returned to prehistoric savagery. By 1914 Germany had come to be widely regarded as one of the most advanced peoples; yet this same Germany was carried into war by a feudal class, which hoped to preserve in this way the privileges threatened by modern economic and intellectual growth. Most of continental Europe, as a matter of fact, has remained feudal and medieval throughout the modern period.

May we say that modern society is distinguished primarily by its democratic form of government, and secondarily by the social, economic, and religious developments that generate and support democratic government? Rather obviously, a society committed to self-government must differ in almost every way from one that does not. The assumptions which require democratic government must have consequences in the domestic, educational, recreational, social, and religious activities of a people.

While it is proper to describe modern society in terms of these distinctive political and social institutions, the word "modern" indicates a direction of social evolution rather than any set of fixed institutions. The American colonies were evidently moving toward democratic government; yet they still retained much that was undemocratic and old-world. Democracy is a direction of thought and life. It is a movement that began some centuries ago, and that will indefinitely continue its transformation of social institutions and human character.

Between this modern movement to democracy and medieval feudalism occurred a transitional period marked by monarchical government. The rapid breakdown of feudal institutions under the stress of new conditions made a temporary dictatorship inevitable. Monarchies were established wherever some able and ambitious feudal lord, supported by a public seeking escape from feudal forms, was able to enlarge his feudal office into that of sovereign. In this way developed nations, or societies centrally organized around the monarch, in whose person was centered and symbolized the national unity. England best illustrates this transition from feudalism to a more modern form of government. Henry VII ended the destructive wars between feudal factions, established royal power, carried through legal and economic reforms, prevented the recovery of the feudal nobility, and encouraged the development of national industry and commerce. He and his Tudor successors exercised virtually absolute powers, which they owed to their able and firm government and to their encouragement of commercial and urban interests which had found no place in the feudal system. The English parliament, a representative but still feudal institution, could not prevent this monarchical assumption of power; but it kept alive the memory of feudal rights, and never acquiesced in the theory and practice of absolute monarchy.

Henry VIII, by cutting the ecclesiastical ties binding England
to Rome and vesting in himself the headship of an established
church, completed the separation of the English nation from
the continental system, and also removed the checks by which
spiritual authority had set limits to secular power.

England's transition to monarchical absolutism was facilitated
by its insular position; but it was also aided by a tradition of
ecclesiastical independence which went back to Saxon times.
The Tudor monarchy protected England from the convulsions
and religious wars which followed the Reformation on the continent of Europe. The ecclesiastical changes initiated by
Henry VIII and continued by his successors were achieved
without violent conflict. The authority of Rome was denied,
the ecclesiastical estates were distributed among supporters of
the monarch, English replaced Latin as the language of religious ritual, and the clergy renounced the rule of celibacy.
There was considerable range of theology and interpretation
within the established church; and the new reformed sects,
although intermittently persecuted, were allowed to establish
themselves. The fact that Spain closely identified itself with
Rome and seriously threatened Protestant England helped to
cement the English people into national solidarity.

It seemed that England had safely weathered the dangerous
transition from feudal to national life; but this peaceful transition was interrupted by the accession of the Stuart dynasty.
The Stuarts claimed powers no greater than those exercised by
the Tudors, but they showed little understanding of public
interests, and they used their office in ways which alienated
almost every class of subjects. Parliament, controlled increasingly by the gentry since the great feudal lords lost power,
gained public support as it become more representative of the
English people; and it intensified its effort, made possible by
its formal control of the taxing power, to limit royal prerogative. The crucial issue, however, which carried the people of
Britain through successful revolution and which initiated the

movement to democratic government, was that of religious freedom. The Stuarts had long resisted the Presbyterian Scotch, who wished to retain the management of the church in their own hands. Finally, when the Presbyterians threw out his appointees, Charles I summoned the English parliament to vote him monies to suppress these rebels. Parliament, itself mainly Presbyterian, voted instead to support the rebels, and declared war against Charles. The parliamentary armies were largely composed of Puritan dissenters officered by Presbyterian gentry; and when parliament moved to make terms with Charles, these soldiers took power into their own hands, set up a tribunal which tried and executed Charles on the charge of high treason, and established the Commonwealth, a form of government which was neither monarchical nor parliamentary.

This English revolution established the political principle of the supremacy of law. Charles I, who had claimed to be above the law, was executed for breaking the law. It is often forgotten that this revolution also proceeded to the establishment of a republican form of government, enabling a people to rule itself directly through its moral and religious leaders. Since the Stuarts had alienated almost every section of society, the revolution against them was variously motivated, economically, socially, and politically, as well as religiously; but it is impossible to mistake the dominantly religious origin, motivation, and outcome of this first of all the revolutions that have modernized society. The British people, having rejected the authority of Rome and subjected themselves to a Puritan discipline of their own making, proposed now to preserve this religious and moral power from royal interference, and to make of it the ruler of their land. It was a Puritan revolution, issuing in a Puritan government.

To be convinced of the moral and religious motivation which impelled the movement to modern democratic society, one must observe that only where the movement of Puritan reform was able to advance with relative freedom did the movement to democratic government complete itself. In Britain the Commonwealth failed, and the Stuart exiles were restored; but the Commonwealth was not dead. During the Restoration period and thereafter there migrated across the Atlantic many thousands of those Puritan reformers whose hopes had been directed upon its moral ideal; and it was on the bleak but hospitable shores of a new continent that arose the self-governing congregations out of which there grew a truly modern society. A third revolution, fought on American soil, was necessary to secure the free development of this free people, which successfully established on new soil the Commonwealth which in the Old World had been choked by the deadwood of feudal habit. Free land alone, without moral and religious faith, would not have generated a free people and a modern society. This is shown by the history of Spanish and French settlements. Only where there moved the reformed Christian faith, in lay congregations which understood and actualized the political implications of their religious convictions and ideals, did those distinctive social institutions originate which we properly call "modern." Modern society is a child of the Puritan Reformation and a grandchild of medieval faith.

Not everywhere, unfortunately, did there proceed from the reformed religion a development of this sort. In Germany, the movement which separated the church from Rome was encouraged by feudal princes, under whose protection the Protestant church became an established and state-subsidized institution closely identified with government; and the free congregation never became there the decisive factor in a struggle for religious liberty against an absolute state. Because a state-subsidized church quickly becomes the vested interest of a governing class, and fails to generate forces directed toward social and political reform, the forces looking to social progress in Germany were directed upon a culture almost purely secular, *i.e.* literary and philosophical. Nor did the reformed faith have liberal consequence in France, where at first it had promised much. There, as earlier in Tudor England, the established clergy sided with the national monarch in his struggle against papal authority; but they later required, as recompense for this support, his persecution of the reformed religion. Here, too, the consequence of the Reformation was to identify an established church with a royalist and absolutistic form of government; and the struggle for political liberty became anticlerical, and in its theory atheistic. The French revolution was accordingly long delayed and unusually bloody and bitter, and the republic which it established was never stable. This has been the history of every libertarian movement which was not supported and strengthened by free religion.

The seventeenth century was remarkable for its production of political pamphlets. This literature was an outgrowth of the religious and theological literature, also tremendous in bulk, which had followed the Reformation. After the failure of the Commonwealth with its Puritan objectives the liberal thinker turned increasingly to philosophical and moral principles in his effort to substantiate his political purposes. The political theory developed during the later seventeenth century was the chief instruction of those who gave to modern society its political constitution; and among these political theorists one name, that of John Locke, outranks all the rest.

The purpose of the creators of modern government was to enfranchise and empower the individual conscience, by making effective in every individual his religious responsibility for all of his fellows. This responsibility, it was now clear, could be fully exercised only through a control of government. Yet how could the freedom and power of the individual be reconciled with the fact of government? How may law, with its restriction upon individual behavior, leave unimpaired the moral power of the individual?

During the Middle Ages this crucial problem had been partially solved by a division of the governing power among feudal ranks and between church and state. The degree and kind of power allotted to an individual corresponded to the social function which he was to exercise. With the breakdown of medieval institutions, there was no agreement as to what these functions were, nor who was responsible for them, nor where the appropriate powers might be located. Life became an interminable and unprincipled struggle for the possession of these powers, and absolute monarchy appeared as the necessary alternative to chaos. Most of the forward-looking thinkers of the Renaissance, accordingly, were ardent supporters of monarchical government. Their monarchical theory was established either upon some religious or theological view, or more empirically upon a study of the conditions and presuppositions of stable government. One such study was that which focused itself upon the concept of sovereignty. Starting from the Greek view that human life can be humanly lived only in the politically organized community or state, the promoters of the concept of sovereignty concluded that there must be in every real and actual state a center or seat, in which the power of the community is definitely located, and from which it is exercised in the prescription and execution of law. The seat of sovereignty might be a monarch, or a council, or some other governing group, monarchy usually being favored. This doctrine of state sovereignty, explicit or implicit, is the historical source of most of the absolutistic political theory of the later centuries, and also of the *Realpolitik* of the last half century. It is absolutistic because it places political authority in some part of society less than the whole—in a king, a governing group, perhaps even in a political majority. It is *Realpolitik* because it defines political authority in terms of power—the authority of government is identified with the actual power of government, and is not justified by being derived from some more ultimate right. This absolutistic tradition, which really identified right with might, has dominated European political theory and practice from that day to the present. It forcefully expressed the new hope of nationalism, the ideal of the strong and solidly organized people, defined in terms of their possession of territory and their political unity. The nonmoral character of this "realistic" political theory is starkly apparent in its two best-known exponents, Machiavelli and Hobbes.

Machiavelli, a Florentine who wrote early in the sixteenth century, was inspired by his too idealistic conception of ancient Rome. He dreamed of a strong and united Italy, and looked enviously toward France and England, which had already achieved national solidarity. Several causes had kept Italy divided into warring principalities, the chief cause, Machiavelli believed, being the concern of the Papacy to keep intact its papal domains. What Italy needed, he concluded, was a prince whose personal ambition would override all religious and other scruples, and whose skill in intrigue and war would enable him to unify Italy by sheer force. In his famous book *The Prince* he presented a manual of advice and instruction for such a tyrant. Machiavelli was a genuine patriot, weary of the political turmoil and the moral corruption which he saw about him; and at heart he was a liberal, one who would revive the virtues of stout and honest citizenship as they had supposedly existed in republican Rome. He assumed, however, that this patriotic purpose justified every intrigue, deceit, and violence. He calls for a ruler whose power over his people is absolute, and who will use education and religion to keep his subjects devoted to himself and to his political ambition. Machiavelli's book, full of sincere, shrewd, yet cynical perception of the baser motives playing into political life, has been for four centuries the guide of unscrupulous statesmen, until its essential doctrine, teaching that the state as the whole source of law and right transcends moral limitations, became the creed of a new tyranny in Mussolini, Franco, and Hitler.

More than a century after Machiavelli, this doctrine of political absolutism was given systematic expression by *Thomas Hobbes* in his book *Leviathan,* still regarded as a classical work because of its bold effort to deal realistically with the forces entering into political life. Hobbes based his political theory upon a materialistic philosophy of nature. The motions which blindly impel the ultimate particles of matter along their courses are compounded in the human individual, he taught, to produce a force which drives the individual toward an unlimited and nonmoral effort to preserve and expand his power. This force, if it acted unchecked in all individuals, would result in interminable conflict and social chaos. The function of the state is to superimpose upon this chaos a stable order or law. This requires the displacement of the natural rights of the individual by powers limited and directed by the state. It requires the elimination of the free or self-determined individual, that is to say, and the substitution of a subject whose behavior is wholly determined by the law of the land.

Hobbes has sometimes been called the founder of modern political science. There is no doubt that he attempted a new and realistic study of the forces working in social and political life, and that his use of the traditional vocabulary current in his day was not intended to justify traditional concepts, but was imposed upon him by the need to communicate unfamiliar ideas in some familiar and intelligible form. Thus he makes use of the language of "natural rights" and "natural law," familiar since Cicero and propagated by the scholastic philosophers; but he gives to these terms quite new meanings. Where "natural rights" in the earlier tradition had been derived from "natural law," which meant ultimately from the eternal law of God, Hobbes means by "natural rights" just those actual forces which inhere in the isolated individual, and which drive the individual to perpetual conflict with his fellows; and these natural forces, he holds, must be transcended and overruled by "rational law," which has its source in the authoritative power of the state, effective in forcible administration. Where, in short, earlier philosophical tradition had tried to reconcile the individual with the state, by teaching that the individual in his rational and moral nature, and the state in its legal structure, equally manifest one and the same law which is that of universal and divine justice, Hobbes defines the individual and the state in such a way as to make their reconciliation impossible. The individual is defined as in his inherent and constitutive nature lawless, wholly belligerent, and nonmoral; and the state thus becomes something superhuman, imposed upon the individual by an external and alien power. Hobbes did not hesitate to call the monarch "a mortal god." His theory is close to that of the Greek sophists, who held all law to be nothing but artificial convention, without real authority and imposed by force or deceit. The concepts of natural rights and natural law have never wholly recovered from this Hobbesian interpretation.

Hobbes' intention, of course, was to justify political authority as the true law, that of reason and morality; but he defined the individual in such a way as to allow no relationship between individual freedom and rational or moral law. Law must be imposed upon the individual from without, by an external force. To justify and explain this imposition, Hobbes gave to another current idea, that which held government to arise out of a contract, a new and strange interpretation. The Epicureans, it may be recalled, had used this contract theory to deny moral authority to the state. The state is in the position of a contractor, they held, commissioned by society to perform certain specified and limited functions. Hobbes, however, describes a strange contract according to which the individuals composing society irrevocably renounce all their inherent powers, and place these without residue in the hands of the sovereign, who undertakes in return to make the good of the state identical with his own good, to maintain law and order, and to delegate to his subjects only such powers as will not disturb the common peace. This implies that all real individual rights, as distinguished from those "natural rights" which according to Hobbes are just lawless powers, derive from the state or the monarch; and this is the constitutive principle of political absolutism. Hobbes' doctrine is as unintelligible as it is immoral. It is impossible to understand how lawless individuals should ever come together and in a moment of "reason" make such a contract; nor could such lawless individuals, of course, ever keep the contract. Hobbes can be made consistent only if we imagine that one or a few lawless individuals impose their will by brute force upon all, and thus make their will the law of the land.

Looking back over the last three centuries, and observing how the theory of political absolutism first elaborated by Machiavelli and Hobbes has revealed its implications in the totalitarianism of today, we realize that these thinkers propagated the heresy of state-worship; for that, it is now clear, is what is taught by a political theory which makes the state or its governors the source of moral rights and the seat of authority. In the seventeenth century Hobbes found few disciples. He wrote his book in Paris, whither he had fearfully fled at the outbreak of the first English revolution; but even the royalists to whom he offered his defense of monarchical absolutism indignantly rejected it. They believed that the monarch is the sole source of law and right, without responsibility to his subjects; but they defined the power of the ruler as a divine right placed in the ruler by God and leaving him subject to divine will. This doctrine at least recognized the responsibility of the state to a higher moral jurisdiction. But in the later centuries, especially on the continent of Europe, Hobbes' materialistic metaphysics with its absolutistic political implications were to have terrible consequence in group violence and legalized massacre.

The second English revolution, which in 1688 replaced the Stuart dynasty by one which accepted the principle of limited monarchy, actually transferred the governing power of Britain to a strongly entrenched nobility; but there is no doubt that the Whig leaders who accomplished this change had the support of the larger public, and that this "glorious revolution" was generally conceived to establish the principle of self-government. In the writings of its spokesman Locke, indeed, this revolution produced the classical exposition of democratic theory.

John Locke, son of a small landholder whose services in the first revolution had depleted his fortune, qualified himself as a physician, but remained at Oxford pursuing scientific and scholarly research until his close relations with certain Whig noblemen caused the Stuart monarch to demand his dismissal. Locke went to Holland, where with other conspirators he prepared the way for the Whig revolution. Following his return to England with the new monarch, he published in rapid succession the political and philosophical works which he had prepared in exile.

Since the Stuarts and their supporters defended absolute monarchy on the principle of the divine right of the king, Locke directed his chief attack against this doctrine, and not against the more systematic theory of absolute government presented by Hobbes; but the positive argument of Locke constitutes a criticism and correction of Hobbes' theory. Rebutting the doctrine of divine right on its own ground, that of scriptural interpretation, he offers a defense of self-government which is independent of religious premises.

Starting as did Hobbes from the concept of the self-determinate individual, Locke immediately diverges from Hobbes in his conception of the individual, whom he finds to be naturally, prior to all government, bound to his fellows in moral association. Thus the initial concept of Locke is really that of a society or moral community, composed of free individuals who are bound to one another by reciprocal friendship and concern. This moral individualism of Locke is often confused with the nonmoral individualism of Hobbes and others; but this confusion leaves Locke's political philosophy quite unintelligible and robs his theory of all moral basis. The initial principle of democracy places all moral responsibility in the individual per-

son, who is held to be the sole source of moral feeling and
insight; and if this moral or social nature of the individual is
unrecognized, it follows of necessity that some institution or
group or class must be invested with moral authority and
ultimate power. All democratic theory and practice, accordingly, flows from this first stark and uncompromising principle, historically derived from the Puritan conception of a
direct relation between the individual and God, which states
that moral authority, or right, inheres in every human individual. It follows that all institutional powers whatsoever must be
derived from these rightful powers of individuals. Neither
church nor state nor any other institution is possessed of intrinsic authority, since all authority ultimately lies in the people
and the individuals who compose it. All institutional authority
is delegated.

To express this principle in language familiar to his readers,
Locke makes use of the concepts of natural law, natural rights,
and contract. By the law of nature, he teaches, man is a moral
being, invested with natural rights which are inalienable because they are identical with his human nature. Individuals live
together naturally, in mutual aid and tolerance, independently
of formal political association; but they find it convenient to
delegate certain of their moral responsibilities to a group of
individuals, appointed by themselves to form a government.
The contractual character of this agreement is evident in the
specification of the powers thus delegated to government, and
in their explicit limitation. The powers so loaned are revocable,
and revert to the people if government should fail in its functions or abuse its office.

There is, strictly speaking, no place in this theory for such
concepts as the state, sovereignty, state's rights, etc. Rights are
moral powers, and these reside inalienably in the people, *i.e.*
in the moral individuals who constitute the people. Governments may be established, and be armed with delegated powers,
subject to the continued consent of the people. It is the inten-

tion of this theory, as it must be the intention of any theory which proposes to invalidate absolute government, to deny intrinsic authority to the state, and to locate all authority and all ultimate power in the people, which is conceived to be independent of the state, to be prior to the state, and to outlast the state.

The foundation of this theory is its affirmation of the goodness of the individual human being. Only if man is moral can he be worthy or capable of self-government. This does not mean that man is always and everywhere incapable of evil. It means that man is essentially or generally good; above all, it means that no line can divide people into two species of beings, one good and therefore worthy of exercising government, the other bad and therefore unworthy to govern. If men are generally good, and all men govern, government will be generally good. But the goodness of man lies finally in his free moral will. It is because man is a free moral agent, able to know and choose between good and evil, that he is invested with inalienable authority. No individual and no group of individuals has the right to deny to another individual or group of individuals the exercise of moral judgment and power. Democracy is the only form of government which does not at some point deny this conception of the moral nature of man.

Since all authority or right whatsoever inheres in the human individual, one cannot exhaustively list the "rights of man." Locke emphasized especially, as natural rights which require a specific limitation of governmental power, the rights of religious freedom and of property. It should be obvious that an individual can delegate to no one else his religious responsibilities; and just government may accordingly exercise no authority of any sort over religious belief. Locke extended this requirement of religious toleration to all save Romanists, who, he believed, were by their allegiance to Rome compelled to deny toleration to others, and thus prevented from entering into the compact establishing free government.

The natural right which Locke most lengthily defended was that of property, his belief being that all other rights would stand or fall with this one. Locke was influenced by English history, which had been a long struggle between monarch and parliament for control of the national treasury and the power to tax. This history made very evident the close relationship which exists between political and economic power. So long as the monarch was financially independent, the people had little or no recourse against his usurpations of power; and Locke believed that government could be kept responsive to popular will only if the people kept in their own hands these economic controls.

This right to property has become during the last half century an issue so hotly debated that it has brought into question the whole doctrine of natural rights, and the justifiability of the democratic form of government established upon them. We should expand our conception of political democracy, some say, into that of economic democracy; and this is to be achieved only by completely subjecting the economic life of a people to governmental control. Without prejudice to the profound and ramified issues which are involved in this problem, we may perhaps venture some discussion of what is required by democratic theory and practice in respect to the economic life of a people.

The intention of democracy is to secure to each and every one of the individuals constituting society a full and equal share in the direction of the common life. This direction is most obviously and immediately effected through the mechanisms which enact and administer law, *i.e.* through government. Democracy aims, therefore, at the full and equal participation of each individual in government, which it attempts to secure by allotting to each individual an identical political power. The broadest function of government is, and always has been, the regulation of economic life—the great bulk of law has, and always has had, this purpose. There can be little question, therefore, of the right of a people to regulate through its government its economic life. Why, therefore, should there be any limit to the extent of this economic regulation? If government is controlled by the people, should not the people through its government exert complete and absolute economic control?

To answer this question intelligently, we should observe that every sort of control exercised in human society is either directly economic, or dependent upon economic means. This is true of the control exerted by a people *upon* its government, as well as that exerted *through* its government. Laws are not effective until they are administered; and the administration of law is effected and controlled by means of monetary appropriations. It is not enough, in order to know the political form of a society, to know its written constitution. The written constitution may appear to be democratic, yet leave government autocratic. The constitution is effective only if it is materially implemented. But we learn the political form of a society unmistakably when we discover the sources and controls of the monies and other economic powers at the disposal of its government.

Thus a government not dependent upon appropriations, ultimately derived from taxes voted freely by property owners, may hire an army which makes it independent of every control—except, perhaps, that exerted upon government by the army itself. Governments are in the last resort groups of men; and to place in the hands of any group of men complete control of the national economy will automatically place those men beyond popular control. This is not only a theoretical deduction. It is also a generalization from facts which have always been apparent. There are countries today in which such complete economic control not only makes government completely independent of public opinion, but places it beyond the threat of popular revolution. Thus the proposal to secure to the people complete control of its economic life by means of government ownership, or unlimited governmental power over economy, is equivalent to the proposal to reestablish absolute government. Do the proponents of economic democracy really intend this return to political and economic autocracy? A people will control its government and be self-governed only so long as it retains individual ownership of its material wealth and resources.

This fact was apparent to the seventeenth-century revolutionaries who established the principles and began the movement of modern democracy. They clearly saw the relation between economic conditions and political practice; and it was because they were "economic determinists" in this literal sense that they emphasized the right of private property, which absolute governments had necessarily and consistently abrogated. But we are more aware today of how certain individuals and groups, by means of their great wealth and their control of economic enterprise, may exert undue pressure upon public opinion and government. It is to prevent this sort of usurpation that some, forgetting the longest and largest lessons of political history, wish to place unlimited and absolute economic power in the hands of elected governors, and to convert an imperfect democracy into what they assume will be a perfectly benevolent autocracy. Yet it should be clear that if religious freedom requires the separation of church and state, economic freedom equally requires the separation of economic and political managements.

What the phrase "economic democracy" really intends is the establishment of something like equality in economic power, both as an intrinsic justice and as the condition of equality in political power. This worthy objective cannot be reached by consolidating all economic power, and therewith all actual political power, in the hands of an absolute de facto government, which once it is established can never be removed. Economic justice can be progressively and approximately reached by means of broad legislation directed to the equalitarian distribution of property. In his assumption of the principle of private ownership, Locke also provided the means which would preserve this principle from abuse. He did this by defining property as the product of labor. Locke meant, of course, every sort of labor, and did not narrow the term, as we unfortunately narrow it, to specify only certain types of economic activity. This principle, taken in its whole meaning, provides a basis for broad legislation securing to all individuals that economic justice which is in fact, most would agree, a condition as well as an objective of democratic practice.

Locke's political philosophy gets its full weight only when it is placed in the context of his general philosophy, which we will consider in a later chapter; but it constitutes as it stands the classical exposition of democratic political theory, and the basis upon which was erected and still is established the constitutional democracy of today. The theory is not affected by any criticism of the concepts of "natural law" and "natural rights," in terms of which Locke presented it. This language, appropriate to Locke's time, only denoted the facts of moral responsibility and moral community which every adequate social and political theory must recognize. There are really only two kinds of political theory and practice. There is democratic theory and practice, which places moral authority in the individual human being and derives all governmental powers and social values from this; and there is absolutistic theory and practice, or the "philosophy of the state," which ostensibly locates authority and value in some institution, but really locates it in some hereditary or self-appointed group of individuals, identified with the state.

Democracy is not one of a number of political forms, among which we may choose that most appropriate to present circumstance. Democracy cannot afford to be relativistic. Democracy is the acknowledgment in theory and practice of the fact of individuality, which fact is the source of all natural moral law. As we shall see later, democracy is the practical application in human relations of those selfsame principles which in science guide us to truth. Men can temporarily ignore this fact of individuality; they can erect dogmas into "absolute truths," they can seek to contain individual behavior by force in some absolute "state"; but particular fact and individual character will not be indefinitely ignored. Because these are real, they will make themselves effective, resistance only making their reaction more violent. Absolute government of necessity generates its own destruction. Democracy is the law of nature and of life, the condition of political stability and the creative agency of human progress. Simply because society is constituted of human individuals, society can exist in health, without unnatural violence and legalized corruption, only in democratic form.

Democratic theory is adequately established, and perhaps best established, upon the basis of the observable facts of human character and human society. Absolutistic theory has usually appealed to a wider metaphysical basis, professedly defining the structure of universal being. Thus we saw that Hobbes, whose political premises have been those of most modern absolutism, justified these by means of a more general theory of mechanistic materialism. It is important, therefore, that democratic theory should be aware of its wider philosophical presuppositions, in order to protect itself against those who proceed from an absolutistic general philosophy to an absolutistic political program. Both the proponents and the opponents of absolute government have sought this philosophical establishment of their political principles. Their desire has been to show that the widest or most basic presuppositions of science require the sort of social and political theory they advocate Hobbes found these largest presuppositions of science in the principles of atomistic materialism. But Hobbes, an acute and intelligent observer of human behavior, remained a tyro in natural science and never attained to an adequate understanding of its method and constitution. Our study of the philosophical basis of democracy therefore requires some appreciation of the development of modern science, allowing us to understand its method and to grasp its presuppositions. This study, which we begin in the following chapter, will be our concern to the end of the book. Just as Greek philosophy was a reflection upon Greek science, so modern philosophy has been a reflection upon the methods and results of modern science, especially in their implications for social and political life.

Notes for Further Reading

1. Sabine, G. H., *A History of Political Theory*. New York, Henry Holt and Company, Chaps. XVII–XXVI, 1937.
2. Figgis, J. N., "Political Thought in the Sixteenth Century." *Cambridge Modern History*, New York, The Macmillan Company, 1904, Vol. III, Chap. 22.
3. Smith, P., *The Age of the Reformation*. New York, Henry Holt and Company, 1920.
4. Machiavelli, N., *The Prince*. Chicago, Packard and Company, 1941, also various editions.
5. Lanquet, H., *A Defense of Liberty against Tyrants*, introd. by H. J. Laski. New York, Harcourt Brace and Company, Inc., 1924.
6. Laski, H. J., "The Rise of Liberalism." *Encyclopaedia of the Social Sciences*. New York, The Macmillan Company, 1930, Vol. I.
7. Gooch, G. P., *English Democratic Ideas in the Seventeenth Century*. New York, The Macmillan Company, 1927.
8. Laird, J., *Hobbes*. London and New York, Oxford University Press, 1934.
9. Hobbes, T., *Leviathan*. Garden City, Doubleday Doran and Company, 1937, Parts I and II.
10. Smith, A. L., "English Political Philosophy in the Seventeenth and Eighteenth Centuries," *Cambridge Modern History*, New York, The Macmillan Company, 1909, Vol. VI.
11. Laski, H. J., *Political Thought in England from Locke to Bentham*. New York, Henry Holt and Company, 1920.
12. Lamprecht, S., *The Moral and Political Philosophy of John Locke*. New York, Columbia University Press, Archives of Philosophy, No. 11, 1918.

12   THE RISE OF MODERN SCIENCE

W<small>E ALREADY TOOK NOTE, IN REFERENCES TO</small>
Grosseteste and Roger Bacon and their successors,
of the first beginnings of modern science. In the teachings of
Bacon is recommended that conjunction of rigorous mathematical analysis with immediate observation of fact which is
the characteristic feature of modern science; and in the writings of fourteenth-century Occam we find clear statements of
some of the controlling concepts, *e.g.* that of inertia, which
have determined the development of modern physical science.
It is usual to date the rise of modern science much later, in the
sixteenth and seventeenth centuries; and it is true that the new
science found its firm establishment, its wide propagation, and
its popular acceptance during and after the Renaissance. The
Latin treatises of the earlier scholars might conceivably have
moldered forgotten in monastic libraries if there had not been
great physicists like Galileo and Newton, and great publicists
like Francis Bacon and Descartes, who convinced the world of
the importance of the new science and secured acceptance of
its method and results.

This development and propagation of science was an important part of the larger but more confused movement we call
the Renaissance. The Renaissance was many things. Initially

and primarily it was an exodus out of the cloister, into the several vernaculars of western Europe, of the Latin learning of the medieval clerics. It was also a recovery and temporary adoration of the classical and pagan cultures of antiquity. But finally and most importantly it was the expression of a new outlook upon nature and man, a new attitude toward fact, and a new enterprise of the human spirit. This new mind eludes definition, but we can perceive and indicate its most important features.

First, perhaps, we should note its great swing to an orientation upon the future, after centuries intellectually focused upon the past. Out of this reorientation was born the most dynamic and creative as well as the most revolutionary and turbulent force in the modern world, to wit the concept of progress. The new vista upon an unlimited human progress is perhaps the deepest meaning of the phrases, such as the Renaissance, the Enlightenment, and the Age of Reason, which men coined to express their satisfaction with and their confidence in the new prospect. This concept of progress was incorporated into and supported by the new science. Greek science, and after it medieval science, had conceived of a completed wisdom, progressive perhaps in its application to new situations and problems, but essentially static and whole. Socrates had not been able to convert men to his conception of science as a *pursuit* of knowledge, something at once less and more than the possession of knowledge; but modern science has conceived itself to be a progressive exploration of nature rather than a final statement of eternal and fixed truth. With this increasing faith in a progressive science has come new faith in the continuous improvement of human nature and the conditions of human life. We find the distant origins of this new faith in the gospel of hope and deliverance announced by early Christianity. Medieval Christianity had fixated Christian faith upon a supernatural and otherworldly goal, to be attained only after death; but the Reformation, returning to earliest Christianity for its inspiration, required the realization of its religious ideals here upon earth. Nowhere, we should observe, but in the Christian west has this faith in progress, with its mental orientation upon the future, dominated human society and revolutionized theory and practice; but this way of thought is so natural to ourselves that we erroneously impute it to every people and to every age. The "natural" orientation of the intellect, a survey of human cultures would force us to conclude, is upon the past; and even today among ourselves, wherever this old-world mentality still rules a "cultured" mind, our restless ever-new modern culture is felt to be raucous and crude, lacking depth, overtone, and resonance.

A second feature of the modern mind is its realism or naturalism. The otherworldliness of late Greek and medieval faith was not so much renounced as transmuted, to become the demand for a progressive realization of the religious ideal. Once we forget the religious background of this modern naturalism we fall into moral confusion, failing to distinguish a naturalism which deifies what is, from a naturalism which sees in present fact the promise of what ought to be and shall be. The intellectual distinction of Christianity, we noted in our discussion of this faith, was its shift to a temporalistic concept in which nature is defined as a temporal creation and an historical progress. One cannot establish modern science and society upon Greek eternalism. To try to do so is to convert all that is progressive, dynamic, and naturalistic in modern life into abnormality, violence, and horror.

But it would be foolish and perhaps presumptuous to attempt closer delineation of this modern mind, which we appreciate only in the full sweep, covering now some four centuries, of its forward impetus. Let us try instead to illustrate its innermost essence, as it is revealed in one who is perhaps the greatest of its exponents! As Aeschylus illustrated for us the deeper-lying mentality of early Greece, so the prophetic soul of Shakespeare informs us of what underlies the modern mind.

The earlier poems and comedies of Shakespeare we may dismiss, since they illustrate chiefly the superficial neoclassicism which is sometimes still identified with the Renaissance, but which was truly only its accident. In this neoclassical art the artist tried, impossibly, to re-create the thought and imagination of Greek antiquity; and he succeeded only in appropriating the archaic mythology and the external conventions of antique art, grasping nothing of the antique spirit. He remained still a fifteenth- or sixteenth-century European, rather ludicrously cavorting in tunic or toga.

The historical plays of Shakespeare, however, already boldly innovate the realism of modern art. If these plays are read in the chronological order of their events, they will be found to constitute a single drama of epical dimensions, telling of the curse with its fatal repercussions which was the War of the Roses, the curse being lifted and the bloody sequence ended through the accession of Henry Tudor. The theme is reminiscent of the great trilogy of Aeschylus; and Shakespeare's new realism appears in this, that where the Greek poet took his theme from mythology, Shakespeare made use of not so distant history to portray the working of natural and moral law. Here in modern art, as in modern science, is a subordination of imagination to historical and particular fact.

But it was in his tragedies, and especially in *Hamlet*, that Shakespeare reached that mental and moral crisis out of which sprang his supremest art, revealing his full and still immeasurable stature. In the earlier tragedies he had still conformed to the medieval roster of virtues and vices. Othello is jealousy, Coriolanus and Caesar are ambition, Macbeth is vacillation, Lear is vanity masked by paternal fondness. But in *Hamlet*, Shakespeare calls into question the moral foundations of the universe. That unusual impartiality, with which in the earlier dramas both heroes and villains are sympathetically understood, now becomes the center of the play.

It is customary to call *Hamlet* a work so profound as to be inexplicable. In the writer's opinion, the play will reveal its meaning to anyone who will compare it with its great forerunner, the drama of Aeschylus. Like Orestes, Hamlet is given the task of avenging his murdered father upon his guilty mother and her paramour. Like Orestes, he is driven mad by inner tension between conflicting loyalties. The psychological situations and the moral problems are identical; but the treatment and issue are significantly different. Hamlet refuses to wield the sword of judgment, he insists that the guilty shall encompass their own destinies, and he accepts madness and death as the price of his filial and human kinship to the ghostly and living protagonists of the play. Is Hamlet so inexplicable, is the question "to be or not to be" really left unanswered? Shakespeare calls to the bar of new judgment all conventional morality, his contempt for which finds voice in many ways, most unmistakably in the figure of the platitudinous Polonius, skewered like a rat skulking behind the arras. *Hamlet* is the first great moral study of modern man. It demands a new and empirical understanding of man, to be reached by a sympathy extended to guilty and innocent alike. It appeals for a merciful kindness that falls like the gentle rain from heaven. It tells us to abstain from judgment, to leave vengeance to God, and to acknowledge always and at every personal cost our responsibility to each and all. Because Hamlet will not be self-righteous and punitive, because he will not avenge murder with new death, he is caught up in the purge by which evil destroys itself; and that, he says when dying, is all right too. Shall we say that Shakespeare first penetrated to the meaning of religious atonement? Only Tolstoi, in modern literature, has plumbed so deep. In the later plays of Shakespeare the moral insight which *Hamlet* discovers in mental crisis generates a vast calm, telling us of the natural goodness of the world and man. This insight is man's peace.

So Shakespeare is the prophet of the inquiring, self-critical, and exploratory naturalism that has been the science, art, philosophy, and ethics of the last three centuries. It is not an irreligious, still less is it an immoral naturalism; but it is religion and morality without dogma, in pursuit of widening vision and creative power.

The intellectual revolution and inauguration which genius such as that of Shakespeare and Buonarroti announced in art had its theoretical parallel in science. To the Pole *Jan Köpernik* (1473–1543) we credit the "Copernican revolution" which was so much more than an astronomical hypothesis affirming the revolution of the earth about the sun. Why did the Copernican theory arouse such dissension, such ardent support and resolute opposition, that intellectual Europe was divided by it into two belligerent camps? From the viewpoint of today, the Copernican astronomy only further applied the scientific method initiated by the Pythagoreans, and cultivated in some measure throughout the intervening ages. Strictly speaking, this solar-centric astronomy constituted only an appropriation of Greek science, with its commitment to mathematical principles and celestial spheres. Copernicus gave to the circular motions a new center in the sun; but this had been proposed by Aristarchus of Samos shortly after 300 B.C.; and we find that Copernicus gave due credit to his Pythagorean sources. Yet this Copernican hypothesis shocked western Europe out of its dogmatic slumber, by requiring a new and strange conception of the world. It returned, after centuries of Aristotle and Aristotelianized Platonism, to the mathematical methods of Pythagoras and Plato himself, ignoring and discrediting the Aristotelian science which was now the basis of scholastic theology and the content of scholastic learning.

Secondly, because the work of Aristarchus had been neglected and forgotten, the hypothesis appeared as a bold and independent advance going beyond all earlier achievement; and thus it established the intellectual parity of living man with antiquity, or even his intellectual superiority. For seventeen or more centuries the conclusions of fourth-century

Greek science had been accepted as the highwater mark of human achievement, and as the eternal content of the human reason itself. Copernicus signaled the close of that long age with its submission to past authority. The tremendous effect of the Copernican theory shows us the character and potency of the sixteenth-century mind, which was shocked by the theory because it was alive to its implications, and willing to entertain these even while it was overwhelmed by them. The Copernican revolution was the work of the mind of Europe, at least as much as it was the work of Copernicus himself. The earth moves, said Copernicus. Men in earlier ages had heard those words, and shrugged their shoulders; but sixteenth-century Europe stood aghast and fascinated before this hypothesis, which tumbled down all the familiar medieval architecture of high heaven and lowly earth, of sacred and profane. It was not indeed Copernicus and his astronomical successor Kepler, who still subscribed to the perfection or divinity of the celestial motions, but other less expert thinkers who felt the shock and consequence of the Copernican astronomy. And because the church set its ecclesiastical authority against the new hypothesis, insisting upon the infallibility of Aristotle in his astronomy as elsewhere, the Copernican hypothesis became the issue between two worlds, one subservient to the past and committed to dogma, the other oriented upon a future which promised new knowledge and free achievement.

Acknowledging the importance of this sixteenth-century astronomer, we must not forget the earlier and more authentic inauguration of the new science by thirteenth-century Bacon and his successors, who much more than Copernicus created the methods, fashioned the concepts, and stated the large outlook upon fact which have distinguished modern science from earlier science. These men announced the governing conceptions which should control the new science, they provided its theory of knowledge, they formally overturned the whole scholastic tradition along with its Aristotelian foundations, and they worked steadily and creatively, in England and later in France, to produce the discipline which has developed into modern physical science. After Occam, who directed the new science on its way, we find Nicholas d'Autricourt applying atomistic concepts, to facilitate the reduction of particular causal sequences to measurable and mathematically formulable displacements. John Buridan fashioned the fruitful concept of impetus or momentum. Albert of Saxony defined the center of gravity of a body and the principle of gravitational acceleration. And Nicholas Oresmus elaborated the mathematical calculi which made possible the applications of these concepts to particular physical situations. These and other medieval thinkers, most of them Franciscan clerics, created the terrestrial physics which in the hands of Newton was to be mightily enlarged, to swallow up the celestial astronomy of Copernicus and Kepler, and to establish the universal yet empirical study of fact which is modern science.

During the fifteenth and sixteenth centuries, however, the new science emerged from the cloister, and was much stimulated by its application to secular and practical uses. Navigators looked to it for new instruments and for a new cartography. Builders of ships, docks, and canals encouraged inquiry into the principles of hydrostatics, discovering the stresses exerted in and by fluids. There was considerable invention of simple machinery applying mechanical principles, and a great development of mining and metallurgy, often scientifically directed. Merchants encouraged the invention of new methods of calculation and bookkeeping. It was a great age, holding in embryo the industrial world which was to come. Most notable of these practical interests encouraging science, it must be confessed, was the desire for new arts of war, which stimulated Galileo's study of the motion of projectiles.

Galileo Galilei of Pisa (1564–1642) owes his popular fame to his confirmation of the Copernican theory, and to his adherence to this hypothesis in face of ecclesiastical opposition. Summoned before the dread Inquisition, and forced to make verbal recantation of the thesis that the earth moves on its axis and around the sun, Galileo is reported to have murmured as he left the tribunal, "But it does move!"

As a student at the University of Pisa, he developed the mechanics of the pendulum; as a young professor there he taught that bodies of unequal weight fall with equal acceleration; and when orthodox Aristotelians challenged this heresy, he confronted them with a demonstration of objects dropped from the famous Leaning Tower. He constructed a telescope which made visible the moons of Jupiter, proving that Jupiter is a planet like the earth. He detected and measured sunspots to demonstrate the rotation of the sun on its axis. He revived the late Greek distinction of primary and secondary qualities, in order to explain the effectiveness of his mathematical and mechanical science.

But quite properly the name of *Isaac Newton* (1642–1727) outtops all others in these annals of modern science. Newton's achievement was to synthesize the diverse but related studies composing the new science into a universal system, so as to establish what seemed at that time a single, compact, and all-comprehensive theory of nature. His success was due to his creative mathematical genius; yet we are right to remember him primarily as the discoverer of the "law" of gravitation, the force which explains the celestial motions, the rise and fall of the tides, and the facts of weight. The principle of gravitation was of a new sort, and presents in a nutshell the radical difference between this new modern science and earlier science. Let us observe and stress this difference, which ultimately, as its whole implication is progressively discovered, makes modern thought incommensurable with all earlier thought! The principle of gravitation is universal in its scope, in that it applies to material being everywhere and always. Yet it is not a rational principle, if by "rational" we mean a principle laid down by the reason itself, as are the principles of mathematics.

The principle of gravitation states that material bodies will attract one another according to the product of their masses and the inverse square of their distance. Why attract, and not repel? Why attract according to the product and not the sum of the masses? Why the inverse square, rather than the inverse cube, of their distances? There is no answer to these questions, except the answer that this is the way in which material bodies observably behave. The principle, in short, is *inductive*, not rational—it is a summary of particular observations, not the deliverance of a prescient reason. Newton, as a matter of fact, entertained many alternative and equally reasonable hypotheses, before he discovered that which exactly conformed to his data.

If we will keep steadily before our minds this character of the principle of gravitation, a principle at once *universal yet inductive* or *empirical*, we shall follow with understanding the whole later development of modern thought. The significance of this principle is its implied teaching that the whole character of nature, even its largest, most ultimate, and most basic character, is to be known by *observation and in no other way*. Modern science accepts this implication. We therefore call it "empirical science," indicating in this way that its conclusions are derived wholly from sense-experience. Because Greek and medieval science believed the largest principles of knowledge to be established by reason alone, and to be applied to experience and imposed upon experience by the reason, we properly call that earlier science "rational" and "nonempirical."

Newton may properly be regarded, therefore, as the chief founder of modern science. In the principle of gravitation he confirmed and securely established the science which his predecessors, from Grosseteste and Roger Bacon onward, had initiated. The later seventeenth and early eighteenth centuries dimly felt this peculiar importance of Newton's science. They saw in Newton the great frontispiece of a new "age of reason," and the source of a new "enlightenment."

Men vaguely felt, but they could not clearly conceive, this empirical character of modern science. They became intellectually confused when they tried to define the distinction between the old rational science and the new empirical science. Their confusion was excusable, in that it has been finally removed only in our own century. This long confusion was partly due to the presence in the Newtonian science of certain intermediary principles known as the "laws of motion," which seemed to connect the empirical principle of gravitation with the rational principles of pure mathematics. Newton's science presupposed the whole of mathematical theory, which constituted a sort of anatomy in the new science; and it was generally conceded that mathematical principles are completely self-evident or rational, neither needing nor allowing inductive proof. "Things equal to the same thing are equal to one another." Observation and experiment can add nothing, it would seem, to this universal mathematical truth. Let us concede for the moment this rational necessity of mathematical axioms! What shall we say of the "laws of motion," stating that action is equal and opposite to reaction, and that a body will move with constant velocity except as it is accelerated by external pressure? Are these propositions self-evident, like the axioms of mathematics? Or do they only summarize our experience of things? At that time they seemed self-evident; and so they seemed to bridge the gap between the rational principles of mathematics and the inductive principle of gravitation, allowing all of these principles, mathematical, mechanical, and gravitational, to be lumped together and confused. Only in the twentieth century has this confusion been removed. For three centuries scientists and philosophers pretended to distinguish between rational and empirical knowledge, when in truth they could not do so. This disability, no longer excusable, is still the chief source of philosophical and intellectual confusions.

Let us look further at this Newtonian science! It was

genuinely empirical, we see; yet it still confused inductive knowledge, reached by observation, with rational principles supposedly inherent in the mind prior to experience. Was it materialistic, or Platonic? It was Platonic in its mathematical approach and in its mathematical anatomy; but did it not seek to explain everything as a consequence of the motions, distributions, and inertias of material particles? In a sense it did; but it recognized also the two infinite media of space and time, which support and condition all this mechanical occurrence; and space and time seem to be immaterial. But are space and time effective? Are not space and time just passive conditions, necessary to but in no way determining mechanical occurrence? Newton himself spoke of space as the sensorium of God, meaning that it functions as a divine medium conditioning everything that happens, but affecting everything equally, so that its effect cannot be measured and may be canceled out of our calculations. Today the physicist inclines to believe that space is effective, and that it conditions material motion variously and therefore calculably; but he is also inclined to explain the character of space at any place as determined by matter at or near that place, and this is again a materialistic view. Today we are aware of radiant energies such as light, which do not conform to the formulas applicable to solid matter; but Newton, who developed this science of light, conceived light to be made up of material corpuscles; and contemporary science now conceives of the transmutability of radiant energy and matter.

We should conclude, perhaps, that the Newtonian science was materialistic, but that it raised the question of the relation between the material constituents of nature and the fixed "laws" or principles which these constituents seem to obey in all of their motions. The question is whether the universal principles are determined by the material motions, or the material motions determined by the universal principles. The seventeenth century was apt to answer this question unhesitatingly, uncritically, and piously. The principles were taken to be the laws which are imposed upon nature by God; and the complete adequacy of these laws, their power to explain without residue even the smallest material change, was accepted as evidence of the omnipotent and omnipresent governance of God over His creation. Thus the success of materialistic science was interpreted in such a way as to demonstrate the truth of a non-materialistic religion.

We will not further debate this problem here. Notice that the new science was in two respects non-Platonic! First, it elevated to universal status and scope inductive principles like that of gravitation; and secondly, Plato called upon "matter" to explain whatever in nature *is not* universally formed and definable, whereas the modern concept of matter identifies matter with what *is* universally formed and defined. We would discover, if we pursued these differences, that Greek science and modern science, in spite of their common use of mathematical techniques and their common pursuit of large theory, constitute two radically distinct ways of thinking about nature.

From this difference springs the central problem of modern thought. The central and insoluble problem of Greek science, we saw, was the relation of form to matter. This problem now seems to disappear, because modern science does not divide existent being into two halves, called respectively form and matter. An existent thing, modern science has supposed, is perfectly and exhaustively conformed to "natural law," it diverges in no respect from the necessity imposed upon it by universal law. It is indeed just a particularized instance of the universal form which is defined in the basic principles of science. But new problems now arise, or rather the old problem resurrects itself in new ways. Just what is added to or subtracted from the universal form, when it is so particularized in existent and individual things? What shall we say distinguishes the particular from the universal, if we cannot appeal to the Greek dualism of form and matter, and say that form effectively shapes things into universal character, and that matter effectively perpetuates itself in the individual uniqueness of things?

Unfortunately these questions have never been put with sufficient clearness by later philosophy. Two habits of mind have worked to prevent a clear discernment of the problem, as it is perpetuated in modified form in modern science. The first of these habits is just the Greek and medieval philosophy itself. Where the thinker did not clearly perceive the difference between modern science and earlier science, namely its departure from the Greek dualism, he did not give up the now obsolete concepts of form and matter, but tried confusedly to make use of them in estimating the results of modern science. The second obstructive habit of mind was that established by the medieval nominalists. Why not say, said the nominalists, that particulars alone are real, and that universal forms are just mental fictions, resident only in the mind? This easy disposition of the problem still appeals to overspecialized and myopic minds. Why not suppose, these contemporary nominalists say, that our scientific theories are only useful mental constructs, facilitating the recall or anticipation of particular sense impressions? Suppose we do say this—have we solved our problem? Do not these mental constructs still *function* as universals, whenever we use them in relation to particular sense-experience? And do they not *exist* in ourselves? We do not solve the problem of universal knowledge by confining universals to the mind. We only renounce all hope of solving the problem, or forbid its discussion. The real problem is still where it was for the Greeks, in the world and not in the mind. To know how and why we can have a general knowledge of facts which in themselves are wholly particularized, we must know how and why particular things or particular events conform, or at least seem to conform, to general and universal principles. Why are things so similar, and similar in just such and such ways?

The result especially of this second habit of mind was to convert a real and genuinely scientific problem, namely the problem why nature so largely conforms or seems to conform to universal law, into the merely *epistemological* problem of how we know, *i.e.* of the relation of general knowledge to our immediate apprehension of particular fact. Modern philosophy became accordingly centered in epistemology. This epistemological emphasis had certain advantages, we shall see, since it resulted in a new appreciation and better understanding of mental processes; but it had great disadvantages too, in that it separated philosophy from science, and often from the external world itself, leaving the philosopher in a mental prison which he himself creates.

But let us return to the new inductive science as Newton established it, in order to sharpen our grasp of its character. To turn from rational science to inductive empirical science is to convert science into a progressive and exploratory work, establishing no conclusion permanently, but advancing always to larger comprehensions of fact, formulated in new and wider theories. The renunciation of absolute rational principles meant that universal principles must often give way to the evidence of observable particular fact. The humblest, smallest, remotest fact, if only it is well enough attested, can break the proudest, largest, and most familiar theory. This makes science more modest, more tentative, less dogmatic. Science does not merely discover a world already known to our reason, as Plato was compelled to conclude. We do not know the world, we are only in process of learning what it is; and our largest descriptions, so far from being most certain, are least certain and most exposed to radical change. But as reward for this new humility before fact, science becomes immensely more powerful; for now each recalcitrant fact, instead of being scholastically dismissed as mere accident, becomes the occasion for new and wider hypothesis, and a clue to what the new hypothesis must be. The new science discovers a new virtue of impartiality, a new sense of justice toward particular fact, a larger righteousness. It is altogether more rigorous, exacting, and self-critical.

Plato pointed in the right empirical direction when he instructed his students to "save the appearances," *i.e.* to work toward the closest conformity of hypothesis to observed fact; but modern science is not concerned merely to save the appearances—it makes the appearances its whole criterion of truth. Modern science is hard put to save the theory. Modern science is faithful to Plato in its pursuit of theoretical knowledge, mathematically formulated; but it conjoins with the Platonic rationalism, first, Aristotle's identification of real being with individual being or particular fact; and second, the Greek atomist's denial of chance, his insistence on complete causal determinism. Nothing in intellectual history is so astonishing, so strange, so disturbing, and also so pregnant, as the successful union in modern science of principles which to earlier thought seemed irreconcilably incompatible, and which to many erudite minds seem so still.

Notice finally that the new science, at least in its Newtonian form, comprised a great philosophy or metaphysic. It postulated the reality of ultimate material particles, moving in the independent and infinite media of space and time, and causally influencing one another according to a definable set of universally effective principles. So universal and comprehensive a conception constitutes a philosophy, a metaphysical system. We can, of course, proceed to further philosophical discussion of the problems which arise in the persistent application of this science, or which dwell in its inherent implications; but this should not blind us to the fact that a science like modern physics is itself a philosophy, at least if we believe in it and accept its results. We cannot simply accept physics as "science" and then have recourse to another science, which we please to call "philosophy," for our preferred truth. If we accept science as scientific truth, we are committed to a philosophy which will comprehend and be relevant to the findings of science. The Newtonian science, of course, has been expanded and modified, recently in very radical ways; but it still at any and every time presents a definable conception of universal nature, *i.e.* a metaphysic.

The Newtonian metaphysic is closer to Augustine than to any Greek metaphysic. With Augustine, Newton held the world to be infinite, as the creation of an infinite Creator. Like Augustine, who taught that the world must be contingent, *i.e.* underivable from any known principle because it is the creation of the free will of an omnipotent God, Newton held that universal principles such as gravitation must be discovered by observation, and cannot be deduced from any known rational necessity.

In this chapter, in order to follow the rise of modern science to its secure establishment by Newton, we have run ahead of our chronological schedule. When Newton published his abstruse and technical treatises, there was a large intellectual public ready to receive and applaud his conclusions. This large public had been created by a number of more popular writers who publicized the methods, hopes, and achievements of the new science. The most notable of these publicists were Francis Bacon (not to be confused with his great predecessor of the thirteenth century) and René Descartes. Newton was a pure scientist apparently rather aloof from social interests; but for the general public the new science was the important harbinger of a new dispensation of faith and hope. The faith in an empirical science which proceeds from observation to a discovery of the anatomy of nature conspired with a practical faith which looked to the reform of every human institution, and to the establishment of government upon a secure and moral basis. Conjoined, this theoretical and this practical faith constituted the characteristic modern faith in human progress. Free to proceed to new and liberating knowledge, emancipated from dogma and past error, and encouraged to reform its social institutions in an expanding and liberal appraisal of human character, this new society felt itself to be the master of its fate and the creative agent of a glorious future.

Until the twentieth century, modern society was upborne by this tide of faith, out of which was generated great strength, high achievement, and a very real sum of human good. In the strength of this faith it transformed itself, not everywhere but in strategic areas, into the great democratic, intellectualized, and industrialized economy we know today. No faith less wide or less ardent can support this tremendous organized economy of life and work. It is not merely the further progress of man, it is the continued existence of modern society that depends upon this faith. The hope and faith of a society is the measure which finally shapes and governs all of its history.

During the nineteenth century, eloquent voices called into question this modern faith. Thoughtful minds became confused and uncertain as the modern age revealed its material potentialities, and there was a loss of nerve. In the twentieth century, intellectual leaders especially in European society began to separate themselves from "the masses" which still adhered to the now familiar faith in a progressive justice and truth. Confused and misled by these leaders, and perverted by more sinister forces, European society became torn by international and social conflicts, which already in our own time have well-nigh completed its ruin. The somewhat perfervid idealism of the earlier centuries gave way to skepticism, pessimism, and moral atavism. To many, it seemed that the science which had promised complete insight had failed to reach objective truth, or had provided only a trivial truth which tells us nothing of what we most need to know. Society appears less like a moral community, it was felt, than a battleground of ceaseless warfare between pressure-groups; and the vaunted movement of progress, it was concluded, is but a foolish and unintelligible dogma, incompatible with a science which finds in nature only a determinate but nonmoral sequence of events.

So time has brought us through another of its apparent circles, setting us again where Plato stood when he defended the intellectual and moral faith of Greece against a sophistry which drew its arguments, it seemed, from science itself. What Plato defended was constitutional society, or government by law, and a theoretical science which confirmed that political faith by revealing in all nature the governance of a transcendental law. Can we similarly restore faith in democratic justice and in empirical science? Does modern science, which grew up as the twin sister of modern government, support modern society; or does it preclude a justice which is also liberty? This is the underlying theme of later intellectual history. It will be shown that modern science, wholly and clearly understood, is still the true complement of modern justice. The demonstrations of this thesis require some understanding of recent philosophy, telling of the titanic struggle which has quickened, expanded, and endangered the life of modern man.

Notes for Further Reading

1. Dampier-Whetham, W. C. D., *A History of Science*. New York, The Macmillan Company, 1929, Chaps. III and IV.
2. Ginsburg, B., *The Adventure of Science*. New York, Simon and Schuster, 1930, Chaps. V–VII.
3. Libby, W., *An Introduction to the History of Science*. Boston, Houghton Mifflin Company, 1917, Chaps. IV–VIII.
4. Mayer, J., *The Seven Seals of Science*. New York, D. Appleton-Century Company, Inc., 1927, Chaps. V, VI.
5. Needham, J., and Pagel, W., eds. *Background to Modern Science*. Toronto, Cambridge University Press, 1940, Chaps. I, II.
6. Sarton, G., *The History of Science and the New Humanism*. Cambridge, Harvard University Press, 1937.
7. ———— *The Study of the History of Science*. Cambridge, Harvard University Press, 1936, contains bibliographies.
8. Singer, C., *From Magic to Science*. New York, Liveright Publishing Corporation, 1928, Chap. II.
9. Thorndike, L., *History of Magic and Experimental Science*. New York, The Macmillan Company, 1929, for reference.

13 THE RATIONALISTIC PHILOSOPHY OF MODERN SCIENCE

IN THIS AND THREE SUCCEEDING CHAPTERS WE WILL discuss the two chief trends of thought, respectively rationalistic and empirical, which were stimulated by the development of modern science, and which proposed to establish more firmly, and to elucidate and explain, the method and presuppositions of the new science.

In pursuing this effort, philosophy becomes increasingly separated from science, at least in name. Earlier, science had been but "natural philosophy." Even in the nineteenth century scientific treatises were still published under this title. We pointed out that Parmenides had distinguished philosophy from science when he concentrated his attention upon the theoretical or logical form of Greek science, in abstraction from its specialized content. But this distinction, although perpetuated in the study of logic (which engages the form of scientific language in abstraction from its content) had not been supposed to involve a separation of philosophy from science.

Today a good deal of confusion attends this subject of the relationship between philosophy and science. Their true relationship is shown, we shall claim, at the conclusion of this book; but for the present we may notice first, that modern science is distinguished by its division into a number of special sciences, each virtually independent of the others. The physicist, the biologist, and the sociologist go their own ways, following the articulations of their respective fields of fact without sub-servience to each other; and modern philosophy accordingly seeks to bring these sciences together, in a single conception of nature. But secondly, philosophy is still, and more so than ever, the effort to understand not so much what the world is like in its detail (that is the task of science) as to understand what is knowledge itself, and what the existence of this knowl-edge implies about the world. If we are going to describe nature comprehensively, omitting nothing, nature must in-clude man; and man's most characteristic activity is his suc-cessful effort to know and describe his world.

Philosophy has therefore this special task of understanding a world which in man intelligently comprehends itself, or at least moves toward such comprehension. Thus the dominant study of the modern age has been a study of theoretical knowl-edge which discovers the form of knowledge, the relation of knowledge to its object nature, and its consequent value as objective truth or something less. In its narrower analyses, this study is often called epistemology or logic; but in its entirety, which must comprehend all known fact, it is truly philosophy. Because this most inclusive study involves a comprehension of man, with his moral and social purposes, it is of general interest and not merely the province of certain specialists.

An easy but illegitimate way of reaching a general or philo-sophical conception of nature, ostensibly covering all fact, is to take some special science and to suppose that its principles cover everything, neglecting and calling "illusion" what fails to come under these principles. Thus Plato universalized mathe-matical physics; Aristotle universalized botany or taxonomy; and Greek atomism universalized principles which today are best illustrated by chemistry. There are still a few thinkers who attempt this impossible inclusion of all fact within a special science. The best-known form of this fallacy is the brand of materialism which would force physics or chemistry to swallow all other science. It should be clear that if the sciences did really compose only one science, scientists would have established this unitary science themselves, by empirical methods. The multiplication of special sciences is conclusive evidence that fact does not reduce to any one special hypothesis; and to insist that it must do so is merely a form of rationalism or dogmatism, an insistence that nature must be what we personally desire it to be.

However, over and above this fact of the plurality of special sciences, there is another and more compelling fact which precludes our elevation of any special science, or even the sum of the special sciences, into a universal comprehension of fact. This is the presence within each science of an apparent contradiction. Modern science rests firmly upon two criteria of truth. One, the primary and dominant criterion, is the shape and character of observable particular fact. The other criterion, subordinate but still indispensable, is logical consistency. Modern science assumes that *some* theoretical formulation will comprehend all the evidence of particular fact in a given field; and it is this assumption which supports rationalism, which stresses the conformity of nature everywhere to logical principles. Modern science escapes dogmatism, in spite of its apparent rationalism, by its readiness to abandon any and every theoretical formulation, even the most comprehensive, which fails to satisfy all of the empirical evidence. This compromise works excellently, and is the generating dynamo of scientific achievement; but it does not explain itself, it constitutes an apparent contradiction. The rationalistic or logical requirement, effectively applied in every pursuit of large theory, postulates some universal character in nature to which all particular fact *must* conform; but the empirical requirement postulates the power and right of every particular thing to be just its unique and individual self, conforming to no known principle.

Out of this effort to justify and explain the compromise between logic and fact arises and develops modern philosophy. Three distinct trends of philosophical thought are observable. The first seeks to ignore the empirical factor in science, or to reduce it to the rational factor; such philosophy only continues Greek and medieval rationalism, but in an aggravated form. We shall call this trend "modern rationalism." The second seeks to ignore or to reduce the rationalistic element in science; and we shall call this "empiricism." For the third trend there is still no accepted name. Its intention is to undercut and explain the compromise, doing justice to both factors. Kant is the greatest representative of this trend; but it appears in many contemporary movements, for example in contemporary realism and pragmatism. The very important practical significance of the long struggle between rationalistic and empiricistic philosophies arises from their implications for political theory and practice. Rationalism, because it is absolutistic or dogmatic, ultimately calls for some absolutistic form of government. Empiricism rejects every kind of absolutism, both theoretical and practical; but it has hitherto failed to establish a theory of liberal government, and has exposed us to the dubious mercy of the political absolutist. Kant's great but unsuccessful effort to synthesize rationalism and empiricism pointed to the solution of the problem, which today, we shall argue, is satisfactorily and rather astonishingly achieved.

Modern rationalism has been almost entirely the work of thinkers on the continent of Europe. Empiricism has been almost entirely the work of British thinkers. America, which took up its philosophical task only half a century ago, looks impartially upon these past traditions, and may inaugurate a philosophy comprehending and reconciling the opposed trends. We consider here the rationalistic philosophy developed in the seventeenth century on the continent of Europe, diverging somewhat to include in its chronological place the work of Francis Bacon.

As we began our account of the rise of modern science with some mention of Copernicus, we may well begin this summary of modern philosophy with Bruno, whose speculation was in many ways an effort to appreciate in its full significance the revolutionary Copernican theory. The life of *Giordano Bruno* (1548–1600) is the vignette of a stormy and religiously convulsed age. Born in Naples, he was early initiated into the Dominican order. From this rigorous discipline he fled to the Protestant church, where he found even less comfort. He then wandered persecuted over Europe, teaching, quarreling, publishing when he could. Finally he was betrayed to the Inquisition, which burned him at the stake for his heresies.

Bruno's blessing and curse was an intellectual imagination willing to draw from the Copernican hypothesis its maximum consequence. If the earth is not the center of the universe, he argued, there is no center, nor any conceivable bound. The universe is infinite and homogeneous, and any part of it is as important and representative as any other part. God is equally manifest in everything—there is no privileged and locable "heaven." The infinite universe displays the infinite being of God. Infinity cannot be extensively grasped. We can know nature only intensively, in its individual items. The item we know best is our individual self, of which we have an immediate and concrete intuition. Reflection discovers in the self a creative activity or moral will which is the microcosm or small edition of the universal macrocosm, the infinite activity of God. Our understanding of reality must be exploratory rather than definitive. Nature is like a face, which we comprehend by appreciating its several parts in their relationship. Our personal lives similarly set forth our souls or characters, because they are the creations of our wills. The infinite character of God is therefore revealed to us, in some degree, in all the visible creation of nature, which it is our duty and privilege to study

. . . Was your burned and blackened body, Bruno, also a revelation of the infinite being of God? Let Bruno serve as the philosopher of the Renaissance, pointing to yet not entering the modern era! He was a great and vigorous spirit, a Michelangelo in metaphysics, from whose genius the better known later thinkers freely borrowed.

The man who probably did most to acquaint the reading and educated public of Europe with the new science, and to propagate enthusiasm for it, was Francis Bacon; and even today it is not unusual to hear this second Bacon referred to—as if his great namesake Roger Bacon had never lived—as the founder and expositor of modern scientific method and the creator of its "inductive logic." We shall see that he was something less than this.

Francis Bacon, Lord of Verulam (1561–1626), was an ambitious Elizabethan, contemporary with Shakespeare. He achieved high office under James I, becoming the king's first minister, from which elevation he fell disgraced, convicted of having accepted bribes. He was a man of great energy, a firm believer in monarchical authority, and convinced of the power and duty of government to undertake large research and beneficent enterprise. The political opposition which finally toppled him had other ideas about the extent and responsibilities of state power.

Bacon was eminently suited for the task to which he appointed himself, which was to turn Europe from its sterile medieval scholarship to an independent, empirical, and productive study of the world. He was widely read in classical and medieval literature, which had early formed his mind; yet he had caught something of the vision of Roger Bacon and Occam, and appreciated the possibilities of the new science in the extension of man's control over nature. In his *New Atlantis* he anticipated the industrialized world of today, with its mechanized transportation and production. His reputation as a writer, established by his early *Essays*, and his ability as a brilliant special pleader, together with his high position, gave him an intellectual authority which was out of proportion to his limited knowledge of science; but his fame and abilities made him the most successful advocate of modern science. Even Bacon's limitations probably served him well—they were those of the European public he wished to influence. A Hume or a Kant would have had less immediate success.

Bacon's work had two sides, respectively critical and constructive. He opened his *Novum Organum* with a blast against all medieval learning and scholastic philosophy. Earlier scholarship, he wrote, had been little else than book learning and intellectual idolatry. It had been subservient to racial habits of mind (the "idols of the tribe"), personal prepossessions (the "idols of the cave"), tradition, especially scholastic tradition (the "idols of the theatre"), and habits incorporate in language (the "idols of the marketplace"). Nowhere had it served truth, which is discovered only by persistent and dutiful observation. Let book learning be the useless tedium of priests! Nature will be the study of men who directly draw from their observation of fact the power to control nature and man.

Later centuries have responded perhaps too readily to this Baconian exhortation to cut oneself off from past intellectual tradition, in order to extract from sheer fact a knowledge which has no presuppositions whatsoever. Admirable in its encouragement of critical and observant habit, Bacon's teaching suffers from its neglect of the continuity of man's intellectual evolution. This weakness becomes apparent in Bacon's description of science. In truth, modern science revived and widened an intellectual tradition which had been preserved for twenty-two centuries, ever since its inception in ancient Ionia; but because he was ignorant or unappreciative of this long evolution, which he knew only in its medieval decline, Bacon failed to grasp the ideal of theoretical unity, which is a source and guide of modern science no less than it was of earlier science.

The title of his work, *Novum Organum* or *The New Method*, shows us that he intended this book to displace the original *Organon*, which was the logic of Aristotle. The new science did make use of a new method or logic, quite other than that of Aristotle and closely related to the mathematical method of Plato; but Bacon shows little awareness of this mathematical element, and no understanding of its function. He still, even in the seventeenth century, refused the Copernican hypothesis; and he seems to have been quite ignorant of the work of contemporary scientists like Galileo and Harvey. That he knew something of his English predecessors is shown by his speaking of the "Laws of Heat" and "of Light," as examples of the sort of "form" the scientist should discover in nature. These "forms" or simple natures, he says, are clues to the latent processes which underlie observable change; and his instructions concerning the use of the inductive method, in a careful comparison of instances intended to discover constant correlations, with regard for negative instances and with constant use of measurement, are cogent enough. But Bacon's description of scientific method would be quite misleading to one who had no independent knowledge of science; and its importance lies more in its intention than in its achievement. Its intention was to describe the new science in its most general character and method; and here, Bacon places too much stress on the collection and classification of instances, and too little on the construction of hypothesis or large theory. From Bacon chiefly comes the misconception, prevalent especially in the English-speaking world, that science is only a collection and cataloguing of "data," and that every such catalogue of facts is a contribution to science. Science is truly an imaginative and constructive art. It is the greatest of all the arts, in its stimulation and restraint of the imagination by realistic attention to actuality or "fact." Those of us who are not creative scientists may accept the formulas of science, using them and noting their implications and presuppositions; but only the creative scientist is qualified to reveal the "method" of science. Since this method is that of genius, it eludes definition, and can be appreciated only in its achievements. Newton is said to have reached his gravitational hypothesis by observing the fall of an apple from a tree; but what was the breadth and content of thought that could read into the fall of an apple the fall of moon to earth and of tide to moon, and pursue this analogy through mathematical labyrinths never traced before? Was that an "induction" from observed instances? In some sort, perhaps; but in what sort?

Bacon's writings, if we may accept the evidence of seventeenth-century literature, were the chief stimulus of the rather facile optimism which called itself "the Enlightenment." The spokesmen of the Enlightenment regarded all earlier time, with some reservations respecting pagan antiquity, as an age of darkness from which reason or science now at last delivered man—and delivered him completely, into perfect light. This curious obliviousness of medieval antecedents was due in part to the linguistic shift from Latin to the European vernaculars; yet Francis Bacon and Descartes, the two chief literary sources of the Enlightenment, were Latin scholars deeply indebted to medieval literature. They gave expression, we must conclude, to a real and widespread desire, current in their time, to shake off all the past and to advance in the power of certain new conceptions of nature and man to an unparalleled future. The writers of the Enlightenment were able to convince their contemporaries, and even the later centuries as well, that reason appeared on earth suddenly and without antecedents, this interesting event occurring in or about the year 1600. Thus we are told to see in Francis Bacon, who owed whatever he knew to medieval predecessors, "the father of modern science"; and Descartes is held up as "the founder of modern philosophy." Seldom has a culture drawn such a veil between itself and its past. Not until the late nineteenth century did modernity begin to suspect its medieval heritage, and attempt to bring filial honor to its intellectual parents.

Only less influential than Francis Bacon in the propagation of this revolutionary desire to annihilate all the past was *René Descartes* (1596-1650). Descartes is the philosophical complement to Bacon, in that he emphasized the rational element in science which Bacon neglected, and overlooked the empirical element which Bacon stressed. Descartes was a mathematical genius of the first order, and the developer of analytical geometry. This mathematical invention, which unites number-theory with geometry to produce a mathematical instrument of tremendous power, has supported all the later development of physical science. Descartes had some reason, therefore, to believe that he had found a key which would unlock every door, and make nature completely transparent to the human intellect. But Descartes expected more than scientific illumination from his new instrument. He believed that the scientific knowledge thus obtained would transfigure human life, and establish human society on a new and stable basis. No modern thinker has been more successful than Descartes in persuading his contemporaries to accept, as an apparent and necessary truth evident to every intelligent mind, his own ideas of the world and man. In one modification or another, the Cartesian rationalism is as influential today as it was in the seventeenth century.

Like Bacon before him and like many a philosopher since, Descartes presented his startling metaphysical theory in the modest guise of a method. We will not take too seriously Descartes' *Discourse on Method.* What the author presents as a new method is nothing more than the procedure familiar to every student of elementary geometry. Break your material up into its elements, get down to the simplest parts and the clearest relationships, and then carefully retrace your steps until the figure is lucidly reconstructed—this innocuous advice was the cover to a new and revolutionary theory of nature, man, and society. What Descartes meant was nothing less than this: Applied mathematics is our sole science, its results are certain and its range unlimited, and all our other beliefs must be established upon or accommodated to this basic and certain knowledge.

Descartes, a frail lad, was educated by Jesuits in northern France. He was there impressed, he tells us, only by his mathematical studies, all other instruction seeming futile. Where Descartes learned his contempt for scholastic philosophy and his inclination to Augustinian and Calvinistic theology is an interesting question. After sampling the salon life of Paris and finding it trivial and hectic, he took refuge in the army. One cold night before a coal fire there came to him the vision of a new science and a new world. Descartes is so modest in his account of this vision that its radical implications are easily overlooked. One sees the cool and lucid rationalist, and misses the social reformer whose utopian optimism has stimulated the most violent social revolutions of the modern age. This new science, Descartes believed, would within the near future place in man's hands a power allowing him complete control over every human condition. Disease, poverty, crime, and war would be eliminated; and human society would be established upon a new and completely rational basis. Until such time as this millennium was reached, Descartes discreetly promised, he would conform to the usual moral conventions and live as other men.

Appreciate first the scientific vision of Descartes! Greek geometry had analyzed static surfaces and volumes, carved out of empty space. The new analytic geometry seemed to lay hold of the properties of motion itself. Given three straight lines at right angles and intersecting at a point, any motion can be described by reference to these three coordinates. A series of such references defines a line, or the path of a motion; and a set of such lines may be used to define any physical situation, or any complex of motions constituting a physical change. We are all familiar with this method, used every day in graphs representing correlations between observable changes, or describing the progress of some temporal change. Descartes believed that his method would permit the complete representation and perfect elucidation of every natural change. The only condition is that all such change should be understood as complex motion in space-time, and nothing else.

He therefore advances a metaphysics, *i.e.* a definition of the universal and eternal character of nature, ensuring that all natural change shall be understood in this way, as merely change of place. This world, apparently so material, dense, distributed, colorful, and otherwise qualitied and diversified, is really none of these things. It is an infinite ocean of homogeneous motion—not of things moving, be it noted, but of pure motion, things being only composite motions. Descartes calls the mobile continuum "matter"; and he says, using scholastic language, that "its essence is extension" or geometrical pattern. But this scholastic language is only a figure of speech, giving him contact with his scholastically minded readers. Descartes' conception is like nothing in earlier thought. It is a thoroughgoing dynamism, in which everything material is swallowed up in motion or energy. The very distinction between matter and space falls away. All space is motion, and what we call "matter" is only some part of mobile space, comparable to a whirlpool or a current in a river. This conception allows all natural character and all natural change to be described by means of a graphical geometry, which is able to represent the directions, velocities, and accelerations of motion. Geometry and its applications become our whole natural science; and it is a science utterly adequate to the description of natural occurrence.

This dynamic conception of nature, which would reduce everything to continuous yet decipherable motion, has sustained itself in physical science for three centuries. It is not, however, the sole conception of nature entertained in physical science, which always supplements this doctrine of absolute mobile continuity with theories presupposing a discontinuity of stuff in nature. Nor is the conception of a mobile continuum itself clear or complete. Physical theory distinguishes many types or species of motion or energy, in its accommodation of this concept of dynamic continuity to the discrete and articulate world which is presented to our senses. Descartes' conception of nature, no less than that of Plato, harbors a dualism according to which a static, universal form, eternally defined by the axioms of geometry, invests the particular motions which variously manifest this eternal form; and as with Plato, the relation between universal form and particular motion must be left wholly unintelligible. Since this dynamic concept of nature is difficult and perhaps impossible to clarify, it is usually replaced by a mechanical conception which conceives nature to be constituted wholly of some sort of clockwork, intricate and infinite. Descartes himself often slipped into this mechanical conception when presenting or applying his dynamic theory.

One great virtue of this Cartesian concept of nature is its rigorous determinism. Everything that happens, at any time and place, even in its most minute features, is held to be completely necessitated by its spatio-temporal context. There is no accident, no chance, no element of formless "matter" in nature itself. Events are accidental or due to chance only in the sense that we are ignorant of their causes and powerless to control these. Perfect knowledge would see everything in nature to be wholly necessitated, and therefore completely intelligible. This mechanistic concept of nature would seem to be the condition of a complete understanding and an absolute control of natural occurrence.

But where does man belong in this mechanistic world? He cannot, Descartes concludes, belong in it at all. The mind of man, which observes, knows, and within its powers controls material nature, must be wholly other than nature, no part of it. Man's body, of course, belongs in the physical world, and consists of determinate physical processes; but his mind, Descartes teaches, is nonphysical and nonspatial, and belongs to another realm. This absolute separation of "matter" and "mind," *i.e.* of the physical and mental realms, constitutes the *Cartesian dualism.* There is the infinite mobile expanse of physical being, which is all of a piece and wholly subject to mechanical necessity; and then there are human minds, somehow in but not of this physical realm, attached to bodies but with no "essential," *i.e.* explicable, relation to these bodies.

Yet these minds, if they are to know nature and to move the physical things which are their bodies, must have some real and causal relationship with nature. The Cartesian dualism breaks down in face of the actual and observable interaction between nature and mind. Descartes deals with his insoluble problem in two ways. Sometimes he moderates his stark dualism —he admits that the physical motions of nature proceed through our sense organs to produce sensations in our minds, and admits also that our minds, which are free wills, may influence our bodily processes, and through them direct the external processes of nature. But all such interaction between mind and nature, he recognizes, is an infraction of his dualistic conception; and his final disposition of the problem is theological. God created the physical world, he holds, in the form it is scientifically known to have; and he created also conscious human beings, endowing them with minds able to know nature and to control it in adequate measure. Our duty, therefore, is to use these endowments, and not to inquire into their mysterious origins, which lie hidden in the inscrutable will of the Creator. It should be enough for us that we have reason, that we can apply reason in scientific research, and that we can scientifically control our bodily movements and so our immediate environment. The limitations of reason do not prevent our fullest use of reason, leading to the rational transfiguration of human life.

Descartes called physical nature "matter," and said that "the essence of matter is extension," meaning that the true form of physical nature is its geometrical pattern. He similarly speaks of conscious experience as "mind," and says that the "essence of mind" is thought or scientific analysis. This language is really a concession to scholastic philosophy, and a source of confusion in Descartes' philosophy; but it was nevertheless indispensable to his system. Our immediate apprehension of nature is wholly unlike that colorless, soundless, perfectly geometrical and mobile continuum which nature becomes in Descartes' science. The really physical characters of things, Descartes believed, are proper to external reality itself; but all color, taste, and other sensible character is wholly in and of the mind, being a mental confusion, due to our intellectual passivity, of the true mathematical pattern of nature. What earlier philosophy held to be accidental and unintelligible in the world, and ascribed to "matter" in distinction from "form," Descartes finds to be an illusion in the mind, where, however, it really exists as sensations, feelings, and other non-rational activities. When reason is active, all of this confused mental material is eliminated or transmuted, to leave us with a rational understanding of the real motions of nature in their purely geometrical character. There is the real physical world, composed of sheer motion; there is the real mind, constituted by a true and rational apprehension of physical motion; and then there is a sort of iridescence, produced by the confusion of physical reality and mind, but truly nothing. The power of the Cartesian philosophy lay chiefly in the simplicity and clarity of its positive teaching. This was, that mathematical science truly portrays external reality. With resoluteness it ignored, or dismissed as illusion, whatever presented difficulties to this doctrine.

Yet what a strange, stark, and really terrible doctrine it is! Man is to be identified with his reason, which finds in external reality only an infinite, colorless, silent waste of physical mo-

tion, meaningful only in its mathematical form. In all this infinite vastness only man lives, knows, feels, esteems, and acts.
All else, including animals and plants, is clockwork. Man is
free to accept or reject his faculty of reason. When he rejects
it, he becomes the passive slave of illusions which are the invasion of his mind by matter, a sort of death. When he accepts
reason, he becomes a disembodied intellect, contemplating
physical necessity and turning it to use. But to what use? There
is no place in Descartes' philosophy for the concept and properties of life; yet do not a matter and mind detached from
living flesh become meaningless? Matter becomes meaningless
motion, mind becomes a mirror reflecting that motion. Descartes
assumes, of course, that man has a life to live, a will to exert,
a goal to gain, a goodness to secure; and he assumes that science
is the instrument of this quest. But there is no place for
these assumptions in his metaphysics. That, literally taken,
makes of the mind the meaningless mirror of a meaningless
world.

Whether or not we call Descartes "the father of modern
philosophy," he certainly was the founder of modern rationalism. The essential faculty of mind, he taught, is its faculty
of rational intuition, or of entertaining "clear and distinct
ideas." The constitutive faculty of science, as we saw, he
held to be an intuition of mathematical pattern in nature. The
source of this faculty is a number of mathematical principles
which are innate in the human mind, although they may not
become conscious and explicit without effort. Descartes in-
sufficiently recognized the contingent character of nature, the
physical properties of which cannot really be deduced from
mathematical axioms, although they lend themselves to mathematical statement. Consequently, he nowhere did justice to the
empirical character of modern science, which reaches its large
theory only with the help of inductions based upon observed
particulars. Descartes thinks of the scientific mind as a sort of
searchlight, which can be focused upon any particular part of

nature, and by virtue of its intuitive power perfectly illuminate that limited area. He thinks of scientific theory as being already completed in mathematical theory, the expansion of science being only the continued application of this theory to ever new areas of nature. He does not conceive of a development of scientific hypothesis, stimulated by widening experience and reaching new basic principles.

Modern rationalism, thus initiated by Descartes, differs importantly from the earlier rationalism established by the Greek philosophers. That earlier rationalism was a dualism of matter and form. It conceived nature to be everywhere dual, each existent thing and process being compounded of two sorts of being, namely of eternal and perfect form, and of shifting matter which is the source of imperfection and change. The Cartesian dualism of matter and mind is something very different. It conceives nature to be everywhere perfectly formed, what seems imperfect or unintelligible being truly an illusion in our minds, which are no part of nature. Yet the distinction between the particular changing detail and the universal geometrical form of nature must still be preserved, although there is now no philosophical place for it; and this seems to introduce again, but now unconsciously and disingenuously, the matter-form dualism which is explicitly rejected. Further, the Greek rationalism was genuinely idealistic. It conceived the universal form of nature to be the goal or end toward which all things strain, and in the reaching of which lies their natural good. Only for minds, according to modern rationalism, does form constitute an ideal of this sort. Nature is perfect in its absolute geometry; but imperfect man must still strain to know this form, the intuition of which is its cognitive ideal. Does this mean that nature is wholly good, that every prospect pleases and only man is vile? Or does it mean that nature is nonmoral, its values arising solely out of its utility for man? Or is nature beyond good and evil, is it a sort of absolute contentment beyond all striving? It is evident that the Cartesian dualism, in departing from the naturalistic idealism of the Greeks, generated new and profound moral problems.

There is a positive as well as a negative side to this Cartesian metaphysic. It "denatures" nature by taking out of nature all the quality and vitality which relates nature to man, in order to define external reality in terms of mathematical or rational necessity. This leaves the relation of man to nature wholly unintelligible, a mystery referred to the inscrutable will of God. But on the other hand, the doctrine recognizes, in a degree never recognized before, the autonomy of moral man. The law of nature, its mechanical necessity, is now no law for man, but only the means by which man exercises his creative moral power in the pursuit of his own ends. But what are these ends, what instructs us concerning them? What is man's true nature? It lies, apparently, in his autonomy or freedom from law. The Cartesian philosophy expresses here the stark and bold ethics of Augustine and of Calvinistic Puritanism, which were to become explicit in Kant.

That Descartes was not uninfluenced by this Puritan tradition is suggested by his large use of Augustinian conceptions. Like Augustine, he instructs us to make use of skeptical doubt in order to reach certainty. We can and initially must doubt everything; but even the largest and most resolute skepticism is finally cut short by the indubitable existence of the doubting and thinking self. *Cogito ergo sum,* I think (or doubt), therefore I am. Thought cannot think away its own activity. Using the arguments of medieval theology, Descartes advances from the evident existence of human thought to the necessary existence of an infinite and perfect God, and thence back to the reliability of the God-given reason and its self-evident intuitions.

The Cartesian philosophy raised more problems than it solved; but they were problems which had to be raised, and which all later thought has duly attacked; for they are implicit in the method and form of modern science. Because it seemed to make the new science simple and rational; because it seemed to offer a much needed ground for intellectual and political authority; because it promised a social millennium in an "age of reason"; because it expressed the high optimism of the Renaissance and seemed to turn its back upon the past; because, paradoxically, it also brought into philosophy certain moral and religious conceptions implicit in the Puritan Reformation; because it verbally bridged the gap between scholastic theology and the new scientific outlook; and, finally, because it was presented in a prose so lucid and effective that it has remained the model of French style ever since—for these reasons, the Cartesian philosophy had enormous influence. It established a rationalistic tradition which developed and modified itself with each succeeding generation, to become a permanent factor in modern thought; and its importance and success were not, of course, without reason, being due to the undeniable rational element in modern science, which cleaves to its theoretical form and everywhere requires the accommodation of fact to the requirements of logic. We shall not be able to estimate the value of the thought of Descartes, consequently, until we have come to some conclusion concerning this relation of empirical fact to logical form. What Descartes too much neglected, we saw, was the empirical element in modern science, this being its most characteristic and important element.

Notes for Further Reading

1. Boulting, W., *Giordano Bruno*. London, K. Paul, Trench, Trübner and Company, Ltd., 1916.
2. McClure, M. T., *Bacon: Selections*. New York, Charles Scribner's Sons, 1928.
3. Wheelwright, P., *Bacon, Hobbes, Locke: Selections*. Garden City, Doubleday Doran and Company, 1930.
4. Kennedy, G., *Bacon, Hobbes, Locke: Selections*. New York, Doubleday Doran and Company, 1937.

5. Fischer, K., *Francis Bacon of Verulam*, trans. J. Oxenford. London, Longman, Brown, Green, Longmans, and Roberts, 1857.

6. Andrews, C. M., *Famous Utopias*. New York, Tudor Publishing Company, 1937. Includes Bacon's *New Atlantis*.

7. Church, R. W., *Bacon*. New York, The Macmillan Company, 1884.

8. Eaton, R. M., *Descartes: Selections*. New York, Charles Scribner's Sons, 1927.

9. Roth, L., *Descartes' Discourse on Method*. London and New York, Oxford University Press, 1937.

10. Veitch, J., *Descartes' Discourse on Method*. La Salle, Ill., The Open Court Publishing Company, 1917.

11. ———*Descartes' Meditations, etc*. New York, Tudor Publishing Company, 1937.

12. Fischer, K., "Descartes and his School," *History of Modern Philosophy*. Trans. J. P. Gordy. New York, Charles Scribner's Sons, 1887.

13. Boutroux, E., "Descartes and Cartesianism," *Cambridge Modern History*. New York, The Macmillan Company, 1909, Vol. IV.

14. Haldane, E. S., *Descartes, his Life and Times*. New York, The Macmillan Company, 1905.

15. Gibson, A. B., *The Philosophy of Descartes*. New York, E. P. Dutton and Company, 1932.

16. Smith, N. K., *Studies in Cartesian Philosophy*. London, Macmillan and Company, 1902.

17. Lévy-Bruhl, L., *A History of Modern Philosophy in France*. La Salle, Ill., The Open Court Publishing Company, 1899.

14 THE RATIONALISTIC PHILOSOPHY OF MODERN SCIENCE

(Continued)

Especially on the continent of europe, the thought of Descartes became the starting-point of many who wished to emancipate themselves from past tradition, and to establish life and society upon a purely rational, indisputable basis. As we have seen, the Cartesian system was by no means so complete a break with earlier thought as he and his contemporaries believed. His mathematical concept of physical nature improved upon that of Pythagoras; his dualism of physical and mental being gave philosophical room to the Christian dualism of world and spirit, the sacred and the profane; his theology was Augustinian and scholastic. But these traditional elements, which allowed Descartes to reach his readers, largely served as a bridge which could be crossed and then burned and forgotten. They constituted a sort of religious background, taking care of the inscrutable and allowing the foreground of thought to be brilliantly illuminated. By most of Descartes' readers, a method so powerful and a reason so lucid was expected to overcome every problem. Men of less genius did not see that his power was the clarity with which he perceived the limitations of his rationalistic method. Descartes was still scholastic in leaving ultimate issues to faith. His followers supposed "method" to have no limits; and the really tremendous metaphysic of God, matter, and free will was reduced first to the stark and unintelligible "Cartesian dualism" of matter and mind, finally to the flat and superficial materialism of the later Enlightenment and the French revolution.

The crux of Descartes' philosophy, the blind spot generating its insolubles, was its failure to grapple with causal relationship. Physical causation was there identified with mathematical identity, in order that every statement about physical nature might be formulated in a mathematical equation. Mental causation, connecting thoughts or ideas, he seems to have identified with rational necessity, or what we would call "logical relationship." But neither of these relationships, he clearly saw, could be substituted for the apparent causal interactions between physical and mental being without erasing the distinction between matter and mind, and thus collapsing the whole system. Therefore he left the relation between matter and mind inscrutable, even as Plato had left inscrutable the relation between matter and form. Some of his followers, developing a late suggestion of his own, argued that bodies might indirectly affect minds, and minds bodies, through the active mediation of God. A physical event, they said, might be only the occasion and not the effective cause of our mental sensation of that event, God producing in us the sensation appropriate to that event. Similarly, when the mind proposes to move the body, it is not the mind but God who actually moves the body. We wish to raise our hand; and God, perceiving our desire, moves the hand for us. This doctrine, known as *Occasionalism*, would make God the direct cause of everything done to or by human beings; and its apparent piety does not withstand scrutiny. Occasionalism served, indeed, to reveal the inadequacy of the Cartesian system, because it finally brought all causal relationship into question. Do we understand how one physical body affects another physical body, the Occasionalists finally asked, any better than we understand how physical body affects mind? To say that the motion lost by one body is only transferred to the body with which it collides allows us to describe such events in mathematical equations; but it does not explain how the transfer of motion takes place. Motion is a bodily property, and how can bodies exchange properties? The causal connection remains unexplained and inexplicable, and we must say that one physical event only occasions another, the true cause being God. The Cartesian doctrine, at first sight so lucid and rational, evaporates into religious mysticism. The French cleric Malebranche welcomed this conclusion. The physical world, he suggested, is but a myth, all our experience proceeding in God, who is the sole agent and ceaseless creator of all that is. This idealistic mysticism was later developed by Berkeley.

But two continental thinkers, Spinoza and Leibniz, made valiant attempts to modify the Cartesian system in such a way as to meet this matter-mind problem without sacrifice of the Cartesian faith in science. *Benedict Spinoza* (1632–1677) attempted a solution by means of the concept of an absolute correspondence or parallelism between physical and mental processes. To every mental condition, he supposed, there corresponds a physical condition; and vice versa. Our will to move and our bodily motion are not cause and effect, but two aspects of one and the same concrete event. Similarly, every sensation is the mental aspect of some bodily condition. The real world, in short, is everywhere at once mental and physical, just as a box must have an inside and an outside, or a curved line a convex side and a concave side. Matter and mind are not two substances; they are two most basic properties of one and the same substance.

This conception of psychophysical parallelism has proved useful, even indispensable, in human psychology; and we cannot doubt that it expresses a biological fact. Also, it suggests a more general conception which is intellectually emancipating.

A single concrete thing, it suggests, may present very different aspects of itself in various contexts. We are thus led to suppose that universal nature may contain a diversity of patterns, not merely one pattern. We shall find many developments of Spinoza's parallelism in later thought. But the idea also multiplies difficulties. For example, if you are fatigued and exerting yourself to rise, both your bodily inertia and your muscular effort must have their mental correspondents, so that one cannot speak simply of the mind controlling the body; and psychologists, openly or surreptitiously, sooner or later inevitably assume psychological control. But the largest difficulties, at least for Spinoza, arise when we suppose this psychophysical parallelism to extend through the whole of nature. We can believe that animals have in some degree mental processes, as well as physical processes; and we may even suppose that plants have some rudimentary sort of sensitivity and consciousness; but does it mean anything to speak of the mental process of an electron, of the Mississippi River, or of the solar system? It is curious to find that Spinoza, famed for his attack upon anthropomorphic religion, really embraces a most extreme anthropomorphic view, that which supposes nature everywhere to be characterized by the body-mind relationship, which is clearly evident only in man.

Spinoza's dominating interests were moral and religious, not scientific. We might perhaps best understand his philosophy by seeing in it an effort to provide a moral science supplementing the Cartesian physics. Descartes believed, as did everyone apparently at that time, that the "pure reason," source of an absolute mathematical science, must deliver itself no less of an absolute moral science; but Descartes nowhere provided this moral theory. There is one great moral principle implicit in his work, namely that man, being free, must use his reason, *i.e.* science, to attain his ends. But he nowhere indicated the practical and moral objectives to the realization of which we should apply our power over physical nature. He assumed that man would regenerate society and establish it on a firm basis; but he nowhere rationally established even this assumption. So Spinoza wrote his *Ethics*, a treatise of rational morality and rational religion.

We possess today a considerable body of theoretical science, the authority of which is seldom seriously questioned; but after three centuries of theoretical research, we have still no authoritative science of ethics. Kant, who was the profoundest student of this problem, concluded there can be none, because freedom and authority are reciprocally exclusive. But Spinoza did not doubt the possibility of a rational ethical theory. His faith was due in part to his need, which would not be denied. He was the son of a Jewish family, driven from Spain to Holland by the persecutions of the Inquisition. In Holland, his intellectual audacity brought him into collision with orthodox Jewry, which excommunicated him from the synagogue. Spinoza needed a rational religion, one that would leave him intellectually free, yet unite him with his fellows despite all differences of confession and race. He became the first modern exponent of a liberal religion which would carry into creative faith the intellectual powers active and creative in science. He had a second ground of faith. Although Spinoza subscribed to the Cartesian science, he was not only nor even primarily a Cartesian. In his youth he had steeped himself in Jewish and other scholastic theology, and he never renounced certain large tenets of scholastic doctrine. The Puritan conception which allows to nature no intrinsic value, but sees in it only a physical mechanism created to serve man's moral purpose, never found lodgment in the mind of Spinoza. Nature was for him what it was for the Stoics, the material expression of universal and divine Being. Both metaphysically and morally, Spinoza is a modern Stoic, one who adapts the Stoic concept of nature to the supposed requirements of modern science. The main outline of his metaphysics is as follows: There is but one Substance, infinite in extent and variety, but absolute in its unity.

Of the infinite aspects or *attributes* of this Substance we know only two, matter and mind. Substance is continuous but diversified, its diverse characters and parts being called *modes*. Some of these modes, *e.g.* motion, are infinite. Some are finite, *e.g.* all individual character and all specific form. Each mode, since it is concrete, will present both a physical and a mental aspect, as in the body and the mind of man. By means of this division of nature into modes, Spinoza brings back into philosophy many pre-Cartesian habits of thought, especially that which saw in every natural thing a striving to realize its proper form or "mode."

This pre-Cartesian outlook conflicts with the Cartesian elements in Spinoza's thought, and leaves his doctrine self-contradictory. Earlier thought had rested upon a dualism of form and matter, allowing a pluralism of individual substances. The Cartesian physics required physical monism and strict determinism. Every individual thing, it insisted, is but some mode, *i.e.* some local part or character, in the universal Substance; and this means that it is completely determined by that Substance. Spinoza explicitly draws this consequence, denying freedom to the individual in any sense that would allow the individual to control his fate. The universe is one vast mechanism, moving as a whole; and its mental pattern everywhere repeats the pattern of physical necessity. It is hard to see, therefore, how human thought can initiate any control either of itself or of physical nature. Yet Spinoza, being a moralist, necessarily insists upon some sort of human freedom, or power to control events. His explicit defense of human freedom is his supposition that man is free when he rationally understands, and therefore willingly and joyfully accepts, his individual destiny as a part of the universal Being which is God. But even this power to choose between rational acceptance of fate and ignorant subservience to it implies a break of some sort in the absolute determinism presupposed by the concept of Substance. It makes the human individual a small but independent substance, in some degree effecting its own mental processes, and therewith its physical processes. And in fact, Spinoza assumes much more than this bare choice. To choose the rational life, he says, is to resist the passions, temptations, and feelings induced in us by our immediate environment, which compel us to pursue pleasure, fame, position, wealth, and other "worldly" goods. To live rationally is to live wholly in and for an "intellectual love of God," *i.e.* a rational understanding of ourselves as mere items in the universal Substance. Spinoza implies that the individual is free to determine his life, and that he will find his true good in an intelligent and voluntary participation in a universal divine Process.

We may accept the ethical purpose of Spinoza, which was to establish a rational and intelligent moral science, without being disturbed by the metaphysical inconsistencies of his ethical theory. In the same way we may accept his call to an independent and intelligent religious faith without identifying ourselves with his specific conclusions, which were determined by his faulty interpretation of science. Spinoza was adamantly opposed to all revealed religion, with its appeal to past authority, its dogmatic persecution of heresies, and its anthropomorphism. The only true God, he taught, is that eternal, immutable, universal Substance, which, wholly unlike our human selves, is omnipotent and infinite, yet accessible to our rational intuition. Spinoza's criticism of biblical sources initiated a new era of critical and scientific religious study, and was the important forerunner of the critical historical science of today. He widened the religious outlook of his age; and his work should have initiated a creative movement, reaching new religious truth by applying to religion the faculties developed by a free and observant science. His achievement remains great, therefore, after we discount his ethical and religious teaching as too rationalistic and intellectual, too solitary and aloof, too unrelated to emotional and social actualities.

The chief philosophical influence of Spinoza, over and above the scientific influence exerted by his determination to apply scientific method in ethics, psychology, and sociology, has been due to his rationalistic monism. No modern thinker has upheld with more fidelity the ancient faith of Parmenides in a unitary Being, accessible to the unitary reason of man. Spinoza distinguished three sorts or levels of knowledge, in opinion, reason, and intuition. Under opinion he included all ordinary experience, hearsay, tradition, etc. By reason he meant a scientific knowledge guided by innate rational concepts common to all men; and by intuition he meant a most ultimate philosophical or religious insight, proceeding from an intuition of the attributes of God to an "adequate knowledge of the essence of things." Insufficient attention has been given to the superrational or superscientific power attributed by Spinoza to this intuitive faculty, which really makes his doctrine one of religious mysticism, in spite of its rationalistic vocabulary. His distinction between reason and intuition revived the medieval distinction between philosophy and theology, which Spinoza brought over into the modern world, where it became the distinction between an exploratory natural science dependent upon observation and logic, and a philosophy ostensibly transcending such empirical science by means of an infallible intuition of absolute and universal truth.

Spinoza's *Ethics* ostensibly made use of this philosophical "intuition." Starting with the intuition of God as "substance," and imitating the form of strict demonstration used in Euclid's geometry, Spinoza first postulates the necessary existence and attributes of God, and proceeds from these to construct a large ethical and psychological theory descriptive of the nature of the world and man. No one today, presumably, would maintain that Spinoza's conclusions necessarily derive from his premises. But in the seventeenth century the requirements of strict logic were vaguely felt rather than clearly understood, and Spinoza's "intuitional" metaphysics became the model of much rationalistic pseudoscience in the later centuries.

The fact was that philosophers had now to reconcile, and if possible to synthesize, two important but quite different intellectual traditions, developing quite distinct concepts of nature and knowledge. One was the Greek and medieval tradition, which drew, so to speak, a horizontal line through nature, dividing every natural thing into a more lowly matter striving upwards toward its true form, and a transcendental form condescending to this lowly matter. The other tradition was this newer Cartesian conception, which drew a vertical line dividing physical reality off from another reality called "mind." Since this physical reality was also usually called "matter," it was mistakenly given many of the properties of the Greek matter; and this led to all sorts of confusion and ambiguity. No one tried more brilliantly, or more desperately, to make sense of this confusion of Greek and Cartesian metaphysics than the German philosopher Leibniz.

Gottfried Wilhelm Leibniz (1646–1716) was, like Descartes, a mathematical genius; and, again like Descartes, he wished to conceive of nature in such a way as to make it wholly conformable to mathematical thory. Descartes, the inventor of analytical geometry, had conceived nature to be wholly fluid and continuous, to be just geometrical motion. Leibniz was the inventor of the infinitesimal calculus, a rather paradoxical theory which requires us to conceive of any finite quantity as being composed of an infinite number of infinitesimally small quantities. The application of this theory requires a conception of nature just the opposite of that of Descartes. Descartes had to suppose that every apparently solid and discrete body is really mobile, fluid, and continuous with its context, its apparent solidity and fixity being due to the constant pattern of its motion. Leibniz, on the contrary, had to conceive every apparent continuity in nature, *e.g.* a line, or path of motion, to be made up of those discrete infinitesimals which compose, when there are infinitely enough of them, finite and visible things.

Could this conception of natural structure, as infinitesimally grained, be made to resolve the difficulties left by Descartes? The crucial difficulty was the relation of mind to physical reality. Descartes had defined physical reality in terms of its property of extension or spatiality; and mind he had defined as pure thought. In those days, people conceived of mind or spirit as something wholly nonmaterial; and this meant that mind would have no spatial properties such as length, breadth, or volume. Now an infinitely large number is a number larger than any number you might name; and an infinitesimal is a fraction smaller than any fraction you might name. Might not an infinitely large number of minds, possessed of no volume, compound to form something apparently possessed of volume —just as an infinite series of points may compound to form a line, a point being defined as "position without size"? This at all events is Leibniz' basic assumption. Reality, he says, is truly an assemblage of nonspatial minds. He calls these spirit-atoms "monads." A visible thing is really an infinite number of these spaceless monads, which when so compounded appear to have size. Even the smallest discernible thing will contain an infinity of monads.

This conception, at first sight startling and somewhat distressing, initiates the doctrine of *modern idealism*, which— quite unlike the idealism of the Greeks—denies the ultimacy of matter and affirms the sole reality to be mind. It allowed Leibniz to escape the problems of the Cartesian dualism, simply by renouncing the dualism. But it raised more problems than it solved, because it required the explanation of everything apparently physical as the appearance of activities really mental. How could the stable physical world, with its universal physical laws, be explained away as an illusion? Leibniz uses two ideas in elaborating his idealism. One is the view that error is some sort of mental confusion; the other is the idea that God, in creating the world, so constituted it as to produce in us the illusion of physical being.

It was Descartes who first taught, in modern times, that our ordinary experience is only a confused version of our clear rational intuition of true being. Spinoza, thereupon, supposed that animals and other subhuman beings are possessed of an even lower and more confused mentality. Leibniz similarly supposes that the extended physical world arises from our confused vision of myriads of nonextended monads which to a perfect vision would be separately and individually known. But the uniformity or natural law which characterizes this extended and illusory physical world is not altogether an illusion. It represents the true character of the constituent monads, which were created by God in such manner as to exhibit, when confusedly seen, these real uniformities instituted by God.

The monads, Leibniz taught, are purely spiritual, indestructible, self-determinate beings. Each monad, from the beginning to the end of time, exhibits only its own successive states, in the order determined by God at its creation. You and I are such monads, temporarily attached to myriad other monads constituting our bodies. Our experience did not begin with our birth, it began with the creation; and it will continue, after death has dissolved our bodies, to the end of time. Since each monad is wholly self-determined, there is no real interaction anywhere. When you see me, I am really here; but your perception of me is not due to my presence, it was instituted in you, and ordained to appear at this time, by God at the creation; and it was then also ordained that I should really be here at the time you see me, so that your perception, although wholly subjective, is nevertheless objectively true. Leibniz is an Occasionalist in this denial of real causation in nature; but it is to the original creation, and not to the present intermediation of God, that he looks for the explanation of all apparent causation.

This doctrine gets impossibly involved. First, we must suppose that a monad really sees other monads, but sees them only confusedly as extended objects, much as separate points are seen fused into a line. This would imply that monads, although of no volume, still are distributed in space. But then we must suppose that the monad sees nothing, but experiences only its own nonspatial states, which it falsely supposes to be those of an external world. "The monad has no windows," writes Leibniz. It is like a cinematograph film, projecting its own story and attentive only to itself; yet the picture it runs off truly depicts, by the grace of God, the scene actually occurring outside of it. This external scene, however, if it were intimately and clearly depicted, would consist of myriads of other films or biographies, not of a landscape with spatial things. The Leibnizian fantasy baffles elucidation, because it consistently denies yet everywhere assumes the reality of some sort of medium in which monads proceed through changing relations. How did Leibniz conceive of this original medium, within which an infinite plurality of monads may remain distinct yet "ideally" related? He thought of it, presumably, as a logical medium, whatever that may be.

Thus all the observable and cognizable relations within nature, and all the observable and cognizable things so related, become for Leibniz a vast illusion which yet informs us concerning relations within unknowable monads, these relations constituting a "preestablished harmony" instituted by God among the monads at their origin. Leibniz recognizes two such preestablished orders. One is that of Cartesian science, which discovers a physical world related by laws of mathematical or physical necessity. The other is that of an organismic and hierarchical science, more like physiology, which discovers levels of organization in nature. Thus atoms are organized into molecules, molecules into cells, cells into organisms, organisms into societies. Although each such unit, *e.g.* atom or cell, consists of an infinite number of independent monads, the monads are "ideally" ordered so that one monad seems to control the whole unit. This is why you, *i.e.* the monad which is you, seem to control your body. The largest unit is the universe, an organic whole "ideally" controlled by the Supreme Monad which is God. Presumably this Monad, which ideally controls all other monads, is another Person than that which actually created all monads whatsoever, including Himself.

The curious, intricate, elusive, and ultimately unthinkable system of Leibniz was the work of a man whose mathematical genius took him into a game with manipulable symbols. These can be thrown at will into all sorts of symbolic patterns; and the problem is then to give to the symbols descriptive meanings. The relationship of these patterns to observable fact may be remote or nonexistent; yet they can be defined with mathematical precision. Leibniz is the *reductio ad absurdum* of the rationalistic dogma, revived by Descartes, that the clarity and distinctness of ideas, *i.e.* their logical manipulability, is their truth. Yet Leibniz applied this faculty of free mathematical invention to very real problems, for example to the problem of freedom in a physically necessitated world, and to the problem—if it be another and not the same problem—of the relation of particular fact to general hypothesis. His conclusion was that freedom and individuality or particularity are real and ultimate, but that natural law and generality are also real in a certain sense, because God so created free individuals that they would seem to behave according to general principles. This conclusion probably amounts to the admission that freedom and individuality are not to be intelligibly reconciled with the concept of natural necessity, but must be affirmed by an act of religious faith.

Leibniz was the greatest logician since Aristotle and prior to Bertrand Russell; and he was the originator of the movement which led to modern logic. His fertile logical imagination generated several ideas which have had profitable applications in science. One of these, already mentioned, was his idea of organic relationship. Another was his notion that space and time, at least in their mathematical formulations, are relational orders of things and not the absolute media which Newton supposed them to be. This notion is now familiar through the physical theory of relativity. He is also, as we noted, the first consistent proponent of modern idealism or mentalism, which denies the ultimacy of matter.

The deepest assumptions of Leibniz, implicit in all of his thought, are revealed in his theodicy, which is his apology for the apparent evil in a God-created world. Leibniz could not argue that evil is just a consequence of individual freedom, because he held God to have created each individual just as he or it is. He argued therefore that this world is the best of all possible worlds, meaning that it is of all possible worlds that which contains most good and least evil. But why any evil? Because, Leibniz argued, the realization of one good thing prejudices that of another, and so entails some evil. You can't have your cake and eat it. This view implied that God, in creating the world, was bound by certain prior necessities of a logical or ontological sort. It presupposed a realm of ultimate possibilities, *i.e.* of ideal entities awaiting realization and already definitely interrelated. God was conditioned, Leibniz assumed, first by this external realm of possibilities, and secondly by his innate goodness which willed the best. His creation was limited, therefore, to the selection of the optimum set of possibilities, the realization of which is our world. This logical idealism is the historical source of the many forms of so-called "realism" which have appeared since the close of the nineteenth century. These later realists have not been aware, as a rule, that they are resuscitating the Leibnizian theology.

Descartes, Spinoza, and Leibniz are the most important initiators of modern rationalism. Rationalism is primarily a theory of knowledge, stating that true knowledge is obtained by the use of certain absolute principles given with the mind and constituting the reason. But rationalism necessarily advances a metaphysics or definition of reality, because it must present the set of selected principles which define the absolute and universal form of reality. Descartes and Leibniz emphasized mathematical principles, their different mathematical systems pointing to very opposite concepts of "reality." Spinoza, less bound by physical science, cultivated a "rational intuition" which apparently, if we may judge by its very different results in different thinkers, allows one to intuit any sort of "absolute reality" one happens to prefer. It is clear, perhaps, that this rationalistic philosophy is cognitively irresponsible. We know today that mathematical theories can be made to order, in such a way as to define any sort of material we may imagine; and this means that mathematical theory, in and by itself, is no indication of the sort of world we actually inhabit. But a free "rational intuition" of Spinoza's sort is even more irresponsible. It does not even conform to strict logic, as does mathematical theory.

Notice, once more, how this modern rationalism differs from the Greek and medieval rationalism! Plato also supposed that true knowledge arises from self-evident principles given to the reason, and that these rational principles define the eternal and universal structure which is discovered by science in the world. But the Greek rationalism did not identify this "reality" with existent nature, as does modern rationalism. It identified "reality" with the form of nature; but it also postulated a material element which is the source of accident, defect, and particularity in nature. Modern rationalism renounces this dualism of form and matter—it takes existent reality to be pure form, and holds that what is not pure form arises as a subjective illusion, due to confusion in the mind.

It is evident that this rationalistic doctrine assumes, but without admitting it, the cooperation of the senses in natural knowledge. Knowledge of universal principles would tell us nothing about *this* world, which is a consensus of particular fact. Only the senses can reveal the particular configuration of nature at any place and time. Geometry could not tell us that there exists a sun with just so many planets, or that Jupiter has four moons, or that you were born and now exist. Leibniz was aware of this particularity or contingency of nature; and it is his effort to do justice to it that compels him, finally, to call all universal character an illusion, although still a "rational" illusion reaching "ideal" truth. We shall conclude, later, that rationalism cannot be made compatible with the particular character of natural occurrence, which requires an empirical theory of knowledge.

If rationalistic philosophy is irresponsible, what makes science responsible, and what would make philosophy responsible? We know today that modern science is responsible not because it seeks mathematical clarity and logical consistency, but because it accommodates its theoretical hypotheses to particular observable fact. This empirical criterion of observable fact hampers somewhat the rational pursuit of logical consistency. It is easy to be consistent and dogmatic if we may ignore conflicting evidence. But it is just this hard struggle between the two criteria of fact and logic that produces scientific hypothesis and generates scientific progress. It is easy to be logical—and dogmatic; it is hard to be empirical and truthful. The rationalistic thinkers did not understand this; and our appreciation of the true nature of modern science is chiefly due to a trio of empirical philosophers who placed their whole emphasis upon particular observable fact, holding that it—and not an infallible reason—is the source of human knowledge. We shall find that these thinkers, in their anxiety to do justice to the empirical element in modern science, did less than justice to the rational element; but it is these empiricists, none the less, who carry forward the largest and most characteristic movement of modern thought.

Notes for Further Reading

1. Malebranche, N., *Dialogues on Metaphysics and Religion*, trans. M. Ginsburg. New York, The Macmillan Company, 1923.
2. Church, R. W., *A Study in the Philosophy of Malebranche*. London, G. Allen and Unwin, Ltd., 1931.

3. Luce, A. A., *Berkeley and Malebranche*. London and New York, Oxford University Press, 1934.

4. Wild, J., *Spinoza: Selections*. New York, Charles Scribner's Sons, 1930.

5. Spinoza, B., *Ethics*. New York, E. P. Dutton and Company, Everyman's edition, 1911. Also other translations.

6. Broad, C. D., *Five Types of Ethical Theory*. London and New York, Cambridge University Press, 1934.

7. McKeon, R. *The Philosophy of Spinoza*. Boston, Longmans, Green and Company, 1928.

8. Wolfson, H. A., *The Philosophy of Spinoza*. Cambridge, Harvard University Press, 1934.

9. Wolfson, A., *Spinoza*. New York, Modern Classics, Inc., 1932.

10. Roth, L., *Spinoza*. Boston, Little, Brown and Company, 1929.

There are also studies of Spinoza by Gunn, Caird, Martineau, Joachim, Pollock, and Duff.

11. Leibniz, G. W., *Philosophical Works*, trans. Duncan. New Haven, The Tuttle, Morehouse and Taylor Company, 1890.

12. Langley, A. G., *The New Essays*. La Salle, Ill., The Open Court Publishing Company, 1896.

13. Latta, R., *The Monadology, etc.* London and New York, The Oxford University Press, 1925.

14. Montgomery, G. R., *The Correspondence of Leibniz*. La Salle, Ill., The Open Court Publishing Company, 1902, 1918.

15. Rhys, E., ed., *Leibniz' Philosophical Writings*. New York, E. P. Dutton and Company, Inc., 1934.

16. Carr, H. W., *Leibniz*. London and New York, Oxford University Press, 1929.

17. ———— *The Monadology of Leibniz*. Los Angeles, University of Southern California, 1930.

18. Merz, J. Y., *Leibniz*. Edinburgh, Philosophical Classics for English Readers, 1886.

19. Russell, B., *A Critical Exposition of the Philosophy of Leibniz*. New York, The Macmillan Company, 1900, 1937.

20. Lévy-Bruhl, L., *A History of Modern Philosophy in France*. La Salle, Ill., The Open Court Publishing Company, 1899.

15 THE EMPIRICAL PHILOSOPHY OF MODERN SCIENCE

WHEREAS RATIONALISM ATTRIBUTES TO MAN A faculty of absolute knowledge, and takes science to be the application of this rational intuition to observable fact, *empiricism* holds that all knowledge is derived from experience of observable fact, so that no principles are true intrinsically, or apart from evidence. Rationalism imposes "self-evident" intuitions upon nature; empiricism advances tentative hypotheses, and submits these to the authority of nature, exerted upon us in sense-experience.

Why did modern science, as exemplified in Galileo and Newton, stimulate on the continent of Europe a movement to rationalistic philosophy, but in Britain a movement to empirical philosophy? One reason is that continental Europe was intellectually centered upon Paris, chief seat of the scholastic philosophy which looked back to Greek rationalism; whereas Britain had largely provided the nominalistic opposition to scholasticism. The new science pointed both ways in its double emphasis upon mathematical unity and observed fact. The physics of Newton, for example, was rationalistic in its dependence upon the mathematical principles incorporated in it; but it was empirical in its establishment of universal principles such as that of gravitation, which had to be reached by observation and experimental hypothesis. It is not self-evident that bodies must attract each other according to just this formula. Reason alone, it follows, does not tell us what sort of a world this is. The nature of nature awaits discovery. Science must continually construct new hypotheses, and retain these only so long as they meet the observable facts.

The principles of rationalistic philosophy can be stated fairly simply. The principles of empiricism are more difficult to expound, because their final implications are obscure and perhaps inexhaustible. How, for example, shall we explain the fact that theoretical science, although it willingly subjects its special hypotheses to factual confirmation or disproof, still assumes that *some* general theory must meet all of the facts? Empirical science still seems to rely upon the self-evident principles of logic, assuring the success of theoretical analysis. The early nominalists, who were the forerunners of empirical philosophy, too easily disposed of this difficulty. Reality is made up of individual and unique things, they said; and theories are merely verbal or mental constructions. We will find that this is by no means the whole truth. Scientific theories are indeed composed of words or ideas in our minds; but if we are to distinguish between a true theory and a false theory, we must suppose that the true theory indicates, and the false theory fails to indicate, a real pattern in the real world, and not merely a pattern in our minds.

Francis Bacon, who instructed his readers to look only to nature for their knowledge, inclined to this nominalistic view; but he cannot be said to have presented an intelligible theory of knowledge. *Thomas Hobbes* (1588–1679), whose political philosophy we have already noticed, served Bacon as a sort of secretary in the old minister's declining years. Hobbes explicitly subscribed to nominalism in his analysis of cognition; but his materialistic philosophy implies a rationalistic theory of knowledge. His intention seems to have been to carry out Bacon's suggestion that the method of the new science should be applied to human behavior, in order to provide a science of human nature—somewhat as Spinoza attempted to apply the Cartesian science to the subject matter of ethics. Hobbes and Spinoza may therefore be counted among the founders of psychological and sociological science. The psychology and sociology of Hobbes was empirical in its attempt to inaugurate a fresh study of human behavior starting from observed fact; but it was rationalistic in its assumption that the basic principles of physical science must account for every sort of natural activity, including human behavior. Materialistic philosophers are apt to be unaware of the metaphysical character of their doctrine. They seem to think that their basic postulate, affirming that reality is just a movement of material particles in space, states a fact which is immediately evident to the senses. In truth, this materialistic conception constitutes a very large intellectual hypothesis. This hypothesis was reached only after centuries of scientific study, it is not at all evident to the senses, and it may be untrue. But the materialist converts this hypothesis into a metaphysical and rational principle when he sets it up as the sole, final, and infallible principle of scientific explanation. It is this unconscious rationalism of the materialist which sooner or later inevitably reappears in the political absolutism characteristic of materialistic thinkers.

Because Hobbes came to mathematics relatively late in life, after his mind had been formed by other studies, he never perceived the significance of the role played by mathematics in the new science. This precluded any adequate study by Hobbes of the nature and method of scientific cognition; but it allowed him to perceive the diversity of science, in its accommodation of scientific theory to different fields of fact. He could conceive of a succession of sciences, proceeding from physical theory to biological, psychological, and social theories, and existing in some independence of one another. This enabled him to avoid the difficulties of the Cartesian dualism and to understand mental processes as manifestations of causal inter-action proceeding between the human organism and its natural environment. Mental process, Hobbes supposed, is only physi-cal process of a special and complicated sort. Psychology ought therefore to pattern itself upon physics. Just as physical science divides into geometry and mechanics—the first defining the static structure of matter and the second describing the inter-active processes of matter—so psychology will divide itself into two studies, one discovering the permanent principles of human behavior and the other describing the temporal proc-esses of human life. This may sound very empirical and scien-tific, but its analogy between physical dynamics and a psychol-ogy of human purpose betrays an irremediable confusion of mind. This confusion becomes apparent when Hobbes identifies the two divisions of psychology respectively with ethics and politics. Hobbes here confused an empirical psychology, which would seek a general statement of how men do in fact behave, with a normative moral code prescribing how men should behave. Hobbes was betrayed by his unconscious rationalism. Because he believed that there are absolute mechanical prin-ciples to which everything must of necessity conform, he could conclude that there are absolute rational principles to which all human beings must of necessity conform; and so he inevitably came to confuse moral principles, which tell us how man ought to behave, with scientific axioms telling us how men must behave. Ever since Hobbes, materialism with its confusion of moral and descriptive principles has hindered the scientific study of man and society, and endangered freedom.

Hobbes did not know, we conclude, what constitutes em-pirical science, in spite of the fact that his fresh and often dis-cerning study of man helped to inaugurate an empirical psy-chology and sociology. Yet when he turned to a direct study of human knowledge, he committed himself very definitely to the principle, out of which issues finally a true empirical philosophy, that the whole source of knowledge lies in immediate sensory experience. Further, he stated, such experience is always of individual things; and the goal of knowledge is a knowledge of the causal relations connecting individual things. Here he recovered the insight reached by Occam three centuries earlier; and through Hobbes these ideas reached a wide public.

Hobbes' psychology is introspective and associationistic. As physical science explains physical occurrences by analyzing them into the irreducible elements which are their component parts or "causes," so mental processes, Hobbes taught, can be analyzed into the simple sensations which are their "causes." These simple and irreducible sensations he took to be the direct effects in the mind of external physical stimuli. Simple sensations are elementary qualities such as red, blue, cold, rough, etc. If sensations comprise the material which is given to the mind by external reality, in order to understand the mind we have only to discover what it does with this material. Stimulated by some present sensation, the mind may recall a past sensation which is "associated" with the present one. Sensations, further, are pleasant or unpleasant, and induce appropriate bodily reactions. Such reaction may be conditioned by a remembered sensation, associated with the present sensation; and when this happens we speak of the reaction as willed or purposeful. Groups of associated sensations may also be associated with words, so that a word comes to stand for a whole group of particular sensations. What we usually call "knowledge" is therefore really a language, indicative of past and present sensations. To improve our knowledge, we should become critical of language, and avoid words which do not indicate actual sensations. There are many such words, devoid of descriptive meaning because they refer to nothing in experience. Meaningless words of this sort are really the disguises of ignorance. "Soul" and "spirit," says Hobbes, revealing his materialistic prepossession, are pseudoconcepts, or meaningless words of this sort.

Hobbes' materialism and the political absolutism which derived from his materialistic principles seem to have exerted considerable influence on the continent of Europe. In Britain his materialistic rationalism and his political absolutism found little response. This was not the case with his psychology and his nominalistic theory of knowledge, which had important consequences. These studies revived the critical attitude of the medieval nominalists who had opposed the scholastic rationalism; and they initiated modern *critical philosophy*, which undertakes a critical analysis, and reaches a very cautious estimate, of the validity and scope of theoretical knowledge. Chiefly through Hobbes there came to be developed that subjectivistic and introspective sort of psychology which studies mental contents in isolation from their physiological and external conditions. Recent psychology has largely freed itself from this subjectivistic and sterile tradition. In philosophy, however, Hobbes' subjectivistic analysis of mind has continued to characterize an introspective "epistemology," which narrows and defeats philosophical speculation. But Hobbes, in spite of his faulty psychology and his absolutistic premises, was nevertheless an important channel through which the critical philosophy of the later Middle Ages came down the centuries to ourselves.

This critical philosophy was primarily directed against rationalist tradition. Its positive purpose, however, was the defense of an empirical science basing its conclusions wholly upon observable fact. *John Locke* (1632–1704) is generally and with reason regarded as the chief founder of modern empirical philosophy. We have already noticed Locke's political theory, which still provides the theoretical basis of modern democratic government. We should see in Locke's general philosophy, published in 1691 in the famous *Essay Concerning*

Human Understanding, an extension and justification of the doctrines presented in his political writings. It is not always remembered that Locke's empirical theory of knowledge had its political motivation. We tend to forget that democratic theory, like every political theory, requires its broad foundation in a general philosophy of nature and mind.

Its political significance, its intrinsic philosophical importance, and also perhaps a certain misinterpretation of its teaching to which we will refer again, made the publication of Locke's *Essay* a major intellectual and literary event. The book seemed to its readers to inaugurate a new era of philosophical science, and even a new way of thought. Yet today, the book is unexciting reading; it is turgid, obscure, disappointingly and consistently prosaic. What to Locke's first readers was new, revolutionary, and stimulating is to the modern reader familiar and commonplace, and more or less taken for granted. But if this is so, it is largely because Locke made it so. Society has come to accept as truisms the method and the conception which Locke had difficulty even in expressing.

Locke's initial purpose, indeed, was a negative one, namely to discredit and to remove from men's minds the rationalistic presuppositions which, he believed, retarded scientific progress. In order that men should desire new knowledge and pursue scientific research, it was necessary to convince them first of man's relative ignorance, and secondly of his power to discover what he does not know. Locke's conception of science is diametrically opposed to that of Descartes, for whom science was the application everywhere of certain self-evident axioms. For Locke, there are no such absolute principles of natural knowledge. Science is not an application of eternal principles to new fact. It is more like a chemical transformation, synthesizing diverse facts into a large unitary hypothesis. It is a productive process, using the inexhaustible material of sensation for the continuous manufacture of new knowledge. The most important feature in this conception is that it refuses to make conformity to some known and supposedly indubitable principle the test of the truth of a new hypothesis. Locke is excusably vague, and sometimes mistaken, concerning just how new truth is obtained.

His *Essay* opens with a critique of dogmatism and rationalism. In his political writings he had attacked the concept of divine monarchical right, because this was the most powerful and widespread of the dogmas which prevented individual assumption of the responsibility of self-government. He now attacks all dogma, and indicts the dogmatic habit of mind itself. There are, he says, no "innate ideas." He means that there are no principles which are innate to the mind, prior to experience, or which need no confirmation by experience. All ideas and all knowledge derive from experience, our surest ideas being those which experience most widely confirms. What rationalistic science takes to be infallible and self-evident principles, he says, are in fact only *nominal definitions*, prescribing certain fixities of meaning and conventional use. They do not amount to *real definitions*, defining once and for all the ultimate natures of things. Such real definition, Locke implies, is beyond our powers. Our knowledge of things is partial, tentative, progressive, never final nor definitive. Locke was a lifelong student of science; he practiced medicine, cultivated the friendship of leading scientists, and kept abreast of scientific invention. He did not confine himself to an appreciation of mathematical physics. He conceived science to be discovery—not a set of theoretical principles, but the inexhaustible generator of theories and principles.

Negative in its denial of self-evident truth, positive in its affirmation of the creative and exploratory power of science, Locke's view is negative again in its denial of universal knowledge, *i.e.* knowledge of the universe in its totality. He was driven to his study of cognition, he writes, by his perception of the fruitlessness of current metaphysical discussions, in which philosophers threw at one another different conceptions of the world and its ultimate structure. These conceptions, he complains, can neither be confirmed nor be disproved; and so they are vain and arbitrary. All actual knowledge, because it summarizes a limited human experience, is necessarily partial and tentative. Locke's purpose was to divert the energies dissipated in metaphysical controversy into productive scientific research. His intention in the *Essay* was to indicate the limitations imposed upon human knowledge, and to chart the domain in which research is possible and profitable.

This explorable domain is determined by sense-experience, which provides the only materials for reflection and analysis. Locke assumes that the mind is possessed of certain powers, enabling it to move from sense-perception to scientific knowledge. He does not mean that the sensory material is itself knowledge. He allows that the mind may compare, break up, compound, relate, and otherwise act upon its sensational elements, and also that it may reflect upon its own processes. Locke's analysis of mental activity added little to that of Hobbes. It relied largely on the distinction between simple and complex ideas, simple ideas being those, it would seem, which resist further introspective analysis. We would say today that many of Locke's "simple ideas" are anything but simple, and that he consistently confuses logical with psychological simplicity. What is psychologically simple may be logically complex, and what is logically simple may be psychologically unfamiliar and difficult. This epistemology initiated by Hobbes and Locke is, we have intimated, one of the more sterile and confused developments of modern philosophy. But in so criticizing it, we must salvage the important distinction which it misrepresented. This is the distinction between sensory material, or "experience," or particular fact on the one hand, and the formulated, organized knowledge which is science on the other hand. Once we lose sight of this distinction, we can no longer distinguish truth from error.

The rationalist also claimed to draw this distinction between sensory evidence and theoretical hypothesis; but in fact he denied it, by relegating all that is not rationally formulated to a limbo of sense-illusion. The distinction between what is perceived and what is conceived lies within science itself. Science includes both clear and explicit theory and the inchoate evidence which is organized by means of theory. We owe to the empirical philosophers the insight that science is the concrete but intelligent apprehension of particular fact, *i.e.* of nature itself as it observably exists. What the empiricists failed to make clear was the relation between these two elements, the formulated theory and the particular observable facts. Somehow the particularized evidence at once distinguishes itself from the general theory, and supports the general theory. But how?

Locke took refuge in the oversimple distinction between primary and secondary qualities, in order to explain the scientist's transmutation of sensed particular fact into scientific knowledge. Nature, he assumed, is a collection of real things or substances, each of which has its real and intrinsic properties. Some of these properties enter into experience unchanged; and in regard to these, our perception is truthful and scientific. But many of the characters of perception are not truthful. They are the effects in us of the actual properties of the thing; and these effects may little resemble their external causes. Locke's suggestion is that science should discover the true natures of things by discerning and reflecting upon the primary properties. (This suggestion is revived in a corrected form in the "critical realism" of today. But Locke's main conception, which states knowledge to arise as the result of a process of comparison, abstraction, and recombination effected upon the materials of sensation, points in a very different direction, leading to modern idealism.) Locke does not, as a matter of fact, provide a single consistent description of cognitive process. Sometimes he is a realist, and holds knowledge to be at least in some degree identical with the substances which it describes;

but at other times he is more subjectivistic, and implies that knowledge moves in another medium than things, and that it can at best refer or correspond to things, somewhat as a railroad schedule may refer to trains although it is no part of the railroad system.

Following Francis Bacon and Hobbes, Locke devotes much attention to language. Here he adheres to the nominalistic view that real substances are inexpugnably individual, so that "universals" are only convenient names for groups of individuals, and do not constitute any real and universal sort of being in the world. Our fixed definitions and absolute demonstrations, he concludes, concern only words with their meanings and implications. Because we create these words as needed, we can define them as we please and then insist that the definitions be respected, for example by means of a dictionary; but we must not suppose that the clarity and distinctness of our ideas, *i.e.* their susceptibility to clear definition, establishes their truth. Our meanings and definitions are descriptively true only insofar as they conform to observable fact. Here Locke establishes the empirical criterion of truth, which lies in sense-experience or particular fact.

This sharp distinction between verbal definition and descriptive knowledge is today fairly generally understood. It would seem to be presupposed in every honest endeavor to evaluate, as true or less than true, our explicit descriptions of nature. Yet Locke was not able to abide consistently by this important distinction himself. In two fields of science, he believed, strict definition and conclusive demonstration are possible. These exceptional fields are mathematical science and moral science. To make such exceptions was to weaken, or even to renounce, the empirical and nominalistic position which Locke elsewhere maintained; and Locke's study becomes increasingly rationalistic in tendency as it proceeds. In his concluding chapters, summarizing the whole discussion, he seems to depart from the correspondence-theory of the earlier chapters. Instead of insisting that truth is the correspondence of idea with fact, he seems to be saying that knowledge is a perception of agreement or disagreement among ideas. Only very cursorily does he now discuss "the agreement of ideas with real existence." These later chapters might have been written by a rationalistic follower of Descartes. Yet Locke may not have meant to say that the axioms of mathematics and the generative principles of morality are innate and self-evident truths, established by pure reason. In attributing absoluteness or certainty to these axioms and principles, he may have meant only that they are the widest, most certain, and best attested deliverances of experience, confirmed by all observation. In spite of many requests that he should do so, it might be added, Locke was never able to present the set of principles basic to a "moral science" paralleling mathematics. He felt, perhaps, that these absolute moral principles were implicit in his political theory. If so, they would comprise an affirmation of the moral, self-responsible, and essentially virtuous character of individual man.

Locke's limitations were also his strength. He was a man of incomparable "common sense," able to state philosophical convictions in language intelligible and convincing to the reader untrained in philosophy. At the same time, he had an intellectual shrewdness and a superlative honesty which led him to the heart of a problem, and which usually saved him, much as he wished to save others, from losing his feet among words and ideas. His intellectual modesty, moreover, relieved him from the necessity of elaborating a completed philosophy, meeting and resolving all of the problems which he himself raised. Locke did not see these problems as clearly as Hume and Kant would later see them. He conceived of the pursuit of knowledge as a campaign which is to be tactically advanced on many fronts, and which neither requires nor allows a global strategy. He did not believe, we noted, in the possibility of a universal, comprehensive study of fact. Yet his very limitations allowed him to establish, more securely than his predecessors had done, the concept of an empirical science released from absolute pre-suppositions, devoted wholly to observation of and reflection upon particular fact, and following particular fact wherever it might lead. If this conception was not new, Locke was at all events the first thinker to put the conception into generally intelligible language and to secure its wide acceptance among educated people. This is why the *Essay*, in spite of all its turgidity, inconsistency, and prosaic diction, was reprinted in numerous editions, translated into many languages, and preserved in every library to become what it remains to this day, the classical text of modern empirical philosophy. The *Essay* helped to deflect and redirect human thought; and Locke stands alongside of Newton as the second of the two great minds who securely anchored the modern intellect to an empirical method.

We spoke of a certain misinterpretation of Locke's *Essay*, which may have had something to do with its immediate success. People referred to Locke's study as one which proposed "a new way of ideas." Evidently, some of his readers supposed him to be saying that the seeker after knowledge may safely neglect the study of things, and confine himself to the study of his ideas, *i.e.* to his own mental content. To do this would be, of course, the surest way to error. Sanity is just the persistent study of an environment which is external to ourselves, and unaffected by what we think about it. The intention of empirical philosophy is to direct thought upon the external environment, the home of particular fact; for this is the object of all science and the sole source of evidence. Yet Locke did in his conclusions seem to be defining knowledge as only an agreement or disagreement among ideas present to the mind.

This unfortunate misreading was to embarrass empirical philosophy throughout its development; and it is in order to escape from it that we are required to advance today beyond the empirical philosophy of the past. But before the error could be removed, it had to be elaborated into a system making clear its whole implication. This was done by George Berkeley, writing not long after the publication of the *Essay*.

George Berkeley (1683–1753), a student preparing for the ministry at Dublin University, was one of those who were entranced by this "new way of ideas." If knowledge is wholly derived from mental impressions or ideas, young Berkeley pondered, how can the knowledge thus obtained discover to us anything peculiarly nonmental, material, and inert? In a brilliant psychological study, Berkeley showed that many of the experienced characters which we unhesitatingly ascribe to material nature are really the action or effect of sensory activities proceeding in the organism. Everything that is directly perceived, he concluded, is conditioned by the nature of the percipient organism, *i.e.* by our own nature. Berkeley realized that this conclusion was pregnant with philosophical consequences; and very soon, while still in his twenty-second year, he published *The Principles of Human Knowledge*, destined to become another of the classical texts of modern philosophy. His thesis is that of *idealism*. A reality that is perceived and known by mind, he argues, must itself be of a mental character, related to that which apprehends it. If reality were completely nonmental, wholly unlike and unrelated to our minds, there could be no real connection between nature and mind, and knowledge would be impossible.

The conscious human organism or mind, Berkeley concludes, enters as a factor into every sense-perception; and if perception is the material source of truth, this mental character will consequently qualify all that we know. The world that we know, he continues, is constitutively determined in all of its character by the fact that it is perceived, *i.e.* by its relation to the perceiving mind. We may not therefore accept a science which ostensibly defines nature, but which does not acknowledge this mental character qualifying all our immediate experience of nature. If the mental character of "being-perceived" necessarily qualifies any and every known thing, this mental character is the most indubitable and universal character of reality.

A good deal of misinterpretation has attended this Berkeleian doctrine. It is sometimes supposed that Berkeley intended to deny the externality, the solidity, the inescapable objective reality of the world about us, and to maintain that only our idea of the world, not the world itself, is real. This is just the contrary of Berkeley's teaching, which is perceptually realistic. Everything that you see, feel, touch, or otherwise immediately sense, he means, is exactly as real and exactly as qualitied as it appears to be. You must trust your immediate contact with nature, provided by your sense-perception. You should not explain away these indubitable and authentic perceptions, by supposing, for example, that the world which seems so solid, so colorful, so diversified into all sorts of things and qualities, is really a fluid, homogeneous, continuous, all-mobile ocean of motion such as Descartes conceived, or a concourse of invisible particles. It is not the senses but reason that deceives. Berkeley insisted that he was the first philosopher ever to profess a true realism, all earlier thinkers having taught that the world we perceive is unreal. This claim was perhaps somewhat exaggerated; but Berkeley could claim to be the first *perceptual realist*, the first thinker who has held, consistently and literally, that only sense-perception delivers truth.

Berkeley tells us to trust perception, rather than intellectual conception. But is not his own philosophy an intellectual conception? What becomes of Berkeley's idealism for a perceptual realist who believes that stones are the heavy solids he feels them to be, skies the blue or gray expanses, and trees and animals the qualitied individuals he immediately perceives? His idealism is itself a conceptual theory, an intellectual speculation professing to reveal the unperceived yet nevertheless intelligible essence of the world. Do we literally perceive minds? Is it not by argument, thought, ratiocination, and hypothesis that

Berkeley establishes his conclusion that all reality is mental? He used his mentalism, indeed, to discredit the materialistic doctrine which teaches that external reality is really composed of unconscious material atoms, moving according to the laws of mechanics. This mechanistic science may explain how physical things interact with and upon each other; but it does not yet explain how things act upon our minded selves, producing mental effects in conscious organisms. The causal connection, Berkeley might have said, presupposes some deep sort of continuity, likeness, or even identity between what is cause and what is effect, *i.e.* between the external world and its effects in conscious perception.

It should be recognized that this idealistic argument is still possessed of force. That there is causal interaction between the living organism and its external environment most of us will readily admit; but we do not always admit that the existence of this causal process requires us to explain the external world in terms of its interaction with animals and men, as well as in terms of its inorganic interactions. The cognitive response of man to nature implies something with respect to nature. We must also explain the living organism in terms of its interactions with the external world; and this duly leads us to a biochemistry and even a psychophysics; but this latter implication Berkeley did not or would not see. His purpose was to make a frontal attack upon materialism of the Hobbesian sort, which, when taken alone, he quite properly saw, invalidates all moral, religious, and intellectual truth, fails to explain our immediate perception of natural quality, and finally makes unintelligible the distinction between living and nonliving things. Both materialism and idealism, we may conclude, are partial truths. The materialist wishes to recognize only such causal relations as connect inorganic substances, ignoring the relations between conscious organisms and their environment; the idealist, on the contrary, recognizes only this latter sort of relation, and neglects the causal processes discovered in inor-

ganic nature. But a comprehensive view must initially acknowledge both sorts of causal relationship, and plumb deeper into
the process of nature.

Berkeley's attack upon materialism and his substitution for
it of idealism were motivated by religious faith and supported
by aesthetic feeling. The world to which we directly respond
in perception is a beautiful world, replete with aesthetic values.
Our aesthetic response to nature is also a moral response,
restraining us from vandalism, the wilful destruction of natural
beauty; and this aesthetic sense is developed by our reactions
with our fellows into a full-fledged moral insight, recognizing
others as kin to ourselves and on a parity with ourselves. But
the aesthetic and moral response in man presupposes an aesthetic and moral character in the environment, which after all is
what stimulates that response; and the conscious recognition of
this environmental stimulus is the source of religious faith. We
may perhaps agree with Berkeley that his perceptual realism,
with its deliberate acknowledgment of the immediately perceived aesthetic qualities of nature, is the condition of moral
feeling and religious belief. Berkeley did not hesitate to carry
this insight to its full conclusion. The external reality which we
call the world, and which he has said to be mental in character,
he identifies with a universal Mind which is God. This would
mean that God is pure and universal perception, and that we,
in our limited human perception, have a measure of identity
with God, seeing as He sees. This beautiful and truly religious
mysticism takes us back to St. Francis and other medieval
mystics; and we now see, through the help of Berkeley, why
this medieval mysticism encouraged an empirical science and
philosophy.

It has usually been assumed that everything we immediately
apprehend through our sense organs in perception is particular
in character. Perception, we suppose, is an apprehension of
present individual being. It is also usually assumed, on the other
hand, that general or nonparticular character—what once was

called "universal form"—is apprehended by the intellect or reason. The medieval mysticism which sought an immediate, even a sensory, apprehension of divine and ultimate Being consequently involved a new evaluation and a rehabilitation of particular fact, which Greek science and philosophy had belittled and neglected. Both assumptions—that we know particular character only through the senses and general character only through the intellect—may be mistaken. The writer believes them to be so. But they are still widely and unhesitatingly affirmed; and they help to reveal to us certain aesthetic, moral, and religious motives which have advanced the development of empirical science and philosophy in the modern age.

Many of Berkeley's subsidiary arguments, applying or supporting his idealistic thesis, are acute and have been confirmed by later thought. For example, he rejects the distinction, at least as it was then made, between primary and secondary qualities. We cannot separate out of our experience, he points out, certain perceived characters which persist unchanged by our perception of them, to leave aside those which are transformed by the process of perception. Every perceived character whatsoever, he shows, is subjectively conditioned—size and shape just as much as color or warmth. In the sense of being subjectively conditioned, therefore, all perceived characters are secondary; and it is further clear that all of those characters which had been elevated as primary and absolutely truthful, such as size and shape, are known to us only by way of the so-called secondary characters. A world without color, without light and shade, and without tactile quality would present no sensible sizes or shapes, but would fuse into inarticulate unity. Berkeley, however, would call all qualities primary, rather than secondary, because he holds that in spite of their being conditioned by the percipient organism, they are the real and ultimate qualities of the world. Today, the cogency of Berkeley's criticism of primary qualities is fairly generally conceded. All perceived characters, it is usually allowed, are subjectively conditioned by the position and the nature of the perceiver. Yet contemporary science still distinguishes between the size of an object as it appears to the eye and its "real" size as measured by rulers, protractors, or other instruments. The scientist, if we may judge by his practice, is a "critical realist" somewhat after the style of Locke. He accepts perceived character as evidence; but he moves from perceived character to a conceptual description of the scientific object which is causally responsible for what he perceives. Molecules are real enough, although they are invisible and known only by inference. He is neither a perceptual realist nor an idealist. His view, if he were to make it explicit, would be found much more complex.

Berkeley in his attack upon materialism also made use of nominalistic arguments. What we perceive, the nominalist assumes, is always *particular* character, and general or universal forms exist only in our minds. Our general concepts of matter, Berkeley also concludes, are only mental fictions, conveniently referring to particular things but not defining anything real. Berkeley acutely counters the rationalistic belief that mathematical concepts necessarily define an ultimate structure in nature, by discriminating between the exact forms defined by mathematical theory and the rough and approximate geometry we actually perceive. No one ever *perceived* a "perfect" circle, a "line without thickness," a "point without size," he points out.

An extreme and unreserved nominalism, denying reality to all general form whatsoever, would invalidate all general knowledge, including such general conceptions as that of Berkeley's idealism. Berkeley's nominalism thus contradicts his idealism. Berkeley excuses this self-contradiction verbally, and rather disingenuously, by saying that our idea of mind is not a concept but a "notion," so that it escapes nominalistic criticism. This distinction between concepts and "notions" is not tenable. Berkeley's idealism is a conceptual system, no less than is materialism; and if we are to allow that idealism is an intelligible doctrine, we must allow realistic truth to concepts and renounce the nominalistic position.

We have now seen several sorts of idealism, and it is important to distinguish them. First, we met *Greek idealism*, which did not deny but emphatically affirmed the reality of matter of a certain sort. Greek idealism was dualistic, it explained each existent thing as a compound of matter and form. It was idealistic in the sense that it attributed to the forms which invest things a high or "ideal" beauty, a supreme rightness and significance—not that it conceived things, or even forms, to be peculiarly mental or immaterial in the modern sense. *Modern idealism*, unlike the Greek, is monistic; it denies the reality of matter, and attributes reality only to mind. Modern idealism has two forms. Rationalistic or Leibnizian idealism defines the mind in terms of its intellectual processes and its conceptual knowledge; and it consequently conceives reality to be some totality of intellectual process. Perceptual or Berkeleian idealism defines the mind as a panorama of sensory experience; and it consequently conceives the universe to be a larger expanse of such experience. Both conceptions are difficult, vague, and ultimately unthinkable. Their value is to remind us that the conscious intellectual and perceptual processes of man really exist. These processes cannot be argued out of court; and they make unacceptable any conception of nature which leaves them inexplicable or unaccounted for. Man, and all that he is, is part of nature, and a clue to nature. But simply to define nature as a larger replica of psychological process seems rather futile, not to say puerile. Plato, whatever his inadequacies, was more mature in his perception of the problem and in his dualistic solution of it.

We noticed that Berkeley's idealistic metaphysics, with its acknowledgment of a "notion" of mind and universal being, required a departure from his nominalistic theory of knowledge. An early *Common-Place Book* in which the young thinker jotted down his daily reflections shows him to have been at first inclined to follow his nominalistic principles to their logical conclusion. A pure nominalism, denying reality to everything connoted by general concepts, finally issues in unrelieved skepticism. Berkeley evidently recoiled from such skepticism. But Hume a few years later would more resolutely pursue the path from which Berkeley shrank back.

Criticism of Berkeley's idealistic metaphysics must not blind us to his importance in the development of empirical thought. Berkeley remains the thinker who has opened our eyes widest to the richness, the diversity, and the articulate design of what we immediately perceive, and who has most forcefully demonstrated the dependence of all thought upon this immediate experience. Berkeley's metaphysical idealism was the result of his effort to do philosophical justice to this spontaneous apprehension of the primacy and plenitude of perceptual knowledge. Justified, surely, was his conviction that the world which we intellectually conceive, and which in our theoretical science we describe, is after all this world that we see, touch, feel, and even in some sense are; and stronger, perhaps, than his formal argument is Berkeley's indication of the religious ultimacy of this naked contact with utter reality, which in perception we enjoy. No writer has so emancipated the thinker from "the pale cast of thought," and so restored to him his lost sense of immediacy with nature, as this brilliant young physician of the mind. Whatever we call Berkeley's realism, however we criticize his formulation of it, it is medicine much needed by an overintellectualized world. It is this insight into man's perceptual immediacy with nature, and not Berkeley's logic or lack of it, that makes him an important exponent of empirical thought, and his book the classic it has remained.

Notes for Further Reading

1. Hobbes, T., *Leviathan*. New York, E. P. Dutton and Company, 1914, Everyman's edition, Parts I and II.

2. Laird, J., *Hobbes*. London and New York, Oxford University Press, 1934.

3. Taylor, A. E., *Hobbes*. New York, Dodge Publishing Company, 1908.

4. Robertson, G. C., *Hobbes*. New York, Charles Scribner's Sons, 1886.

F. J. E. Woodbridge, M. W. Calkins, G. Kennedy, P. Wheeling, and others have edited selections from Hobbes.

5. Locke, J., *An Essay Concerning Human Understanding*. New York, E. P. Dutton and Company, Inc., 1901.

6. —— *The Essay*, ed. A. C. Fraser. London and New York, Oxford University Press, 1901.

7. Lamprecht, S. P., *Locke: Selections*. New York, Columbia University Press, 1928.

8. Calkins, M. W., *Locke's Essay: Selections*. La Salle, Ill., The Open Court Publishing Company, 1905, 1920.

9. Morris, C. R., *Locke, Berkeley, and Hume*. London and New York, Oxford University Press, 1931.

10. Alexander, S., *Locke*. New York, Dodge Publishing Company, 1908.

11. Green, T. H., *Introduction to Hume's Treatise*. Several editions.

12. Fowler, Th., *Locke*. New York, The Macmillan Company, 1906.

13. Fraser, A. C., *Locke*. London and New York, Oxford University Press, 1890, 1901.

14. Gibson, J., *Locke's Theory of Knowledge*. New York, The Macmillan Company, 1917.

15. Berkeley, G., *Works*, ed. A. C. Fraser. London and New York, Oxford University Press, 1871.

16. Calkins, M. W., *Berkeley: Selections*. New York, Charles Scribner's Sons, 1929.

17. Fraser, A. C., *Berkeley*. London and New York, Oxford University Press, 1899.

18. Hicks, G. D., *Berkeley*. London, Ernest Benn, Ltd., 1932.

19. Johnston, G. A., *The Development of Berkeley's Philosophy*. New York, The Macmillan Company, 1923.

20. Wild, J., *George Berkeley*. London and New York, Oxford University Press, 1936.

16 THE EMPIRICAL PHILOSOPHY
OF MODERN SCIENCE

(Continued)

IN *David Hume* (1711–1776) WE MEET THE MAN
whose thought plumbed most deeply the implications of modern science and most forcibly influenced this
modern age. It is unfortunate that this forceful and revolutionary thinker is still chiefly known as a skeptic. Skeptical of
much he was, and from him flows a stream of skeptical thought,
at first narrow but ever widening, which today seems to
threaten the intellectual faith of man. But does this designation
of Hume as a skeptic more reveal the thought of Hume, or dis-
play the failure of those who so label him to grasp his thought?

Certainly David Hume did not set out to be a skeptic.
Seldom has a mind started forth upon the great adventure of
thought with surer faith, more confident of man's intellectual
powers. Hume was an ambitious young Scot whose reading
had infected him with the dream pursued by Bacon, Hobbes,
and Locke—the vision of a science of human nature complementary to the new science of physical nature. Nor did Hume
ever recant that optimistic faith—his whole life was devoted
to its service, and his name stands high among those whose
labor and vision inaugurated the social sciences. But it is not

as a pioneer of psychological and social science that Hume is chiefly remembered and most assured of immortality. He is remembered as the destroyer of that rationalistic tradition, which ever since the time of Parmenides, Plato, and Aristotle had wet-nursed the human intellect. It was a tradition which still constrained thought when Hume wrote, and which even today from certain strongholds seeks to assert its dominion. But because of Hume the iconoclast, a dogmatic rationalism can scarcely reign again. So soon as it asserts itself openly, it is met by the stern gaze and the unanswerable question of Hume, and it retires defeated. This is not to say that Hume rid us completely of dogmatism—there is still plenty of that in the world; but dogmatism exists henceforth by inadvertence, in disguise, or armed with brutal force.

Dissatisfied with life as a shipping clerk, David Hume took his small competence to La Flèche, the little French town where Descartes had been educated; and there, after three years, still a young man in his middle twenties, he completed his first and greatest work, the *Treatise on Human Nature*. Note its title, and also its subtitle, which reads: *an Attempt to introduce the Experimental Method of Reasoning into Moral Subjects*. We would not regard this book, today, as being primarily a study of human nature; we would discover in it no experiments; and we would say that only its less important chapters treat of morals. Its more important parts treat of causal relationship, a concept basic to every study of nature. By the "experimental method of reasoning" Hume meant, if we may judge him by his work, a science not committed to rationalistic prepossessions; and under "Moral Subjects" he included the whole range of human activity.

There is no doubt that Hume's initial purpose was to extend to the field of human behavior the sort of analysis so magnificently applied by Newton to the field of physical nature. Newton seemed to have shown that all material change is explicable in terms of atomic particles, interacting according to the laws of motion and gravitation. How might this tremendous conception, Hume inquired, be carried into the mental realm? Hume's question is naively dualistic; and no less naive is his initial hypothesis. Let there be mental elements, he suggested, which correspond to the particles of matter; and let there be forces of attraction among these mental elements, corresponding to the mechanical forces among material particles! Given these assumptions, we may proceed to unravel the mental processes of man by an analysis similar to that of physical or chemical science. And to know these mental processes will be to understand human behavior and "human nature."

This naive atomistic psychology, to which contemporary psychology allows little cogency, was the device which enabled Hume to emancipate himself from rationalistic prepossessions which even Locke had been unable to escape, and to advance an empirical theory of knowledge which all later science and philosophy has substantially confirmed. Following Hobbes and Locke, Hume conceived the mind of man to be constituted of "ideas," simple and complex. The "simple ideas," or sensations, are the irreducible mental elements which correspond to the material particles of physical nature. Certain forces of association among these simple ideas correspond to the gravitational attractions among material particles; and the action of these forces by and on simple ideas is supposed to explain the mental processes generating complex ideas and knowledge. Hume's theory may also be summarized as follows: The patterns of direct experience, impressed upon us in perception, may be analyzed introspectively into irreducible sensations, the "simple ideas." We may think of these simple ideas as being juxtaposed, like the parts of a jigsaw puzzle or the small tiles composing a mosaic; only they are juxtaposed in time as well as in space. These original relations of spatial and temporal contiguity persist as forces of association among the ideas, after the perceptions fade back into memory. Hume

THE EMPIRICAL PHILOSOPHY OF MODERN SCIENCE

thinks of knowledge as a pattern of ideas which is centered in a perceptual nucleus actually present, but supplemented by ideas recalled from memory. His purpose is to show how such recall occurs, and what sorts of conceptual knowledge it generates.

It seems clear that we do call to mind from memory those ideas which are *similar* to the ideas now present to us. Our most basic and initial thought process is recognition, whereby present perception is supplemented by memory, *i.e.* by recalled earlier perception. Evidently there is among ideas this relation or associative bond of similarity, over and above the association of contiguity described above. Ideas are associated, Hume says, by contiguity and by resemblance. Thus an idea present in perception may call to mind a similar idea, earlier perceived; and this earlier idea may bring along with it other ideas, contiguous with it in the earlier perception. You see Brown, you recognize him because your present perception is associated by resemblance with your earlier perceptions of him, and you are now reminded of Brown's dog which has usually accompanied him.

This is the simple sort of analysis, known as associational psychology, by means of which Hume proposed to explain every mental process, and to develop the empirical doctrine which states that knowledge comes wholly from experience. It is generally considered today, among psychologists, to be faulty in its introspective method and inadequate in its constitutive hypothesis, although the facts of recall, which Hume explained as the result of "associations," are evident enough. Contemporary empirical psychology either avoids introspection altogether, or supplements it by a behavioristic study which places mental processes in the context of their bodily conditions and the external environment. Although Hume's analysis undoubtedly assisted the progress of psychological science, it did this by elaborating an introspective psychology which finally made apparent its limitations and its nonempirical character.

But it becomes evident, fairly early in the *Treatise*, that Hume's interest in the advancement of empirical psychology was secondary to another interest. This was his desire to establish in some way his empirical assumption, holding that all authentic knowledge derives from experience, and that it does not arise, as rationalistic thinkers supposed, from absolute self-evident principles. Hume's two purposes, respectively psychological and philosophical, conflicted. Suppose, for a moment, that we actually possess an adequate theory of mental processes, showing how all mental content derives from experience, and allowing us to trace back any idea to its perceptual sources. Necessarily this theory will explain hallucinations, dreams, and errors as impartially as it explains what we accept as authentic knowledge. It will not of itself explain what distinguishes truth from error; it will show how both truthful and untruthful conceptions derive from experience. Hume committed a fallacy when he supposed that a psychological analysis can reveal to us the methods of science or the criteria of truth; and it is a fallacy that has confused much subsequent thought. When a psychologist explains, as he often may and does, how an individual comes to harbor an illusion or error, he does not reveal to us why that error is error, but only how it arises. The stigmatization of the idea as illusion or error is based upon other special evidence, appropriate to the subject matter of the idea. Of course, if we know to begin with what is truth and what is error, then we may as psychologists usefully classify mental processes into those reaching truth and those involving error; and by studying these separately, we may discover certain general sources of error. This presupposes, we repeat, an independent knowledge of reality and of the truths and errors studied.

Hume proceeded from his study, however, to very definite conclusions concerning what is true and what false in human knowledge; and it is evident that his analysis, although it was begun as a psychological study and expressed itself in psychological terms, became something else than psychology. The name "epistemology" has been used to designate this type of study, which seeks to understand the relations which hold between conceptual knowledge, immediate perception, and their objects. The chief philosophical value of Hume's psychological analysis lay in its concept of association, which allowed him to appreciate certain important relations among ideas— or among things—which had hitherto been neglected.

The concept of association of ideas, like most of the other concepts of Hume's psychology, came to him from Hobbes and Locke. Both of those thinkers had defined knowledge to be the result of a correct apprehension of relations among ideas. They had characterized true knowledge as a perception of relations intrinsic and proper to ideas, and indicated that error arises from the chance or contingent association of ideas in the mind. Thus the idea of triangle, they taught, is intrinsically and intuitively related to the ideas of three intersecting straight lines, of three enclosed angles, etc., and one cannot entertain the first idea without the others. However, one may associate the idea of triangle with a musical instrument of that shape, or with sandwiches which are often triangularly cut; and such associations are due merely to personal experience, and reveal nothing of the constitutive nature of triangles, musical instruments, or sandwiches. Hume's predecessors did not perceive—as some of his successors have not perceived—that in justifying the first sort of relationship as real and in defining the second sort, the associations, as the source of error, they were reestablishing philosophical rationalism, in spite of their philosophical conviction that knowledge comes only from experience. It was Hume's genius to perceive the significance for our knowledge of nature of these chance or contingent associations. He had the intellectual audacity to make these associations, and not the "rational intuition" of "intrinsic and necessary relations," the source and substance of natural knowledge. The whole of our natural knowledge, he taught, is only a tissue of associations of this contingent sort. This is what it means, he argued, to be an empiricist who is consistently critical of rationalism.

He did this by means of an analysis of the most general concepts of science, especially the concepts of substance, causation, and identity. Rationalistic philosophy had been uncritical of these concepts. It had supposed them to be somehow constitutive of the reason, to be applicable of necessity to every sort of fact, and to be, in some profound but unexplained way, appropriate to the universal constitution of nature. But Hume asks, in the confidence given to him by his new appreciation of associations among ideas: Just what is a substance? A certain group of simple ideas, which we may symbolize as *abcd*, recurs again and again in experience, until we recognize it easily and come to think of it as a natural unit. If we see part of this pattern *abcd*, we will infer the hidden presence of the rest. What looks like a bell (*ab*) will sound like a bell (*c*) and feel like a bell (*d*). We come to believe that we have a rational intuition into this unity; and we call it a "thing" or "substance," and suppose that we perceive some intrinsic and necessary bond holding its elements together. Yet all we know is that the complex *abcd* has often occurred, so that we expect the same grouping to occur again. We know of no reason why *ab* should not henceforth occur only in conjunction with *ef* instead of *cd*. Dogs have always barked and cats mewed, and so we refuse to contemplate a future of mewing dogs and barking cats. The necessity of such recurrence, however, lies only in our subjective expectations. These are induced, it is true, by past experience; but we have no intuition of any necessity internal to nature, requiring nature to perpetuate these familiar patterns, or, indeed, any sort of substantial pattern.

A similar analysis is applied to the concept of causation, which Hume suspected, one may say advisedly, to be the most central and pivotal category of natural knowledge. As science advances, probing ever more deeply into natural processes, it describes things less and less in terms of their visible appearances, and more and more by inference from their causal actions and reactions. But what is causal action? Rationalism had consistently confused the concept of causation with the concept of substance, by supposing that the action of a thing is wholly due to the substantial nature of that thing. Rational insight into substances was accordingly supposed to carry with it a rational insight into causal necessities within nature. Hume perceived that in the new science, causal connection meant particular interaction among particular things, although the same *sort* of causal connection may recur again and again. What can we mean, he asks, by causal connection? Can we discover any necessary connection, *i.e.* any rationally intuited relation, between a cause and its effect? He finds none; but he has a very simple explanation of causal connection in terms of associations. When A has been followed sufficiently often by B, he says, the appearance of A will induce in us the expectation of B. The reason for this expectation is that A and B, having occurred often contiguously, are now firmly associated by contiguity. The reoccurrence of A arouses past memories of A, and these bring with them associated ideas of B, which we now expect to be realized again in perception along with A. The character of causal necessity which we impute to nature is really, it follows, a subjective character, resident in ourselves. The same sequence, repeated again and again, generates in us a habit of expectancy, such that the reoccurrence of A suggests the reoccurrence of B. Thus we come to believe that A necessitates B, independently of ourselves; and we proceed to a belief in universal natural necessity. Actually, however, we neither perceive nor understand any such necessity. So far as we know, A may recur without B, B may recur without A, AB may never occur again. We try to establish our faith in specific causal necessities by appealing to a universal principle of necessity, which states that every event must have its cause; but this is arguing in a circle, because we have no

ground for this general principle in established particular
necessities. So far as we know, events may occur without intelligible causes or without discernible effects. The principle
of universal and exact determinism is pure assumption. Certain
regular sequences there have been in our past experiences; but
that these sequences, or any regular sequence, must of necessity
recur in future experience is a gratuitous assumption.

Finally, Hume points out, all causal and substantial analysis
of fact depends upon the postulation of identities in nature;
and the most we are justified in assuming is similarities. Take
personal identity, for example, since that is where we are
most assured of identity. We are aware, much of the time, of
a certain continuity between our earlier and later states; and
we may feel, although we know that we change, a certain
similarity between our earlier and later selves; and this continuity and similarity between earlier and later states of mind
is what we call personal identity. Our experience of anything
not ourselves is, of course, much less continuous; and it is the
close similarity of discontinuous perceptions, supported by intervals of continuity while we observe a thing, that we accept
as evidence of the identity of a thing. We have no evidence
of absolute identity in nature; and without absolute identity,
all the other absolutes fall to earth.

The gist of Hume's argument, then, is the now widely accepted view that all knowledge of natural processes finally
resolves into generalizations based upon observations of particular processes. Hume's reduction of substance and causation to
associations of ideas inducing expectancies, although it neglects
the large element of rational construction in science and is too
psychological in its phrasing, has withstood attack for two
centuries, and has led to an ever clearer appreciation of the
empirical character of natural knowledge. All description of
nature, from its largest range to its most microscopic detail,
depends in some way and in some measure upon our perception
of repeated sequences in nature. If, as Hume was able to show,

we cannot reduce this relation between cause and effect to some intuitively known and rationally understood relation, but must accept it empirically and as we find it, then it follows that natural knowledge can do no more, in the last resort, than summarize observable fact.

What are the consequences of Hume's conclusions concerning natural knowledge? There are two sorts of consequence, respectively critical and constructive. The critical or destructive consequences are the surer and the more important. They might be summed up as a recognition of the contingency of nature. To acknowledge the contingency of nature means that we acknowledge the impossibility of deducing the content or character of nature from anything we know prior to our observation of nature. We must discover nature by observation and by study of observable fact, and we may not impose upon nature our preconception of what nature should be or must be. Since what we observe is always some particular situation, natural knowledge will consist of generalizations which summarize particular facts. And since our experience of particular fact is of necessity limited to what we or others have actually observed, our generalizations must be asserted modestly, and not exaggerated into definitions of "absolute reality." All natural knowledge is probable knowledge. Its probability may be very high, practically equivalent to certainty and theoretically close to certainty; but it cannot reach absolute certainty. For example, all human experience supports the belief that the earth will continue to turn on its axis, and that the sun will again rise tomorrow in the east. But we have no proof that the earth must continue so to turn; or if we could deduce this rotation from some general mechanical principle, then this principle in its turn would be indemonstrable and only empirical. Our widest, surest, and most basic knowledge of nature is still only a generalization from observed particular facts, and rests upon empirical evidence, *i.e.* upon observation. Even the most basic principles of natural science are of this sort; and they consequently do not constitute absolute and necessary principles, intuited by the reason. We do not know why the world is the sort of world it is. We do not know what sort it is, except as we have observed it. Our actual observations cover only the sort of fact we can observe; and they include only a part of this, because we cannot attend to everything we see. And we have reduced to generality, of course, only a small part of all the particular fact we have observed. It follows that all scientific generalizations, even the most comprehensive and stable of them, remain tentative, capable of improvement, less than certain.

Other thinkers had indicated the contingent character of nature; but Hume was the first thinker to expound fully and clearly its consequences for our conception and estimate of natural knowledge. Others before him had challenged the rationalistic view which held knowledge to be rooted in absolute principles of reason, and which conceived science to be only the application of these rational and necessary principles to particular observed situations. But these earlier empiricists had not clearly distinguished the sort of knowledge that is reached by factual generalization from the sort of knowledge that would issue from absolute rational principles. Hume was led to do this, we saw, by his psychological conception of the causal relation as a habit of mind induced by past experience; but his willingness to accept this conception of causation as a sufficient basis for natural science shows us that he had understood the philosophical implications of the Newtonian science. Plato, Copernicus, Descartes, even Newton himself—all of these men had conceived science to be the application of absolute mathematical principles to the particular and observable facts of nature. But Newton differed from the first three in that he placed between the absolute and universal principles of mathematics and the particular observed facts a new sort of principle, best illustrated by the law of gravitation. This principle is not rational or necessary, it is one that could not have been predicted and which had to be discovered by observation. Yet it is a very general and perhaps "universal" principle, and not itself a particular fact. All the principles of natural knowledge, Hume is saying, are of this sort. The whole of science, including its largest principles, is obtained from experience; and it is subject, therefore, to change, modification, and growth.

But what of the mathematical principles still incorporated in the Newtonian science? Are they not still rational, necessary, and universally applicable? Hume could not show that they are not; and it is evident that they embarrassed him, because they seemed to preserve a rational element in natural knowledge which he could not argue away. He dealt with the difficulty in two ways. Sometimes he showed that the basic concepts of mathematics arise, just like any other concepts, as the result of associations among ideas; and this would imply that mathematical theory is no more absolute than other theory, *e.g.* physical theory. At other times, he frankly recognizes that mathematical science arises from absolute rational axioms; but he assumes now that its principles do not apply perfectly to observable fact, which is consequently still free to be what it will. Hume's honesty appears in this equivocal treatment of mathematics; for we know today that both of his two views, contradictory though they seem, are correct. A science like geometry includes two elements: an empirical element which is really descriptive but only probable, and a rational element which is certain, but not necessarily descriptive of anything in nature.

Hume's general conclusion was, then, that authentic knowledge must be identified with a natural science reaching generalizations possessed of greater or lesser probability, and that principles which are supposedly possessed of intuitive certainty are on that very account suspect, and to be denied descriptive truth. This conclusion invalidated—with some reservation as regards mathematics—all so-called rational knowledge. Most emphatically it excluded all rationalistic philosophy, which Hume called "metaphysics." We should accept as valid, he said, all established knowledge of matters of fact, *i.e.* all empirical science, and also mathematics; but all other "knowledge," especially metaphysics, should be "consigned to the flames." It is this critique of rational knowledge in the interests of empirical science that makes Hume the most important and the most characteristic thinker of the modern age. By invalidating rationalism, he opened the way for an empirical science which might be completely free in its hypotheses concerning the structures and processes of nature.

There were also consequences from Hume's study of a constructive sort. Hume's initial purpose, we saw, was to show how the concepts of science are obtained, namely as the result of a combination by association of present and past perceptions. This side of Hume's work has been developed by many later thinkers, but it is more difficult to judge the value of this Humian epistemology. The proposal to establish the truth of scientific knowledge by an introspective epistemology would seem, indeed, to contradict the critical view which holds that authentic natural knowledge consists wholly of generalizations from particular facts. The empirical view would seem to imply that the hypotheses and concepts of the special sciences are established wholly and solely by the particular evidence supporting them. This would mean that no philosophical analysis, dealing with fact and science as a whole and universally, can add to or subtract from this evidence. To accept the empirical view, in short, is to suppose that empirical science with its methods and results establishes itself; and to assume that empirical science needs or allows of some philosophical foundation is to demand, once more, a rationalistic basis for natural knowledge. However this may be, a succession of thinkers have elaborated the Humian epistemology, attempting to show how scientific concepts, or the objects conceived by scientists, are "legitimately" constructed. Their conclusions have been diverse, dubious, and of uncertain value; and it should be remembered that Hume's critical work is not prejudiced by the failure of Humian epistemology. It is the scientist, not the philosopher, who establishes the concepts of science.

Hume's statement of his conclusions was unnecessarily subjectivistic and skeptical. He was satisfied to say that causal knowledge, and therewith all natural knowledge, consists of habits of expectancy induced in us by past experience; and he did not further inquire—being prevented by his subjective psychological approach—into the implications of this statement. The statement implies, surely, that mental habits are effects of the more constant configurations of nature, continuously effective upon us in perception. The relation of knowledge to nature is at least that of effect to cause. This conclusion meets a difficulty which Kant was to exploit, since it conceives of a nature lying outside of experience, causing experience—and how, if all knowledge is derived from experience, should we know a nature which lies beyond experience? In the writer's opinion, the problem is apparent rather than real. The empirical doctrine states that knowledge is derived from experience; but it does not exclude the realistic hypothesis that experience is the direct effect of a reality lying beyond the mind, and that experience consequently provides clues to the character of that reality. This hypothesis is a legitimate one, and one that is confirmed by all experience and analysis.

Hume's central thesis, that knowledge is the sum of mental habits induced by past impressions, is so broad and simple that it would cover animal as well as human psychology. This was its great value. It indicated certain characters of knowledge so general and so obvious that they had escaped attention. But it is also clear that Hume, in establishing the empirical basis of knowledge in observable fact, neglected the rationalistic elements which distinguish science from ordinary knowledge and animal habit. Mathematical reasoning and other sorts of reasoning which Hume would have called "metaphysical" have a most important auxiliary function in science. This much is clear, although we are almost as far from an adequate psychology of the reasoning processes today as was Hume. Contemporary philosophy, we shall see, is able to do justice to the rational element in science without endangering the empirical foundation of science, and without recourse to psychological hypotheses which only confuse the issue.

Although Hume was wont to call himself a skeptic, and has usually been so called, we can see today that he was skeptical chiefly by contrast with the prevailing habit of mind, which was still rationalistic in its conception of knowledge. If knowledge means absolute, certain, universal knowledge, standing upon absolute intuitive principles, then Hume was of course a skeptic, because he admitted only an empirical knowledge generalizing from experience and reaching high probability. But to establish empirical knowledge as he did was to establish faith in the power of the mind to explore and describe nature. The skeptic of rationalism is the great advocate of an empirical science, a science which, just because its conclusions at any time are less than final, is capable of indefinite progress. It is impossible to state within a sentence the liberation of science effected by Hume; but we are all aware of it, and our conception of science today is just what Hume showed it might be and ought to be. We regard present scientific theories as "habits of mind," justified by past experience and liable to modification; but we have multiplied the conceptual and experimental methods by means of which past experience can be summarized, present experience enriched, and hypothesis diversified and confirmed.

Hume's popular reputation as a skeptic is probably due more to his writings on religion than to his critique of rationalistic metaphysics. His criticism of theology, however, was primarily a criticism of the rationalistic philosophy which since the second century A.D. had incorporated itself into orthodox faith; and his *Dialogues Concerning Natural Religion,* so shocking when he wrote them that he withheld their publication during his lifetime, might be defended today as only a proper demand for intellectual independence in the pursuit of religious truth. With regard to revealed religion, Hume rejected miracles, along with whatever else cannot be brought into conformity with observable fact. But Hume's attitude toward religion is that of the honest inquirer, not that of the atheist. He opened the way to an independent and creative study of religious fact; and it is most to be regretted that the later centuries, which have turned Hume's empiricism to good use in every other field, have tended to place religion outside of the intellectual pale, either as a truth too sacrosanct for impartial study and creative hypothesis, or as an error better left alone. It is a pusillanimous and ignoble compromise, ultimately destructive of science and religion both, which has left to each of these two faiths one half of the mind and a peculiar social domain.

Of next importance in Hume's work, after his establishment of empirical science and method, was his application of this method to human and social fact. Hume did not follow Locke, who believed moral principles to be fixed and universal. He taught that moral knowledge too is derived from experience. But like many thinkers then and since, Hume did not sufficiently distinguish a psychological analysis of feelings, affections, and emotions, as motives of human behavior, from moral theory. "Reason is and ought to be," he wrote, "the slave of the passions." In this revolutionary rejection of all earlier teaching, Hume attacked the divorce of "moral reason" from the emotional life of man. He recognized quite properly the dependence of action upon feeling, and the instrumental function of thought in analyzing and guiding our emotional responses. But in his moral theory as elsewhere, he did less than justice to the rational element in man. The source of all moral distinctions and preferences, he taught, is ultimately the experience and anticipation of pleasure and pain, these qualities attending all our states or "ideas." Hume applied this hedonistic doctrine liberally, not egotistically. It is everyone's pleasure and pain, and not only our own, that we should strive to increase or diminish. Such courses of conduct are to be preferred on the ground of their general *utility*. But utility for what, to what end? Hume did not ask this question, because he conceived pleasure and the avoidance of pain to be the sole values or ends of conduct. We are naturally sympathetic, he believed, to such a degree that others' pleasures and pains are felt as our own. (But the moral question is not whether we do, but why we should, consider others' feelings.)

Hume's ethics is humanitarian and humanistic. It is established upon the facts of feeling, sympathy, and human affection. Its weakness is that it everywhere assumes, but nowhere explicitly requires and sanctions, a moral ideal starting from these facts of human feeling, and intelligently and systematically proceeding from them to a large and steady conception of what human life and society ought to be. To take Hume literally would suppose him to mean that our feelings of pleasure and pain, together with our sympathetic susceptibilities, comprise our moral faculty; and this is to imply that thought or reasoning plays only a minor and incidental role, and has no constitutive part in morality or ethics. Just as Hume confused a psychological account of how the mind reaches knowledge with a philosophical study of what constitutes truth, so he confused an empirical account of the moral nature of man, as it actually exists, with an ethical study of the objectives or ideals which are implicit in man's moral nature and which should explicitly direct his behavior.

Yet Hume does in one place distinguish this "natural" morality of man, effective in his immediate personal relations, from the "artificial" morality which man explicitly formulates and deliberately exercises. Justice, Hume agrees when he comes to deal with political matters, is an ideal which is reached only when the spontaneous affections of men are extended and organized by means of conscious volition and thought. If

Hume had given more attention to this transition from "natural" morality to "artificial" justice, and begun his ethical study with a consideration of government, he would have importantly amplified both his ethical and his political theory. But when he proceeds to his study of politics, he is once more the student of the natural growth of social institutions, intent upon showing how the natural impulses, widened by sympathy and strengthened by education, suffice to explain the long development of legal and political institutions. He regards the concept of a social contract, by means of which Locke had established government upon the natural and inalienable rights of the individual, as a convenient but rationalistic fiction symbolizing the long development of organized society out of men's natural needs and dispositions. He does not seek the principles which had implicitly determined this development. Hume left ethics in a confusion which can be removed only by an analysis superior to any attempted in the past.

Thus there is a positive and a negative side to Hume; and we should see both sides clearly and estimate them objectively. The positive side is his empiricism and his naturalism. His empiricism brought science back to its proper and necessary starting-point, which is observable particular fact, and cut down everything which might obstruct science by separating the scientist from observable facts. What most obstructed science was the retention, as absolute rational principles, of "metaphysical" concepts which were after all only the largest or most firmly established principles of Greek and medieval science. The Newtonian science had already broken away in some respects from these principles; and Hume, perceiving this, saw further that no scientific principle should or could be allowed such absolute authority. He quite properly concluded that all scientific principles which describe nature are but large generalizations from observed particular fact. In his application of this empirical theory of knowledge Hume becomes a naturalist, which is to say that he finds in nature something which exists in its own right, which goes its own way, which is more than appearance or illusion, and which has its own real, objective, and intelligible design. In this naturalism Hume escaped both from Greek metaphysics, which saw in nature only a confused and deteriorated version of the true reality envisaged by the theoretical reason, and from medieval theology which had taught that this world is but the purgatory of an otherworldly spirit whose true home is elsewhere. Such naturalism need not be irreligious—one of the chief sources of modern naturalism, we have seen, was the religious mysticism of the Middle Ages, which proceeded through Franciscan scholars to Occam and thence to Locke, Berkeley, and Hume. A free and creative religion, no less than a free and creative science, must start from an open-minded and appreciative naturalism, willing and able to exhaust the resources of our human experience of fact—historical fact as well as present fact, be it emphasized.

The negative side of Hume's teaching was due to the necessity he was under of combating the dogmatic rationalism of the past and of his contemporaries. In his empirical theory of knowledge he failed to appreciate how large is the role of logical analysis in the construction of scientific hypothesis. He consequently failed to see that science arises and develops only where there exists a will to knowledge, which presupposes first a specific and distinct scientific interest, and secondly some conception, however vague and mutable, of what distinguishes scientific truth from erratic opinion. These preconditions of science might be summed up as a faith in logic. The scientist assumes his power to construct logical and self-consistent hypotheses; and he supposes, further, that the world will reveal itself to persistent logical analysis. He assumes, in a word, that the world may somehow be reconstructed in thought.

We shall see how later thinkers have attempted to correct Hume's neglect of this rational element in science, some praiseworthily advancing an empirical rationalism, others desperately relinquishing the empirical insight of Hume and returning to rationalism; but Hume's doctrines, too uncritically and literally taken, have sometimes produced a sort of scientific obscurantism which only inverts the "fundamentalism" of the religious dogmatist. The earlier rationalism had its most popular expression in the concept of natural law. There are certain absolute principles, said the rationalistic philosopher, which must of necessity be applied in all scientific study, such application constituting science. There are certain absolute laws, said the popular version of this view, which all natural things must obey, as a result of their inclusion in the cosmos. Hume's devastating criticism of rationalism has finally destroyed this faith in natural law; and there is no doubt that the old concept of natural law, which conceived material things to be necessitated by such laws as that of gravitation, must be replaced by the insight that material things do in fact, but not by any observable necessity, conform to scientific formulas. Consequently, it is concluded, there is no law in nature, neither natural, nor moral, nor of any other sort. Things do what they please, without regard to any universal context or environment; and it is simply an accident, with no implications of any kind, that things so conveniently conform in those ways which science successfully describes. The possibility of science, its existence and its continuous extension, it is concluded, carry simply no implications whatsoever regarding nature.

Now this is an error as disastrous to science, and also to society, as was the earlier dogmatism. Science has not ceased to be rational in becoming empirical. It still makes demands upon nature, although these demands have emptied themselves of all save logical content; and the plasticity of fact to the demands of logic is still a character of fact, carrying implications about the world at large. We will not develop this theme here; but we shall see, in our concluding chapters, that the true effect of Hume's criticism was not so much to invalidate the concept of natural law as to widen it and carry it further back, to a place where it could still support, but not fixate or limit, scientific hypothesis.

And similarly in moral theory, where Hume's naturalism profitably reminds us that the sources of moral judgment lie in human feeling and affection, a too literal and uncritical acceptance of his teaching has propagated the view that there are no authentic moral principles. Here, too, we shall find that Hume's criticism of rationalistic morals did not really invalidate the moral law, but widened it and carried it back to a place where it still requires, but cannot stereotype or limit, our definition and pursuit of moral ends. And we shall agree with Hume that the moral nature of man has its "artificial" extension, *i.e.* its full and rational development, in the pursuit and progressive achievement of social justice.

But Hume's influence and importance, whatever these corrigible defects in his teaching, cannot be exaggerated. All subsequent philosophy, even where it perversely returns to the dogmatism which Hume struck down, has had to start from Hume's inescapable conclusions; and consequently Hume's monument and true epitaph is the further course of human thought itself, which he so forcibly impelled upon its new path. Hume is the narrows through which the tide of modern thought was channeled, and by which it was accelerated and directed toward the future. He was a man of two worlds. In his diction and conceptual thinking he was true to his age, that eighteenth-century "age of reason" which loved the clear and distinct, the flat and low, the broad foreground and near horizon. But in his imagination he was of the turbulent romantic group who found easement in mountain and torrent, who sought remote vistas and loved only the new and unstereotyped or the far-away and long-ago. Explicitly, he loved reason and measure, and distrusted "enthusiasm"; yet his was the mind that was to free men from fixed categories and immutable precepts. In his heart he was the greatest rebel of his age; for what was Rousseau's rebellion, which unleashed hysterical revolution in France, compared with this rebellion which has challenged and still challenges every intellectual and social institution that cannot continue to justify its claim in terms of human experience? When Hume showed that the bond between cause and effect is no necessary bond, but a bond primarily of mental habit induced by past experience, and subject therefore to change in the light of new experience or experience better encompassed, he did no less than liberate human thought from human inertia. And in emancipating thought, he emancipated also action, to free at last the human race itself. Seldom, only occasionally as in his *Dialogues Concerning Natural Religion*, does that mighty imagination escape the rein of firm and even harsh restraint; but when it does, we realize that Hume liberated human thought in virtue of his own imaginative vision. He envisioned a nature that is free, moving, and intent, not to be deprived of its great leaping-times. It was a mystical adoration of natural freedom, of liberty in all nature, that moved Hume to cut those intellectual bonds which had confined the thought of man through earlier time.

Notes for Further Reading

1. Hume, D., *A Treatise on Human Nature*, ed. Green and Grose. London and New York, Longmans, Green and Company, 1874.
2. —— *Works*, ed. Green and Grose. London and New York, Longmans, Green and Company, 1874.
3. —— *A Treatise on Human Nature*, ed. Selby-Bigge. London and New York, Oxford University Press, 1903.
4. —— *The Enquiries*, ed. Selby-Bigge. Oxford, The Clarendon Press, 1894.
5. Hendel, C. W., *Hume: Selections*. New York, Charles Scribner's Sons, 1927.
6. Green, T. H., "Introduction to Hume," *Treatise on Human Nature*, ed. Green and Grose. London and New York, Longmans, Green and Company, 1874. A critical study.

7. Hendel, C. W., *Studies in the Philosophy of David Hume.* Princeton, N. J., Princeton University Press, 1925.
8. Laing, B. M., *David Hume.* London, Ernest Benn, Ltd., 1932.
9. Laird, J., *Hume's Philosophy of Human Nature.* New York, E. P. Dutton and Company, Inc., 1931.
10. Smith, N. K., *Philosophy of David Hume.* Toronto, The Macmillan Company, 1941.

17 THE REVIVAL OF
POLITICAL ABSOLUTISM

In the writings of locke, berkeley, and hume we see the development of an empirical philosophy which in its theoretical and practical teachings expresses the outlook most characteristic of modern man. It is emphatically a liberal or libertarian philosophy. In its study of science it elevates particular fact, which is an apprehension of individual being, into the chief criterion of truth. In its moral and political teaching, it makes the human individual the source and seat of authority, and the welfare of individuals the objective of government.

This empirical and democratic development has proceeded freely and unobstructed chiefly in the English-speaking world, *i.e.* in Britain and America. It has not, generally speaking, characterized the thought and practice of continental Europe. European thought has remained bound by rationalistic habits long induced by medieval scholasticism, and never completely renounced; and European governments have been for the most part feudal, monarchical, or otherwise absolutistic. The intellectual and political collapse of continental Europe in our century is the consequence of this failure to advance from absolutistic to liberal forms of thought and government. The old ways of thought and life will not combine with, and cannot compete with, the new; and the effort to force them to do so leads to social disintegration. It is very important, therefore, to recognize the forms in which absolutism perpetuated itself in Europe; for it was apt to make use of liberal vocabularies which disguised its tyrannical purpose, and even gave it entrance into liberal societies.

We have seen how Descartes, Spinoza, and Leibniz transformed scholastic rationalism into a new and even more rigid discipline. This modern rationalism relies upon a small nucleus of mathematical axioms, to which are added certain metaphysical principles such as definitions of substance, causation, etc., for its theoretical support; but it is inevitably driven to expand this nucleus of rational knowledge into a system coextensive with the total body of scientific and moral truth. Everything that is structural in nature and man, the rationalist must finally conclude, is known in virtue of principles which are somehow incorporated in the reason and thereby raised above criticism; and it is only transient and accidental character that is discovered by experience. The empiricist holds, to the contrary, that truly descriptive knowledge derives, by way of generalization, from our immediate experience of particular character.

We shall conclude in our final chapter that empiricism issues from a faith in the ultimacy and value of individual being. Where we possess and apply this faith, we are empirical in science and democratic in government. Where we lose or fail to apply it, we immediately become dogmatic in thought and absolutistic in political practice. For the rationalist, individual being is possessed of intelligible and valuable character only in virtue of some larger structure, which imposes its form upon the individual, molding the latter into its own design; and this larger structure, in its manifestation in human character, is usually identified with the body politic, or the state with its body of sanctioned law. Thus rationalism inevitably leads to political absolutism; and the forms of political absolutism so generated are many and diverse.

In Britain and America, the movement to democracy was initiated by the first English revolution, which resisted the violence done by an absolute monarch to his subjects' religious convictions; and this first revolution gave to all the later political development a religious significance and support. On the continent of Europe, the revolutionary movement proceeded under different auspices to a different outcome. The Cartesian philosophy, in spite of the idealistic efforts of such men as Spinoza and Leibniz, tended to become a physicalism or materialism which sees in existent reality only a universal physical mechanism. The Cartesian concept of natural science was usually the resource of progressive thinkers who desired to carry society out of medieval darkness into truth, and to strike off feudal shackles which were clamped ever more oppressively upon continental peoples, the more the inadequacy and injustice of feudal forms became apparent. In France, the materialistic tendencies of Cartesianism were further strengthened as a result of the ecclesiastical support given to the monarchy, which bought this support by extending protection and privilege to the established clergy. The reform movement became anticlerical, and from anticlericalism it was easy to proceed to materialism and atheism. The result was a confusion of progressive and religious currents which has defeated political progress on the continent of Europe from that day to the present. The struggle between progressive and conservative factions became extraordinarily bitter, and revolution became unnecessarily bloody, cruel, and the cause of social vendetta.

At first, the Enlightened intellectuals who led the party of reform gave some recognition to religious faith. Voltaire, Helvétius, and other liberal thinkers professed *Deism*, a view which held God to have created the world, but which rejected the conception of revealed religion that a divine providence works in or upon man at all times. According to the Deist,

God had created a world wholly subject to mechanical law, and had endowed man with a knowledge of this law which placed human destiny wholly in human hands. Reason or science, consequently, rather than religious faith, should be man's reliance in both theory and practice. Voltaire, to offset the religious interpretation of human history presented by Bossuet, elaborated a universal history which held man's gradual emancipation from theology and religion to have been the chief cause of human progress. Deism used the concept of a divine creation of the world to discredit revealed religion; and soon its pretense was dropped. Diderot and De la Mettrie frankly taught that human life may be comprehended within the universal mechanism which is nature; and Holbach and Cabanis honestly admitted and sturdily emphasized the atheistic implications of their materialistic philosophy. The most successful account in mechanistic terms of human behavior was that of Condillac, who described how a statue, endowed only with a sense of smell, might be supposed to be led by this initial olfactory endowment to a full intellectual life.

The question of whether a mechanistic explanation of human behavior is possible is too large to be decided here. It is clear that the immediately perceived qualitative characters of experience, *e.g.* color, are in some sense discontinuous with the structural character, *e.g.* wave motion or geometrical structure, of which we learn by scientific inference. The mental processes can be correlated with physical processes, as Spinoza suggested; but no one has yet succeeded in *reducing* mental processes to physical processes, as mechanistic philosophy would require. However, the possibility of such reduction is an empirical or scientific problem, and not a philosophical one. But just because this question must be left open, we may and do quarrel with the materialistic metaphysician who asserts that the principles of physical science, as these are formulated today, must *of necessity* explain human behavior, along with every other natural process. This assertion is dogmatic because it goes beyond the empirical evidence, and in some respects contradicts that evidence. It would seem, for example, that just as physical theory was importantly modified when it was extended to cover the analysis of chemical phenomena, so it will again be modified when it is extended to cover organic and mental phenomena. A physical science developed to the point where it could be made to comprehend all fact whatsoever would explain the phenomena of human morality and religion; and so comprehensive a science would need to distinguish, and could not reduce to a common physical level, the activities of moral man, of sensitive animals, and of inanimate bodies.

In France, rationalistic thought delivered itself of its absolutistic political implications in the teachings of *Jean Jacques Rousseau* (1712–1778), whose writings were perhaps the chief inspiration of the leaders of the French revolution. Rousseau was an unhappy, neurotic, expatriated Swiss, whose gift of impetuous eloquence made him the spokesman of oppressed and unhappy France. His chief political work, *Le Contrat Social,* incited the French people, as later it incited other peoples, to revolt against their feudal and monarchical forms of government. But Rousseau's book also provided the concept upon which was established the absolutistic political theory of the centuries which followed.

The most distinctive feature of Rousseau's political teaching is this concept of the *general will,* by means of which he intended to reconcile individual freedom with absolute state power. The political unit should be small enough, he taught, to allow its citizens to meet together in general assembly, to participate individually in debate, and to reach their decisions by majority vote. But what is it in the majority vote that carries authority over all the members of the community? The majority vote has this authority, Rousseau says, because it expresses the *general will.* This is the will of the community as a whole, shared by all citizens including even those who voted against the measure. The majority vote expresses the "essence" of the community. Rousseau may have meant to indicate by this phrase only the will to live in community with others, which presupposes a real appropriation by the individual of the interests of other individuals; but what he actually presents is an organic concept of the community, which he conceives to be a living organism, possessed of its own mind and will and moving by its own power to achieve its purpose. If this concept is fully elaborated, it will be found to leave the individual with no original rights. The individual will enjoy rights only as a member or part of the state, within which he is, so to speak, a cell or atom. The general will, the will of the state as determined by majority vote, says Rousseau, is the true or real will of the individual; and this implies that the individual really exists only insofar as he is exercising functions identifying him with the state of which he is a citizen.

Thus Rousseau draws the full consequence of the political conception of Hobbes, who first explicitly gave to the state this absolute status, and made it the source of all moral authority and all rights. In Hobbes' theory, the state is identified with the monarch, whose will is rightfully imposed upon all of his subjects as the condition of peace and security; in Rousseau's theory, the state is identified with a political majority whose will, expressed in its elections, becomes the true life of all its members, leaving all nonpolitical activities either worthless or reprehensible. Rousseau's theory is thus an important historical source of the political totalitarianism which, coming to complete and undisguised expression only in our own time, makes of the state the guardian and controller of every human activity and relationship. Nor did Rousseau balk when he perceived this implication of his doctrine, attributing to the state supreme moral authority and unlimited power. *"Each of us puts his person and all of his power,"* he wrote, *"under the supreme direction of the general will . . . If the state is a moral person whose life is the union of its members, and if the most important of its cares is the care for its own preservation,*

*it must have a universal and compelling force . . . The social
compact gives the body politic absolute power over all its
members . . . The voice of the people is the voice of God."*

This is very far, we should insist, from the political theory
upon which our own democracy is established. We agree with
Rousseau that the ballot is the fairest and most expedient means
of determining public opinion and electing an administration;
but we do not believe with Rousseau that the use of this
method requires us ever to renounce our individual judgment,
and to accept the vote of a majority as the voice of our "real"
conscience. If an Aryan majority should vote to exterminate
a non-Aryan minority, if a white majority should vote to
enslave a Negro minority—is that the voice of God? It is
not Rousseau's faith out of which grew our American institutions. These were established to define and to limit the powers
of the state, to protect minorities, and to place moral sanctions
wholly and forever in the individual conscience. But Rousseau's
concept of the general will was the faith out of which must
grow, steadily as the decades pass, absolutism such as we see
growing in our world today. We must know that there is no
general will. There are only individual wills.

Several things conspired to disguise from Rousseau the absolutism implicit in his theory, or to reconcile him with it. He
proposed to limit the size of the state so radically that no established government, possessed of permanent power, would be
needed. The whole community could in this case gather in
general assembly to exercise its political responsibilities; and
this would tend to prevent the alienation of political power
from individual citizens to some well-entrenched caucus or
political machine. But the proposal to limit states to small
townships is wholly impracticable. The irresistible movement
of civilized society is toward states of continental size, exerting
highly concentrated power. It is the more important therefore
to define governmental powers, and to secure the principle of
individual and minority rights. In the large modern state it is

inevitable that a well-organized minority will occasionally out-vote a confused and divided majority; but the difficulties peculiar to democratic government should not wean us from democratic theory and practice. Real democracy is activated by the moral resolve to extend to each individual his right of self-government, whatever may be the consequences; and we may insist that democracy, whatever may be its defects, has proved itself to be the least imperfect and most stable type of government yet devised. Shortcomings of democratic practice should keep steadily before us the original and permanent aim of democracy, which is human liberty; and liberty is the freedom of the individual to exercise to a maximum degree his individual judgment, both in his political capacity and in his other capacities. The liberty of the individual on Rousseau's theory would be ultimately that of the member of a totalitarian state, who may enjoy almost despotic power if he will identify himself with the ruling group, but who is either enslaved or liquidated if he cannot do this. Progress, incidentally, is always initiated by minorities, who finally persuade the majority to accept their view.

But Rousseau was driven to his absolutistic conception of the state by force of logic. He came to his study of government with premises which made absolute government the condition of political unity. These presuppositions are revealed in his other writings. In his earlier *Discourses*, Rousseau had expressed a revulsion against civilized society so intense and uncompromising that it amounts to social nihilism. That social injustice was intolerable in eighteenth-century Europe is true; but it is not true that everything was wrong, that no betterment was possible, and that civilization needed to be dug up root and branch like a noxious weed. Rousseau's antisocial vehemence sprang as much from his neurosis, which finally became insanity, as from any objective estimate of the society about him; but it roused a response in minds less tortured but also less intelligent than his own, to inculcate a violence of social and political revolt that was to incite a no less violent reaction; and the path of social progress in France became tortuous and difficult.

Like the Cynics and Cyrenaics of ruined Greece, Rousseau sought refuge from social ills in the ideal of the "natural man," emancipated from all social convention and completely good in his original nature; but where the Greek reformer identified this original nature with reason, Rousseau identified it with feeling or sentiment. This appeal to feeling made him a prophet of romanticism, and one of the forerunners of the later "revolt against reason." Thus Rousseau's social rebellion initially indicted the whole development of civilization, with all of its moral and intellectual outcome. He held up the "noble savage" as the proper ideal of a humanity freed from the corruptions and diseases of civilization. (This ideal was of course a sheer fiction. Primitive or "savage" man is far more bound than are we by tabu and social convention, and the history of civilization is that of a progressive emancipation of the individual; but it was a fiction giving forceful expression to a revolt against moral and intellectual restraint which has moved underneath all later European life, and which finally broke through the surface of moral "convention" to perpetrate the massacres and brutalities of the last three decades.) By replacing the natural and spontaneous relations among men with a wholly artificial structure, Rousseau taught, civilization induces an unhealthy growth in which man grows progressively more corrupt. With his natural sentiments deformed by unhealthy arts, and with his native intelligence destroyed by a cold and artificial intellectualism, man developed an industrial economy which divided society into the wealthy and the poverty-stricken, and then established a tyrannous state which sanctified and perpetuated economic injustice as political "justice." Civilization and the intellect, he concluded, are all our woe, our progress is truly a progressive decay, and health is to be regained only by sweeping out of existence the whole corrupted fabric of civilized society and starting a new growth. Genghis Khan, had he written books, might so have justified his effort to exterminate civilized man.

That there is an element of truth in Rousseau's furious indictment of civilized society we should not deny. Since civilization is an enlargement of the potencies of man, its evils will be more heinous, even as its virtues and goods are greater, than those of a simpler society; and the effort to return to the simplicity and "naturalness" of an earlier day, in spite of the complexities of civilization, is necessary and good. Rousseau is an important source, accordingly, of the naturalism which today presents social and moral ideals as only the spontaneous aims of our deeper or more common human nature. But we should not let this naturalistic truth blind us to the sinister and destructive side of Rousseau, whose naturalism and romanticism were to be a source of Russian nihilism, of the doctrine of class warfare, of European anti-intellectualism, and of the cult of racial supremacy.

The social conception which conditioned Rousseau's political theory is further illustrated in his pedagogical novel *Emile*. The chief means by which civilized society propagates its diseased and decadent forms, Rousseau believed, is formal education, whereby children innately good are debauched and deformed into the corrupt habits and hypocritical morals of their elders. A true pedagogy, he taught, will make its chief purpose the insulation of the child from the society about it. Simply by protecting the child from this corrupt environment, it will provide the conditions of a free, natural, and healthy development realizing the individual potencies of the child. The educator will accordingly avoid all formal instruction, withhold all artificial punishment and reward, exert no moral pressure, and strive only to abet the natural propensities of the child, who needs only this opportunity to reach his full and beneficent development.

Rousseau's *Emile* is the classical and extreme statement of the thesis which is fundamental to "progressive education" to-day. Its attack upon a too formal education, and its concern for the vital development of the individual child, have never ceased to be provocative of educational reform. There is moral and religious significance in its rejection of the doctrine of original sin, a tenet of the Calvinistic faith which originated in Rousseau's birthplace, Geneva. Yet this pedagogical theory, like most of Rousseau's thought, is equivocal. To remove children wholly from adult influence, say by letting them grow up to-gether in the woods, would be to produce something neither animal nor human, and nothing like what Rousseau envisaged as "the natural man." Any and every educational program, whether it be progressive or formal, will provide an environ-ment which is stimulating in some ways and restraining in others, and which will importantly condition the child's de-velopment.

What Rousseau and the progressive educator really pro-pose, therefore, is to study the child as a growing organism, and as a unique individual, and on the basis of this understand-ing to provide stimulation and opportunity adapted to the individual child; and such education may go far beyond that casually provided by the adult society which is the child's en-vironment. A pedagogy of this sort will indeed be more effec-tive, and determine the character and personality of the pupil much more deeply and strongly, than a formal and stereotyped education. Such education requires, of course, a more intimate understanding and closer care of the individual child by the educator, with more effective direction of the child's develop-ment. The result of such education will depend almost wholly upon the character and ideals of the educator. A liberal educa-tor will produce liberals, a revolutionary will produce rebels, and a reactionary will produce reactionaries. The progressive educator is self-deceived, unless he is of the sort that just turns his pupils out to grass, if he thinks of his pupils' development as in some peculiar way a natural growth. He himself, with his character, pedagogy, and ideals, is the most effective director of that growth. But his naturalistic vocabulary may deceive him in his estimate of himself, by hiding from him the moral and religious traditions which molded his own character and outlook. The progressive educator, so far as the writer's experience goes, is usually a man or woman molded by a religious tradition which may have been forgotten or discounted, but which still works in families and individuals and in our larger society, in the moral or spiritual habits of thought which it inculcated.

Rousseau's doctrine of the general will has been presented here as an important source of the absolutistic theory of the state later developed in Europe. This presentation will incur criticism which in some respects is justified. Rousseau is widely regarded by men of liberal leanings as one of the great protagonists of political liberty. The writer earlier shared this view, and still respects it. Unquestionably the writings of Rousseau inspired the French people to revolt against feudal and other oppression. Unquestionably his writings have strengthened such revolt in other lands. There is no question of Rousseau's democratic intention. But today our study of Rousseau may not stop with an appreciation of his attack upon feudal and monarchical absolutism. Our concern today must be to preserve in the libertarian movement itself a liberal character. Much as monarchy saved Europe from feudalism to become a worse tyranny, so the popular government which replaced monarchy may generate new forms of tyranny, if it is not enlightened and controlled by the will to do justice; and this requires insight into justice, widely propagated by true political theory. Rousseau did not provide this theory. His controlling concept of the general will did in historical fact give to the enemies of equalitarian justice just what they needed for their violent defense of political absolutism. Rousseau's concept provided a basis for that "theory of the state" which identifies the state with some larger or smaller part of the people, less than the whole people; and this ascription of absolute moral authority to one part of society, that expressing its "will," necessarily requires the extension to that part of an absolute authority recognizing no limits to government. A group or class so empowered could never be justifiably nor successfully challenged. The town meeting can no longer be our government. The democratic spirit of the town meeting had to be built into the Constitution of the United States, setting limits to government in the interests of individual liberty.

It should be remarked that the political theory of Rousseau has nowhere, neither in France nor elsewhere, supported a stable and healthy democratic society. To affirm that men are basically good is not to affirm that any and every majority is necessarily and absolutely right, so that not to accept its decision is to convict oneself of immorality. If there is a general will, why must it locate itself in a given majority? Why might it not locate itself in an intelligent, specially trained, intensely patriotic, or hereditarily privileged minority? The absolutists seized upon Rousseau's concept, and discovered the general will to reside in aristocratic national tradition (Burke), in a feudal monarchy (Hegel), in racial or national exclusiveness (Fichte), in the sheer will to power (Nietzsche), in imperial ambition (Mussolini), in a divine emperor (Japan), in the proletariat (Marx and Lenin.) The doctrine is just what democracy must and does reject. Constitutional democracy secures the absolute rights of *all* individuals, allowing to government only limited and delegated powers. Political absolutism secures absolute power to some group, ostensibly the vehicle of the "general will," and therefore identified with "the state." For democracy there is no state or states, there are only individuals and their governments.

Notes for Further Reading

1. Hibben, J. G., *Philosophy of the Enlightenment*. New York, Charles Scribner's Sons, 1910.

2. Lévy-Bruhl, L., *A History of Modern Philosophy in France.* La Salle, Ill., The Open Court Publishing Company, 1899.
3. Stephen, L., *History of English Thought in the Eighteenth Century.* New York, G. P. Putnam's Sons, 1876.
4. Sorley, W. R., *History of English Philosophy.* London and New York, Cambridge University Press, 1937.
5. Lange, F. A., *History of Materialism.* New York, Harcourt, Brace and Company, 1925.
6. Macdonald, F., *Studies in the France of Voltaire and Rousseau.* London, T. Fisher Unwin, 1895.
7. Morley of Blackburn, J., *Works.* New York, The Macmillan Company, 1923. Essays on Voltaire, Diderot, Rousseau, etc.
8. ——— *Diderot and the Encyclopedists.* New York, The Macmillan Company, 1897.
9. Rousseau, J.-J., *The Confessions,* pref. E. Wilson. New York, Alfred A. Knopf, 1923.
10. ——— *Emile,* trans. W. H. Payne. New York, Thomas Nelson and Sons, 1909.
11. ——— *The Political Writings of Rousseau,* ed. C. E. Vaughan. New York, The Macmillan Company, 1915.
12. ——— *The Social Contract,* trans. Tozer. London, G. Allen and Unwin, Ltd., 1924.
13. Andrews, C. M., *Famous Utopias.* New York, Tudor Publishing Company, 1937. Includes *The Social Contract.*
14. Gauss, C., *Rousseau: Selections.* Princeton, N. J., Princeton University Press, 1920.
15. Macdonald, F., *Jean-Jacques Rousseau.* New York, G. P. Putnam's Sons, 1906.
16. Rolland, Romain, *The Living Thoughts of Rousseau.* Boston, Longmans, Green and Company, 1939.
17. Hendel, C. W., *Jean-Jacques Rousseau, Moralist.* London and New York, Oxford University Press, 1934.
18. Höffding, H., *Rousseau and His Philosophy,* trans. Richards and Saidla. New Haven, Yale University Press, 1930.
19. Babbitt, I., *Rousseau and Romanticism.* Boston, Houghton Mifflin Company, 1919.
20. Cobban, A., *Rousseau and the Modern State.* London, George Allen and Unwin, Ltd., 1934.

18 KANT: CAN RATIONALISM AND EMPIRICISM BE RECONCILED?

WE HAVE NOW SEEN THE TWO OPPOSED INTER-
pretations of modern science. Descartes and his successors perpetuate the rationalistic interpretation in a modified
and more exacting form. They hold that reason is equipped
with certain absolute principles or concepts which apply un-
failingly and of necessity to every detail of particular fact.
Natural science accordingly is just the continued application
to existent fact of these absolute principles defining the ultimate
structure of the universe. The empiricists, on the contrary, insist that natural knowledge is derived from experience, and
consists of empirical generalizations summarizing observed particular facts. Their criticism of rationalism culminates in
Hume, who concludes that even the best-established principles
of natural science fall short of absolute certainty, and possess
only a high probability as habits of mind determined by past
experience.

It would seem that neither of these opposed views can be
completely discounted. Rationalism failed to explain such
principles as the law of gravitation, which seems to be universal in scope although it is not a self-evident or rational

principle, but is clearly derived from a study of observed facts. Yet the empirical philosophers did less than justice to the rational element in science. After all, the whole of mathematical theory is somehow compounded into physical and other science; and even the most empirical scientist seems to be dogmatic in his insistence that particular facts must conform to *some* theory. It would seem that the senses and reason somehow conspire together to produce theoretical science. Why must nature, which to observation is everywhere individuated in particular fact, always conform in some way to general or universal theory? The animals, living by instinct, may merely expect to find the sort of things they have been conditioned to expect by past experience; but science seems to go beyond such animal expectation, and to require nature to submit to general law and to yield to theoretical analysis. Is reason not active at least in this demand, that nature shall conform to some general hypothesis? And does not this mean that we cannot think about nature without already attributing to nature this most general character of susceptibility to theoretical description? Our task, therefore, is still to show how nature can be particular in all of its observed detail, yet general or universal in its large structure. Empiricism and rationalism must somehow meet.

Among modern thinkers, Kant most honestly desired this reconciliation, most resolutely attempted it, and most nearly achieved it; and, in his mighty effort to comprehend the issues and outcome of human knowledge, he built up a philosophy which is still, many might agree, the supreme intellectual construction of the human mind. This is not to say that Kant succeeded in his attempt, or that his great construction is acceptable today. Kant failed in his compromise and his synthesis because he started from false premises. But because he so clearly saw and so broadly comprehended the fundamental problem of modern thought, Kant remains the greatest mind of this modern age, and perhaps the best introduction to contemporary thought. If we will return to the spirit or intention of Kant, while renouncing his false premises, we shall succeed where he failed. We shall reach a conception at once rational and empirical, able to embrace the largest insights of past philosophy.

Immanuel Kant (1724–1804) lived the uneventful life of a professor at the remote University of Königsberg in northern Prussia. He had some Scottish ancestry, awareness of which may have made him more susceptible to Hume. His family was Pietist, a fervent sect similar to our Quakers. His education was of the very formal, scholastic sort then prevalent in Germany. This education gave him a horrendous vocabulary; but it strengthened his conviction in the integrity of the largest intellectual tradition of western thought, that which came from Greek antiquity.

The philosophy imbibed by Kant in his school education consisted chiefly of a scholasticized version of Leibniz; and it is evident from Kant's *Inaugural Dissertation* that this study had already made him aware of certain difficulties in the rationalistic philosophy. He had learned from Leibniz that the general principles of reason could never disclose anything concerning the location in space and time of a given event. Even if we were to suppose all of the general principles of physical science to be given to us with the reason, these principles would never necessitate the existence of a solar system, with a sun having just this mass and just so many planets. The general laws of matter would never reveal how matter is distributed in space and time. This meant, Kant saw, that all actual knowledge requires experience, and that the world in its concrete content is a contingent world. But it was the study of Hume, Kant tells us himself, that "awoke him from his dogmatic slumber." Kant was the first, and remains one of the few, to grasp the full implication of Hume's criticism; and it was because he comprehended Hume's teaching that he realized its inadequacy as a description of human knowledge, and set himself to correct or supplement it. Out of this effort grew the three great critiques, *The Critique of Pure Reason, The Critique of Practical Reason,* and *The Critique of Judgment,* upon which rests Kant's immortal fame. It is chiefly in the first *Critique* that Kant attempts the reconciliation of rationalism and empiricism. The second *Critique* is a study of man's moral insight; and the third *Critique,* if it had succeeded, would have synthesized science and morality, to reach a metaphysical or religious comprehension of nature and man.

The word *Critique,* retained in the titles of all three major works, shows that Kant conceived his philosophy to be essentially that of the empirical philosophers, who had criticized the scholastic rationalism and later the Cartesian rationalism. In all three works, Kant is bent upon rejecting the dogmatic metaphysics of his continental predecessors. In the first *Critique,* for example, he rejects a "pure reason" which is supposedly aware, independently of experience, of the ultimate plan or design of the universe. He denies the possibility of such "metaphysics" as emphatically as Hume. Yet Kant will not allow, with Hume, that natural knowledge is only a generalization, or a sum of expectancies, induced by past experience. There are, he insists, rational principles of universal scope which quite validly impose themselves upon experience; but these principles, he allows, do not of themselves constitute knowledge of nature. To provide knowledge, they must be complemented by experience. Actual knowledge always involves experience of fact, as well as knowledge of universal principles.

Kant was qualified to speak concerning science. He was a physicist and astronomer of repute, who early advanced the hypothesis that the evolution of the solar system may be explained on purely mechanical assumptions. In his science, moreover, he was wholly committed to the Newtonian physics, which conceived nature to be an assemblage of material particles contingently distributed through space and moving or reacting according to known mechanical laws. Kant did not share the view of the earlier empiricists that scientific method may be applied to human nature, to produce a science of human behavior. In his conception of science, he remained Cartesian and dualistic. There is physical nature, subject to mechanical law; and there is the human mind, which faces and knows a physical nature of which it is no part. Leibniz had written, in a late work critical of the empiricism of Locke: "Yes, everything in the mind is derived from experience—except the intellect itself!" Kant subscribed to this view. The mind is not merely a part of nature. It has its own constitution and its peculiar sort of activity; and this intellectual constitution enters into all our knowledge. Kant's problem was to show how the intellect with its fixed principles combines with the empirical material provided by the senses, in such a way as to do violence to neither element. It is clear, he believed, that the most basic intellectual principles cannot be derived from experience. They are and remain authoritative, and to deny their authority is simply to end in skepticism. Hume might say that there is no necessary causal connection in nature, that a stone flung into the air might just as easily—that is, for aught we know—fly up to the moon as sink to earth. But suppose that just one stone, so flung, did not fall to earth—would not the scientist look for a cause? Would he not reclassify stones into gravitating and nongravitating substances, and persistently seek until he had found the deeper law, or the underlying natural necessity, which rules both? Science affirms causal determination in nature; it does not merely affirm a subjective determination of human expectancies. Science has never had to retract this demand, nor could it retract the demand without committing suicide. Not to require causal connection in nature would be to suppose that anything, or nothing, may cause anything. It was in the interests of empirical science itself, we should see, that Kant took issue with Hume.

So Kant will establish empirical science and philosophy in a new way, one that will not deny the dependence of science upon experience, yet that will leave to science its authority, and show the most basic principles of science to be incumbent upon us. On the one hand stands a dogmatic metaphysics which simply advances its concept of nature as a rational endowment, a sheer intuition into universal being. On the other hand stands the skepticism which holds all knowledge to be just subjective opinion or instinctive feeling. Between the Scylla of dogmatism and the Charybdis of skepticism moves empirical science, requiring nature to disclose its intelligible structure, yet yielding always to the evidence of observable particular fact. How is this science possible? What is its procedure, what are its instrumentalities?

Kant begins his study of this problem by asking what is implied by the inclusion of mathematical theory in all physical knowledge. We saw that the empiricists were always embarrassed by mathematical theory; for it could not be denied either that mathematical principles are self-evident and certain, *i.e.* rational, nor yet that they seem to apply everywhere in nature. From the time of Pythagoras to the present day, the universal applicability of mathematical theory has been the chief evidence for rationalism; for here, in such truths as "four is two pair," is knowledge which seems to be wholly self-evident and also true of fact. And such knowledge is just what is meant by "rational knowledge."

Kant does not simply take for granted, however, this rational yet descriptive character of mathematical science. He attempts to demonstrate it, or to disclose it clearly and incontrovertibly, by showing that mathematical propositions are at once *a priori* and *synthetic*. An *a priori* proposition is one that is necessarily true, and that discloses its truth to rational inspection. An *a posteriori* proposition, on the other hand, is one that depends upon empirical evidence. That two and two are four is *a priori*, since no experience could disprove it, and none is required to prove it. But that gold is heavier than iron is *a posteriori*, since this is the sort of proposition that could be wrong, and is established only by empirical evidence, *i.e.* by observation or experiment.

Mathematical propositions, then, are a priori and rational; but do they constitute real knowledge, or are they, as the empiricists implied, only a knowledge of words or ideas? Kant recognized that there are such purely nominal definitions, merely disclosing what is meant by a word. Thus the sentence "a dog is an animal" is necessarily true, but it is true only because the word "dog" means a certain sort of animal, and what is not an animal could therefore not be called a "dog." Such propositions Kant calls *analytic*, because they only analyze the meanings of words, and do not necessarily tell us anything about the world. "Angels are bodiless spirits" is a perfectly good analytic proposition, because it correctly defines "angels"; but it tells us nothing about the world if we have no empirical evidence that angels exist. If the propositions of mathematics are of this analytic sort, their absoluteness is of little importance, since they need describe nothing in the world. (This was Berkeley's view, and at times Hume's.) But Kant holds mathematical propositions to be *synthetic*. They cannot be reduced to nominal definitions, he says, because they do more than state the meanings of words. The word "triangle," for example, may necessarily mean three intersecting lines; but it does not logically imply that the angles of a triangle sum up to 180°. One might know the meaning of "triangle" without knowing this. Yet everyone believed, when Kant wrote, that a triangle necessarily contains angles to the sum of 180°. Thus Kant reaches his conclusion that the propositions of mathematics are at once a priori and synthetic. They are necessary, certain, absolute, universal in their truth; and yet they constitute a knowledge of fact, *i.e.* of things, and not merely a knowledge of words and their meanings.

How, Kant asks, is such a priori synthetic knowledge possible? How can we have an intuition into the universal, absolute, necessary constitution of the world, such as seems to be provided by mathematical science? We believe that nature must everywhere obey these mathematical necessities, both where we have observed nature and where we have not. Can you conceive of a future, Kant would ask, producing triangles the angles of which do not sum up to 180°? Or of a nature in which five and seven are not twelve? To explain such knowledge, Kant took the only path open to him. These principles, he concluded, are the conditions of any experience of nature, in such sort that we can experience nothing which does not conform to them. *It is the mind which imposes these principles;* and it imposes them upon everything that enters into the mind. Everything that comes into the mind is transformed and organized by the mind itself, which in this way transmutes fragmentary and chaotic sensations into an intelligible design. The mind is like a librarian upon whose desk pours a stream of new volumes of all sorts, and who even in receiving these books catalogues and shelves them according to a preconceived plan. Mathematical science merely makes explicit this plan, which is the very constitution of our mind, so that it enters into every possible experience.

And now Kant proceeds to an exhaustive study of the mind, in order to find out everything he can about this mental constitution that enters of necessity into all experience. He finds three levels of mental organization, those of perception, understanding, and reason. The first level we have already considered, since it is that which organizes sensations into the forms defined by mathematical science. There are two *forms of perception*, Kant says. The first is that of time, which is defined by arithmetic; the other is that of space, defined in geometry. Kant thinks of time as a succession of moments, to distinguish and count which would produce the order of number. These forms of time and space inform all perception of nature. Even animal perception is so informed, although of course animals do not abstract and define these forms, as we do in mathematics. They see numbers, but do not count and name them.

The second level of mind is built upon the first. It produces an order defined in the *categories of the understanding,* such as relationship, causation, substance, etc. These categories play into all our ordinary thinking; but they are most consistently applied in science, which carries further the modes of thinking used in common sense. These constitutional forms should not be thought of as passive or inert. They are the forms of our conscious activity in perception and intellection. They are fixed and definable ways of organizing, ordering, and cataloguing sensations.

But why, and by what right, does the mind organize its sensations first into temporal succession and spatial order, and then into the more complicated and specific spatiotemporal patterns we call "causal processes," "substances," etc.? The librarian, cataloguing his books as they arrive, follows a general plan of some specific sort. He may catalogue them alphabetically, or according to the date of their publication, or by their subject matter, or in some complicated way using all of these orders. What plan does the mind follow? Its ultimate aim, Kant says, is unity, a single all-comprehensive system. Evidently, the sort of pattern that results will be determined in some degree by the sort of sensory material that is to be organized; and we can accordingly specify, in some degree, the sort of pattern that is reached. For example, all of our sensations whatsoever belong in the time-order; but only some of them enter into the space-order, while others do not. Those which are spatially ordered we attribute to external reality; and our effort to organize these into unity is guided by our idea of a completed world. We never actually complete this organization, so that *the world* remains only an ideal, always in the making. Those sensations which cannot be spatialized Kant attributes to our internal reality; and these are organized in view of an idea or ideal of *the self*, which again, of course, is never completed so long as we live. But finally we strive to relate together these two organizations of experience, *the world* and *the self*, in the light of an all-comprehensive ideal, which Kant calls *the Idea of God*. So these three ideals or *Ideas of reason*—the self, the world, and God—are the goals and directives of all thought, and the generators of all knowledge. They comprise the third and highest level of mind, that of reason.

Kant developed this description of mental activity at length and in great detail, because it was his belief that the whole constitution of the mind, which appears again in the structure of all our knowledge, could be clarified and defined in this way once and for all. We will not follow him into this lengthy analysis. To do so would only obscure the large conception of knowledge which is thus elaborated. We have seen the motives and assumptions which determined Kant's "reconstruction of knowledge." They lay in his desire to do justice to the presuppositions of science, which insists upon bringing every particular fact under some general law, and in his conviction that mathematics provides a knowledge which is at once rational (a priori) and descriptive of nature (synthetic). We want to know the largest consequences of his study.

These consequences are of two sorts, positive and negative. If natural knowledge is the product of mental activity, which builds the sensations given to the mind into a great architecture determined by principles constitutive of the mind itself, Kant will have no difficulty in establishing the truth or cogency of natural science. We need not hesitate to assume that the largest structure we attribute to the world will necessarily continue to inform all of our experience. This largest structure, Kant has shown, does not merely comprise a generalization from past experience, as Hume supposed; it constitutes the very form which all experience nesessarily manifests even in becoming experienced. An experience which does not conform to the orders of time and space, for example, could not be even a perception, because perception is composed of sensations so ordered. Similarly, we may be sure that every perceived event will have its determinate causes and effects, and take its place in the physical order revealed by science. Science is established, consequently, upon a solid basis of rational and necessary truth. Its basic categories are beyond dispute.

However, there are important negative consequences flowing from Kant's study. These rational principles are really principles of mental procedure. We cannot change them, because they are constitutive of thought; yet they do not, as they stand, describe anything outside of the mind. They cannot be called "principles of absolute being." They become descriptive only when they are actually applied in the organization of sensory material. Our knowledge stretches, therefore, only as far as our experience extends, or perhaps as far as human experience extends, if we may believe what others have seen. It follows that although the principles are universal and absolute, the knowledge which they produce is not so, because it extends only as far as a limited human experience. "Concepts without percepts are empty, percepts without concepts are blind," wrote Kant in a justly famous phrase.

Kant seems to have reached his objective, which was to reconcile the apparently opposed claims of rationalism and empiricism. The rationalist is correct in his defense of absolute principles, but wrong in his claim to absolute knowledge. The empiricist is right in claiming that knowledge derives from experience, but wrong when he denies absolute principles. The truth is, Kant holds, that we have actual knowledge when the material provided by experience is properly organized by means of absolute principles—and only then. Knowledge is more than a summary of past experience; but it is less than an insight into universal being. Knowledge is the integration of a limited experience in the direction of an ideal of unity which lies beyond experience. If we could integrate all experience, we might achieve this ideal, and know absolute being; but experience is of necessity incomplete—it flows in upon us at every moment in new sensations, nor can we ever intellectually exhaust past experience.

Kant was quite as determined to disestablish metaphysical absolutism as he was to establish empirical science. He spoke of his view as *critical philosophy*, meaning that it was essentially a criticism of the older rationalism, which attributed to the reason a power to intuit the totality of being. Kant allows to the mind a power to impose upon all of its concrete experience a certain structure, namely that which results from its organization of sensations into articulate experience; but because the content of experience is provided by sensations which come to the mind from outside, and which constitute a contingent and unpredictable element in experience and knowledge, the definition of this permanent and rational structure is something less than knowledge of reality. We can be sure that experience will always be temporal, spatial, mathematically ordered, and causally determined; but many sorts of worlds would be compatible with an experience so structured. Only science, therefore, which describes what is actually observed, and not metaphysics, which claims to define the whole of reality, constitutes knowledge.

Kant concludes, as Hume had concluded, that a knowledge dependent upon experience can never comprehend reality, nor reach a final and absolute description of reality. The principles of reason are blank checks until they are given the cash content of particular fact, which is provided by sensations. But Kant goes further than Hume in his critique of rationalism. Hume showed the notion that the principles of reason describe reality to be gratuitous; but Kant seeks to show that it is self-contradictory and therefore positively erroneous. Rationalistic metaphysics refutes itself, he says. To abuse the concepts of reason by supposing them to be descriptive of reality is to abut on certain self-contradictions which Kant called *the antinomies of pure reason*. Reason would compel us to assume that nature

is infinite in time and space, yet also finite; that nature had a
first cause or beginning, yet that every beginning had its earlier
cause; etc. The principles of reason in this way themselves
prohibit or rather protest their abuse. They are regulative principles, not descriptive truths. They work well so long as we
use them in the description of some limited part of nature,
i.e. apply them in the analysis of particular fact. But they collapse when we try to make them the pillars of a knowledge of
absolute, universal being. The reason, as Locke saw, has its
inherent limits. It is the indispensable servant of empirical
science; but it is useless when divorced from experience, as it
is divorced in all metaphysics.

But at this point we must ask: Do we not begin here to
undermine the power or validity of empirical science, as well
as that of rationalistic metaphysics? Should we not suspect that
principles which collapse when we work them too hard are
less than reliable even where they seem to serve well? How do
we know that the regulative, organizing principles of the mind
give us knowledge of reality when we apply them circum-
spectly, in actual experience? We cannot know, Kant replies.
The world that appears to us in perception, and that is described by empirical science, is a *phenomenal* world. It is something we ourselves construct; and since we can never get out of
ourselves, to see the world without looking at it and to know
the world without thinking it, we can never know the relation
of our knowledge to that *noumenal reality* which is reality-in-
itself. We are like a person who is given a few of the
fragmentary words or syllables which, in their totality, compose a story, and who is challenged to reconstruct the story.
We know certain rules of composition, and we do our best; but
there is no one who knows the original story, to tell us how
nearly we are reproducing it. Is our version at all creditable?
Or, dreadful thought, is there no original? Do we compose only
our own dream? Is science *re*construction of the real, or is it
merely a human construction or artifact?

Why not just assume that science is a true reconstruction of physical reality? Is there positive evidence against this? Yes, there are the antinomies of reason. Kant's rationalistic and realistic successors would override these self-contradictions; but Kant was too honest to do so, and to by-pass in this way the incontrovertible analysis of Hume. He was also persuaded by his moral sense, which required him to affirm freedom, that the concept of physical necessity presupposed by science must be something less than ultimate. Science, he concluded, gives us knowledge of phenomena or appearance. Knowledge of ultimate being is something else than science.

So, we see, Kant's reconciliation of rationalism and empiricism and his establishment of empirical science were bought at the price of a rather lowly estimate of science, which Kant will limit to a knowledge of phenomena or appearances. This conception has been called *phenomenalism*, also *positivism*. The reason for the first name is obvious, because "phenomenon" means "appearance." The name "positivism" indicates that although science alone is positive or valid knowledge, yet science reaches something less than a description of reality-in-itself. Science discovers the true pattern of phenomena; it allows us to describe, calculate, and predict what we experience; but it cannot claim to describe a world lying outside of experience. We do not penetrate in our science through appearance to reality.

This phenomenalistic or positivistic conception of science seems plausible at first sight, and it has satisfied many; yet it will not withstand steady inspection. Why should we claim more than a knowledge of phenomena? We may not know what real fire is, but we do know the phenomenon or appearance of fire; we know that this phenomenon is apt to be followed by certain disastrous phenomena like second-degree burns or gutted homes—and so we hasten to put the fire out. What more should we desire than this knowledge of phenomenal uniformities? But notice, *it is the real fire we put out*, not the phenomenal fire merely. The appearance of fire we could extinguish merely by closing our eyes or moving elsewhere. Thus we move in a real world, we act upon real things, yet we see and know only appearances! And what is more, we know the difference between extinguishing the fire itself, and removing its appearance! Somehow, therefore, we do distinguish between phenomena and noumena; and this involves knowledge of both. The positivistic doctrine, moreover, becomes immoral when it is applied to living organisms. We must believe that a dog's yelp indicates real pain in the dog, not merely the phenomenon in our minds. We must believe that our sympathy helps a real person to forget a real sorrow. As Kant will recognize in his study of morality, moral insight must penetrate through appearance and reach reality, if moral judgments are to be valid. But moral judgments are conditioned by factual judgments, and are valid only if these are true.

We may conclude, perhaps, that Kant's study of knowledge reveals its own failure by thus issuing in phenomenalism. We may not buy our faith in science at so high a price. But Kant's study is valuable even in its failure. It has revealed to what degree science is an elaborate edifice, constructed by the mind. Kant, following the empiricists, has invalidated the old naive realism which took knowledge to be a direct reflection of an external reality in the eye or mind. Further, he has shown that the effort to retain universal rational principles, at least if we accept also the empirical view that natural knowledge comes from experience, leads to a new sort of skepticism, namely phenomenalism. It would seem that any regulative principle which is imposed by the mind upon experience, and which introduces into experience its own structure, must have this outcome. To avoid this skeptical outcome, we would need regulative principles which merely open the mind to what lies outside of the mind. To see, we must open our eyes. To know, we must open our minds. What would such principles be, requiring us to open eyes and mind?

It is interesting to compare Kant's view with the views of his two great predecessors, Plato and Descartes. In Platonism, reason is held to intuit ideal forms which regulate and inform all the processes of nature. For Kant, the ideals of reason, or *Ideas*, are objects or objectives posited by the mind; they regulate and inform cognition, but we may not attribute to them any power over nature outside of the mind. This leaves nature without intrinsic value, if indeed we can speak of "nature" at all. Yet Kant never relinquishes his faith in a reality external to the mind. This reality is for him still the source of our sensations; it provides all the material which is informed by mind. In this devaluation of nature, as in the absolute estimate of mathematical physical science which required it, Kant resembles Descartes. He might be said to have compounded the Platonic idealism with the Cartesian dualism; but the result is almost a mentalism, affirming mind to be the creator of all articulate form.

What did Kant mean by "mind"? Evidently not the individual mind. He takes science, the creation of many minds, to be the chief manifestation of mental activity. His *Critique* is not a study in empirical psychology, generalizing from individual behavior. Did he mean the mind of man? Yet he speaks in his nebular hypothesis of the evolution of the solar system from an elementary matter, before man was; and he inclined to an evolutionary conception in respect to the organic species of nature. He did not mean literally, therefore, that the physical world became organized only when the mind of man arose to organize it. Mind is for Kant, it would seem, a sort of Absolute, coeval with nature; yet to say this, of course, is to violate Kant's prohibition of metaphysics. Thus, some sort of absolute external reality providing sensations, and also some sort of absolute mind, are presupposed by Kant's view, although he explicitly prohibits such presuppositions. The problem left by the Cartesian dualism, that of the relation of matter to mind,

reappears in the Kantian dualism of phenomenon and noumenon, appearance and reality.

These difficulties or inadequacies in the Kantian philosophy
were apparent in Kant's day, not least to Kant himself; but
they were inescapable then, and for long afterwards. Once we
suppose that certain principles, for instance those of mathematics, are at once absolute or rational and necessarily descriptive of the world, we are caught in Kant's dilemma and impelled toward Kant's conclusions. *The great value of Kant's
philosophy is first to have clearly defined, in its definition of
a priori synthetic propositions, the essential core of rationalism; and then to have shown the inevitable consequences of
rationalism, in phenomenalism or positivism.* No one has shed
so much light upon the intellectual process, with its rational
and empirical elements and their relationship, as did Kant.

But today this foundation of a priori synthetic knowledge,
upon which Kant established his whole study, no longer exists.
Within the twentieth century, advances in logic, mathematics,
and physical science have shifted the weight of evidence against
Kant's basic premise stating that the propositions of mathematics are a priori yet synthetic. Physicists now treat geometrical theories as physical hypotheses, modifying them as required by the observed facts; and this means that geometrical
propositions are synthetic or descriptive of fact, but not absolute nor a priori. Logicians, on the other hand, have shown that
the axioms of arithmetic may be regarded as analytic propositions which merely define the uses or meanings of symbols.
Thus *the evidence today no longer supports the premises upon
which Kant's study was based.* When Kant wrote, all extant
evidence supported his belief in the existence of a priori synthetic propositions. Today, if this belief is not conclusively
falsified, it is at least shown to be dubious and precarious. This
shift of evidence in Kant's disfavor does not imply that Kant
was mistaken in his acknowledgment of a rational element in

science, nor that he was ill-advised in attempting to define this
element and to appreciate its working and consequence. But it
does mean that we cannot accept Kant's definition and estimate
of the rational element, and that the problem needs to be
attacked and solved anew. We will return to this problem in
our concluding chapters.

Kant lived into the nineteenth century, and he was a widely
read man, sensitive to the cultural movements of his time; yet
he remained in his basic philosophical outlook identified with
the early eighteenth century, or even the seventeenth. His
basic outlook was not, we saw, very different from that of
Descartes, who so radically separated the mind from physical
reality. Kant could not or would not sympathize with the
efforts of Hume and others to extend the methods of empirical
science in empirical studies of human behavior and social fact.
He did not believe (and herein lay his power) that the human
individual who knows and judges nature is merely a part of
nature. He was willing, therefore, that nature should be defined
in purely mechanical terms. He accepted the science of Newton as definitive; and he therefore regarded the descriptions
of the biologist, for example, as only preparatory to a more
incisive and authentic description of organic processes in physical terms. The study of moral man, on the other hand, he
regarded as no part of empirical science. Nature, he allowed,
is everywhere bound by causal necessity; but man, he believed,
is free. In his second great work, the *Critique of Moral Judgment*, he turned his extraordinary analytical powers upon man.

In this ethical study, Kant was even more critical of moral
absolutism than he had been of absolute metaphysical theory in
the first *Critique*. In his study of science, he did arrive at certain absolute principles, although he strictly limited the application of these to observed fact; but he finds no corresponding set of moral axioms. He therefore concludes that there
exists no rational moral science—a most revolutionary conclusion, because everyone, except Hume and his utilitarian dis-

ciples, had believed in absolute moral principles. Kant finds no
a priori and synthetic moral truths, corresponding to those of
mathematics in science. Because he had established all scientific
knowledge upon this basis of a priori and synthetic principles,
he is compelled to deny the possibility of every sort of moral
science, even or especially an empirical moral science such as
the utilitarians pursued.

What then is moral insight, if there is neither a rational
science establishing absolute moral principles, nor an empirical
science deriving moral knowledge from experience? Is moral
judgment arbitrary and irrational? No, Kant replies; it is, on
the contrary, the only sort of judgment that might be called
absolute and wholly rational. Moral judgment, Kant believes,
penetrates through the curtain of phenomena which veils us
from reality-in-itself, and really grasps, in full and naked immediacy, its noumenal object in reality. Kant is recognizing here
that although we may fail to describe ultimate being in conceptual formulas, we are ourselves real and ultimate in our
movement and conduct. Correct moral judgment is therefore
right conduct, intelligent practice. An act is right, Kant believes, if it is motivated wholly by good will; and in our conscience we have awareness of our motives. We cannot see into
other hearts, and know their motives; and so we do well not to
judge others' conduct. When we are motivated by good will,
Kant implies, we have true insight into the individual situation
upon which we act. Conscience is a sort of knowledge; but
because it is an individual awareness of a unique particular
situation, it does not provide general principles nor moral
theories. What has been prescribed as general precept and
moral code, Kant says, truly amounts only to a classification of
the material situations in which the moral drama plays. We may
speak of cases of honesty or dishonesty, kindness or cruelty,
etc. But what makes an act honest or dishonest, kind or
cruel, is its activation of an individual moral insight which is
never duplicated. The noumenal reality which appears in the

moral act, Kant seems to mean, is so completely individuated that it baffles analysis and escapes classification. In his moral teaching, Kant is a nominalist.

Yet, strangely enough, Kant's rejection of moral science itself constitutes a sort of moral doctrine and allows the statement of certain universal principles. The moral individual is absolute, noumenal, real; his conscience is his true being; the phenomenal world is a stage for the moral drama which alone is real and substantial. Influenced presumably by his pietistic upbringing, Kant gives to us the starkest, most protestant, and most otherworldly ethics in the annals of philosophy. No book, no code, no church, no priest, no law, no state, not even God himself may be supposed to mediate between an individual and his conscience, or between the individual and his fellows. Yet this uncompromising moral individualism does not issue in moral isolationism; and it consequently generates certain universal principles. It allows an ultimacy of being and value to the moral individual, *i.e.* to the individual defined as the seat of moral judgment and of moral or immoral choice. But there are many such individuals, each possessed of ultimate and inalienable value; and this fact imposes upon each individual certain principles of conduct. We should act, Kant concludes, in such a way that we might wish our act to be a law henceforth for all mankind. We should strive, that is to say, to be exemplary. We should deal with our neighbor as we would have all men dealt with and as we would be dealt by. We should never use a person as a means to an end, but always as an end in himself. We should see in other persons moral beings, like and equal to ourselves. These are only different ways of expressing one and the same truth; and it is a universal truth. Kant calls this truth the "*categorical imperative,*" meaning that it is what must bring all acts and situations into the moral category and under moral judgment. It is the law that there shall be law in human behavior. It is the fact that we live as members of a society composed of free responsible moral beings.

Kant's moral doctrine has been much debated since he presented it to the world, some accusing it of being empty, others proceeding to infer from it a whole code of moral precepts. In the writer's opinion, such debate is today out of place. Kant's formulation of moral doctrine was based upon the conclusions of the first *Critique*; and these conclusions required the absolute separation of judgments of fact from moral judgments. But we no longer accept the assumptions, and therefore we escape the conclusions, of the first *Critique*. However, Kant's doctrine is far from being empty. It presupposes a plurality of persons or human individuals, each an end or ultimate value in himself, and each possessed of individual rights and of responsibility for all other individuals. It is, in short, the moral theory of Locke, upon which was established democratic society; and the writer confesses that he has found no other doctrine upon which democratic justice can be established.

It is in truth a metaphysical doctrine, affirming that human beings are ultimate, irreducible, plural, and individual—or it would be a metaphysical doctrine, if this irreducibly individualistic pattern of human nature were extended to all of nature and made universal.

If Kant's ethical doctrine provides the indispensable foundation of democratic practice, Kant's political theory falls short of what we might reasonably expect from him. It is true that he explicitly locates moral responsibility in the individual, and denies that the state has an intrinsic value and authority; yet these explicit statements are prejudiced by the admission that the state is a necessary condition of moral conduct and individual freedom. This view would ultimately compel us to allow to the state an unquestionable and absolute authority. This conception, we have seen, goes back to Rousseau and Hobbes, who also conceived the state to be the necessary source of all morality. It is not consistent with the Kantian ethics, which defines the human individual as a moral being, independent of any political organization. Truer to his ethical insight is

Kant's teaching on the ideal of international peace and the conditions of its realization. It is illogical, he writes, to hope for international justice among states which do not practice domestic justice. How should a state which oppresses its own subjects act justly in its intercourse with other peoples and their governments? Our quest for world peace is really a pursuit of justice throughout the world. The condition of world amity is the establishment everywhere of democratic government. Kant asks that history should be written so as to show how all human progress has been the movement toward this ideal of universal justice. We should know from our own experience, if not from Kant, how intimately and effectively the foreign policies of a government are conditioned by the internal policies maintaining that government in power; and we should not look for honest dealings from tyrants.

The first and the second *Critiques* shed light upon each other and are really complementary. Reality, we now perceive Kant to mean, is not the waste of physical motion portrayed by a science limited to the description of "phenomena." Reality is a concourse of spiritual beings, of absolute moral individuals. The phenomenal world is the object of our intellectual judgment; the noumenal world is the medium of moral behavior. Kant has taken important steps toward the voluntaristic and skeptical anti-intellectualism which moved under the surface of the nineteenth century, to explode into open and terrible violence in the twentieth century. Kant was probably not aware of this largest tendency of his thought, because his initial purpose was the salvaging of the intellectual heritage of the past. His whole purpose was to establish the authority of science in matters of fact, and the authority of moral insight, or conscience, in matters of conduct. Yet each purpose prejudices the other. A science which portrays nature as a physical mechanism has no moral significance, and therefore has to be deprecated as only phenomenal; and a moral judgment which is allowed to make no use of the intellectual categories of science becomes ineffable, and can express itself only in action. Knowing and doing must proceed in different worlds. Science and morality face opposite ways.

Kant, it seemed, had wholly sundered science and morality. Yet in his first *Critique*, Kant had taught that our knowledge of the world and our knowledge of the self should ultimately be brought together in a comprehensive synthesis of experience, under the regulation of the Idea of God. In his third and last *Critique* he attempted this synthesis.

The *Critique of Judgment* should have been the crown of Kant's philosophical study and the keystone of his great architectonic; but it was in fact a supreme and tragic failure. All of its great enterprises tail off into negative conclusions. Kant pays in this book the full price of the errors of the earlier *Critiques*. And yet, through this explicit failure, there shines like a great promise the suggestion of what the book would have been if it had succeeded. Here, as always, Kant's genius lay in his grasp of the speculative problem and the right approach to it, and not in his attempted solution of it; and in this third *Critique*, the problem attacked is the last, most ultimate of all problems, namely the relation of human life with its effort, its conscience, and its consciousness, to the world environing and generating that life.

Let us first appreciate the *Critique of Judgment* in its grand plan; and only then consider why the vast projection failed! The book proposed what seemed impossible, a synthesis of the first two *Critiques* bringing together the two domains of scientific and moral cognition, which had there been defined in such a way as to exclude each other. With the simplicity characteristic of genius, Kant points out that the only likeness between a scientific judgment and a moral judgment is that both are judgments. If we knew, therefore, what is involved in any act of judgment even as such, we should have a clue to the connection between science and morality. What, he asks, are the presuppositions of any and every judgment?

A scientific judgment brings some particular thing, event, or situation under some law. "That," we say, "is an instance of gravitation, or of catalysis, or of the law of diminishing returns." Similarly a moral judgment brings a particular act under the moral law. "That," we say, "was right," or "that is what ought to be done." The particular thus brought under a law must possess some quality or character, allowing it to become subject to judgment. This character cannot be provided by the mind, because it is what instructs the mind to lay hold on that particular. For example, we do not in science call just anything a particular instance of law. Three crows in an oak tree together with a cow in a barn do not comprise an instance of anything. Nature or experience falls into natural unities, like a crow, an oak tree, a cow, a star, a storm; and such unities are presupposed by all analysis, and even by all perception and reaction. Things catch and hold our attention in virtue of some character intrinsic to themselves; and this intrinsic character belongs to things prior to and independently of the informing action of the mind. If a particular may be barely apprehended in this way, before we have brought it under any law, this apprehension comprises a rudimentary kind of cognition, telling us of the presence of particulars or individuals. Kant speaks of this faculty as *aesthetic* apprehension, to distinguish it from cognition proper. There is an aesthetic faculty of mind, corresponding to aesthetic character in experience or nature.

The aesthetic faculty may be active to such an extent that we speak of the character apprehended by it as "beautiful." "Beauty" is unusually impressive aesthetic quality; but all our experience, Kant means, has some aesthetic character, positive or negative. We feel such character to be objective and real, although we might be hard put to it to convince another by argument of its presence. The music which enchants you may have no charm for me. Kant proceeds to a study of aesthetic character. He distinguishes the merely beautiful from the sublime; and in works of art, he distinguishes talent from genius and technical facility from aesthetic insight.

What more can one say concerning this character of aesthetic value or beauty? What is its claim upon us? It does not incite, but rather discourages, intellectual analysis and formal classification. We feel that the beautiful object is consummate, that it fulfils itself and beggars description. It makes and meets a claim, it realizes a need which is not ours but its own. All beauty, Kant concludes, is apprehension of some realization of individual being. We love the thing for its own sake, not for our sake. This quality of beauty, this mark of individual self-realization, seems to be wholly objective and independent of our minds.

At the root of all judgment whatsoever lies this aesthetic apprehension of objective individual being; and presumably all science and all morality, in their movements to comprehend experience and enrich judgment, do no more than integrate or synthesize this basic and primary aesthetic aspect of reality. Nor does there seem any limit within experience to this aesthetic quality. Nature is beautiful in our widest perception of it, for example in the night sky with its illimitable distances. Does all scientific and moral conprehension of fact only formulate our aesthetic apprehension of reality? Can we say that nature at large realizes itself, and thus manifests purpose and aim? Do science and moral insight conjoin, to reach this final insight into a reality which in its largest design, even as in its most particular detail, reveals a single purposive intelligence? This would indeed make science and morality consummate, by showing them to be respectively the theory and the practice of a religious apprehension of universal being.

This is the sort of synthesis that is suggested in the third *Critique*; but the plan is not carried out, because at each step some obstacle arises to prevent its advance. Thus Kant will not allow cognitive status to aesthetic insight, because he finds no a priori aesthetic principles regulating aesthetic judgment. We feel that the quality of beauty is independent and objective, that it is imposed upon us and not imposed by us, so that everyone must acknowledge its presence; but since there are no a priori synthetic principles in this field, we can state no necessity compelling judgment. We cannot argue about beauty. So Kant concludes that in spite of, or even just because of, the peculiarly external and objective character of aesthetic quality —just because it determines us and not we it—we cannot attribute finality to aesthetic quality. Consequently he deals with aesthetics narrowly, as a faculty exercised in art but not in science and morality; and so he perpetuates the error of a protestant culture which first proscribed beauty, and then, when it relented somewhat, acknowledged beauty only furtively, and sought it in a suspect and amoral art. Nor could he, of course, establish principles of aesthetic judgment even in the sphere of art. Our concepts of beauty, he says, are merely intellectual stereotypes without aesthetic content. We may debate whether the play *Hamlet* is well put together, because technique is an intellectual faculty adapting means to end; but we may not debate whether *Hamlet* is a work of genius. The domains of beauty, of truth, and of goodness, it would seem, are all reciprocally exclusive.

Nor will Kant allow that our aesthetic appreciation of natural beauty, which does seem to argue a realization of individual purpose in the individual thing, supports any conception of larger purpose in nature. Here, he says, we must be faithful to mechanistic science, which requires everything that happens to be mechanically predetermined, and precludes all teleological explanation, *i.e.* the explanation of events in terms of their later outcomes. This prohibits the ascription of purposiveness to nature. Kant admitted that the biologist requires purposive concepts, as well as mechanistic concepts, in his descriptions of organic activities; but he held such concepts to fall short of scientific rigor. Nor will he accept the view that nature, although a mechanism, may serve a cosmic purpose much as a mechanical clock serves the purpose of its maker. We have no right, he says, reverting to the arguments of the first *Critique*, to make statements about a completed universe, since experience is but fragmentary. If nature provides the conditions of human life, it is no less true that man helps to provide the conditions of plant and animal life. Kant concludes that the apparent beauty and the seeming purposiveness of nature are no argument for religion. Religion stands or falls as a necessary presupposition of moral conduct. Because virtue evidently receives no reward on earth, Kant means, belief in God and immortality is required to make moral effort reasonable. No rational establishment of religion is possible. Religion has no intellectual defense, no relation to science, none to art.

Two motives influenced Kant in this destructive third *Critique*, which suggests a rational conception of religion only in order to invalidate that conception. One motive was his desire to leave absolute authority to moral judgment, which he feared would be weakened by any dependence upon aesthetic or even religious presuppositions. The other was his inability to conceive of a science not identified with mechanistic physics, or to modify in any way the assumption and conclusions of his first *Critique*. The first and third *Critiques* do in fact collide head on, in such wise that the insight of the one precludes that of the other. The first *Critique* was concerned to establish universal principles supporting science; and to do this, Kant was compelled to deal with particular character as a mere filling or content, wholly subjected to and articulated by these principles. The third *Critique* aimed, however, to explain the relation between particular character and these universal forms of judgment; and this required some appreciation of particular character as such, in itself. Kant recognized the ubiquity of particular character in experience, and the aesthetic faculty by means of which we immediately apprehend it; but he could not develop this empirical theme, nor allow particular character to mold the principles and shape the larger concepts of natural knowledge, without sacrificing the rationalism of the first *Critique*. He preferred, therefore, to close again the doors which he had opened, and to return to the phenomenalism from which his enterprise had promised escape. We who are not bound by the presuppositions of the first *Critique* may follow to their full consequence the fruitful suggestions of the third *Critique*.

The *Critique of Judgment*, if it had fulfilled its aim, would have synthesized science, morality, and art in a religious appreciation of the world and man. It would have shown science to be moral, morality to be intelligent and scientific, art to be truly a medium of intellectual and moral cognition; and it would have compounded all of these activities within an intelligent and progressive faith. We are aware today that the failure to bring science into creative interaction with moral and practical life is the greatest failure of our civilization and the source of its deepest ills. The failure of the third *Critique*, therefore, is of much more than academic or historical importance, if it reveals to us the cause, at first sight strangely remote, of our failure to reach mental and moral integrity. The cause lies in the strain or tension, which reappears in every field of human activity, between the material of experience which we call particular fact and the larger designs of cognition and action which arise with thought or reason. This tension, misunderstood or mismanaged, easily becomes disruption, and results in intellectual chaos and social conflict. Particular fact and universal theory have each their rights. When general principles override particular fact, we get a sterile and dogmatic rationalism, which in its practical applications is absolutistic and overbearing. When particularity is allowed to discredit faith in general knowledge, we get an intellectual skepticism which has its practical consequences in social and political chaos.

We shall consider, in our final chapters, how Kant's great effort to reconcile the empirical and the rational elements in human thought may today be brought to a successful conclusion. But between Kant and ourselves lies a century of social and intellectual development which has rather radically reoriented thought. We must know something of this recent history if we are to understand the contemporary mind. In reviewing this history, we should not forget that behind it there still stands the great issue, which we have followed since the beginning of our study, between those rational and empirical tendencies of mind which in their composition are creative thought, and in their disruption intellectual and moral skepticism. Kant's problem still remains, essentially as he stated it in his three immortal works. One may "get around Kant," as some contemporary philosophers advise—but only to return by some detour to this crucial nexus of intellectual life, which Kant faced so squarely, and which he failed to untie only because of his fidelity to what seemed at that time the undeniable fact that natural science stands upon a rational system of absolute mathematical knowledge.

Notes for Further Reading

1. Kant, I., *The Critique of Pure Reason*, trans. J. M. D. Meiklejohn, M. Müller, N. K. Smith. New York, The Macmillan Company, 1914.

2. —————— *Prolegomena to Metaphysics*, ed. P. Carus. La Salle, Ill., The Open Court Publishing Company, 1902.

3. —————— "The Critique of Practical Reason," *Theory of Ethics*, trans. T. K. Abbott. Boston, Longmans, Green and Company, 1898.

4. —————— *The Critique of Judgment*, trans. J. H. Bernard. New York, The Macmillan Company, 1931. Trans. J. C. Meredith. London and New York, The Oxford University Press, 1911, 1928.

5. —————— *The Inaugural Dissertation, etc.*, trans. J. Handyside. La Salle, Ill., The Open Court Publishing Company, 1929.

6. —————— *Perpetual Peace*, trans. M. C. Smith. New York, The Macmillan Company, 1917.

7. Greene, T. M., *Kant: Selections*. New York, Charles Scribner's Sons, 1929.
8. Smith, N. K., *A Commentary to Kant's Critique of Pure Reason*. New York, The Macmillan Company, 1918, 1923.
9. Lindsay, A. D., *Kant*. New York, E. P. Dutton and Company, 1934.
10. Broad, C. D., *Five Types of Ethical Theory*. London and New York, Cambridge University Press, 1934.
11. Garnett, C. B., *The Kantian Philosophy of Space*. New York, Columbia University Press, 1939.

There are other studies of Kant in English by Adamson, Caird, Clark, Fischer, Green, Lovejoy (in *Essays in Honor of William James*, Cambridge, Harvard University Press, 1936), Paton, Paulsen, Prichard, Royce (in *The Spirit of Modern Philosophy*, Boston, Houghton Mifflin Company, 1899), Sidgwick, Wallace, Ward, Watson, Weir, Wenley, etc.

19 DIALECTICAL IDEALISM

WE CONSIDER IN THIS CHAPTER THE THOUGHT OF Hegel, and so take up issues which are very much alive today, when they are the subject of controversy which has moved from the lecture hall to the field of battle. From Kant, as from Socrates in antiquity, radiated movements in several directions, sometimes diametrically opposed. The most important of these movements, viewed in the perspective of today, is that which culminated in the dialectical philosophies of Hegel and Marx.

To understand dialectical philosophy in its historical sources, we must turn to a passage of Kant's *Critique of Pure Reason* entitled "transcendental dialectic." Here Kant warns against the abuse of a priori principles. These principles are properly used empirically, *i.e.* in the organization by the scientist of perceptual experience or observed fact; and apart from this use, they are empty and describe nothing. Kant believed that when these organizing principles are taken to be descriptive in themselves, independently of factual content, they lead to self-contradictions and absurdities. For example, logical principles are indispensable to the construction of intelligible hypotheses, descriptive of natural processes; but we must not suppose that the rules of logic constitute of themselves, prior to their applications to fact, a description of nature. To assume that they do would be to issue in the absurdities revealed by Kant in his "transcendental dialectic."

What is dialectic? Before Plato, the word "dialectic" signified just logical debate, detecting and removing logical fallacies in argument. Plato gave the word a special use. He called "dialectic" the ascent of the thinker from mathematical principles to higher metaphysical truths, leading to an intuition of the eternal Unity which transcends all difference and change. This would be a "transcendental dialectic." Aristotle returned the word to its earlier use; and during the Middle Ages "dialectic" continued to mean the study and detection of logical fallacies. Kant combined both uses when he chose the word to designate the study of those fallacies which, he believed, follow from Plato's proposal to leap by sheer thought, without the help of experience, from the regulative principles of reason to still higher transcendent truths.

In this way, the word "dialectic" might mean any study of principles or concepts as such, in their logical or other relations with one another. The empirical scientist studies the relations of principles and concepts to observable fact, seeking to determine their truth or falsity; the dialectician would study the relations of principles and concepts amongst themselves. Dialectical study of this sort is an important part of logic. The scientist also, of course, may concern himself with the logical or "dialectical" relations of concepts used in his field. The mathematical physicist, as distinct from the experimental physicist, is concerned wholly with such conceptual relations, so that he is primarily a logician. Logical analysis is the business of every thinker whatsoever, not only of the professed logician or philosopher.

But the followers of Kant, starting with Fichte, elaborated by means of "dialectic" a system of concepts peculiarly their own and claiming to cover the entire field of human knowledge. Dialectical philosophy usually refers to the conceptual system elaborated by these post-Kantians.

The chief propounders of this dialectic were Fichte, Schelling, Hegel, and Marx. We will shorten our discussion by considering only very summarily the first two of these men. *Fichte* appropriated the Kantian vocabulary so thoroughly that an early essay was mistaken by the printer for a work of Kant, and published as such. The degree to which Fichte appropriated the thought of Kant is at least debatable. He distinguishes science which is merely empirical, and which he equates with materialistic philosophy, from a dialectical "science" which he called *Wissenschaftslehre* (theory of knowledge). The *Wissenschaftslehre* presents an idealistic metaphysics discounting the material world as only phenomenal or illusory. The illusion is projected by the Self or Will (the "transcendental Ego"), as the condition of moral or spiritual activity. The will is said to project "matter" in order to have something to work on. When the moral will slackens, this phenomenal projection of the Self hardens into a material world, ruled by mechanical inertia and reducing those who believe in it to slavery. Our duty is to throw off this illusion of mechanical necessity, and to liberate the true Self, creative in moral activity. According to the manner of man you are, Fichte said, you will choose between a mechanical science which enslaves you and the *Wissenschaftslehre* which enfranchises the creative Self. Fichte was also the ardent patriot whose *Addresses to the German Nation* helped to arouse Germany to resist the invader Napoleon. He assured the German people of their cultural unity and of their mission to spread this superior culture through the world. As a means to national unity, he advocated "the closed economic state." Fichte's exaggerated nationalism may be excused as a reply to foreign invasion; but there is no doubt of the historical continuity between his teaching and the national socialism of Nazi Germany.

Schelling was the philosophical spokesman of the literary romanticism current in his time. He follows Fichte's dialectic, but he sees the transcendental Ego unfold itself in the creations of poetic genius, rather than in the activity of the moral will. Organic nature, and even physical nature, he says, are the more primitive manifestations of that creative urge which comes to full self-consciousness in poetic genius. Nature is art or artist.

We have dealt cursorily with these thinkers because what is of lasting importance in their thought was given incomparably clearer statement by *Georg Wilhelm Friedrich Hegel* (1770–1831), whom we must acknowledge today, in the light of his consequence for subsequent history, to have been the leading philosopher of his time. Directly, or indirectly through Marx and others whom he influenced, Hegel has importantly shaped the course of later political and intellectual history.

Our brief mention of Fichte and Schelling said nothing about their dialectical method. Although Kant explicitly condemned metaphysics, with its effort to mount to ultimate truths by purely logical analysis, unchecked by observation or "experience," a great deal of his own work is undeniably a logical exercise of this kind. He proposed to systematize, exhaustively and forever, the eternal categories of the human reason; and he attempted this by means of a reflective study of knowledge which did not merely advance probable hypotheses, but claimed to reach absolute and final conclusions. Whether one calls the system of concepts reached by such reflection "a system of metaphysics," or "epistemology," or "logic," is perhaps a verbal matter. Kant would not call it metaphysics, because he insisted that the question whether this conceptual system truly depicts external reality must remain unanswered. Such a system, however, would have all the authority claimed for metaphysics, because it would define forever the anatomy of human knowledge, and determine forever the limits of human thought.

Kant's successors rejected his equivocal stand on the metaphysical issue. They advanced the idealistic thesis that the most basic principles of reason, presenting the constitution of the mind, must of necessity be taken to define the objective structure of reality. This thesis is not improperly named "Objective Idealism," because it claims that all the objects we know are mental constructs. Kant's logical or dialectical analysis of the mind and its concepts was thus converted into a rationalistic metaphysics, claiming to discover by purely logical and non-empirical study—by a sort of intellectual introspection or "reflection"—the ultimate Being which is universal reality. The post-Kantian dialecticians variously modify and develop Kant's analysis of the categories of thought. Dialectical philosophy is a new, more extreme and more powerful form of the rationalism which claims that final, absolute, and universal knowledge is the achievement of an intellectual intuition, going beyond a merely empirical science which is able to advance only to probable hypothesis. Dialectical philosophy is a return to the rationalism of Plato, without his dualistic reservations.

To evaluate justly this powerful modern rationalism, one must consider the following facts. First, conceptual analysis of this logical sort is indispensable to every science, because science rightly seeks to bring into theoretical unity its diverse hypotheses. Only one science, physics, has as yet explicitly acknowledged this responsibility. The mathematical physicist is the "dialectician" who seeks to systematize the special hypotheses advanced by experimental physicists. It is all-important to observe, however, that the mathematical physicist does not ascribe finality to his comprehensive formulations. He recognizes their tentative or hypothetical character; and he expects the experimental physicists to apply his theory to observable fact, and to confirm or disprove it by this empirical test. This is a proper use of logic or dialectic. It leaves logic within science, subject to the empirical method of science to which it is auxiliary. Every science might do well to follow physics in this division of labor between experimental scientists and logical analysts.

Secondly, we must acknowledge a place for the thinker, whether we call him a scientist or a philosopher, who attempts a synthesis of all the sciences. This is properly a responsibility of science, because it calls for the qualifications of a scientist. The post-Kantian dialecticians, not themselves scientists and usually contemptuous of science, could usurp this responsibility only because scientists ignored it. Their contempt of science was not altogether unwarranted, so long as scientists evaded this responsibility for large synthesis.

Thirdly, we must see that a scientific synthesis of the sciences will necessarily differ from and thus "transcend" the limited conceptualization peculiar to special fields. Large and bold speculation is scientifically legitimate; nor will science make important progress without it. All hypothesis is speculative; and dialectical philosophers will always rush in where over-timid scientific angels fear to tread.

Fourthly, there is little question that dialectical philosophy correctly anticipated the large conception which alone can implement such a synthesis of the sciences. This is the conception of natural evolution. The dialecticians were not evolutionists—Hegel was contemptuous of evolutionary hypothesis. Nevertheless, their dialectic anticipated evolutionary explanation, and in some measure did service for it.

So far, we have presented dialectical philosophy as a pseudo-science, professing and anticipating a synthesis of science which only competent scientists will achieve. But finally we must do justice to the dialecticians for their philosophical integrity. They preserved faith in a truth peculiarly philosophical, a truth which science universally acknowledges and applies, but which no scientific hypothesis—not even that last hypothesis which would comprehend all hypothesis—can explicitly state. This philosophical truth is a presupposition, not itself an empirical hypothesis because it cannot be specifically confirmed or disproved, which conditions all scientific hypothesis whatsoever. It is the postulate that real being is identical with individual being. This philosophical truth is today well established, as will be shown in the concluding chapters of this book. Dialectical philosophy substituted for this truth the rationalistic error: Real being is universal being. We shall show how this error generates the confusion of mind which is dialectical philosophy. But we stress here that the dialecticians were justified in their pursuit of a truth transcending empirical hypothesis. There is indeed the absolute and final truth which supports and justifies all scientific hypothesis. There is scientific faith; and this needs philosophical establishment.

And now, after having appreciated these justifiable motives of the dialecticians, we must be rather severely critical. Fundamental to their systems is the false presumption that a reflective and merely conceptual analysis, unchecked by experience, can disclose the complete anatomy of universal nature. To reach their large definitions of universal structure, they simply borrowed the concepts of science current in their day, and wove these into a verbal pattern. They ignored or abused logic, pretending that their dialectic constituted a superlogic. The dialectic, they said, discovers necessary synthetic propositions, where ordinary logic discovers only analytic propositions. This dialectical "logic," using its "infallible rational intuition," is supposed to generate all scientific concepts in their true order, and to reach an absolute, all-comprehensive, and completely rigorous system of knowledge. This claim was really discredited by the dialecticians themselves; for their "dialectical logic" and "rational intuition" disclosed to different philosophers different systems, shaped to their personal predilections.

The Hegelian system still remains the superlative example of dialectical construction. Hegel despised Fichte and Schelling for the slovenliness of their analysis; and he certainly produced a far more closely knit and impressive architectonic. He starts with the blank concept of *Being*. Reflection upon this concept, he says, generates its opposite concept, *Nonbeing*. Tension between these opposite concepts then generates their synthesis in a third concept, that of *Becoming*. This concept *Becoming* is now made the subject of reflection; and it is found to imply its opposite or antithesis in *Quality*; and the tension between *Becoming* and *Quality* generates the synthesis of these two concepts, which is the concept of *Unity*. In this way Hegel proceeds, impelled by what he says is a logical or dialectical compulsion, to generate, clarify, and order the fundamental concepts first of mathematics, next of the physical and biological sciences, then of political and moral science, and finally of philosophy itself. There is no question that this Hegelian reconstruction contains many a shrewd perception of logical and psychological relationship; but no Hegelian living today, it is safe to say, would maintain that the system provides a last conspectus of human knowledge. It is too obvious that the system only reorders the concepts of eighteenth-century science. If dialectical philosophy is to persist, it must undergo continuous reformulation, keeping pace with the progress of scientific hypothesis. Such reformulation would require the thinker to be fully abreast with every science at once, which seems impossible.

What would the Hegelian of today find permanent, and seek to preserve, in the thought of Hegel? He would probably insist, with Hegel, that reflection upon science and its procedure does elicit a rational truth which is of another sort than scientific hypothesis itself. We shall see, as already intimated, that this claim may be allowed. He might also retain, if he does not subscribe to the dialectical materialism inaugurated by Marx, the large idealistic framework of the Hegelian dialectic. In the final stages of the dialectical procession of concepts, there appear the largest concepts of philosophy. These, Hegel says, constitute a final synthesis of all that has gone before. In this philosophical synthesis, Being is revealed to be Absolute Mind. This Mind has gradually unfolded its real but implicit content in all of the stages of physical and organic being; it comes to provisional consciousness in human intelligence; and its final and complete realization is philosophical understanding. Fichte identified ultimate reality with will; Schelling identified it with aesthetic insight; now Hegel identifies it with intellectual process. In his vast dialectic, Hegel tried to give meaning and plausibility to the idealistic thesis which states that reality is Mind. His philosophy has remained the chief resource of idealistic metaphysics.

The contemporary thinker may also return to certain Hegelian insights which are broader than the dialectical system, and perhaps independent of it. Some would say that Hegel's greatest work is not his *Logic*, presenting the dialectic, but the epistemology presented in his *Phenomenology of Mind*, which is a sort of preface to his more systematic writing. This is indeed a brilliant critique of the Kantian philosophy, and possibly the most brilliant defense in any literature of rationalistic doctrine.

It was necessary for any German thinker who did not identify himself with Kant to meet and overcome the Kantian critique of rationalism. We saw that Kant accepted the empirical teaching that descriptive knowledge derives wholly from experience, that he allowed to the pure reason only the task of ordering sensations entering the mind from outside, and that this sharp dualism of sensational material and rational order finally drove him to a skeptical positivism, limiting science to a knowledge of phenomena and allowing no claim to an intellectual grasp of "reality in itself." In the *Phenomenology*, Hegel criticizes Kant's absolute separation of sensation and concept. The "sense-manifold" of Kant, he shows, is unthinkable, and evaporates into nothing when subjected to scrutiny. The relation between sense-experience and knowledge is not just the relation of chaotic material to articulate conception. Perception itself is already perfectly articulate. Content void of form is as meaningless as form void of content.

The difference between sensations and thought, Hegel suggests, is one of degree rather than kind. Animal perception is superficial, in that there only a narrow range of experience determines the quality and character of what is perceived. But the objects of human perception are more full and rich, in virtue of the larger experience which suffuses and shapes them. Finally, to the philosophical and reflective mind, there is possible a perception which is to ordinary human perception what this latter is to animal perception. In philosophical intuition, the object of perception becomes something absolute and universal. It is informed with the whole of experience, so that it becomes nothing less than the universe itself, as this appears and exists in the perceived object. Says Hegel in a magnificent affirmation: *"The Real appears."* Such an object, replete with all experience and informative of universal Being, he calls a "concrete universal."

Kant was therefore mistaken, Hegel concludes, when he distinguished the phenomenal world which is open to inspection from a noumenal reality which lies beyond sense, and which is inaccessible consequently to every sort of intellectual cognition. The noumenal reality appears in the phenomena. There is only the real world, at once phenomenon and noumenon. Even in perception we know absolute reality; but we comprehend it, according to our intellectual stature, in larger or smaller volume.

A contemporary school or movement known as *Phenomenology* develops this direction of thought; but many contemporary realists are more or less conscious exponents of this realistic Hegelian thesis. If the foregoing paragraphs reproduce in some degree the thought of the *Phenomenology*, the reader will understand the power which Hegel has exerted over thinkers able and willing to grasp his thought. In Hegel, the rationalistic mysticism of Heraclitus, Pythagoras, and Parmenides is masterfully restated, in such a way as to meet the attacks upon it of Locke, Hume, and Kant. Shall we subscribe to the power of that thought or succumb to its plausibility? Let us insist, for the moment, that science apparently cannot subscribe to it! The scientist must still separate his conception, *i.e.* his theory or hypothesis, from the particular sensed material which suggests and confirms his thought. How else could particular sensed fact confirm or disprove hypothesis? The scientist, moreover, must esteem sensed fact even more highly than he esteems the most comprehensive hypothesis; for otherwise the observed fact could not, as it does, overtopple the great theory which collides with it. Our question becomes: Is there a rational knowledge transcending science? This question we shall answer affirmatively, but not in Hegel's sense—there is no rational knowledge of the universe, comprehended in its eternal design.

We have not yet mentioned a certain aspect of dialectical philosophy which is what gives to this movement its present hold over the public mind. The modern intellect is now passing through a great metamorphosis, a change so profound, and in its symptoms so critical, that we may wonder whether the crisis will be successfully endured. We may indicate the nature of this change by saying that it is the transition from a spatial to a temporal orientation upon fact. The development of evolutionary science, and also perhaps the physical theory of relativity, give some indication of this profound reorientation of thought; and the popular appeal of dialectical philosophy is due to the popular assumption, partly correct but partly mistaken, that dialectical philosophy is an evolutionary doctrine, depicting the course of nature as it has evolved in historical time. We shall not be able to deal at length with this question here—that would require a separate volume; but we must stress the equivocal character of the dialectic, in its presentation of an "evolution" which at once is and is not a temporal progress. The dialectic requires us to conceive of an "evolution" which is fully completed, yet which eternally goes on.

Fichte, Schelling, and Hegel all make use of the word "evolution"; and Schelling often reads like a post-Darwinian who accepts the evolutionary hypothesis. The dialectic itself is easily mistaken for a summary account of evolution, because it seems to show how the forms of physical fact emerge from earlier forms, and in their turn generate the organic forms designated by biological and psychological concepts. These dialecticians began to write at the turn of the nineteenth century, when the evidence for the hypothesis of evolution was becoming irresistible, and when the idea of evolution was everywhere just below the surface of explicit thought. But the dialecticians did not mean to affirm, rather they meant to reject, the hypothesis of a temporal or historical emergence of inorganic forms and living species. They did not mean what we mean by "evolution"—they did not mean that the dialectic discloses the historical sequence of emergent physical, organic, and social forms. What did they mean? Hegel, explicitly rejecting all evolutionary hypothesis, certainly conceived the dialectical procession to proceed eternally, in all its parts coeval. The dialectical necessity which directs the movement from thesis, through antithesis, to synthesis is certainly postulated as a logical necessity, similar to implication. It does not constitute a causal necessity, holding between earlier and later events.

To clarify completely the pseudo-concept of dialectical necessity would require an analysis showing how rationalistic philosophy perpetuates a profound confusion of mind with respect to two relationships, namely, the relation of logical implication and the relation of causal connection. The former relation is timeless, whereas causal connection is essentially a temporal relation. The concept of dialectical necessity was intended to evade the demonstration of Hume that the clear distinction of these two relations deprives rationalism of its whole basis, which lies in their confusion. But the effect of the dialectic, although it advances no causal hypothesis, is nevertheless to suggest an evolution of the world in time. The dialectic moves "by necessity" from simpler to more complex forms of being, and suggests a serial emergence of inorganic, organic, and human nature. One might in fact regard dialectical philosophy as an impossible and disingenuous effort to affirm evolution implicitly, even while denying it explicitly. We are asked to conceive of nature "as if" nature had evolved, even while denying its evolution. Reality, says the dialectician, can be understood only as a process of evolution; yet because the evolution is that of a timeless thought or reason, it is not a temporal nor an historical evolution. The evolution must be supposed eternally completed and eternally self-sustaining. The evolutionary process does not newly create, it only re-stores what eternally is. The dialectic really restates Neoplatonic philosophy; and it compels us to face the question whether nature is in fact an eternal re-creation of this sort, or a temporal creation still generating new species. If Darwin was right, and if species originate in time, the dialectic has no basis in fact. (It might be still defended, perhaps, on the curious supposition that animals and men always existed somewhere, on other planets or worlds, before they emerged on earth.)

But, in the writings of the dialecticians, this disingenuous "evolutionism" seems to lose its equivocal character when the last stages of dialectic, which deal with human society, are reached. In his social dialectic, Hegel drops the pretense of eternalism, and boldly outlines in dialectical terms the historical development of human government. He understands by human progress the long pursuit and achievement of liberty, which he defines as the perfect adjustment of the individual and the state. This part of the dialectic is given separate treatment, in a work frankly entitled *Philosophy of History*; and it was this social application which interested the general public, and which led to large appropriation of Hegel's thought. Hegel sketches at considerable length the rise of the state, in the form of an absolute despotism such as that of ancient China; and he follows its dialectical progress through Hindu anarchy, oriental empire, the Greek and Roman republics, Roman empire, medieval anarchy, feudal organization, modern monarchy, and modern republicanism. Despotism and anarchy are conceived to be the limiting extremes of a zigzag progress, from despotic thesis through anarchistic antithesis to liberal synthesis, which approaches ever more closely to an identity of individual and state rights. The individual is said to achieve true realization in the degree to which his activity is a service to the state. Hegel taught that the republicanism of the Enlightenment, most clearly manifested in France, was too extreme a reaction to the thesis of monarchy; and he looked to Germany to provide a true political synthesis, in a mixed form of government preserving monarchical and aristocratic privileges along with some popular franchise.

As the years passed, this social or historical dialectic became the most important and influential part of Hegel's thought, pushing his larger system into the background. This was inevitable. First, the interpretation of social history was of interest and importance to everyone. The dialectical method claimed to provide, at long last, what modern society had sought since Bacon and Descartes—a rational science of man. But also, the dialectic seemed in its social teaching to be frankly evolutionary, progressive, creationistic; for one could scarcely suppose Hegel to mean that the procession of governments from ancient China to contemporary France and Germany had all existed simultaneously or coevally. Here Hegel seemed to advocate a temporal progress of man; and the inconsistency of this view with his dialectical eternalism went unnoticed. Finally, Hegel's assumption that political form has been the determinative factor in social history gave expression to the deepest conviction of western society. From its beginnings, western society has been characterized by its pursuit of justice, and by its appropriation and use of political power in the interests of human well-being. With these largest aspects of Hegel's philosophy of history many of us will be wholly sympathetic.

Few, however, will accept the specific conclusions of his

dialectical interpretation of history. We will not agree that the individual finds his whole self-realization in the exercise of his functions as a national citizen. We will not agree that the state has a "reality" equal or superior to that of the individual, nor that the state should have absolute control of education, religion, and every cultural exercise. We will not accept the totalitarian principles, nor the state-worship, which are implicit in Hegel's political theory. Nor will we accept one very large implication of this political interpretation of history, namely that human progress has been advanced exclusively or even primarily through war. Hegel teaches that the cosmic mechanism, by which the succession of dominant cultures generates itself, is that of civic dissension and militant conquest. In spite of his idealistic homage to Absolute Mind or Spirit, Hegel presents the evolution of human society in terms which make of it a very militaristic, material, and unspiritual pursuit of power.

It is unfortunate that so gifted an intellect should have been circumstanced and conditioned as was that of Hegel. Hegel looked to Prussia to unify Germany, and to support the new German nation against the pressure of its European neighbors. He became thereby, in spite of his liberal inclinations, the chief intellectual spokesman of the reactionary movement which followed the debacle of the French revolution. The totalitarian "theory of the state," by which Hegel intended to make the unity and security of Germany the controlling objective of every German and the ruling principle of German life, did in fact guide Germany through several aggressive wars and to enormous power; but the final issue of this teaching is political collapse and moral ruin. Unfortunately, the extreme nationalism which engenders, and which is again fostered by, this "theory of the state" has spread to every people. The immediate intention of the Hegelian political realism is to support unjust privilege, by attributing to those actually in political control, the de facto government, a mystical identity with the "spirit" of the people and a sanctified power.

This reactionary Hegelianism had its own dialectical compulsion (for there is indeed dialectic error, every half-truth suggesting its "dialectical" contrary). It engendered its inevitable antithesis in the dialectical materialism of Marx and his followers; and to this doctrine, both on account of its philosophical importance and because of its tremendous role in contemporary political history, we next turn.

But we should not let Hegel's rationalistic and moral limitations blind us to the largest intention of his idealistic thesis. After we have discounted his political conservatism and his dialectical abuse of logic, his system remains one of the great affirmations of the power and destiny of intellectual man. The dialectic is majestic in its account of the march of that Absolute Being which is Mind through mathematical labyrinths and physical and chemical tortuosities, over organic hills and dales, by social and historical advance and decline to its apotheosis in modern man, self-conscious and reflective and politically creative of his future. Perhaps this is the vision of Lucifer, the angel who fell from heaven; and perhaps, in the ruin and humiliation of the greater Germany he helped to shape, we see the fall of that proud spirit, avid of absolute rule. But, even so, we must give the devil his due. Vision it was, able to incite a people to such struggle as the world had not seen. And even in its large error, it helps to clarify and secure a larger Truth. Corrected, chastened, and redirected, the idealism of Hegel may yet conquer.

Notes for Further Reading

1. Fichte, J. G., *Addresses to the German Nation*, trans. R. F. Jones and G. H. Trumbull. La Salle, Ill., The Open Court Publishing Company, 1922.

2. ——— *The Vocation of Man*, trans. W. Smith. La Salle, Ill., The Open Court Publishing Company, 1925.

   (The two works above are also included in *German Classics*, Vol. V. New York, G. E. Steckert and Company.)

3. —— *The Science of Ethics,* trans. A. E. Kroeger. London, K. Paul, Trench, Trüber and Company, 1897.

There are studies of Fichte in English by Adamson, Everett, Thompson, Talbot, Royce (in *The Spirit of Modern Philosophy,* Boston, Houghton Mifflin Company, 1899), and Pringle-Pattison (in *From Kant to Hegel,* listed below).

4. Mead, G. H., *Movements of Thought in the Nineteenth Century.* Chicago, Chicago University Press, 1936.

5. Pringle-Pattison, A. S., *From Kant to Hegel.* New York, G. E. Steckert and Company, 1924.

6. Hegel, G. W. F., *Phenomenology of Mind,* trans. J. B. Baillie. New York, The Macmillan Company, 1931.

7. —— *Science of Logic,* trans. W. H. Johnston and L. G. Struthers. New York, The Macmillan Company, 1929.

8. —— *Logic of World and Idea,* trans. Macran. London and New York, Oxford University Press, 1929.

9. —— "Logic and Philosophy of Mind," trans. W. Wallace, *Encyclopedia of the Philosophical Sciences.* London and New York, Oxford University Press, 1892.

10. —— *Introduction to the Philosophy of Fine Art,* trans. B. Bosanquet. New York, Harcourt, Brace and Company, 1921.

11. —— *Philosophy of History,* trans. J. Sibree. New York, Colonial Press, 1902.

12. Loewenberg, J., *Hegel: Selections.* New York, Charles Scribner's Sons, 1929.

13. Mure, G. R. C., *An Introduction to Hegel.* London and New York, Oxford University Press, 1940.

14. Stace, W. Y., *The Philosophy of Hegel.* New York, The Macmillan Company, 1924.

15. Croce, B., *What is Living and Dead in the Philosophy of Hegel,* trans. D. Ainslee. London, The Macmillan Company, 1915.

There are also studies in English of the Hegelian metaphysics and epistemology by J. M. E. McTaggart and H. A. Pritchard.

16. Hobhouse, L. T., *The Metaphysical Theory of the State.* New York, The Macmillan Company, 1918.

17. Foster, M. B., *The Political Philosophies of Plato and Hegel.* London and New York, Oxford University Press, 1935.

18. Reyburn, H. A., *The Ethical Theory of Hegel.* London and New York, Oxford University Press, 1922.
19. Cooper, R., *The Logical Influence of Hegel on Marx.* Seattle, University of Washington, 1925.
20. Hook, S., *From Hegel to Marx.* New York, Reynal and Hitchcock, Inc., 1936.
21. Marcuse, H., *Reason and Revolution.* London and New York, Oxford University Press, 1941.

20   DIALECTICAL MATERIALISM

IT IS PERHAPS A GOOD SIGN, INDICATING A GROWING realism, that the contemporary mind entertains in dialectical philosophy a faith which, although it proceeds from rationalistic premises, nevertheless submits itself in the end to the test of empirical fact. The dialectic claims to show a necessary sequence in social history, a fatalistic direction discernible in past history and dominating of necessity the movement from present to future. This is to give to philosophy the role of prophecy, and to make the power to predict our final criterion of truth. One cannot consider dialectical philosophies purely academically, without reference to the social history which they claim to describe and foresee. This is the way society did, does, and must go, says the dialectician; and we are challenged to look and see whether it is in actual fact the way society goes.

The Hegelian dialectic took the national state to be the organ of social progress. For the impetus of progress, it looked idealistically to the intelligence of a people, effective in its intellectual elite. When we speak of history, we usually mean political history; and Hegel only conformed to orthodox opinion when he made the state the agency of social progress, this being the implicit assumption of most historians prior to Hegel and of many since. Can history be written except politically, in terms of nations and empires, their rise and fall?

The Marxist reads history very differently. He overrides national boundaries. He sees in governments and international conflicts only local accidents symptomatic of very broad movements of economic change—as if governments were in literal fact "ships of state," but ships helplessly adrift on currents they cannot influence, much less control. The political historiography of the past becomes for the Marxist a meaningless chronology; but it is one which can be made significant, he says, if it is taken as an index to the economic forces and the real economic movements of the past. For him, governments and political or intellectual elites are only the passive vehicles of social economic forces, which raise these groups to power and again demote them. The forces which govern political history in this way are conceived to be blind forces, working whether men sleep or wake. This is a startling and unorthodox view, and at first sight it seems a terrible one; yet no one who has read Marxist literature intelligently, and taken thought, will ever again be satisfied with a merely political history, nor see in wars merely the collision of national ambitions. Neither the Hegelian nor the Marxist dialectic is true; both are false. Yet each contains some truth; neither is wholly false.

The economic interpretation of history followed the merely political interpretation; and this suggests that it may be the more discerning. The Marxist has at his disposal all that the political historian has written; but in addition he has the insight of Marx into economic power and its political consequences. This is true; but at the same time we should perceive the deep contradiction which arises the moment we make this Marxist reading of history the sole basis of our understanding of past and present occurrence, or the guide of our future program. Just because we are now explicitly aware, chiefly through Marx, of the economic forces which shape political events, we are able to control in some degree the economic forces themselves. If economic fact determines political fact, we can determine what in our society shall be economic fact. We can regulate the national economy by means of political action; and this is to invert the Marxist view, and to revert to the Hegelian position. And now we perceive that political leadership was never so unaware of the Marxist truth that it omitted to secure some large control of the national economy. Throughout all history, governments have existed primarily for this purpose. Do not Marxists agree that any government which fails to do this is on the way out? The simple truth is that "the nation" is a political-economic system. The science of government is neither political history nor economic science, but political economy. What the Marxist correctly perceives is that the economic organization of society has increasingly overborne national boundaries, until it is no longer subject to political control. There grew up a new and large economy which today is world-wide. Our present convulsions are the effort to bring this larger economy under political control. Economic change gives rise to new political problems; but the solution of these problems is the creation of political institutions bringing economic change under new control. Economic activities condition political activities; and the result of political activity is to recondition economy.

We need, accordingly, a new social science, one that can appropriate both of the two half-truths which respectively support the Hegelian and Marxist dialectics. This science must, of course, undercut the error which is the dialectical method itself. Dialectical philosophy violates the first principle of science, which is the requirement of *causal* explanation. The dialectic, we said, arises out of the confusion of causal connection with logical implication. This is really a confusion of fact with language—the very confusion which the nominalistic founders of empirical science hoped to eradicate.

Our initial purpose here must be to do intellectual and moral justice to the Marxist philosophy of dialectical materialism. We

should distinguish Marx from Marxism; and in Marx himself
we should distinguish Marx the social scientist from Marx the
dialectical philosopher and social reformer. *Karl Marx* (1818–
1883) stands today alongside of Darwin as one of the two
outstanding figures in nineteenth-century science. As a philosopher, he must be rated a poor successor to Hegel. His place
as social reformer, however, is unquestionably higher.

Marx revolutionized social and historical science by compelling the scientist to attend to the economic factors working
in social history. He was not original in this emphasis. In the
sixteenth century Thomas More, the leader of parliamentary
opposition to Tudor absolutism who was beheaded for his
refusal to acknowledge Henry VIII as head of the church, had
published a communistic *Utopia.* In the late seventeenth century John Locke had made patent the dependence of self-
government upon popular control of taxation and of the national economy; and Harrington, a most influential writer in
his time but since forgotten, had shown that the form of government depends upon the distribution of property, and that
republicanism requires a wide distribution of the national
wealth. In the eighteenth century Rousseau magnified and
distorted this theme, when he taught that government originated in the successful effort of those who first seized property to entail their booty. Early in the nineteenth century the
French liberals who were disillusioned by the failure of the
French revolution turned to Saint-Simon and Proudhon for a
deeper social analysis, looking below the political surface to
the economic factors which determine political history; and
it is there, in the political disillusionment of post-Napoleonic
France, that we find the sources of the state socialism or communism of the later nineteenth century. But it was Marx who
made use of this thesis, stating that the political history of a
people must be understood in relation to its economic development—of which it is in high degree an effect—a scientific
hypothesis capable of large confirmation, and henceforth ob-

ligatory upon the social scientist. Very much as Darwin transformed all biological science by establishing it upon an evolutionary basis, very much as Newton established physical science upon universal laws of motion, so Marx inaugurated an empirical social science when he multiplied evidence of the casual connections relating social institutions to the social economy which conditions them.

There is some controversy today as to whether Marx himself was an "economic determinist" of the radical sort, who sees in all political and ideological fact only the manifestation of economic process. Neither party to the controversy has difficulty in finding passages in the writings of Marx to support its view. Neither party is mistaken, because Marx the social scientist was not an "economic determinist," whereas Marx the dialectical philosopher of necessity was this. Marx frequently and emphatically states the intelligible and true thesis that economic conditions constitute the most ubiquitous, constant, and dominant factor in social history, *causally working upon* the other political and ideological factors. Writing as a social scientist, Marx takes causation seriously and offers a truly scientific hypothesis. The economic factor could not be a causal factor, it would have nothing to work upon, if there did not exist in society other relatively independent factors in political and other institutions. But when Marx is writing as a dialectician he foregoes causal explanation in order to indulge in dialectical or "logical" explanation; and now the economic pattern becomes not merely the essential and dominant factor which it in fact is, but the constitutive and substantial Being of society, manifesting itself indifferently in economic, political, ideological and other forms. Here we relinquish the causal analysis of science, in order to pursue rationalistic metaphysics with its pseudological explanations.

If we reflect upon this contrast of Marx the scientist with Marx the rationalist, we shall discover the radical confusion of mind which generated dialectical philosophy, and which still paralyzes human thought today in many fields. Consider society just as it exists at a given time, taking it out of all historical context! It should be possible and it is possible to analyze this complex social process, discovering causal relations among its particular parts, and reaching causal generalizations which may be synthesized into a broad social hypothesis, providing an authentic social theory. This theory could then be applied to society at other times and places, and the result would be a continuous enlargement and betterment of the theory. Such social theory is a legitimate and proper objective of social science. It would allow us to describe society at any place and time in terms of our most general knowledge of society, much as physical theory allows us to describe any physical occurrence in terms of constants which appear in all physical occurrence. It would do this by attending only to the uniformities which are observable in social occurrence. It would present any and every social phenomenon as a variant manifestation of one and the same social pattern, namely, that defined by the social theory. It would not be interested in social variation as such; it would be interested in social change only insofar as this change manifests social constants or "laws." The historian might be interested in presenting a succession of social epochs or periods, each of which would manifest in its particular way the unchanging social pattern defined by the social theorist. The theorist would not be interested in this history, except insofar as it revealed to him new constants, variously present in every society and epoch. If he discovered in it uniformities hitherto overlooked, he would enlarge his theory to include these. In this way he would approach an ever more comprehensive description of social structure, as this exists always and everywhere in every society.

Now we must acknowledge that a comprehensive social theory of this sort has not yet been achieved. There are many cogent social generalizations, there are some well-established social hypotheses; but there is as yet no comprehensive and authoritative social theory comparable with physical theory. It is because of this paucity of established social theory that we have recourse to social history; for we correctly conclude that the course of history provided by the responsible historian indicates causal processes which the theorist has not yet elucidated and defined. Social scientists are at present divided into two groups, one of sociologists devoted to social theory, and one of historians seeking to enlarge history. What we need today is greater cooperation between social theorists and social historians. This cooperation will scarcely be smooth and fruitful without clear understanding of the relationship between social theory and social history. Should sociology swallow up historical science, the historian becoming a collector of historical data useful to the social theorist? Or is history an independent study, proceeding without the help of theoretical guidance, and providing real knowledge of social process in spite of its nontheoretical character?

The distinction between social history and social theory lies in their respective uses of causal explanation. Both provide causal explanation; but the theorist explains the causal sequence of events as the manifestation of some known general principle, whereas the historian discovers causal connections to exist among particular events, whether or not the causal sequence illustrates some general principle. We meet here once again the ancient question which divides the rationalist and the empiricist: Do general laws actually *cause* particular events to emerge as they do? Or is all causation particular causation, the so-called "laws" being only our summaries of many observed particular causations? Be it observed that there is no quarrel between the theorist and the historian on this point. Both agree, as all scientists today agree, that "causation" means particular causation, and that generalization only discovers similarities among particular causal sequences. There is no "law" which necessitates particulars to be what they are and to act as they do. But the theorist is interested in particular events insofar as they repeat familiar sequences, defined or definable; whereas the historian is primarily interested in the historical chain of particular causal sequence. Social science, whether it be theoretical or historical, is today empirical in its adherence to the principle of particular causation, which has stood unquestioned by scientists since Newton. The particular earth gravitates to the particular sun *according to* the principle of gravitation, but not as an effect of the principle of gravitation. The principle does not effect anything; it is not a factor in the formula which it states.

Now the dialectician is a rationalist, who proposes to reinstate the principle of universal necessity—as distinct from particular causation—in a new form. The earlier rationalists had conceived the "universe" to necessitate the particular in all of its character, so that each and every particular only "manifests" the "universe" at that place and time. The new dialectical rationalist still conceives the "universe" to determine utterly the particular; but he now conceives the "universe" not to be eternal in space, but as extended in something like time, so that it proceeds as a whole through a necessary "dialectical" evolution. For him, consequently, it is the historian, rather than the theorist, who has insight into universal causation; and just as the old rationalists claimed to possess in *theoretical* intuition a faculty defining the absolute and eternal *structure* of the universe (something far transcending the tentative hypotheses of theoretical science), so the dialectician now claims to possess in his *historical* intuition an absolute and authoritative knowledge of universal history (something far transcending the tentative histories advanced by the geologist, the biologist, and the social historian). "Dialectical science" is just historical rationalism rejecting empirical history, exactly as the earlier rationalism was theoretical rationalism rejecting empirical theory. The dialectic, it becomes clear, is a confusion of eternal structure with moving evolution.

One may reject dialectical method, yet still accept the historical hypothesis advanced by Marx, describing how the economic processes of medieval and modern society did in fact help to determine political and other history. We may distinguish Marx the scientist from Marx the dialectician, and judge his tremendous historical hypothesis impartially, taking it out of rationalistic polemics into empirical science, where it can be confirmed or disproved by factual evidence.

Marx took his communistic principles from post-Napoleonic France. His reading of European history was influenced by his long sojourn in industrialized England. But he was still conditioned in his thought by his earlier life in Germany; and as his thought matured, it took a form directly antithetical, and therefore in its largest character similar, to that of Hegel. Marx, it must never be forgotten, was a Hegelian. Hegel had conceived history to be a drama centered in the political evolution of government; and Marx never really rejects this political orientation. But Hegel had conceived only of a national state controlled by a privileged intellectual elite and advancing by way of national expansion; and this political orthodoxy had made him the spokesman of world-wide reaction against the universalistic principles of republicanism. Marx challenged this intellectual Goliath; and to defeat Hegel on his own ground he accepted Hegel's dialectical premises and also his political orientation, diverging in order to place the ultimate controls of political history in the people instead of in a privileged elite. This was the primary aim, we may perhaps agree, of the Marxist doctrine. Marx wished to show that it is the actual labor of the worker in the field or the shop, something he called the "mode of production," that finally dominates all economic, political, and intellectual life.

The rationalist, like the Aristotelian philosopher, must radically distinguish the essential form of a thing from the nonessential matter which it informs. The essential form of a thing is ultimately the universe working in that thing, and controlling its development and destiny. For Hegel, the essence or form of society is its governing elite, and the people at large are the matter of society which "realizes" itself only through its subservience to that government. Rousseau had attempted a rationalistic defense of liberty by locating the "essence" of society in the general will, identified with a political majority. Marx defines this "general will" more precisely by identifying it with the working class, which in an industrialized society constitutes the "proletariat." This would imply that the laboring class of society is always its true "essence," and that privileged minorities have really existed to serve the laboring class and to be shaped by its demands. This statement belies the facts. It is the sad truth, and the truth which Marx most intended to emphasize, that past history is the story of exploitation by privileged and powerful minorities. We need scarcely document this thesis.

But Marx confuses the issue by moving from political to economic fact. The whole structure of society with all of its institutions, he shows, is rooted in its economic structure as this is determined by the mode of production of material goods. He distinguishes three stages of economic evolution: the agricultural, the commercial, and the industrial. He shows first how the mode of production conditions all political and social occurrence; and second, how each mode of production moves to and issues in the next, so that the whole social structure is successively transformed. This is the social "dialectic."

This is excellent social analysis, so excellent that after all criticism is done, Marx has claim to undying fame; but just because it is excellent description of social process, it neither seeks nor establishes any moral conclusion. Is an agricultural society inferior to or less happy than a commercialized society, or the latter inferior to or less happy than an industrialized society? This is a question of fact; and the answer will vary as we observe different societies of each sort. However, if life be good, its multiplication is a good. Let us agree that this evolution from agricultural to industrialized society supports an increase of population, and that this is good. We must still observe that the mode of production, although it may condition every social institution, is only one of many factors. Czarist Russia with its serfdom, early New England with its freehold farms, and the colonial South with its slave plantations were all agricultural societies; yet how different their political patterns! Twentieth-century Russia, Germany, and the United States are all industrialized; yet how different their governments! Marx confused the fact that economic activities *condition* political activities with the supposition that economic form (the dominant mode of production) *determines* political form (the constitution of a society). This supposition cannot be defended. Liberty and tyranny are both possible in every society, whatever its economic mode of production. Economic progress does not necessarily entail political progress.

Marx was misled by the old fallacy of a *necessary* human progress. This fallacy is a rationalistic misstatement of the truth that there has in fact been much human progress, both economic and political. Economic progress is increased economic efficiency, which may be measured by the weight of product produced by one hour of human labor. This mightily increases as we move from agricultural to industrial society. There has been great economic progress. Political progress should be measured by the degree to which each and every individual participates in government, thus securing due control both of his individual economy and of the political economy. There has also been political progress. But there is no *necessary* relation between economic progress and political progress, nor is there any *necessary* progress of any sort. Russia by political means advances the economic progress of its vast domain, Germany by political means would have kept much of Europe agricultural. It is very clear to the discerning historian that the history of modern civilization is primarily the story of how economic and political progress have stimulated each other, and how failures of political progress have retarded economic progress. Political inertia is the cause of economic backwardness. Economic progress may suggest, but does not itself produce, political progress. It seems rather evident that the primary determinants of modern political-economic history are to be found in science and religion. Science has provided the means to economic progress; but only those Protestant peoples who emancipated religious faith moved to the creation of political institutions which allowed the unhindered development of economic resources. Is it not unwarranted, in view of three centuries of political-economic stagnation in all of the non-Protestant world, to suppose that national economies just grow like Topsy, and produce of themselves their political counterparts and conditions? Is it not evident that authoritarian religion everywhere imposes upon society a quasi-feudal form of government, and seeks to perpetuate such government by preventing economic change? Must we not conclude that man must progress on all fronts, economically, politically, scientifically, and morally, if he is to progress at all?

There is no true dialectic because there is for human society neither necessary progress nor necessary decline. Nothing is necessitated in this way. Simply to discover in past history a fatal decline or direction is to be empowered to overcome that decline and change that direction. The dialectic is morally blasphemous in its subscription to fatality, which is the denial of freedom. In the eighteenth century, when science might seem to depict a world ruled by mechanical necessity, this rationalistic blasphemy was perhaps excusable. If the human individual were in dread fact wholly subject to a universal physical necessity, then we would need to look like Hegel to some imagined necessity incorporated in human history and able to meet, absorb, and transcend that physical necessity. Or, if we could not stomach Hegel's dismissal of science and scientific method, we might turn to the dialectical materialism which tries to see in physical necessity itself a god in disguise, taking Protean shape in biological, psychological, sociological, or other necessity. But in the twentieth century, when modern science has long been freed from its rationalistic swaddling clothes, and when every scientist and every intelligent and informed person knows that physical and other scientific "laws" are not universal natural necessities, but only our latest summaries of observed similarities, this residue of medieval rationalism has no place. We cannot change the physical habits of astronomical nature, and so we must accept its "laws"; but we certainly can change, and every day do change, the social habits of men and women. We do this by means of legislation, education, example, and persuasion. Society knows no law which it does not make itself, except that utter moral law which is the rule of all that exists, and which we have yet to elucidate.

We have considered dialectical materialism only in its social application, and have not referred to its larger doctrine, professedly showing how material being by dialectical necessity proceeds to unfold its implicit content of physical, organic, and, finally, social pattern. Nor shall we summarize this larger doctrine, if only because it can scarcely be said to exist, neither Marx nor any authoritative Marxist having troubled to elaborate it. Its materialism is a vague verbal gesture, dismissing idealism. The gesture is necessarily vague, because the concept of dialectical necessity is incorrigibly idealistic in its confusion of causal connection with logical explanation. Marx seems to have thought that his emphasis on material production required a materialistic metaphysics—as if the production of material goods by human labor were somehow only a physical process, and not as biological, psychological, and moral a process as writing poetry, devising political systems, or elaborating rationalistic metaphysics. But further, the discussion of contemporary materialism, including that of Marxists, would require allusion to Darwin and later science. It must be emphasized that Marx was not an evolutionist in the scientific sense. His system, fully matured when he wrote the *Communist Manifesto* in 1848, was a counterblast to that of Hegel; and, like that of Hegel, it is irrelevant or contrary to the scientific hypothesis of evolution.

We should not leave this discussion without acknowledgment, once more, first of the incomparable importance of Marx to science for his discernment of the economic aspect of the social pattern, which at last makes possible an empirical science of society, and secondly of his even more important work as a social reformer who called upon society to make use of its political-economic power in order to secure an equalitarian justice. It is logically and factually demonstrable that political equality requires something like an equitable distribution of economic goods, and that a people politically free cannot tolerate an enormous private wealth which gives to its owners a preponderant political power. Nor, we should see, is political liberty compatible with state socialism and government ownership. Political liberty requires equitable ownership by the people of the national wealth.

Nor do we wish to leave dialectical philosophy, which Hegel and Marx have made a commonplace of thought, without acknowledging its contribution to the future development of man. This rationalistic doctrine is the forerunner of the true evolutionism or historicism which must be the future science of man. Just as the theoretical rationalism of the great Greeks preceded modern empirical science, so this historical rationalism which is the dialectic points to an empirical historicism, in which science will fully apply that great hypothesis of evolution with which Darwin shook humanity out of its theoretical slumber. And finally, even in its rationalistic error, the dialectic does honor to that eternal and universal moral law which underlies, supports, and curtails all existence, no less in vast nature than in man.

Notes for Further Reading

1. Marx, K., *Capital,* trans. Aveling. New York, Charles Scribner's Sons, 1925.
2. —— *Capital, etc.,* ed. M. Eastman. New York, Modern Library, Inc., 1932.
3. —— *The Essentials of Marx,* ed. A. Lee. New York, Rand Book Store, 1931.
4. —— *A Handbook of Marxism,* ed. E. Burns. New York, International Publishers Company, Inc., 1935.
5. Engels, F., *Ludwig Feuerbach and the Outcome of German Classical Philosophy,* ed. C. P. Dutt. Moscow, Cooperative Publishing Society, and New York, International Publishers Company, Inc., 1934.
6. Lenin, N., *Materialism and Empirico-Criticism,* trans. D. Kvitko and S. Hook. Moscow, Cooperative Publishing Society, and New York, International Publishers Company, Inc., 1927.
7. Lewis, J., ed. *A Textbook of Marxist Philosophy.* Moscow, The Leningrad Institute of Philosophy, 1938.
8. Plekhanov, G. V., *Fundamental Problem of Marxism,* ed. D. Ryazanov, trans. E. and C. Paul. London, M. Lawrence, Ltd., 1929.
9. Bukharin, N. I., *Historical Materialism.* New York, International Publishers Company, Inc., 1925.
10. —— and others, *Marxism and Modern Thought,* trans. R. Fox. New York, Harcourt, Brace and Company, 1935.
11. Bernstein, E., *Evolutionary Socialism,* trans. E. C. Harvey. New York, B. W. Huebsch, 1909.
12. Seligman, E. R. A., *The Economic Interpretation of History.* New York, Columbia University Press, 1924.
13. Lindsay, A. D., *Karl Marx's Capital.* London and New York, Oxford University Press, 1931.
14. Laski, H. J., *Karl Marx.* New York, League for Industrial Democracy, 1933.
15. Hook, S., *From Hegel to Marx.* New York, Reynal and Hitchcock, Inc., 1936.
16. Cole, G. D. H., *What Marx Really Meant.* New York, Alfred A. Knopf, 1934.
17. Haldane, J. B. S., *The Marxist Philosophy and the Sciences.* New York, Random House, Inc., 1939.

18. Eastman, M., *Marxism, Is It Science?* New York, W. W. Norton and Company, 1940.

19. Russell, B., and others, *The Meaning of Marx*. New York, Farrar and Rinehart, Inc., 1934.

20. Wilson, E., *To the Finland Station*. New York, Harcourt Brace and Company, 1940.

21. Sabine, G. H., *A History of Political Theory*. London, George G. Harrap and Company, 1937. Chaps. XXXII, XXXIII.

22. Bober, M. M., *Karl Marx's Interpretation of History*. Cambridge, Harvard University Press, 1927.

23. Stalin, J., *Leninism*, trans. E. and C. Paul. New York, International Publishers Company, Inc., 1928.

24. Coker, F. W., *Recent Political Thought*. New York, D. Apple-London, Reeves and Turner, 1880.

21 THE NINETEENTH CENTURY

OVER MUCH OF THE EARTH'S SURFACE, THE nineteenth century was a period of economic, political, and scientific progress such as the world had never seen. In Europe and the continents settled by its emigrants there was vast increase of population and of wealth. The indigenous populations of Asia and Africa were in effect subjugated by Europe, and not yet inclined to revolt. It was a century of relative peace, a long lull between the world war against Napoleon and that in which Germany would seek world empire. Politically, it was the century of imperialism. Britain was able to police the seas at little cost; and its power was tolerated because its policy of free trade made its hegemony profitable to all. The Americas and Russia were busy with internal expansion, France had moderated its imperialistic ambitions, Germany was not yet ready for its great gamble; and so peace was had by default.

We see today that it was an interim period, a last calm before the storm which in terrible convulsion would end that imperialistic age, and begin a new world no longer centered in Europe. But the nineteenth century dreamed of no such cataclysm. It looked forward to an indefinite future, in which its pattern of life would spread to the world at large. It supposed that its formula of scientific, industrial, and political progress was established for all the future. The rumblings below the surface of European life were discounted. The rest of the world was written off as a benighted area awaiting the European gospel, to be propagated perhaps by European gunboats.

When we consider to what the nineteenth century led in our own time, we become critical of its thought. We conclude that it lacked realism and moved in a warm, myopic haze. What was its real faith? Why did the century of greatest scientific achievement end in reaction against science? Why did the century in which democracy was most largely realized breed revolt against democracy?

Approaching the second of these two questions, we perceive that although in Britain, the United States, and certain other countries there was great advance in democratic practice, there was also growing uncertainty with respect to democratic principles. The theoretical basis of democratic faith had been the concept of natural law, sanctioning natural rights located in individual persons. But the criticism of Hume and others had undermined the concept of natural necessity; and it was not understood that the concept of natural rights, which places moral responsibility wholly in individuals, was derived from the Greek concept of a moral governance of the universe, and not from the modern concept of absolute physical necessity. Kant, it is true, had strictly separated the physical domain of nature from the moral domain of the individual will; but Kant was little known outside of Germany, and inside of Germany his doctrine was perverted by the dialecticians.

Political progressives in Britain had turned in the later eighteenth century to the ethical theory known as *utilitarianism* for their intellectual defense. Hume had found in utility an empirical criterion of truth and value. The French thinker Helvetius had given this doctrine a mechanistic form, by means of a psychological study explaining human behavior hedonistically, as a pursuit of private or special interests. The aim of the state must be, he said, to satisfy private interests by their union in public interests, and to educate its citizens by persuading them of this identity between private and public interests. The character of the individual, he taught, is determined wholly by the social environment; and moral character should be shaped by the state, which is thus the source of individual morality. The best state is that which seeks "the greatest good of the greatest number."

This conception is almost irrelevant to democratic theory. It defines aims which might be those of any government; but it says nothing about the sources and controls of governmental power. Democratic theory is distinguished from all other political theory by its location of responsibility in the moral individual, *i.e.* in all individuals. It is a political and moral faith, not a psychological theory nor an ethical doctrine. Democratic society may seek to realize through its appointed government any specific moral end; and its objectives will vary at different times and places. The utilitarian conception becomes definitely antidemocratic when it is conjoined with the view that the state is the source of individual morality. Jeremy Bentham introduced Helvetius' formula into British thought, in a utilitarian program which demanded for government an unlimited legal sovereignty; and he roundly repudiated the principle of natural rights. The sole test of law, Bentham argued, is its utility in securing the *general* welfare. This Benthamite movement helped to bring about the extension of democratic suffrage; but it did this as a means necessary to the passage of legal and other reforms, and not as an acknowledgment of democratic principles. Following the year 1832, when conservative reaction broke down, this reform group gave to Great Britain a century of progressive and liberal leadership; but democratic thought never fully recovered its grasp of the principle of individual responsibility, upon which alone democracy can be intelligibly and firmly established. Thus a century which tre-

mendously extended the practice of democracy at the same
time undermined democratic theory and helped to destroy
democratic faith. The liberals who had extended the suffrage
in order to empower industry and wealth could become the
conservatives who opposed legislation designed to curb economic privilege. What was worse, authentic democracy was
left without a creed.

There was no great political thinker in this century other
than Marx, nor was there a great philosopher other than Hegel.
Empirical philosophy had gained its immediate objective—
empirical science now met little organized opposition in its
advance to unparalleled achievements. Yet empirical science
itself rested upon a foundation wholly insecure. Science still
made mathematical theory, a rational system rooted in self-
evident principles, the basis of its description of nature, although at the same time it called itself "empirical" and required its hypotheses to conform to observable particular fact.
Kant had perceived clearly, and attacked with complete honesty, the problem of a science at once rational and empirical in
its method. This dual character of science had forced Kant to
positivism; but because he thought the matter through, his
positivism was a clear and sturdy faith, establishing the authority of science as well as the limitations of science, and
establishing also the inviolability of the moral will of man. But
few followed Kant, at least with understanding. The empiricism
of the nineteenth century was a rather sickly faith, which held
up empirical science as probable truth, yet limited its insight
to "phenomena," *i.e.* to something this side of reality. It is
this unrealism, surely, which makes the nineteenth century, so
great in its scientific and practical achievements, appear as an
age which lacked resoluteness, honesty, direction, and will. And
in fact it harvested everywhere what it had not sown. Almost
everything progressive and good in the nineteenth century had
its sources in the preceding century, and applied a vision not
its own, a vision it could honor but never quite recover. So

the high optimism it had inherited steadily thinned and vulgarized itself, losing its impetus, until the confused impulse to faith was ashamed of faith, and retracted to a more honest skepticism. Schopenhauer, who saw the beginning of this century, was prescient of its end.

Arthur Schopenhauer (1788–1860) was a contemporary of Schelling and Hegel; and his greatest work, *The World as Will and as Idea*, was written in 1818 when he was thirty years old. Yet in his thought Schopenhauer was closer to ourselves than to his German contemporaries. Like those men, he moved from the great Kantian criticism to a form of metaphysical idealism; but his sojourns in France and England, together with his wide reading, had made of him a cosmopolitan thinker whose writings can be intelligibly rendered into any language. At first ignored, Schopenhauer before his death received wide recognition, and became something of a popular idol. His direct influence was upon the general public rather than upon professional philosophers; and this has perhaps obscured from us how great his influence was.

His first contribution was a simplification of the Kantian philosophy; but this simplification rather profoundly modified Kant's system. Kant had called space and time the two forms of perception; and he had made causation a category of the understanding. Schopenhauer taught that the two concepts of space and time of themselves compose the concept of physical causation, a view which finds some support in contemporary physical theory. He concluded that the spatial-temporal-causal pattern of fact is generated in perception alone, without help from the understanding. What then is the understanding and the scientific knowledge which it produces? The understanding, Schopenhauer says, seeks an abstract summary or generalization of causal relationships immediately perceived. Perception alone provides factual truth; but the understanding provides, in science, a useful schedule or compendium of perceived fact. With the help of this schedule, we can predict and control the courses of particular occurrence which appear to us in perception. We must not suppose that a scientific formula describes nature, *i.e.* possesses *descriptive* truth. Its value is practical, not cognitive. Science is our supreme tool, everywhere applicable and superlatively useful.

In this doctrine, Schopenhauer advances a pragmatic positivism widely current today. He was a century ahead of his age in proceeding to these conclusions (which is not to say that they are correct). He was a positivist in that he denied the descriptive truth and the cognitive value of science. He was a pragmatist because he conjoined with this skepticism of science a lively appreciation of its practical or instrumental utility.

With Kant, Schopenhauer dismisses "the pure reason," *i.e.* rationalistic metaphysics, as a collection of fallacies arising when we suppose the basic forms of science to define absolute reality. Unlike Kant, he ascribes to the perception of particular fact an authentic and real, not merely a "phenomenal," truth. This is close to the familiar nominalism of earlier thinkers. Schopenhauer seems about to leave us with no real knowledge except what is provided by our immediate and unmediated perception of particulars—that is to say, with no general knowledge of any sort.

However, he does not stop with nominalism, but strikes a new direction. Kant had taught in his second *Critique* that the moral will, which is ultimate or "noumenal" reality active in ourselves, penetrates through the curtain of sense-phenomena, so that moral judgments provide real contact or even identity with reality. Schopenhauer has already said, we noted, that particular perception itself constitutes such contact and such truth. He holds, moreover, that it is the will which is active in this perceptual contact. Perception is the will, nakedly meeting and struggling with the reality about it. But it is not the moral will, he continues, that is so activated and "objectified" in our perception of objects. It is the sheer will-to-live. Perception is the collision of our will-to-live with other things, with resistances, with other wills. All nature is this endless battle-field of conflicting wills. What we perceive is what threatens or supports our will-to-live. What is irrelevant to our personal survival we do not perceive. So, after first contrasting the falsity of systematic science with the truth of perception, Schopenhauer now tells us that perception also is a pragmatic and utilitarian faculty, and not an authentic, objective cognition; for our perception is the "objectification" only of our subjective purpose, our personal will-to-live; and it reveals, consequently, only a private perspective, in terms of our will or our vital needs. Perceptual cognition is true but subjective.

This conception is close to that elaborated by Bergson early in this century. Bergson makes science and ordinary perception the projection into nature of our practical and vital needs. In both thinkers there is this curious self-contradiction, that they at once dismiss science as an instrument not intended to provide descriptive knowledge, yet unconsciously appeal to science for the evidence for their conclusion. Does not science, Schopenhauer argues, demonstrate nature to be a conflict of interacting forces? Is not this concept of force the ground principle of modern science? What are forces but wills, and what are wills but forces seeking self-furtherance? But immediately, forgetting this involuntary and illogical appeal to science as a descriptive and true portrait of nature, Schopenhauer returns to his doctrine that natural science and theoretical philosophy only depict our personal perspective upon nature, which is determined by our private character and needs.

Thus the will, after all, although it is noumenal or real, provides no knowledge but only useful illusion—useful to the amoral, wholly egoistic will-to-live, which seeks its own furtherance against all other wills. This skeptical conclusion expresses the profound pessimism which is rightly attributed to Schopenhauer and which was widely inculcated by his writings. But Schopenhauer himself seeks to transcend this skepticism and pessimism. We have, he says, a third faculty, one which is distinct both from the perception of existent fact and from conceptual understanding. This is our aesthetic faculty. In the disinterested contemplation of beauty we are emancipated from the selfish will-to-live, and completely devoted for a fleeting moment to something other than our private selves. (The reader will remember the source of this teaching in Kant's third *Critique*. It is also the conclusion of Bergson.) Thus Schopenhauer seeks to recover, in the aesthetic faculty and in the art which is its deliberate exercise, the intellectual, moral, and religious faith he had intellectually lost. Aesthetic insight is our sole truth, our true reason. It alone is moral, it alone is true, and it alone is unselfishly motivated and inspired by love of other being. And now, Schopenhauer claims for this aesthetic faculty the cognitive power that earlier thought had ascribed—in his view falsely—to the understanding and the reason. Ordinary perception, he says, sees only the particular. Ordinary understanding substitutes an abstract stereotype for the group of perceived particulars. But aesthetic insight, he claims, discloses in the particular that universal Form which is beauty. It is the same beauty, the self-identical Form, that we appreciate in each and every rose. In this way Schopenhauer returns to the Formism of Plato; but he converts Greek idealism, which was scientific and theoretical, into an aesthetic idealism, fostered by art. Music, he says, is the truest art, taking us most directly to those Forms which are the essence, the true substance, of all being. Music is the perfect, naked penance of the will. Later, in his discussion of the relations between the sexes, he explains the sexual passion as the possession of an individual by the power of the species, which makes of the individual an instrument for the procreation of the species. In this striking application of the doctrine, similar to that of Plato in the *Symposium*, the specific Forms aesthetically reproduced by the artist are depicted as the generative forces of the cosmos.

There is much that is suggestive, original, and perhaps true in Schopenhauer's verbally inconsistent system. The self-contradictions spring from vacillation with respect to natural science. Science is sometimes abruptly rejected as error, sometimes used to establish Schopenhauer's own doctrine. These inconsistencies might be overcome, perhaps, if we allowed biological science, rather than physical theory, to represent natural science. Schopenhauer, like Kant, identifies natural science with physical science; but his emphasis upon the will-to-survive, upon specific form, and upon the individual's self-sacrifice to the needs of its species suggests the initial step toward a new approach to natural process. The complete removal of Schopenhauer's contradictions, however, would be effected only by a study explaining the essential and fundamental role of aesthetic apprehension in all science, physics as well as biology—it would require, that is to say, the successful rewriting of Kant's third *Critique*.

Schopenhauer's writings helped to propagate the voluntarism, the anti-intellectual pragmatism, and the vague aestheticism which ran under the surface of nineteenth-century thought, to erupt in explicit end extreme forms in our own century. Like Fichte, Hegel, and Marx, Schopenhauer helped to widen a growing disruption in the modern mind. Fichte set philosophy against science; Hegel set people against people; Marx set class against class; and Schopenhauer now sets art against science, and the will-to-live against the disinterested intellect. What was the source of this unhappy division of the human mind against itself? A fatal malcontent inspires these philosophies. In the cases of Fichte and Hegel, this malaise comes to light only in the destructive political results of their teaching; but in Schopenhauer, it is conscious and explicit. From this world, with its unholy struggle for survival and power, he intimates, we find release only in complete abnegation of the will-to-live, *i.e.* in death. Even more strange, from the pen of this worldly cosmopolitan aesthete, is the intimation that salvation lies in the sacrifice of the individual for his kind, which is a sort of atonement for the sin that is the world. The other-

worldliness of Greek and Christian religion make their first
modern reappearance in the aesthetics of this irreligious man
of the world.

From Schopenhauer, the errant but groping genius who was
the intellectual father of Bergson and Nietzsche, we turn to the
more superficial talent of *Auguste Comte* (1798–1857),
propagator of the words "positivism" and "sociology." Kant,
we said, was positivistic with respect to science; but Kant
called himself a "critical" philosopher, and the two words con-
note different conclusions drawn from the same premises.
Kant denied the ultimacy of phenomenal knowledge in order
to establish the ultimacy of moral judgment, or conscience.
Comte used this denial in order to discredit all faith in ultimate
truth. The knowledge which reaches phenomena, he taught,
is no knowledge of the real; but it is nevertheless the only
knowledge we may hope to have.

The first third of the nineteenth century was dominated by
reaction against the French revolution with its bloody excesses,
its quick transformation into vapid imperialism, and its failure
to establish republican government. It was a period of anti-
intellectual and vaguely religious romanticism, productive of
much second-rate poetry and worshipful of poetic genius.
Comte represents the effort to return, with appropriate changes,
to the earlier intellectualism. His positivism is eighteenth-century French materialism, shorn of its metaphysical postulates.

The argument of Hume, that science discovers only regulari-
ties in nature, or uniformities in phenomena, was by this time
widely known and accepted. This insight, Comte argues, re-
leases us from the urge to discover "reality," known in an
ultimate "truth." We can henceforward accept the formulas
of science as final, because we can know nothing beyond them.
Looking back over human history, Comte says, we see three
stages of intellectual development. Earliest man was mythological, theological, and animistic, in that he attempted to explain nature as the manifestation of anthropomorphic deities.

From this subjectivistic fantasy he advanced to a legalistic or metaphysical stage, in which absolute principles or "laws" were supposed to rule over nature. Today, at last, men recognize the subjectivism of these philosophies which seek vainly to penetrate through appearances to "reality." Men now accept sensible appearances, or phenomena, as the sum of knowledge, and seek only to classify the regular sequences observable among phenomena. Awareness of such uniformities permits calculated prediction, giving to man some control over natural occurrence; and with ultimate knowledge he may now dispense. This is Comte's *positivism*.

In truth, this modest and empirical estimate of human knowledge is largely window dressing, intended to attract the scientific mind and to make formal renunciation of the older and now discredited scholastic metaphysics. Comte's positivism is really supported by unconscious metaphysical assumptions. This metaphysical framework makes its appearance as a classification of the sciences. The sciences naturally fall, Comte points out, into a definite sequence, proceeding from the mathematical sciences, through the physical and biological sciences, to the sciences which deal with man and society. The sciences antecedent in this order are presupposed in and instrumental to those which follow; and the sciences accordingly culminate in sociology, which telescopes into its theory all the principles of the other sciences. Because of this relationship, the sciences become more complex and difficult as we proceed in this order, from mathematics to sociology; and this is why they were historically developed in this order. Comte regarded himself as the originator of empirical sociology. He may have invented the name; but his social analysis is less empirical and scientific than that of many of his predecessors.

As we have seen, this "order of the sciences" reflects primarily the fact of natural evolution on this planet. Comte was no evolutionist. For him, consequently, the order of the sciences constituted an ultimate metaphysical fact, not to be empirically

explained. But Comte's metaphysics remains unconscious, so
that he nowhere seeks to justify it. He was also more wrong
than right, the historian of science would insist, in his supposition that this order of the sciences is the order of their historical
appearance and development. Chemistry, which occurs quite
early in Comte's sequence, in fact arose centuries later than
biology and psychology, which were importantly developed
by the Greeks. But it is more important to see that Comte's
whole conception of an order of the sciences was not an empirical hypothesis, pointing to an observable uniformity in
nature. It was a philosophical conception, intended to unify
and systematize all the specialized knowledge gained by the
special sciences.

What sort of metaphysical system does this "classification
of the sciences" comprise? This question cannot be definitely
answered, the philosopher's presentation of it being too casual
and vague. It involves, certainly, a logical appreciation of the
diversity of the sciences, with some appraisal of their interrelations; and it further involves a desire, similar to that which
controlled Hegel, to explain the larger order of nature in
terms of the order of man's discovery of nature—as if the
architecture of nature only reflected the architectonic of
thought. These idealistic implications are masked by Comte's
emphatic, but only verbal, empiricism.

A determining factor in Comte's conception was his interest
in the establishment of social science. Much as Descartes the
mathematician invented a cosmos which would be completely
accessible to mathematical analysis, so Comte the sociologist
advanced a system which would make his special study of
social process the culmination of natural knowledge. Comte's
own social studies reveal a curious combination of rationalistic prepossession and empirical hypothesis, and show how
inadequate was this thinker's conception of empirical method.
His basic approach to social fact, indeed, is just that of
Hobbes two centuries earlier. He divides social science into

"social statics" and "social dynamics." In physical science this division into statics and dynamics has meaning. Physical statics deals with stresses in bodies at rest, whereas physical dynamics is the study of bodies in motion; and the two disciplines apply the same basic principles to two sorts of physical situation. This distinction cannot be simply translated to sociology. What Comte calls "social statics" is a study modeled on physical dynamics. It seeks a social theory defining the constants always and everywhere conserved through social change. What he calls "social dynamics" is really an historical study of human progress, in no way analogous to physical dynamics. This error is worth noting, because it makes unusually explicit the long confusion which has obscured our conceptions of social and natural evolution. Comte correctly distinguishes the historical study of human progress from the theoretical study which defines the social structure which is supposedly preserved throughout this evolution; but he incorrectly conceives of these two studies, respectively historical and theoretical, as the two halves of a single theoretical science analogous with theoretical physics. This is only another version of the error committed by Hegel in his dialectic. The dialectic "progresses" from a beginning to an end, like a history or an evolution; yet it claims to be a theoretical system, defining the unchanging and absolute structure of the world. We will return to this problem in our study of evolutionary doctrine.

We have already mentioned Comte's outline of man's intellectual evolution as proceeding through three stages, from animistic mythology through metaphysical speculation to positivistic science. His elaboration of this doctrine is suggestive; it is, in fact, the prototype of the social dialectic of Marx. Each stage, Comte says, produces its characteristic social institutions. The earliest theological stage is marked by the development of ecclesiastical and military institutions; the metaphysical stage is characterized by the establishment of constitutional governments and of legalistic forms of social control. We still live, he complains, in this intermediate stage of evolution, although intellectually, *i.e.* in our science, we have advanced to the third positivistic stage. And here Comte advances the teaching which was the motive of all his thought. Science, he says, must be given its authoritative place in the world, and be made the true government of society. This is to be done by placing the political and economic management of society completely in the hands of scientists, who as absolute rulers will regulate the national economy and regiment the national life. Comte elaborates this socialistic and technocratic utopia in great detail. He even arranges for an organized "religion of Science" with a positivistic ritual, a calendar of "Saints," and a scientific priesthood, all inculcating the worship of Science. In these more extreme proposals, Comte perhaps reveals symptoms of the mental sickness which later destroyed him.

We understand Comte best, perhaps, by seeing in his socialistic positivism an effort to resuscitate the motives and outlook of the French Enlightenment, after these had been widely discredited by the excesses of the French revolution and its imperialistic aftermath. The worship of "Science," considered not as an aspiration for truth but as a set of formulas, continues the dogmatic worship of "Reason"; for Comte's conception of science, in spite of his empirical protests against metaphysics, is really no less absolutistic than that of the earlier rationalism. This philosophical absolutism reappears in the political authoritarianism of his socialistic technocracy. New and of value is his emphasis upon the economic forces which condition political evolution. Comte's teachers were men who believed that the failure of the French revolution arose from its neglect of underlying economic conditions, and who wished to turn society from political objectives to an economic revolution establishing a communistic state. What we should most especially observe is the source of this intellectual and political absolutism in the failure to advance to a truly empirical and evolutionary science of nature and man.

Herbert Spencer (1820–1903) exhibits this same failure. Spencer was long regarded in English-speaking countries as the chief philosophical exponent of evolutionary doctrine. In truth he belongs to the early nineteenth century, with Hegel and Comte, in his explanation of evolutionary facts in terms of nonevolutionary principles. His extensive system, elaborated in a small library of volumes the writing of which occupied his long life, reveals his dogmatic and unempirical method, which resembles that of Hegel in its mechanical imposition of a verbal formula upon the diverse materials provided by the special sciences. He is like Comte, however, in his ostensible repudiation of metaphysics. He prefaces his system with a call to agnosticism, warning us not to pursue knowledge of the "Absolute," which is beyond human comprehension. We are limited to knowledge of phenomena and their uniformities. But having thus eliminated the word "absolute," Spencer turns to the construction of a universalistic metaphysics which is absolutistic in all but name, and which closely parallels the dialectical metaphysics. There are, he says, a number of a priori and absolute principles involved in our recognition of "phenomena"; and the most important of these is the principle of necessary development, according to which matter proceeds to its spatial reorganization by an inherent necessity, from the most simple physical patterns to increasingly complex inorganic, organic, and psychological patterns. The sciences, arranged in their proper order, exhibit the successive stages of this material development of nature; and all Spencer need do, or does, is to present the many concepts of inorganic, organic, and human science as arising from this "necessity," under which "matter" labors, progressively to complicate its spatial pattern. It need scarcely be pointed out that this Spencerian "matter" corresponds in no way to what modern science has understood by this word. The reader will perceive Spencer's revival here of the Aristotelian and scholastic concept of matter, which was defined as the potentiality to realize form; but the dualism of form and matter, which made sense of Aristotle's doctrine, is submerged and unconscious in Spencer's system, which becomes self-contradictory nonsense when its scholastic elements are explicitly stated.

Nothing could be less evolutionary in thought, as we shall see when we consider the scientific concept of evolution, than this Spencerian "deduction" of all natural forms from a blanket definition of "matter." We should note that Spencer's mind was formed, and his system already outlined, before the publication in 1859 of Darwin's *Origin of Species*. There is every reason to suppose that if the evolutionary hypothesis had never been advanced, Spencer's system would have been in no whit different from what it was, even to its "evolutionary" vocabulary.

More empirical in his conception of scientific and philosophical method was *John Stuart Mill* (1806–1873), the intellectual spokesman of the liberal party in his time. Mill's political writings, all published around the mid-century, long remained the accepted texts of liberal theory. Through his father James Mill, and also directly, Mill inherited the utilitarian and hedonistic doctrine of Jeremy Bentham. Bentham was an ardent advocate of legal reform, whose endeavors helped to initiate the long period of legal and political reconstruction beginning in the early thirties. But Bentham's own political principles, as we noted, were something less than liberal, in that they ascribed to the state an unlimited power and authority, which might be turned, he hoped, from harmful to beneficial uses. Mill, in his political teaching, tends to return to the individualism of Locke's political theory. His *Essay on Liberty* defends freedom of speech as the condition and symbol of all other freedoms; and his defense of minorities, in *Views on Representative Government*, implies a recognition that individual moral responsibility, carrying with it inalienable individual rights, provides the only adequate basis of democratic justice. Mill's political theory, however, has usually been understood as an application of a more general ethical theory; and in his ethical writings, Mill remained vacillating and inconclusive. He was not satisfied with the utilitarianism of his father and Bentham; yet he seriously considered no alternative, and his effort to modify its hedonistic axioms only left them meaningless and inapplicable. Pleasure is the objective of every human act, he hedonistically agreed, and the good is therefore to be defined by a hedonistic calculus, correctly calculating the maximum sum of accessible pleasures. He insisted, however, that pleasures must be estimated qualitatively, as well as quantitatively. Mill, and after him other hedonists, never clearly perceived that a rational calculation of pleasures—and still more, of course, a qualitative estimate of pleasures as higher or lower—appeals to ethical criteria lying beyond the immediate feeling of pleasure. Assuming that pleasure is the object of an instinctive and rightful urge, how shall man direct and control this instinctive pursuit of pleasure, to gain from it its optimum outcome? Even to ask this question involves the postulation of some intellectual ethical criterion over and above that of pleasurableness.

A similar vacillation appears in his political writings. Mill supported the consequences which flow from the principle of inalienable rights; yet he feared what might result from the full application of this principle. His defense of minorities, for example, was motivated by his fear that an electoral majority might oppress minorities. Such half-hearted allegiance to democratic principles did not strengthen liberalism. British liberalism was largely a creation of the antimonarchical but still aristocratic Whig party, which supported an extension of political suffrage to gain popular support against the Tory opposition. A genuine liberalism (and we should not let the inadequacies of earlier liberals rob us of this word) is established upon faith in the individual man, and is incompatible with fear of "the masses" and with the very concept of "the masses." Liberalism is our faith that the individual human being is good, morally responsible, and therefore invested with the inalienable rights and duties of government. No one who fears "the masses," or who even applies this repulsive term to groups of his fellow men, has much understanding of liberal and democratic principles. Liberty and democracy know no "masses" and no "classes." Because British liberalism lost sight of its own moral sources, British conservatism was able to wrest the doctrine of individual rights away from liberalism, and use it as Hegel had done in the interests of political privilege.

More forceful and consistent was Mill's defense of scientific empiricism. Here, his chief concern was to distinguish *deductive* method, which discovers only the implications of verbal statements, from the *inductive* procedure of scientific hypothesis. The latter is concerned not so much with statements as with facts; and it moves from the observation of particular facts to a grasp of general truths. Mill's problem was that left by Hume. By what right do we proceed, on the strength of these generalizations of observed facts, to predictions about facts as yet unobserved? Mill did not perceive the full force of this question, which leads us finally to discover a certain rational presupposition involved in all science; for the scientist, in order to pursue any theoretical inquiry whatsover, must assume the commensurability of fact with logic. The real question, therefore, asks why logic successfully implements science. That Mill dimly felt the significance of logic in science, and the importance of logic for science, is shown by his use of the phrase "inductive logic" to distinguish his description of scientific method, and by his effort to formulate axioms of scientific method, much as Aristotle formulated those of deductive logic. In Mill, as in Aristotle, the identification of scientific method with logic betrays ignorance of the true relation of logic to scientific hypothesis. Mill's famous rules of induction are an improvement upon those of Francis Bacon; but they do not define the "method" of scientific hypothesis. They only conveniently summarize certain deductive procedures involved in the scientific analysis which is auxiliary to hypothesis. The true method of science is the creation of hypotheses; and this eludes definition.

Our justification for applying a generalization from past facts to facts as yet unobserved, Mill says, rests upon the largest generalization, which is derived from the sum total of past generalizations. Having made many successful inductions in special fields, we now make a general induction, stating that nature is evidently amenable to inductive study. This largest generalization Mill calls "the principle of the uniformity of nature." It was immediately pointed out that this reasoning is circular. The specific inductions are "successful" only if we grant their necessary applicability to unobserved fact, and this is what needs proof. What proof is there that nature is uniform?

Mill's teaching may be summarized as follows: Our only problem, he assumes, is to distinguish genuinely causal sequences from merely casual or chance repetitions. The *method of agreement* compares an observed sequence with earlier observed sequences. The *method of difference* instructs us, if *abc* has always been followed by *def*, to see whether the absence of *f* in the consequent does not entail the absence of *c* in the antecedent, in which case *c* is presumably the cause of *f*. The *method of residues* says that if *abc* is the uniform antecedent of *def*, and *ab* the uniform antecedent of *de*, then, once more, *c* is the cause of *f*. And the *method of concomitant variations* tells us that where one factor varies quantitatively with another, the two factors are probably causally connected. The occasional admiration of a scientist for these trivial definitions of "scientific method" reminds one of the surprise and pleasure of Monsieur Jourdain, when he was assured by his tutor that he was able to speak in prose, and indeed always did so speak. If this is scientific method, then who is not a Newton? "Inductive logic" has cheapened our estimate of science; and those who would have science receive the intelligent respect which is its due should protest this abuse in no uncertain terms.

Only when the element of creative hypothesis in science is clearly and understandingly distinguished from the logical symbolism which implements science can we appreciate what is creative, and what merely mechanical and formal, in scientific activity. Candid, modest, sober, and wholly without vision, Mill was the noblest representative of an unilluminated age.

It is a far cry from these epigones of the nineteenth century to the commanding figures of Hume and Kant. Let us acknowledge that drama, poetry, science, and philosophy have their great epochs and their declines. These nineteenth-century thinkers had forgotten what were the issues of the controversy they believed themselves to be pursuing. That controversy between nominalism and realism in the Middle Ages, and between empiricism and rationalism after Descartes, was a very real one. The nominalistic and empirical tradition emphasized the ultimacy of particular and observable fact as the criterion of truth, and tried to explain away the rational element in science. The realistic and rationalistic school, on the contrary, emphasized this rational element, which they correctly saw to be the source of the systematic ideal and the theoretical form of science; and they tried either to explain away as illusion, or to absorb into the rational element, the empirical element which is particular observed fact. Hume and Kant squarely faced this problem presented by the dual character of science, which is somehow at once empirical and rationalistic. Both were forced to skeptical conclusions, by which they honestly abide. But these later thinkers, verbally accepting the arguments of Hume and Kant, revert by some simple detour to the dogmatic metaphysics which they ostensibly reject. Evidently they did not understand, and could not therefore take seriously, the criticism of theoretical knowledge advanced by their great predecessors.

We can excuse their confusion, perhaps, if we understand its sources. These lay partly in the conventional use of the word "metaphysics," which had come to be identified with

Aristotelian metaphysics, as this was perpetuated in the scholastic theology and philosophy. These modern thinkers believed themselves to be rejecting all metaphysical speculation when they emphatically rejected the scholastic metaphysics; yet they unconsciously introduced new metaphysics of their own. Their own metaphysics they disguised as a "method." They were unaware that every method, if it is advanced as universal in its applicability and authoritative in its results, implies certain absolute assumptions which provide the generative nucleus of a body of metaphysical doctrine. Descartes and Spinoza, who initiated the most extreme rationalism the western world has seen, conceived themselves to be free from metaphysical assumptions and to be advocating only a "method." But similarly the nominalists and empiricists, who rejected the Cartesian along with the scholastic metaphysics, were the proponents of a metaphysical view, resting upon absolute axioms, but disguised as only scientific method. *Nominalism asserts the absolute and ultimate reality of individual being, as observed in particular things and occurrences; and this is a metaphysical affirmation. Empiricism likewise, although it allows only probability to its general statements, makes observed particular fact the ultimate and sufficient criterion of truth; and this is to subscribe to the nominalistic axiom. But it has never been perceived with sufficient clarity that the empirical realism which is modern science, like the rationalistic realism which was Greek science, constitutes a metaphysics. We need not wonder at the growing confusion of empirical thinkers who were not aware of their own first principles, presupposed in all their method.*

As empirical thought bogged down into confusion and triviality, there inevitably appeared a reaction against it, and a new appreciation of the clarity and forthrightness of rationalistic thinkers who openly confessed to their metaphysical postulates. We cannot follow nineteenth-century thought through all of its many movements; but we may note its course in Britain. Kantian idealism was early introduced into England by the romantic poet Coleridge, but only in the vaguest sort of language. Later, more competent philosophers became aware of the depth and cogency of the Kantian criticism; and about 1865 *Thomas Hill Green* made absolute idealism the orthodox creed of Oxford University, at that time the citadel of British conservatism. (It was not that when Grosseteste, Roger Bacon, Scotus, and Occam there inaugurated modern science.) Green issued his idealistic manifesto in a critical *Introduction* to a new edition of Hume's great *Treatise*, which was still too little and too inaccurately known. Green justifiably attacked Hume's psychological atomism. Experience is not comprised, he correctly pointed out, of "simple ideas" which can be connected only by some extraneous mental habit. These "ideas" are in many indicable ways intrinsically interconnected; and these interconnections are as much a part of experience as are the terms which are related by them. Thus we immediately see a cat—we do not perceive gray color, softness, warmth, solidity, weight, etc., and then put these items together by a mental and intellectual effort. Similarly, the causal and other connections which science pursues are intrinsic to particular fact; and not to predicate them of reality is gratuitous skepticism. Whatever knowledge we have of nature is real knowledge, knowledge of real being.

Green's objections were justified, but they missed the point of Hume's criticism of theoretical knowledge. Admitting that we do lay hold of natural pattern in perception, it must finally be insisted that science goes beyond perception. We do not *see* the universal force of gravitation, we do not see even the planetary orbits, we see at most particular bodies moving or at rest. Our knowledge of large motions and causal principles is therefore either an absolute and rational intuition, or it is probable conjecture, well-confirmed hypothesis. If it cannot be established as the former, it must be accepted as the latter; and Hume's conclusion, that "reason" provides no absolute knowledge of universal natural principles, is not invalidated by criticism of his atomistic psychology. But Green assumed that his discovery of flaws unessential to Hume's central argument invalidated Hume's whole conclusion; and he returns with a leap to an absolute, universalistic, and idealistic metaphysics. Because the elements of experience are not isolated atoms, he concludes that a perfected experience contains no separations, no fragmentary character, no elements of any sort. The whole of experience, he claims, is somehow inherent in every part of experience. The whole mind, with its whole knowledge, informs our every judgment. Yet having so argued, Green must retreat in order to acknowledge the limitations of human knowledge, the lapses of mind, the lacunae and errors of human experience. It is not your or my imperfect mind, he allows, which has this perfect organization and this transparent wholeness and unity. But such is Absolute Mind, of which our minds are imperfect and fragmentary parts, and of which all fact is the infinite and unified content. Similarly, our particular actions and our individual wills are the real modes of a universal, eternal, and absolute Will. Reality is an organized Whole; and in organized human society we intend, so far as our limited and modal nature allows, a proper subjection of our individual will to the absolute Will which is God.

The two most notable British exponents of absolute idealism were Bradley and Bosanquet. *Francis H. Bradley* (1846–1924) was the profounder of the two. Because he probed deep, he brought again to the surface of thought the insoluble problems which Kant had acknowledged and clearly marked, but which Kant's absolutistic successors had overridden. Bradley resurrects, and remains inextricably caught in, those antinomies or self-contradictions which Kant had shown to be latent in absolute and universal metaphysics. How, Bradley inquires, can the limited human mind, analyzing a finite experience, hope to establish principles of universal and eternal validity? If Reality, as absolute idealism implies, is an organic Whole, to know any part of Reality we must literally know every part; and this is impossible. Like the post-Kantians, Bradley had to choose between universalistic metaphysics and logic. Like them, he chooses metaphysics, and lets logic go. But unlike them, he does not pretend to discover a new logic, transcending ordinary logic. In place of a pseudologic like the dialectic, he advocates the rehabilitation of a certain mystical intuition, which carries us from the self-contradictions of philosophical analysis to an aesthetic and religious identity with Absolute Being. So Bradley, somewhat like Schopenhauer, proceeds from the Kantian criticism to a mystical faith. In Britain, a mystical Platonism has always had its devotees. We have noticed Eriugena, the mystical and empirical Franciscans, Berkeley, and now Bradley. Its best-known contemporary advocate is Dean Inge, who frankly subscribes to the pagan philosophy of Plotinus of Alexandria.

Bernard Bosanquet (1848–1923), Bradley's colleague at Oxford, is the Hegel to Bradley's Kant. The question is not, he stoutly replies to the skeptical Bradley, whether we humans can grasp Absolute Being in its extensive infinity; it is whether those parts we do know are adequately known. Are we phenomenalists or realists? Do we grasp Reality in knowledge, or is our knowledge only a projection of ourselves? He assures us that we do engage the Absolute, and that any further experience can only extend, and does not transform, what we now know. His argument is essentially that of Kant, namely that what is articulate and structural in experience is determined by our mental constitution, so that it necessarily appears in every experience, and consequently has universal validity. But where Kant rightly moved from this subjectivistic premise to a skeptical estimate of scientific knowledge, Bosanquet shortcuts to the Hegelian realism. Our judgments, he says, even those judgments which state only particular facts, are in strictness judgments about absolute Reality. When we say, "This is a whale," we mean to say, "Reality is such as to be here and now a whale." If we err, and say, "The whale is a fish," when better acquaintance would classify it as a mammal, our error is one of extent, not of intent. Wider experience would classify the whale as a mammal; but in the context of a narrower experience, the whale is truly a fish. Bosanquet is insisting here that our knowledge of nature is in sort geographical, and that the extension of science by new and often strange hypotheses does not really discredit the older and narrower hypotheses which are displaced. It *was* true that the sun moves round the earth; it *is* true that the earth moves round the sun. Some such view, apparently self-contradictory, is implied in every absolute and nonempirical realism; for this doctrine ultimately requires the literal identity of ideas with things.

Idealistic philosophers made use of a distinction between *external and internal relations*. If the relations discovered by the intellect are "external" to the things related, then some of the relations of a thing may be correctly known even while we are ignorant of others. Thus you may know that your friend has an older brother, but be unaware that he has a younger sister. If all relations are "internal," however, then real acquaintance with anything, *i.e.* knowledge of its character, includes knowledge of all its relations. Knowing your friend, you know he has a sister. It is clear, perhaps, that for common sense and empirical science, the distinction between external and internal relations cannot be ultimate. We proceed as if relations were external, discovering now this and now that causal or other connection, as best we can. It is in the light of these causal relations, however, that we progressively define the character of a thing, so that the relations which initially were external are finally internal. Thus we study a salt, discern its color, its specific crystalline form, etc.; but we fail to determine from these data its solubility. We discover by experiment that it dissolves in any acid; and from this "external" relationship we learn something of its internal constitution, so that the relation becomes "internal." The absolute idealist holds all relations to be "internal"; and this is equivalent to saying that reality is an organic system any part of which is a sufficient index to the whole. To hold that all relations are "external" would be to embrace a pluralism so radical as to reduce reality to chaos. But the student will discover that no philosopher, whatever his formal profession, consistently abides by either view. Bosanquet argues from the internality of relations to a metaphysical monism or *organicism*; but his realistic epistemology, which argues that we may know the part absolutely even though the whole be beyond human comprehension, implies the externality of relations. Bradley was more consistent when he flatly rejected external relations. This idealistic and monistic realism was the impossible effort to adapt the scholastic realism of the Middle Ages to modern science. The doctrine of "internal" relations only perpetuates the scholastic doctrine of "essence," which taught that the reason, acting independently of the senses, grasps the true and controlling natures of things; but that Greek realism required the dualistic metaphysics of matter and form, which can scarcely be accommodated to modern empirical science.

This modern idealism is a peculiarly unstable doctrine, as we observed in its sudden transformation from idealistic Hegel to materialistic Marx. If we suppose, with absolute idealism, that all fact constitutes only a single, universal and concrete, yet intellectually definable pattern, then it is very difficult not to identify this pattern with that defined by physical science; for only physical structure observably extends through all nature—human, organic, and inorganic. It is questionable whether Bosanquet's teaching more inculcated idealism than it prepared the way for a materialistic "physicism." What is not questionable is its direction of British thought toward a pluralistic form of realism, which we will call the "new realism." By arguing very implausibly for "internal" relations, while his realistic theory of knowledge tacitly depended upon the doctrine of "external" relations, Bosanquet revealed more damagingly than any of his critics the inherent weakness of absolute idealism. But discussion of this new realism belongs to our review of contemporary thought.

Looking back over this summary of nineteenth-century philosophy, we find little that is important and philosophically new. The thinker rings the changes of eighteenth-century thought, usually with less vitality than his more creative predecessors. Where reflection starts from Kant, there is a fatal development of "Neo-Fichteans," "Neo-Schellings," and "Neo-Hegelians." Where the thinker starts from Hume, he may either be led to discover Kant, or flounder into a verbal positivism that really returns to a rationalistic metaphysics disguised as an absolutistic "methodology." There were at least two good reasons for this intellectual failure. The first was that the problem which faced this age baffled the inquirer. Mathematical physics, loyal to the mechanical principles of the Newtonian physics, seemed to indicate the dependence of science upon absolute mathematical axioms; and this discouraged a radical and consistent empiricism; yet, on the other hand, science everywhere, no less in physical inquiry than elsewhere, proceeded from observed data to large hypothesis, and in this way affirmed its empirical faith in the ultimacy of particular fact. The nineteenth century lacked the data allowing escape from this deadlock; and the profoundest and only completely honest thinkers were, perhaps, those who saw this problem as Kant had seen it, and accepted Kant's phenomenalism or positivism with respect to natural knowledge, and his noumenalism or moral realism with respect to action. Fortunately the twentieth century was to provide the data freeing human thought from this impasse.

The other reason for the failure of philosophical genius was the shift of public interest from philosophy to science, and, after the mid-century, to the mind-shattering hypothesis of evolution. It was in empirical inquiry that the genius of the nineteenth century exhibited its power. Never had there been such achievement in science—this greatest, perhaps, of the creative arts of man. And worthy to stand by the side of Anaximander, Pythagoras, Roger Bacon, and Isaac Newton is Charles Darwin, the thinker who shook the human intellect as it had not been shaken since the Greeks established theoretical science. The hypothesis of evolution staggered and benumbed the speculative intellect; nor have we yet recovered from that blow. Seldom, as we shall see, has the thinker been able to contemplate the fact of natural evolution, and calmly comprehend its whole implication, without losing his intellectual balance. So let us try to appreciate at least what the scientific hypothesis of evolution did and did not say!

Notes for Further Reading

1. Schopenhauer, A., *The Four Fold Root of the Sufficient Reason*, trans. K. Hillebrand. London, G. Bell and Sons, 1889.
2. —— *The World as Will and Idea*, trans. Haldane and Kamp. New York, Charles Scribner's Sons, 1923.
3. —— *Selections*. New York, Harcourt Brace and Company, 1917. (Editions by Bax, Parker, Mann)
   There are studies of Schopenhauer in English by Wallace, Whittaker, Zimmern, Caldwell, Simmel.
4. Comte, A., *General View of Positivism*, trans. J. H. Bridges. London, Reeves and Turner, 1880.
5. Martineau, H., *Comte's Positive Philosophy*. London, K. Paul Trench, Trübner Company, Ltd., 1853.
   There are studies of Comte in English by Mill, Caird, Watson, Whittaker, Lévy-Bruhl (in *History of Modern Philosophy in France*, La Salle, The Open Court Publishing Company, 1899) and Gunn (in *Modern French Philosophy*, New York, Dodd, Mead and Company, 1922).
6. Mill, J. S., The works of Mill are available in most libraries.
   There are studies of Mill by Baine, Courtney, Douglas, Watson, Whittaker, MacCunn (in *Six Radical Thinkers*, London, E. Arnold, 1910), Stephen (in *The English Utilitarians*, New York, G. P. Putnam's Sons, 1900) and Albee (in *History* of

English Utilitarianism, New York, The Macmillan Company, 1902).

7. Spencer, H., Works available in most libraries. See especially his *First Principles,* New York, D. Appleton-Century, and his "preface" to Collin's *Epitome of Spencer's Philosophy.*

8. Sidgwick, H., *The Ethics of Green, Spencer and Martineau.* New York, The Macmillan Company, 1902.

9. Ward, J., *Naturalism and Agnosticism.* London, A. and C. Black, 1915.

10. Watson, W., *Comte, Mill, and Spencer.* Glasgow, J. Maclehose and Sons, 1895.

Other studies of Spencer by Hudson, Macpherson, Royce, Taylor, Thompson, Harrison.

11. Green, T. H., "Introduction to Hume," in *Treatise on Human Nature,* David Hume, London and New York, Longmans, Green and Company, 1875.

12. —————— *Prolegomena to Ethics.* London and New York, Oxford University Press, 1883.

13. —————— *Principles of Political Obligation.* Boston, Longmans, Green and Company, 1895.

Studies of Green by Fairbrother, Johnson, Sidgwick, Muirhead (in *The Service of the State, Man versus the State as a Present Issue, London,* G. Allen and Unwin), Ritchie (in *Principles of State Interference,* London, Social Science Series, 1891), MacCunn (*op. cit.*).

14. Bradley, F. H., *Principles of Logic.* London and New York, Oxford University Press, 1883.

15. Bradley, F. H., *Appearance and Reality.* New York, The Macmillan Company, 1902.

16. —————— *Essays on Truth and Reality.* London and New York, Oxford University Press, 1914.

17. Rashdall, H., *The Metaphysics of Bradley.* London, Gerald Duckworth and Company.

18. Bosanquet, B., *The Principle of Individuality and Value.* New York, The Macmillan Company, 1912.

19. —————— *The Value and Destiny of the Individual.* New York, The Macmillan Company, 1913.

20. —————— *The Meeting of Extremes in Contemporary Philosophy.* New York, The Macmillan Company, 1921.

21. Sorley, W. R., *A History of English Philosophy.* New York, G. P. Putnam's Sons, 1920.

22. Rogers, A. K., *English and American Philosophy since 1800.* New York, The Macmillan Company, 1922.

23. Perry, R. B., *Philosophy of the Recent Past.* New York, Charles Scribner's Sons, 1926.

24. Höffding, H., *Modern Philosophers.* New York, The Macmillan Company, 1915.

25. Muirhead, J. H., (ed.) *Contemporary British Philosophy.* New York, The Macmillan Company, 1924, 1926.

26. Howison, G. H., *The Conception of God.* Berkeley, University of California, Bulletin 15, 1897. *The Limits of Evolution.* San Francisco, Murdock Press, 1902.

27. Bowne, B. P., *Personalism.* Boston, Houghton Mifflin Company, 1908.

28. Royce, J., *The Spirit of Modern Philosophy.* Boston, Houghton Mifflin Company, 1885.

29. ────── *The World and the Individual.* New York, The Macmillan Company, 1900, 1901.

30. ────── *The Philosophy of Loyalty.* New York, The Macmillan Company, 1908.

31. ────── *The Problem of Christianity.* New York, The Macmillan Company, 1913.

32. Hocking, W. E., *The Meaning of God in Human Experience.* New Haven, Yale University Press, 1912.

33. ────── *Human Nature and its Remaking.* New Haven, Yale University Press, 1923.

22 THE CONCEPT OF EVOLUTION IN SCIENCE AND PHILOSOPHY

IN ANTIQUITY, ANAXIMANDER AND EMPEDOCLES advanced evolutionary hypotheses which were evidently based upon study of the organic species. Early Greek science was as much concerned to understand the generation or evolution of nature as to learn something of the permanent structure of nature. Science was usually presented, indeed, as an inquiry into the *physis*, *i.e.* into the coming-to-be or generation of nature. Today the word "physical" carries no such evolutionary connotation, and this change of meaning testifies to a radical change of interest and outlook. Perhaps by Pythagoras, certainly by Parmenides and Plato, scientific interest was focused upon the constant structure or morphology of nature; and the historical or evolutionary character of nature was henceforth neglected. This neglect of natural history was required by the ever clearer distinction of theoretical or systematic knowledge from more casual knowledge, which did not aim at theoretical unity; and it was encouraged by the increasing dependence of analysis upon mathematical theory. In other words, the development of mathematical physics prevented the development of a science centered upon the facts of organic and evolutionary nature. A logical and mathematical interest displaced interest in natural knowledge. When Aristotle tried to return to a biologically oriented science, he could do so only by a compromise which explicitly rejected the concept of natural evolution, and which established science firmly upon the dogma of the immutability of natural species. This concession to "staticism" made possible the conception of a closed system of nature, confining every motion and change within specific limits. Thus it was allowed that individuals might move and change; but any motion or change which trespassed the cosmic design of immutable species was held to be aberrant or monstrous, and scientifically negligible.

The historical aspect of nature which was thus ignored by theoretical science and philosophy later became the central concern of art and religion. The evolutionary Greek cosmogonies became part of the mythology of poetry and drama; the Greek mystery-religions looked back to quasi-divine heroes, historical figures lost in legend; Thucydides and later historians helped to develop a literary public interested in past human history; the Hebrew people converted their national history into a religious epic; and finally this concern for the historical past and future found expression in the Christian scriptures, and was explicitly formulated by Augustine in his religious "philosophy of history." Pagan science and philosophy were unaffected by this historical literature. Pagan thought, indeed, possessed itself of Christian theology, and once again dominated the European intellect. Therefore modern science and modern philosophy, when they first arose, also focused attention upon the structural pattern of fact, which is accessible to purely theoretical description, and still neglected the larger temporal progress of nature, which requires an historical or evolutionary description.

During and after the Renaissance, the appreciation of historical form was developed in respect to one section at least of nature, namely in respect to human history; and this historical appreciation finally became explicit in the concept of human progress. Although given a name only in the late eighteenth century, the concept of progress underlay and supported the whole development of modern science and society. Science was conceived to be the intellectual wedge which opened the way to political and other progress; and no institution nor system has yet been able to rob modern man of this optimistic outlook upon an expanding and progressive future.

But it was seldom seen, and it still is inadequately understood, that this conception of human progress commits us to a temporalistic or historical conception of nature at large. Quite illogically—if by "law" we refer to the fixed and definable principles of nature—men spoke of a "law of progress." By an inherent natural necessity, said the first advocates of progress, man has continuously progressed in wisdom, goodness, and power. This is, of course, untrue. Human decline is unfortunately as evident as human progress; and it is clear that progress depends first upon the human will to progress, and ultimately upon a number of factors into the nature of which we would do well to inquire.

The philosophical systems elaborated during the late eighteenth and early nineteenth century show a curious half-awareness of history, a sort of effort to accept, without explicitly acknowledging, their mental orientation upon historical and evolutionary fact. We have seen how the post-Kantian dialecticians, and the systems of Comte and Spencer, tried to do justice to the largest consequences of natural evolution without accepting the hypothesis of evolution itself. And, in a deeper manner, the whole development of thought from Hume and Kant onwards prepared the way for an evolutionary view of nature. Both Hume and Kant made time, not space, the widest and most ultimate category of knowledge. Reality, this would mean, is in the last resort a linear, progressive sort of being. But although these two thinkers were somewhat skeptical concerning theoretical knowledge, they did not explicitly conclude that the priority of time as a category of thought establishes the priority of historical character in the external world. Kant's idealistic followers took a step in this direction when they identified the evolution of concepts in the reflective mind with the dialectical order of universal forms in nature; but they hastily retreated from a literal interpretation of this doctrine, by denying the fact of temporal evolution, and by saying that their dialectical pattern "transcends" actual historical change. Increasingly, during the nineteenth century, German philosophers marched up to and reestimated the significance of the historical dimension of nature; but in their last conclusions they invariably became fearful, and by some subterfuge returned to a safe transcendentalism which denies the reality of both time and space.

The actual advance to an evolutionary concept of nature was consequently accomplished by empirical scientists, not by speculative philosophers. Charles Darwin and his fellow scientists brought to a close the long era which had begun when Pythagoras established a science which sought to define, by means of a single theoretical system, the permanent structure of the cosmos. Darwin inaugurated the long era of evolutionary science which is to come, and of which we can as yet only dimly conceive the direction and shape.

We can see today that Plato's science, if it had been remembered in its purity, might have permitted, although it would scarcely have encouraged, the appreciation of evolutionary progress. The principles of mathematics alone, we now perceive, would not preclude the mutation of the specific forms of nature. To call these mathematical principles absolute, as did Plato, would not necessarily imply the fixity of species. But Aristotle, dissatisfied with so abstract a mathematical science and seeking more concrete but still eternal and universal forms, very forcibly insisted upon the fixity of species. He made the definitions of species, stating the morphological relations of species to one another, the basis of all description.

This Aristotelian doctrine, either directly or through its incorporation into Platonism, soon elevated the fixity of species into a primary dogma of the human intellect.

For ourselves, recently emancipated from this dogma, even a cursory study of the species of plant and animal life points to the fact of organic evolution. Why else should the species fall into a natural classification which takes on the form of a genealogical tree? By the close of the eighteenth century, there was ample and conclusive evidence for the hypothesis of geologic and organic evolution. Yet the hypothesis was stoutly resisted or even contemptuously dismissed, often by sincere and competent scientists. These irreconcilables felt, obscurely but correctly, that the evolutionary hypothesis contravened certain fundamental assumptions accepted by earlier science; and they feared that it would discredit the whole achievement of science, and invalidate its method. So they rebuked or ignored Lamarck, who first gathered the evidence for evolution into a unified and really conclusive argument. Condemnation of the Lamarckian hypothesis was the easier, because Lamarck gave to his exposition an Aristotelian and vitalistic interpretation. The mutation of species, he said, is the consequence or manifestation of a vital force inherent in the organism, which in its pursuit of existence may develop new characters transmitted to its progeny. The biologist rejected this view, because it implied that organic changes are self-caused. This would violate the principle basic to mechanistic causal analysis, which holds all change to be reaction to some external action or condition.

Half a century later, in 1859, the scientific world generally applauded the publication of Charles Darwin's *Origin of Species*, although there persisted some minor opposition to its teaching. During the interval between Lamarck and Darwin, geologists like Lyell and Hutton had familarized scientists with the evidence provided by fossil remains of the progressive evolution of the earth's surface. Darwin used this geological evidence in the interests of the hypothesis of organic evolution; and he added much biological evidence, overwhelming in its sum. But further, Darwin cleared the doctrine of its vitalistic elements. The mutations of the species, he taught, are gradual, and proceed cumulatively as the result of minute chance variations in individual organisms. The organism reacts only to its environmental conditions; but some organisms are favored, and others again handicapped, by their small individual variations which in the mass determine survival or death, and so determine the lines of reproduction. Darwin was careful to explain that by "chance" variations he meant not uncaused changes, but variations too small and irregular to be causally explained.

The details of Darwin's doctrine have been challenged and importantly modified. These small variations, it was objected, would scarcely affect survival; and the Darwinian view seemed to require some reproduction in the progeny of effective variations. The development of genetics later transformed the whole conception of organic mutation, by showing how the constitution of the germ plasm determines organic development. The causes of mutation are today almost as mysterious as they were a century ago. Yet Darwin's doctrine, in its essential teaching, stands more firmly than ever. It is generally agreed that the organic species did originate in time, that once there was on this planet no life such as we know it, and that all the organic species have evolved from one or a few original forms of life. Biology, in short, has become an evolutionary or historical science, instead of the purely theoretical science, classifying and interrelating types of form and function, which it was before Darwin. The largest picture of organic nature is this portrayal of organic evolution. The structure of organic nature is not fixed; it may and does change in historical time.

In this way, the concept of human progress was extended and confirmed in a conception of organic progress. Should this evolutionary approach be carried further, to cover the domain of inorganic nature? When Darwin wrote, geologists had already sketched an outline of geologic history, presenting the characteristic features of successive periods of geologic evolution. But beyond geology there stood the purely theoretical studies of chemistry and physics, which still seem to define a universal structure immune to change. Can we conceive physical matter to have evolved, or suppose physical laws such as those of gravitation or the conservation of energy to be variable? Very recently, radical innovations in physical science have transformed the physicist's conceptions of physical structure. It is conceivable that matter might have originated as a modification of certain radiant and nonmaterial forms of energy; and it is also conceivable that physical theories, however useful they may be in prediction, need not correspond to objective structures in the physical world.

Into these difficult and speculative matters we will not enter. Our purpose here is only to perceive, and not to resolve, the new problem which was precipitated by evolutionary science. For thousands of years science had been nonhistorical, nonevolutionary, purely theoretical in its pursuit of the permanent, once-and-for-all definable *structure* of nature. It had sought "laws," principles, formulas applicable here and everywhere, now and always. But with Darwin science advanced to a new genetic method, explaining nature in terms of its origins and historical routes instead of in its "permanent" and "universal" structures. These two methods, the one modeling itself upon human history and moving via organic evolution toward physical creation, the other starting from astronomical and physical theory and extending itself into biological and psychological theory, overlap and reciprocally support each other; yet at the same time they engage apparently incommensurate and incompatible aspects of fact.

The evolutionary approach would explain all natural structures as emerging in time, and as being conditioned by what immediately preceded and surrounded them. Evolutionary science is geographical and historical. It explores a nature which has no known limits, but which has ever-extending accessible ranges in space and time. The theoretical approach, on the contrary, would explain every evolutionary or historical genesis as only the instance of some universal structural principle. To take either approach seems finally to be persuaded into the other. Which shall we enthrone and make definitive? Are there fixed principles in nature which require matter everywhere to transform itself into soil, plant, fish, worm, vertebrate, mammal, man, twentieth-century society? Has this singular evolution repeated itself many times in the distant stars? This seems incredible. Is, then, our planetary evolution unique? Did the universes conspire to nurse life? Did this progress determine itself? This seems, perhaps, no less incredible.

These questions, inevitable yet still unfamiliar, tell us that Darwin ended one long era of philosophical speculation, and inaugurated another which is so young that it has still no voice, no articulate speech. All the old answers, the answers still often thundered from rostrum or pulpit, had assumed the fixity of natural structure. They had implicitly sanctioned the Greek vocabulary of eternalism, of fixed universals, of universal theoretical formulability. They were, in short, just Greek rationalism attired in modern clothes. This collision between theoretical and evolutionary science is perhaps the deepest source of our intellectual confusion today. It is a confusion that threatens the human race, not metaphorically but literally, in that it has helped to drive whole peoples to suicidal wars. In what follows, we will observe some philosophical expressions of this intellectual vertigo that threatens our civilization and our species.

Before turning to these "philosophies of evolution," we should note that the evolutionary hypothesis has really been implicit in modern science since modern science began, and that it only carries further the conceptions and the approach which we have identified as "empiricism." This empirical development was distinguished by its emphatic affirmation of the reality of individual being and the ultimacy of particular fact, and by its opposition to a rationalism which affirmed the reality of universal being and the absoluteness of universal principles. To say that individual being is real is to say that individual being is effective, or truly and finally determinative of what happens in the world. And to say that universals are abstractions is to say that universal being is ineffective, unreal, fictitious. But the structural principles, supposedly effective in keeping species fixed, were universal principles, definitive somehow of universal being; and if there is no universal being, the structural principles are not effective, and we know of nothing which might fixate the species and types of things. To be consistent, we must attribute this mutability of specific form also to inorganic nature. We cannot conceive of organic evolution taking place in a nonevolving cosmos. Yet against all this reasoning is the argument that science, even an historical or evolutionary science, seems to depend upon the affirmation of constants, structural principles, theoretical formulations—in a word some form and some degree of realistic rationalism. A nature that is exclusively individual, wholly unspecific, and incorrigibly fluent could never, it would seem, be known nor intellectually understood.

We will engage this problem in our concluding chapter. Now we turn to certain philosophical speculations which are important not for their solution of the problem, but for their growing recognition of it, and for their oversharp statement of it.

Only in the closing decade of the nineteenth century do we find thinkers who perceived the more radical implications of evolutionary science. One of the first of these was Nietzsche. *Friedrich Nietzsche* (1844–1900) is in ill repute today, at least in democratic society; for he was the proponent of the doctrine of the *superman*, a doctrine which undoubtedly helped to inspire the creators of Nazi Germany. It might be argued that

Nietzsche was better than these degenerate disciples of his. However this may be, Nietzsche first formally promulgated the view that the ambitious individual is his own law, and may properly ignore every moral code and sanction. The casual reader was encouraged by Nietzsche to "emancipate" himself from every moral scruple.

The titles of his books—*Beyond Good and Evil, The Will to Power, The Genealogy of Morals, Antichrist*, and *Thus Spoke Zarathustra*—reveal something of the intention of Nietzsche's teaching. Nietzsche indicted western civilization both for having been lax in its pursuit of moral ideals, and for having pursued false ideals. Justice, mercy, democratic liberty, loving-kindness, pity—above all, pity—these, he wrote, are virtues appropriate to slaves. At the end of a century which over large areas had politically liberated man, Nietzsche claimed that democratic liberalism perpetuated only a slave-culture. What were his reasons for this moral nausea, this revulsion against all traditional ideals and established moral objectives? There is a diseased individualism in Nietzsche, of the sort that marked his spiritual forerunners, Hobbes and Rousseau. The individual will, he argues, is the sole reality, and consequently the sole and sufficient sanction of conduct. It is the duty of the individual to emancipate himself from all convention and social tradition, and to determine in complete solitude and independence his incomparable goal. Nietzsche only intensifies here the voluntarism we noticed in Fichte and Schopenhauer. According to the manner of man you are, said Fichte, you will choose between an immoral material science and my moral transcendentalism. Your duty, Nietzsche says, is to be your incomparable self. Realize your unique being, and make humanity material to your autonomous will! Those who dare to be thus wilful, he seems to say, constitute an heroic aristocracy, which justly makes the more subservient population its slaves.

This stark amoral individualism Nietzsche seems to have learned from certain Greek sophists whom he much admired.

But he gives the doctrine an evolutionary twist, in that he portrays the heroic and aristocratic individual as the protagonist of a new mutation of the human species, bringing into existence the "superman." We remember how Schopenhauer depicted sexual passion as the involuntary servitude of the individual to the ends of the species. Now Nietzsche, a generation after Darwin, suggests that the amoral "hero" enthrones himself in order to establish a new species, and to fulfil the design of a cosmic evolution.

To understand Nietzsche's error, we should appreciate his half-truth. He is telling us that the will of man is the dynamo of his creative evolution, productive of new and higher forms of existence. Moral insight, like scientific insight, must break through and progressively widen the formulated codes of the past. Morality too must evolve. We may forgive Nietzsche his indictment of Christian civilization and his caricature of Christian morality, when we learn what a flaccid, formalized, sepulchral "Christianity" surrounded the boy Nietzsche in his father's parsonage. We can also understand Nietzsche when he sanctifies only one virtue, that of courage; for courage is most needed by those who would themselves pursue and in others arouse a living faith. What we cannot excuse in Nietzsche is his moral snobbishness, his contempt for humanity. Stupid provincialism, from which in his superficial cosmopolitanism he fled, still blinded him to all but an obscure Greek episode of the human past. He had no large prospect upon man's moral progress. Nietzsche, an obscure and lonely neurotic, spent his last years in an asylum for the mentally diseased. That did not prevent the propagation of his equivocal gospel, which was couched in as luminous a prose as the German language has produced. Symptomatic of a mind diseased, perhaps, was the cult which looked to Nietzsche for its medicine.

Nietzsche's doctrine is philosophically noteworthy for its affirmation of radical discontinuity in nature. Human progress, it implies, proceeds by inexplicable leaps from an older pattern or structure to a new and incommensurable form. Quite correctly, we would say, Nietzsche defines human society in terms of its prevailing moral ideal, which determines the largest pattern of human activity. In exhorting us to go "beyond good and evil" Nietzsche is proposing to establish a pattern of behavior wholly dissimilar and discontinuous from the present pattern. He conceives of this leap as a mutation of the human species from an old to a new specific form. If we generalize from this teaching, we would reach the conception of a natural evolution which has proceeded, and which must still proceed, by incomprehensible shifts through discontinuous stages which present no logical nor intelligible relation to each other. So long as a species retains its characteristic form, its behavior pattern will present an intelligible and definable structure; but if the species should mutate, it will present in its new activity another behavior pattern, different from the earlier but again unified and definable in itself. Indefinable, however, is the movement or change from the old to the new structure. This movement, Nietzsche suggests, conforms to no principle, eludes analysis, and neither allows nor seeks justification.

This conception, taken alone, would break nature up into a plurality of worlds, each describable in itself but in no way intelligible as part of a larger natural pattern. What Nietzsche has done is to hold firmly to the idea of definable structure or specific form as the basis of our understanding of nature, while denying the existence in nature of any larger-than-specific pattern, in terms of which the species would fall into some sort of intelligible relationship. He accepts the large fact of natural evolution, and agrees that the species of nature have originated in time by mutation from earlier species. Man, he says, should now mutate into a new "heroic" model. But he rejects the idea of genetic explanation, which explains the character of things in terms of their genesis and continuous development. The genesis of species and the evolution of nature, he implies, transcend understanding. He cannot conceive of an evolutionary, genetic, historical form of knowledge. The transcendentalism to which Fichte and Hegel gave a rationalistic form, and to which Schopenhauer gave an aesthetic formulation, becomes in Nietzsche a sheer anti-intellectualism, a voluntarism unmediated and unmoderated by anything whatsoever. The will, void of scruple and intelligible direction, must carve its destiny. It is this sheer voluntarism, this abandonment to the paroxysm of action, which became the false strength and deeper weakness of Germany. Blind to the world about it, Germany refused all adjustment to its environment, and gave to its neighbors the alternatives of destroying, or being destroyed by, a people gone berserk. Nietzsche might have learned from the Greeks that whom the gods would destroy they first make mad. There is moral sanity, one and the same forever.

A curious doctrine of Nietzsche's, but one which casts light upon his limitations, is his revival of the Greek cyclicism. Everything that happens, he wrote, is the fatal return of what has already transpired an infinite number of times; and it is the mark of the heroic superman that he can contemplate this eternal recurrence without losing his reason. In this fantasy we see a contradictory return to the eternalistic and universalistic outlook which in his main doctrine he emphatically renounces. He intimates, that is to say, that the new insight of the "superman" is just that comprehension of all time and space which Plato had accorded to the reason.

Henri Bergson (1859–1941) is a philosopher of evolution who has seized the other horn of the dilemma presented by the fact of evolution. If we agree that nature radically evolves, so that even the most basic structures of nature are subject to temporal change, shall we suppose with Nietzsche that nature jumps by a transcendental act from one structural block in the moving evolution to another; or shall we, as Bergson advises, make no appeal to structural knowledge, but try instead to understand the evolutionary progress as sheer motion, or

ceaseless and continuous change? Where Nietzsche affirms
the temporal discontinuity of nature, an assumption which
ultimately requires spatial and every other sort of discontinuity,
Bergson denies all discontinuity and defines natural occurrence
as just continuous but intelligible change. It is true, Bergson
agrees, that the theoretical intellect, seeking to define natural
processes in terms of fixed structures, ends with a plurality of
unrelated structures. The structures of physical activity, of
organic activity, and of social activity are evidently incommensurable or logically discontinuous, in that they require
different theories for their description. It seems likely, indeed,
that every natural species and even every individual, if we
proceeded far enough with our analysis, would require special
principles for its description. But it is nevertheless a fact,
Bergson reminds us, that the species have evolved by way of
continuous causal process. There is a causal continuity in nature
that underlies and invalidates every division of nature into distinct types of being. To appreciate this continuity, however,
we must go deeper than theoretical science. Fortunately we
possess another faculty, that of intuition or immediate insight,
which penetrates into the true nature of nature and grasps its
object where the theoretical intellect loses its hold.

We may, perhaps, assent to the proposition that our immediate perception of fact contains much which eludes theoretical definition. Such definitions are, after all, general statements definitive of common character. They are necessarily abstract in their neglect of what distinguishes particulars from
one another. Individual character, for example, eludes exhaustive definition in terms of universal principles. There is a
sense, accordingly, in which perceptual knowledge, the admitted source of conceptual knowledge, remains incommensurate with conceptual knowledge; and this we saw to be the
insight and justification of empiricism. But Bergson, a penetrating and often cogent critic of theoretical science, came to
his study with an antiscientific bias, and perhaps with a par-

tiality for art. Torn in his youth between poetry and philosophy, he made philosophy his career; but he allowed to poetry its revenge, in that he used philosophical analysis to discredit theoretical knowledge in the interest of art and aesthetic intuition.

This invidious teaching was not without antecedents in post-Kantian philosophy, which was now widespread. Bergson gives to the post-Kantian criticism of science, especially to the pragmatic positivism first enunciated by Schopenhauer, a new and incisive formulation. The theoretical intellect, he writes, is not a cognitive faculty motivated by a desire to know nature and intent upon a faithful description of nature. The theoretical intellect serves practical ends. It developed as an agency of survival, and its function is to provide some practical control of our environment. Nature is incorrigibly individual, its every item is unique and incomparable; but the theoretical intellect grasps only those aspects of fact which recur again and again, and in the recurrence or prevention of which we are vitally interested. Bergson suggests, indeed, that the intellect does not so much discover these constant or recurrent characters within nature as construct them and project them into nature, thereby obscuring the true individual pattern of natural occurrence. Theoretical knowledge, he concludes, really tells us only about our own organic needs. It is incorrigibly subjective and deceptive.

Something like this conclusion had been implicit in modern philosophy ever since Hume and Kant attempted to explain how knowledge arises as the result of mental process. Bergson's study of this constructive process is unusually penetrating. Earlier epistemology, he points out, had confused the category of time with one of the three dimensions of space. Time was conceived as a linear order of instants, by analogy with space which was conceived to be a three-dimensional order of positions. But in truth no such homology or similarity exists between time and space, because time is irreversible. Time is everything that space is not. The theoretical intellect likes to think of time as an empty medium to which nature gives content; but an empty world would be timeless. The "time" of which science speaks is not merely an abstraction, it is a mental fiction. Real time, Bergson concludes, is material change itself; and measured time, *e.g.* an hour, is always some spatial interval, such as the distance traversed by the hand of a clock or the angle described by a plane of the rotating earth. It is an hour from here to there. So measured time is only space; and to "real time" Bergson gives the name "duration" (*la durée réelle*).

The rather obvious difficulty with Bergson's conclusion is that it leaves us no way of distinguishing measured time from measured space; yet every calculation of natural events makes use of this distinction, without trouble and with great profit. What Bergson really shows is that measured time and measured space are both constructions. The world is just as various in space as it is changing in time; and if we speak of *la durée réelle*, we should speak also of *l'espace réel*, "real space," geography. But Bergson's emphasis upon the irreversibility of time, *i.e.* the irreversibility of natural change, is one of the important features of recent thought. It signifies that a temporal world must be apprehended historically, and that evolution must be made the widest and most basic category of natural knowledge. Bergson is proposing, one might say with unnecessary violence to theoretical knowledge, to transform natural science into evolutionary science.

The violence of the intellectual revolution proposed by Bergson lies in his mistaken and unjust dismissal of theoretical science as a noncognitive, merely utilitarian enterprise. He shows us that mechanistic science is an abstraction, constructed by thought out of the materials provided by perception. This is true; but it does not signify that this abstract knowledge is motivated solely by practical interests, and not by a desire for truth; nor does it signify that theoretical science fails to reach truth. Modern science does not fail, as Bergson claims, to grasp continuous change. Mathematical science is today equipped to deal with the fact of continuity—it is able to define the continuous line, surface, volume, motion, change. It is only this mathematical grasp of continuity, indeed, that allows us to appreciate and to describe exactly what is discontinuous in nature. Yet Bergson tells us that natural science replaces the continuous evolution of nature by a calculating machine, made up of jointed parts which creak and jerk in a mimicry of nature that is caricature or satire, not truth. It is because he caricatures theoretical science that Bergson must prefer art to science, which is truly the greatest of human arts.

Bergson's studies are rich in incidental insights. In his thoughtful *Matter and Memory* he compares the intellect to a grid, which allows to enter our minds only those elements of "pure perception" which are practically relevant to our vital needs in responding to the given situation. Because the mind automatically preserves in memory every past perception, this grid must suppress those memories which are irrelevant to the present situation. Thus the intellect acts as mediator between the inexhaustible materials of "pure perception" and our similarly inexhaustible personal memory. Science arises at the intersection of environmental geography and personal history. This conception, although unnecessarily subjectivistic, suggests its own expansion in a new understanding of the relationship between time and space. Bergson, it seems, would emancipate both "pure perception" and memory from the intellectual grid; and Proust, Joyce, and other "stream of consciousness" novelists inspired by Bergson show us the consequence of this emancipation in an art which, whatever its surface iridescence, seems to lack purpose and plot.

Bergson's best-known work is his *Creative Evolution*, a metaphysical study of the facts of organic evolution. This study is prejudiced by Bergson's earlier dismissal of theoretical science as a perjured and deceptive account of physical nature; for Bergson cannot now do justice to the causal connection between organic evolution and its environmental context, and his account of evolution becomes vitalistic and unscientific. Yet he cannot simply ignore the environment which has conditioned the evolution of life. Bergson has here reached an *impasse*, because he must take seriously material and inorganic nature. This he had dismissed as a fiction of the practical intellect; but it now must be explained as something real and effective, conditioning life. His attempt to escape the contradiction is interesting. The physical or material world, he says, is the inert residue and reversion of the irreversible movement of life, which he calls *"élan vital."* This living movement he imagines to be a single great impulse, which is broken up by the inertia and resistance of matter, its own reversal, into the multitudinous species of nature. Thus a mechanistic science, Bergson now suggests, correctly describes the downward movement of matter, while an intuitive art grasps the upward movement of life. Bergson owes much in this work to the *Enneads* of Plotinus which described the cosmos as a fount of form dispersed into a material medium. Original and curious is Bergson's suggestion that the deepest division of the universal *élan* is that which separated it into the routes culminating respectively in man and the insect. Whereas man developed intellect, he says, insect life developed a faculty of sympathetic intuition, or instinct; and it is now man's privilege, by a deliberate effort, to appropriate this intuitive faculty also, and by combining it with the intellect, produce a more powerful instrument of cognition than nature has yet evolved. Here, as in Nietzsche, that contempt for past human achievement which has injured modern thought since the Renaissance is so far exaggerated as to become a sort of imbecility. What would be this new wisdom, compounded of the cognitive faculties of men and insects?

Vitiating Bergson's critique of the theoretical intellect is his failure to recognize the imaginative and intuitive faculty which has always marked the true scientist, and which is exercised in every creative hypothesis. Bergson identifies science with the scientific formulas generated by the creative scientific mind, formulas which any mediocre mind can memorize and mechanically apply. This error may in its turn have been due to Bergson's narrow conception of intuition, which he identified with perception. We need not suppose that immediate perception is our whole intuition of truth, and that we possess, in addition to this perceptual faculty, only a power of verbal classification and abstraction. Knowledge is advanced by large intuition suggesting new hypothesis, this latter being the source of all descriptive theory. Somehow we must rehabilitate our real faculty of cognition, the true and creative "intuition" which is the generator of all science and all true art.

In his ripest study, *The Two Sources of Morality and Religion*, Bergson is more sober. He finds two distinct factors working in social evolution. One is the moral insight which has inspired the great teachers and prophets; the other is the codes and institutions which preserve and apply these prophetic insights. His fantastic proposal to synthesize the instinct of insects with the theoretical intellect now reappears in the wise proposal that we should deliberately bring a critical moral insight to bear upon our social institutions, continuously reforming and ultimately transforming these. So the most brilliant Jewish thinker of his century would once again reconcile the law with the prophets, and fulfil the law in an ampler justice.

As the Nazis exploited Nietzsche, so the teachings of Bergson have been exploited by reactionary political opportunists, who read into his intuitionism the justification of a violent *activisme*, and who use his pragmatism to justify the abuse of institutional mechanisms and orthodox loyalties. Much as the Greek sophists prostituted the critical method of Greek science, by transforming it into a cheap and scurrilous diatribe against "convention" and morality, so these modern sensationalists have cheapened the modern criticism of science, by converting it into an apology for amoralism and social violence.

A third philosopher of evolution is *Benedetto Croce* (born in 1866). In both Nietzsche and Bergson we noted a fatal disposition to identify truth with the cognition of present fact. Nietzsche is the more subjectivistic of the two thinkers, in that he identifies truth with the will-to-power which, realizing itself in present fact, makes reality its projection. Bergson teaches that pure perception alone, unfraught by memory of the past, identifies the mind with external reality. This idolatry of the present comes to even more extreme expression in Croce. We will not summarize Croce's system, which retains in its formal outline much of the Hegelian philosophy by which he was early influenced. Better known and more important is his aesthetic doctrine of *expressionism*, which teaches that the work of art only objectifies the thought or intention of the artist. This doctrine is innocuous or trivial until it is taken to exclude the more realistic doctrine of classicism or formalism, which states that aesthetic objects are universal and objective forms, the artist only discovering these forms and creating their images in his material productions. According to expressionism, our appreciation of a work of art is only an acknowledgment of the artist. In the classical doctrine it is an acknowledgment of the eternal and absolute form which could inspire the artist because it exists in nature itself.

Croce's most original thought is an extension of this expressionism. Like Schopenhauer and Bergson, he dismisses empirical science as a merely practical instrument devoid of cognitive power; but like Hegel he has high regard for a superempirical philosophy able to transcend empirical science. In Croce this transcendental idealism acquires a new and strange form as a result of his special interest in historical knowledge. He was, before proceeding to philosophical speculation, a distinguished historian of art.

For Croce the historian, time is a category of being as fundamental as it is for Bergson; and history, he concludes, constitutes our basic, most philosophical comprehension of fact. In his estimate of history, however, Croce is misled by his subjective idealism, which does not allow him to distinguish history as it occurred in the past from history as it is recovered by the present mind. He is misled also by his expressionism, which holds every product of mental activity, including written history, to be only an expression of the mind which produced it. So Croce tells us that the materials of history, *i.e.* the data recovered by historical research, do not constitute history until they are organized, synthesized, and informed by the living mind of the historian. It is only here and now, in its actual entertainment by some mind, that the past has reality. What therefore is the past? It is a dimension of the present mind, which somehow projects its own distinctive form as "the past." Our ordinary conception of the past is in this case diametrically opposite to the truth. We think of the past as determining the present, whereas in truth the present determines the past. More correctly, history is the full realization of our present selves. The essential work of mind, *i.e.* of absolute being, is the continual reformation of its historical retrospect, and a perpetual rewriting of history.

It is questionable whether a subjectivism so extreme as Croce's does not collapse into meaninglessness. We ordinarily suppose that the documents and other data used by the historian actually preserve certain characters possessed by them when they originated. We believe that we read the very words inscribed by Caesar in his remote encampment, or dictated by Queen Elizabeth. But no, Croce tells us; your perception of the document is a present perception, is it not? And similarly your interpretation of the document is a present hypothesis? What is there here that is past? There is only your present mind, which generates that "past." But if we accept this conclusion as true and sufficient, what meaning can we give to the words "history," "the past," "yesterday," "tomorrow." Time evidently demands more objective treatment—Croce's violent embrace destroys its object.

It is disturbing to find reputable historians—in America, for example, Charles Beard and Carl Becker—subscribing to this subjectivistic and relativistic view, which finally robs history of meaning and historical science of truth. The explanation of such adherence is that Croce's view, as we shall presently acknowledge, contains a certain half-truth. But for the moment let us clearly see that a view which denies the causal determination of the present by the past very evidently reduces all science, historical as well as theoretical, to nonsense, and leaves the intellect impotent. Croce's historical subjectivism helped to inspire the theatrical and belligerent Mussolini, who dreamed himself Caesar and called upon the Italians to think of themselves as imperial Rome, since so to think, he told them, is to be that Rome. Croce himself is a courageous and consistent liberal; but his subjectivistic philosophy is grist for every fantasy that seeks escape from fact.

Nietzsche demands a future radically discontinuous from the past, and wholly unconditioned by it. Bergson describes a duration or "real time" which escapes all general formulas in its incomparable novelty. Croce reverses our usual concept of natural causation by conceiving the past to be only a creation of the conscious present. All three thinkers seek a new conception of time and causation; and the compulsion which drives them, consciously or unconsciously, is an evolutionary science which teaches that even the most basic characters of nature are subject to change. Earlier, these basic characters were supposed to be immutable. Science had explained particular change as only the manifestation of this deeper and wider immobility, as only an "instance" of some uniform and constant principle. Does an evolutionary science require us to deny this earlier conception of natural uniformity and causal determination? And if it does, what does it offer in its place? Can we conceive, with these "philosophers of evolution," a world wherein later events are not completely and inevitably determined by earlier events? Can we conceive of any historical causal succession that will not manifest, in its particular way, some general or even universal principle? Would it not be paradoxical if the hypothesis of evolution, which is the largest possible application of the conviction that what occurs later is the causal resultant of what existed earlier, should finally invalidate the concept of causation on which it rests?

The mechanistic concept of causation, which requires later occurrence to be exhaustively explained as the determinate effect of earlier occurrence, has been the governing principle of modern science, and it has been the anchor since time immemorial of common sense and human sanity. We can really conceive of no other sort of explanation of fact. All that has ever pretended to be another sort of explanation either collapses upon careful examination into nonsense, or reveals itself to be only a verbal disguise of mechanistic explanation. Thus philosophers long spoke of teleological explanation, by which they meant an explanation of earlier occurrence as being somehow determined by what it brought to pass later. We cannot avoid this sort of explanation in our dealings with conscious and purposive behavior. The reason or cause of a purposive act, we are wont to say, is the future effect which it intends. And so, the teleologist argued, we may suppose every occurrence, and finally the whole cosmic process, to be determined by that last supreme event which is its ultimate issue. The future explains the past; and it does this only because it determines the past, of which it is the reason or cause. But the scientist, faithful to his principle of mechanistic causation, will easily elude this argument for teleology in nature. The statement that purposive behavior is determined by the end which it seeks to realize, he will say, is elliptical. The purpose does envisage an end, and action is guided by that prospect; yet the purpose, the prospect, and the end envisaged are themselves already determinate, and determined in fact by past conditions. Purposive behavior is thus only a peculiarly complicated sort of mechanistically determined activity.

It should be noted that the mechanistic principle is ethically indispensable, as well as scientifically necessary. All intelligent and purposive behavior presupposes the power to control events; and events are controlled only by providing the antecedent conditions which will cause to happen what we intend to happen, or prevent from happening what we would prevent. Only if mechanistic causation rules, can purpose be effective. But it may well be that mechanistic causation is a more complex and subtle relationship than has been supposed. In respect to any particular situation, we must insist that what occurs later is wholly determined by what occurred earlier. But how do we proceed when we attempt a causal analysis of the situation? This particular situation *s*, we say, is of the general type *S*; and we know from past experience that situations of this type *S* result from conditions of the types *A*, *B*, *C*, etc. Such causal knowledge allows us to bring about, or to prevent, situations of type *S*. In pursuing this sort of analysis, we finally come to understand things and situations in terms of typical causal processes; and it is in the light of this knowledge of typical causation that we define and name things. But when we reflect upon this procedure, we find that it ultimately entails the naming and defining of things in terms of what they do, *i.e.* in terms of what they effect under given conditions. Thus sugar is what will dissolve in water, melt at a known temperature, produce on dissolution so much water of crystallinity, etc. As Hume made clear, the causal relation *connects* antecedents and consequents; but it does not itself disclose the nature of the connection which it is. The use of causal analysis, with fidelity to mechanistic explanation, instructs us to predict later events as the effects of earlier and observed causes; but it also instructs us to understand and define things and events in terms of what they will do and become. Thus *mechanistic explanation means understanding earlier and later events in terms of each other, along the dimension of time.* It does not require any further doctrine, stating that everything was determined at some first moment, or that everything is determined by its last issue. Hume's conclusion still stands—we know of no universal necessity in nature. Every moment is real and effective, not only the first or last moment; and the later moment is no less effective than the earlier moment.

Now the hypothesis of evolution exhibits this truth, first glimpsed by Hume, in a striking and tremendous way. We discover on this planet a progressive mutation of natural form from inorganic, through organic, to human character. There is material continuity in this progress, the inorganic matter becoming organic, and organic matter becoming human. We are required, therefore, to seek some sort of causal explanation of the progress; and it is this explanation which eludes our philosophers of evolution and drives them to speculative frenzy. Nietzsche concludes that the evolutionary mutation is inexplicable, that it is externally unconditioned, and that we can therefore mutate into anything we please. Bergson concludes that evolutionary change is explicable, but only by a sort of explanation that eludes scientific statement and that finds its expression in the symbolisms of art. Croce concludes, astonishingly, that the very distinction between past and present, upon which all causal explanation rests, must be renounced, in which case, of course, the problem disappears; but this means only that we are prohibited from asking any intelligent question concerning natural change.

One more "philosopher of evolution" will help us to grasp the nature of this problem, presented by evolutionary science. *Samuel Alexander* (born 1859) seems to have been early influenced by the dialectic of Hegel, but to have refused Hegel's idealistic epistemology. He is realistic in his acceptance of the theories of natural science; and he makes his chief concern the progress of natural evolution, especially in its movement from physical or inorganic matter toward organic form, and finally toward human intelligence.

In his chief work, which is entitled *Space, Time, and Deity,*

Alexander describes chemical, organic, and human forms as arising not by any dialectical or other necessity, but freely or contingently, out of an original being which he calls "space-time." This original being is a ceaseless nonmaterial motion which conforms always to a fixed pattern or structure, namely that which is approximately defined by mathematical science.

First to evolve out of this mobile matrix is material being, which is characterized by new qualities, *e.g.* color and sound, of the sort earlier contrasted as "secondary" with the "primary" properties of physical being. But Alexander realistically assigns these secondary qualities to external nature. He does not dismiss them as subjective effects in the mind of physical motions outside of the mind. Such matter, possessed of these qualities, is already *sensate*; and from this sensate matter proceeds organic or living being, which has in addition to physical and sensate characters the tertiary qualities we call "feelings." Finally, out of organic matter proceeds minded matter, individuated and self-conscious, and with further new properties. The evolutionary progress, however, does not stop with mind; it proceeds from mind to Deity; for we already see the first appearances of this next stage of being in human society, with its synthesis of individual minds generating new moral properties.

Alexander's rather technical presentation of this doctrine, together with his realistic epistemology, has tended to disguise the sources of his thought and the remarkable, not to say fantastic, character of his conception. His hypostatization of nonmaterial physical motion as the matrix out of which all material evolution proceeds looks back to the Platonic dualism of shifting motion and immutable form. The conception of "sensate" matter arising from a purely mathematical motion, and proceeding by certain combinations to the new synthesis which is organic matter, really only rephrases the Hegelian dialectic. Yet Alexander takes very seriously the hypothesis of evolution; and this leads to radical departures from his Platonic and Hegelian models. There is for him no eternal, overreaching or indwelling Form, working upon nature and persuading it into that form "as far as necessity allows"; but the diverse forms of sensate, organic, minded, and deific nature arise spontaneously—or rather, given certain complications of the earlier form, the later form its thereby also present; and here we are reminded of Spencer, who taught that the organic and human forms of nature are nothing else than progressively complex distributions of matter. These sudden and inexplicable appearances of new forms or qualities Alexander calls "emergences," and he exhorts us to accept "with natural piety" this potentiality of matter to re-create itself in new forms. "Natural piety," it would seem, requires a moratorium on inquiry and curiosity. It is just the nature of nature, we are told, to evolve, and to evolve specifically yet unpredictably into the mineral, organic, human, and social forms which we observe. Alexander does suggest the effective and universal presence in nature of a certain "nisus," *i.e.* a tendency or direction, leading from forms of less value to forms of more value. This nisus, a sort of ghost of the Platonic Good or the Hegelian Absolute, escapes definition, and is presumably the object of a transcendental apprehension. We have here a mystical conclusion, similar to that of Bradley.

Alexander's system is valuable for its clear presentation of the problem it undertakes to solve. If we accept the analyses and results of the several theoretical sciences as a final and definitive description of nature, it is shown, then we must admit the effective presence in nature of relationships and changes which simply elude theoretical explanation. Theoretical physics defines physical structure, theoretical chemistry defines chemical structure, theoretical biology defines organic structure, theoretical psychology defines human nature, and theoretical sociology will define, as they eventuate, the activities which Alexander attributes to "deity." But no theoretical analysis will grasp the evolutionary changes which transform physical motion into chemical interaction, this into organic growth, this into mental activity, and so on. These transformations constitute "emergences," *i.e.* unpredictable and causally indeterminate appearances; we must accept them "with natural piety," *i.e.* without asking for causal explanation. We may appreciate the succession of emergent evolutionary forms as aesthetically and morally significant, but as pointing to a dimension or direction in nature which eludes intellectual study and scientific statement. Alexander in this teaching envisages nature as made up of a plurality of great blocks, each wholly intelligible in itself, but not intelligibly related to anything else. There is no intelligible world, no set of principles universally applicable. The principle of causal determination finally breaks down, because it applies only to limited fields of fact.

The concept of *emergence* has been rather widely appropriated by contemporary philosophers and scientists. Its virtue is to allow us to be completely realistic and intellectually confident with respect to the descriptions provided by the theoretical sciences in their current hypotheses. The structures defined by these theories are held to be real, ultimate, and wholly objective; and if we are unable to relate them to one another, this intellectual impotence corresponds to something illogical or inexplicable in nature itself, and not to any failure or incompetence in our intellectual grasp of nature. The doctrine of emergence means, accordingly: first, that we identify science with our several definitions of diverse natural structures; and second, that this identification of science with theoretical definition precludes forever a scientific understanding of the process of evolution.

These conclusions, in the writer's opinion, are quite unacceptable. First, they dogmatically assign a permanent limitation upon human knowledge, and place a prohibition upon a certain type of inquiry. Second, the hypothesis of evolution is itself a scientific doctrine, supported by evidence; and it already establishes the fact that the mutations in the evolutionary progress are causally determinate, and therefore intelligible and explicable. And third, the doctrine of emergence only revives the discredited fallacies of rationalistic philosophy. It revives in its hypostatization of primary and secondary qualities the Cartesian dualism; but it proceeds to widen this dualism into an absolute pluralism, by adding tertiary and quaternary qualities. Yet we know of many causal relations between physical actions and organic reactions, between physiological conditions and mental processes, between individual thought and its social environment. Why should we arbitrarily insist that causal relations are intelligible when they occur *within* physical, organic, mental, and social processes, but unintelligible when they occur *between* these processes? Science cannot respect so arbitrary a distinction.

And finally, when we examine more closely this doctrine of emergentism, we discover that it is only a rather belated recognition, obscured by rationalistic prepossessions, of the truth announced by Hume. Hume showed that *no* causal connection is intelligible in the sense that the effect can be *deduced* from the cause. In all causal analysis, we finally reach types of causal sequence which just *are*, and which we must accept as the way of the world, as the basis of all scientific explanation of particular occurrences and as the source of our definitions of things. But this finality of causal connection holds of all causal connections, not only of some. If the causal effect by which a physical object stimulates in ourselves a mental perception is inexplicable and "emergent," so is the causal connection by which a physical object influences the motion of another physical object. This even the seventeenth-century Occasionalists knew. But Alexander either does not understand, or will not accept, the demonstration of Hume that all causal process whatsoever is "emergent" in its contingency. He is really a belated Cartesian, lost in an evolving world. He tells us that there are four or five absolute substances, namely physical motion, chemical matter, organic matter, mind, and society. He admits that the earlier substance produces the latter. But he rationalistically identifies science with an intuition of absolute substance; and therefore he concludes that there can be no intelligence of the process of evolution which generates these "absolute" substances one from another.

We have now noticed four philosophical efforts—and they are perhaps the most notable efforts up to the present—to accommodate thought to the disturbing fact of natural evolution. The first three thinkers advise us to put no faith in the theoretical intellect, to accept the results of theoretical science only for their practical utility and not as descriptive of actuality, and to seek truth by means of some nonintellectual faculty of volition, perceptual intuition, or imagination. The fourth thinker would retain scientific theories as being truly descriptive of the specific structures of nature; but he too concludes that this scientific knowledge fails to grasp the process and meaning of evolution. We observe evolutionary change, he agrees, but we can know nature only insofar as it does not evolve. Alexander's conclusion only makes unusually clear and explicit the attitude of most contemporary scientists, who accept the *facts* of evolution in all of their detail, but make no effort to pursue these facts in a large study of the implications of the hypothesis of evolution for our conceptions of nature and knowledge.

This impotence of recent thought in face of the fact of evolution is due to the failure to see that evolutionary science, which initiates a new conception of nature, finally requires a new and enlarged conception of natural knowledge. A strictly theoretical science, it is true, cannot expect to provide exhaustive explanation of a radically evolving world. A strictly theoretical science makes its whole business the ever more exact definition of general structures, whereas an evolutionary science discovers and seeks to explain the transformation of these structures one into another. We will not try to show at this point the implications of evolutionary science, because these are better appreciated in the light of certain recent and revolutionary advances in logic and physical science. But we may insist here that we cannot legitimately accept the common conclusion of these "philosophers of evolution," who tell us that evolutionary progress is scientifically inexplicable because it eludes a purely theoretical analysis. Science is not necessarily limited to theoretical analysis; nor, as we shall show, has it ever been so limited. Science has always been more than its theoretical descriptions; and only because this is so could it arrive at and seriously entertain the hypothesis of natural evolution. Science is eternally committed, however, to the principle that all natural occurrence whatsoever is causally determinate, and therefore scientifically intelligible and explicable. If we will only hold fast to this principle of sufficient causation, which is the root of human sanity, we may come through the dark forest of intellectual confusion and know again the light of reason.

Notes for Further Reading

1. Frazer, J. G., *Condorcet on the Progress of the Human Mind*, London and New York, Oxford University Press, 1933.
2. Morley of Blackburn, J., *Biographical Studies* (Turgot, Condorcet). New York, The Macmillan Company, 1923.
3. Bury, J. B., *The Idea of Progress*. New York, The Macmillan Company, 1921, 1932.
4. Dewey, J., *The Influence of Darwin on Philosophy*. New York, Henry Holt and Company, 1910.
5. Osborn, H. F., *The Origin and Evolution of Life*. New York, Charles Scribner's Sons, 1917.
6. Morgan, C. L., *Emergent Evolution*. New York, Henry Holt and Company, 1923.
7. Boodin, J. E., *Cosmic Evolution*. New York, The Macmillan Company, 1925.
8. Hobhouse, L. T., *Development and Purpose*. New York, The Macmillan Company, 1913.
9. Baitsell, S. H., ed. *The Evolution of Earth and Man*. New Haven, Yale University Press, 1929.
10. Conger, S. P., *New Views of Evolution*. New York, The Macmillan Company, 1929.

11. Morgan, T. H., *The Scientific Basis of Evolution*. New York, W. W. Norton and Company, Inc., 1932.

12. Huxley, J., *The Living Thoughts of Darwin*. Boston, Longmans, Green and Company, 1939.

13. —— *Evolution, the Modern Synthesis*. New York, Harper and Brothers, 1942, 1943.

14. Henderson, L. J., *The Fitness of the Environment*. New York, The Macmillan Company, 1913.

15. Bergson, H., *An Introduction to Metaphysics*, trans. T. E. Hulme. New York, G. P. Putnam's Sons, 1912.

16. —— *Matter and Memory*, trans. Paul and Palmer. New York, The Macmillan Company, 1912.

17. —— *Creative Evolution*, trans. A. Mitchell. New York, Henry Holt and Company, 1911.

There are studies of Bergson in English by Carr, Chevalier, Elliot, Gunn, LeRoy, Stephen, Wilm, and others.

18. Boutroux, E., *The Contingency of the Laws of Nature*. La Salle, Ill., The Open Court Publishing Company, 1916.

19. Croce, B., *Aesthetic as Science of Expression*, trans. D. Ainslee. New York, The Macmillan Company, 1922.

20. —— *History, its Theory and Practice*, trans. D. Ainslee. New York, Harcourt, Brace and Company, 1921.

21. Carr, H. W., *The Philosophy of Benedetto Croce*. New York, The Macmillan Company, 1927.

22. Nietzsche, F., *Works*, ed. Levy. New York, The Macmillan Company, 1925. Also ed. and trans. Tille, Common, and others. 1896f.

There are selections from Nietzsche by Mencken, Mann, and studies by Brinton, Carus, Ellis (in *Affirmations*, Boston, Houghton Mifflin Company, 1922), Flaccus (in *Artists and Thinkers*, Boston, Longmans Green and Company, 1916), Foster, and others.

23. Alexander, S., *Space, Time, and Deity*. New York, The Macmillan Company, 1920.

24. Miller, H., *History and Science*. Berkeley, University of California, 1939.

III   CONTEMPORARY PHILOSOPHY

23 REALISM

WE NOW REACH THE END OF OUR SURVEY AND approach the goal for which we undertook it, namely, an understanding of contemporary life and thought. Some of the thinkers noticed in the preceding chapter are either still living or only recently deceased; and certain of the nineteenth-century movements earlier described are still influential, although usually in somewhat modified form. Our study of these thinkers and movements accordingly already introduces us to contemporary thought. Yet there is a sense in which the twentieth century, especially the period following the First World War, has drawn a line between ourselves and earlier speculation. Contemporary philosophy makes new starts in new directions. This independent and rather revolutionary attitude affects the way in which earlier doctrines are understood and developed today; and we best appreciate the new outlook by observing those contemporary movements which are still in process of formulating their doctrines, and which bring this outlook to sharpest expression. We will consider the movements known as the new realism, pragmatism, and logical positivism; but it should be remembered that every such classification is oversimple and somewhat misleading. Today the whole pattern of traditional thought is undergoing a sort of kaleidoscopic transformation, so that familiar doctrines seem to become their opposites, and positions formerly defined in contrast with one another seem to support one another or to merge into one another; and we do not know how the immediate future will transmute the "isms" of the present. Few contemporary thinkers are willing or able to identify themselves with just one movement or doctrine. A realist may lean to pragmatism, a pragmatist to positivism, a positivist to realism. Yet in order to understand, we must distinguish and classify, remembering that our distinctions are subject to change.

We will first consider the new or revived realism of the present, because this movement slightly preceded and thus set the stage for the other two movements. The new realism was initially a negative or critical doctrine, rather than a positive system of thought. It would be difficult to find a set of principles affirmed by all contemporary realists; but it would not be so difficult to point to certain conceptions rejected by all of them. During the latter half of the nineteenth century, the sort of speculation developed by the post-Kantian idealists had established itself in most colleges and universities. The profundity of Kant's critique of natural science was slowly but steadily appreciated; and the *volte face* by which his rationalistic followers turned this critique of natural knowledge into a transcendental metaphysical system was widely accepted as the sole escape from skepticism and as a legitimate development of Kant's more constructive paragraphs. In Britain and America, and to some extent on the continent of Europe—there especially among Catholic scholars—this post-Kantian idealism stimulated strong reaction, culminating in organized rebellion; and it was out of this rebellion against Kantian philosophy that the new realism was born.

The motivations for the rebellion were scientific, political, and religious. Absolute idealism, we saw, started from the Kantian critique of science. Kant had intended to establish the validity of natural science, while pruning "reason" of its metaphysical pretensions; but the idealists transformed this criticism into an invalidation of science, in the interests of a superscientific metaphysics. The scientist who is intent upon particular fact, it was urged, reaches only a tentative, conjectural, and incorrigibly partial or fragmentary knowledge; but the reflective philosopher carries the stumbling and blinkered effort of science to its true goal in an unrestricted knowledge of absolute, universal, and unitary being. Only in such absolute knowledge do we find the complete interrelationship of fact which science haltingly depicts in its empirical hypotheses. Perhaps we may agree that science does point beyond its present formulations of fact to a more inclusive knowledge. But the scientist would like to advance to this better knowledge himself, with due regard for scientific method and rigor. He is not satisfied to be told that his method is by definition incompetent, and that another "transcendental" knowledge, which he would call empty and verbal, must supersede his empirical study of fact. So science was increasingly and quite properly hostile to this philosophical transcendentalism.

Further, the political implications of this absolutistic philosophy aroused fear and distrust, especially when it became the creed of conservative opposition to a liberalism which seemed to have lost its intellectual bearings. Starting from the apparently innocuous and liberal-sounding doctrine of individual self-realization, the absolutist could portray this self-realization as a movement by which the individual person ultimately identifies himself with Absolute Reality, the One or All, and proceed to discover the chief actualization of this Absolute in the state. This conclusion may appear farfetched; yet it is historical fact that all absolutistic political theory has grounded itself upon some form of absolutistic metaphysics.

Finally, the doctrine of metaphysical absolutism, even where it was ostensibly advanced as the theological bastion of religion, repelled many a religious mind and probably contravened the creeds of most religious confessions. Christianity especially has always preserved, even in its theology but much more in its implicit prepossessions, pluralistic assumptions which cannot be made compatible with an uncompromising monism like absolute idealism. Moral insight and religious faith finally set limits to the pursuit of unity, system, and certainty.

In Britain, the growing reaction against absolute idealism found a center at Cambridge University, which had for some time cultivated the sciences and been critical of classical piety and transcendental philosophy. The Cambridge realists found support in the Scottish universities, where since the eighteenth century a form of "common-sense realism" had been advocated as the basis of intellectual faith, offering a way of escape from the too subtle analysis and consequent skepticism of Hume. The most essential doctrine of *G. E. Moore*, initiator of the Cambridge movement, stated that the objects of knowledge, whether these be perceptual qualities, conceptual objects, or values apprehended by aesthetic or moral insight, may be quite independent of the mental processes involved in our cognition of them. Moore argued that the white color of a flower, the rectangular shape of a table seen in perceived perspective or diagrammatically conceived, the properties of a chemical agent, mathematical functions, or the qualities of mercy and justice are objects open to direct intellectual inspection, and that such inspection does not change them in any way. We are continually, in sense-perception and in thought, apprehending by discovery such real qualities, relationships, things, and other objects. These objects are not generated by cognition. They have being in their own right; their character and relationships are there to be discovered; and when they are discovered, they constitute a knowledge which can be invalidated by no epistemological criticism and by no psychological analysis. The senses first, and after them the theorizing intellect, are reliable witnesses, and provide authentic knowledge of real being.

This doctrine has usually been called "realism" in view of its opposition to transcendental idealism, nominalism, positivism, and other movements which hold that the mind in some way constructs and in some degree generates its cognized objects. The doctrine is indeed realistic in its insistence upon the identity of cognized objects—qualities, things, relationships —with reality itself. Yet the name "realism" is not very helpful to our appreciation of its distinctive teaching. Medieval scholasticism was realistic when it taught that the reason intuits the true essences or specific forms of things. Nominalism was realistic in respect to sensed fact, if it insisted that our immediate perceptions of particular character, but not our abstract conceptions, infallibly apprehend reality. And absolute idealism in Hegel or Bosanquet was realistic when it accorded to the concepts generated by transcendental reflection an absolute validity and an identity of some kind with universal being. The idealistic postulate of absolute idealism, affirming the identity of Reality with Mind, was used to establish the realistic postulate that the objects constructed by mind may have the status of absolute reality. In what, then, did this new realism distinguish itself from older forms of realism? Wherein was it more realistic than these other doctrines? The new realism distinguished itself from earlier realism in two ways. First, it was impartial with respect to the realistic claims of perception and conception, or the senses and the intellect. Both, it held, may directly and truly apprehend real being of some sort. Secondly, it was unusually clear and outspoken concerning the nature of such cognition. The perceived or conceived object, it said, enters the mind without alteration of any kind, without shadow of change. Cognition differs from many processes known to us, in that the cognized object is unaffected by its mental context, or by the process of becoming cognized. The object as it is apprehended is exactly what it was before it was apprehended, and what it will be after it is out of mind again.

A primary intention of this doctrine was to protect scientific knowledge from the various kinds of criticism it had undergone since Berkeley and Hume. If both perception and conception may be realistic and ultimate in their apprehension of fact, then the results of the scientists' careful and systematic use of these faculties may be accepted, and are immune from philosophical criticism.

Yet it is surely obvious that much of our perception is sub-jectively conditioned. If you and I stand a few feet apart, we have different visual perspectives of the same scene. It is equally obvious that our conceptual understandings of the same situa-tion may vary. Scientists working in the same field and accept-ing the same data may entertain different conceptual formula-tions of their material. The new realist had to show, therefore, just how, and when, and in what respects, perceptual and con-ceptual objects are indubitably real. My vision of the clock is a real and objective perception, not affected by what I think about it; but if I am peculiarly astigmatic, the clock I perceive is peculiar to me. Copernicus and his geocentric predecessors used the same mathematical theory; yet they differed in their applications of mathematical concepts to perceived fact, and so reached different conceptions of the solar system. A vast amount of realistic effort has been devoted to showing how, and in what carefully defined respects, the realistic postulate may and should be upheld; but today, after thirty years of exacting epistemological study, there is little consensus of opin-ion among realistic epistemologists. Occasionally, experimental psychology is able to apply scientific criteria to the study of cognition, and so bring debated issues to a decision; but for the most part, the realist is dependent upon an introspective faculty, if faculty it be, which is not amenable to scientific criteria. It would seem that the new realist, in attempting to establish the truth of science by means of a realistic epistemology, must appeal, even as do his idealistic opponents, to a sort of analysis other than that of science, and ostensibly more basic. Yet his intention was to set empirical science upon its own feet, as an autonomous study reaching truth.

The ablest adherent of G. E. Moore, and the outstanding

proponent of contemporary realism, is *Bertrand Russell* (born 1872). Russell in his successive writings has attempted such diverse approaches to the problem of knowledge, and reached so various and tentative conclusions, that a résumé of his teaching is scarcely possible. Noticeable is his distinction, both in his earliest and in his latest writings, of two domains of "real" knowledge, *i.e.* of absolute and necessary judgments. One of these is the perceptual domain of sensed quality. We indubitably perceive colors, shades of the "same" color, and relationship among colors. Orange is *necessarily* placed between red and yellow. Here is the domain of indubitable, immediately apprehended fact which provides the material—not only in its qualities but also in its relationships—for all conceptual knowledge. The other domain is that of logical and conceptual objects, *e.g.* mathematical entities. Here also we have immediate and indubitable insight. The problem is to see how these two domains of absolute knowledge, which appear in many ways incommensurable, conspire to give us the hypothetical or probable knowledge which is empirical science. Russell attacks this problem again and again, but never claims that he has solved it.

Russell's lasting fame, which will increase as the centuries pass, depends less on these inconclusive epistemological studies than on his reform of logic, to which we referred in our study of Kant. For more than two thousand years, logic had remained much what Aristotle left it—a study of sentences of the form *A* is *B* (all *A* is *B*, some *A* is *B*, no *A* is *B*, some *A* is not *B*) and of syllogisms composed of pairs of such sentences and their implications (no *A* is *B*, some *C* is *A*, so some *C* is not *B*). Philosophically minded logicians had produced large tomes which elaborated this primitive logic as a basic definition of the "laws of thought," and discussed with some acumen and vast labor its relationship to factual material and ultimate being. But modern science had long since forgotten this Aristotelian logic, and developed its own ways of thought and intellectual procedures. These were altogether more complicated and more powerful than the naive formulas of the Aristotelian logic; and they could not be "reduced" or made conformable to Aristotelian logic except by very artificial and inadequate devices. It is rather astonishing to realize that modern empirical science had already advanced for some four centuries, and produced achievements which dwarfed all earlier science, without any codified "logic" or set of rules regulating its procedures—a situation shocking to the pedantic mind but not unpleasing, perhaps, to the liberal mind.

But today we know that modern science did in fact possess its logic, a logic that is superior to and inestimably more potent than the rudimentary organon of Aristotle. *Mathematical theory has functioned as the logic of modern science.* First in physical science, and later in the biological and social sciences, mathematical theory has borne increasingly the weight of cumulative scientific hypothesis; and where empirical description remained non-quantitative, and therefore resistant to mathematical treatment, it has modeled itself upon physical theory, which is preeminently quantitative and mathematical. Any sort of hypothesis which could conceivably be given mathematical formulation, even though the data may not yet allow of such formulation, is accepted as logically valid, *i.e.* consistent, verifiable, and intelligible.

This understanding of the logical function fulfilled by mathematical theory in modern science we owe chiefly to Bertrand Russell; and we shall see that it makes possible a philosophical insight larger than any attained by the human intellect since Thales and his Greek successors established theoretical science twenty-five centuries ago. In 1910, collaborating with his mathematical colleague Alfred North Whitehead, Russell published the first volume of his *Principia Mathematica*, which established the new "modern," "mathematical," or "symbolic" logic. This work, although not conclusive and in some of its analyses already modified, will remain a classical text of the logic of the future. It transformed the discipline of logic, vastly extended it, and made possible a new understanding of the nature of logic and of its relation to empirical knowledge and to fact.

This revolution was not the work of a day, nor yet of two men. Russell leaned heavily on the contributions of earlier mathematicians and logicians, such as Leibniz, Frege, Peano, and Boole; but he consolidated and developed these earlier studies, and, above all, he made the intellectual world aware of them and their significance. The *Principia Mathematica* formally announced the close of one long era of intellectual development, and the inauguration of a new philosophical era, in which the inquiring human intellect casts loose from certain fixed moorings to which it had earlier been anchored. Henceforth the thought of man must sail the open sea and find, instead of the old landmarks, stars by which to navigate its course.

This prospect which is opened up by the *Principia Mathematica* we shall discuss later. Here we take note only of the contribution of this work to logic. The authors show conclusively enough that the propositions of pure mathematics can be restated without loss of cogency in strictly logical terms. Mathematical theory becomes a compact but tremendous symbolic system, the purely logical character of which can be made explicit by a meticulous and rather tedious process of analysis and symbol definition. The forms and operations of thought, it follows, are not to be identified with the rudimentary code sanctified by traditional logic. They are at least as many, as various, as flexible, and as capable of development as are the operations and symbolizations of a creative mathematical science.

Russell undertook this inquiry into logical form in the interests of realistic philosophy. It was, he assured the writer, expressly to undercut and to discredit the assumptions of Kant concerning mathematics, that he proceeded to this laborious reduction of mathematical to logical statement. Kant, it will be recalled, had distinguished mathematical propositions as *synthetic* from the purely *analytic* (and therefore trivial) propositions of traditional logic. An analytic proposition, Kant meant, is one which merely makes explicit in its predicate term what is implicit in its subject term. For example, the sentence *seven is a number* merely explicates in the predicate a property of *seven* which is involved in the definition of *seven*, so that the addition of the predicate adds nothing new. But propositions like *seven and five are twelve*, Kant argued, cannot be reduced to analytic statements, since the definitions of *seven* and *five* do not logically imply that their sum is *twelve*. Kant therefore concluded that mathematical propositions, in their undeniable necessity and in their factual truth, demonstrate our possession of a faculty which is neither merely logical, reaching analytic propositions, nor merely empirical, reaching synthetic generalizations which are only probable. The basis of all natural knowledge, he insisted, is this mathematical knowledge, constituted of propositions which are absolutely and universally valid, yet which are not merely definitions of meanings, but statements describing the world we know in experience. It was from this Kantian conception of a "pure reason," able to make absolute statements about the necessary and universal forms of experience, that the metaphysicians who followed Kant proceeded to their transcendental and superempirical "science."

By showing that the propositions of pure mathematics are, after all, analytic propositions merely expanding definitions, Russell discredited transcendental metaphysics at its source. In this way he confirmed the empirical direction of thought which had been initiated by the nominalists, developed by empirical science, and philosophically clarified by Hume. In this empirical view, there are only two sorts of propositions. On the one hand, there are analytic propositions which define meanings, or perhaps words or other symbols; and these propositions are absolute, necessary, and certain only in the degree that they are firmly adhered to. We can define meanings and symbols as we please, and uphold our definitions by fiat—for example, in a dictionary the authority of which we enforce. On the other hand, there are synthetic or descriptive propositions which make statements about things and natural processes; and these propositions, based upon our limited perception and our partial understanding of nature, are subject to change. These propositions are less than absolute, being only probable in their truth. As Hume had shown, we have no absolute or certain knowledge of matters of fact. The absolute certainty of a proposition is sufficient evidence of its purely logical and nondescriptive character.

Mathematical science, ever since the time of Pythagoras and Plato, had seemed to constitute a knowledge at once absolute and certain in its truth, and universally descriptive in its applicability to nature; and the existence of this mathematical science had seemed to demonstrate the possession by man of a rational faculty able to reach such absolute and universal knowledge of fact. The reduction of mathematical propositions to symbolic definitions ended this long error, by sharply demarcating the sphere of free or arbitrary logical construction from that of scientific hypothesis; and it thus ended, presumably for perpetuity, the era of rationalistic metaphysics. However, this clear demarcation of the fields of logic and science does not solve, but only makes more acute and definable, the problem of the relation between freely constructed symbolic systems, such as mathematical theory, and the descriptive theories of empirical science, within which mathematical theory is somehow incorporated. Does physical science, for example, with its intimate dependence upon mathematical theory, endow this incorporated logic with descriptive meaning and truth, and show the commensurability of pure logic with material fact? Or does our awareness of this purely logical structure in physical science warn us that physical theory is a human construction, which may not be accepted as the sheer description of an external reality? Why do these elaborate logical constructions implement an empirical and descriptive science? Why does nature submit to or conspire with our faculty of symbolic construction? How and why is language possible?

This was Kant's real question; and Russell has not answered it. He has widened and more correctly phrased the question. Kant asked: How is mathematical physics possible? We must still ask: How is any theoretical science, implemented by symbolic logic, possible? Russell himself, returning to this problem after his epoch-making excursion into logic, has remained faithful to the introspective, quasipsychological sort of analysis cultivated in Britain since Berkeley and Hume. In his analysis of "experience," he seeks irreducible elements of sensed quality, which he supposes to furnish the infallible materials of knowledge; and, in his study of the logical structure of knowledge, he defines logical classes constituted of pluralities of particular propositions. His problem is to discover how these two domains, made up respectively of sensory atoms and of logical atoms, come together in factual knowledge. The positive results of this inquiry are meager; and Russell's addiction to this introspective analytical epistemology may have prevented him from perceiving the largest consequences of his epochal work in logic.

In his social and political writings, Russell is the defender of an extreme moral and political individualism. His guiding objective is the emancipation of the individual from every restraint, freedom from which would not demonstrably injure other individuals. One must admire the courage with which Russell has preached and practised this view, and one may sympathize with the view itself in a period which tends to overlook the individual in the pursuit of massive well-being and social uniformity. Yet we may ask whether the psychological atomism which defeats Russell's epistemological inquiry does not blind him to the positive responsibility of the individual, as the member of a social community, for the lives of others than himself. The human individual lives as a member of society, in the political government of which he necessarily participates; and his responsibility is not limited to an abstention from injury to others. His political power, just insofar as it is exercised, makes him the guardian of others. Inevitably, he is his brother's keeper. His right use of political power makes him the creator of other lives, his abuse of it makes him the destroyer of other lives. Moral and political responsibility therefore constitutes a positive responsibility for others' good; and our insight into what is good for others presupposes our interest in others and our love of them. An atomistic individualism, limiting individual responsibility to a negative withholding of injury from others, will not indefinitely support democratic government. This requires the positive assumption by each individual of the responsibilities of a governor of the social and moral community, within which each life is determined and by which it is shaped.

But we should be satisfied, perhaps, to leave to the future an estimate of this most important thinker of his generation, whose tremendous effect upon thought will be patent as long as intellectual curiosity impels the human mind. We will return to further consideration of Russell's influence in our treatment of contemporary positivism.

Alfred North Whitehead (born 1861), Russell's collaborator in the *Principia Mathematica*, proceeded from this same logical study to farreaching metaphysical speculations. It is interesting to observe how these two men were so differently influenced by that study, and to speculate on the reasons. Russell, trained in philosophy and favorable to the empirical British tradition, was confirmed in his suspicion that logic is an empty or "trivial" knowledge, having to do chiefly with symbols and their manipulation. Whitehead, an able and creative mathematician, was confirmed in his belief that conceptual construction is the heart or dynamo of thought itself, and was encouraged to trust to his logical talent in an attack upon the largest problems of philosophy. Where Russell perpetuates the critical empiricism of Locke and Hume, Whitehead continues the speculative tradition of Leibniz, who was inspired by somewhat the same facility in logico-mathematical construction.

We recall that Leibniz initiated the logical studies which culminated in the mathematical logic of the *Principia Mathematica*. His constructions were suggested by tendencies of seventeenth-century science, tendencies which have maintained themselves since his time. Leibniz' doctrine of monadism was devised to explain how a reality really composed of ultimate, distinct, and irreducible individuals might be described by a physical science which assumed the continuity of natural motion. Leibniz' monads reappear in the "*occasions*" of Whitehead; and the continuities of space, time, and motion reappear in Whitehead's "*process of reality*."

These occasions, we are told, are the real and individual events of which nature is composed. Each occasion has its peculiar organic unity, its distinct quality or substantiality. Unlike the monad, which was eternal, the occasion endures only so long; but much as the monads were so related as to produce the effect of continuous matter, the occasions conspire in virtue of their reciprocal "ingredience" to produce a continuity of natural process. Scientific theories explicitly formulate these relations of ingredience, which synthesize smaller occasions into larger occasions, until all occasions are finally synthesized in "the process of reality" itself. We understand this relationship of ingredience most intimately, Whitehead tells us, by an introspection into our conscious selves; for we are constituted of processes of this sort, composed of individual experiences or events which are reciprocally ingredient, and which compose into our character and our career. These personal occasions, ingredient in one another in our unitary life-process, are ingredient also in other occasions external to ourselves. Experienced events have relations both to one another and to nonexperienced events. This dual relationship

allows us, therefore, to infer the relationships among nonexperienced events; and it is these we seek to define in theoretical
knowledge. Such knowledge is abstract and indirect; but because our intellectual cognition is itself an occasion, directly
ingredient with our immediate perceptions and, through these,
indirectly ingredient with external events, natural knowledge
is incorporate with its object, the external world; and this is
how the Cartesian dualism of mind and matter is overcome.
We are hereby assured that experience and knowledge, although not to be identified with nature, are homogeneous with
nature. Experience is the stuff of which nature is made; and
nature is also the stuff of which experience is made.

Whitehead's metaphysic is in many ways superior to its
model, the Leibnizian monadism. It is extraordinarily versatile,
flexible, competent in its interpretation of science. It is never
without a philosophical answer; nor will the answer strain
credulity although Whitehead's terminology may tax the
memory. Leibniz needed both a *deus ex machina* to set the stage
of nature, in God the Creator of the monads, and a *deus in
machina*, in God the Supreme Monad. Whitehead, like Samuel
Alexander, requires only a deity who works as an active and
universal principle of realization, moderating and informing the
careers of those who freely cooperate. For Whitehead, individual being is authentically free and indeterminate, and not
predestined. Almost certainly, there never was so ingenious a
metaphysical system as this of Whitehead; and not impossibly
it may continue indefinitely to be just that—the last metaphysical system to end metaphysical systems.

Why has this brilliant speculative construction, so ingenious
and plausible, which at so little cost saves so much—all the
freedoms, all aesthetic qualities and moral values, the two
criteria of science, and religion along with science—why has
this genial philosophy elicited so little intellectual response, and
not become the rallying point and credo of all honest and
reverent intellectuals? Whitehead's vocabulary is somewhat

difficult, but not more so than many another; and his style is fluent, and often poetically beautiful. Is our indifference to his achievement the proof that we have already entered a dark age, ignorant of truth because indifferent to it? It may be that skepticism has destroyed our capacity for large faith, however reasonable and well-evidenced that faith may be. But it is also possible that Whitehead in his facile construction, like Leibniz before him, has failed to perceive the motive and real burden of modern thought, which ever since the Middle Ages has rejected such metaphysical solutions of the problems of life and knowledge.

In our discussion of Leibniz, we found the Leibnizian system to presuppose a realm of logical possibilities, out of which God selected for actualization, at the creation, those which synthesized into "the best of all possible worlds." What is that realm of logical possibilities, which limits all reaction and sets bounds to God and man? Is it more than a fantasy, the projection as "most ultimate being" of the present finalities of human experience or thought? The nominalist and the empiricist have held it to be no more than this. In the system of Whitehead this logical realm of essence, which was the explicit or implicit postulate of all the rationalistic systems of the past, reappears in a realm of *eternal objects* which constitute the ultimate and irreducible material of all occasions. The end of all analysis, if analysis could be consummated, would be just this eternal realm of essences, which is incorporated in, yet unaffected by, the toil and joy of individual life and temporal progress. It is the reality of this realm of essence, Whitehead holds, that makes possible and true our understanding of all particular fact and individual existence. This is Whitehead's realism. Apart from these eternal objects, particulars could not truly instance general types, types could not be related to compose theories, nature would be inchoate, and natural knowledge would be impossible.

Shall we call this conception rationalistic or empirical? It is certainly not the old rationalism, which identified its rational intuition of eternal essence with a theoretical knowledge of the cosmic process of nature. In Whitehead's system, the essences provide only the atomic elements, out of which existent actualities are composed; and because the elements are infinite in number, they can compose into an infinite variety of existent worlds, so that the character of existent fact is contingent and must be discovered by observation. Whitehead's conception is therefore consistent with empirical method; but does it illuminate and justify, or does it on the contrary make inexplicable and dubious, an empirical theoretical science? In what sense is our science descriptive of *this* world, if its theory would equally well apply to innumerable other worlds, variously compounded of the same essences? And how can we conceive of the relation between these two realms—the intuited realm of subsistent essence, and the experienced and lived world of particular existence? Does this sort of realism ignore the real problem, which is the relation of general knowledge to particular existential fact? Does it know the creed and share the burden of a genuine empiricism, which intends to affirm the ultimacy and the intelligibility of individual being? Or does it, like Plato, leave inexplicable the relation between the actual and the ideal, and lead us toward skepticism?

Russell, although he too affirms the cognitive ultimacy of ultra-individual essences, such as are reached by an introspective epistemological analysis, is no longer inclined to give them metaphysical status, but leaves their relationship to existential reality problematic. It is questionable whether contemporary realism, in trying to save theoretical science from its critics by insisting upon the identity with "reality" of the objects described by theoretical analysis, leaves science more securely established or more exposed to rationalistic distortion or skeptical dismissal. Presupposed in all philosophical realism of this kind is the assumption, conscious or implicit, that some sort of analysis other than scientific analysis is needed to establish the veracity of science; and a discipline which could assume authority *for* science in this way would also enjoy authority *over* science. Science itself, it would seem, claims no such infallibility of judgment as the realist claims for it; yet its arguments are more cogent, and its conclusions more probable, than the purely speculative results of an introspective epistemology.

The realistic reaction which we have just observed in certain of its British exponents was widespread and took various forms. On the continent of Europe, it appeared in a revival of scholastic philosophy which, although long dormant, had always opposed the conclusions of Humian and Kantian epistemology, as well as more empirical interpretations of natural science. *Neo-Scholasticism* has maintained the chief tenets of the Aristotelian metaphysics and epistemology; but it adapts them where possible to the teachings of contemporary science. Like the new realists, the Neo-Scholastic holds that the objects of knowledge are not affected by the fact of becoming known; but he ascribes this power of real cognition only to the intellect or reason, to which he attributes an insight into real substances and their specific or essential characters. With St. Thomas, the great medieval scholastic, Neo-Scholasticism sees in rational science the servant of a higher truth given by religious revelation; but this subordination need not preclude an objective analysis of scientific fact. The scholastic thinker is interested chiefly in that pattern of specific form which Aristotle had made the most ultimate structure of nature, but which modern science, centered in quantitative physical study, has for the most part overlooked.

Influenced by the scholastic and Aristotelian realism, but also importantly modified by the context of nineteenth-century idealism, is the German movement which culminated in the *Phenomenology* of Husserl and his followers. This movement originated with Bretano's realistic conception, developed by *Alexius Meinong*, of the cognitive act as an independent apprehension of real objects. Cognition, in this view, has a peculiar status, and may not be treated as a merely psychological process, integrally part of the context of natural processes which are the object of cognition. The objects of cognition, Meinong taught, may or may not exist—they must include, indeed, objects which cannot possibly exist, as well as objects which do exist and objects which might exist. Thought, in a word, is something distinct from, and more extensive than, the nature which is thought about. It is essential to thought that it should be able to contemplate and define certain "objective realities," whether or not these "realities" exist. Meinong is led to affirm the being of a realm of subsistents, *i.e.* of real and intelligibly interrelated objects which transcend the realm of existent things. This "objective" realm of essences he finds to be the basis or substance of all scientific and ethical theory.

Edmund Husserl (born 1859) has defended, elaborated, and applied a related conception in the studies known as *Phenomenology*. This name would appear to derive from Hegel's realistic study *The Phenomenology of Mind*, which claimed that an intellectual cognition of perceptual phenomena, or appearances, discerns those universal yet "concrete" forms which are the substance of ultimate reality. (*The Real appears!*) Husserl, however, distinguishes phenomenological cognition as a peculiar sort of act, neither merely perceptual nor yet metaphysical in Hegel's sense. For Hegel, cognition is rational and absolute because it comprehends a particular phenomenon as an integral part of the universal and absolute whole, which alone is real being. For Husserl, the absolute rational cognition grasps only its present object—a view which does not involve metaphysical assumptions of a monistic sort. Phenomenology thus belongs to the new realism in its postulation of a vast plurality of real objects, known directly and with absolute certainty by the mind. It differs from other forms of new realism in stressing that these objects are real and objective *only for a conscious subject*. As its origins suggest, it is a realism which leans toward

idealism, and which tries to combine the motives of both movements. It is a pluralistic idealism close to scholasticism.

In America, the new realism has had notable proponents.
William James, of whom we will speak again in our review of
pragmatism, expounds in some of his writings a realistic epistemology; and by his teaching at Harvard University he stimulated a broad movement of realistic thought. James joined the
British realists in their attack upon monistic and absolutistic
idealism; but his approach to philosophy differed from theirs.
James was influenced at once by his studies in empirical psychology, which seemed to require a clear distinction between the
processes of mind and the external environment which stimulates mental activity, and by his study of continental thinkers
such as Renouvier, Lotze, and Mach. Ernst Mach had conceived
of a realm of elements which are neutral to mind and matter,
these neutral elements being the irreducible material out of
which both physical reality and psychical reality or composed.
The difference between mind and matter, Mach taught, is a
difference in the organization or relational pattern imposed upon
these irreducible elements—somewhat as very modern music
and classical music may differently compose the same elemental
sounds. James' thought was tremendously stimulating; but it was
never given systematic clarity, its many striking and original
conceptions were never synthesized, and it eludes classification
and summary. From him there proceeded in America both a
realistic school of thinkers and a pragmatic movement which
we will consider later.

The men who were stimulated by James, or who later joined
the realistic movement, have proceeded along various routes.
They are united by their common rejection of idealistic epistemology, and by their agreement that thought, to reach truth,
need not claim knowledge of total reality. Knowledge may be
partial and plural, and yet be authentic. But once the common
enemy, absolute idealism, had been unhorsed, the ties which
united these thinkers became less evident than their differences.

Most widely known of this realistic group, perhaps, is *George Santayana* (born 1863), whose mellifluous style and literary skill give to his writings an appeal apparently irresistible to the reader untrained in philosophy. Santayana's earliest realism was of a Platonic sort. In his *Life of Reason* he invited the reader to the contemplative life, in the enjoyment of an interminable play with eternal essences mathematical, physical, and aesthetic. From this Platonic heaven Santayana seems to have fallen without a parachute upon an earth inconsiderately hard and material. We live, he writes with infinitely cadenced complaint, torn between heaven and earth, and strung between the "life of reason" and a sordid "animal faith." This is Santayana's statement of the problem of the relation between the realistic essences which are open to rational cognition, and the empirical knowledge of existent fact which is obtained by way of observation and probable hypothesis. The problem itself he never directly attacks; but he unceasingly bewails it, in a poetic prose which charms, perhaps because it lulls, the philosophical neophyte.

A sturdier representative of American realism is *John Elof Boodin* (born 1869). Boodin's empirical or "functional" realism consistently avoids that dualism of essence and existence which remains the insoluble residue of more strictly realistic theories of knowledge. Boodin's primary business with epistemology, it might not unfairly be said, is to get rid of it with its apparent insolubles, in order to advance from the latest findings of the special sciences to more comprehensive and unified speculation about the world. His "functional realism" sets the mind in material interaction with its bodily setting and with the external environment, the result being that natural knowledge remains functionally corporate with its object nature, yet specifically distinct from it. This conception of functional relationship is further developed in a metaphysics of organization. The many individual and overlapping energy-systems which comprise reality reveal an unstable yet enduring hierarchical organization, the lower and more material levels of the hierarchy supporting the more highly organized systems of living and intelligent activity. In this modernized Aristotelianism, we are finally told of a highest and most universal Form, which influences and conditions, yet is again supported by, all the more partial organizations of matter. This divine Form is said to be immanent in nature, however, and not transcendental; although Boodin is sometimes inclined, like Newton, to conceive space to be the universal, all-pervasive mind which conditions the material energies and preserves the cosmic order of the world. In his *Cosmic Evolution*, Boodin suggests that this most ultimate Form, the underlying and universal law of nature, may itself change in time. Boodin's speculation is realistic in its fidelity to the facts of nature, as these are described in the empirical sciences. His idealism is of the metaphysical sort of Plato, not the epistemological idealism of the nineteenth century. His profoundest study, perhaps, is an early monograph on the nature of time. Time is identified with the destructive principle which eats into natural structures, and thereby falsifies our judgments of "what is."

We have selected Santayana and Boodin for mention here not because they are typical of the thought of American realists, but rather because they show its wide range. A more complete review of contemporary realism would indicate the significance of the realistic movement both in the context of contemporary social movement, and in its place in the historical development of thought. Realism, in one form or another, has been the major tradition of western philosophy. Its purpose, ever since its first resounding statement by Parmenides, has been the establishment of theoretical science against skeptical criticism. In Greek realism, theoretical science and theoretical philosophy were scarcely distinguished. Philosophy was felt to be only a clearer and extended statement of the method of natural science, clarifying its constitutive assumptions. But Greek realism was explicitly rationalistic, because it held the structures defined by theoretical science to be intuited by the pure reason, the sensory perception of particular fact serving only to illustrate, not to discover, these real structures. Modern science, nominalistically influenced, has emphasized the role of perceived particular fact, which it allows to be the criterion of theoretical truth and the whole source of theoretical knowledge. The Cartesian philosophy, in its defense of theoretical science, renounced the dualism of matter and form which had made Greek realism intelligible; but it affirmed the realistic creed more emphatically than ever, by identifying the concrete being of nature with the structure defined by geometrical theory. This Cartesian realism failed, we saw, to explain the facts of time, motion, and particularity, which were earlier taken care of by the Greek concept of matter; and the empirical attack seemed in the eighteenth century to have discredited all realism. Then came the bold attempt of the post-Kantians to save realism by attributing realistic truth not to observant empirical theory, but to a "reflective" philosophical theory. These men were quite serious in their denial of cogency to empirical science, and in their excogitation of a new "philosophical science." It soon became evident to other serious men, however, that this return to realistic faith at the price of abandoning empirical science saved only the form and not the substance of that faith. Either the results of theoretical science had to be surreptitiously reestablished by the theoretical philosopher, or his "philosophical science" lacked all cogency and even meaning. And so we are brought to contemporary realism, which is a fresh effort to establish the cogency of theoretical science, by affirming again and in some new way the identity with ultimate reality of the objects defined by science.

How far does this latest effort succeed? Contemporary realism usually admits that the special theories of science are reached by hypotheses based upon a study of particular fact. The realist is empirical in his admission that the descriptive theories of science are only probable hypotheses. We have no rational intuition, he would agree with the nominalist, of the law of gravitation. The forms of nature are contingent, in the sense that they could conceivably have been other than they are found to be; and this means that we must discover them by patient observation of particular fact. It is difficult to know just what the realist is reaching after, in his insistence that theoretical description provides knowledge which in some respect is identical with its object in reality. That science is our best knowledge, most of us would agree. That it reaches ultimacy, or identity with its "real" object, seems to make inexplicable, and perhaps impossible, the advance to better theory. It is significant that after thirty or forty years of intensive analysis, philosophical realists have little in common.

The strongest argument for realism, not conclusive but weighty, is that the evidence which we accept in science as the *criterion* of truth must be indubitable, and in some sense identifiable as "real." Science applies a double criterion. First, there are perceived characters, which provide the data suggesting hypothesis and also the data by means of which hypothesis is confirmed. Second, there is the criterion of logical consistency, applied in the theoretical construction of hypotheses. If we allow ultimacy to these perceptual and logical elements, how does this admission establish or require the thesis that the objects of theoretical knowledge are in some respect identical with reality? From these elements there can be constructed false and fantastic doctrines, as well as sound empirical theories.

What science requires is that a scientific theory, to be judged true, must satisfy all the extant evidence. This is less than the realistic requirement that authentic knowledge must define objects identical with reality. In going beyond the requirement of science, realism may endanger science; for in his quest of objects identifiable with reality, the realist finally arrives at essences or elements far removed from the objects described by science; and in this way he suggests that scientific objects have only a dubious relation to reality.

The value of realism, responsible for its strong appeal, is its intellectual faith. Realism affirms the power of thought, and calls upon us to accept as truly descriptive of nature the conclusions of an intellectual study of nature. The reality which science aims to describe, however, is existent nature; and the reality which realism finally establishes is that of subsistent being, a realm of essence the relation of which to existence remains mysterious and inexplicable. We will suggest later that all realism, old or new, fails to grasp the chief motive of empirical thought, and does less than justice to the empirical science of today. The realism of science is something else than this philosophical realism.

Modern science rejected Greek and scholastic realism, we may say, because it was necessary to reject the finality of all merely general and theoretical knowledge, in order to allow the continuous progress of theoretical science in the light of new evidence. The concept of scientific progress, we shall find, requires an advance to a new and larger conception of scientific truth. But this advance cannot renounce that faith in the descriptive power of science which realism seeks to uphold. The philosophy of the future must be an enlarged realism. We may not, in order to do justice to particular fact and empirical science, renounce our faith in the descriptive truth of knowledge; yet this is what the philosophies of pragmatism and positivism, to which we now turn, would seem to require.

Notes for Further Reading

1. Moore, G. E., *Philosophical Studies*. New York, Harcourt, Brace and Company, 1922.
2. —— *Ethics*. New York, Henry Holt and Company, 1912.
3. Russell, B., *Philosophical Essays*. London, Longmans, Green and Company, 1910.
4. —— *The Problems of Philosophy*. New York, Henry Holt and Company, 1912.
5. ——*Mysticism and Logic*. Boston, Longmans, Green and Company, 1918.
6. —— *An Analysis of Mind*. New York, The Macmillan Company, 1921.

7. Russell, B., *An Outline of Philosophy*. New York, W. W. Norton and Company, Inc., 1927.

8. —— *An Inquiry into Meaning and Truth*. New York, W. W. Norton and Company, Inc., 1940.

9. Alexander, S., *Space, Time, and Deity*. New York, The Macmillan Company, 1920.

10. Broad, C. D., *The Mind and its Place in Nature*. New York, Harcourt, Brace and Company, 1925.

11. Whitehead, A. N., *The Concept of Nature*. New York, The Macmillan Company, 1920.

12. —— *Process and Reality*. New York, The Macmillan Company, 1929.

13. James, W., *A Pluralistic Universe*. Boston, Longmans, Green and Company, 1909.

14. —— *Essays in Radical Empiricism*. Boston, Longmans, Green and Company, 1912.

15. Mach, E., *The Analysis of Sensation*, trans. C. M. Williams, 1897. La Salle, Ill., The Open Court Publishing Company, 1914.

16. Holt, E. B., and others. *The New Realism*. New York, The Macmillan Company, 1912.

17. Perry, R. B., *Present Philosophical Tendencies*. Boston, Longmans, Green and Company, 1912.

18. —— *General Theory of Value*. Boston, Longmans, Green and Company, 1926.

19. —— *Philosophy of the Recent Past*. New York, Charles Scribner's Sons, 1926.

20. Santayana, G., *Scepticism and Animal Faith*. New York, Charles Scribner's Sons, 1923.

21. —— *The Realms of Being*. New York, Charles Scribner's Sons, 1942.

22. Sellars, R. W., and others. *Critical Realism*. Chicago and New York, Rand McNally and Company, 1916.

23. Findlay, J. N., *Meinong's Theory of Objects*. London and New York, Oxford University Press, 1933.

24. Husserl, E., Article "Phenomenology," *Encyclopedia Britannica*, 14th ed. London and New York, 1929.

25. Laird, J. *Recent Philosophy*. London, Thornton Butterworth, Ltd., 1936.

24 PRAGMATISM

As CONTEMPORARY REALISM IS THE CHARACTER-
istic outlook in British philosophical circles, so pragmatism has had its center and widest following in the United
States of America. There have been pragmatic thinkers in
Britain and Europe; but only in this country has pragmatism
been a movement or school effectively propagating a common
outlook and faith. And pragmatism remains, in spite of its occasional appearance elsewhere, a philosophical movement largely
identified with America.

It was only in the twentieth century that American thought
attempted to find for itself a distinctive vocabulary and formulation. Colonial America had preserved a motley of theological, philosophical, and moral creeds brought from Europe,
especially from England and Scotland. It was to follow these
creeds without hindrance that many American colonists had
crossed the Atlantic and settled in the New World. Calvinistic
and Lutheran theology, Puritan zeal, the political philosophy
of John Locke, and the "common-sense realism" cultivated in
the Scottish universities had satisfied a colonial society which
was not so much indifferent to philosophical ideas (indeed, it
was somewhat unusually committed to them) as absorbed by
the practical business of creating out of great material resources

485

a new economic and political world. The aid given by France
during the American revolution doubtless heightened awareness of French thought; and young America, in its reciprocal
sympathy with revolution in France, imbibed something of the
materialistic philosophy of the French emancipators. But this
French materialism, although ingredient, did not shake American thought from its traditional cast, which was the thought
of seventeenth-century Britain modified and developed by the
new environment. To understand American mentality, one
must remember the origins of American society lying in the
sixteenth and seventeenth-century struggle for the reformation
of church and state, and its effective separation, psychological
as well as geographical, from eighteenth- and nineteenth-
century Europe.

During the nineteenth century, there appeared in America
poets and essayists whose thought is noticeably "new world."
The poetry of Walt Whitman reflected the breadth of the
American landscape and the tumultuous tide of American life.
But for the most part these writers still looked to Europe for
what philosophy they used. Emerson used the language of
German transcendentalism to express an individualistic faith
in the propriety of the human spirit to its universal environment. Thoreau's call to nature and simplicity, and to the solitude wherein the individual can find self-integrity, was Greek
cynicism at its best, with overtones from Montaigne and
European naturalism; but Thoreau's naturalism is less the revulsion from a decadent civilization than the discovery of woods
and field in their primeval beauty and their own right.

During the last quarter of the nineteenth century, American
scholars who visited Europe were impressed by the efficiency
of the German universities; and on their return, they sought
with some success to pattern higher education in America, now
entering a period of tremendous expansion, upon this German
model. Scholarship was made methodical, research was organized in the seminar, and thought became meticulous and

formalized. To what degree American scholarship will retain these German borrowings remains to be seen. Along with German pedantry came a good deal of German philosophy, usually that of the post-Kantian idealists; and for a time it seemed as if German transcendentalism might take root on American soil. Its ablest exponent was *Josiah Royce*, a son of California pioneers, and long the colleague of William James at Harvard University. Royce was a very independent disciple of his German teachers. He never confused the Absolute with human experience; and he remained very empirical in his emphasis on individual being, and in his refusal to transcend temporal and spatial relations. Where the German absolutists tended to see the supreme actualization of the Absolute Mind in the political state, Royce found it in the religious community of mankind. In such ways, he eliminated those aspects of German absolutism which made it least acceptable to the American public; but he was nevertheless to witness the realistic and pragmatic reaction which virtually swept absolute idealism from the lecture halls of America.

The leader of this reaction was *William James* (1842–1910). James came to philosophy late, by way of art, medicine, and psychology. To this training he owed his most fruitful conceptions; but it may have prevented him from appreciating the historical development of philosophy, and its fidelity to certain root problems apart from which it loses its importance and even its identity. James' study of psychology, a new and adventurous discipline still in search of a "method," quickened his perception of the empirical and experimental character of science, and made him impatient with every sort of formalism; and these tendencies were strengthened by what he found in his study of psychical processes. In his *Principles of Psychology*, a work no longer authoritative but still the most stimulating of psychological texts, James moved from the introspective associational psychology which had been current since Hume to a functional and biological analysis of behavior. He refused to separate the conscious and intellectual processes of the mind from their context in the concrete bodily life. It was because he realized that this psychological orientation was more than the new hypothesis of a special science that his interest moved from psychology to philosophy. A functional psychology, he saw, undercuts the Cartesian dualism of mind and matter, a conception from which the whole long development of modern philosophy had consciously or unconsciously moved.

The mind, as the seat of human intelligence, has evidently two distinct relations to nature. As the vehicle of knowledge, it faces nature. Nature is the object of knowledge, and mind is the knowing subject. Yet it is also true that the mind is stimulated by nature, and reacts within and upon nature; and in this interaction the mind is integral with nature, and does not merely contemplate an external world. As an empirical scientist seeking a veridical description of nature, James emphasized the first of these two relations; and when he did this he inclined to realism, which insists upon some sort of correspondence or identity between what is mentally cognized and reality itself. But as a psychologist observant of human behavior, and also as a sensitive human being acutely responsive to his fellows, James emphasized the second relation; and it was this emphasis which came to expression in his *pragmatism*.

Although human behavior is what we are most interested in and familiar with, it is the latest of the processes of nature to be scientifically studied. The name "psychology" still suggests that we are dealing here with something else than the visible activity of people. In order to get started upon his empirical psychology, James had to demolish a traditional psychology which ostensibly studied purely mental states, introspectively observed in isolation from material nature. We must renounce, he said, this conception of mind or experience as an independent stuff, which can be cut up like a patterned tablecloth into snippets of sensation, idea, or what not. Mind is activity. It is dynamic process. Mind is our name for the continuously changing process which integrates the organism into its environment. In man, this process happens to be conscious and intelligent; but consciousness is not something additive to the process. "Consciousness as such" does not exist. Concepts are only fixities or uniformities of interaction, appearing in this vital process of adjustment. They are only relative constants, subject to change. It is because we rigidly and artificially separate this vital process into two incommensurable parts, a substantial world and a substantial mind, that there arise the insoluble pseudo-problems of which metaphysical theories are the pretended solution. If our knowledge of the world is our functional adjustment to the world, knowledge is conditioned both by what lies outside of us and by what transpires within us. If this is so, we cannot suppose that knowledge defines a reality wholly independent of ourselves, a thing-in-itself which needs only to be realistically inspected and described. Nor, on the other hand, should we conclude that knowledge is therefore wholly nondescriptive and subjective. The cognitive process is real enough, wherever it proceeds and whatever it be; and it involves both external nature and human activity in its content and structure.

James rightly believed that this functional conception, which sees in cognition an adjustment or relation between man and his environment, requires a new conception of what constitutes truth. Earlier philosophy had never wholly renounced the familiar assumption that knowledge is true insofar as it describes a structure which is intrinsic to nature itself, and independent of the mind. The philosopher might realistically affirm the identity of the cognized object with ultimate reality; or he might claim only that a certain correspondence exists between what is cognized and what is real, much as a photograph represents the thing photographed; or, failing to demonstrate even such correspondence, he might lapse into skepticism. But James struck a new and bold course. If cognition is man's adjustment to his environment, he said, then true knowledge is what best secures this adjustment. The truth of an hypothesis, he concluded, lies in its practical consequences, in its usefulness as a guide, in its vital service. The belief that justifies itself in use is the true belief, constituting knowledge; and the belief which breaks down, or which misleads when it is applied, is error. The truth-value of a proposition or theory, James boldly announced, is just its cash-value, *i.e.* its practical service to those who use it.

James gave Charles S. Peirce, a mathematician and logician, credit for the origination of this pragmatic concept of truth. Whether Peirce was a pragmatist is debatable. In any case, it was James himself who brought to the concept its large significance and who was responsible for its wide popularity. The thought of Peirce was dominated by Kantian and other European influences. James became the thinker most characteristic of America because he brought to philosophical expression, in spite of his sojourn in Europe, the mentality of a people long separated from Europe, and developed by a very different natural and social environment. The intellectual tradition which governs contemporary American thought is that which came from thirteenth-century Roger Bacon, sixteenth-century Francis Bacon, and seventeenth-century John Locke. All of these men had been pragmatic in their conception of knowledge, although not in their definition of truth. Knowledge, they had taught, is power; and the essential function of knowledge is not a contemplative description of nature, but an experimental control of nature. This conception had reappeared in the utilitarianism of Hume and his successors; but in the Old World it had never dominated philosophical speculation, always being subordinated to a more realistic conception of truth.

We will do best to see in American pragmatism, therefore, a revival and new formulation of the earlier empirical philosophy, and we should not identify American pragmatism with any European form of pragmatism now current. As a continuation of the earlier empiricism, American pragmatism is primarily a critical doctrine, antagonistic to rationalistic metaphysics. Its power and its purpose are never apparent to the thinker who fails to appreciate this fact, and who demands from pragmatism a systematic doctrine. The pragmatism of James was essentially his criticism of European rationalism. The pragmatism of Dewey and his followers extends this criticism to certain current forms of realism, which are shown, the writer believes correctly, to involve rationalistic implications. And if American pragmatism perpetuates the empirical opposition to absolutistic philosophy, it is also the expression of a liberal faith which continually opposes absolutism in practical life. Institutions, it teaches, are made by man for man; and they are therefore subject to perpetual criticism and continuous modification by those who use them.

In America pragmatism gives new voice and fresh application to the moral and intellectual faith which has generated modern science and modern society. It is the philosophy of the liberal and progressive thinker; and it claims to have found a more just and effective statement of the moral and philosophical truth which inspires modern man. But although pragmatism preserves a tradition carried from its parental source some centuries ago, and only now given new and forceful expression, the pragmatist is not oblivious of what has transpired since then; and he is especially aware of the philosophical significance of evolutionary science. It might almost be said that pragmatism is a form of empirical philosophy which identifies science with evolutionary biology, whereas earlier empiricism had identified science with physical and chemical theory. This and other shifts of approach appropriate to contemporary thought make pragmatism a doctrine difficult to define; and this difficulty is increased by the critical or negative character of the doctrine, which leaves its positive affirmations fluid and elusive.

James' initial statement of the doctrine, that truth is the cash-value of a proposition, meaning that the truth of a proposition is to be measured by its service to the practical endeavors of man, was striking but somewhat superficial. It exploded like a bombshell in intellectual circles, where it provoked a storm of opposition which was only partially based on misunderstanding. Surely it is obvious, his critics exclaimed, that a belief may work successfully without being true. A man may back his false belief that a horse can win a race, and collect his bet because the other horses are disqualified; but the false belief is not made true because it led to success. The Chinese people long imbibed tea as a preventive of disease, when what kept them well was not the tea, but the boiling of the water incidental to the infusion. Shall we say that their false belief was pragmatically "true." Pragmatism, said these critics, is only the familiar fallacy *post hoc ergo propter hoc*, according to which whatever follows a certain antecedent must be the effect of that antecedent. But does sunset bring about the rise of the stars, because it precedes their ascent?

James attempted to meet his critics by narrowing and sharpening his thesis, but he never achieved a satisfactory statement, and in some respects only confused the issue. In his most famous essay, *The Will to Believe*, he forcefully argues that our belief in a proposition may be a condition of the happenings which confirm its truth. Faith in yourself or in a friend may inspire the conduct and secure the results which justify that faith. And, similarly, a religious faith augmenting hope and courage may be the cause of the beneficent consequence which justifies or confirms the faith. This argument is cogent in its appreciation of human faith as a causal factor in the world; but it is confusing and misleading if it is taken to be an argument for the pragmatic concept of truth. Because man shapes his environment in accordance with his desires and purposes, the character of this man-made environment must be understood as a function or consequence of human purpose. If we desire a smoke-free city, our belief that the city can be rid of smoke is a condition of the city's becoming free of smoke; and here, belief may help to create its own evidence. But does our belief that the moon causes the tides help to make this belief come true? Or is this belief true simply because it states a fact which is wholly independent of whether the fact helps us or hurts us, and of whether it is believed or not? Can we, where King Canute could not, retard the tide by refusing to acknowledge its advance? James' pragmatism seemed to collide with every sort of realism—not only with philosophical realism, but with the realism of science and common sense.

The defense and development of pragmatism was undertaken by *John Dewey* (born 1859), who has remained its most fluent and influential advocate. Dewey brought to this crusade arguments and conceptions derived from nineteenth-century European philosophy, especially from the post-Kantians. Like James, he was influenced in his approach to philosophy by his study of psychological and biological facts. He placed knowledge in its concrete matrix, the progress of individual and social life; and he viewed it as an instrument of adjustment, serving the organism and society by bringing each into adjustment with the other, and also into adjustment with nature at large. But Dewey was also early and profoundly influenced by the thought of Hegel, which determined his epistemology and his philosophical method; and if we would understand contemporary pragmatism, which is that of Dewey, we must appreciate its relation to the Hegelian metaphysic, in spite of the fact that few pragmatists seem to be aware of this influence and that Dewey himself has forgotten it.

How could the Hegelian system, which we saw to be the most absolute of rationalisms, be converted into a doctrine which is extremely empirical, and critical of every sort of rationalism? Hegel, we remember, had created what he called a "new logic," namely "dialectical logic." Ordinary logic, he said, is purely abstract, trivial, and nondescriptive—its definitions are merely nominal or verbal; but there is a "concrete logic," the dialectic, which allows the thinker to penetrate to the real substance of things, and to reach real definitions, absolute in their truth yet descriptive of the world. The use of this "concrete logic" makes possible a philosophical or metaphysical science far superior to the ordinary empirical science which is elaborated by scientists. This metaphysical science provides a conspectus of universal Reality, within which every observed fact and every existent thing may be known, in its ultimate and absolute character.

We have already noted the errors of this Hegelian doctrine. Dewey does not follow Hegel into these errors. But he does accept from Hegel the notion of a "concrete logic," *i.e.* a logic which is not formal and abstract, nor composed merely of verbal definitions, but which is a method of thought, and which contains in its implicit procedures true and universal presumptions about the world. According to Dewey, this "concrete logic" is not productive of a metaphysical system superior to science. It is just the method of empirical science itself. It is the "inductive logic" which carries science from narrower hypothesis to wider hypothesis, inclusive of more fact and new fact. Science does not, Dewey implies, merely proceed from a set of given facts to an hypothesis supported or required by these data. It invariably proceeds from earlier hypothesis, which is beaten upon by new facts compelling the advance to new hypothesis which comprehends these new data. Thus knowledge is a growth, ever feeding upon new experience, and sustaining and re-creating itself by absorbing new fact. Its "concrete logic," one might say, is this process of intellectual metabolism or growth; and the power of "logic" or scientific method is just this generative principle or direction of growth, which is the deepest and most ultimate character of experience.

Dewey is led by this appeal to "concrete logic" to refuse to recognize the problem of the relation of human knowledge to the world which that knowledge describes. The relation which he likes to discuss is that between later and earlier knowledge.

The actuality he sees is the process of knowledge itself, integrating mind and nature. This process does, of course, absorb and digest the new facts which continuously come into the mind; but this involves for Dewey no realistic conception of an actuality external to the mind, and independent of it. The new facts which enter the mind are not to be conceived as existing in their own right, because they derive their character as "facts" wholly from their relationship to old and new hypothesis. Dewey's pragmatism, in short, is a new and empirical version of the post-Kantian idealism. It seems to attribute reality or actuality only to the process and content of mind. It avoids any realistic discussion of the relation of knowledge to an external world, a reality which is not knowledge but the object-which-knowledge-describes. It allows us to discuss only old-facts-as-known, hypothesis or knowledge, and new-facts-as-known. It confines us within human experience.

It should be perceived that the idea of a "concrete logic" necessarily involves an idealistic metaphysics. Logic is truly the study of explicit knowledge, wherein logic distinguishes the most general form from the varying content. If logical forms are "concrete," in the sense that they still contain all their particular factual content, then we cannot hope to distinguish what is general knowledge of nature from what is particular fact, nor from whatever it is that appears to the mind as particular occurrence. We cannot distinguish mind from nature. But pragmatism seldom acknowledges its idealistic presuppositions. It obscures these by its definition of knowledge and intelligence, which it identifies with the organic process of adjustment to environment. This definition itself implies, of course, a realistic and nonidealistic conception of nature, since it separates the organism from its environment. But the bodily organism, it is then said, is itself just the process of intelligent readjustment. The body is its life, and the life is its intelligence. This implicit idealism is further obscured by the pragmatist's dominating concern with the social environment. The most important environment of the human individual, the pragmatist rightly insists, is society, composed of other human intelligences. Having shown that social readjustment is the reciprocal adjustment of life to life and mind to mind, pragmatism easily and unconsciously extends this conception to the relations between the organism and inorganic nature. Thus the exposition of the doctrine, essentially idealistic, may proceed in naturalistic and even materialistic terms, and appear to be only a sober and scientific description of the bodily progress which is human life. And in large degree pragmatism is a psychology of this kind—except that it is presented as a philosophy, covering not only human behavior but everything whatsoever. It is biology and psychology converted into a philosophy of nature and science.

William James used to divide philosophers into "tough-minded" realists and "tender-minded" idealists. One of the most tender-minded and idealistic of men, he prided himself on his tough-minded realism. Pragmatism continues this appealing self-deception when it disguises its idealistic assumptions under a naturalistic vocabulary. So it appeals to a people of whom James is still the most representative philosopher, and which admires a kind heart under a rough exterior.

But how does Dewey avoid the dogmatism of the Hegelian idealism? The "concrete logic" of Hegel was a body of dialectical dogma, a hard tissue of "concrete universals." Pragmatism avoids dogmatism because it is empirical and nominalistic in its overt epistemology. For it there are no universal truths (except, of course, its own unconscious preconception, requiring us to define life and existence to be the continuous, intelligent, knowledge-implemented interadjustment of individuals to their environment). Pragmatism does not allow us, in its unconscious idealism, to discuss this environment itself, in its independent character. The process of organic readjustment is an intelligent *progress*, of which explicit knowledge is the instrument. Knowledge, as a function of the progressive life of man, is in radical evolution, and submits to no fixities of statement. Even if we were to conceive of a fixed physical environment conditioning man, knowledge would still be fluid and progressive, never definitive; for each intelligent readjustment of the organism to that fixed environment would constitute a change of organic character, this would establish a changed relationship of organism to environment, and this would generate new facts requiring new hypothesis. In Hegel, we saw, the conception of natural evolution was degraded into that of a fixed dialectical system. By Dewey, evolution is given its rightful character; but Dewey still, like Hegel, presents the evolution idealistically, as that of intelligence or concrete mind. The needed readjustment of a thing to its environment is described as constituting a "problem"; the thing's reactions to the problematic situation are a trial and effort applying implicit or explicit hypotheses, which apprehend the character of the situation in its relation to the thing; and the true hypothesis is that which effects the readjustment, producing satisfaction. The satisfaction is only temporary, because the new readjustment will sooner or later generate new problems.

Pragmatism originated, we saw, in the pragmatic definition of truth. The truth of a proposition was said to be its beneficent consequence, or the character of the proposition which conditions this beneficent consequence. The truth of a belief is the good it does. To say this is to subordinate all factual judgment to moral judgment. This is the great virtue and appeal of pragmatism, that it converts all factual and scientific truth into moral truth. Kant had been compelled to distinguish scientific knowledge, as only phenomenal, from the true insight which is conscience. The post-Kantians had attempted to convert this moral intuition into a systematic philosophy, transcending a merely descriptive science. Dewey, rejecting the rationalistic presuppositions of Kantian thought, flatly identifies moral intuition with scientific intelligence. If science speaks truth, then its affirmations are those which effect beneficent consequence, and which bring about what ought to be. Scientific and moral judgment are one and identical. In this way, pragmatism recovers the faith of the seventeenth-century Enlightenment. The Enlightenment looked to science for moral guidance, vaguely identified the necessities of natural law with the laws of God, and expected to establish an earthly paradise with the help of science. Much as the seventeenth-century Enlightenment was the utopian faith of a society morally instructed by religion, but faced by a religious actuality which had hardened into dogma and institutionalism and worked for division instead of social unity, so American pragmatism is today the moral resource of people still informed by religious faith, but unable to find religious expression in creeds and institutions which have become obsolete, ineffective, and a sectarian cause of social disintegration. Pragmatism, like the Enlightenment, is critical of religion and religious institutions; but it is nevertheless the child of religious faith, seeking to apply faith. The son of the preacher teaches pragmatism in the college. What will *his* son teach?

If morality is scientific intelligence, then science should be not only a description of nature, but a program of social reform. Pragmatism accordingly becomes a social and political movement, calling for the fullest application of science and its most intelligent effort in every field of human activity. Dewey has been a prolific writer, and his applications of pragmatic doctrine to the various fields of human endeavor have made him the foremost teacher of his generation. The initial effect of his teaching is to encourage the laborer in every field, by presenting practical work as the noble exercise of human intelligence in some special domain. Work is at once dignified and exhorted to greater and more intelligent effort. The second effect of pragmatic doctrine is to inspire the worker to creative effort, and to guard him against stereotyped habits, professional prejudices, institutional loyalties, intellectual inertias of every sort; for practice is identified with intelligence, and intelligence is defined as being progressive and creative. More specifically, Dewey has convinced the jurist that law is but the instrument, continuously renovated, by which society readjusts itself to changing economic and intellectual conditions, so that law exists to serve life and not to control it; and jurists have turned to an empirical and pragmatic jurisprudence. He has told the statesman and citizen that governmental institutions may not be more fixated than the social actualities which generate and use government; and pragmatism becomes the faith of the political radical. In pedagogy, the educator is warned against formal disciplines, and inspired to a "progressive education" which will develop the native powers of the pupil, by exercising them in ways preparing him for the actualities of contemporary life. By a pragmatic criticism of art, the artist is weaned from classicism and the pursuit of art for art's sake, and led to make his craftsmanship the instrument of social reform and the dignifier of human labor and the common life. In matters religious, the believer is directed toward a liberal modernism which makes little of formal creed and institutional tradition, deprecates sectarian differences, and translates theological metaphysics into ethical doctrine and sociological instruction. "Science" and "society" become terms quickened by one another into new significance; and "Science and Society" becomes the slogan of a reformatory program which will recreate every human activity, not least by bringing the too specialized departments and institutions of human life into reciprocal stimulation and readjustment, in the acknowledgment of a common social responsibility.

All of this is high achievement; and surely no empiricist, nor any liberal, moral, and progressive thinker, would desire to diminish or undo the stimulating influence which pragmatism has exerted and will continue to exert upon American society. Pragmatism is a complex, rich, and many-sided doctrine. It revives and empowers the largest and most liberal tradition of modernity, going back to the earlier sources of this tradition, but bringing into it certain philosophical and scientific developments of the later centuries.

Yet pragmatism has this liberal character chiefly in America, where it owes its power to forces which it does not generate itself, but which it borrows from a more realistic faith. When pragmatism directs us to live intelligently, and to make science the instrument of human progress, it relies upon the existence of a science which owes its instrumental power to its realistic faith. And when pragmatism advises us to make the successful realization of a practical program the justification of the means used and of the end sought, it assumes the program to be one which our moral judgment can endorse prior to its prosecution. Pragmatism, in short, always silently accepts and applies realistic criteria of truth, prior to its application of the pragmatic criterion; and then, forgetting this initial realism, it enlarges the place of pragmatic utility.

It is clear, surely, that any and every application of the pragmatic view involves a realistic acceptance of knowledge as truly descriptive of being. A hypothesis is true, we are instructed by the pragmatist, if it is instrumental to the large business of living, and secures the adjustment of the living being to the social and physical environment. Let us agree with the pragmatist that a feeling of discomfort may apprise us of some maladjustment, and that a renewed feeling of comfort is evidence of successful readjustment to our environment. We must still realistically accept these feelings as symptomatic of real relations existing between a real organism and a real environment. Only upon this assumption will the feeling of discomfort lead us to the perception of a definable problem. The source of pragmatism was, after all, a realistic empirical psychology. Only upon that realistic assumption can theoretical hypotheses and practical proposals be relevant to the problem, and remedial of the discomfort which generates the problem. Only upon that assumption is the achieved satisfaction the consequence of the hypothesis and its application. In order that knowledge should be instrumental, and that we should perceive and establish its instrumentality, we must have descriptive knowledge of a real world, made up of existent persons and things.

If pragmatism has meaning only for one who is at heart a realist, what does pragmatism add to the realistic theory of knowledge? Our actual knowledge at any moment comprises a comprehensive summary of observed past occurrence. Pragmatism reminds us that this knowledge is not final nor absolute, but may be modified by future experience. We use our present knowledge when we hazard predictions, and the observation of the predicted occurrence confirms the knowledge on which the prediction was based. The pragmatist comes to regard this future confirmation of present knowledge as the sole verification of knowledge. The truth of the hypothesis, he says, lies wholly in its relation to the future occurrence which verifies it, *i.e.*, makes it come true. But, in sober fact, the truth of any actual hypothesis lies wholly in its relation to past and present fact, and to no degree in its relation to future fact. It is past occurrence, so far as known, which establishes an hypothesis; and the future occurrence which may confirm the hypothesis cannot do this until it too has occurred, and is past. Further, the prediction which later confirms an hypothesis need not be and usually is not some practical application of the hypothesis. It may be a purely scientific prediction, concerned only to test scientific truth. Knowledge is not made true by being used. Its descriptive truth lies in its comprehension of observed particular fact; and its instrumental value derives from its descriptive truth.

In its conception of truth, pragmatism still does unconscious service to the idol of absolute knowledge, a service which finally leads to skepticism. If the truth of a theory lay in its future consequence, knowledge would never be possessed, it would always be only anticipated. The pragmatist is led to identify knowledge with verified particular prediction because

he supposes that the occurrence of the predicted occurrence
removes all possible doubt. Yet a false hypothesis may occasionally implement a successful prediction. Nor is any hypothesis
placed wholly beyond doubt by its particular verifications. To
repeat, what establishes any hypothesis is the sum-total of
known particular fact, and not its confirmation in some one
application, however important that application may be.

One consequence of pragmatic doctrine threatens the efficacy of pragmatism in respect to its two chief purposes. Pragmatism wishes to stress the moral significance of science, and
also to defend empirical science from absolutistic and rationalistic attack. We can defend empirical science, however, only
by showing that its two criteria of abstract logic and observed
particular fact effectively secure truly descriptive knowledge.
The moral significance of science does not derive from its
practical utility. It derives from its justice or impartiality toward particular fact, such fact being the index of real being,
and also from its provision of the disinterested knowledge
which alone can reveal moral problems and implement their
solution. This intimate relationship between science and morality will be clarified in our concluding chapters, which will
show that morality is the application in conduct of those two
criteria of descriptive knowledge which govern scientific inquiry. Here we suggest that to look only to future consequences for the verification of an hypothesis or the justification
of a program would leave present thought and enterprise unenlightened and unintelligent. The wisest hypothesis, based on the
largest evidence, would have no priority over the most foolish,
if the whole test of truth lay in the future. The most immoral
enterprise could be preferred to the most moral, on the ground
that only our future experience of the practical consequences
of the two enterprises can decide their respective merits.

In this way, pragmatism threatens to put a moratorium on
intelligence and science. In America, pragmatism has worked
for good because it has inspired men of realistic common sense,

and because it has quickened moral ideals nurtured by centuries of moral and religious education. Already, however, pragmatism begins to reveal its inherent inadequacies. It begins to infect the scientist with skepticism, by destroying his faith in the descriptive power of theory, and by persuading him that his theories are merely mental constructs implemental to prediction. And it begins to foster an unhealthy jurisprudence, willing to overlook the absolute and eternal requirements of justice, and to question the constitutional securements of justice, in too plastic an accommodation of legal principles to local and transient pressures. In Europe, pragmatism has been the resource of violent and reactionary groups, who defend their unscrupulous and tyrannical programs of action on the ground that the success of these programs, that is to say their forceful actualization, will pragmatically justify them. Pragmatism was the *activisme* of the reactionaries who betrayed France, and of the chauvinists who marched on Rome. "Just think this new Rome," cried Mussolini, "believe in it, and the thought will be made fact and verify itself!"

There is one other argument for pragmatism, however, which should not be overlooked. We have concluded that the only criteria of truth are logic and observed fact, which is to exclude the pragmatic criterion of practical utility. In strictness, the criteria of logic and observed fact do not suffice to single out just one hypothesis as true, invalidating all others. The same body of factual evidence will always support a plurality of self-consistent theories; and the ground upon which we prefer one of these alternative thories is in fact some pragmatic consideration of convenience, familiarity, or simplicity. Thus there is and will always remain a pragmatic element in knowledge. But is this an argument for or against the descriptive cogency of knowledge? We can use it in several ways. We can argue that science is never quite descriptive, since it involves some consideration of human convenience. We can say that the alternative theories are descriptively equivalent, since they equally satisfy the requirements. But we might also argue that convenience constitutes a third criterion of knowledge, namely an aesthetic criterion postulating the beauty and rightness of nature. But all such argument is perhaps rather trivial, so long as we hold the primary and effective criteria of truth to be logic and factual evidence, and not elegance nor utility. The scientist will never prefer an elegant theory to one that better meets the facts or attains to greater consistency. The aesthetic and moral character of science is to be seen in its fidelity to logic and to fact rather than in its service to human convenience. Knowledge must direct practice, and not be subservient to it.

Notes for Further Reading

1. Peirce, C. S., "How To Make Our Ideas Clear," *Popular Science Monthly*, 1878.
2. ———— *Chance, Love and Logic.* New York, Harcourt, Brace and Company, 1923.
3. Buchler, J., *Charles Peirce's Empiricism.* New York, Harcourt Brace and Company, 1940.
4. James, W., *Principles of Psychology.* New York, Henry Holt and Company, 1923–31.
5. ———— *The Will to Believe and Other Essays.* Boston, Longmans, Green and Company, 1912.
6. ———— *Pragmatism.* Boston, Longmans, Green and Company, 1907.
7. ———— *The Meaning of Truth.* Boston, Longmans, Green and Company, 1909.
8. ———— *Collected Essays and Reviews.* Boston, Longmans, Green and Company, 1920.
   H. M. Kallen and E. Rhys have edited selections from James' writings.
9. Schiller, F. C. S., *Humanism.* New York, The Macmillan Company, 1912.
10. ———— *Formal Logic.* New York, The Macmillan Company, 1912.
11. Dewey, J., *How We Think.* Boston, D. C. Heath and Company, 1910.

12. Dewey, J., *Democracy and Education*. New York, The Macmillan Company, 1916.
13. —— *The Quest for Certainty*. New York, Minton Balch and Company, 1929.
14. —— *Reconstruction in Philosophy*. New York, Henry Holt and Company, 1920.
15. —— *Experience and Nature*. La Salle, Ill., The Open Court Publishing Company, 1925.
16. —— *Liberalism and Social Action*. New York, G. P. Putnam's Sons, 1935.
17. —— *Logic, the Theory of Inquiry*. New York, Henry Holt and Company, 1938.
18. Dewey, J., and Tufts, J. H., *Ethics*. New York, Henry Holt and Company, 1908.
19. Dewey, J., and others. *Creative Intelligence*. New York, Henry Holt and Company, 1917.
20. Ratner, E. ed., *The Philosophy of Dewey*. New York, Henry Holt and Company, 1928. Selections.
21. Moore, A. W., *Pragmatism and Its Critics*. Chicago, University of Chicago Press, 1910.
22. Mead, G. H., *The Philosophy of the Act*. Chicago, University of Chicago Press, 1938.
23. Otto, M. C., *The Human Enterprise*. New York, F. S. Crofts and Company, 1940.
24. Laird, J., *Recent Philosophy*. London, Thornton Butterworth, Ltd., 1936.

25 POSITIVISM AND THE
PHILOSOPHY OF SCIENCE

AT THE BEGINNING OF THIS TREATMENT OF CON-
temporary philosophy, the reader was advised that
rubrics or " 'isms" should not be taken too precisely. Few contemporary philosophers would wish to be rigorously confined
within any one system, or narrowly identified with just one
movement. Thus, most pragmatists have realistic leanings and
many realists would admit the pragmatic conception of truth
as supplementary to their own. It is similarly doubtful whether
any leading thinker today would accept the label "positivist."
Yet a group of writers, heading an important movement of
thought, are best distinguished from realists and pragmatists
as being positivistic in their approach to philosophy and in
some of their conclusions.

We are already acquainted with several sorts of positivistic
philosophy. Hume was at once positivistic and pragmatic in
his suggestion that abstract concepts are mental constructions,
preserved on account of their utility but not necessarily descriptive in their statement. Kant was more explicitly positivistic,
when he concluded that empirical science, the sole authentic
natural knowledge, describes only a phenomenal realm, lying

506

this side of ultimate reality. But the term "positivism" was chiefly propagated by nineteenth-century Auguste Comte. Comte agreed with Kant that science is the sole authentic knowledge, and that it is still only phenomenal; but he refused to appeal beyond science, as did Kant, to a faculty of moral cognition able to grasp noumenal being, *i.e.* reality itself. Comte wished to revive the rationalistic faith of the eighteenth-century Enlightenment; but he was sufficiently influenced by the empirical criticism of Hume and Kant to be desirous of avoiding metaphysics. His proposal was to moderate the claim of science, by allowing that empirical or natural knowledge reaches conclusions which are less than absolute, and which describe only the phenomenal realm accessible to direct perception; yet at the same time he wished to establish science as the sole reliable cognition accessible to man. This estimate of science he called "positivism," intending to distinguish scientific method, as the sole approach to positive and verifiable knowledge, from the methods used by the theologian and the metaphysician. As Touchstone modestly said of Audrey, "A poor virgin, sir, an ill-favored thing, sir, but mine own," so the positivist deprecates any claim to realistic knowledge, yet ascribes exclusively to natural science whatever knowledge man may possess.

This positivistic outlook persisted throughout the nineteenth century, being especially favored among scientists and those close to science. In Germany, shortly after the mid-century, it was given a new formulation. *Albert Lange* used positivism as his basis for an attack upon materialistic metaphysics. Accepting as his initial postulate the critical positivism of Kant, Lange proceeded to show that materialism violates Kant's prohibition of dogmatic metaphysics, in that it carries the categories of science beyond human experience into pure speculation; but he then diverged from Kant in his naturalistic account of the origin of the categories. For Kant, these categories were fixed forms of thought, transcending the variable content of

mind; but for Lange, they arise within the mind and are determined by psychological processes. This implies that the
science of any epoch may be peculiar to that epoch, even in its
most basic statements; and in this new limitation of science,
the positivism of Lange goes far beyond that of Kant.

A number of thinkers followed Lange, whose effort was to
purify science of all a priori and metaphysical elements carried
over from the theological and philosophical past. Scientific
statements, it was proposed, should affirm only what is actually
observed and confirmed by the scientist. One should not attribute to scientific formulas a universality, nor to the objects
defined by them a reality, over and above that which is established by observation itself. These men proposed a minimum
statement, or a maximum economy of statement, in respect to
what is affirmed by science.

Ernst Mach (1838–1916), a physicist teaching at Prague
and Vienna, accordingly taught that physical processes and
psychical processes should be regarded as only different combinations of the same neutral or common elements; for this
hypothesis obviated the metaphysical dualism of physical and
psychical being, or of matter and mind. The physical object
is only an integrated sum of sensible apprehensions, said Mach.
The sensed weight of a body obviously reduces to a complex of
sensations and their interrelations—a large cork ball feels light,
a small lead ball of the same weight feels heavy; but the calculated mass of a body, which is a theoretical constant, may
also be reduced to a complex of interrelated sensations. The
"constant mass" of the body is just a shorthand formula for
certain complicated relationships among sensations. Mach did
not mean that we should dispense with scientific concepts such
as "mass," or cease to define scientific objects such as "the
earth" or "an atom." He meant that we should know what these
concepts and objects really denote. We think of them as
denoting the characters of a "real physical world," existing
independently of the mind; and we then think of our ideas of

these physical entities as existing in another psychical realm, not that of the physical entities themselves; and so we proceed to an absolute dualism of mind and matter, with its insoluble problems. But in fact, Mach meant, we know directly only one sort of entities, namely immediate sensations with their interrelations; and both "physical" and "psychical" facts belong in this one realm.

We need not appeal, therefore, to an external reality lying beyond the realm of experience, and other than it. Our usual supposition, which is that we explain phenomena by showing them to be the effects of real things lying back of phenomena, is quite unnecessary, and presumably false. We are justified in believing only what is actually observed and attested by science—all further belief is gratuitous and "metaphysical." We need to postulate, therefore, only the phenomenal realm.

Mach also pointed out that definitions of scientific objects are conditioned by the experimental procedures pursued in their study. He recognized three criteria of scientific truth. First, we should accept as true only those relational complexes, *i.e.* theories, which can be reduced to sensational elements. Second, we should require logical consistency, even though this requires theoretical constructions going beyond what is strictly verifiable in experience. And third, our hypotheses should attain a maximum simplicity, economy, and utility as the agencies of precise description and accurate prediction. In these three requirements, Mach recognized the three aspects of cognition which have variously led to realism, idealism, and pragmatism; but because he balances each aspect against the others, preferring none, he identifies himself with no one of these views.

Similarly complex and inclusive is the positivism of other late nineteenth-century thinkers. The most notable and brilliant of these was *Henri Poincaré* (1854–1912), the leading mathematician of his time. The logical element in knowledge is found by Poincaré to arise in mathematical intuition, which is a priori and universal. The empirical or experimental element Poincaré seems to identify with the act of verification, which finds predictions based upon universal hypothesis to be in correspondence with observable fact. But between the rational intuitions of mathematics and the empirical verifications of science occur the all-important processes of hypothesis-making; and here Poincaré, like Mach, has recourse to the aesthetic or utilitarian criterion of economy, simplicity, and elegance. He shows that wherever one hypothesis is found to be internally consistent and empirically verifiable, a host of other hypotheses can be constructed to meet these same requirements. Our choice among these equivalent hypotheses, therefore, is dictated neither by logical necessity nor by observable fact. It is not, it follows, dictated at all, but is subject to our convenience; and so the third factor in knowledge is subjective, arbitrary, and conventional.

The notion that civic and moral law, and finally all human opinion, is established solely upon human agreement or social convention was a familiar doctrine in ancient Greece, where it was propagated by the sophists. This sort of conventionalism has been revived in various forms during the last half century. We met it in Bergson's last work, a social study which sharply distinguished between the moral intuition of the prophet and the established institutions which conventionalize and perpetuate the prophetic teaching, sometimes in a distorted fashion. Conventionalism has been seriously and emphatically advocated by the school of French sociologists led by *Emile Durkheim* and *Lévy-Bruhl*. These thinkers ascribe ultimate reality and specific character to societies. Each society, they teach, generates and develops institutional forms peculiar to itself, in ways not reducible to any universal formula. Science or knowledge, too, these men say, is only a social institution, arising literally in a "collective mind" which perceives and thinks in definable ways. This common, impersonal, collective mind, not the variable individual mind, they say, is the true subject and host of knowledge, and the legitimate seat of intellectual and political authority. The moral sense of the individual, felt as obligation to God or mankind or moral law, is really a subconscious awareness of society, induced by the pervasive force which is exerted by society upon individual thought and conduct. Sociology is the study of this ultimate, real, and authoritative being which is society. Religion, law, moral theory, art, economic theory and practice, science, and even logic are all, according to this "*sociologisme*," only the instruments and expressions of the "collective mind."

This doctrine looks back by way of Comte's sociology to Rousseau's doctrine of the general will. In the writer's opinion, it is one of the more perverse and dangerous fallacies of our time. The "collective mind" can be used to justify extreme nationalism, racialism, or other immoral and antisocial prejudice. In the name of science, this collectivism denies the objectivity of scientific truth, and teaches that every society must have its peculiar science rooted in a peculiar logic. As the fount of morality, it would erect the collectivistic state, exercising an absolute authority which is implicitly accepted, it says, even in the individual's deepest sense of moral obligation. In the name of religion, it denies the objective truth of religion, and makes religious faith only conformity to collective opinion, or loyalty to one's tribe. A similar doctrine, pursued by the German exponents of *Kultur-philosophie*, encouraged the movement to Nazism. Nowhere is the moral confusion of European society so evident and so disastrous as in this pseudoscientific sociologism.

Yet we have to recognize that this aberrance of thought, with its deification of society and convention, is a groping effort to do justice to the moral basis of knowledge, which is not to be so unhappily identified with "convention." It is this moral basis which gives to science its universality, and prevents it from becoming provincial, racial, national, and "sociological." It is this moral basis, we shall see, which upbears and justifies the rational and empirical criteria of science.

One may perhaps identify as *contemporary* positivism, however, an outlook which has little in common with the sort of conventionalism we have just described. This new movement looks back to earlier positivism and to Mach; and it is faithful to the original intention of positivism, which was to justify faith in natural science, even at the price of some sacrifice of scientific objectivity. Contemporary positivism received its greatest stimulus from the revolution in logical science precipitated by the publication of *Principia Mathematica*. Its chief study is the relationship of the logical structure of knowledge to the empirical content of knowledge; and its main tenet is the primacy and universality of logic, adherence to which unites all thinking men into one intellectual community. For this reason it is sometimes described as *logical positivism*.

In our discussion of the work of Bertrand Russell, it was mentioned that Russell undertook the reduction of mathematical propositions to logical propositions in order to undercut the Kantian philosophy, which was established upon the view that mathematical knowledge is independent and irreducible. Russell succeeded beyond his hopes; but the sword which he fashioned for use against Kantian idealism, in the interests of new realism, was a double-edged weapon. He was able to show that mathematical propositions are not synthetic, because they are demonstrably equivalent to sets of logical propositions. These latter are purely analytic or *tautological*, in that they are established by the definitions of symbols. Every logical proposition, and consequently every mathematical proposition, may be understood as a complicated way of saying "*A is A*." Algebraic identities, where the logical equivalence of the two members is hidden by complications of algebraic symbolism, may illustrate these analytic or tautological propositions. It is not obvious to the beginner that $(a + b)^3 = a^3 + 3a^2 b + 3ab^2 + b^3$; yet when he considers the meanings of the symbols as these are defined by his manual, he finds that the two sides of the identity are only different ways of saying the same thing. Thus the identity is an *analytic* proposition because it only reveals, upon analysis, the meanings of the symbols as defined; it is a *tautological* or self-evident proposition because it follows of necessity from the definitions of the symbols used.

To show that mathematical theory can be reduced to logical theory, *i.e.* to definitions of symbols together with the results of logical operations upon the definitions, was to show that mathematical theory is not a descriptive science making statements about the structures and processes of nature. Mathematical systems can be constructed *ad libitum*, and they may be of any sort we please. If we do not like irrational numbers, we may construct a theory in which these will not occur. If we are not satisfied with the three dimensions of height, breadth, and depth, we may construct a geometry with four or forty dimensions. Thus the apparent necessity or certainty of mathematical propositions (two and two must be four, cannot be five) stems initially from our fidelity to the meanings we have allotted to symbols. "Two" *means* "one and one"; so "two and two" means "one and one and one and one"; but "one and one and one and one" means "four." If we had originally defined "one and one and one and one" to be "five," then "two and two" would be "five," and "two and two are four" would be nonsense.

Because Kant had based his whole conception of science upon the mistaken premise that mathematical propositions are at once necessary and descriptive, the *Principia Mathematica* did in fact undermine and explode both the Kantian philosophy itself, and the metaphysical absolutisms which had depended upon it. But *to demolish the Kantian philosophy was not to remove the indubitable fact which Kant's philosophy had endeavored to explain.* This indubitable fact is the *theoretical* or systematic character of scientific knowledge. Science proceeds from the diverse and chaotic data provided by perception to organized and unified theories, such as those elaborated by mathematical physics. Mathematical theory is the chief agency facilitating this organization and unification of natural knowledge. If mathematical theory is shown to be logical theory, then logical theory becomes the indispensable instrument of science; and logic seems to provide the firm anatomy or structure of descriptive science, which builds its specific hypotheses upon logical theory. Nor can descriptive science advance, nor express itself at all, without recourse to language and logical system.

If, then, the immediate consequence of the new logic was to invalidate absolutistic metaphysics, its more lasting effect is to heighten our appreciation of the rational structure of natural knowledge, to which Kant, in spite of his mistaken premises, effectively called attention. Logical positivism is the effort to do justice, once again, to the logical anatomy which gives to theoretical science such unity, such consistency, and such generality as it undoubtedly possesses. After three or four centuries dominated by empirical thinkers who were inclined to nominalism and somewhat skeptical of theoretical knowledge, there now occurs a swing of the pendulum; and we enter a period which places emphasis upon the logical and rational character of knowledge, and which asks what is implied by this ineradicable logical structure.

The effort to answer this question has only just begun, speculation is still tentative and groping, and to attempt to predict its outcome would be premature. But because this newest form of rationalism starts from a fresh and deep insight into the nature of logic, viewed both in itself and in its relation to theoretical science, it is certain to lead to important developments, and to become the broadest approach to philosophical speculation in the future. Because it was initiated largely by thinkers influenced by Mach and Lange, and through them by Kant, it is not surprising that its first conclusions should be positivistic in tendency. But this positivistic stage seems already to be approaching its close.

The categories of science which support the superstructure of natural knowledge, said Kant, arise from and express the mind's essential function, which is to integrate human experience. We cannot, accordingly, simply attribute to external reality itself the structures defined by these categories. If the structures initially express a unity which is imposed by the mind upon experience, they need not define a unity in external reality. There is good reason, Kant said, to deny to the categories this external reference; because if we assume them to possess it, we are led to antinomies or self-contradictions. Today, the function which Kant ascribed to the categories is seen to be fulfilled by the faculty of logical improvisation, which generates symbolic systems such as mathematics; but because these logical systems are made at our pleasure, without resort to empirical verification, there seems to be no reason why they should describe anything external to ourselves; and when we do impute to them such descriptive cogency, we are led to nonsensical or meaningless statements which parallel the antinomies of pure reason discovered by Kant. This is the argument of the logical positivist; and it is not mistaken to see in it a modernized and corrected form of the Kantian criticism of absolutistic metaphysics.

Like Kant, however, the logical positivist entertains a lively sense of the importance, the inescapability, and the self-integrity of this logical structure in knowledge, in spite of the difficulties which it may raise with respect to our faith in thoretical description. Only where experience is so integrated into theoretical unity, the positivist says, do we have authentic knowledge. The ideal or objective of science, accordingly, is a theoretical system which would include all experience, at least insofar as this is theoretically conceivable. To this ideal of a "unity of science" the logical positivist calls all intelligent and well-meaning men. All scientists, all scholars, all educated minds, he says, belong to one and the same intelligent human community, which is united by its allegiance to this ideal of unitary and integrated knowledge. This ideal and this faith is the answer to the skepticism and anti-intellectualism which the positivists see, not without good reason, to threaten science and civilization. In this teaching, they continue the intellectual tradition both of the earlier positivism and of the eighteenth-century Enlightenment.

But contemporary positivism does not escape, and in some of its conclusions it emphasizes, the skeptical implications which are inherent in this rejection as metaphysical doctrine of all final realistic statement. To perceive these implications clearly, we must look more closely at the positivist's conception of logic and of the relation of logic to fact. Some system of logic is implicit in every theoretical description of natural process. In physical description, for example, this logical element is largely provided by mathematical theory. Mathematical symbolism enters physical science as a working tool; but it remains incorporated in scientific theory as a logical structure. The *Principia Mathematica* had shown that mathematical systems are a priori, in the sense that they rest upon arbitrary definitions which state only the agreed-upon meanings of symbols, and neither require nor allow of empirical verification. Logical form seems, therefore, to constitute a nondescriptive element which is incorporated into every scientific description of fact. And the logical positivist is able to show how this logical element can be extracted from descriptive science, and studied and developed independently of science (as had always been done, incidentally, by "pure" mathematics). The question arises, then, as to the relation which exists between this separable logical element in science, and the descriptive, empirical, or "material" element which gives to natural knowledge its reference to things or facts. Shall we regard the logical element as extraneous to the factual knowledge of things, somewhat as the color of an etching may be irrelevant to what is depicted?

Or shall we insist that the logical element, because it is integral with the theoretical description, is part of the factual knowledge, and therefore invested with descriptive meaning? Is logic, as Kant would have inquired, at once self-evident and descriptive?

On this issue, the three dominant philosophical traditions again make themselves felt and arouse controversial debate. The realist argues for the descriptive cogency of logic, and affirms its power to define an objective and real structure in the world. He may assert that the separation of logic from the descriptive material of science can never be quite complete, so that logical theory remains a widest and most abstract descriptive knowledge. The pragmatist takes a middle position. The logical theory, he says, is the agency or instrument used in problem-solutions, just as is all scientific theory; and it will develop and shape itself as conditioned by the matrix of concrete knowledge. Logic is therefore neither extraneous to the material facts, nor itself a statement of material fact; but it summarizes operations of analysis by means of which problems are solved. The positivist, at the other extreme position, holds that logical structure is separable and has been separated, and that its independence of the factual material to which it is applied, and within which it is incorporated to produce "knowledge," constitutes a very real problem, which realism and pragmatism do not take sufficiently seriously. Contemporary positivism, in short—and this is its great merit—insists upon a fresh and thoroughgoing examination of the relationship of the rational element to the empirical element in knowledge; and it insists that this examination must start from the new grasp of logical form achieved in our own time.

This inquiry was advanced by a group of men sometimes known as the "Vienna circle." (Mach spent his later years in Vienna.) In his *Tractatus logico-philosophicus*, Wittgenstein pointed to certain difficulties which would seem to prohibit a realistic theory of knowledge. Every system of logic, he concluded, contains statements which refer only to linguistic usage, and which cannot be given meaning when we suppose them to refer to something in the world outside of language. These linguistic usages are merely conventions, necessary to speech but without necessary reference to what is spoken about. To be realistic about knowledge, therefore, is to insist that these arbitrary linguistic conventions constitute part of the structure of universal reality. Yet to suppose that human language can impose a law upon universal nature is surely the extreme of egoism. Wittgenstein argues that all metaphysical propositions do in fact, as Kant had taught, commit this egregious egoism; and he is led, therefore, to prohibit every sort of metaphysical speculation, and to renounce every form of realistic faith in the identity of scientific objects with "reality." He is the most positivistic member of this group.

Rudolf Carnap, formerly of Vienna and now resident in America, one of the ablest students of the new logistics, attempted an ambitious "reconstruction of knowledge" which aimed to purify science from the metaphysical residues left by the confusion of linguistic conventions with natural fact. The difficulty which faces such efforts to purify science of metaphysical elements is the impossibility of speaking about the material element in knowledge without introducing the formal element. It is possible to abstract, and to present in symbolic notation, the logical forms utilized in scientific description; and Carnap's most beautiful analyses are devoted to this abstraction. But what remains when these forms are removed? There is left, the positivist assumes, only the actual material of sense-experience itself; for science is the sheer union of logical form with material content. But how shall one speak of this purely empirical content without introducing into our description of it the logical forms which are necessarily incorporated in all articulate speech? Carnap proposed that a material made up of "protocol-sentences," somewhat like the staccato phrases of a policeman's bare description of what he saw and heard at the scene of a crime, might do service here. But it is evident that even the barest description of empirical fact must contain not only logical structure, but a good deal of everyday opinion or scientific hypothesis. There is no direct way of stating what is left in natural knowledge, when all theoretical form is taken away. The logical form and the empirical content of knowledge are not simply glued together, it is evident, in natural knowledge. It is upon the false supposition that the two elements are so simply related that logical positivism breaks down.

Already, however, the thinkers in this group are attempting new approaches to the problem of the relationship of logic to fact. Any scientific or other description of fact (or, for that matter, any fantasy) is the rendition into communicable language of something which is not language. We may, therefore, study language itself, and especially scientific language, as a sort of medium in which knowledge occurs. Much as the geometry of space enters into every material configuration existing in space, so the pattern of language will enter into every verbal description. We may turn, therefore, to a study of language-pattern, and discover in this way the linguistic structure which is incorporated in all explicit knowledge. This structure can be isolated, and reveals itself to be constituted of several elements. First, there is *syntax*, of which we learn something at school in our study of grammar. But school grammar is peculiar to one language, and we need a universal grammar. We possess this in the highly developed grammar or syntax of scientific language. The propositions which make up syntax consist wholly of statements about symbols and their relations. They refer to nothing outside of language. Thus a syntactical system can be elaborated which has no meaning in the ordinary sense, because it refers to nothing outside of itself; yet it is precisely definable and completely intelligible. All pure mathematics, *e.g.* algebra, is such syntax. Syntactical systems can be given descriptive meanings by a process of *interpretation*. We first elaborate a purely algebraic syntax, and then we agree that certain of its symbols shall refer to the actual properties of the space about us; and now the syntax is transformed into a system of descriptive geometry. There will always be within syntax, however, certain logical statements which refer only to words or symbols, and which cannot be given an intelligible material interpretation. As these statements are carried into the interpretation, we cannot say that a descriptive theory is wholly intelligible as a statement of material fact.

But the logician further distinguishes in language certain elements which he calls *semantic*, having to do with the relations of symbols to the things spoken about. And he finds still other relationships, which he calls *pragmatic*, which have to do with the relation of words to their speakers or hearers. All of these sorts of relationship, of words to words (syntax), of words to things (semantics), and of words to the users of words (pragmatics), may enter into the meaning of a word. This kind of linguistic analysis promises interesting results, some of which may have significance for philosophy; and it suggests a development which will combine the positivistic, realistic, and pragmatic theories of knowledge.

Logical positivism seems to be developing, therefore, into a broad study which seeks to establish no particular set of philosophical tenets, but which is chiefly characterized by its new approach to new problems. This approach is opened by the new and increasingly clear understanding of the role played by logic or language in human cognition. Partly because of their Kantian antecedents, in the writer's opinion, this group of thinkers excels in its perception of the philosophical significance of the recent revolution in logic. It is true, as the empiricist and pragmatist insist, that logic has grown up within science, and developed with the growth of natural knowledge; yet it is also true, as the realist insists, that logical terms have some sort of meaning in their own right. The movement we have called "logical positivism" would overlap these two opposed views.

It constitutes really a new and corrected rationalism. It agrees with the empiricist that logical study only abstracts the formal structure of empirical knowledge; yet it also agrees with the realist and rationalist, who holds that logical or rational form constitutes something which regulates and conditions knowledge, and which is not to be identified with the empirical content of knowledge. This movement raises again, in short, the issue which has long divided thinkers into the opposed camps of rationalism and empiricism; and it does this with the intention and the promise of reconciling their differences.

As yet, the proponents of this new and empirical rationalism are still somewhat uncertain of their way. They are embarrassed by their antecedent tradition, namely the nineteenth-century positivism which stoutly rejected all final "metaphysical" statement. They do not see that their clarification of the nature and function of logic may rid metaphysics of its terrors, by leaving wholly free and unconditioned the progress of empirical hypothesis. In our concluding chapters we will develop this possibility. Here we are concerned only to estimate and do justice to the important insight of logical positivism. This movement again makes clearly evident the a priori and formal element which abides in all theoretical knowledge, and indeed in all explicit description that makes use of language. Syntax, grammar, "the word" are always with us; and to use language is to affirm certain presuppositions of language, which impose themselves in this way upon all thought.

So we are brought back after a full circle to the point where philosophy began in Greek antiquity. "In the beginning was the Logos"—there is no thought which is independent of logic. How shall we explain, what shall we deduce from this ubiquity of logical form? Shall we say that the dependence of thought upon logic is the Achilles' heel of thought, because logic is merely verbal convention, just language, an arbitrary and subjective structure peculiar to man and human nature? This way leads to skepticism. Or shall we say that nature itself finds voice in human speech, that the logic of science is the logic of nature itself, and that in our recognition of logical form we lay hands upon the eternal anatomy of the world? This way, Parmenides said, leads to truth. And we shall find that we can agree with him, and do so without sharing his distrust of the senses and empirical fact. Logic in its application to fact, it can be shown today, is the servant and protector of empirical truth, and not its master.

Notes for Further Reading

1. Vaihinger, H., *The Philosophy of 'As If,'* trans. C. K. Ogden. New York, Harcourt, Brace and Company, 1924.
2. Durkheim, E., *The Rules of Sociological Method*, ed. G. E. G. Catlin. Chicago, University of Chicago Press, 1938.
3. Alpert, H., *Emile Durkheim and His Sociology*. New York, Columbia University Press, 1939.
4. Lévy-Bruhl, L., *Ethics and Moral Science*, trans. E. Lee. Paris, F. Alcan, 1905.
5. Mach, E., *Analysis of Sensations*, trans. C. M. Williams. La Salle, Ill., The Open Court Publishing Company, 1897.
6. —— *Popular Scientific Lectures*, trans. T. McCormack. La Salle, Ill., The Open Court Publishing Company, 1898.
7. Poincaré, H., *The Foundations of Science*, trans. G. B. Halsted, Charles Scribner's Sons, 1921.
8. —— *Science and Hypothesis*. New York, Charles Scribner's Sons, 1906.
9. Laird, J., *Recent Philosophy*. London, Thornton Butterworth, Ltd., 1936.
10. Ogden, C. K. and Richards, I. A., *The Meaning of Meaning*. New York, Harcourt, Brace and Company, 1923.
11. Wisdom, J., *Problems of Mind and Matter*. London and New York, Cambridge University Press, 1934.
12. Ayer, A. J., *Language, Truth and Logic*. Toronto, Ryerson Press, 1936.
13. Broad, C. D., *Scientific Thought*. New York, Harcourt, Brace and Company, 1923.
14. Eddington, A. S., *The Nature of the Physical World*. London and New York, Cambridge University Press, 1928.

15. Planck, M., *The Philosophy of Physics*, trans. W. H. Johnston. New York, W. W. Norton and Company, Inc., 1936.
16. Wittgenstein, L., *Tractatus Logico-Philosophicus*. New York, Harcourt, Brace and Company, 1922.
17. Popper, K., *The Logic of Discovery*. Vienna, J. Springer, 1935.
18. Carnap, R., *The Unity of Science*, trans. M. Black. London, George Routledge and Sons, 1934.
19. ――― *Philosophy and Logical Syntax*. London, George Routledge and Sons, 1935.
20. ――― *The Logical Syntax of Language*. New York, Harcourt, Brace and Company, 1937.
21. ――― *Introduction to Semantics*. Cambridge, Harvard University Press, 1942.
22. ――― *The Formalization of Logic*. Cambridge, Harvard University Press, 1943.
23. Reichenbach, H., *Experience and Prediction*. Chicago, University of Chicago Press, 1938.
24. ――― *From Copernicus to Einstein*. Boston, Longmans, Green and Company, 1942.
25. ――― *Elements of Symbolic Logic*. New York, The Macmillan Company, 1947.
26. Morris, C. W., *Logical Positivism, Pragmatism, and Scientific Empiricism*. Paris, Hermann and Company, 1937.
27. Lewis, C. I., *Mind and the World Order*. New York, Charles Scribner's Sons, 1929.
28. ――― *Symbolic Logic*. New York, D. Appleton-Century Company, Inc., 1933.
29. Lewis, G. N., *The Anatomy of Science*. New Haven, Yale University Press, 1926.
30. Frank, P., *Between Physics and Philosophy*. Cambridge, Harvard University Press, 1941.

26 THE SIGNIFICANCE
OF THIS HISTORY

WE HAVE COMPLETED OUR SURVEY OF SOME twenty-five centuries of intellectual effort. We may now digest this study by drawing its consequences for present thought. What light does this history cast upon contemporary fact?

First, let us look back once more upon man's intellectual evolution in order to grasp its major theme and its controlling direction. This retrospect will tell us where man stands today, after twenty-five centuries of pondering upon himself and the world, and how he states his problem. This we do in the present chapter. In the following chapters, we will see how he is compelled to solve the problem so stated, and allowed to arrive, at last, at philosophical truth.

The major theme of intellectual history has been man's progress to a free science supporting a free government. The outcome of this evolution is a society both intellectually and politically emancipated. We need two words to indicate this liberty, and we necessarily think of the movements, toward intellectual freedom and toward political liberty, in some separation from each other. Yet they are truly one movement, seen in two of its aspects. We could not say that every scientist has been a political liberal, nor that every political advance has consciously premised itself upon science. But on the whole, scientific and political progress have supported and stimulated each other. Together they have defined and propagated the sanity which is liberalism in thought and conduct.

It is still convenient to divide the evolution of western civilization into three epochs, ancient, medieval, and modern. In some respects, the modern period does return to the intellectual ideals of antiquity. It again pursues a theoretical science, and establishes a constitutional form of government. But modern civilization is more different from antiquity than like it. Antiquity was rationalistic in its science and conservative in its politics. Modern society is empirical in its science and progressive in its moral and political practice. Modern thought has recovered and absorbed ancient thought, but has subjected it to relentless criticism. This radical difference between modern and ancient society has its cause and explanation in the medieval centuries.

When we say that the science of antiquity was rationalistic, we mean that science was then conceived to possess a core of absolute axioms, which supposedly were known to the reason independently of experience. This core of axioms was *science net*. *Science gross* contained in addition the many applications of this rational truth to particular fact. The human reason provided science, the animal senses provided the material which was to be scientifically understood. And when we say that modern science is empirical, we mean that science is now conceived to consist of all of the generalizations which may be garnered from sensed fact. These generalizations may be woven together into organized theories; but the theories remain summaries of experienced fact, they are not regarded as rational and absolute truths. Whereas Greek science made rationally intuited principles the test of truth, modern science makes observed fact the test of truth. In this respect, the modern intellect inverts the Greek intellect. It proceeds upward from fact to theory, whereas the Greek intellect descended from theory to facts.

Similarly, in the political sphere, Greek government subordinated the individual to the law, whereas modern government subordinates law to the individual. There was certainly frequent revolt among the Greeks against this legalistic subjection of the individual, just as today there are movements which would make the individual again subject to absolute government. We are speaking, of course, only of the largest, most definitive features of modernity and antiquity; and these rather strikingly contrast. Modern man, in accepting from Greece the instrument of theoretical analysis, has used it to generate a progressive empirical science, whereas the Greeks used it to perpetuate a dogmatic rational science. Modern man, in accepting from Greece the instrument of constitutional government, has made it the servant of social and legal progress, whereas the Greeks made it an agency of conservatism and reaction.

This, chiefly, is what we have to learn: How and why does modern theoreticism escape from the limitations of Greek theoreticism, and how does modern constitutionalism escape from the legalism and conservatism of Greek constitutionalism? If these two questions are not confidently and clearly answered today, it is because we do not see that they are really one question, the two parts of which must be satisfied by one and the same answer. In the following chapter we will present an answer, not without confidence and we hope with clarity. In this chapter, our purpose must be to see just how, today, the question must be stated, so that it may find an intelligible answer.

It is clear, to begin with, that we must escape from the Greek error which made liberty incompatible with progress. When we first meet the ancient Greeks, historically speaking, they already possess free government. Some centuries earlier they had deposed their kings and made the law their governor, with themselves the executors of the law. They were aware that their political liberty distinguished them from the "barbarian" peoples about them, who still submitted to the personal despotism the Greeks have taught us to call "tyranny." Yet these tyrannies finally destroyed Greek freedom; and it is significant that the downfall of Greek liberty was due not to military defeat, but to certain internal weaknesses in Greek society. The Greeks could defeat imperial Persia; and they would have similarly repelled every invader, if they had not been destroyed from within by disunity and internecine strife. What defeated them was their failure to make their free and constitutional government the agency of political progress.

The rise and expansion of imperial Persia was not merely a military threat to the Greek cities. It was also a moral threat. There were those within the Greek cities who spontaneously prostrated themselves before that imperial might, and counseled their fellow citizens not to attempt resistance, but to appease and ally themselves with the irresistible invader. It required a loyalty religious in its intensity and almost fanatical in its courage to defy that advancing Persian tide. So the Greek leaders called upon their peoples for a religious faith in their institutions; and to establish or confirm them in their faith, the Greek statesman became a thinker, a scientist and philosopher. He taught the Greeks that in defending their constitutional governments they only did what true religion required of them. The whole cosmos, he argued, is a constitutional polity, ruled by a divine and universal law. In all of its motions, the cosmos manifests this eternal and immutable law. And to establish this religious truth, the Greek thinker created a natural science moving from observable fact to a theoretical knowledge of that cosmic structure which, he said, is natural and divine law. The *Logos*, he taught, is the true God. The civic constitution is the *Logos* in its human context, and loyalty to constitutional law is therefore a religious duty. Law is the responsibility which is allotted to all things, and which finally is authoritative over all things.

Thus arose theoretical science, a quest for the enduring structure which inheres in the diversity and change of observable occurrence. Historically speaking, natural science emerged as a by-product of Greek government, in a somewhat anthropomorphic interpretation of natural structure by way of its analogy with the Greek constitution. And we shall find that natural science is still and forever the child of political faith, and that it collapses as soon as it forgets its living source in moral and political truth.

This new faith—for such it really was—finally established itself in that world, but not without arousing opposition which succeeded in seriously impairing its form and import. The new science outraged the orthodox, who would have new wine only in old bottles, and who were faithful still to the Homeric pantheon of anthropomorphic deities. These orthodox people wished to be politically free, yet to remain morally and intellectually subject to a monarchical deity and his feudal retinue of lesser gods. The new faith also challenged, of course, all those who openly or secretly admired imperial tyranny, and who plotted to overthrow their civic constitutions and to establish tyrannies or sub-tyrannies in their place. But it must also have offended some progressives who saw the necessity of adapting Greek law to changing conditions, and who therefore feared this analogy between civic law and the eternal constitution of nature.

Opposition to the new science appeared in the persecution by established authorities of leading scientists; and criticism became vocal in the sophists, pilloried by Plato. These men taught, as do our sophists still, that society is not ruled by any external, transcendent, moral, or divine compulsion, but is observably controlled by forces internal to society, forces generated and exercised by ambitious individuals and social groups. Politics is always pressure-politics. A successful faction imposes its will upon society, and claims for its legislative acts a moral or religious sanctity which does not invest them, its actual authority being just sheer power. Law, they concluded, is only convention, a usage or imposition without real authority. Justice is the rule of the stronger; and the stronger may be the unscrupulous but skilful tyrant, the self-willed but able oligarchy, or the majority, individually weak but strong in their number. And the sophist was perhaps more willing than his opponent to put his thesis to the test of observable fact. Look at nature, he said, and you will see everywhere the rule of the stronger, the survival of the fittest, and the extermination of the weak. Nature is war, society is war, peace is a truce or a temporary balance of powers. There is no moral foundation for government because there is no moral law in nature—unless we give the name of moral law to this natural propriety by which the strong compels the weak. But in truth, according to the sophist, nature knows no law. Science has no authority. Only power has authority.

The Greek thinker, struggling to meet and defeat this sophistry, never perceived its full strength. Failing to distinguish the half-truth which lends it plausibility, he failed to detect clearly its error. The half-truth in sophistry, Greek or modern, is its recognition that *power lies in individual things*— and ultimately only there. The sophistic error was to deduce from this correct premise the mistaken conclusion that the power of the individual precludes moral law and civic justice. The Greek thinker, in his effort to combat the sophistic error, threw out both the error and the truth. Convinced of the cogency of his science, he now examined that science more intently, to discover wherein lay its generative insight. What he discovered was the theoretical form of science, which gives to science its unity, its stability, and whatever else distinguishes it from casual opinion. The error of the sophist, Parmenides decided, is that he trusts his senses. He sees individual things, and so he believes that individual things are real. If they were real, Parmenides conceded, all that the sophist concludes would follow. In this case, there could be no absolute science, disclosing an eternal law. Each man would have his individual perspective on nature, and his conclusions would be true only for himself. Yet science is equally cogent for all men. In science we transcend individual difference to share a single, common truth. How is this possible? Because in science we do not function as individuals, reacting to individuals. We react as rational beings, or rather as rational Being. As reasoning and reasonable beings, we humans are an unindividuated One. Similarly, in the Object which reason knows, all individuality and difference vanish. We know the One, the Absolute, which is what science defines in its absolute and unitary theory. Even the difference between subject and object vanishes, and the knower becomes identical with what is known. We know the One because we are the One. Reason, completed, is mystical identity.

In this way, to combat sophistry and skepticism, natural science was transformed into rationalistic metaphysics. This was a mortal blow to science, which lives only as a continual progress, absorbing ever more particular fact into its empirical generalizations and its growing theories. A universalistic metaphysics cannot progress. What it presents is presented as the infallible intuition of a single, self-identical reason, apprehensive of a single, self-identical Being. And what is the value of a "science" which, confronted with the evidence of particular fact, turns aside saying, "Mere sense-illusion"! How should we apply such "science," or test it, or communicate it? What Parmenides really did, of course, is what every later metaphysician has done. He took the science of its day as it came from the scientific observer; he abstracted its widest and most general statements by means of logical analysis; and then, mistaking this logical analysis of what is known for the empirical discovery which is science, he announced that his abstract conclusions are established by a rational intuition, and that even in their near-emptiness they depict the concrete substance of truth.

Plato made a valiant attempt to correct this Parmenidean metaphysics by compromising with the sophistic irrationalism. With Parmenides he agreed that the reason apprehends the eternal One; but natural science, he said, arises when this rational intuition is applied to the changing and particularized world of things. Science is thus the rediscovery of eternal and universal form in the sensed particular changes of nature. This theory of knowledge, Plato sometimes implied, requires a dualistic view of nature, which is properly conceived as being compounded of two sorts of being. One is the immutable Form, which Plato called "Being"; the other is motion itself, called by Plato "nonbeing." In this Platonic dualism, the senses are allowed to provide the material of existent fact, in which the Being apprehended by reason is variously, incompletely, and transiently manifested. So sensory knowledge and empirical science are not sheer illusion, but a confused and imperfect version of rational knowledge.

Plato seemed to have saved the Greek faith in the "intellect," *i.e.* in theoretical reason. He turned back the tide of overt skepticism, which did not rally again for two thousand years. Because this Greek metaphysics also defined eternal Being as divine and Good, it saved also the profounder Greek faith in the identity of intellectual and moral truth. The reason, intuiting the Being which is the origin of all intelligible structure in the world, discovers those true forms which are the proper destinies or ends of natural motions. Everything seeks to manifest its true form; and since these forms are all reciprocally adjusted, as aspects of the one Being, this effort of things to realize their forms sustains the vast and eternal economy of nature.

But if Greek metaphysics saved the letter of intellectual and moral faith, it did not save natural science, which is the full confession of this faith. It allowed the senses to illustrate the sublime truth known to the reason; but it did not allow the senses to generate knowledge, nor to confirm or disprove the edicts of reason. For two thousand years, accordingly, natural science languished; and it was supposed, except in a few obscure corners, that reason had spoken its piece in Greek metaphysics, which needed henceforth only to be memorized.

This failure of Greek science, which after two short centuries of rapid progress was paralyzed into Greek metaphysics, is related to the political failure of Greece. Natural science had arisen and developed as an extension of the faith of the Greeks in their political achievement. Because the Greeks identified their constitutions with the detailed usage or law of their particular city-state, they could not conceive of a Greek liberty which was not committed to the sovereignty of the city-state, and to the preservation of every jot and tittle of its law. Yet the Greeks were now surrounded by great and powerful neighbors, and the prime condition of their independence was a merger of the city-states into a Greek nation. Their failure to confederate was their doom; and the tragic struggle between those who treasured local independence as the substance of liberty, and the progressives who fought for local readjustments with too little care for justice and its preservation, destroyed the political faith of Greece. When Plato came to maturity, the doom of Athens was written on the wall; and so, renouncing a political career, Plato turned to a metaphysical idealism that made justice a regulatory idea, a faith which might influence and ameliorate the course of human injustice, but which could never be realized, except perhaps by a miracle, in the actualities of government.

And so, except for minor amendments, the Greek testament stood. There is a truth, it said, accessible to the reason; but this truth defines an object not of this world, although what is intelligible in this world is so in virtue of that transcendental truth. There is a Good, it said; but that, too, is not of this world, although it is the measure of all natural goodness. The profound pessimism investing pagan civilization, which evinced itself in a nostalgia for the remote and golden past, finally possessed itself of the Greek spirit in this otherworldly, transcendental Platonism. The later Greeks, in particular the Stoics, no longer distinguished ideal justice from universal cosmic law; and this had the advantage of detaching the concept of justice from the city-state, to make it the concept of a universal moral law, antecedent to all government and independent of it. But the "blessed city of God" of the Stoics, although it contained all who acknowledged its moral government, was still an invisible realm, not to be sought in political actualities. Greek metaphysics was the consolation of a defeated and conquered people, who magnified their dream of a justice they could no longer hope to possess.

This consolatory metaphysical dream became philosophy, became even "science," and remained this for two millennia. No wonder that under later antiquity a rebellion moved against the Greek formalism that had become so unrealistic. Christianity made this rebellion vocal and effective, when it turned from theoretical to religious symbolism, in order to announce its optimistic gospel of salvation come to earth.

Greek metaphysics seemed to weather this storm of religious revolution. It emerged again in Christian theology and in a scholastic philosophy auxiliary to theology. Early Christianity had looked beyond the law to prophetic revelation, beyond the state to the congregation united by *caritas* or love, and beyond cosmic structure to the creative power which fashioned structure even in creating matter. But Greek legalism restored itself in a feudal ecclesiasticism, Greek formalism restored itself in a Platonic theology. Finally, however, in the Reformation and its consequences, the Christian revolution against pagan thought was consummated, to produce the science, the political theory and practice, and the emancipated society of the modern world.

There was really but one reform, one rebirth, one revolt, ushering in this modern world. It was the revolt which transferred authority of every sort from institutions to individuals; and this required the transformation of every human institution, however humble, however august. It transformed the family, the school, the church, the trade and profession, the social economy, the state, the creed, science and philosophy, the human intellect, even the human heart and soul. Let us not pretend that modern civilization is comparable with anything that went before, that it is to be judged by the same norms, esteemed for the same values, subjected to the same necessities. It is a new world created and inhabited by a new man. The new world is a revolutionary world—it has made revolution the peaceful order of its progress. The old world conserved institutions. The new world makes institutions the instruments of human progress, creating them at need.

First to be transformed was the church, which became the free or non-authoritarian congregation. In these independent but self-disciplined congregations, modern man first appropriated and exercised authority. In them was first established the characteristic practice of modern society, that of free government. Modern society is the reformed congregation writ large, writ into all humanity, writ into all space. For the transformation of the church required, even as it intended, the transformation of all else. Next to be reformed was the state, which had usurped the authority let fall by the church, and now in the person of the secular monarch presumed to regulate religion. The first political revolution struck down this royal thief. The free congregations rebelled—let this history for once be truly spoken—the free congregations rebelled, and established a republican Commonwealth which was not so short-lived nor so soon forgotten but that it fathered modern government. From that first political revolution there proceeded the movement to modern democracy. It proceeded primarily on the American continent, but with occasional repercussions elsewhere. Three centuries of continuous change, peaceful or violent, reconstructed society upon a new basis. That basis is the sovereign person. Authority is inalienably invested in the individual, and it is invested there because it is in the individual person, and only there and always there, that moral responsibility resides. This basis of individual authority is the foundation of the new man who is the modern world.

The first English revolution established the supremacy of the law over its executive officers. It did this by arraigning and executing Charles I for treason against the realm. But how should the sovereignty of the individual and his supremacy *above* the law be established? John Locke attempted this, using as his theoretical basis the concept of natural rights. By natural and divine law, he said, the individual is invested with inalienable authority. Only in the moral individual is authority to be found; and all other authority is consequently derivative, revocable, loaned. All final responsibility lies in the individuals who constitute "the people."

This theoretical justification of democratic justice, convincing in its day, became a source of intellectual and moral confusion when, half a century after Locke, the concept of natural law was apparently overthrown by David Hume. We discover, Hume showed, no natural necessity in the world. We discover only uniformities of behavior. So far as we know, nothing in nature is compelled, regulated, or subjected to any legal or moral necessity. Things move as they are determined to move by their individual natures; and scientific formulas only register the ways in which they spontaneously behave.

If there is no natural law, what are "natural rights" invested by "natural law"? Political theorists have increasingly subscribed to the conclusion that criticism of natural law must carry down with it the concept of natural rights. As the implications of Hume's criticism were grasped, it was felt that democracy lacked adequate theoretical foundation; and modern political science has steadily gravitated toward Greek sophistry. Rights can be derived, it begins to be believed, from the actual needs, the shifting movements, the changing conditions of society. The source of all rights is society itself. The individual derives his rights from his membership in society; he has no individual rights, and seldom has he individual powers. Look about and see for yourself—where does the individual enjoy powers? He enjoys powers only as he is identified with some irresistible social movement, only where his individual power becomes a drop in the momentous current, only where he goes with and does not breast the tide that is determined by prevailing conditions. And it is only where his small powers are so identified with those large powers, which in their sweep possess themselves of government and thus make themselves authoritative, that his powers become "rights." "Right" is power enthroned and able to exert authority. "Right" is might.

To secure the political rights of the individual, modern society established a fundamental law in the democratic constitution. The intention of the constitution is to secure political authority to the individual. A democratic constitution is one which establishes the political mechanisms needed to implement individual authority in government, and to prohibit whatever might usurp that authority. But what if constitutional restrictions upon government should seem to oppose the tide of social movement, which seeks to translate its pressures into legislation and executive command? Must not the constitution be made completely plastic to actual need, present condition, prevailing opinion? Should there be limits to what a duly elected government may do? Does not every such limit flout the will of the people, and subordinate public interest to private interest?

This is the dilemma, making private interests and public interests seem to be incompatible, to which we, like the Greeks, have come. The dilemma is aggravated by the mistaken supposition that individual rights derive from natural law, so that if natural law is a fiction, individual rights are fictions too. Yet how should individual rights, which are powers inalienably pertaining to individuals, be derived from anything whatsoever? "Natural rights" means underived and absolute powers. The concept of natural law may conceivably be derived from the concept of individual rights—whether it can be so derived is a question. But neither the concept of natural rights, nor the actuality of natural rights, is derivable from the concept of natural law. What our fathers meant, when they used the familiar verbiage of natural law to establish natural rights, was that the existence of individual rights is an absolute and non-debatable axiom. The individual is defined as the possessor of inalienable rights.

We are now beginning to see how the problem facing modern society must be stated. We must ask: How does one establish this principle of individual natural rights? The founders of modern government believed the principle to be a rational intuition, self-evident and infallible. They placed it beyond debate, exactly as we place beyond debate the truth that one and one are two. Yet we see that it cannot literally be placed beyond dispute. It is even now disputed; and there seems to be some evidence, provided by a scientific and empirical study of social process, against its truth. Can this evidence be outweighed? Or, even better, can it be analyzed, and discovered not to disprove, but to confirm more surely than ever, the principle of individual rights upon which modern justice has established itself?

It can be analyzed and shown to confirm the democratic principle. But to do this, we must undertake an analysis which goes deeper than what is ordinarily called scientific analysis. We must undertake philosophical analysis that probes to a truth which is implicitly obeyed and applied by all science, and which is indeed generative of science. We have to penetrate to philosophical truth. Our motive in seeking this truth is political—we wish to assure ourselves of the righteousness of democratic government. But we find that philosophical truth also conditions our faith in science. Democratic theory or practice, we find, is not subject to criticism upon any ground of scientific evidence. The reason is that the generative principle of democracy, and the presupposition upon which is established all scientific truth, are one and the same. Consequently, to accept scientific evidence and subscribe to scientific truth is to stand upon the principle of democratic justice. The principle of natural rights, that is to say, is not merely a political principle, nor is it merely a moral principle. It is the absolute principle supporting all knowledge, scientific as well as political and moral.

When David Hume discredited the conception of universal necessity, which is what is usually meant by "natural law," he did not discredit, but on the contrary he confirmed, the faith of science and of common sense that things react upon one another according to their individual natures. This is the conviction which supports all scientific inquiry into nature, and apart from which no intelligence of any sort is possible. It is also the implicit presupposition of Hume's criticism of universal necessity. It is because things are determined to react according to their own individual character that they cannot be bound by any universal necessity. Yet the scientist must also assume the amenability of particular fact to theoretical description; and this seems to imply some basic compatibility between individual things and general principles.

Now this last assumption, which seems necessary to science, precipitates the same sort of dilemma as that noted earlier in our consideration of political theory. We say that the individual is free, that he is the source of all government; and yet we limit the political action of the individual by a constitution which requires or prohibits certain types of behavior. Similarly we say that science must abide by the evidence of particular fact, and may not dictate to particular fact. Yet we also say that particular fact must be amenable to theoretical description —that the facts must conform to some theory. This demand that fact shall be amenable to theoretical formulation is enforced by the use of logic. The scientist requires all particular fact to submit to the necessities of logic, such submission being the necessary and sufficient condition of the theoretical formulation of fact in science. But *how*, on the showing of Hume that we find no necessity in nature, *do we justify this seeming assumption that nature is subject to logical necessity?* Is not this predication to nature of logical conformity just a convenient fiction? What evidence is there that nature is somehow inherently logical? How do we harmonize this rational demand, that particular fact shall always conform to some theory, with our empirical insistence that particular fact may be anything we observe it to be?

Modern civilization seems to stand rooted in paradox. The individual, we say, is sovereign; yet he is, of course, bound by a constitution which prescribes and limits the exercise of his sovereignty. Particular fact, we say, is the source and criterion of true theory, even as the individual is the source and the criterion of just law; yet particular fact may not transgress the requirements of logic, nor reject the conditions of its theoretical comprehension by the scientist. The constitution still limits individual freedom, logic still limits hypothesis and fact. We live in self-contradiction, holding the individual to be at once free yet bound, holding particular fact to be and not to be the sole criterion of truth.

Might we not say that this self-contradiction has worked well, and justified itself in practice? Has not the democratic constitution supported a century and a half of liberal and progressive legislation? Has not the logical constitution of science permitted the fullest accommodation of theoretical hypothesis to particular and observed occurrence? Why worry? Why not accept, as a mystery which somehow supports all that is intelligible and good, this self-contradiction at the root of science and society?

Because this paradox which has underlain modern theory and practice is today the source of intellectual, moral and political confusion, to a degree that threatens civilization itself.

This self-contradiction begins to destroy us. It makes our scientists skeptics, it blinds us in our pursuit of justice. It undermines moral and intellectual faith; and when faith is gone, hope and purpose are gone too. But further, we are vaguely aware that to solve this problem and to remove the paradox will be to reach insight wider and more profound than any wisdom of the past.

All that is of importance in modern thought has centered itself upon this problem. First, in the thirteenth century, there sprang up the nominalists who established modern science upon the principle that only individual being is real. They evaded the problem of theoretical knowledge by saying that general ideas are in the mind only. They did not ask by what miraculous and inscrutable power science is able to defer at once, in one and the same genuflection so to speak, to universal logic and to particular fact.

Descartes took the problem more seriously. The true logic of science, he believed, is mathematical theory. Why does mathematical theory always and without residue apply to particular fact? Why should fact always accommodate itself to mathematical description? Because, he answered, mathematical structure is the real, eternal, and universal structure of nature. God created material nature, giving to it just that structure; and he also created man, endowing him with the mathematical reason which is competent to cognize that structure in particular things. Do not question the inscrutable will of God, advised Descartes. Do not ask how you came by your rational intuition, your science. Use your reason, extend it in scientific application, and apply it to better your world.

But Newton invalidated this Cartesian rationalism when he established the empirical principle of gravitation. Hume thereupon challenged all rationalism. Every natural or descriptive principle, he showed, is like the gravitational principle in that it is an empirical generalization inferred from observed particulars. Reason tells us nothing of universal and eternal structure. Our best reason is our most comprehensive summary of particular facts.

There is no doubt of the truth of Hume's contention, and no defense against his critical polemic. Yet if his truth were the whole truth, there would be possible no distinction between human science and animal cognition. The higher animals whose sensory faculties most resemble our own should also be physicists and chemists, and speculate concerning canine or other freedom. What Hume neglected was the agency in science of language, with all that language implies. He overlooked the cognitive interest, and did not appreciate the logical instrumentalities which this interest has generated.

So Kant attempted to correct Hume's error without sacrifice of Hume's truth. Science, he said, is the effort of the cognitive will to unify experience. It brings to this task the agencies which are reason. These are internal to mind; and we may take note of them in the explicit and necessary axioms, *e.g.* those of mathematics, which are basic to all description. Science is compounded on the one hand of contingent and particular fact, but on the other hand of the rational forms which bring this material into theoretical system. But on what evidence do we believe that this imposition of mental forms produces a science truly descriptive of external reality? There is no evidence, Kant concluded. We cannot suppose that science describes reality as it is in itself. The world described by science is a phenomenal world; it is appearance, not reality. The true or noumenal reality is known to us only in moral judgment. This is immediate, final, and absolute; but it grasps only the particular situation regulated by the moral act. Kant did justice to the rational element in science, but only at the sacrifice of our faith in the power of science to describe reality.

There followed the metaphysicians, who made Kant's failure to establish scientific truth their excuse for a return to dogmatism. Hume and Kant have shown, they argued, that empirical science reaches only phenomenal knowledge, which is to say illusion. But Kant himself pointed the way to an absolute rational science. If the mind necessarily imposes its formal requirements upon all possible experience, we may safely abide by its rational edicts, assured that every experience of particular fact will conform to these. Rejecting the checks placed by Kant upon "pure reason," these thinkers allowed to it an absolute power. They elaborated verbal systems which, in the absence of any empirical check, could be anything the metaphysician pleased; and what the metaphysician usually preferred was a system which would subordinate the individual person to the absolute authority of the state, even as particular fact was systematically subordinated in his rationalistic reconstruction. From these post-Kantian metaphysicians proceeded the political absolutisms which would make Europe a graveyard, and menace every liberty under the sun.

Skepticism, it seemed, had conquered, first by destroying faith in the power of natural science to describe reality, secondly by opening the way to a metaphysical dogmatism contemptuous of science. We are perhaps too little aware of how deeply this skepticism, with its dreadful corollary in political and intellectual absolutism, has eaten into the modern mind. The absolutisms fathered by the Humian and Kantian skepticism, especially that of dialectical philosophy, are widely mistaken for science itself. Today every schoolboy learns that the concepts of natural law and natural rights are fictions and historical curiosities; and to suggest that there still underlies all natural and human existence a universal and moral law is to be met in intellectual circles with pained and uncomprehending surprise. Yet what probability can we allow to the hypotheses of science, if we are less than certain concerning the assumptions upon which science proceeds in its calculations of probabilities? And how shall we attempt to be just in our dealings, and hope to make at least some approach to justice, if we are dubious and confused with respect to the very distinction between what is just and what is unjust? Even to pursue scientific truth or to attempt justice, we must be able to say what "truth" and "justice" mean. And to define these terms in such a way as to leave truth and justice accessible to man is to say something absolute and incontrovertible about this world, in which truth is sought and justice aspired to. What is this absolute or philo- sophical truth which makes reasonable the pursuits of scientific knowledge and justice?

We are now ready to undertake successful assault upon this problem, which has hitherto defeated philosophical inquiry. Its solution, we have learned, requires us to establish the identity of the empirical and logical criteria of truth, the false distinc- tion of which has hitherto prevented the reconciliation of rationalism, emphasizing the logical criterion, with empiricism, emphasizing the criterion of fact. Science requires hypothesis to be at once logically self-consistent and consistent with observed particular fact. We need to know that these two demands can both be fulfilled in a single hypothesis, and that the satisfaction of one demand does not preclude that of the other. What we shall show is that there are not two demands. There is in truth only one requirement, which is at once rational and empirical. Logic, we shall show, only implements the empirical requirement that hypothesis shall conform to *all* observed fact. It is the word "all" that generates logic—logic secures impartiality and comprehensiveness of hypothesis. The logical requirement is the demand that the empirical require- ment be fully satisfied, and not satisfied only in part. The solu- tion is as simple as that. This is the conjunction of reason and sense, fulfilling the moral requirement of justice or impartiality.

So we shall bring to an end the ancient controversy between rationalism and empiricism, and establish at last the truthful- ness of science and the power of the human intellect to reach a realistic knowledge. The controversy was not fruitless, because it was the necessary preparation for this reconciliation. The reconciliation demonstrates the simple but solemn truth, stated long ago by Socrates—that intelligence and righteousness are one, so that all evil-doing is ignorance. Science, our impartial acknowledgment of fact, is the proper foundation of justice, our impartial acknowledgment of individual being. Science and justice alike are the fruits of that philosophical truth, now in our time at last confirmed, which asserts the identity of real being with individual being.

27 THE ESTABLISHMENT
OF PHILOSOPHICAL TRUTH

IN THIS CHAPTER WE BRING THE DEVELOPMENT OF philosophy to a successful issue by resolving the problem which has defeated past thought. Science requires hypothesis to conform to fact, yet seems also to insist that fact shall conform to logical necessity. Democratic government affirms the sovereignty of the individual, yet seems also to require that the individual submit to law. Why should particular fact defer to the requirements of logic? How should a sovereign individual submit to law?

There can, we intimated, be only one resolution of this problem. The two requirements, apparently contradictory, must resolve into one and the same requirement. This has usually been perceived, and the philosopher has attempted to show either that the logical and legal requirement includes the other (rationalism) or that the logical and legal requirement is not valid (empiricism). But this contempt of one or the other requirement led only to interminable controversy between opposed schools of thought.

In modern times the problem has been beclouded by a misconception common to both schools. Because it was clear that

545

philosophy, being a critical study of science, is something other than scientific hypothesis, it was supposed that philosophy must dispose over some material evidence not accessible to science, or at least over some method peculiarly its own. Both rationalists and empiricists succumbed to this error, and proceeded to elaborate those awesome "epistemologies" which today meet the student aspiring to philosophical truth, convincing him that philosophy is something truly horrendous, probably surpassing understanding, and certainly not for him. Those "epistemologies" are really rationalistic or nonempirical psychologies, in which "introspection" and dogmatic assertion do service for observation and verification. Incidentally, they deliver the empiricist into the hands of his rationalistic opponent, because to assert their truth is to imply the existence of some other sort of knowledge than empirical knowledge —which is just what the empirical philosopher wishes to deny.

In truth, there is no descriptive knowledge other than empirical science, and no other method than scientific method. The rationalist may call his dialectical method "logic," or the pragmatist call his psychological description of the knowing process "logic"; but in fact, what logic is, is no longer a matter of dispute; and logic certainly does not comprise a special method of cognition or research. On the contrary, logic is an aspect or part of all scientific method, which is the sole cognitive method. Yet this fact does not prevent us from studying scientific method, and determining by means of logical analysis just what are its implicit and universal presuppositions.

We come, then, to the nub of our problem, namely what is implied by scientific method itself. It begins to be understood that the last forty years have witnessed a scientific revolution, as radical as that by which Newton established modern science upon his justly famous "laws of motion," and perhaps as that by which Thales in ancient Ionia first set science on its path. But few are aware of the character of this revolution, or have inquired into its philosophical implications. The inertia of past intellectual habit makes such inquiry difficult, even for those whose labors initiate the new conception. Usually a generation has to pass, and another generation grow to maturity in the new way of thinking, before the full implication of a revolutionary hypothesis is seen.

The revolution we refer to is popularly associated with the name of Einstein, and properly so, although many others have participated in it. We may define it as a departure from certain of the principles of the "classical" science of Newton. It might be called the inauguration of romantic science, using the word "romantic" somewhat in its literary or aesthetic sense.

We are not concerned here, fortunately, with the whole current and consequence of this revolution in physical science. Our concern is limited to one point, namely the implication of the new science for our conception of the relation between mathematical theory and the science of physical nature. The effect of the Einsteinian hypothesis is to provide a new and liberating insight into the relation of physical science to mathematical theory. Since the time of Parmenides, *i.e.* the fifth century B.C., it had been assumed that physical hypothesis must defer to mathematical theory. The axioms of mathematics were held to be absolute self-evident truths vouched for by the reason itself. We must agree that these axioms seemed self-evident; and prior to Einstein there had been established no instance calling into question their exact applicability to nature. Plato, it is true, allowed that nature, because of its material element, might fall short of exact conformity to mathematical necessity; but Descartes and the moderns were more strict, and required the exact conformity of observable fact to mathematical principles. It is this uncompromising rigor of modern science that has led to the correction of its ancient error.

Until our own century, then, mathematical rationalism seemed invulnerable. Mathematical axioms seemed rational and self-evident, and nature everywhere bore them out. This precluded any forthright empiricism, since it is clear that if the axioms of mathematics necessarily apply to nature, many other rational axioms may be similarly applicable. Science would stand rooted in an absolute rational knowledge, and the only question would be how far such absolute knowledge extends, and whether it might not replace empirical science altogether. Kant tried to circumscribe the field of rational knowledge, in order to enlarge the role of empirical inquiry; but such circumscription is of necessity arbitrary—who shall decide whether a truth is or is not "self-evident"? Kant was compelled to call "self-evident and a priori" the basic definitions of physical matter; and because his distinction of self-evident principles from material hypotheses finally involved him in skeptical phenomenalism, his successors enlarged the sphere of "self-evidence" to include all the more basic concepts of science. This would imply that introspection, not observation and hypothesis, is the correct scientific method.

Mathematics has always included two intimately associated but distinct theories, indicated by the names arithmetic (with which belongs algebra) and geometry. The implications of the new science of Einstein primarily concern geometry. Since Euclid of Alexandria around 300 B.C. systematized Greek geometry, this theory had retained its basic axioms unchanged throughout its further development. But early in the nineteenth century certain European geometers subjected the Euclidean system to logical experiment, by asking what would happen if the rather dubious or mysterious axiom which defines parallel lines were simply ignored. The result was an astonishing explosion of Euclidean geometry into a number of non-Euclidean systems, each self-consistent, yet each very different from the others. There was now not one geometry, but an indefinite number of geometries; and Helmholz showed that these new geometries were really empirical hypotheses, because they were conceivably subject to empirical confirmation or disproof. But

they were strange and difficult to handle, the minute measurements testing their approximation to fact were not at that
time practicable, and Euclidean geometry satisfied every scientific need; therefore they were placed on the shelf of mathematical curiosities. However, even the construction of these new
geometries was disproof of Kant's contention that Euclidean
geometry rests on a priori synthetic principles; for the new
geometries rest equally upon "self-evident principles," identical
with those of the old geometry; and the several geometries,
new and old, cannot all be true.

This conclusion was empirically confirmed early in this
century when Einstein and his successors revived the non-
Euclidean geometries, using them as alternative and divergent
hypotheses in the description of physical fact. It was found
that Euclidean geometry sufficiently defines physical motion
only in certain limited cases; and the physicist in his most
general hypotheses now creates his geometry to order, in the
light of empirical fact. Geometry, in short, is henceforth physical hypothesis, not rational intuition of self-evident truth.

This removed geometry from the domain of "rational
science"; but arithmetic remained. It could still be argued that
arithmetical principles constitute a domain of rational knowledge, necessarily applicable to all particular fact. If so, arithmetic would still provide the needed evidence that there exists
a faculty of rational intuition, independent of and superior
to empirical hypothesis.

That arithmetic does not comprise a science of this sort was
shown by Russell and Whitehead, whose logical studies were
contemporaneous with the development of the physical theory
of relativity which so transformed geometry. These two
thinkers invalidated Kant's contention that arithmetical propositions are at once a priori and synthetic, which would
mean that they are self-evident or necessary truths descriptive
of universal nature. The *Principia Mathematica* showed that
number-theory can be reduced to, or replaced by, a system of

purely analytic propositions, *i.e.* verbal definitions. Geometry had been shown to belong to empirical science; and now arithmetic was shown to comprise a system of pure logic, consisting of analytical definitions of symbols together with innumerable propositions obtained from these definitions by means of purely logical operations.

These two advances, respectively in physical science and in logical theory, revolutionize our conception of natural knowledge. There had been logic, mathematics, and empirical science; and, in this trilogy, the conception of mathematics, as a study like logic in the self-evidence of its truth, yet like empirical science in its power to describe nature, had importantly determined the conceptions both of logic and of science. This trilogy suggested that knowledge is the expansion of a core of self-evident logical truth, first into mathematical truth and finally into the whole of science. It implied that logic is only the most abstract form, and empirical science the most detailed form, of a single knowledge of reality. It suggested that logic and mathematics are sciences no less descriptive of fact than is empirical science, and that empirical science is no less rational and self-evident in its intuition than is logic. It perpetuated the illusion, in short, of a knowledge at once rational or self-evident and descriptive of fact; and such knowledge would be absolute.

Henceforth there is no such trilogy. There is only analytical logic and empirical description. Mathematics has divided down the middle, so to speak, arithmetic moving over into logic and geometry moving over into empirical science. More strictly speaking, there is only one real or descriptive science, to wit, empirical science, reached by observation and hypothesis. But we may, by means of logical analysis, detach the symbolic or linguistic form of any empirical theory, and consider this abstract form in separation from the material of observable and particular fact organized by that theory. When we do this, we are logicians pursuing logic. We may consider geometry to be such a symbolic system, and develop geometrical symbolism purely as logicians and without thought of the descriptive truth or falsity of the system; and such study is "pure geometry" or "mathematics." But we may also consider geometry as descriptive hypothesis, and study its conformity to physical or astrophysical fact; and when we do this, we are empirical scientists. This profitable division of labor into analytical and experimental studies should be exercised in every theoretical science, the logician developing symbolic systems, and the empirical scientist applying and testing these systems in field and laboratory.

But we are not so much concerned with the new scientific developments opened up by this recent intellectual revolution, important though these are, as with its implication for philosophical truth. Its immediate philosophical consequence is its decisive verdict against rationalistic philosophy in favor of empirical philosophy.

There is, it makes clear, no self-evident rational knowledge, at least of the sort pretended. Our only knowledge of nature is empirical knowledge, comprised of hypotheses of high probability. Logic and mathematics are not natural knowledge, but constitute an art of symbolic construction or notation; and any descriptive character they may possess derives from the empirical material from which their logical elements were originally abstracted. It will be some time, perhaps, before this implication is widely perceived and becomes a commonplace of thought. Old errors live on, and rationalistic metaphysicians will still advance a "concrete logic." But there can be little doubt of the issue. The newly enfranchised science and the expanded "mathematical logic" are here to stay; and their implications will steadily become evident.

But this is only half the story. Admitting that neither logic nor mathematics nor any other "rational science" may confine scientific hypothesis or prescribe to empirical science; admitting that language, with the logic which is the syntax of language, must make itself wholly plastic to fact in the interests of descriptive truth; admitting, let us say, that logical form carries just no information whatsoever concerning the universal form of nature, and that if it did so, this would prejudice the power of descriptive science to mirror nature in language—admitting all this, must we not still ask what function logic has in science? It does not follow, because logic defers to fact, that it in no way conditions and directs the pursuit of fact, and that it does not in spite of all its deference exercise a sharp jurisdiction over all scientific statement of fact. It very obviously does so. The logical criterion of truth is as authoritative as the empirical criterion, which is observed fact. What then exactly is its authority?

The function of logic is to require theoretical statement, to ensure that scientific description shall be in terms of large theory. It is the guardian of theoretical form. By means of logic, the thinker constructs and perfects large systems or theories, which the empirical scientist may then interpret as empirical hypotheses descriptive of natural structures and testable by experiment and observation. The crucial point in this cooperation between logical theorization and empirical observation is the exceptional case in which the theory apparently collides with some patent fact. The simplest possible statement of some observed fact may stand in logical contradiction with the theory. For example, physical theory, applied to observed astronomical fact, may require the prediction that a planet will appear at a given moment at a prescribed place in the sky; but when the moment arrives, the planet may be observably elsewhere. Now logic registers this contradiction, and demands its removal. It does not, like Plato, allow the neglect of that exceptional case as an "aberration of nature." It does not require that the theory be saved by some disingenuous sort of interpretation. Logic simply indicates that the contradiction is there to be removed, so that fact and theory may become truly commensurable. But this requires that the theory be modified, and replaced by a new theoretical hypothesis consistent with the recalcitrant fact.

Thus the effect of logic, stated in its simplest terms, is to ensure that all observed fact shall have its due place in the symbolic construction which is scientific theory, and that no particular fact shall be disfranchised. The symbolic construction which is the logic of a science does not express a concern for logic and symbolization as such. These are only means to scientific impartiality toward fact.

Logic implements empirical impartiality toward observed particular fact. This is its sole scientific function, as is demonstrated in two ways. First, the scientist holds no brief for any specific hypothesis as such, but he is always willing, just insofar as he is an authentic scientist, to relinquish a theory which fails to meet all of the evidence. He is not interested in theory as such, he is interested in theory only as a device enabling the impartial accommodation of fact. Secondly, the scientist does not insist upon, and no longer expects to find, a single theory covering all fact. Modern theoretical science is incorrigibly pluralistic, advancing physical theory, biological theory, social and psychological theory simultaneously and in independence of one another. This relinquishment of the old rationalistic goal of a single universal theory implicitly affirms the auxiliary character of theoretical form and the instrumental character of logic. If logical unity were an end or objective in itself, the plurality of theories would be an indictment convicting science of error—which is just what the rationalist frequently considers it. But modern science, subservient only to evidence, has substantially established the truth that natural processes present diverse structures requiring for their description many theories, not only one. There is, science increasingly assures us, no single theory of nature.

We reach here the momentous fact that is the solution of our problem. The two criteria of truth, logic and particular fact, are really one and the same criterion. True rationalism *is* em-

piricism, empiricism is altogether rational. The logical criterion
is nothing else than the empirical demand, explicitly extended
to require deference to *all* particular fact. The rationalism of
the past was never more than a halfhearted rationalism. Really,
it fell short of logic, in order to prefer some particular facts,
and to neglect certain other particular facts, namely those
which could not be accommodated to the metaphysical system
which the rationalist misrepresented as "logical truth." The
long controversy which is the history of philosophy comes
now to an end, in the elucidation of a philosophical truth
which is rationalistic even in the absoluteness and universality
of its empirical regard for fact.

Most of us have always known fundamentally that the scientific pursuit of knowledge is a moral undertaking, and that
this moral character appears in the scientist's impartiality
toward observed fact. Science is man's honesty, his prime
virtue. But we became confused in this matter, because it
seemed that science, in describing actuality as it actually proceeds, discovers no moral bedrock in nature itself. Things are
what they are, and not necessarily what they ought to be. Even
to be impartial, it seemed, science must divest itself of all moral
prepossessions, and depict a world in which might and not
right, power and not justice, holds sway. Therefore it was that
the rationalist arose, to insist that the virtue of nature resides
in its unity or wholeness, that this unity is at once the presupposition and the objective of scientific inquiry, that the "laws
of logic" state and apply this insight into nature's moral unity,
and that an empirical science which does not discover this
unity must yield its place to a "rational science" which does
discover it.

We can now correct this error and salvage its half-truth.
There is no virtue in unity or universality as such. Does the
subservience of all material nature to "mechanical necessity"
make nature good? Would a homogeneous nature be superior
to a heterogeneous, infinitely diversified nature? Virtue and

value, we know, are characters of real being, and real being is individual being. It follows that real value is by definition differentiated. Value is difference, not sameness; nonconformity, not orthodoxy. Individuality alone has value. The rationalistic identification of value with likeness or structural unity, which in modern times has generated the absolute and totalitarian state, is finally a blasphemy against justice, truth, and God. Justice looks beyond sameness in order to appreciate individual character, truth looks beyond identity in order to perceive particular difference, God knows each creature in its individual uniqueness. Yet the blasphemy was well meant; and it was correct enough in its assumption that logic somehow indicates the moral nature of nature, and implements our apprehension of the morality of nature. The rationalistic error was to mistake the nature and function of logic. It is not logic, we saw, which requires the comprehension of nature under a single theoretical hypothesis. Neither logic nor the logician requires nature to be unified, homogeneous, same. Logic demands nothing in the way of description or definition of nature; it ensures only that our statement of fact, whatever it be, shall neglect no fact. Or rather, it ensures this impartial comprehensiveness of fact if we will first, prior to all analysis, set ourselves to do justice to all fact. If we will be just and empirical, logic will implement our will; but if we want to be dogmatic and unjust, logic will no less subserve the elaboration of rationalistic systems, which may be imposed upon facts and upon men as sanctified truth. Logic is indifferently the tool of truth and of error. But we would be unjust to logic if we emphasized its susceptibility to abuse at the expense of our appreciation of its great service. Given the will to truth, logic implements that will. Thus is justified Augustine, who established a new civilization upon the primacy of the will.

What is the will to truth? It is the will to do justice to each and every particular fact. What is particular fact? It is our apprehension of individual being at some time and place. All real being is individual being, as Aristotle taught. Science is the will to do rightly by all individual beings, in cognitive acknowledgment of their existence. To acknowledge the reality and worth of individual beings requires us to identify value with difference, and not with sameness; but it does not preclude the recognition of sameness. The similarities of things are real; and very often we can do approximate justice to many things at once, by concentrating on their similarities. We require, for example, that each human individual, in virtue of the moral responsibility which attaches to all of us alike, shall have equal political power. This collectivistic method leads to error, of course, if we insistently ascribe similarity where it does not exist but is replaced by difference. In loading an airplane we may classify passengers and goods indifferently as to weight, but not as to needed space. Scientific and other formulas are devised to implement our acknowledgment of individual things insofar as these bear approximately the same characters. They implement injustice when used blindly and mechanically, to make us overlook real difference.

So far we have used the function of logic in science only to indicate a moral law which is incumbent upon man, and which resembles Kant's categorical imperative. Thou shalt do justice to all individuals, first in the scientific acknowledgment of individual being apprehended in particular fact—thus we might rephrase Kant. And why, it might be asked, should we be just? From this blatant rejoinder Kant could only weakly appeal to an afterlife, in which the patent injustices of this world will be personally rectified by God. But is God mocked? May one with impunity do injustice in this world? Why is it incumbent upon us to deal justly with individual beings in this life? Because individual being is real and alone real. If this is not so, empirical science is a barking up the wrong tree. But if it is so, then every crime done to individual being is folly on the part of the criminal. To say that individual being is always and alone real is to say that it alone and always is effective. Reality is effectiveness, power. The force and quality of every particular action determine those of the particular reaction. Common sense and justice equally require a respect for particular fact and individual being. Prudence and kindness are ultimately one. Every injustice done to individual being of necessity recoils upon the doer; and every mercy blesses him that gives no less than him who takes.

This is the moral law of nature, as it is that of society. It is the meaning of the metaphysical truth which affirms the reality of individual being, and in consequence denies the reality of "universal being." These last two words are meaningless, unthinkable; they comprise a self-contradiction. *There is no universal being*, there are only individual beings which in some respects, but in no case in all respects, may be similar. The respects in which things are similar or dissimilar must be determined by observation and experiment; and that is why empirical science must be the rule of life, of society, and of God.

After six centuries, we have justified the doctrine of the medieval nominalists whose real work, we remember, was the establishment of empirical science. The nominalist denied the reality of universal being in the interests of individual being; but he was unable to do justice to the power of theoretical knowledge. General ideas, he averred, exist only in the mind; and this was to leave science without claim to objective truth. We correct this error when we acknowledge the existence of real similarities among individual things. If similarities are not real, how should specific and individual differences be real?

We discover herein the integrity of modern thought. Since Roscellinus, Grosseteste, Roger Bacon, Duns Scotus, and their successors initiated modern thought, there has moved forward this single faith in the absoluteness and primacy of individual being. Out of it has been built an empirical science and an industrial economy. Out of it has been generated a democratic society, pledged to equalitarian justice among men. These two developments are truly one. A society which industrializes itself without enfranchising itself is doomed by its internal contradictions, its production of unchecked and unchartered powers. A society politically free will inevitably pursue and apply in its economy that empirical science which is its just acknowledgment of the nature which environs it.

This theme could and will be infinitely documented; but perhaps we have said enough in its establishment. It is a simple truth that affirms the identity of real and individual being; but its simplicity does not prejudice its utter profundity, nor limit its infinite variety of use. It is ultimately a religious thesis, and the source of all true religion. To acknowledge the sanctity of individuals is true religion. The men who made this truth the dynamo of modern civilization were religious men, able, as was St. Francis, to see God in sky and earth, and know men and women illuminated by the holy light of truth. But our business is the translation of this mystical light into verbal utterance and creative doing.

So far as philosophical doing is concerned, the establishment of philosophical truth ends the fruitless but unavoidable controversy of the past in order to direct philosophy to its real task. This truth was implicit in the Greeks, who created constitutional government and theoretical science; it generated Greek justice and Greek science. But when it sought explicit statement it fell prey to the error that "in the beginning was the word," the word incarnating itself in nature. The word is a human device—nature is not language given flesh. But the Greek philosophers who mistook word and stereotype for real being, and thereby fell from truth, correctly divined the true problem which arises the moment we are apprised of this truth. To say that individual being is real being is to say that reality is radically differentiated, so that the existence of difference is no problem. One never need, and never can, explain why things are different. One can and should discover why things are similar. Reflect upon any special science for a moment, and you will see that its pursuit is always the discovery and causal explanation of specific similarities. There arises the question, still empirical but philosophical in its breadth, why there should be similarity at all, of any sort. The Greek philosophers asked this question, but would not wait for an answer. They replied at once: It is of the essence of nature to present similarities; for nature is truly one, and its identity appears, compounded with difference, in similarities.

But this is false. The true essence of nature is individuality or difference of character. Similarity is overlaid. That the inquiry into the causes of similarity is a significant, possible, and profitable inquiry is demonstrated by every causal hypothesis; but it was given a new and striking significance when Darwin showed that every organic similarity is the consequence of the mode of reproduction of living organisms, as these are influenced by their environment. By asking this philosophical question about similarity in one special field, Darwin revolutionized biology. But the question must be carried into every field, and be asked finally of nature at large, until we learn at last something of the creative power that has moved in all things to fabricate this world. For we are intended to know even as God knows, in naked truth, and not "see through a glass, darkly."

28 SCIENCE AND GOVERNMENT

AT THE INTRODUCTION OF THIS STUDY IT WAS stated that philosophy is everybody's business, because political liberty can be established only upon a philosophical foundation. We are now able to expand this statement by showing just how political liberty is secured by philosophical truth. We can do this best by showing how science and just government are parallel activities, respectively theoretical and practical, inspired and directed by this fundamental truth.

Belief in democratic government has hitherto been an expression of faith, and this of course it will continue to be— most of us instinctively *feel* that democratic government is right and just, and tyranny a crime and shame. But it is doubtful whether strong feeling alone will indefinitely support the vast and ever more audacious enterprise of democracy. Our forefathers were accustomed to distinguish faith from reason. This distinction was necessary and proper in an age when "reason" meant a truncated Aristotelian science buttressed by metaphysical dogma, and when "faith" meant acceptance of a religious teaching which, whatever its limited scriptural letter, expressed a truth surpassing that of "reason." The founders of modern democracy drew their political conviction, in respect both to its intensity and to its objective, from their free religion, which imposed upon the individual a religious and moral responsibility not to be delegated to king or governor. Accordingly, the revolutionary founders of the first modern republic, the short-lived Commonwealth, stated their political faith in religious terms. Such statement would still be fitting. We still hold liberty of conscience and thought to be the primary freedoms, generating all others; but the religious terminology would be invidious and misleading today, especially among peoples still intellectually dominated by authoritarian religion.

It is this selfsame religious faith, however, which finds its authentic statement in philosophical truth. There is but one Truth, capable of infinite variety in its formulation. Religious mysticism, which is what most moderns mean by religion, is the illuminated perception of the holiness which everywhere invests individual being, *i.e.* reality. Philosophy corrects rationalistic theology when it translates this ineffable mystical experience into the sober statement, "Reality is individual being," and proceeds to enlarge this simple truth into a descriptive science. We still expound in this science the faith of those who inaugurated modern government; but the word "faith" now loses its equivocal meaning. It no longer means a belief transcending reason, knowledge, science. It means the truth which generates reason, knowledge, and science.

It scarcely need be elaborated further that philosophical truth, so far from being something that eludes demonstration, is implicitly demonstrated in every demonstration of fact whatsoever. Every scientific hypothesis applies this truth, and in its confirmation confirms it; nor does any description of fact have meaning or truth except in virtue of that one truth. Every practical program has moral claim and final efficacy in the degree to which it is an acknowledgment of all of the individuals affected by it. Every work of art owes its beauty and significance to the artist's perception and successful communication of some character of being revealed to him in an individual scene, situation, or thing. Even animal faith, active in the animal's spontaneous and differentiated response to the particularity which stimulates it, is this truth; and, in the inorganic world, each thing reacts in its particular character to the particular reagent, assuring us that there too only individual being is real. The measure of thing, animal, and man is the increasing scope of action without loss of this discriminating reaction to individual difference. This truth, we said, is the moral law of nature, and the only necessity known to us. What does not in its degree obey this law, reacting individually and infallibly to individual being, is in that degree nonexistent, its failure so to react being the token of its demise. We were told that the wages of sin is death, but in literal truth the sin itself is the wage. The measure of a life is the scope of its reaction to individual beings.

Righteousness and justice are the efforts to carry this truth, with its obligatory acknowledgment of individual being, into human relationships. There is consequently observable in all past history a living connection between science and government, *i.e.*, between man's conception of nature at large, or reality, and his social pattern. And, as we should expect, any advance in the grasp of truth has first been effected in social morality and government, before it generated an explicit science describing the larger environment. However, social institutions and instituted intellectual habits have diverse inertias; and we should not press the parallel between science and government too hard. In a declining society, for example, the intellectual habits of an earlier progressive period may overlap political decadence. Greek philosophy outlived Greek liberty; and Germany could turn scientific technique to evil and terrible abuse.

Yet the parallel remains true, and is often striking. We saw how the intellectual leaders of Greek antiquity created theoretical science in order to confirm their countrymen in their political achievement. The great universe itself, they asserted, is a political community ruled by natural law. Significant, surely, is the parallel between the political decline of Greece and the transformation of this Greek science into an unrealistic metaphysics. It is because Parmenides suspected, and Plato saw, the failure of Greek government that these men looked beyond an empirical science descriptive of actuality to a transcendent science descriptive of a Being which "is" yet does not exist. Because they witnessed political decline, they renounced that faith in actual justice which had inspired the earlier scientists. They could not or would not see that the cause of Greek distress was the smallness of their sovereign city-states, and the confined and obstructed justice which this entailed. They could not agree, accordingly, that the doom of their cities, admittedly inevitable, was also just. And with this failure of moral realism went a failure of cognitive or scientific realism, a hardening of empirical inquiry into an impressive but sterile metaphysics.

The parallel is seldom quite so clear in later times, chiefly because the intellectual habits of the Greeks (or should we say their vocabulary?) were retained by peoples politically undeveloped. We should see that Greek morality, as this appeared in their political institutions, was as astonishingly beyond that of other peoples as was their science. Yet there is observable a loose but discernible connection between the feudal and ecclesiastical hierarchy of the Middle Ages and the medieval predilection for Neoplatonic and Aristotelian hierarchies of forms. Again apparent and striking, however, is the historical connection in the modern period between the developments of empirical science and democratic government. Our purpose here is not to review this historical parallel, but to diagnose and understand it as it works today.

Modern democracy differs from Greek democracy in that it places the individual above the law as the maker of law, whereas liberty meant to the Greeks a common and equal subjection to law. It is true that the Greek assemblies multiplied their laws; but the Greeks never thought of law expect as something structural and permanent, embodying the fixed character of their city. They had no conception of continuous legal progress. Their conservatism is excusable in view of the relative superiority of their constitutions; but it was nonetheless their doom, because it precluded advance to a larger political unity. Greek science reflected this fatal weakness in that it aimed, despite its realistic and empirical study of fact, at a knowledge whole and complete, a final and absolute wisdom. Only Socrates among the Greeks seems really to have understood that science is a progress out of ignorance, a pursuit, not a possession, of knowledge.

We have been able to clarify this Socratic teaching. Knowledge of an absolute sort, or wisdom, we do possess in the philosophical insight into the identity of real with individual being. But this truth says nothing specific, it is blankly universal; and knowledge as ordinarily understood, or science, is an endless application, implemented by expanding general hypothesis, of this absolute principle. Science in its formulas is not so much knowledge as instrument to knowledge, science becoming knowledge only in its applications to particular fact. The cognitive will to acknowledge particular fact is wisdom. This effort we saw to be implemented by logic, which ensures, *if we will have it so,* the impartial acknowledgment of particular fact. It would not be wrong, accordingly, to speak of logic as the constitution of science. Just as the political constitution of a democratic society secures to each individual his effective participation in legislation and government, so logic, intelligently and morally applied, secures to each particular fact its due weight in the shaping of scientific hypothesis. And just as the sharp distinction between logic and hypothesis is the condition of scientific impartiality and scientific freedom, so the separation of constitutional law from other law is the condition of justice and political liberty.

We have seen how the past confusion of logic with empirical hypothesis has limited and confined science. So long as geometry was conceived to be "pure mathematics," *i.e.* a study resting on absolute and self-evident axioms, its postulates were incumbent upon the scientist, and hypothesis had to remain within its framework. No hypothesis might be advanced, none was conceivable, which violated those principles. When scientists broke through this confinement by their acceptance of non-Euclidean geometries, they demonstrated that geometry is not pure but applied mathematics, *i.e.* empirical hypothesis; and this ended at least the old confusion of the logical or theoretical form of geometry with the descriptive material so informed. "Pure mathematics" we now see to be a synonym for "logic," a study of symbolic systems viewed in their formal clarity and in abstraction from any consideration of these systems in their descriptive use. To distinguish in a scientific theory the logical or formal element from the descriptive, empirical, or material element is to liberate hypothesis; because one and the same logic can now be compounded with an indefinite number of descriptive elements, to produce a variety of self-consistent descriptive theories. These theories are then alternative hypotheses, susceptible to confirmation or disproof in the light of observable fact.

The confusion of logic with descriptive theory limits hypothesis to an "orthodox" field of speculation; but what are the positive effects of this confinement, and what suggests or motivates the confusion? Generally, it is just the result of intellectual inertia, and has no positive motive. It is difficult, even or especially for the scientist, to change those broadest descriptive principles which have directed all past analysis. To change these requires him to create new intellectual habits. Yet, because science is finally motivated by love of truth, it is chiefly scientists who have escaped from dogma and initiated new ways of thought. It is usually others than scientists who have sought to confine empirical hypothesis and intellectual progress by fervently and resolutely confusing logic with science. The false "logics" are invariably the work of men who call themselves philosophers, and not the work of scientists. What is their purpose? Evidently it is not scientific, not cognitive. We must suspect that it is usually social or political. Their intention is to confine society, and to keep human behavior and political organization within certain limits. They are moralists who insist upon certain fixed precepts, which they confusedly identify with "logical necessities," and present as the permanent and sufficient condition of social and individual health.

What shall we say of this purpose? It would be a mistake to condemn it out of hand—that would be to throw out the baby with the bath water. The dogmatic moralist usually means well. His error is that he does not penetrate to the true dogma, namely the philosophical truth which ends dogma. He stops short of this truth, in order to set up as absolute certain of its past applications. Philosophical truth may be identified with no specific social order, no specific form of political organization, no specific code of human behavior. It requires only that any and every form of activity shall acknowledge the existence and character of all the individuals affected. But, of course, this universal principle must be given specific applications, proper to time and place; and the dogmatist's error is to set up these specific applications as themselves the permanent and universal law, not to be departed from. This is the error which destroyed antiquity and every other past civilization.

The dogmatist is not necessarily a social conservative protecting vested interests, *i.e.* goods gambled on the perpetuation of current modes of thought and behavior. The progressive radical too may be a dogmatist. He may insist that a certain social pattern which does not yet exist, but which should exist, is the one mold in which society should forever be contained. To distinguish the dogmatist from the true reformer, we have only to ask whether the dogma itself involves or excuses injustice. In intellectual matters, this judgment is usually possible.

There the confusion of logic with descriptive hypothesis is seen to involve the neglect of some body of particular fact, in the interests of some favored body of fact. In practical matters, judgment is seldom so easy; but the dogmatist usually betrays his prejudice by admitting that his dogma involves injustice to some individuals, and arguing that this is excused by some larger good consequent upon it. But justice, which is philosophical truth, forbids such casuistry. It requires the full acknowledgment of *every* individual claim, not only of some or of most. It requires acknowledgment of individuals past and gone, of individuals now living, of individuals yet to be. The principle acknowledges no limitation of time and space. The only limit is the actual one, our relative ignorance of individual being. But this confession of ignorance excuses no dismissal of known fact. Moral responsibility is absolute and uncompromising.

To defeat dogma and enthrone justice, modern society created the democratic constitution. As the intention and effect of logic is to secure living contact between hypothesis and particular occurrence, so the intention and effect of this constitution is to secure the living repercussion upon government and legislation of the individuals governed. To understand its efficacy, compare the democratic constitution with nondemocratic constitutions. Every people has its political constitution, written or unwritten, because "constitution" means the habitual procedure determining the appointment of government, the sources and limits of legislation, etc. The constitution of a nondemocratic society is quite simply one which intrusts the responsibilities and powers of government to some group fewer in number than the whole people. It is perhaps irrelevant to justice whether this group rules wisely or foolishly, benevolently or malevolently, in order to preserve hereditary privilege or in order to inaugurate utopia. Such government is unjust, however "good" or "bad" it be, because it violates the first requirement of justice, which is that every human being has the right and duty as a moral individual to participate in government. Will anyone deny that government enormously determines the destinies of the governed, that it is the most potent single factor in civilized society? It has therefore enormous responsibility to and for man. But whose is this responsibility? It is that of every individual, who is morally responsible to and for all of his fellow humans. Each of us is his brother's keeper. It follows that every government which is not self-government is a refusal and denial of this responsibility, not on the part only of those who exercise such tyranny, but on the part of all who tolerate it. The moral individual subjected to tyranny must be in continuous revolt; and not to revolt is criminal.

Nondemocratic society attempts to live a self-contradiction. It acknowledges its duty to abide by the law and to support the imposition of this law upon all; and only in virtue of its dutiful support can the law be imposed, and govern the lives of all concerned. Yet that same society will not accept responsibility for this law—this responsibility it delegates to some hereditary aristocracy, some priestocracy, some bureaucracy. Were the Greeks right when they held those barbaric peoples around them, who were unaware of their moral responsibility for government, to be something less than human?

Similarly, of course, the governors of a nondemocratic society live in self-contradiction when they require obedience to law as a moral duty, yet at the same time deny to many their real moral responsibility, which is that of government itself.

The democratic insight into the foundations and conditions of justice has many evident implications. First, it sets limits to government. It is evident that no individual should seek to impose upon his fellows by force—and government is whatever finally applies physical compulsion—much that he would like to see done. Much human activity, perhaps the bulk of human activity, is of such sort that compulsion and regimentation would injure or destroy it. Our first objective in government should be minimum government, leaving a maximum sphere to freedom, persuasion, and education. However, there can be set no formal limits to government. The intention of the constitution should be to secure to every individual his participation in government and his voice in legislation. The conditions securing this franchise will vary with social progress. What provides these conditions belongs in the constitution; what does not has no place in the constitution. Constitutional law is not in its formal prescription eternal law. What is eternal in it is its purpose, which is to secure the conditions of self-government. If it should be found, for example, that an extreme maldistribution of wealth defeats the intention of the constitution, then the legal correctives of that evil should appear as constitutional amendments. It is not debatable, however, that government should be limited in its every dealing by "due process of law," because whatever violates that edict is done arbitrarily and illegally. Just government is necessarily constitutional government, or government by law; for there exists no device other than legislation which allows a plurality of individuals to establish and enforce a cooperative decision. It follows, finally, that the final arbitrament must be that of the court of law, because it is there, and only there, that the law of the land, including its constitutional law, is called into effective operation. The division of government into three branches is not a device to limit government by reciprocal checks and controls; it is the necessary mechanism by which a people makes, implements, and applies its law.

Democratic government is today the chief means by which the individual exercises his moral responsibility. This responsibility is not limited by national boundaries, it is to and for all men everywhere. It is evident that our political acts affect the lives of individuals in other nations. In a democratic world, national polities would be jurisdictional districts and not sovereign states. There is truly no sovereign state, there is truly no state, there are only individuals and their governments. This is involved in the very conception of democratic justice, which exists to implement the universal truth that every individual is responsible to and for all. The sovereign national state must indeed wither away, if man is to be just and free. In the meantime, democrats cannot but be cautious in their relations with governments which are tyrannies, alliance with which could make them co-partners in injustice. America was not created to be supreme among the "great powers." It was created to inaugurate the transition of human society to just government. It is a missionary institution, propagating a gospel to all men.

Challenging the statements of this paragraph stands the political philosophy known as "the theory of the state." Most explicitly announced by Hegel, this theory places sovereignty in the national state, which is to place it in those who are able to seize and to hold the controls of government by any means, their power and office being their whole sanction. This theory has sanctified the unbridled nationalism which at last destroys Europe and threatens us all; and protected by an umbrella of rationalistic dogma, it has spread to democratic countries, and more effectively than any fifth column confuses democratic faith and sabotages democratic progress.

It was said that the advance to moral truth makes itself apparent first in those practical political activities which are everybody's business. The Greeks first created government by law, and then came the thinker who developed the conception of a universe governed by natural law. It might be more difficult to demonstrate that the revolutionary movement which established democratic government in modern times similarly preceded and directed the intellectual revolution which established the freedom of hypothesis and empirical science. The thesis may however be defended. Although the origins of modern science go back to thirteenth-century Bacon and his successors, this new science was confined to a narrow clerical circle until the late sixteenth century; and the reformatory movement which in Britain and America proceeded to political revolution, it may be argued, had its wide origins in the popular spread of the Franciscan brotherhood in the thirteenth century. However this may be, there is no question of the fact that the establishment of democratic liberty by means of a written constitution preceded by more than a century the complete enfranchisement of science. This latter has occurred only in our own time. It is only today, in virtue of the clear and explicit distinction between formal logic and descriptive science, that empirical hypothesis is finally freed from the last dogmatic shackles which confined it.

Now that science is finally freed from the sheath of dogma which had protected its immaturity, science may properly be the support of intelligent practice. Its first assignment is to illuminate our understanding of the relation of constitutional to other law. If we lose faith in the democratic constitution, it will be because this constitution seems to require "interpretation" dictated by what is vaguely referred to as "different social philosophies." This is the vocabulary of intellectual and political skepticism; and there is no question that a succession of court majorities widely diverging in "social philosophy" and in their consequent legal decisions will weaken faith in democratic justice. Yet what is the alternative? So long as our own Constitution is fixed, must it not by some expedient be made to fit the facts, *i.e.* conform to social actualities? Of course it must. Not to conform would be finally to become discredited as an agency of justice, and to be thrown off. Yet how can it be thrown off? A people ruled by law must abide by law. It must somewhere, either in a Supreme Court or in some lower court, accept the jurisdiction of law. To throw off the Constitution would be to live by no constitution, and no longer live by law; and this means, whatever one pleases to call it, a personal dictatorship by some permanent or transient group usurping justice.

Our error has been to think of the Constitution as fixed, and to mistake its letter for its intention. Once we acknowledge and abet the intention of the Constitution, which is the security of the individual in his responsible political power, we need not prostrate ourselves before its letter. It is not the office of the Supreme Court to change or twist that letter—its business is to apply the Constitution in its letter. It is the duty of the whole people, gathered in representative Constitutional Convention, to revise periodically its Constitution, bringing it up to date by rewriting, deleting, or expanding its clauses, in such manner that it effectively fulfills its intention, which is the equal distribution of political power among all individuals. We need today a new political science and a new political literature devoted to the continuous betterment of our basic constitution. To this study should be called our ablest minds, and to its propagation our ablest publicists. How long will American liberty persist if it confines itself, not to the wise purpose, but to the literal knowledge of those who established it? Let the wisdom of the founding fathers live again in us their progeny.

Empirical science illuminates this study. It is fidelity to logic, we saw, that invigorates science, compelling attention to exceptional cases and thus requiring the invention of larger hypothesis and the continuous advancement of science. Similarly the democratic constitution, by enfranchising minorities and individuals, generates the pressures and forces which compel progressive legislation. But is not logic fixed? Is it not just because logic is fixed that it had to be separated out of science proper, and distinguished from the descriptive hypothesis which the fixity of logic would otherwise paralyze?

No, logic is not fixed, there is no eternal logic. Its constancy is relative to hypothesis, which does and should progress more rapidly than logic. We may, we said, detach by logical abstraction the largest form of scientific description, its so-called logical form; and then we perceive that a variety of descriptive hypotheses may be cast in that same form, and this is to liberate hypothesis. But speculative hypothesis is not henceforth to be confined within that one form or logic. It is free to cast new forms, even new logical forms. Let us establish this last freedom!

We said that geometry had disclosed itself to be empirical hypothesis, whereas arithmetic had disclosed itself to be a purely logical system or notation. This statement was roughly correct, but not the whole truth. The several geometries differ in certain only of their generative postulates, other postulates remaining formally identical in all. These identical postulates, disclosed by formal analysis, comprise the "logic" of such geometry as we now have. This does not mean, however, that there is no other logic or notation useful in the description of physical nature. As a matter of fact, physical science makes very great use of nongeometrical logic, for example in quantum mechanics; and the next rather terrifying responsibility of the physical scientist, to which Einstein and others already devote themselves, is the creation of a single notational system or "logic" which will replace these two notations now in use.

Similarly we should not suppose that arithmetic or number-theory, whatever its "purely logical" status, defines forever the largest outline of numerical form. Mathematicians such as those who develop the theory of groups already explore beyond these confines. There was a time when mathematical logic, or arithmetic, forbade the notion of fractions not to be expressed as a ratio of two integers, forbade the notion of nothing, forbade the notion of negative quantities, and forbade many another notion now familiar to the mathematical student. Arithmetical progress has been a continuous re-creation of notational logic—the only sort of logic we know.

So it is with the democratic constitution. The modern form is not that of the Greeks. The Constitution of the United States is not the original Constitution, which has been subjected to amendments each of which modifies the meaning of the Constitution as a whole. What we need accordingly is a political science which will do for constitutional law what the mathematician has done for the logic of physical and other science. The political scientist will replace the disconnected sequence of clauses and amendments by a logically consistent instrument, setting forth what at this time are the conditions and mechanisms required to allow the full participation of each and every citizen in the process of government. The Constitution as it stands is the good beginning of this work; but in comparison with what it might be, it resembles Cartesian geometry in relation to twentieth-century mathematics. A Constitution so reformed would establish a maximum freedom in a society using science not to regiment but to enfranchise the diverse powers of man.

IV   THE FUTURE

29 THE FUTURE OF SCIENCE

Not the least of the profits derived from
philosophical truth is its enfranchisement of science,
through the complete liberation of empirical hypothesis. Even
the astounding scientific achievement of the last half century
proceeded under a rationalistic handicap. This was the assumption that science is a superstructure built upon a fixed foundation of obligatory principles, or committed to a single definable "method." Many books are published professing to present scientific method; but examination reveals these to be only a confused conglomerate of logical formulas and current hypotheses, cemented by vague discussions of probability, induction, and verification. In truth, the only conditon imposed upon scientific speculation is conformity to the two criteria of knowledge, logic and fact. Sufficient understanding of formal logic may allow the scientist to estimate within his special field the powers and limitations of current scientific language, a perception which might enable him to extend the scope of his hypothesis; but the scientist is seldom hindered by any incapacity of logical power. The physical scientist obtains in his mathematical training a competence in logic surpassing that of any save the most expert logicians; and every appropriation of scientific theory involves large understanding of logical

form. Nor does the contemporary scientist need reminder of his responsibility to observable fact, or of his obligation to confirm hypotheses by continuous verification. What would most help the scientist is a philosophical understanding of the relation of logic or syntax to descriptive hypothesis. This would assure him that the "method" of science, at least that of the creative scientist, is nothing else than audacious imaginative speculation, subject only to the requirements of intelligibility and observable fact. The "method" of science, in short, is the method of genius in any and every field. It is not technique merely. Science is the creator of techniques, not their creature.

In spite of the tremendous achievement of modern science, its large provision of well-being and security, and its indispensability as the intellectual and material foundation supporting contemporary civilization, there is growing discontent with science. In Europe, this discontent became a widespread and violent revolt; and it is quite possible that science will never again on the continent of Europe be the vigorous, generously supported activity it once was. Why this revolt against reason? Are those peoples unaware that without science they must decline into small and impoverished economies, such as marked the feudal past?

Animus against science is usually animus against the political implications of that moral truth which all true science confirms and propagates. The discreditors of science are usually the seekers of social and political privilege, desperately resisting the tide of liberal effort that is quickened by science; and in this defense of social privilege they are only too often supported by scholarly and other defenders of intellectual privilege, whose estate is also threatened.

But the arguments which have been advanced against science are often very plausible, and they are widely accepted. So they need to be squarely refuted. They center in the assertion that science advocates a mechanistic conception of nature which involves a materialistic conception of man, and that these conceptions blind us to individual quality, and thereby destroy society.

What is the truth in this assertion? There is no truth in it. We have seen that the primary principle of science is its empirical regard for particular fact, and that this regard for particular fact activates a moral reverence for individual being. If there is any way of thought which does not mechanize thought and which properly esteems individual character, that way of thought is thereby scientific.

Why therefore does the lie flourish, whence derives its plausibility? Its plausibility derives from a confusion of scientific thought with scientific formulas. Scientific theories are large and complex generalizations, defining certain widespread characters of natural processes. Necessarily, general theory abstracts in its statement from much particular difference. The moralist, who is no scientist busy with the creation and application of theoretical hypotheses, and whose knowledge of science is culled from hearsay or textbooks, may suppose science to present its theories as themselves a final description of nature; and if he does so, he may well conclude that science abstracts from particularity and individuality. If the moralist really were the logician he sometimes pretends to be, he would know that no general theory pretends to describe anything. The theory is just a symbolic notation. Scientific description is the use of this notation in the description of particular situations; and this necessarily involves the greatest deference to particular or individual character of which the human intellect at any time is capable.

Science in its applications, as in its creation of knowledge, is intrinsically and immaculately moral—it is nothing else than the moral regard for individual being. Every sort of statement classifies individual things under general terms indicating common properties; but it is only science which subjects general statement to particular verification and which expertly adapts it to the individual case. This is the very definition of science, deference to particular character being just the scientific approach to fact. The engineer who applies physical theory must adapt its formulas to the particular materials he uses and to the particular situation he proposes to control. Any mechanization of his thought, any blind application of formula is a failure of scientific intelligence.

Abetting this confusion of science with scientific notation is the undeniable fact that the powers given to man by science are susceptible to abuse; they can indeed be used to serve immoral ends. How is this possible, if science be the application of moral truth by the moral will? Obviously, a nation can use its industrial power to wage oppressive war; a corporation can use scientific machinery to produce and distribute the apparatus of vice; an industry can estimate its human personnel as so much property, to be bought and exploited like coal or iron; an agency can hire psychologists to prepare deceptive advertising. What is happening here where science sells its soul?

What we see here is a failure of science which is made possible by the departmentalization of science, its division into a plurality of sciences or theories. Scientific industry is necessarily moral in respect to the nonliving materials which it exploits. If it had no respect for the character of these materials, its machinery would not function and would break down. But the industry which respects its material property may be blind and unintelligent with regard to its human personnel; it may bring to its laboring employees habits of mind developed in its dealings with inanimate matter. This is not science but the absence of science—science never overlooks specific difference. But what of the psychologist who lends his knowledge to the exploitation of laborer or consumer? Does not this imply a malevolent potentiality residing in science itself? Does not the advertiser or propagandist sometimes exploit for evil ends a scientific knowledge of human character? Admittedly he does; but his crime is still a failure, not an achievement, of science. Psychology and social theory are still immature studies, which in their praiseworthy effort to emulate the theoretical achievement of physical science, have retained some of the conceptual and mental habits of physical science. As the scientific study of human behavior perfects its theory, it will necessarily rid itself of concepts and habits ill-adapted to its specific material, which is living, intelligent, and individuated human beings. There, too, it will be seen that action directed by scientific knowledge is of necessity moral action, in this case controlled by respect for human character; and it will become a truism that an industry which injures or deceives human beings destroys the capital on which it lives.

However, this mature and developed sociology does not yet exist. What shall we do, in the meantime, to prevent the blind application of the physical and biological sciences to problems requiring a science of man which we do not yet possess? It is this unintelligent application of science, and this lack of social science, which support and even in some degree justify the attack upon science as a mechanistic and materialistic faith destroying the human spirit. Turn from science to art or to religion, say these critics of science—there alone you will find a sort of knowledge which does justice to what is specific and individual in man.

We must discern the element of truth in this criticism. It lies in its recognition of *the specificity of nature*. Knowledge of physical, vegetable, and animal process does not comprise a knowledge of what is specifically human. The difference between man and other beings is more important, scientifically and morally, than his likeness to other things. We still suffer even in contemporary science from that seventeenth-century rationalism which identified reason with a single theory of reality, the error which empirical science in all of its development has steadily invalidated. *It is that very rationalism which is mechanistic and materialistic.* There is, says the rationalist, really but one universal Being, possessed everywhere of the character defined by self-evident principles of reason; and individual things are valueless except as they manifest this universal homogeneity. Is this to assert that individuality is value? It is to deny it. And what does it help that the rationalist calls himself an idealist, names his "universal Being" mind or spirit or God? Does not everything we know assure us that if there be such universal Being, its character must be that defined by the largest principles of physics, so that Reality is physical matter? It is only if rationalism is a false doctrine that specific and individual characters have value and real being.

Empirical philosophy, with its issue in empirical science, exists to restore to specific and individual character its reality or value. It is theoretical science, not rationalistic philosophy, which demonstrates the impossibility of reaching that single theory of nature which would transcend all difference. It is science, not rationalistic philosophy, which establishes a plurality of theories, describing respectively the most general characters of physical, biological, and social fact, but stopping far short of unity. But can science indefinitely stop short of unity? Must it not forever seek to comprehend its plurality of theories in a single, all-embracing, theoretical system?

We reach here the real problem of the contemporary intellect, to which all that has been written here or elsewhere is preparatory. It is evident today that science is a plurality of theories. It is no less evident that it seeks their synthesis. Is this effort vain? Is it praiseworthy or reprehensible?

These questions indicate a certain confusion of mind. The comprehension of fact sought by theoretical science in no way retracts the necessary pluralism of science, nor prejudices the reality of specific difference. Suppose that we possessed a physical theory, allowing us to describe all organic and human activity in physicochemical terms? Would not this theory require the clearest possible distinction between those several physicochemical processes which we call respectively inorganic, organic, and human? Would we not have reached this most abstract theory only by taking with utter seriousness the specific differences which distinguish things, plants, animals, and men? Would not psychological theory and biological theory be special variations of that most abstract theory? Science would still be plural; psychophysics and biophysics would not be descriptive of geologic and astronomic fact.

We may accredit to Samuel Alexander, Lloyd Morgan, and other "emergentists" the discernment of this ineradicable pluralism of science. Theoretical analysis, say these men, has definite limits. The reduction of organic process to physico-chemical process (*i.e.* the description of living behavior in physicochemical terms) does not affect the reality of those specifically organic characters which distinguish organic from inorganic matter; and similarly the reduction of psychological fact to biological fact does not erase the qualities distinguishing man from other animals. There is still required a plurality of distinct theories describing respectively physical, organic, and human structures.

This is true; and so far as it goes we applaud the emergentist for his insight; but if we stop with emergentism, we discredit science more profoundly, and undermine scientific faith more effectively, than does any anti-intellectual critique of science. The emergentist still identifies science with its general theories, he is still a rationalist in his conception of truth. For he goes on to say that science and the human intellect are eternally limited to this analysis of fact into incommensurable sorts of fact, respectively physical, biological, and psychological or sociological. In virtue of our physical, biological, and psychological theories we are enabled to discern in natural process some three variant structures, and so reach causal explanations of fact; but just for that reason, according to the emergentist, we must refrain from all effort to explain causally the relation of these differently structured processes, or their generation one from another. We may not seek to explain fully how metabolism transmits inorganic matter into vegetable and animal flesh, nor how inorganic matter generated a living world.

Certain physical complexes, produced by intelligible causal mechanisms, are found to be accompanied by new properties which we distinguish as organic; but we must accept this emergence of organic properties by an act of faith, simply as a fact, not inquiring into it because it is by definition inscrutable and inexplicable. Alexander calls this faith "natural piety." It is certainly not scientific piety. Science forbids any definition which leaves nature causally inexplicable, and therefore unintelligible.

The immediate source of the emergentist's error is his false conception of causation. Causal connection may be affirmed, it is implied, only where we are aware of constant and widespread structure allowing us to confirm and describe causal process. Where we lack knowledge of causal structure, our affirmation of causal connection is meaningless. Physical causes have intelligible physical effects, organic causes have organic effects, but the ascription of organic effects to physical causes is meaningless. Yet, if we know that inorganic matter is in fact transmuted into organic matter, we must accept this fact which transcends causal explanation. Must we do this by an act of blind faith?

What the emergentist does here is to deny the existence of causal connection wherever the character of causal connection cannot be precisely defined in general terms. This error is due to his identification of science with current scientific theory; and this error in its turn arises from a residual rationalism, a confusion of scientific truth with the symbolic systems or "theories" which implement description. The emergentist no longer looks for a single universal theory definitive of "universal Being"; he verbally accepts the pluralism of science; but he still insists upon a small number of theories, three or four, eternally defining three or four eternal sorts of "universal Being." He is still a rationalistic philosopher who takes the current theory created by empirical hypothesis to constitute an eternal intuition into universal Being.

The simple truth is, we know, that the scientist must postulate the presence of causal connection *before* he theorizes about it. The emergentist would require the scientist to have his theory perfected, even before he starts to construct theory or to entertain empirical hypothesis. The emergentist forbids all original speculation, all new hypothesis. This would fixate current theory, much as Greek metaphysics made dogma of Greek science. But, to repeat, the source of his error is the fallacious notion of general or universal causation, exerted by general or universal Being. It is true that a primary postulate of science has been the universality of causal connection; but this postulate refers to *particular* causation, not to general or universal causation, of which science knows and will know nothing. The causal postulate is already affirmed in the truth which generates science, and which asserts that real being is individual being. "Real," by definition, means causally effective. The rationalistic error, we conclude, is to see in the observed similarity of particular causal processes a condition of the existence of such causal process. In truth, the similarity of causal processes is only the condition of our knowledge of specific causal process. We know that events are caused, whether or not we can describe their causes. We may not define nature in terms of the limitations of human knowledge.

But what is the correction of the emergentist's error? Its full correction is philosophical truth, postulating the universality or ubiquity of necessary *particular* causation. Without this postulate all scientific inquiry stops, and scientific knowledge evaporates into mere verbiage. But its more pointed correction is a perception of the implications of this truth for current and future science. Science must and does postulate the complete and intelligible determinateness of the process of evolution; and as a matter of fact it already inquires, not without success, into the causal processes transmuting inorganic into organic matter. There is no reason why the evolutionary process should be cut for purposes of theoretical analysis at just two or three points. We may properly select for causal analysis just this transition from inanimate to living matter. But, more largely, we must acknowledge that the whole evolutionary process is the work of *particular* determinations, *i.e.* of individual things. All the "structures" of nature have originated in individual variants—all individuals are variants, for that is what "individual" means. We will always continue to seek and find similarities of particular causation, defined in new theories; but we must not let rationalistic dogma nor loyalty to theoretical analysis blind us to the fact that all of the crucial causations determining evolutionary progress have been unique differentiations, or dissimilarities, which by subsequent repetition and diffusion have established new types. *The future task of science is to do justice to the nonconformities of nature which have determined evolutionary progress. To do this is to complete the work of theoretical analysis, which discovers natural uniformities.*

This insight into the full requirement of philosophical truth, which is the transformation of theoretical science into evolutionary science, frees us from the rationalism which would confine all future science within the limits of current theory. But it also mightily expands and transmutes the scientific concept of nature; for we now see that every type of being, *i.e.* every similarity discoverable among individual beings, is the result of the particular differentiations in which it originated. This holds of human types, of organic species, and of the inorganic sorts which we call "physical." The creation of the world was and is and forever shall be the work of individuals. This perception radically reforms both our conception of nature and our science of nature. It replaces the old eternalism and universalism by an awareness of the creative progress which is reality. Into this new science will come every perception we have ever had of the efficacy of individual beings in the creation of the world.

30 THE FUTURE OF PHILOSOPHY

IN THE PREVIOUS CHAPTERS PHILOSOPHY HAS BEEN
presented as a study politically motivated, inquiring
into the implications of natural knowledge for the opposed
postulates of necessity and freedom. The postulate of natural
necessity has been shown to support the doctrine of absolutistic
government, and democratic self-government has been shown
to require the postulate of natural freedom. Long controversy
between rationalistic philosophers affirming necessity and empirical philosophers affirming freedom is closed by the victory
of empirical philosophy, achieved in our own century.

But now that the long controversy is over and the victory
of liberal theory assured, it is necessary to turn back to do
fuller justice to the rationalistic philosophers who defended
the idea of natural necessity. What was the intention of these
thinkers who so long and so fervently maintained their rationalistic dogma? They were motivated by fear of social chaos,
and by their desire for some absolute foundation for social institutions. The authority of church or state, they felt, must be
absolute. Sovereignty must be one and indivisible. Otherwise,
they thought, there can be no authority, no sovereignty, no
assurance of law and order. To this practical consideration was
added the desire for some absolute foundation supporting

science. Human experience is limited, we see only a part of
the surface of things, and what we see is shifting, diverse, and
disconnected. How can the scientist claim to reach authentic
knowledge from the fragmentary clues of sense, how can he
jump to universal theory from a few sense data, if he has no
initial assurance that there really exists a universal form or
Being, manifested in or through the fragmentary sense data?
These practical and theoretical considerations supported one
another. Let it at least be absolutely certain that there is universal Being! Then we may allow sensations to be data, indicative of the permanent character of reality; and we are at the
same time assured that the most constant elements of human
life, namely, its moral laws and political institutions, are ver-
itably absolute, being the moral law and divine constitution of
eternal nature itself.

If the myth of universal Being is rejected, some other way
must be found to support the induction from particular fact to
general theory, and to allow sovereign persons to live together
in political unity. First, what supports scientific induction? By
what right does one proceed from fragmentary evidence to
comprehensive and unified theory? Why may one believe that
generalizations based on past occurrence will be honored in
future occurrence?

Induction is predicated, as J. S. Mill said, on the postulate of
natural uniformity. What is meant by "uniformity"? Nothing
more, it would seem, than the observed likeness or similarity
of things. We perceive certain similarities among things; and
as the scientist ponders upon these, he is led to deeper and
wider similarities. He may finally conclude that all things are
physically similar, and that physical science therefore describes
a universal physical structure, common to all things and preserved in nature through all time.

Clearly, theoretical analysis presupposes some sort and degree
of uniformity—its whole aim is the discovery and elucidation
of uniformities. The likeness or uniformity of things is thus a

postulate of theoretical science. But science, we have seen, postulates also the particularity or difference of things, underlying or accompanying their similarity. This is the meaning of the scientific emphasis upon particular fact as the criterion of general theory. Why, if things are radically different, should it be assumed that they will always present similarities? Why, if things are free and not necessitated, should they necessarily present any universal structure? Why should the physical structure inferred from yesterday's facts hold of tomorrow's facts? Why should things conform at all? Why should nature not be chaos, devoid of large and lasting order?

A possible reply to this question would be to say that nature may indeed be chaotic, and the apparent order of nature only a mental framework which we project into nature. This Kantian reply we cannot accept, because it destroys all scientific and moral faith. Another possible reply would be to say that since science does exist, and supports itself upon the postulate of natural conformity, the existence of science establishes the fact that nature is uniform and must be uniform. This is to claim too much. Science discovers much uniformity in nature, it is true; but it discovers no reason why there must be uniformity. In its acknowledgment of particular character as most real and ultimate, science implies that the order of nature rides upon a deeper disorder or chaos; and the physical scientist, in his recent researches, has demonstrated that this chaos or indeterminacy exists, and that it sets limits to scientific description. Why should chaos not increase, and devour whatever of order there is? Human society occasionally falls prey to chaos. Why should nature at large not do so? What keeps things similar, what makes them more similar than they were, or similar in new ways?

The philosophy of the future will make its first principle the radical individuality of things; but it must also do justice to the uniformity of things which makes theoretical science possible, and to the community of persons which makes government and civilization possible. To what is due the similarity of things and the reciprocal social adaptation of persons, if there is no absolute necessity compelling similarity and adaptation? This is today a very practical question. Society has reached the place where a few individuals may destroy the human population of this planet, and conceivably even all planetary life, by means of the lethal instruments devised by science. The condition of human survival is peace; and peace requires the transcendence of the nationalistic exclusiveness which leaves us in political and cultural chaos. The human race must be brought into social community, something it has never known. How does order come out of chaos? How is cosmos generated?

This, we may remember, was the question which science originally arose to answer. The earliest Greek thinkers hoped to comprehend the *physis*, or the generative force which creates nature. It was the later thinkers, Pythagoras and Parmenides and Plato, who limited their objective, and who asked only how nature is sustained, not how nature is created. This shift of scientific interest corresponded to a shift of political interest. The earliest Greek thinkers hoped to create a Greek nation; the later thinkers saw this hope defeated, and sought to return to the old civic constitutions. This effort to perpetuate inadequate institutions destroyed Greece, even as the effort to perpetuate our own past with its unabridged national sovereignties would destroy modern civilization. But what is the clue, where can we get insight into the generative principle of nature? How can order be created out of chaos? We have today good evidence that nature has evolved, producing all of its cosmic order out of itself. How has this evolution been determined?

The Greek error was to believe the orders of nature and society to be fixed, when in fact all cosmic order has evolved and still evolves. Aristotle taught the fixity of species. Plato seems to have believed in an absolute geometrical order. The consequence of this error was a failure to appreciate the *effective* reality of individual character. The notion of fixed species, for example, requires the notion of a superindividual force working in or upon individuals, and confining their activities within specific limits. In fact, however, the species effects nothing—all that happens in this world is the result of individual interactions. Why a species or type persists is something that calls for explanation. It is not explained by the existence of the species. It is known that the continued existence of a species means that the species is adapted to its environment. What do we mean by "adaptation"? To say that a species is adapted means that the individuals comprising the species are adapted to one another and to the other things affecting them. Each individual thing exists in interaction with other individual things. Each individual is dynamically dependent upon the other individuals to which it reacts. It is evident that the reactions of a thing may be destructive or preservative of the things which stimulate its reactions. If its reactions are predominantly destructive of these stimuli, the thing will no longer be stimulated, it will no longer react, it will cease to exist.

In this way, we are led back to the true insight which underlay the Greek error. The Greeks saw that nature comprises an economy, composed of things so adapted to one another that their reactions to one another preserve them all. *There is an economy of nature, even as there is an economy of man.* The Greek error was to suppose that this economic pattern is fixed, and that it preserves itself. In truth, the economic order is not fixed, it continually evolves; and it does not preserve itself, but it has been created, perpetuated, modified, and enlarged by the individuals dependent upon it for their existence. This is the true moral law of nature, embedded in the very conditions of individual existence; and out of this basic and original moral fact have proceeded, "in the order of time" as Anaximander said, all the orders and uniformities of the world. The individual entities composing nature are by definition different, and they are not necessitated to conform or to be uniform. But they do largely conform; they remain in many respects similar or uniform. Our problem is to learn how there arise these uniformities, which persist because they preserve a reciprocal adaptation of thing to thing, and so constitute the economy of nature. How has nature evolved? What is the sufficient condition of human progress, which most patently advances the evolution of nature?

When we approach the problem of evolution seriously, resolved to solve it, we grasp some remarkable facts. We have been astonished for some time at the striking evidences of symbiosis, or interdependence of plants and animals, which are daily revealed by the biologist. But let us now ask what a really well-adapted vegetable or animal character would be? Within a few thousand years, the surface of this earth will presumably be populated only by those plants and animals which serve man. Wilderness will have vanished, and new species created by scientific ingenuity will cover the earth. Really adapted were and are only those organisms, the issue of which man has domesticated or will domesticate.

The centerline of plant and animal evolution is that which points to the human economy. We are merely being literal and scientific, we are not being idealistic or vain, when we see the organic evolution of earth to be a progress directed toward man, and most largely determined in all of its history by factors which become fully effective and visible only in the human economy of today.

Can we see what character it was which gave to man his dominance among the organic species? Presumably, man became man when he achieved the domestication of animals and plants. This liberated him from "the state of nature," in which the organism is dependent for its provision upon wild products. The domestication of food must have removed natural checks upon the human population, which would so increase as to become socially congested, and find new checks in violence and exterminatory war. The same causes produce the same effects today. Out of this chaos of human violence, we must believe, arose the first political institution, possibly the clan system. The large and congested population was organized into a number of clans. The individual identified himself only with his clan, which protected him from the mass-excitement and violence generated by the larger population. The individual could know his small clan, and he could accept its rather rigid regulation of his behavior as a condition of peace. Among the clans was preserved a minimum of necessary intercourse, carefully controlled. By the clan system an amorphous and delinquescent population was crystallized into a viable pattern.

That political institutions originated somewhat in this way is suggested by the ritual and symbolism of the clans. Each clan identified itself with some plant or animal species; and the first "gods" appeared in mythical Wolves, Bulls, Oaks, and Fishes whose "life" was the enduring life of the clan. The clansmen were "children of the Bull"; and for them beef was *tabu* except when eaten ritually, with awe and trembling. What was the spell of these symbolisms, which have persisted through all the centuries of civilization down to today? Did the congested war-diseased population look back with nostalgia to the "state of nature," which disappeared with the domestication of plant and animal food? Did men long to be again just an animal species sharing the natural economy of the wilderness? And did the clan system profess to be a return to that state of nature, in its solemn pretence that humans are "really" wolves, cattle, sheep, and fish? Again and again, in later history, we see populations which have outgrown their political economic institutions rise in social convulsion, and attempt a "return to nature." How can man return to nature, what does the nostalgia for nature mean? Man returns to nature only by his creation of political-economic institutions which remove congestion, and allow populations larger than have existed before to live together in peace. His nostalgia for nature is his need for a justice which will obviate violence, by securing some consideration of each by all.

In fact, of course, the conception of the clan system was quaint, artificial, a product of the creative imagination. The clansmen were not wolves, there was no Great Wolf imbuing with his immortal vigor the tribe who solemnly ate of the wolf meat. It was because these symbolisms were human creations that they had to be so rigidly and dogmatically upheld. For there was in fact a clan; and the clan owed its unity and strength, its prosperity, and finally even its existence to the symbolism which identified the individual with his clansmen. The human population of this earth must still and always live in virtue of some symbolism, assuring the individual of his kinship with his fellows and with nature. The only question is what sort of symbolism it shall be. If man lives in the strength of symbolic art, shall this art be myth or science?

It is significant, surely, that the first symbolism to create a political-economic system should have deified animals and plants. Man had raised himself to human status by his domestication of animals and plants, a practice which presupposes an unusual interest in and attention to other species. We may guess that domestication was initially noneconomic, being motivated by a kindly and playful love of living things, such as still makes children identify themselves with pets. It was this same spontaneous affection for species different from the human which bore fruit in the symbolism supporting the clan economy. Later, the divine Sheep became the Lamb of God, and still later the good Shepherd who gave his life for the sheep.

The domestication of animals and plants, and the consequent creation of political and religious institutions, occurred long ago; but today there occurs a change as far-reaching and unsettling as that which took man from his wild Eden, and made of him a social being dependent for his existence upon political invention. Today, we see the domestication by man of his physicochemical environment, this advance being usually spoken of as "the scientific and industrial revolution." For a century, there has been enormous human increase, leading to social congestion, mass-excitement, and exterminatory wars. Once again we seek new political institutions, partitioning humanity into viable groups and regulating the intercourse of these groups. And once again men turn, in their search for a symbolism supporting this new order, to a myth suggested by those interests which led to the congestion from which they must be saved. It was scientific interest in physicochemical nature which initiated the industrial revolution, with all of its social consequences. So there appears today the symbolism of materialistic philosophy, assuring us that if we will only believe that men are (not wolves or sheep or fish but) physicochemical mechanisms, the social future will be secure. This materialistic philosophy is usually presented as nothing but science itself; but materialism is metaphysical myth, and not science. The physicochemical processes constituting the human being are to be understood more by way of their difference from other physicochemical processes than by their likeness to these. Whatever overlooks or denies specific or individual difference is a myth. Science is just the consistent refusal to neglect specific and individual differences. From science we deduce, in place of myth, the truth that respect for individual being is the foundation of all human and natural economy.

When we survey the large course of evolution, we see that it has proceeded by great leaps or abrupt departures from type. This is what allows us to classify things into species, genera, orders, etc. Consider, for example, the chemical elements, each type of atom clearly demarcated from its ninety-odd fellows. Why is nature not qualitatively continuous, in such a way that between any two known types there will be found a third? Why is nature specific? The answer of science is that nontypical individuals have existed, but have failed to survive and reproduce themselves. This still does not explain why new and very different orders have emerged, and established themselves as preeminently adapted.

It used to be supposed that sudden changes in the physical environment conditioned the great departures of organic evolution; but the physical environment has been remarkably stable, and the biologist finds that the greatest diversification of organic species occurred in the periods of greatest physical stability. The appeal to changing physical conditions as the cause of organic evolution was really a hang-over from pre-Darwinian thought. The physical environment was given the role of creator, because men still hesitated to affirm the creative power of life itself. But one has merely to observe the morphological and other relationship of organic species to learn that life is preeminently conditioned by other life. The fact that organic evolution has proceeded apace in eras of maximum physical stability suggests that the chief condition of specific change is congestion, due to the rapid increase of the organic population under favorable physical conditions. The most potent environment of a living organism is the life-environment, constituted of other living organisms. When physical conditions are stable and life multiplies rapidly, the individual is subjected to new pressures exerted upon it by a mass of its own kind; and these new stimuli will elicit new sorts of response. Most of these responses will be destructive in effect, and result in depopulation with temporary relief from congestion. But occasionally there will occur a novel response, one which is preservative and not destructive of its stimulus; and individuals so responding will be favored above their fellows, and become the progenitors of a new type.

To speak more generally, evolutionary progress may be conceived to be at once the result and the condition of natural increase. Nature is not quantitatively fixed, in such a way that there is always the same number of the same sorts of things. Whatever is exceptionally well adapted will multiply, and this multiplication will automatically produce a new condition of congestion, in which things otherwise well adapted are over-stimulated by things of their own kind. The individual is no longer adapted to members of its own species. There occurs in all of nature the violence and destruction which in human society is war or massacre; but there also may occur those creative responses which initiate new sorts of adaptation supporting an increase of being. These creative responses are the reactions which have established new types and species, and advanced the progress of cosmic evolution. The whole course of evolution may be understood as a creation of material nature, with continuous increase in the number or quantity of existent things, this increase requiring the continuous readaptation of things primarily to things of their own kind. Evolutionary progress is a qualitative progress, advanced by the rise of new and more deeply adapted types of being; but the qualitative progress is also a quantitative progress, the new type being "higher" just insofar as its reactions tolerate and support an increase of being. Thus the progress of human character is to be measured by the increase in human life which it makes possible; and human progress is accordingly most easily appreciated in terms of the development of the political economy, by means of which man has supported in health and security a steadily increasing population. Materialism was right in its quantitative emphasis; but it overlooked the fact that the size and security of a population is dependent upon the character of the individuals composing it. Idealism was right in its emphasis upon quality; but in rejecting quantitative measure, it deprived itself of all objective moral criteria, and inevitably became arbitrary and prejudiced. Use the quantative measure; but discover the quality which conditions the quantity of life or other existence!

There is every reason to believe that human progress illustrates the principle which has determined the evolution of nature at large. Human progress is conditioned by the appearance and spread of new qualitative character, which sooner or later effectively reforms the political-economic organization of society, this new economy supporting an increased population. Can we perceive the working of this principle in subhuman nature, and learn how there appeared and multiplied living organisms, mineral compounds, and even physical entities? Does the political economy of man only make apparent a power of economic organization which can be pursued into the smallest grain of nature, and which has generated the cosmos itself?

Consider how the evolution of the earth's surface has pivoted itself upon the peculiar properties of water! One may conceive the whole evolution of vegetable and animal life to be a device by which the waters of sea and sky were spread over the dry land masses of the earth; for living matter is chiefly water, and is distinguished by its power to retain water in various chemical combinations. The most distinctive property of water is its moderation and stabilization of temperature. But temperature is the measure of heat, and heat is rapid molecular vibration. Too rapid vibration causes the disintegration of molecular matter, the last stage of material decomposition being the reduction even of atomic matter into radiant energies such as light. The stabilizing properties of water provide the needed clue to the evolutionary mechanism of universal nature. The creation of the material cosmos, in all of its physical, chemical, organic, and social organization, is the progressive induction of energy into temperate and nondestructive motions. There is always violence or destruction, potential or actual; but there has been also a progressive establishment of patterns of interaction which preserve and increase the sum of material being.

Does this natural progress constitute a mechanistic process? The evolution of nature is mechanically necessitated in the sense that each establishment of novel adaptation will lead to an increase of material existence, this material increase subjecting each material thing to new and disturbing conditions. But the progress is not really mechanical, because this incidence of violent disturbance need not of itself effect the moderation of violence, by means of an advance to some new form of organization. This transcendence of old forms by new forms is unpredictable and mechanically inexplicable. How can it be explained, if not mechanically?

Mechanical explanation means the exhaustive analysis of any particular occurrence in terms of uniformities or similarities already known to invest entities of the sorts involved in the occurrence. But the appearance of a new type or species, establishing a new pattern of interaction among things, by definition escapes reduction to earlier uniformities. The new type is "emergent." Darwin rightly attributed to chance the individual variations which he saw to be the condition of specific change. He did not mean, he said, that these variations are uncaused, but only that their causes escape detection. Biological science through its genetic studies has advanced far beyond Darwin in its knowledge of the mechanisms of heredity; but it must still statistically attribute to "chance" the origin of what genetic combinations shall occur, to determine the character of a living population. Recourse to statistical methods involves a renunciation of strictly mechanical explanation. The latter seeks to determine causal relations among individual entities, whereas statistical analysis seeks only to determine approximate uniformities of group behavior.

It should not be supposed that the use of statistical methods prejudices the scientific conviction that everything happens by due cause. On the contrary, statistical science establishes this causal postulate more firmly. When the empirical philosopher challenges the postulate of universal necessity, he means to deny that particular events must necessarily conform to some universal design. He does not deny, rather he most emphatically insists, that particular events are causally necessitated by other particular events. His intention is to affirm particular causation, and to say that all effective causation is the work of individual entities interacting upon one another. This means, individuals being by definition different in their characters and reactions, that particular occurrence will always elude exhaustive description in general terms. This was the insight of Darwin, when he wrote that the individual variations supporting evolutionary change are duly caused but nevertheless escape theoretical formulation. The individuals which establish a new type or species are individually different from anything that has existed before; and it is just this individual difference which is reproduced and repeated, to become the defining character of a new type.

Several conclusions have now been reached concerning the evolutionary progress of nature. They may be summarized in the following hypothesis. The successful adaptation of individuals of a given type to the things around them will result in an increase of population, with consequent congestion, destructive violence, and depopulation. The better a type is adapted to environing types, the worse will become the maladaptation of individuals of that type to one another. (Thus man, the supremely adapted animal species, is most subject to social maladjustments, or failures in the adaptation of man to man.) This diseased or maladjusted condition will persist either until the population is much reduced, when the whole unhappy cycle will begin over again, or until, to use the language of Plato, some individual variation "by good fortune" originates a new sort of adjustment. This novel adaptation will support an increased population; but it, too, will eventually produce still further increase, with new congestion, and new need of novel adjustment.

The foregoing conception of evolution allows an answer to the question with which this chapter opened, demanding some ground or source of the observable uniformities of nature. If things are not necessitated to conform, they evidently conform freely; and our problem is to discover how things have come to conform and how they may be persuaded to conform in new ways. The conformity of things, evolutionary science informs us, is more than bare uniformity. The conformities or uniformities preserved by nature are ways of reciprocal adaptation among things, these reciprocities constituting a natural economy. The specific types of nature are due to the multiplication, spread, and persistence of certain individual characters which proved to be preeminently adapted. The classification of natural species points to a natural history, which, if we could know it, would inform us of the individual entities in which these species originated. There has been an historical succession of individual characters establishing new and better adapted types. These individuals have advanced natural evolution from its physical and chemical beginnings, through its mineral, organic, and social stages, to what is supremely human in man today. These potent individuals are the true creators of the world.

It is for the philosophy and science of the future to elaborate and propagate this truth. Only individuals are causally effective; and the total achievement of effective individuals is nothing less than the creation of the cosmos. It may some day be scientifically demonstrated that henceforth the hub of cosmic creation lies in the human life on this planet, in that the activities of human life proceeding on earth exert just that small but decisive influence which makes the difference between cosmic health and cosmic decay. In this case, man would literally become the creator and providence of the world. However this may be, fact and logic compel the conclusion that nature is and always has been the creation of its individual constituents. It is a democratic world that we inhabit, the divine government of nature being wholly that of the things in it.

This insight into the individual origins of natural uniformities revolutionizes man's concept of nature. It provides full and final release from the dogma of material necessity, and opens our eyes to the creative power which always has invested and always will invest the things of nature. There is no "law of progress," mechanically necessitating progress; but all evolution and progress is the work of free individuals, freely responding in their own character to what stimulates them. This thought is both inspiring and chastening. To know that nature from the beginnings of creation has itself met and mastered the problems which it generated is most encouraging. But it is sobering to know that there is no underlying necessity guaranteeing the solution of these problems and the continuance of creation. Human destiny at least lies wholly in human hands; and possibly in human hands lies the further destiny of all creation.

Long ago, Plato in his dialogue *Timaeus* suggested how the cosmos may have been created from chaos by a divine Artisan, who eternally persuades the originally unordered elements to accept an ideal pattern. An evolutionary science might confirm this conception of cosmic creation out of chaos. Chaos means the absence of constant order and uniformity. A plurality of interacting individual entities, among which there persisted no constant and definable relations, would be in fact chaotic. Within such chaos, there might occur individuals so reciprocally adapted that they were able to persist, and steadily to extend into other things, by causal interaction, a similarly adapted character. From this beginning of cosmic order, as a result of the increase of these adapted beings and their interstimulation, might proceed the evolutionary changes which have created the diversified but specified world of today. In a real degree nature remains chaotic, because the differences among its individual constituents persist under all of their conformities; and at any time such difference may reproduce itself, to establish a new conformity. But modern evolutionary science requires no *deus ex machina*, such as the demiurge of Plato. The creative power is that of those individuals who have responded to their stimuli in new, better adapted ways.

Human memory, in historical science, brings some acknowledgment to the seers, statesmen, scientists, and saints who by word and deed have established new adaptations of the human individual to his human and natural environment. Behind these heroes are the anonymous and unsung individuals who inspired them; and back of human history is the unrecorded past, human and subhuman, no less rich in individual achievement which carried energy from its immaterial beginnings, through its chemical, mineral, and organic stages, to man and his civilization.

We cannot develop this theme here. To do so would be to transform science into the religion it ought to be and some day will be. For what we shall learn is this: Creative love alone has from the beginning engineered this world; and if man abjures this religious love, the very stones will cry aloud their adoration, and take up the creative work which man lets fall. But we shall not let it fall. There lies ahead of man a heaven that shames all prophecy. That heaven, or annihilation, is his destiny.

Philosophy in this way finally returns to the deeper truth of religion such as that of the New Testament, or of art when it points to a mercy and love which is the deeper fount of all justice. Political institutions, whatever their form, will not give us security and peace if they are observed only in the letter, and not in the kindly spirit which created them and which they were created to serve. No more than logic provides scientific truth if it is not the instrument of willing attention to all particular fact, does a democratic constitution secure justice if it is not used to implement a kindly and loving goodwill toward all human individuals. Let democratic society lose its lovingkindness, let it confuse the machinery of democratic government with the tricks of power-politics, and very quickly a political majority will by harsh and autocratic action incite some offended minority to justified rebellion. The democratic constitution will secure justice if it makes effective in legislation and administration that love of one's fellows which purifies the heart from hatred, and which constitutes, whatever it be called, the true religion of man. The justice which has generated the cosmos is itself an instrument of creative love. When will intellectuals again be humble enough, and bold enough, to speak aloud this name of love, and to make it the head and corner of their symbolic art?

INDEX

605